LEIGH
MATTHEWS

THE
NATIONAL
BESTSELLER

LEIGH
MATTHEWS

AUTOBIOGRAPHY

ACCEPT THE
CHALLENGE

EBURY
PRESS

An Ebury Press book
Published by Random House Australia Pty Ltd
Level 3, 100 Pacific Highway, North Sydney NSW 2060
www.randomhouse.com.au

First published by Ebury Press in 2013
This edition published in 2014

Addresses for companies within the Random House Group can be found at
www.randomhouse.com.au/offices

National Library of Australia
Cataloguing-in-Publication entry

Matthews, Leigh, 1952–
Accept the challenge / Leigh Matthews.

ISBN 978 0 85798 210 0 (pbk.)

Matthews, Leigh, 1952–
Australian football players–Biography.
Football players–Australia–Biography.
Australian football–Biography.

796.336092

Cover design: Blue Cork
Front cover photo: Getty Images
Internal design by Midland Typesetters, Australia
Typeset by Midland Typesetters, Australia
Printed in Australia by Griffin Press, an accredited ISO AS/NZS 14001:2004
Environmental Management System printer

Random House Australia uses papers that are natural, renewable and recyclable products
and made from wood grown in sustainable forests. The logging and manufacturing
processes are expected to conform to the environmental regulations of the country of
origin.

CONTENTS

Foreword		vii
Preface		xi
1	In the beginning	1
2	From Chelsea to Glenferrie	11
3	Growing up fast	16
4	A first flag	23
5	First coach, biggest influence	32
6	Huddo	41
7	The best of times, the worst of times	50
8	Brothers in arms	57
9	Living in the '70s	62
10	Scott, Tuck and Matthews	68
11	A new era	75
12	Personality profiling	84
13	The coach of coaches	93
14	An amazing talent	105
15	Crossing the fine line	111
16	The Bruns incident	117
17	The end is near	129
18	The final curtain	137
19	Heading to Victoria Park	144
20	A club in transition	164
21	Rebuilding	171
22	The launching pad	182
23	The jigsaw pieces begin to click	191
24	A tough decision	209
25	On the cusp of history	219
26	The agony is over	235

27 A special bunch   248
28 Hangover   262
29 The window is closing   270
30 Buckley in, Shaw out   282
31 My time is up   295
32 Jumping the fence   308
33 Too good to refuse   323
34 Building the base   331
35 The honeymoon begins   345
36 The sordid search for a competitive edge   368
37 The premiership turning point   376
38 2001: Reaching the tip of the pyramid   392
39 2002: A game of seconds and inches   418
40 2003: Defying the football gods   426
41 You can't beat City Hall   443
42 Knowing your time is up   464
43 From then till now   485
Acknowledgements   499
Career highlights and statistics   501
Index   507

FOREWORD
BY BRUCE MCAVANEY

It's exciting to be invited to the birthday party of a legend, especially when it's a milestone to be celebrated – and you count them as a friend.

But it's not easy finding a present for an icon.

In March 2012, Leigh celebrated his 60th birthday and the Australian Football League rose to the challenge. They presented him with a permanent premiership cup inscribed: 'The AFL Commission and Administration pays tribute to the wonderful service given to the game by Leigh as one of the initial 12 legends inducted into the AFL Hall of Fame in 1993, considered one of the greatest players and coaches of all time.'

I believe it's the only occasion the AFL has given this prize to an individual. Could any person receive a more resounding endorsement from the governing body?

Leigh has noted that turning 60, together with a more sombre moment nine months earlier, were the catalysts that enabled him to 'let go' when it came to coaching. It's a massive event affecting the psyche of any elite sportsperson – that 'saying goodbye' to the challenge, the battle that's been the reference point for the duration of their career: in Leigh's case, for close to 40 years.

Having worked closely with him for more than a decade, I'm not completely convinced that Leigh has become completely non-competitive. He certainly goes about his role as a football analyst with a lot of pride and a fair chunk of passion.

And when I reflect on Leigh's playing career, it's comparable to any of the greats in Australian sport. He transcends the Australian game and sits proudly as one of only three AFL players to date who are given the status of 'legend' in the Sport Australia Hall of Fame. (Ted Whitten and Ron Barassi are the other two.) I believe that's the highest honour a selection committee can bestow on any sportsman or woman.

The first occasion I spent any real time with Leigh was as host of the *Talking Footy* program that started on Channel Seven in 1995. He was our first guest on our second-ever show. After a poor Collingwood performance, he'd created the back page headline on the morning of our Monday program. After the show, he gave me a lift home and my lasting memory was surprise. Because this was a gentle soul, not the lethal player I'd seen on the field, nor the ruthless coach I'd imagined.

I know it's a revelation for others when they first meet Leigh.

After coaching Collingwood, he joined Channel Seven. This was pre-Brisbane Lions, and we've spoken since then on a regular basis most weeks; always about football, often about horse racing. I've learned a lot.

Leigh's written about the rare occasions he felt joy as a coach. We've seen memorable vision of him striding proudly and powerfully onto the ground, celebrating Collingwood's drought-breaking premiership in the dying minutes of that 1990 grand final – and again in the coaches box as Brisbane were about to win another flag during that modern-day historical 'three-peat'.

But the most emotional I've ever seen him close up was at Eagle Farm race course when his favourite colt, Sizzling, won a Group One race. It was, I think, one of the great thrills of his life.

When the Lions were on a winning run, I knew within a few minutes what time the phone would ring on a Monday. I'm sure it was as much about keeping a routine and satisfying his superstitious streak as it was about any need to chat to me.

Leigh's revelation that he would have skipped the experience a coach goes through on grand final day – that unbearable tension that comes with the occasion – just to know the result, good or bad, is balanced by his realisation of what he was missing when his team weren't there on the big day.

It's a bit like the experience of Luke Nolen, jockey for the famous unbeaten Black Caviar, who found racing periods overwhelming but every time she went for a spell, he'd miss her and pine for her return, despite the mental angst he knew to expect.

Leigh begins this book with a quote from General Patton about that balance between the rewards of success and the dread of failure, which I'm sure challenges all the greats at some stage. Think Kieren Perkins in Atlanta in 1996, where his only hope for victory was to lay it all on the line right from the start, and take the chance that he mightn't be good enough, knowing there was no excuse.

I've always felt that Leigh has the loudest voice when it comes to AFL matters and he has used that status wisely. Leadership is a buzz-word in sport these days. Few have led more successfully. He's analytical, deals in facts, gets to the bottom line.

His acceptance of responsibility is a lesson we can all learn. Consistency, honesty, respect. They're all words I associate with Leigh Matthews.

The argument of who is the greatest is always difficult but a lot of fun. Federer or Nadal? Carl Lewis or Usain Bolt? LeBron James or Michael Jordan?

Leigh could be the greatest player in AFL history. He may well be the most significant single person the indigenous game has seen – and for somebody who knows him and has enjoyed a friendship, that's a very exciting thought.

PREFACE

Accept the challenge without reservation or doubt and risk the depression of losing, so you may experience the exhilaration of victory. – General George S. Patton

It was early in the week leading into the first game of the 1990 finals series. As Collingwood coach, the pressure was building on me to make a better showing in our third consecutive finals.

After bombing out of both the 1988 and 1989 finals series without winning a game, the team's terrific effort to finish second at the end of the home-and-away season would quickly become just another failed year if we didn't win at least one final. No individual player is ever held as responsible for the team performance as the coach, so I was sitting in my office in the bowels of Collingwood's home ground at Victoria Park, pondering how best to approach the task ahead.

A couple of letters from the daily mail delivery were dropped onto my desk. Through 20 years of coaching in the Australian Football League, I received many letters from keen supporters – some complimentary and some critical, but always emphasising the enormous emotional stake supporters invest in their favourite footy team. I always read them because I have a natural curiosity and you never knew when you might stumble onto something worthwhile. That day, one of those letters contained a quote that we used during the Magpies' ultimately successful September and October premiership campaign that year. It also encapsulated what football has been to me for what seems like my entire life.

After a sequence of nine grand finals without winning a premiership since the last Collingwood victory in 1958, this particular letter writer was a lady who was one of the tens of thousands of Collingwood supporters who were desperate to see their beloved team break the 32-year premiership drought. The writer – whose name I wish I could remember in order to give her due credit – sent a quote she thought might be useful as a theme for the upcoming finals.

As a coach always eager to find that something extra, the words struck an immediate and resounding chord with me. If I had one objective as a coach, it was always to simplify the message and this General Patton quote was brief, clear to understand and seemed to outline the very essence of competition – particularly under the heightened emotions that accompany the pointy end of the season.

I used this quote from General Patton as part of Collingwood's 1990 finals campaign, which ended with one of the game's most famous drought-breaking premierships. It has stayed with me throughout the years that followed.

These words became something of a creed to me. When I think back, the attitude has always been there throughout my lifetime journey as both player and coach – then, now, and on reflection even more so earlier in my playing days. Hence, it provides an apt title for a book about a life spent in the extreme competitiveness of elite AFL football.

Everything we do and really care about starts with accepting the challenge. 'Challenge', 'depression' and 'exhilaration' are big words. They're exaggerated extremes, but together they're the tripod of performance, and cornerstones of what competitive sport at the top level is all about. It involves embarking on difficult goals and ambitions, because if the task isn't difficult it simply is not a challenge. (I should add here that I don't mean to confuse feeling down and depressed after a football loss with the debilitating and serious illness of depression.)

If you put yourself on the line and accept the challenge that comes with high goals and lofty ambitions, then there's an emotional price to be paid for failure, but there's also the reward of succeeding. Being addicted to the challenge of competition has been, on the upside, my driving force, and on the downside my cross to bear. The urge to compete and win was like a hole within that I could never fill.

Football has been very good to me and, while it might sound corny, I love the game. Footy has been a constant companion throughout my life; family aside, it has provided my most treasured moments and memories.

After 37 years and 793 games in the AFL as a player and coach, I had the good fortune to be involved in 12 grand finals and eight premierships in a career split between 17 years as a player at Hawthorn (1969–1985), 10 years coaching Collingwood (1986–1995) and then another decade at the Brisbane Lions (1999–2008).

While my career was pretty successful, the teams I was part of had a win-to-loss ratio of only 62.1 per cent. The message I draw from this is that, no matter how successful you might be, in the AFL competition over the long term it never gets much better than losing every third week. This is a sobering thought for anyone involved in football. (Even for someone like Joel Selwood, who in his first five years with Geelong, prior to the 2013 season, enjoyed a winning ratio of 105 wins from 125 games, an amazing 84 per cent. No way will Joel's winning ratio be above 70 per cent when he eventually retires.)

For me, the pain and despair of losing lasted so much longer than the joy of winning. The losing feeling was deeper and hurt more, while the winning feeling quickly turned to the next week and the next opponent. Reminding myself that it's only a game provided little consolation. The logical part of my brain always knew that a game of football should never be treated as life and death, but I'm afraid my heart never agreed. The post-game few hours after losing entailed a kind of deep mourning – even more so in my coaching days – that defied any logical explanation.

There's always that awful nagging fear of failure for the competitor to deal with, but the bottom line, as General Patton said so well, is that if you don't have a go and risk losing, there's no possible chance of winning. So that's the challenge. Accepting that losing is part of winning and still totally committing every part of your being – mind, body and soul – that is the simple first prerequisite of success.

The many and varied ways of applying this mindset practically – the lessons, the methods, the people, the observations, which led to a set of beliefs and principles I formed over my 40 years in elite team sport – these are what I regard as the building blocks of success. This is primarily what this book is about.

It is also about my great belief that life is a series of sliding door and crossroad moments. There are so many seemingly unrelated and random events, some good, some bad, some earned, others unearned, but all of them undoubtedly contribute to the twists and turns that meld together to determine the direction of our lives.

Having been invited a few times over recent years to write a book about my football life and declining the opportunity, a couple of crossroad moments changed my mind. In July 2011, Leigh Smith – a childhood mate and one of my closest friends – died suddenly of a heart attack. He was the same age as me. In March 2012, I turned 60. And sometime late in 2011, I completely accepted that I was totally and utterly finished with the thought of coaching again.

From the moment I ended my coaching stint with Brisbane in 2008, I'd had no specific desire to coach again, but deep within I probably knew that if any club had tried hard enough to headhunt me, then the possibility of coaching was still there. It was a faint but still flickering ember, like a smoker choosing not to smoke but always with the urge to have a cigarette.

Not any more; I now know that the coaching phase has finished forever.

So as they say, if you can, do; if you can't, teach; if not, then write a book. I'm now ready to remove myself from my natural inclination to live in the moment and look back on a life spent largely in and around football clubs – a life that has allowed me to live out most of my boyhood dreams.

In the 2000 Academy Award-winning movie *The Shawshank Redemption*, set in a brutal prison during the 1940s, there's a moment when an ageing old crim (Morgan Freeman) – convicted in his youth of a vicious murder – fronts the parole board for the umpteenth time. When Freeman's character, 'Red', is asked about the young man who committed the brutal crime, he replies that he doesn't know or empathise at all with his younger self. This reminds me of how I feel when I reflect on my early playing days.

Now, as a middle-aged grandfather, when I look back at the

relentless, driven, hungry, win-at-all-costs young man I was in my 20s, I almost shudder. On the football field that was one scary ultra-aggressive dude, with a ruthless and brutal approach more in keeping with waging war than playing a game of sport. Just as Red said, he seems like a totally different person.

To be totally honest, I don't particularly like much of my playing football persona. It might well have been necessary in order for me to succeed, but playing footy brought out the dark part of my soul, or so I thought.

In researching this book, I stumbled across an old documentary produced in the early 1990s about my playing days and my early years in coaching. It included an interview with my parents in which they both said of me: 'He loved to win.' My mum even added that, as a kid, if I couldn't win I'd cheat. Thanks for the honesty, Mum!

As much as it sounds embarrassingly distasteful, it probably wasn't too far from the truth. When I look back, I have always been very goal-oriented and probably enough of a chameleon to shape my actions to best achieve the goal and basically do whatever it takes. And as much as winning fairly was always good, I've always thought it better to be a rule-bending winner than a squeaky-clean loser. So, if you're thinking this book will be something of a moral compass, it's probably best to think again.

Apart from a bit of bad conscience about deep down being individually very selfish while playing a team sport, my main regret about my playing days is the brutal and often illegal physical punishment I dished out. If I could, I'd take back those occasional rushes of blood. Maybe at the time it was considered part and parcel of the game – and it would be easy to pass it off accordingly – but when you impose the football moralities of the 21st century on football in the 1970s, it paints some unpleasant pictures.

That later-in-life soul-searching aside, my life in football has largely been very good to me, both in personal and team achievement senses. Grand final day at the MCG has provided many euphoric moments, irreplaceable memories and the highest of highs: seven grand finals as a player and four premierships; five grand finals as a coach and four premierships.

Being part of premierships with three different clubs has been a great privilege, but the price is a split allegiance that means I don't barrack specifically for any one club.

Individually, there's no denying I would have loved to win a Brownlow Medal, because it's the AFL's official best player award, but I received plenty of individual recognition and plaudits – though never enough to be completely satisfied. I remember making a comment a few years ago about retiring Brisbane champion Michael Voss that also applied to me, that we both had an 'achievement hole' within that no amount of success can ever fill. That still applies to Vossy, I'm sure, but at this stage of my life I'm more into smelling the roses than riding the emotional roller coaster that is part and parcel of top-level AFL footy.

My media work with Channel Seven and 3AW is well enough paid, but I'm now very much working at my hobby, because I still love going to the footy. Getting paid to talk about it without the stress and worry of winning and losing at the end of the match is no chore at all.

The evolution of the game is never-ending and while the on-field spectacle has changed enormously since my first game back in 1969, physical contact team sport at the elite level must be the closest thing there is to civilian war. Maybe that is just a personal view from a footy warrior of yesteryear, but I think not. I'm convinced that a successful footy team needs the same fabric of trust, respect and role-playing discipline as an army would going into battle.

As I reflect on 37 years at the front, and a further seven years in the media, it has left me with a string of beliefs and principles that I believe are paramount in the make-up of successful sportsmen and sporting teams. This book will explore these key characteristics, such as leadership, motivation, communication and teamwork, and identify key lessons I've learned in each area that are fundamental to success.

One thing I certainly believe is the old chestnut that 'the harder you work, the luckier you get'. But I also believe there is good and bad fortune which will help or hinder things along the way. For example, in my 17 years as a player at Hawthorn we had only three coaches: John Kennedy, David Parkin and Allan Jeans, all outstanding Hall of Fame coaches. I'm so grateful to have had the benefit of their vast knowledge and teachings.

While clearly nobody can control random good and bad fortune, there are always a number of factors you can control by maximising performance through thorough preparation. One of my favourite Allan Jeans quotes is that 'Success is where opportunity meets preparation.' You can't always control opportunity, but you can control your own preparation.

I remember many years ago hearing a presentation from Debbie Flintoff-King, the Australian gold medallist who won the 400 metres hurdles at the 1988 Seoul Olympics. She told how she took a suitcase of food to the Games. Now, if anecdotal evidence is at all reliable, the food hall at any Olympics will serve any and every food imaginable, but Debbie's attitude was simply not to take any chances: she chose to take control of the situation and took with her all her essential nutritional requirements.

For me, the most essential articles in a footballer's arsenal on match day are his football boots. Uncomfortable footwear will always spell disaster for any competitor in a running athletic sport. While every AFL club has a boot-studder who's responsible for bringing the players' boots to the game, I wasn't prepared to risk even the remote possibility that something might go astray. I always took my boots home after our final training session and took them with me to the match.

Ultimately, football is about playing. It's about the people who put on the show – the players who put mind and body on the line whenever they run onto the field, whenever they cross the white line that separates the doers from the watchers.

Coaches are not remembered in the same way as the players and neither should they be, because nobody sees what they do. The only visible part of the coaching job is the press conference and, believe me, talking a good game is far easier than coaching one. As soon as one coach finishes and is replaced, there is no video highlights package to remind fans of his work. No, the coaching role is very much: 'The King is dead, long live the King.'

As a player, at least you generally have control over your own performance and all that goes with it. From the moment the ball is bounced, it is all about you and your team. You win or you lose as a group, and you share the emotions.

From siren to siren, a coach is largely a glorified spectator, even more so under the current interchange frenzy where the positioning of the 36 players is changing every few seconds. The most valuable work is done in the months, weeks and days leading up to the contest. Win or lose, generally speaking, as soon as one game finishes his mind will immediately turn to the next challenge. Most wins bring a feeling more of relief, or at best satisfaction, rather than any sense of extreme joy.

In the 461 games I coached, I only experienced that rare but addictive exhilaration experience at the final siren perhaps one out of 10 games – maybe 40 times altogether. Aside from premierships and special occasions, it was business as usual. It was about next week. Where can we learn from the game? What can we do better next time? If we won, the players had done it, but if we lost you felt and accepted total blame for the team performance. I guess in politics they call it ministerial responsibility.

In 2001–2004, when the Brisbane Lions played in four consecutive grand finals, strangely the most vivid memory of those years was the final 'alone-time' in my room at the team's Parkview Hotel on St Kilda Road waiting to get on the team bus and head to the MCG.

Ninety-five per cent of the coaching job was done. I would have loved it if there had been a supreme Coaching God to check in with: Had I said enough? Had I said too much? Was there anything that needed doing?

No coach ever knows the exact answers to those questions, which always leaves the nagging uncertainty. Hardest of all for the coaching control freak is that, on the biggest day of all – the one day of the year when a premiership was up for grabs – control would, as normal, shortly be handed to the players. When the game started, it would be the players' performance that would determine the outcome and the incredibly emotional peak or trough that the result would bring.

As the waiting tension built and the gnawing knot in the pit of my stomach grew, I knew that six hours later there would be an absolute extreme of emotions – the ultimate exhilaration of winning a premiership, or the devastating depression of losing. I can tell you honestly that I wished I could have bypassed the next six hours of tension and gone straight to the post-game when, one way or another, the performance pressure would be over.

Yet at 11.30 am on grand final day in 2005, when the Lions had failed to qualify for the big game, my mind wandered back 12 months to that nervous and lonely wait to board the bus to have a crack at a premiership. And where did I want to be? Back in my hotel room at the Parkview, of course, living with that same uncomfortable knot in my stomach but never feeling more alive – every sense on edge and alert as the contest approached.

Sometimes what you hate about something, you also love. It's all about accepting the challenge and risking the depression of losing so that you might experience the exhilaration of victory.

That is the essence of competition.

1

IN THE BEGINNING

I remember once asking my dad what he'd give me if
I won five Brownlow Medals in a row. Suffice to say,
I never lacked ambition.

It has always intrigued me how and why we become what we are.

Embarking on writing this book has necessarily involved a lot of reminiscing about my formative years, and a type of cathartic self-counselling. The by-product of looking back into the 60 years of my life is a bit of a soul-search about that very subject. While we generally accept that it's a combination of nature (what we're born to be) and nurture (how our environment and experiences mould the end person), the percentage contribution of each has no definitive answer.

I guess the starting point to the nurture part must be our family background. Some people have a horrid childhood through no fault of their own and still survive and thrive into productive, well-adjusted adulthood. Others seem to have been born into good families but for one reason or another they still go astray.

Every individual has a unique story; this is mine. As a middle-aged grandfather looking back at my childhood, the belief that is reinforced from my experience is that being cared for and about is far more valuable than having wealthy parents.

I was a much better provider to my daughters, Tracey and Fiona, than my parents were for me and my two brothers, but a single-minded focus on my football career, particularly in the part-time era when training was an after-work activity, meant my girls tended to think that basically footy came first and family came second. Thinking back, and to my regret, they were probably right. However, even with my time over again I couldn't say I would have done it differently. Sometimes success has a very big price.

I'd describe my family's financial circumstances during my childhood as lower working class; certainly not on the poverty line, but we lived a pretty frugal existence. The school shoes might be re-soled next pay if we could afford it; until then the cardboard inner soles had to suffice and you hoped it didn't rain in the meantime.

That aside, my childhood in Langwarrin, a few kilometres from Frankston on Victoria's Mornington Peninsula, and my teenage years in Chelsea on Port Phillip Bay, a bit closer to Melbourne, were very normal and free of trauma. The Matthews family home in Centre Road, Langwarrin, now outer south-east suburban Melbourne but very much country during the 1950s, was where I spent the first 10 years of my life.

It was positively archaic by modern housing standards. Forget about dishwashers, computers, new-generation mobile phones. In 1952, when I was born, our little cement-sheet, two-bedroom home on a three-acre plot of land attached to my grandmother's dairy farm had no electricity, had only tank water – no running hot water – an outhouse toilet, wood stove, no phone and no TV.

With no electricity for refrigeration, the old ice chest with big blocks of ice delivered each day kept the food cool. These ice blocks were central to one of my very earliest memories. As a toddler one hot summer's day the temptation was too much so I climbed up on a chair and licked what seemed to me like a big cold Icy Pole. My tongue stuck to the frozen surface and naturally when I yanked it clear a bit of skin was pulled off my tongue, which then started to bleed.

When I think back to this painful childhood event, very early in my life I got to taste my own blood, discovered I didn't like it and just maybe decided that if someone was going to bleed, it wasn't going to be me!

We led a pretty carefree life, running around barefooted, and in my primary school days my biggest concern each summer was not stubbing a toe on the exposed tree roots that surrounded our house.

The radio was the only contact with the outside world, but we knew no better at the time, so we survived just fine.

I have no doubt that because of the many communications distractions that exist in modern life – multiple TV stations, the internet, Facebook, Twitter, every second kid with a mobile phone – the influence of the immediate family environment has been diluted compared to previous generations.

These modern gadgets didn't apply to the Matthews family growing up in country Langwarrin in the 1950s, when external influences were negligible. There was my dad, Ray, mum, Lorna, and the three boys. Russell was five years older than me and my brother Kelvin 20 months younger.

Mum and Dad gave all their sons heaps of love, care and, importantly, time, particularly later in our teenage years when sporting opportunity required parents to become voluntary taxi drivers; but I never remember them being at all goal-driven or particularly aspirational, certainly not in their middle-aged years. As parents, they were supportive and encouraging, but never crossed the line of being pushy or overbearing.

I don't think the drive and ambition that was part of me for as long as I can remember was inherited from my mother and father; I think the intense competitive urge that developed through my growing years came more from having a sibling rival and competitor in Kelvin.

While I was older, he was always more physically advanced for his age. For instance, I made up the numbers as a winger in the Victorian under-14 schoolboys team; in his year Kelvin was captain. Playing for Chelsea seniors as 16-year-olds – me in 1968 and Kel in 1970 – I did okay, but Kelvin won the club championship.

As we grew from toddlers to teenagers, we were of similar size and shape, so there was always someone not only to play kick-to-kick with but an opponent for some very physical backyard one-on-one, normally umpired by our elder brother, Russell. Russell tells me that even when we were very young our backyard footy ground at Langwarrin was quite a battleground, because Kel and I never wanted to play kick-to-kick, always preferring the hurly-burly of a match. As umpire, he would crack it with us for not playing by his rules during our often fierce battles.

It was not something that I was aware of at the time, but the subconscious rivalry and competition with Kelvin when we were youngsters was invaluable in developing a strong will to win and the relish of physical contact. Having coached twin brothers Chris and Brad Scott, I suspect they too benefited from having this combined playmate and rival in the same household.

The common denominator in the Matthews household was a love of sport, particularly football. It's a sad reality that we only ever remember our parents from middle age onwards. From that time, Mum and Dad really only shared the same house and there was not much affection in their relationship. I often say only half-jokingly that they liked footy more than they liked each other. Family and sport were their common interests.

As personalities, Dad was friendly, non-confrontational and out-going while Mum was a reserved homebody, so Dad spent a lot of time going to events alone. I'm not sure if that worried Dad much, because he would just strike up a conversation with whoever hap-pened to be sitting or standing nearby.

My mum was a conservative pessimist, a glass-half-empty type of person. I think this is a quality that I inherited from her. In sport, at least Dad got out and had a go, which despite the conservatism from my mother was something that I took from him. Mostly I accepted the challenge of having a go, although the fear of failure bred into me from my mum was my main motivation to succeed.

Footy was in my blood for as long as I remember and there was never a time when I didn't want to play it at the top level. I just always did. And not just as any old footballer. As a kid, I wanted to be the best footballer there ever was. I remember once asking my dad what he'd give me if I won five Brownlow Medals in a row. Suffice to say, I never lacked ambition.

What I did have was a family in which football played a gigan-tic role. My father, Ray, was a useful country player who played at senior level for Langwarrin in the Nepean League and Frankston in the Mornington Peninsula League. He was no star, but he under-stood the game and he captain-coached Langwarrin and coached the Frankston under-19s.

Dad didn't barrack for any particular VFL club but my mother, Lorna, grew up in Essendon and was a very keen Bombers fan. I grew up barracking for North Melbourne, because they wore the vertical royal blue and white stripes of the Langwarrin footy club. Russell and Kelvin inherited Mum's affection for the red and black.

For most of his working life, Dad was a linesman with the old PMG, the forerunner to Telstra. He served in the Australian Air Force in Papua New Guinea during the Second World War, involved with the engineers corps building airstrips around Port Moresby. It wasn't long after he returned from the war that he was married and began a family.

My father died in 1999 and when we went through Port Moresby to walk the Kokoda Track with the Brisbane Lions in 2005, I wished I had talked to him about the time he spent there 60 years ago as a young man. I'm embarrassed and regretful to say that I never had those conversations when he was alive. It's a lesson for us all to find out about our parents' early life before they're gone.

One thing we never lacked was attention. We were always loved and always cared for in a way that made us feel special. We were fortunate when it came to things that mattered. Where Mum and Dad were concerned, Russell, Kelvin and I were always top of the list.

During the school week, the Matthews boys would ride their bikes about five kilometres to Langwarrin Primary School, a bit of a hazardous journey in the spring, when dive-bombing magpies would use us for target practice. It was a small school, with four classrooms and four teachers. There were always a couple of years grouped together, depending on numbers. While I wasn't a bad student, my favourite times were before school, at lunchtime, and after school when we could kick the footy or practise our cricket.

On Saturdays in football season the whole family would pack up and go off to watch Langwarrin or the nearby Frankston. Kelvin and I would take a passing interest in what was going on out in the middle while counting down the minutes to half-time, when we could get out and have a kick ourselves. Once or twice a year, Mum and Dad would take us to the MCG to watch the then VFL.

It was Melbourne's home ground, so they were always one of the teams. The 1960s was still the era of black and white TV, so after watching the colourless television replays I was most surprised one time when Collingwood were playing to discover that Des Tuddenham had ginger-coloured hair.

In our plentiful spare time, because there was not a lot going on in Centre Road, Langwarrin, we spent countless hours kicking a football in winter and playing cricket in summer. A fortunate by-product of living on acreage was that there was a lot of open space for footy, with trees for goalposts which could double as cricket wickets as required. We had to make our own fun, because there was rarely anyone else around – no next-door neighbours, no corner shop within walking distance and the closest shopping centre was at Frankston, a 15-minute drive away.

There were family farms dotted along Centre Road, but none within a few hundred metres and no other boys around our age. The Matthews dairy farm owned by my grandmother was about a kilometre away and if we were really bored we could wander down and watch my Uncle Trevor milk the cows.

So was born a fear of boredom that would stay with me throughout my life. I hated the prospect of having nothing to do. So football and cricket it was. All you needed to occupy your time in a worthwhile manner was another person, and the three Matthews brothers all had a love of sport. Hour after hour we'd play footy, or in summer our own version of Test cricket.

After work, Dad would get involved too, firing bullet-like stab passes at us from about 10 metres as we'd try to mark it. The old footy turned sandy-coloured and rounded with age. It's a great memory. I can still feel the thud of the ball on my chest. I played the odd inter-school game of football in my early years at Langwarrin primary school, but there was no organised under-aged club football back in those days.

Then came the big move. It seemed like the end of the world at the time. In 1962, late in my fifth-grade year at school, the Matthews family paid the princely sum of £3500 for a new home in Glenbrook Avenue, Chelsea. Chelsea was closer to Dad's work and my parents thought moving into suburbia would afford their boys better opportunities as they grew up.

Funny what you remember as a kid. On my first day at Chelsea Primary School, Kelvin and I sat together in the playground at lunch-time crying, because we didn't want to leave Langwarrin. It was what we knew and what we were comfortable with. Again, it was an early pointer to my adult personality. I was naturally conservative. I liked my comfort zone, liked being in control, and didn't particularly relish change.

The Chelsea house seemed like luxury compared to Langwarrin, but it wasn't all that different – still cement-sheet walls, only two bedrooms but with a bungalow out the back, a small kitchen, dining room and living room, and a small laundry. We were very fortunate a couple of years later when we got internal plumbing and could do away with the backyard toilet.

What we did have was a terrific thickly grassed backyard footy ground about 15 metres long by about 10 metres wide. On one wing was the weatherboard bungalow and on the other the paling timber fence adjoining the neighbouring property; the back of our house hemmed in one end, while the outhouse surrounded by a six-feet-high hedge was at the opposite end. Goals were the gap between the house and the fence at one end and the space between the bungalow and outhouse at the other.

The bungalow had an outside light globe, which gave us the opportunity to play night footy as well, although regular stray footies meant that the solitary globe needed replacing every second week.

Boy, did Kelvin and I go at it in our personal backyard battle-space! It was a perfect venue for fair dinkum matches in those few years late in my primary school days. We used the timber fence like a wrestler would the wrestling ring ropes. The ageing timber structure had a fair bit of give in it and we learnt that, if you go into contact hard, you can bounce off it and back into play very quickly. It was an early lesson that stood us in good stead when flesh and blood opponents replaced that rickety side fence.

The move to Chelsea meant we enjoyed a big change in lifestyle. There was no more isolation; we had playmates everywhere. The Williams family, with four children, lived on one side of us – Sue, Julie, Paul and Shane (who coincidentally became the head trainer at the

Brisbane Lions during the 1990s). Michael and Peter Luff lived on the other side. Glenbrook Avenue had a street full of youngsters. It was not unusual to have a couple of dozen kids wanting to play when we'd put the rubbish bin out on the road for a Test match, or get out the plastic footy for kick-to-kick.

Not that we didn't have a good leather football. As was always the case, Mum and Dad made sure we had the important things. But you didn't kick the leather footy on the bitumen, because there was no new one each year. That was reserved for the grass in the backyard, or the nearest oval.

As a cricketer, I was a batsman/wicketkeeper but not nearly as good as Kelvin, who was a batsman/bowler. We played in the same Chelsea under-14 team and he was captain, even though he was two years younger. We played on matting and if you made a 50 you'd receive a cap. I never got one. I once got to 45 and Dad made me retire. There was occasional tough love in our household.

Dad was a keen bike-rider in his youth, and our other occasional Saturday night treat was an outing to the long-defunct Melbourne Velodrome at Olympic Park, now the home of the Melbourne Storm rugby league team. I can still hear the clatter of the bikes on the board track. I loved watching Australian great Sid Patterson compete against international visitors in the sprint races.

We learn lessons in our youth all the time. Whether we know it at the time or not, many of these events affect our thinking and attitudes. In Year 6 at Chelsea Primary School, I ended up being captain of the school, the cricket team, the football team and the athletics team. At the school presentation one lunchtime, I got given a certificate for each of those four roles. When we went back to our classroom, in a display of being a smartarse kid, I spread the certificates vainly across the top of my desk.

My teacher, Mr Fred LeDeux, who had played a few games with Geelong footy club in the 1950s, seeing what I was doing, sarcastically and embarrassingly began to call me Cappy. The lesson has stayed with me: there is never any excuse for big-headedness, showing off or getting too carried away with yourself. None of the other kids ever called me Cappy, but Mr LeDeux continued to use it as a friendly reminder that humility is important. I thank him for emphasising that lesson, which has stuck in my mind ever since.

I was 12 when I played my first full season of club football with the Chelsea under-15s. It was a new team. Until that year, the youngest level of organised competition on the Mornington Peninsula had been the under-17s, so the timing couldn't have been better for me. We wore Geelong colours and I was just the little kid playing on the wing, relishing the chance to put into practice the countless hours I'd spent in kick-to-kick and backyard one-on-one with Kelvin.

Captain of the Chelsea under-15s was Glenn Murphy, whose girlfriend at the time was our next-door neighbour Julie Williams; so that was the moment my junior footy began with the Chelsea Football Club – if it hadn't been for getting to know Glenn, I might have joined the Luffs, who played at the neighbouring Bonbeach Footy Club.

We won the premiership that year, but late in the grand final I got belted by an opponent and finished the game being carried off on my team-mates' shoulders a sobbing mess. Amazing how the last grand final I played in, over 20 years later in 1985, I was again a sobbing mess – for vastly different reasons – as a retiring 33-year-old veteran.

That game as a 12-year-old might have been the basis of my long-held belief that if there is a choice between hitter or hittee, being a hitter wins every time!

The following year, a few of us Chelsea kids decided to try out for the Mornington Peninsula under-15 schoolboys' team. After the first trial game, the coach read out the list of players who were still in contention. My name was not on the list, but my mate Robert Judd, who came down with us, was.

Robert was getting instructions for the next training session and I was standing next to him, waiting for us to go home, when the coach saw me and said, 'Oh, young Matthews, you can come back next week as well.' The disappointment of rejection was suddenly replaced with the thrill of still being in contention.

I ended up making the peninsula squad and from those state championships was selected in the under-14 schoolboys Victorian team that year. If I hadn't been in the right spot at the right time, that opportunity to get a junior Big V jumper would never have eventuated – an early example that, whether we like it or not, random and uncontrollable good or bad fortune will intervene in our lives to a much greater extent than we'd like to believe.

We travelled to Canberra, where I was billeted with the Rutter family. On the last Saturday, we played Western Australia in the grand final at Manuka Oval on a day I'll never forget – and, happily, would never replicate. It had snowed heavily on the Friday night and when we arrived at the ground it was six inches deep in snow. Just to get a result, we played four five-minute quarters of the most bizarre football I can remember. And somehow we won.

Twelve months later, although still eligible for the same Victorian side because the age bracket was increased to under-15s, I missed out on selection.

2

FROM CHELSEA TO GLENFERRIE

*Going from under-15s straight to the VFL was like jumping
the Grand Canyon.*

The reality of my first training session at Hawthorn on that hot
summer day in the middle of January 1968 was vastly different from
the fantasy I used to have as an impressionable youngster dreaming
of playing VFL footy.

Each club had its own suburban ground back then and there was
nothing more suburban than the Hawks' headquarters. The MCG it
was not. The oval was squashed in between the railway line on one
wing, Linda Crescent lined with houses on the other wing and the
Glenferrie Road shops immediately behind the eastern end goals. At
the opposite end was a relatively modern concrete grandstand, but the
striking feature of the ground was the main grandstand, which was
constructed with vivid red house bricks. I don't think I have ever seen
anything similar and it looked very old even back then.

Underneath the big red stand were the dressing rooms. From the
dirt car park at the back, big double doors led into the spacious cavity
that doubled as the warm-up room, small weights area and overflow dressing section, with hanging pegs around the wall. There was
nothing big-time about my first look inside the Hawthorn footy club;
while bigger, the rooms were no more flash than those at Chelsea.

It was only when none of the faces looked familiar, none of the
household names were anywhere to be seen – no Peter Hudson, no
David Parkin, no Bob Keddie, no Peter Crimmins – that I realised
the senior established players had their own locker room positioned

at the end of a forbidding-looking corridor. Getting an invitation to summer training was one thing, joining the big boys was obviously another thing completely.

Talk about a fish out of water. The previous season I had captained the Chelsea under-15s and here I was walking into Hawthorn's Glenferrie Oval with the 40 or so senior squad from the season before, most of whom I had only ever seen on TV, and 50-odd young hopefuls who had received that momentous letter inviting them to try out with the Hawks.

Be there at 5 pm on Monday, 10 January (there was no pre-Christmas training back then), and bring your training gear – that was about the extent of the information provided. It didn't matter to me; that's all I needed. Opening that invitation to train with a league club was just the most incredibly exciting time. The sobering fact that I was only an average-sized 15-year-old going to train with a senior VFL club didn't seem to register, so any thought that I was too young to go was quickly dismissed.

My lift from Chelsea to Hawthorn was courtesy of Mr Anstey, the father of Noel Anstey, another invitee who lived in Frankston. Although I can't remember the connection, the Ansteys were kind enough to pick me up on the way through. The plan was to have a meal at the Hawthorn social club after training, which seemed in keeping with my idea of a new talent being suitably feted by the eager recruiter.

Training that first night was essentially circle work, with about 80 players chasing a handful of footballs, nothing like the one football to two players ratio of recent decades at AFL club training. Needless to say, I didn't get leather poisoning that night. A bit of running to finish the session, a quick shower, and over Linda Crescent to the Hawthorn social club and that much-anticipated free meal. The glamour and romance that I had built up in my mind, the fulfilling of a lifelong dream to play league footy with all its associated perks, was suddenly put on hold that evening when I discovered that this was no freebie. We had to pay for ourselves.

The realisation came to me – after my one and only training session at Hawthorn in 1968 – that this young teenager was nowhere near ready to be a VFL senior player. Back to Chelsea I went until I grew up a bit more.

There must have been many other completely unready youngsters turning up at training sessions all over Melbourne in that period, because this was when the zoning system was in place. Introduced in 1967, it involved the whole of Victoria being split into areas assigned to individual VFL clubs who all fielded seniors, reserves and under-19 teams. In the late 1960s, it was not like the modern era of selective drafting, when only a dozen or so new draftees and rookies will come into the AFL team's initial training squad. Back then, it was more a scatter-gun approach and any young player in the zone area who was showing promise would at least get an invitation to summer training.

Fortunately, 12 months later I was back for the start of what ended up being a 17-year career in the brown and gold, although getting into the senior players' dressing-room came only towards the end of that first season, when I broke into the first 18. It seemed quite a step forward at the time. The concept of achievement and success can come in many forms and often starts with baby steps.

It was an important year for me back at Chelsea, because I moved on from under-age football and into the senior team, playing against men. Amazingly, in the modern era the well organised and lavishly funded AFL elite development programs churn out 18-year-old draftees who have mostly never played against adults. No wonder the draft system remains an art rather than a science.

Going back to Glenferrie Oval the following January, I was still only 16 but the jump from Chelsea seniors to Hawthorn's training squad was manageable. Going from under-15s straight to the VFL was like jumping the Grand Canyon.

It's always a conundrum about whether to play the highest standard possible as a developing junior or whether the struggle to compete above your level has an ongoing negative effect on confidence and belief. Like most things in sport, it depends on the individual. There's no definitive answer, but from my observations I'd say the strong will survive and be strengthened by struggle, whereas the weak may shrink under too much pressure.

I had played three seasons with the Chelsea under-15s and going into 1967 was still eligible to play a fourth season at that level, when the under-17s coach Tom Gray asked me to join his team, so the family and I had a choice to make.

Mum and Dad were fine with moving me up an age group, but I had reservations. The year before, I had gone through an enormous growth spurt. At least I grew the 10–15 centimetres to become average height for my age, when I had always been quite small, but the growing pains and aching thighs had made it a tough footy year for me.

That bad season and being sick of being the little kid in the team led me to decide to stick with the under-15s. It was nice to be the bigger fish in a smaller pond for that one season. It was a fun, confidence-building footy year. I played centre half-forward, was captain, won the competition best and fairest, and we won the premiership.

I'm sure Tom Gray thought I didn't like him, because the following season it was time to be fully tested again and I went straight from the under-15s to the Chelsea senior team. Playing that season against men was challenging and more than once I felt out of my depth with the physical aggression the odd opponent decided to apply.

At Hastings one day, my opponent Robert Mayes, who was only a year or two older, was threatening all types of violent retribution if I got another kick. Nothing untoward occurred and I survived to live another day, but it was one of the few times I've felt uncomfortable on a football field. The fact that it sticks in my mind so many years later underlines it was a pivotal moment in my attitude to playing footy – that you can never allow an opponent the emotional ascendancy and that being the victim was not for me.

I'm sure the experience of mostly playing above my age as a teenager and being smaller and lighter than most opponents was also a very good development tool for me, because it taught me that momentum was about weight multiplied by speed. Even as a lightweight, if you attacked the contest at top speed it maximised your chances of holding your position and coming out with the football – or, if necessary, knocking an opponent out of the way.

While I'd gone to Hawthorn intending to stay, I still had to make the final list selected in March, and there was one last game I was scheduled to play with Chelsea. It was a pre-season promotional practice match organised between the previous year's Victorian Football Association premiers Dandenong and the Mornington Peninsula League premiers Chelsea.

The VFA competition was played on Sundays (all VFL games were on the Saturday), with the main match televised by Channel 10. Many of its players became very well known, and it was a much higher standard league than the MPFL. Still, back to Chelsea to play with my mates I went, fully aware that we probably had a thrashing coming. While the big defeat predictably occurred, another pivotal moment in the game was a personal turning point for me.

Dandenong's team included a big fireman carrying the tag of 'Big Jim' McNamara, who had quite a well-earned tough-man reputation. At one point during the game, he was playing the ball along the boundary line in front of the dressing-rooms wing and I happened to be coming towards the play from the centre square direction. While Big Jim must have weighed around 100 kilograms and I was only about 75, the opportunity was presented for a heavy bump and I took it. Armed with the element of surprise – I'm sure he didn't see me coming – I barrelled into him at top speed and my momentum knocked him off his feet and sent him sprawling over the boundary line into the interchange area.

This act of physical bravado against the opposition enforcer made me quite a hero with my Chelsea mates and added to my growing belief that attacking the contest at top speed is critically important, and that in footy the meek do not inherit the earth.

3

GROWING UP FAST

Hawthorn were well in front and my main recollection was being in a kind of nervy haze wandering onto the field – more akin to being in a dream than a real game of footy.

Walking into Hawthorn training in January 1969 was very different from the fleeting visit of 12 months earlier; for one thing, a season with Chelsea seniors playing against men was a big progression from junior footy. Although I desperately hoped it would be the beginning of a successful career, my initial challenge was simply to make the Hawks' final training list, which would be selected in March. While still a 16-year-old teenager about to start my Year 12 schooling at Bonbeach High School, over the previous year I had become something of the feted recruit, more in line with my boyhood dreams and the picturesque, suburban Glenferrie Oval setting was no longer a totally foreign destination for me.

I'd done that one night's training the January before, had played a trial practice match there during the mid-year school holidays in 1968 and later in the season the family and I were invited as special guests to watch Hawthorn play Richmond.

It was a memorable day being around the match-day inner sanctum of a VFL club for the first time. It was made even more so by Hawthorn's surprising selection decision to pluck 18-year-old schoolboy Kevin Heath straight from Assumption College to make his VFL debut. That the first-gamer lined up at centre half-back against the great Richmond centre half-forward Royce Hart was even more remarkable, even given that back then the gap between the elite VFL level and the lower grades was not as gigantic a chasm as it is today.

By modern standards, it would be like picking a schoolboy to play his first game on Jonathan Brown – talk about giving the kid an impossible task – but he performed quite well in a beaten side to get a game the following week. This began a fine career that included 140 games and the 1971 premiership at Hawthorn and 78 games with Carlton.

In the January leading into the 1969 season, the Hawks had taken only two recruits – me and a young ruckman from Carrum by the name of Ron Stubbs – on their pre-season training trip to Sydney, where we stayed at the Star Hotel on famous Bondi Beach. Still 16, for me it was quite an intimidating experience being around the established players I'd only ever seen on television replays and hadn't met before. They were all friendly, but I'm sure they must have wondered why they'd been lumbered with this young kid plonked into their group. It might not have had the glamour of the modern Collingwood-to-Arizona type overseas excursions, but around Chelsea and the Matthews household the Bondi trip was a very big deal at the time.

Still, while not a complete stranger, walking into Glenferrie Oval for the first group training session of 1969 was a pretty nerve-racking experience. Only a handful of the many hopeful recruits would earn a spot on the senior list and despite my reasonable senior season at Chelsea the year before, I wasn't exactly brimming with confidence.

That apprehension of starting at the bottom was reinforced when I was again directed to the large overflow warm-up area to get changed for training. The senior players' more private locker room was still out of bounds.

Also in this large secondary dressing area were probably 40–50 other young zone players, and among them was a tall, blond-haired, athletic-looking kid from Longwarry by the name of Peter Knights. It was the start of an incredible shared journey. We would start our footy careers at Hawthorn on the same night in 1969 and both end our playing days 17 years later on grand final day of 1985.

Very few youngsters of any era waltz into an elite football club without feeling a large dose of insecurity, and that was certainly my emotional state. It's like going to secondary school from primary school, where you start at the very bottom of the status-and-experience ladder, and from there have to work your way up.

I guess the attitude of never expecting and never assuming was part of my personality, even back then as a raw teenager. I'd never take anything for granted and the fear of failure was always lingering in the background.

Getting to training from Chelsea was a practical issue in itself. It was about an hour's drive from Glenferrie Oval and I was way too young to have a driver's licence, let alone a car. This was where my former Chelsea team-mate and first under-15s captain, Glenn Murphy, came into the picture. He'd made his debut for Hawthorn in 1968 and had offered to give me a lift.

We change a lot over our life's journey, but even as a teenager I didn't like the feeling of being out of control. I hated having to rely on someone else to get me to training. Every Tuesday and Thursday afternoon I'd wait for Glenn, worried he'd forget me, or would be delayed in his job as a painter, which would happen quite often. It was an early symptom of the control freak that I would become – even more so in my coaching life a couple of decades later.

The biggest names at Hawthorn in 1969 were undoubtedly senior coach John Kennedy, captain David Parkin, vice-captain Rod Olsson, rover Peter Crimmins and half-forward Bob Keddie. The marquee player was champion full-forward Peter Hudson, who had kicked 125 goals the season before.

Apart from normal training leading into the intra-club practice games in March, there was one notable diversion. Training camps around footy clubs have been many and varied over the years. That first pre-season Hawthorn went to the Portsea training venue run by Percy Cerutty, best known as coach of the unbeaten mile runner and Rome Olympics gold-medallist, Herb Elliott.

Vice-captain Rod Olsson picked me up from Chelsea on the way through and, while I quickly learned that what happens on trip stays on trip, I don't mind saying I was surprised to learn quite a few of the senior players had stopped in at the Portsea hotel for a few drinks before making their way to camp. It's funny how some things stick in your mind. I can still remember being most impressed that Rod could taste the difference between Courage beer and the Carlton and United brand. The inedible breakfast surprise served up at the Cerutty camp the following morning of muesli to be eaten dry without milk was not such a good memory!

Running up the infamous Portsea sandhills was very tough, but the unforgettable highlight was Cerutty's, for want of a better word, 'lecture'. I was a kid who accepted authority and was eager to learn, but I have to say that to describe Percy as eccentric would be a compliment. To this day, I'm not sure what Percy was talking about during his address, which was delivered in a small horse-paddock-type area adjacent to his Portsea home. We were seated around the edge, while he galloped around showing us how to express a throaty grunt, which he said would release the tension in our bodies. It was impossible to take him seriously, and not laughing out loud was the greatest challenge.

That athletes make coaches is truer than vice-versa. I suspect the great Herb Elliott would have made any coach look good.

The pre-season came and went without incident, I started Year 12 at school and achieved that first big step of making the Hawthorn senior list, which meant financially, if I played reserves all year, I would earn around $200 for the season. To put that in context: when I started work as a trainee cadet with Dunlop Automotive 12 months later, I earned $32 per week.

Footballers didn't play for the money back then; it was only a few dollars on top of a normal job, so the challenge and pressure of footy being both your passion and livelihood that exists for the modern professional player was not in play for the part-timers of generations past.

You always remember your first game quite vividly. My first in a Hawthorn jumper was playing on the wing in the reserves curtain-raiser against Collingwood in round one of 1969 at Glenferrie Oval. It was certainly not a burst-onto-the-scene moment, and the challenge of getting into the senior team wasn't going to be easily achieved.

I played the next couple of months in the reserves and was going okay, but my White Diamond football boots were giving me bad blisters on my heels, which meant painful second halves during matches and limited training weeks to let the blistered skin recover between games. Whatever protective taping I tried, nothing was helping.

One Friday I was in Frankston shopping centre when I spied a pair of three-striped, low-cut Adidas boots in the display window of the local Melbourne Sports Depot store. That was a critical moment for me, because when I went into the store and tried a pair on they fitted perfectly, and thereafter my blistered heels came good and were no longer a problem.

Almost bizarrely, a couple of years later I ended up being paid a significant fee to wear the Adidas footwear that had solved my heel blister issue and allowed me to run comfortably pain-free. It was like being paid to eat or breathe.

After a couple of months in the reserves, it came to round nine against St Kilda at Moorabbin, when during the second quarter an opposition player fell across my left knee as I kicked the footy. Down I went in a screaming heap. In many respects, footy has always been a game of seconds and inches, because if the cruciate ligaments had been damaged it would have been a quick end to a budding career.

Back in 1969, effective reconstruction surgery was like mobile phones – yet to be invented. While I was on crutches for a week, fortunately it was only my medial ligaments that had been damaged, and after six weeks off I was ready to play again. It was the worst injury and longest absence from playing that I'd suffer in my entire career. In the injury stakes the footy gods smiled on me.

After a couple of games in the reserves after the knee injury, in round 16 the big day came. The dream of getting my first senior game arrived when I was selected to play against Melbourne and, to add to the excitement, the venue was the MCG. The Hawks sat third on the 12-team ladder but the week before had lost narrowly to ninth-placed Footscray at Western Oval.

The teams were broadcast on Thursdays at 9 pm on the now-defunct 3DB radio station and being perched around the old box radio listening and hoping to hear your name as an 'in' had become the Thursday night ritual. When my name was announced, it was an unbelievable buzz. My first game! I can tell you, I slept very little that night.

There was even greater excitement when a photographer from *The Sun* newspaper came to my classroom at Bonbeach High the day before the game to take some shots of the fresh-faced Hawthorn first gamer. It was even more thrilling when the photo of this 17-year-old schoolboy was plastered across the front page of the paper. I reckon my extended family must have given the sales of *The Sun* a real boost that particular Saturday.

In those days, there was no special treatment for players included in the team, and no protecting a first-game youngster from the media. After all, VFL clubs of that time probably only had a full-time staff of one or two.

On Saturday, 26 July 1969, I made my VFL debut against the Demons. Having driven to the game with Mum, Dad and older brother Russell (Kelvin was playing with Chelsea), I walked nervously down into the old visitors' rooms, located under the grandstand at the Punt Road end.

The interchange system was not even a twinkle in Kevin Sheedy's eye back then. There were substitutes, a 19th and a 20th man – of which I was one, which meant I sat on the bench until the last 10 minutes of the game, eventually getting the call to go on and play forward pocket.

Hawthorn were well in front and my main recollection was being in a kind of nervy haze wandering onto the field – more akin to being in a dream than a real game of footy – when a long kick into the Hawks' attacking goal square at the Punt Road end fell off the pack straight into my hands. Without thinking, I spun around and snapped a goal.

That first goal didn't provoke the kind of reaction we'd see in today's footy. Team-mates enthusiastically swamping a youngster after he'd kicked his first goal wasn't yet in vogue; wild celebrations also weren't part of sport back then. It was a 'Well done' from those within earshot and then resume positions for the next centre bounce.

My joy after that first goal was quite mild anyway, but keeping my feelings inside was the way I played footy all through my career.

We won by 36 points. Peter Hudson kicked nine goals and Ross Dillon four for the Demons, who were entrenched at the bottom of the ladder.

Personally the net result of the day was quite dismal, as I'd sat on the bench all day, and had only one touch, despite it being a goal. However, playing that long-dreamt-about first game of top-level footy was the highlight of my life to that point.

It ended up being a memorable day for a totally different reason as well. After getting showered and changed, I joined my family waiting outside the rooms and headed home, where I met up with some of my Chelsea mates for a Saturday night out at the Southern Aurora Hotel in Dandenong. Actually, not for the first time, I broke the law that night because I indulged in a bit of under-aged drinking by having a few beers. Hotels checking that you were 18 and allowed to drink legally in licensed premises was haphazard at best in those days, so you took the chance and if you got kicked out, so be it.

Again, one of life's sliding-door moments intervened. I struck up a conversation with a girl I'd never met before by the name of Maureen Wooller, who not only lived in Chelsea but in Derby Parade, which happened to be the street next to the Matthews home in Glenbrook Avenue.

From that chance meeting at the Southern Aurora Hotel on the night after my first senior game, one thing led to another and we ended up getting married in the middle of the following year.

It was to be a period of great change. Before I'd left my teenage years I had, in chronological order, played that dreamt-about first game, got married, become a father, played for Victoria, played in a premiership team and won my first club championship.

Both personally and footy-wise these couple of years were a life-altering period in which I was forced to grow up fast. But I've never regretted being a young husband and father. In fact, the stability this provided would be a terrific aid to my football career.

4

A FIRST FLAG

*All a team can do up until grand final day is stay alive while,
one by one, others drop out of the race. Hawthorn's 1971
campaign taught me that most valuable of lessons.*

Three-quarter time in any close game provides a brief physical respite and a chance to mentally regroup before that one last burst to the final siren. At this late stage of the game, players are coping not only with the scoreboard situation but the baggage, either good or bad, of their performance to that point of the match.

My personality type meant I had a natural tendency to withdraw into myself to quietly summon up the forces to finish the game strongly; for me it was a short period of introspection. Even in this my first grand final – as a 19-year-old – that was the psychological mode I dropped into. Each player is a little different, but generally speaking it's hard to focus – minds are muddled and all over the place. When that short break leads into the one quarter in the season when a premiership will be decided, this distracted emotional state is exaggerated many-fold.

At three-quarter time in the 1971 grand final, in wet, miserable conditions, Hawthorn trailed St Kilda by 20 points. We were in big trouble. After dominating the season and finishing on top of the ladder with a 19–3 win–loss ratio, our flag ambitions were sinking fast. We were learning a football lesson the hard way: that while premierships can be lost during the season, they can be won only on grand final day.

Our problems didn't end on the scoreboard. We'd used our 19th and 20th men, and our number-one strike weapon, Peter Hudson, was concussed and had half his ear hanging off from a bad knock he received earlier in the game. Never did a 20-point deficit seem so big, and there was a feeling of pessimism as we gathered in the traditional huddle around our coach, John Kennedy.

Players can rarely remember in any detail the coach's instructions at the breaks in play, so while I can't recall his precise words, the message from the coach wasn't so much about how we were going to win but more about fight and dignity – to make sure we played the game out to the final siren. If we were going to lose, do it honourably; not to drop our bundle and let the margin really blow out.

However, as the players broke up, ruckman Don Scott pulled us back in and delivered his own message, which I can remember precisely. Refusing to accept what looked inevitable, his words were emphatic and graphic: 'What's he fucking talking about? We're going to win! Follow me!'

That was Scotty at his belligerent, bombastic best. Only 23, and playing in his 93rd AFL game, he had the most incredible never-say-die attitude, and such was the power of his character that he dragged others along with him. He point-blank refused to contemplate defeat, demonstrating a fighting spirit that would rear its head a couple of decades later in 1996 when he became the figurehead for the anti-merger campaign that enabled the Hawks to continue as a stand-alone club after almost joining forces with Melbourne.

As we headed out to our positions, that live-in-the-moment zone essential to any footballer meant that nothing but the game was occupying my thoughts. If some reflection had been allowed, I might have remembered having not been at the MCG the previous season but listening on the radio as Carlton came from 44 points down to overhaul Collingwood. What a difference a year can make.

With a quarter to go, a Hawthorn premiership was still possible, which was a huge progression from the situation 12 months earlier, when we'd finished a lowly eighth with only 10 wins, and on grand final day in 1970 we were already a month into our post-season break.

The improvement from 1970 to 1971 was massive for the Hawthorn football club and was mirrored by their 19-year-old second rover. For me it was a period of enormous change in my personal life, which I'm sure contributed hugely to a big lift in my playing performance.

After five games in my debut season in 1969, I'd played 16 senior games in 1970 but was always tuned in to the Thursday night team announcement, because I was certainly not an automatic selection. Going into my third year in 1971 still with only 21 games under my belt, there was little indication that I'd progress from a player battling to maintain a position in the senior team to not only playing twice for Victoria, but by year's end winning the Hawthorn club championship. It was a transformation that came quickly and unexpectedly.

Off the field, big changes were also in train. Before the 1971 season had even kicked off, on 3 February at Frankston hospital, my wife, Maureen, gave birth to our eldest daughter, Tracey.

Maureen and I were both teenagers who were growing up fast; we now had the responsibility of having our own little family. I can vividly remember going to pick up Maureen and Tracey when they were ready to leave the hospital a few days after the birth.

The head nurse walked us out to our car, a red EH Holden with the P plates still on mandatory display, which was a tell-tale sign of a very young driver. I had Tracey in the carry basket and, as we reached the car, I could see the nurse's worried look and could almost read her thoughts: 'Two kids with a baby – what chance has this poor little thing got?'

She looked me in the eye and said: 'Make sure you take good care of your daughter; you've got responsibilities now.' That concerned comment has stuck in my mind ever since. Maybe there has been an element in my subconscious determined to prove her misgivings wrong.

While still in my late teens, life changed from living the single social scene to the settled existence of having a wife and baby. No-one in their right mind would suggest teenagers should become parents, but for me becoming a very young husband, father and provider was a lifestyle change that helped my footy enormously.

Later in life when I became a coach, I was always pleased when my young players had a steady girlfriend and even happier if they got married and became fathers. Leaving behind the young bucks' lifestyle always seemed to help them mature and in turn helped their footy.

While my personal breakout year in 1971 came out of the blue, just as unpredictable was Hawthorn's climb from non-finalists the year before to the top of the ladder, with 19 wins and a fantastic percentage of 153.7.

Our great full-forward Peter Hudson had kicked 146 goals in 1970, so expecting better from him was unrealistic. The one boom recruit was centreman Robert Day, from South Australia.

What transpired was what usually sparks a hugely improved season: career-best years from the experienced core and the 40–80 games group, and a few next-generation youngsters who progress from their football apprenticeship to become valuable regulars. With the great benefit of hindsight, Hawthorn was a club coming through a period of great changes to its playing stocks, and the fruits from an extremely productive recruiting zone were coming into maturity.

If we use 80 games (usually five years at the club) as the experience cut-off point, entering the season there were only a handful in this category. Captain David Parkin (151 games), ruckman Ken Beck (125), half-forward Bob Keddie (92), wingman Des Meagher (90), centreman Ray Wilson (88) and rover Peter Crimmins (83) were the very experienced core and there was a group coming into their prime, of which Scottie and tough nuts Norm Bussell, Ian Bremner and Mick Porter were the most notable.

This was a very brutal era of footy and it was a great comfort for us young fellas to have these guys on our side. Even Peter Hudson had only 77 games under his belt, although he'd kicked a remarkable 391 goals over the previous three seasons.

Yet the biggest difference was the emerging next-generation bunch. For most of 1971, full-forward Hudson aside, our goal-to-goal line was a bunch of kids with only 20-odd games' experience going into the season. Fullback Kelvin Moore, centre half-back Peter Knights and centre half-forward Alan Martello all started the year as promising youngsters and graduated into terrific contributors and bona fide stars in a team that dominated the season.

Then there were the other second- and third-year players Leon Rice, Bruce Stevenson, Les Hawken and myself. This was a third of the team that was just starting out.

The end result was an unbelievable season. We won the opening five games, lost by six points to the Bulldogs at the Western Oval in round six and then won our next 11, to be 16–1 after round 17.

Then our domination waned; if the premiership had been played mid-season, we would have bolted in but, as footy teaches us over and over again, all a team can do up until grand final day is stay alive while, one by one, others drop out of the race. Hawthorn's 1971 campaign taught me that most valuable of lessons.

We lost a couple of our last five games and in the second semi fell in by two points against a fast-finishing St Kilda. Even that win was off the back of Huddo kicking seven of our 12 goals. The reliance on our champion goal-kicker as our form tailed off later in the season had become decidedly unhealthy. We knew it and our opponents knew it, which meant that, in the dog-eat-dog grand final to come, if you stopped Hudson you would probably stop Hawthorn.

We also suffered a major blow in the second semi when Peter Knights fell awkwardly after a marking contest and damaged his knee sufficiently to miss the premiership-decider.

In the old final-four system of that time, the top two played off, with the winner going to the grand final and the loser to the preliminary final. St Kilda beat Richmond easily in the preliminary, which set up the rematch.

Saints coach Allan Jeans had prepared his side for a real dogfight, and it was that and more. We'd led by one point at quarter-time but had been forced to replace an injured Les Hawken with 19th man Ken Beck after he'd injured his ankle. At half-time, we were two points behind and were down to 18 players after replacing a concussed Robert Day with 20th man Ray Wilson. Robbie was deemed to be in a marginally worse condition than Huddo, who had been flattened by St Kilda's Kevin 'Cowboy' Neale in the first quarter with a round-arm blow that split the right ear of our champion spearhead and briefly knocked him out.

Earlier in the week, Huddo had finished equal runner-up in the Brownlow Medal to Ian Stewart, who had become the fourth player to win the game's highest individual honour three times and the first to win it with different clubs – after switching from St Kilda to Richmond in sensational circumstances earlier in the year.

On grand final day, our gun goal-kicker was chasing his own piece of history, needing four goals to break the single-season record of 150 set by South Melbourne's Bob Pratt in 1934. The pair had spent much of grand final week together with the media, discussing a milestone which was hotly favoured if Huddo proved anything like true to form in the grand final. Only three times in 23 games that season had he kicked less than four goals, averaging 6.3 goals a game.

It wasn't to be. He got two early ones and a third shortly before half-time but he wasn't quite the same after his altercation with 'Cowboy' and was battling with double-vision. As legend has it, it might not have been entirely accidental. Word from the St Kilda camp – later to become a bit of footy folklore – was that when 'Yabby' Jeans had spoken to his playing group about how they would combat the Hawthorn champion, 'Cowboy' had mumbled from the back of the room something to the effect that 'He can't kick goals if he's unconscious.'

After a low-scoring four-goal-apiece opening half of brutal hand-to-hand combat footy, the old black and white footage clearly depicts an ordinary game for skill but a level of contact which would be regarded as shocking in the modern era. The Saints surged over four goals clear in the third term and our only goal for the quarter came just before the siren when Leon Rice slotted a difficult long-range snap. Importantly, it was the last goal before three-quarter time and got the margin back to 20 points.

It was time for a change. For probably the only time in his illustrious career, Huddo was shifted away from the goal square and our half-forward Bob Keddie was pushed into full-forward.

With the few words from John Kennedy, and Don Scott's defiant passion ringing in our ears, we got an important adrenalin rush as we resumed our positions. The challenge in this heightened emotional state was to still think clearly and get back to living in the moment. Any thoughts of projecting half an hour ahead would become a major distraction and had to be resisted. To maintain that short burst of energy-producing adrenalin, we needed something positive to happen. Otherwise, that slight up feeling quickly becomes an energy-sapping downer.

This is where words must be followed by strong actions and Scotty delivered both.

At the bounce to start the final quarter, Scotty charged in like a raging bull against St Kilda ruckman Brian Mynott and thumped the ball towards centre half-forward. In the following contest, I was awarded a free kick for holding the ball against my opponent, Wayne Judson. It was outside my normal drop punt range of 50 metres maximum, so to try and get the extra 10 metres required I was forced to unload with a hit-or-miss torpedo punt. For once, I hit it sweetly, the ball sailed through and we were away. The margin was suddenly a seemingly manageable 14 points.

We kicked three goals in five minutes, with Bob Keddie and Peter Crimmins following my long torpedo, and when Bob added a fourth at the 12-minute mark we'd hit the front. With Scotty dominating in the ruck, it was an epic final quarter. Bob added another goal, and then another after a controversial umpiring decision to disallow a goal to Huddo. The replacement full-forward had kicked four goals in 16 minutes in one of the great final-quarter performances in grand final history.

Scotty wasn't exactly a copybook kick, or a prolific goal-kicker, but he got in on the act with what even he described as a pure fluke. As he put it, he scrubbed a left-footer that bounced over the heads of a couple of players and then bounced a couple more times before going through.

The goal-kicking record was a subplot within the titanic struggle for the flag. Three times Huddo could have bettered it. Once he kicked into the man on the mark from only 15 metres out after fellow Tasmanian Barry Lawrence conned him as to where the mark actually was. Another time, he actually kicked the ball through for a 'goal' after receiving a Keddie handpass but it was called back because umpire Peter Sheales had called time-on. Then, late in the match, he raced into an open goal but kicked the ball out on the full. Fortunately, perhaps, he cannot remember anything much of the second half.

After kicking just five goals in the first three quarters, we posted seven unanswered goals in 20 minutes to get 19 points up. It was a 45-point turnaround, and not even two late St Kilda goals could stop us hanging on by seven points.

In any close game, the sound of the siren sparks extreme emotions and when the siren sounded with us in front to win the premiership, the feeling of joy was magnificent. The exhilaration and euphoria were overwhelming. I remember jumping into Peter Crimmins' arms and we gave each other an almighty bear hug. There is plenty of man-love around post-game for the premiership team.

Back then, it was traditional for the premiership cup to be presented in the grandstand. And so it was. But by the time captain David Parkin had returned to the playing arena for the traditional lap of honour with his team-mates, he'd done a little damage. During the game, Parko had injured the top knuckle on one of his fingers trying to tackle St Kilda's John Bonney. In those days, the shorts waistbands had metal buckles to enable you to tighten them and they could be quite dangerous. Parko received the cup without any problems, but just as he was about to re-enter the ground he caught the same finger on the edge of the cup and dropped it. As it crashed onto the concrete, it smashed the filigree work and it had to be rebuilt. It was a premiership cup nevertheless, and at 19, after just 43 senior games, I'd fulfilled a lifetime dream to win a premiership medal.

I remember vividly the post-game message from John Kennedy, telling us to think of what the team next door was going through and to be sure to behave with dignity and respect. It was a lesson well-learned.

Later, we had a team dinner at Isabella's in Russell Street before returning to Glenferrie Oval, where we were introduced with the cup to the Hawthorn supporters. On Sunday, the celebrations continued at the Baron of Beef in the Dandenongs, and on Monday we were entertained by the Mayor of Hawthorn at the Town Hall. Parko was made Lord Mayor for the day, with Crimmo appointed Town Clerk. They took a photo of the group in formal mayoral robes to begin a Hawthorn tradition which would continue for each premiership side. It was still going when they won their 10th flag in 2008.

The 1971 season had also been a real breakout one for me. To be selected for Victoria and to get that fantastic Big V jumper was a massive highlight. State football has largely disappeared as the national AFL competition has evolved, but every state should still pick their best team each year and award each player his own state guernsey.

My first game wearing the Big V was against South Australia at the MCG, with Tom Hafey as coach and Des Tuddenham as captain and we won comfortably. My second, against Western Australia later in the year, was one I'd happily forget, because I ended up the centre of attention for all the wrong reasons.

It involved an incident with Western Australia rover Barry Cable and was probably my first act of on-field brutality. Basically, I was running at top speed at the ball and was on a collision course with Cable, who was coming from the opposite direction. I took my eye off the ball, jumped over the footy and crunched him. Suffice to say I wasn't too popular with the Perth fans, and it would have earned me a fair suspension in the modern game.

The other by-product from the year was being tagged 'Lethal Leigh' by *Sun* newspaper columnist and Collingwood premiership captain Lou Richards. Boy, has that stuck!

Still, by the end of the 1971 season it seemed a long, long way back to the schoolboy who'd played only five games two seasons before. I now felt that I belonged in the side and could be a valuable contributor at the top level.

Being confident of your place in the team is the first step to playing consistently well. I've heard the theory that fighting for your position in the team is motivating and will keep you on your toes, but from my experience it's the exact opposite. While a constant reality for fringe players, uncertainty of selection makes players anxious and is a negative to getting their best performance.

Being entrenched in the team was good for my stress levels as well, because being nervously camped around the radio waiting for the Thursday night team selection became a thing of the past.

5

FIRST COACH, BIGGEST INFLUENCE

The Kennedy influence on his players and, in fact, his football club was a classic example of the truth that, to speak it with credibility, you must live it with conviction.

Football has undergone a multitude of changes over the 40-odd years since I played my first game for Hawthorn. One of the few remaining common denominators is the immense effect that the senior coach will have on the impressionable youngsters who come under his direction. Maybe that effect has been diluted a bit in modern full-time footy, where the senior coach is only one voice among the ever-increasing numbers on AFL coaching panels, but the boss is still the boss and remains the main individual influence.

When I joined Hawthorn as a raw, inexperienced teenage boy, the coach was the intimidating presence that was John Kennedy. Since finishing my club-level involvement and after time to reflect, I find myself having an increasing appreciation of just what extraordinary good fortune that was.

After some time around him, it became obvious that, despite the fearsome reputation, John was not the alpha male power leader who filled a room with his confidence and bravado. If anything, he was unassuming and maybe even a bit shy. He had a definite aura, but it came from an inner strength and disciplined self-control without any pretence of needing to be anything other than himself.

The Kennedy influence on his players and, in fact, his football club was a classic example of the truth that, to speak it with credibility, you must live it with conviction. Everything he ever asked of his players in a physical or emotional sense, his whole uncompromising attitude to football competitiveness and his team-first mantra, were not only words; they were integral to every fibre of his being.

No figure in the history of the game is more a father of his football club than John Kennedy has been to the modern Hawthorn.

It always seemed to me that the Kennedy football persona was honed by his experience during the period when the Hawks went from perennial losers to fierce and successful competitors. After entering the VFL in 1925, when John went to Hawthorn to play in 1950 the club had never been in the finals and was perennially anchored near the bottom of the ladder.

Nothing changed in the short term. In the 164 games that he played until retiring in 1959, the Hawks won only 59 times, so losing was the norm rather than the exception.

When you lose a lot, you tend either to give up or develop a determination to fight back and find a way to win, or at least never lose easily. For the John Kennedy who shaped his players' attitude to competition, it was certainly the latter.

Maybe the adversity of being part of a struggling team was the springboard for his incredible will to fight to the death, and the ever-present fear of losing meant complacency when we won was simply a foreign concept. This competitive spirit and a seemingly ego-less team-first philosophy was the way he lived his life and was gradually ingrained into the players he coached.

I must admit that as a young player I had a very individualistic drive to succeed, but under the John Kennedy example I felt guilty for feeling that way and embarrassed if that selfish attitude bubbled to the surface in my actions. Particularly in those early impressionable years when I went from being a teenage boy to a young man, I think this coaching influence was very important for me: to accept – albeit sometimes begrudgingly – that in a team sport, if the crunch comes the individual must always submit to the team cause.

After he took over the coaching job in 1960, 'Kennedy's Commandos', as they were known, won Hawthorn's first premiership in 1961, but after being runners-up to Geelong in 1963, the rest of the decade failed to produce another finals appearance.

In 1967, the zoning system was introduced where the whole of Victoria was split into areas and allocated to each of the 12 VFL teams. This system proved to be a godsend for Hawthorn in the years that followed. An extremely productive zone and the recruitment from Tasmania of a young full-forward by the name of Peter Hudson were the start of an inflow of talented players into the brown and gold guernsey. Importantly, the Hawks had John Kennedy to mould that talent into an effective, cohesive team.

I've often said, only half-jokingly, that what he taught us about footy could be written on the back of a postage stamp, but what he taught us about life and competition was priceless.

Having said that, John did have his tactical successes. When the great Peter Hudson arrived, it became obvious he was unbeatable in one-on-one contests, so that individual strength – added to playing in the crowded confines of the skinny Glenferrie Oval home ground – meant the other forwards were pushed up field to give him plenty of space to work his magic. The best tactic is always to exploit an existing competitive advantage, which John did with clearing the full-forward space for Hudson.

Particularly at centre bounces, there was a mass of players crowded around the contest, which was the catalyst for the introduction of the diamond that eventually became the centre square, which was restricted to four players from each team.

The search to find the next competitive advantage is never-ending, which led to a practice game played in the pre-season of 1973 against Glenelg at their home ground in Adelaide.

The centre diamond was being introduced and rather than play the normal six forwards, six midfielders, six defenders positioning, John decided to play no designated forwards, the mandatory four in the centre square, six players on each wing, with Peter Knights and Kevin Heath positioned as zoning defenders. It would be revolutionary today, let alone 40 years ago. I'm sure the Glenelg players and the few thousand spectators couldn't believe their eyes.

We heavily outnumbered the opposition around the contest, so we won first possession almost every time, and then the idea was to run and link up with handball to maintain possession of the footy. With no forwards to kick to, the by-product was a lot of long, running shots at goal, which resulted in an inaccurate 1.11 at quarter-time. The experiment was abandoned then and never repeated, but it taught me a lot about our natural fear of change.

Pushing players up field, congesting around the contest and often no-one in the forward half, looked a lot like the footy we see today. John was a tactical genius a few decades before his time!

Having won the Hawthorn club championship the previous two seasons playing as a forward pocket and second rover changing on-ball with Peter Crimmins, the thought of altering our traditional position structure and, more importantly, the role that was working very well for me was totally unappealing. In fact I was extremely miffed and negative about the whole idea.

Much later, in my coaching days, I often mentally referred to that Glenelg match experience. Change is always a bit scary, because it's going from the comfortable known to the uncomfortable unknown and if players are to commit to change – and change is inevitable – they must be sold on the potential value to both the team and, just as importantly, to the individuals themselves.

From my observations, leaders tend to be somewhere in between authoritarian at one extreme and collaborative at the other. When I was a 17-year-old embarking on my footy career, John Kennedy was only 41 but he seemed very old to me and was very much the authoritarian coach. He was a school principal by profession and a school principal in coaching style.

Training was only Tuesday and Thursday after work, or school for me in that first year, so players spent very little time at the club. Consequently, one-on-one communication was minimal and what he said to the team as a whole was the theory content of coaching in those bygone years. That authoritarian style wouldn't work in today's era, in which most players need a lot of TLC and anything remotely negative is taken to heart.

Back then, playing was simple. If the coach told you to do something, you did your best to do it. And if the coach yelled at you, you didn't like it but at the same time didn't take it too personally because he yelled at everyone.

However, it was not the John Kennedy style to rant and rave. While he always spoke with an eloquent passion and delivered with ear-splitting volume, the communication was minimal in words and strong in message.

My first experience with John – even in print I have trouble calling him by his Christian name, he was always Mr Kennedy to me – was at a nondescript trial game between two groups of schoolboys from Hawthorn's zone played at Glenferrie Oval in 1968, during the mid-year school holidays.

After the match, John addressed the teams and at one point he looked at me and said, 'Young Matthews, you didn't do so well today, but I've heard you have a bit of a cold.' I guess I was already a well-regarded future recruit and the comment was typical of the honesty-with-diplomacy Kennedy communication style. Deliver a put-down but not too cutting, not too personal and with a slight get-out.

He was a magnificent orator and in the 1960s and '70s, when pre-game planning was minimal and the emotional stimulation of the pre-game pep talk was still important, his Hawthorn players had the great benefit of regular stirring and inspirational addresses.

At training, John always wore his flea-bitten long-sleeved Hawthorn jumper from his playing days, perhaps even from as far back as the 1950s. Standing in the middle of Glenferrie Oval, he'd yell instructions in his big, booming voice. There was never a chance of players not hearing and in the coaching years that followed I used to regret my squeaky little voice, which by comparison was hard for players to hear if they were more than 30 metres away.

On match days, he'd wear that gabardine overcoat for which he became famous, and at home games he'd take up his position on the slightly elevated wing on the Linda Crescent side of the ground, just above where the 19th and 20th men would sit until they were called into the game. There was no such thing as a coach's box back then, or even a runner. He'd use the head trainer to deliver the occasional move, but if he desperately wanted to send out a message he'd just use that booming voice for which he was so well known.

Training under John never varied too much. We did a lot of circle work without opponents, and a lot of competitive match practice in pairs around the ground, usually in an anti-clockwise direction. As David Parkin, my first captain, used to say, John's idea of variation to a training drill was to do it in the opposite direction. Back then, coaching was a lot less about tactics and a lot more about getting the basics done well.

The Kennedy addresses were always strong, emotive and passionate. And yet, unlike most coaches, who'll occasionally toss in an expletive to make a point, he never swore. The old coaching chestnut of dropping in the f-word for ultimate emphasis was not him.

Believing strongly that less was usually more when it came to talking, he didn't waste his words and chose the few he said very carefully. One day after a game in which he wasn't especially pleased with the officials, he said something to the effect of: 'Normally, I can't comment on umpires ... Well, today I definitely can't comment on umpires.'

Many a comment from John Kennedy has gone down in football folklore. For instance, what he said to the Hawthorn players during the 1975 grand final: 'At least do something. Do. Don't think, don't hope, do! At least you can come off and say, "I did this, I shepherded, I played on. At least I did something."'

Sometimes the 'do something' comment had its backfires, like his instruction to ruckman Ken Beck one day when we played St Kilda down at Moorabbin. He told Ken that when an opposition player was taking a kick at goal and he was on the mark, he shouldn't just stand there, but do something unusual to try to put the opposition player off. So, when Carl Ditterich was lining up a shot at goal, Ken did a handstand and a cartwheel. Ditterich promptly ran around the man on the mark and kicked a goal from closer range but, as the coach said to Ken afterwards, at least he'd done something.

This wasn't the only time Ken did something unusual. After the 1971 premiership, we went to Perth to play the WAFL premiers. I was rooming with Ken and Peter Hudson and as we settled into our room, Ken pulled out a fruit cake his wife, Judy, had made for him to take on the trip and said: 'There's three of us and we're here for three nights, so I'll cut it into nine bits so we can have it for supper.' Not quite the typical wild premiership celebration people might have expected!

In the years that followed the Kennedy coaching career, even beyond his 80th birthday, whenever he took to the microphone it was always worth listening to, because he had such a great command of his audience.

However, playing under John did have its difficult times. Initially I was a disciple, but in my early 20s that all changed for a season or two. He just seemed so harsh and tough all the time and I had the odd nightmare where I told him where to go. Looking back on those years, that probably said more about me getting a bit full of myself than it did about him.

His players learned very early on that if you wanted to play under John Kennedy you had to commit to the team cause. There was no better example than the coach himself. He was a man of no ego. Never did he put himself ahead of the team.

I came to believe over time that individuals are in it for themselves, and that players don't sacrifice for the team without getting something in return. But under John I learned very early on that it's much easier to play well in a good team than it is in a struggling team, so it was smart to invest yourself in making the team better.

You don't have to play a lot of team sport to realise that it's much better to win than lose, and if you help the team to win, you receive the reward of shared team success and the reflected glory that follows. This was something he drummed into his players relentlessly, and was to underpin the very philosophy I adopted when it came to coaching.

The other absolute non-negotiable for John was that you had to be fierce in your attack on the ball. Habits were formed by the way you trained, so training was always very physical.

As I mentioned, before I got to Glenferrie Oval the Hawthorn teams were known as Kennedy's Commandos, because of the dawn pre-season commando-type training they did on the Yarra River at Bulleen in Melbourne's eastern suburbs. Rightly or wrongly, there was a belief that part of the reason the club had won the 1961 premiership was because they were much fitter than the opposition.

Even though things had changed a little by the time I arrived, there was always a very strong physical component to our training;

and while John was never critical of skill errors, he jumped all over anyone for a lack of effort, or a lack of hardness at the footy.

Although it contradicts totally the modern-day focus on head injuries and concussion, John worked on the basis that injuries above the neck didn't count, and that blood streaming from a cut eyebrow or a broken nose should never stop you from contesting for the footy. Back then, a little blood was a badge of honour, although obviously that idea went out the window when the AFL introduced the blood rule.

John drilled into his players never to let the opposition know you were hurt. If you got knocked over, you always had to bounce straight back up again. I was fortunate that I was only ever knocked out two or three times in my career, but whenever this happened I came out of that unconscious fog standing up. That was because it was so deeply ingrained in me always to get back up.

Even though he was well into his 40s by the time I was established in the senior team, John was still wonderfully fit. He used to love running around Glenferrie Oval, occasionally bare-footed, and often said how he loved the feeling of mud squelching up between his toes. He was a great endurance runner and he would beat the majority of his players on the 6–7-kilometre runs we used to do so often. When he'd send us off on a run around the streets of Hawthorn on a Sunday morning, he'd always run in the opposite direction, I suppose to make sure no-one was tempted to take a short cut on the way round.

He set very high standards and was unforgiving in the quest to get the best from every player in the team, but he always measured each player against their individual abilities, and didn't expect anything more than they were capable of. One of his favourite sayings to emphasise this point was that what we need is 'from each according to his ability'. This might be a familiar quote to followers of the German philosopher Karl Marx, but also to the Collingwood and Brisbane players I coached.

To John, football was an impersonal game. Once we put the Hawks jumper on, it was footballers versus footballers, our team versus their team, and individual identities had to be sacrificed in the process.

When he was critical, you never felt as if he was being personal. He said what he had to say to the player as a member of a team – not as the player who was a private individual. He was demanding and uncompromising but never blunt and insulting, even if a lot of players used to think, 'Gee, he's a hard old bugger.' John was a coach who gave tough love and he was not into positive reinforcement.

He was never forthcoming with too much praise. It was not something that came naturally to him and he preferred to work on the basis that if you'd played well you knew it and your friends and family knew it, so you didn't need the coach telling you.

That's not to say there wasn't an understanding and sensitive side; it's just that his players didn't see it very often. I did once.

In 1973, we'd started training on Wednesday nights in addition to the normal Tuesday and Thursday. My wife, Maureen, was a very young mum with two young children. I was leaving home for work at 7 am and getting home from training after 9 pm, which was putting a bit of pressure on the home front. So, one day I summoned all my courage, took a deep breath, and broached the subject with him. We discussed the situation and eventually he said that for the time being I wasn't required at Wednesday night training. Although I suspect there were a few team-mates who wondered why I was getting special treatment, John's sensitivity to a personal situation was an indication of his caring nature, which I'd seen probably for the first time.

Whatever I was born to be and whatever was nurtured into me up until the time I went to Hawthorn, being under the coaching influence of the great John Kennedy during that most impressionable of times, from teenager to mid-20s, was undoubtedly the single biggest factor in how my competitive attitudes were formed.

6

HUDDO

To watch him was like watching a magician.

Every year the media part of the football industry spends much of its time prognosticating what will happen in the season ahead, because the fans seem to love that kind of footy chat. Under questioning and to market their clubs, even coaches and players occasionally get caught up in this useless exercise in crystal ball gazing.

Working in the media, I too am guilty of joining the prediction industry when my basic instincts are that in a heavy physical contact sport like footy the most predictable aspect of the game is its extreme unpredictability. No-one ever really knows what's about to come.

In 1971, Hawthorn had a dominant year, won the premiership losing only three games for the season and, with a young age demographic, another flag looked there for the taking. Nothing had happened over the summer to alter that optimistic view.

Then came round 1, 1972. It was Hawthorn versus Melbourne at Glenferrie Oval on a bright, sunny afternoon. Shortly before half-time, our champion goal-kicker, Peter Hudson, already with eight goals in the bag, took yet another mark. His ninth goal looked a certainty, until suddenly we realised something was wrong.

Huddo had led out for the ball in front of Demons fullback Ray Biffin, while their back pocket player Barry Bourke had attempted to spoil by coming in from the side, but he was a step late. The contact from behind and from his right-hand side unbalanced our great spearhead, and as his left foot landed on the turf, the twisting pressure on the planted leg caused his knee to buckle and collapse. Medical staff came from everywhere and inspected the injury for what seemed like ages before he was stretchered off.

It was April Fool's Day, but this was definitely no joke. His season was over. It was a defining moment, not only in our defence of the 1971 premiership and in the career of the champion full-forward, but in the very history of the game.

Peter Hudson was the glamour player in football at the time. He was the Wayne Carey or the 'Buddy' Franklin of his era. Only 26 and in the prime of his career, he was coming off an extraordinary four-year run in which he'd kicked season totals of 125, 120, 146 and 150 goals in 1968–71. In 84 games, he'd kicked 541 goals at an average of 6.44 goals per game. Who knows what he might have finished with in the season-opener of 1972 and beyond had he not been injured.

Sadly, he was never the same again. Good enough, still, to kick eight goals in a one-off comeback game in 1973. And good enough six years later to kick 110 goals and top the 1977 goal-kicking list. But he was never again the consistently dominant player who had rewritten the goal-kicking record books from 1968 to 1971.

While statistics often don't accurately reflect the full sporting picture, in this case they do. In his golden four-year run, Huddo kicked six or more goals 51 times in 84 games. Fifteen times he kicked six, there were six bags of seven, nine bags of eight, and eight bags of nine. Eleven times he topped double figures – four 10s, two 11s, two 12s, two 13s and a 16.

The associated problem was that he kicked almost half the Hawks' score: he kicked 45 per cent of our goals in 1968, 40 per cent in 1969, 44 per cent in 1970 and 40 per cent in 1971. Opposition teams had no counter for him. If they could put him down for six goals prior to the first bounce, they'd take it without a moment's hesitation.

He was a phenomenon.

At one point, a jokester put his own spin on a big billboard outside a church in Hawthorn. The huge sign posed the question: 'What would you do if God came to Hawthorn?' The wag wrote below in large writing, 'Move Peter Hudson to centre half-forward.'

Huddo was a freak, and yet in so many ways he was athletically normal. He was not overly tall at 189 centimetres, not overly bulky at 92 kilograms, not overly quick by foot and had terrible endurance. He would have been a dismal failure at any sort of draft camp testing. What he had and what made him great wasn't measurable off the footy field: he was extremely agile at ground level, had lightning reflexes, quick reaction time, fantastic body use and the ability to read the flight of the ball superbly. It was a joy to look up with ball in hand and know that if you could kick the ball so as to give Huddo front position between the flight of the ball and his defensive opponent, he'd end up with the footy nine times out of ten. A 60/40 chance was all he needed.

Of course, on the other hand, he was the forward target every time – which created an unhealthy reliance on one player to kick most of the score. If he failed, which was rarely, Hawthorn automatically lost.

I'd seen first-hand just how good he was, even before playing my first senior game. It was round five in 1969. I'd played in the reserves at Glenferrie Oval and was sitting with my curtain-raiser team-mates up in the old red brick grandstand watching the seniors. Coincidentally, it was against Melbourne too, and Huddo put on a clinic.

That day, only 23 and playing in just his 41st game, he kicked 16 goals, including six in the final quarter. The entire Melbourne side could only manage 14 as Hudson bagged what was to be a personal best. He was two short of the VFL/AFL record of 18, set by Melbourne's Fred Fanning in 1947, and one less than the 17 that Jason Dunstall would kick in a Hawthorn game in 1992. But for an impressionable young fella like me at the time, it was the most mind-blowing performance I'd seen.

There's nothing more exciting in a game of footy than a champion goal-kicker racking up a big bag. This match, and particularly the last quarter, still vividly sticks in my memory over 40 years later. Every time the ball went into Hawthorn's forward line there was almost a hush, a collective bated breath, that was punctured by a gigantic roar as Huddo took another big grab and kicked yet another goal. The anticipation was enthralling.

To watch him was like watching a magician. You'd see him lead to a contest and think he was out of position, but suddenly he'd come up with the footy. Or it'd take a lucky bounce and fall into his arms.

Except it wasn't luck. His judgement of the ball in the air and his ability to anticipate where the ball was going and get there before anyone else was remarkable.

He was an unfashionable kick, but was deadly accurate. Whereas in the modern era players will generally use a drop punt, or occasionally a torpedo if a long way from goal, Huddo used an ugly flat punt. It was a style of kick that disappeared from the game shortly thereafter, along with the old stab pass, but nobody could question its accuracy when Huddo had the footy in his hands.

One day during the 1971 season, we played St Kilda at their Moorabbin home ground with a howling northerly wind blowing straight down the ground. At one point, Huddo had a set shot, right foot to the boundary, deep in the dead pocket at the northern end, where the stiff breeze was blowing the ball forcefully away from the goals he was aiming at.

Hudson took the kick and it was marked by an opposition player in the opposite pocket. Just as the St Kilda defender was preparing to take his kick, we looked across to see the goal umpire waving his flags to signal a goal. Quite incredibly, the football had gone through the goals before the wind had blown it back out into the field of play. It was the type of freakish act that added further to the aura of genius that became part of the Peter Hudson legend.

Until that fateful opening match of 1972 when bad injury cruelled his career, whenever Hudson was playing I used to think the footy gods smiled on him, and although it wasn't luck, it sure looked that way at times.

One of those times was against Footscray at the old Western Oval, when his opponent, Peter Welsh, took off with the ball. Like most of us deep forwards, Huddo wasn't particularly keen on chasing, but with nobody else in sight he ran after the Bulldogs' full-back. With every step, Welsh got further away as Huddo chugged along behind. One bounce, two bounces. And then on the third bounce, almost as if the ball had a mind of its own, it bounced straight up over Welsh's head and into Huddo's arms. He was too far from goal to have a shot – even for him – and so he passed it to Don Scott alone in the goal square. I wouldn't say it was the only time Huddo ever chased out of the full-forward line, but it was one of not too many. It was also quite possibly the only time I saw him have a kick that was not a shot on goal, because he was always within scoring range.

It's an unfortunate evolution in the game that the stay-at-home full-forward position has become largely redundant over the last few years. The full team defence of recent seasons has meant every player has to get up into midfield to help in the defensive effort. Unless these big targets could be trained up many notches, Peter Hudson and other champion forwards of his ilk, even the greats like Tony Lockett and Jason Dunstall, are blasts from the past. It's a sad fact that we can no longer watch these one-position goal-square-based full-forwards thrill us with their occasional double-figure tallies – another unfortunate by-product of the fully professional era of massive coaching intervention in the game.

Back in the early 1970s, when there wasn't anything like the saturation media coverage that modern football commands, Peter Hudson and the other 100-goal-a-year forwards of his time, Peter McKenna, Alex Jesaulenko and Doug Wade, were the rock stars of their era.

In the publicity stakes, however, Huddo had them all covered. For instance, in late 1973 there was what became known in footy folklore as the 'helicopter' match, when he made his VFL comeback against Collingwood at Waverley. It was almost 17 months after that ill-fated day in 1972 when he'd blown out his knee against Melbourne, and he'd trodden a quite unbelievable path back to the football spotlight.

At the time of his initial injury he'd tried to train several weeks later. He found he was alright running in straight lines, but as soon as he tried to change directions he was no good – classic symptoms of needing what we now call a knee reconstruction – and ultimately at the end of 1972 he'd had surgery to repair his cruciate ligament. This kind of surgery was really bad news back then.

Huddo knew he wasn't going to be playing a lot of football any time soon, so he'd headed back to Hobart and switched his focus to business. As a genuine Tassie hero who'd made it big on the mainland, he was offered the extremely attractive opportunity to take over the Granada Tavern, a very big pub that within a few years had 60 people on the payroll. It was a full-time commitment and he hadn't even been doing any football training when, late in 1973, he got a call from Hawthorn coach John Kennedy asking if he'd be interested in coming back to play. That was another opportunity too good to pass over and, on the strength of a little personal training for two or three weeks in Hobart, he was picked for Hawthorn in round 21 against Collingwood at Waverley.

However, there was a problem. The well-known comic character Norman Gunston was the live act at the Tavern on the Friday night, so Huddo couldn't leave Hobart until the Saturday morning. He caught a domestic flight to Melbourne and, in one of the more bizarre things I've ever seen, he was flown by helicopter from Tullamarine out to Waverley and landed in the middle of the ground at half-time in the curtain-raiser match.

After round 20, Hawthorn were seventh on the ladder with 40 points and a healthy percentage of 109.5, trailing fifth-placed St Kilda on 44 points and 107.8, and sixth-placed North Melbourne on 42 points and 98.1. We were still in with an outside chance of grabbing the fifth finals berth, so it was a good time for the club to pull the old number 26 jumper out of mothballs.

I was out injured that day, so like thousands of other spectators, I was there with great interest to see the Hudson comeback sideshow.

While I don't remember many short-term injuries, I do recall this one because it was an experience that gave me some understanding of an event that would occur more than 30 years later, when Brisbane's Nigel Lappin would play in a grand final with broken ribs.

In the round 20 game against St Kilda at Glenferrie Oval, I copped a couple of broken ribs courtesy of a knee in the back from Saints defender Barry Lawrence as he used me as a stepladder to take a mark. For three or four days, I thought I was going to die. I couldn't do anything without excruciating pain – couldn't sleep, couldn't cough, couldn't even take a deep breath. But, as was the case with Nigel all those years later, after three or four days I started to come good. As it turned out, I only missed one match and played the next week in round 22.

But back to that infamous helicopter game. Hudson was sporting a mullet haircut and looked very overweight and unfit. In fact, he looked a bit like one of those old European violinists. Playing his 103rd game at 27, he was like the Andre Rieu of the 1970s. Yet almost as if to underline his greatness as a ball-getter who could convert from anywhere within 50 metres, he mesmerised the Collingwood defence and kicked eight goals. He did it all by superior judgement and his freakish ability to pick up the flight of the ball and get in the right spot to either mark it or win possession via a second effort at ground level. It was eight out of 13 as the Hawks lost 13.10 (88) to 16.10 (106). Nobody did it better than Huddo.

However, with St Kilda beating North the same day, our finals hopes were dashed, so there was no point bringing him back the following weekend for the last game of the season. Also, he'd done a bit of fresh damage to his knee cartilage in the first quarter and wasn't moving very well anyway.

It was all part of an incredible comeback game story that even back then was bizarre and in the modern football world seems too crazy even to contemplate.

Still living in Hobart, Huddo played the first two rounds of the 1974 VFL season with Hawthorn, but his knee still wasn't right, so he gave it away. In 1975–76 he played in Hobart, and in 1977 he made a full-scale comeback with Hawthorn – or as much of a full-scale come-back as is possible if you're still living interstate. He would train on his own in Hobart during the week and fly to Melbourne on a Friday to play Saturday and fly home on Saturday night. He played 21 of 22 home-and-away games plus three finals and kicked 110 goals. He had 99 at the end of the home-and-away season, posted his century in the first final as a 31-year-old, and kicked just one goal in his last game – a 5.15 (45) to 16.16 (112) preliminary final thumping from North Melbourne. It was the fifth time he'd topped the century. Only Tony Lockett and Jason Dunstall, with six tons apiece, have cracked triple figures more often – and they played 281 and 269 games respectively. He could have gone on, but the challenge to play again had been satisfied. With a business to run in Hobart, he called it a day.

At Hawthorn Huddo finished with 727 goals from 129 games. His goals-per-game average of 5.64 is the best in league history, ahead of John Coleman's 5.48 goals per game for Essendon back in 1949–54.

Huddo was the first real footy superstar I knew. He was always a marquee player in my eyes, and yet from the moment I met him as a teenage recruit, he was just a normal, friendly bloke with no special airs or graces. It was a sporting tragedy that his career, like many others over the years, was cut short by injury.

He left an indelible mark not only on the football world – he is an official AFL Legend – but on me personally, because he gave me the nickname that everyone at Hawthorn has called me ever since. It was in my first season in 1969, when he was watching the reserves play the curtain-raiser. He passed comment to those sitting around him that he thought I ran like Barney Rubble of Fred Flintstone fame, and pretty soon thereafter I was known simply as 'Barney', or more particularly 'Barn'.

There was a distinct correlation between the presence of the great full-forward at Hawthorn and the club's success. He'd helped us become a premiership side in 1971, but when he left the club's success rate fell noticeably. In 1972, without our one-man forward line, we finished sixth with a 13–9 record and missed the five-team finals series. In 1973, we finished seventh with an 11–11 record and again missed the finals.

Many would say the Hawks had an unhealthy reliance on one player to kick them to a winning score, and they were right. Forty years on, the same dilemma exists. As much as it is great to have a player of Huddo's goal-kicking feats, coaches are reluctant to rely so heavily on one player for fear of what will happen if and when they're not available or have a bad day.

Personally, my career probably thrived with the absence of our champion goal-kicker. The gun marking forwards draw the ball to them all the time and without Huddo in our forward line the rest of us got more of a look-in. The big payday came against Essendon at VFL Park on Easter Monday of 1973.

As a forward pocket rover, I played mainly deep forward and went onto the ball when our first rover Peter Crimmins wanted a spell. That was my assigned role in this round-three match-up.

It was also the weekend I developed a special affinity with choco-late chip pavlova. On the Sunday night, we visited very good family friends the Judds in Chelsea and in the days of a much less strict nutritional regime I indulged in a nice big piece of chocolate chip pavlova. That pavlova may have had nothing to do with what happened the following day, or maybe it was a late present for my 21st birthday the month before, but for me that Easter Monday game came straight from heaven.

Whatever the cause, that match – of the 332 games I played for the Hawks – was the best. The special feeling of being in the zone and perfectly in tune with the game is a serene and unforgettable time. That was where I spent those two hours of football. The footy seemed to follow me around that day. I had 40-odd kicks and kicked 11 goals.

It was a game to remember forever and chocolate chip pavlova has been a favourite dessert ever since.

The photo taken that night, which was on the front page of the *Sun* newspaper the following morning, of me with my two young daughters – Tracey, who was two years old, with ten fingers outstretched, and Fiona, who was still a toddler, with the one pointed finger – remains one of my very favourite mementoes of a very memorable occasion.

7

THE BEST OF TIMES, THE WORST OF TIMES

The challenge was simple: if the Kangaroos couldn't score, they couldn't win.

The 50-metre line didn't exist back when I played. I wish it had, because the back line wasn't a place I often visited as a player and this ground marking would have served as the start of my no-go zone.

While maybe I embellish my lack of defensive push-back just a little, the fact is my playing style was very much of a midfielder who pushed aggressively forward. Although getting the ball upfield was part of my role, kicking four goals a game was my own break-even point to have played well.

However, in the final quarter of the 1976 grand final, that charge-forward mentality was put on hold.

It was a case of the match situation demanding an alteration to natural instinct. Even for someone like me, who was essentially an offensive on-baller, when you get to a grand final all individual wants and needs are easily forgotten. They don't matter. It's all about the team – especially in the final quarter of the game that decides the flag.

At three-quarter time of the 1976 grand final, we led North Melbourne by 10 points and I adopted a 'protect the lead' mentality. I figured we'd worked so hard to get ourselves in front that we had to do whatever it took to prevent the Kangaroos from grabbing back the lead. That meant stopping them from scoring, even if I had to take on a foreign role of playing midfield back. If the ball was locked in our forward line, they couldn't score, so the positioning I adopted was to help win the centre bounce clearances, get the ball into our forward line and then be an extra midfielder to stop the ball getting into the Kangaroos' scoring range.

It was a Hawthorn side hell-bent on revenge after what had happened 12 months earlier. There's no greater motivation than the memories of a grand final loss, and we'd been smashed by North in 1975. The memory of that bitter taste of defeat, of getting so close and then failing, is a fantastic motivation for the following year. Having won in 1971 and lost in 1975, the vast difference in the post-game feeling was still starkly entrenched in our collective psyche and the determination to experience that winning feeling again was a powerful force.

Three-quarter time in a close grand final is when you metaphorically take a deep breath and regroup for that hectic sprint to the finish line, and those completely opposite experiences of either exhilaration or depression. After a long, drawn-out season, a mere 30 minutes will decide which of those extreme emotions will come with the end result; the challenge as always is to live in the moment and do what it takes minute by minute, without getting stressed or distracted by the end result.

North had gone into the grand final without potential match-winner Sam Kekovich, who was injured in their preliminary final win over Carlton, and they were soon carrying a wounded Barry Cable, who was a top-notch rover and one of my very toughest opponents. It had been a fairly even contest. We led at each change, but our poor kicking had kept North in the game. It was 10.18 to 10.8 as we huddled together at the final break and I set myself to play a road-block role behind the ball.

Hawthorn had finished second in the home-and-away season with 16 wins, half a game behind Carlton. We beat third-placed North by 20 points in the qualifying final and Carlton by 17 points in the second semi-final before taking on North in the grand final.

It was the year when another unfortunate injury had struck our great centre half-back, Peter Knights. He suffered a broken collar-bone mid-season and still finished a narrow runner-up to Essendon's Graham Moss in the Brownlow Medal, despite playing only once in the home-and-away season after round 13. But he was back for the finals.

In the qualifying final against North, I'd had a day out and kicked seven goals. It was 7.6, in fact, and this led to an unusual assignment in the grand final. As I lined up at the first bounce, I had a new tagger – North skipper and 1974–75 Brownlow Medallist Keith Greig.

It was probably the only time in his career the Kangaroos' champion was given a stopping role, but as it turned out it was a job that didn't last too long. About midway through the first quarter, it happened that Keith won possession on the Kangaroos' half-back flank in front of the two coaches' boxes situated in the MCC members' area. With the ball in hand, he tried to baulk me. He got past my body, but he couldn't get past my right-hand coat hanger.

I was immediately reported by umpire Bill Deller. The report sheet incorrectly said I hit him with a left fist, when it was actually my right. The tribunal let me off on the technicality of an incorrect report, with the words that justice must be seen to be done. I don't imagine that slight technical error would prevent a two- or three-week suspension under the modern match review panel system.

With the great benefit of hindsight, 1976 was slap bang in the middle of a five-year premiership window that Hawthorn enjoyed from 1974 to '78. My simple definition of being in a premiership window is reaching the preliminary final, because if a team gets that far then they qualify as a potential flag-winner. North beat us by five points on a rain-soaked MCG in the 1974 preliminary final and belted us by 55 points in the 1975 grand final.

Personally, it was my peak period; I was in what I believe is a footballer's prime. Going into the 1974 season, I'd played five seasons, 84 games, and was still only 22 years of age. I had the experience and the physical resilience and – with almost no injury interruption over the next five years – I played 113 games, kicked 353 goals and won four club championships.

Team success came too: we won 81 of the 113 games I played, got into three grand finals and won two premierships.

Life was good, or it should have been. The fact was that the nagging fear of failure, that ever-present reality that misfortune can arrive at any time, made enjoying the successes a largely forlorn hope. There was always next week or next season to worry about.

It's the price of the raging competitive beast within to never achieve inner peace or contentment, except for the occasional and fleeting moments that then pass all too quickly. I was fortunate to have plenty of individual and team success through my playing and coaching career, but the addiction I suffered – having an unquenchable need to succeed – was an affliction that was never under control.

There had been no premiership window around the 1971 success. That flag came on the back of one isolated outstanding season, with no finals either the year or two before or after that premiership-winning year.

So 1976 was about taking our chances, because being in the premiership window is no guarantee of actually winning the big one. St Kilda and the Western Bulldogs of recent years are examples of being very close to football's holy grail but not being quite able to go all the way.

As usual, I can't remember what was said by John Kennedy, but as we went out to our positions after the three-quarter-time break my personal strategy as the on-ball rover was clear: win the centre bounces, get the ball into our forward line and lock it in. Along with our captain and ruckman, Don Scott, and ruck-rover, Michael Tuck, the three of us did our best to form a wall behind the footy. The challenge was simple: if the Kangaroos couldn't score, they couldn't win.

There were only three goals kicked in the last term of the 1976 grand final, all of them by Hawthorn and one of them by another Matthews – my younger brother, Kelvin – whose goal late in the quarter helped seal the victory. After Kelvin came to Hawthorn in 1971 we'd played 83 games together going into the game and this was to be the one premiership we shared.

His bulky frame charged out from the full-forward line, took possession of the bouncing ball, turned sharply to drop off his trailing opponent, straightened onto his right foot and slotted the goal. That turn and shrug of the hips was reminiscent of those games of backyard footy in Chelsea, but instead of me being that dropped-off tackler, this day I was a team-mate applauding from midfield. The big number four that Kelvin wore was all I could see as he ran in to kick that decisive goal. It was a beautiful sight.

A 30-point win and a second premiership was ours to celebrate.

As a raw teenager in 1971 in only my third season, the premiership was a bit of a blur, because it happened so quickly. At the time, there was little understanding of the difficulty involved; this second one coming five years later and after a couple of near misses was a moment to really savour.

The football wheel turns rapidly and the changing of the guard since 1971 had been enormous; only Kelvin Moore, Ian Bremner, Leon Rice, Alan Martello, Don Scott and myself were able to be there again in 1976.

The message of never confusing the make-believe highs and lows of football with real-life drama was highlighted emphatically a few days later with the tragic passing of our much-loved former captain Peter Crimmins.

Despite being extremely ill, Crimmo had sent a telegram to John Kennedy which was to be read out to the players before we took the field in the grand final. It read: 'Good luck to all you boys. It will be a long, hard 120 minutes. I will ride every bump and tackle with you and I'm sure you will be there at the end.' It was signed 'The Little Fella'. The challenge on grand final day is to avoid getting over-hyped by the occasion and those words from a person we all liked and respected so much were of great inspiration and comfort on what can be an emotionally overwhelming day.

Crimmo had been club captain in 1974–75 and was struck down by testicular cancer and hadn't played at senior level since round seven of 1975. He made an ill-fated attempt to get up for the grand final that season but was not deemed match-fit enough to be selected. Thereafter, he didn't play at all in 1976 as his health deteriorated badly throughout the year.

The Deputy Premier of Victoria, Lindsay Thompson, had offered him a chauffeur-driven transport to the grand final, but he was just not well enough to attend. A group of the players took the Cup around to Crimmo's home at Croydon around midnight. I wasn't part of it and didn't actually learn of the visit until afterwards, but the players who did go and see him were hit with a bit of a shock. They hadn't seen the little fella for a few weeks and he was fading away. He died three days later at a far too young age of 28.

I was at the sports store I owned at the Brandon Park Shopping Centre in Glen Waverley on the Tuesday after the grand final when the terrible news came through. It was a shock to us all because, while we knew he was very ill, I didn't realise the end was so close. It was a huge loss for the club, because he'd been such a wonderful character around the place and was one of those guys who was genuinely liked and respected by everyone.

At times like this, the loss to us of a well-known footballer was insignificant compared to the loss suffered by his wife, Gwen, and children, Ben and Sam, the wider Crimmins family and his many friends.

Crimmo was vice-captain to David Parkin when I arrived at Hawthorn. I had a special relationship with him because we were roving partners. He was very much the senior partner and I was really just the young inexperienced forward pocket who had an occasional run on the ball. As I started to settle in, I got a little more actual roving time, and bit by bit that grew. But during the early years he'd often say to me as we'd break up from the three-quarter-time huddle each week: 'I'll start on the ball – you go forward and kick a few goals.' And I was quite happy with that.

When I think of Crimmo, I think of someone like Hawthorn premiership rover John Platten, or more recently North Melbourne champion Brent Harvey. Only 173 centimetres tall and 72 kilograms, he was tiny yet wonderfully resilient and incredibly brave – quick, skilful and always able to lift his side through his personal example.

Looking back on our partnership, as the aggression in my game bubbled over into outright brutality on occasions, there was a bit of Luke Skywalker and Darth Vader about our pairing. To most footy fans, even the Hawthorn ones, Crimmo represented the much-admired fair-haired good of Luke Skywalker, while I probably engendered grudging praise at best. As a footballer, I was more representative of the powerful but dark side of his fierce *Star Wars* rival.

Everyone loved Crimmo. He was the little guy with spunk, and when I think of him it also reminds me of the old saying that it's not the size of the dog in the fight that counts, but the size of the fight in the dog. It didn't get any bigger than the Little Fella.

He was a real bonding influence among the playing group. Not only was he a very good player himself, but he was so enthusiastic and effervescent that he helped keep everyone else up. He was happier doing something for someone else than he was looking after himself, and it was commonplace for him and Gwen to have team-mates around to their home on a Saturday night after a game. We always felt very comfortable in their company, and it really rocked everyone when he passed away in what should have been the prime of his life.

It was a sad and sobering time, which made the unbridled joy of the premiership victory a few days before seem very superficial and unimportant by comparison. At times like this, we're reminded that football is only a game.

8

BROTHERS IN ARMS

*Frankly, apart from the brother thing, meeting Kelvin head-on
wouldn't have been a very healthy thing to do.*

After the 1971 flag, and more particularly the Peter Hudson injury,
we'd fallen away badly. We just missed the finals in 1972, finishing
sixth with a 13–9 record, but slipped to seventh at 11–11 in 1973.

In 1974, we bounced back to finish third in the home-and-away
season at 15–7 and third overall, losing to eventual runners-up
North in the preliminary final. In 1975, we topped the home-and-
away ladder at 17–5 but, after beating the third-placed Kangaroos
by 11 points in the second semi-final to be the first team into the
grand final, we faltered in the game that decided the flag.

We lost to North by 55 points in the big one after they kicked 7.2
to 2.6 in the last quarter. Arnold Briedis kicked five goals and John
Burns and Doug Wade four apiece to help give the Kangaroos their
first premiership. It was the last game for Wade and North's captain
Barry Davis.

In one of the oddities of Hawthorn history, it was the second game
and also the last for 21-year-old full-forward Michael Cooke. He'd
become the first Hawthorn player to debut in a final when the coach had
decided to play a slightly out-of-sorts Michael Moncrieff at full-back in
the semi-final. Cooke had played well in the reserves in partnership with
his brother and centre half-forward Robert, and when he kicked four
goals in the low-scoring semi he held his spot for the big one. Unfortunately, he was replaced without having touched the ball in the grand final.
He never played at senior level again and finished his career at Olinda.

My memories of the 1975 grand final are scarce and perhaps subconsciously I'd wiped the whole thing from my mind. Even in my junior days at Chelsea, I had the good fortune to play only in winning grand final teams. In five years, we'd played in four grand finals for four wins, and my only other grand final, at Hawthorn in 1971, had also produced the right result.

However, I do remember vividly John Kennedy having an earnest conversation with Bohdan Jaworskyj in the rooms after the match. The German-born half-back flanker had announced prior to the match that it would be his last for the club, but on a day when most of us had a shocker, the man we called 'Bugs' had been pretty solid, and in the immediate aftermath the coach had tried desperately to convince him to abandon an earlier decision to go back to North Adelaide. He'd played 63 games for Hawthorn from 1973 to 1975 and at 28 he could certainly have played on. Instead, he returned to the club where he'd played in the 1971–72 SANFL premiership sides and would later be named in their Team of the Century. For once John didn't get his way.

It's an inevitable process at football clubs that, as players move on, other players arrive to take their place. After the 1971 premiership, a string of players who would become senior standouts wore the brown and gold for the first time. The Hawthorn zones were like a very productive gold mine with a conveyor belt of talented players emerging year after year. Add effective recruiting from outside Victoria and the mix created a golden era for the decades ahead.

Many of us had the good fortune to lob at Hawthorn at a very opportune time. Premiership players continually replenished the team; like Alan Goad, John Hendrie and Michael Tuck in 1972 and Geoff Ablett in 1973. Robert DiPierdomenico, David Polkinghorne, Barry Rowlings and Alle De Wolde were first-gamers in 1975; followed by Rodney Eade, David O'Halloran and Ian Paton in 1976; and by Peter Russo and Terry Wallace in 1978.

It was a continuation of the influx that occurred in the late 1960s through the debuts of Peter Knights, Kelvin Moore and yours truly in 1969, Alan Martello and Leon Rice in 1970 and Michael Moncrieff in 1971. And it would happen again in the next generation, with the likes of John Kennedy junior in 1979, Peter Schwab, Colin Robertson and Chris Mew in 1980, and Dermott Brereton, Gary Buckenara and Richard Loveridge in 1981.

My brother Kelvin was another player who arrived at the club during this era. He'd actually joined Hawthorn in 1971, after winning the best and fairest at Chelsea as a 16-year-old in 1970. He didn't play a senior game in his first year at Glenferrie, but did pick up the club's 'Most Promising Player' award chosen from those who didn't play senior football. He was also surprised to pick up the paper the day before the 1971 grand final to learn that, although he hadn't played a senior game and hadn't been advised, he was actually an emergency for the premiership decider.

Kelvin, who had played such an important role in my childhood development, played his first senior game for Hawthorn as an 18-year-old in round five of 1972 against Footscray at Glenferrie Oval. Peter Knights, who would top the club goal-kicking list that year, kicked five goals as we won by 28 points.

It was a very proud day for Mum and Dad to have two sons playing together at senior level for the first time. There would be another similarly proud day for my parents in 1974, when Kelvin and I played together for Victoria against Western Australia.

Not that it was enough to get Mum to the match; after seeing every game we had ever played as we grew up, watching her sons go out to battle in front of big crowds was a stress she decided to do without. Dad would have seen just about every senior game we played, but Mum didn't see a solitary one.

Just as injury had cut Peter Hudson down in his prime, so it did to Kelvin. He'd kicked a career-best eight goals against Fitzroy at the Junction Oval in round 5 of 1977. He was at the peak of his career, and by round 10 had reached 93 games for the club.

It all came to a shuddering halt a few weeks later at a Saturday morning training session at Camberwell Football Club before a Monday game against Essendon in round 11. It was an innocuous mishap – nothing terribly traumatic, just a misplaced step that seemed to jar his knee. He tried to keep training but was forced to call it quits. After a few weeks of physio and some failed attempts to prove his fitness at training, the diagnosis of a damaged cruciate ligament was finally confirmed.

Knee reconstruction surgery was in its infancy back then. The procedure to repair the cruciate ligament meant Kelvin spent two weeks in hospital with his entire leg in a plaster cast, and afterwards he was about six weeks in a splint to keep his leg straight, resulting in massive wasting of the thigh muscle because it was inactive for such a long time.

Nowadays, after cruciate repair surgery, players are on their feet after a few days and normally playing again within 12 months. Back in the 1970s, though, it was virtually an insurmountable blow to a footballer's career.

Kelvin got back and played a few games in early 1978, but it was evident to all close to him that things weren't going especially well. It was at this time that a long-time family connection kicked in.

Back in 1969, when Rod Olsson was vice-captain of Hawthorn, he'd picked me up and driven me to my first training camp at Portsea. Thereafter, Rod and his wife, Elle, had become quite good friends with Mum – so much so that a few years later when Rod was coaching in Tasmania, Mum went over to Hobart and stayed with Rod and Elle for a weekend.

It was fortuitous that in 1978, when Kelvin was battling a little in his post-knee injury period, Rod was in his third year of a four-year stint as senior coach at Geelong. I've got no doubt his relationship with our family and with Hawthorn made him aware of Kelvin's situation and had at least encouraged the Cats to explore the possibility of getting him.

This was during the era when there was a transfer window in June each year, and Kelvin traded in the number four jumper in brown and gold stripes which he'd worn from his second season at Hawthorn after starting in number 28. In its place, he picked up a number seven jumper in blue and white hoops. He played his first senior game for Geelong against Richmond in round 14 eight weeks after his last game for Hawthorn, and in round 21 we played against each other for the first time, which created a dilemma for the allegiances of the Matthews family.

Hawthorn won that day by two points, but it was to be the only occasion we got the better of a Geelong side in which Kelvin played. Oddly enough, two of the four subsequent times Kelvin played against the Hawks I didn't play, and in the other two games in which we were opposed the Cats won by 80 points in round 15 of 1980 and by 14 points in round 17 of 1981.

There wasn't a lot of contact between us on the field because we were both playing midfield forward, so were generally at opposite ends of the ground. Frankly, apart from the brother thing, meeting Kelvin head-on wouldn't have been a very healthy thing to do.

If I was a little tank, as I was sometimes called, Kelvin by this stage of his career was a big tank. I'd never forgotten the day at Princes Park in the early 1970s when his younger version hit Carlton's Vin Waite with a bone-rattling shirtfront (they were legal back then), after Waite had flattened David Parkin. That's why later, when we were in different jumpers, I was happy to have an entire field between us and was in no hurry to resume the one-on-one battles of our childhood.

Kelvin played a total of 58 games for Geelong before retiring at the end of 1982, aged 28. In total he played 155 games, including nine finals.

9

LIVING IN THE '70S

In 1973–1974, when I was earning about $5000 a year playing footy, I was making nearly $20,000 selling trucks.

By the turn of the century, the evolution from part-time to full-time footballers was complete. From the mid-'80s, senior coaches had gradually given up working outside their football jobs, and by the time the 1990s ended assistant coaches were total footy full-timers as well.

Currently, over the 800-odd players on AFL lists, the average salary is almost $300,000, with first-year draftees guaranteed $50,000-plus and Gold Coast Suns marquee recruit Gary Ablett the top of the heap, earning almost $2 million a year.

Where football earnings were by comparison to working a normal job is highlighted by the progression of payments through my 40 years in footy. When I went to Hawthorn in 1969, I was doing Year 12 at Bonbeach High School. I played 11 reserves games and five senior matches and earned around $400 for the whole season.

The following year, through a contact at Hawthorn, I went to work as a trainee cadet at Dunlop Automotive with a starting salary of $32 per week or $1664 per annum. I played 16 senior games for the Hawks and earned about $600.

That's a ballpark summary of where earnings were four decades ago.

Many champion players such as Collingwood's Bob Rose and Hawthorn's Graham Arthur would head to a country club as player-coach because they could earn significantly more than they could by staying in the VFL.

Footballers back then didn't play for the money; it was our hobby and passion with a few bucks for our trouble. Many footy careers were cut short because of work priorities. My 1971 premiership team-mate Ray Wilson retired after the following season to pursue business interests. Financially, he most definitely made the right move. Terry Gay, the Hawks' promising young centre half-forward of the late 1960s, retired in his early 20s to embark on a medical career. Terry is now one of Melbourne's most highly regarded cardiologists.

After becoming a senior regular in 1971, winning club champion-ships in 1971, 1972 and 1974, and representing Victoria most years, my football salary crept up to around $5000 per annum.

Prior to the 1976 season, I retained the services of my solicitor, Isaac Apel, to help negotiate a better deal. The player manager concept was revolutionary back then and the Hawthorn board didn't take kindly to being backed into a corner when Isaac threatened legal action to gain a clearance if the club didn't pay me the princely sum of $13,000 a season for the next three years.

To put that amount in context: when North Melbourne in 1972 recruited Geelong's Doug Wade, Essendon's Barry Davis and South Melbourne's John Rantall, they were reputedly on $10,000 per season. That's peanuts by modern standards, but was big money in the early 1970s. After a little angst, Hawthorn eventually agreed to our demands. The same process was repeated three years later after I'd won the 1976, 1977 and 1978 club championships and the Hawks had won the flag in 1976 and 1978.

By then, the dollar demands had gone up appreciably. There were a few approaches on the table from other clubs, with Essendon topping the rest with an offer of $75,000 per year and Carlton putting on the table $60,000 per season for a three-year contract. A clandes-tine meeting at the Hallam Hotel in outer south-eastern suburban Melbourne with a couple of the Blues' influential supporters was the closest we got to considering their offer, but it established the market rate.

The demand to Hawthorn was set at $40,000 per season. There was no way I wanted to leave and happily, after a few weeks of negoti-ation, the club agreed. I played seven more years from 1979 onwards and in my last few years was pushed up a little to $50,000 per season.

It's fair to say that I was underpaid during most of the 1970s but quite overpaid for that last struggling swan-song year in 1985.

That was the modest progression of my football earnings; fortunately, my off-field income had a few lucky breaks.

After being selected in the Victorian team in 1971, I was contacted by Adidas executive ex-Olympian Ron Clarke and met with him and their Australian boss Jan Van Hoboken at the Bird and Bottle Restaurant in Croydon. Apart from Ron reminding me to cut the fat off the lamb chops I was having for lunch, the big surprise was their offer to pay me $20 a week to wear the three-striped footwear, plus as much Adidas gear as my family and I could wear.

That was the rent for a small flat in Chelsea, so my wife Maureen and one-year-old daughter, Tracey, who had been living with her father, George, and younger sister, Deb, could afford to shift into a place of our own. The Adidas deal was the windfall that made this possible. I say windfall, because, as I've mentioned, I was wearing Adidas boots by choice, so getting a week's rent as payment was a total bonus.

With the work at Dunlop going nowhere, my next sliding-door moment was through former Hawks player and then reserves coach, Roy Simmonds. He was a truck salesman with Bill Patterson Cheney and told me they had a spot for a new salesman. With Simmo's recommendation, I got the job.

Again, my timing was spot-on. My mechanical knowledge was nil; if my car broke down, I called the RACV to get me going. My selling ability was no better than my knowledge of trucks. However, Bill Patterson Cheney had the exclusive Bedford brand dealership and the six salesmen, including me, each had an area of Melbourne. Basically, I didn't sell trucks; more accurately, I took orders.

There was plenty of business and plenty of orders to be taken. In 1973–1974, when I was earning about $5000 a year playing footy, I was making nearly $20,000 selling trucks.

In mid-1975, when the truck orders were petering out, another opportunity presented itself. One day, I happened to walk through the Hawthorn reception on the way to training and was introduced to an elderly gentleman by the name of Arthur Hamilton, who had come to the club looking for a player to become his business partner. Arthur had the option on the lease for the new sports store that was to be part of an extension to the Brandon Park Shopping Centre out near the VFL Park football stadium. He asked if I was interested in going into business with him.

Neither of us had any experience in the industry, but I was good friends with former Hawthorn player and club selector Jack McLeod, who had a sports store and Toyworld franchise at Croydon.

With Jack's offer to help, we decided to give it a go. Selling trucks was out and selling footy boots to kids was in. Initially, the shop was not really worthwhile as a partnership and after the first year Arthur agreed to be bought out and went into full retirement. My elder brother, Russell, came in as manager and we had one other full-timer. The business thrived and by the late 1970s it was generating a profit of around $40,000 a year – about the same amount I was getting for playing footy.

I reckon the comparative figures these days for a full-time player would show that I'd be earning $800,000-plus just to play footy. That's an increase of 2000 per cent, or multiplied by 20. Today, a small sports store like my Brandon Park business would be doing well to generate a $200,000 per annum profit, an increase over the same 30 years of around 500 per cent. That in a nutshell highlights the massive inflation that has run rampant in the AFL over the past couple of decades.

In the early 1980s, half the then VFL teams were broke and the introduction of the player salary cap helped protect the competitive, ever-ambitious clubs from poaching players from their opposition and bankrupting themselves in the process. During this period, the recruiting war between Collingwood and Richmond wrecked them both.

Fitzroy's inability to survive in its own right and being forced to merge with the Brisbane Lions in 1997, and the near forced merger of Hawthorn and Melbourne around the same time, are the extreme examples of when spending exceeds income.

The emergence of full-time players during the 1990s and the subsequent need for full-time coaches, conditioning experts, medical staff, and other ancillary employees, have created the latest surge in club spending, and the strain of keeping up is clearly showing.

The financial competitive edge enjoyed by the rich and powerful clubs, such as Collingwood and the West Coast Eagles, is making life very difficult for clubs at the opposite end of the financial power scale. Many clubs are heavily in debt and struggling to make ends meet without help from AFL head office.

Here are some basic numbers. In round figures, around the year 2000 both Collingwood and North Melbourne were spending about $10 million each on their footy departments, including player payments. A decade later, the Magpies were spending almost $20 million, the Kangaroos only around $15 million. Unless Collingwood are unbelievably wasteful, that must give them a competitive edge.

Here's another telling set of numbers. Over the six years from 2004 until 2010, total football department spending across the competition increased from $175 million to $260 million. This kind of footy inflation is led by and manageable for the wealthy upper-class clubs, but is killing the financial battlers.

The AFL administration and the AFL Commission have done a fantastic job in managing and growing the sport, which is almost totally funded by the earnings of the national competition.

Yet for all the terrific initiatives they've put in place over the last 25 years, I'm very critical that the sport's governing body hasn't repeated the salary cap concept of limiting player payments by limiting other footy spending. The result has been a massive increase in footy department spending over recent years.

The AFL's refusal to put a cap on football department spending has created a competition underclass that needs subsidies from head office just to survive. The term 'unequal distribution' is the AFL's tag for this subsidy payment to those in need.

Sometimes, for all their great work, I wonder whether the AFL head office understands footy at club level. In the nitty-gritty, hand-to-hand combat that tends to best describe the intensely competitive life at AFL clubs, millions are being spent in the attempt to find a competitive advantage over the opposition.

The AFL concept of subsidising the poor clubs to achieve a

satisfactory minimum football department spend is folly. The competitiveness that drives footy at club level means the financial envelope will always be pushed to the limit and usually beyond. Increasing minimum spends for the financial battlers won't work. If an even competition with 18 self-sufficient, financially viable clubs is ever to be achieved, what needs to be introduced is capping the maximum football department spending. If it is good enough for player payments to be capped, so should the non-player expenditure.

10

SCOTT, TUCK AND MATTHEWS

*It would be easy to think that Hawthorn's Team of the
Century on-ball brigade, who played side by side in a couple
of premierships, had to be best buddies. Not so.*

When Hawthorn Football Club announced their Team of the
Century in 2002, they did it individually, starting with back pocket
Gary Ayres. One by one, the first 15 players were announced and
celebrated. However, when they got to the final three positions – the
on-ball division of ruck, ruck-rover and rover – there was a change
of tack and it became a group thing. The three players were introduced as one: Don Scott, Michael Tuck and Leigh Matthews, or to
Hawthorn insiders 'Scotty', 'Tucky' and Barney.

It just made sense, because we were always regarded as a team
within a team. After all, we'd been together as the first ruck division at Hawthorn for a very successful period in the club's history. A
bit like the Three Amigos, we went together like bacon, lettuce and
tomato, or reading, writing and arithmetic. Whenever you picked
up the paper on a Friday morning, there we were named as the
Hawthorn on-ballers and when the match started we were alongside
each other at the opening bounce.

When I joined Hawthorn in the late 1960s, many Hawks players
were freebie guests at the Baron of Beef restaurant in the outer
Melbourne suburb of Monbulk, owned by keen Hawks supporters
Jack and Renee Farr. They had been lifelong fans, but as they got to
know personally the many and varied people who were part of the
Hawthorn team there was one slightly sad reality.

Renee often commented that as a girl she loved watching the team run out onto the field before a match. Fit and strong, oiled arms shining, in a really tight pack, they looked like 20 brothers, she'd say. With a closer involvement, she was a little disappointed to discover that players being all best buddies was more a myth than a reality. She found out a basic fact about team life: that this player didn't particularly like one of his team-mates, so-and-so's wife didn't particularly like another team-mate's wife – all the normal vagaries of group life, whether it be a football team or a business team.

My Channel Seven and 3AW colleague Brian Taylor put it very well when he described elite-level footy as a game of forced relationships. Players and coaches, and by association their families, are recruited into their clubs because of their talent, not because of existing friendships. As Renee Farr discovered, some members of the playing group were best buddies, others were friends, some were like work colleagues and some didn't particularly like each other.

It doesn't matter as long as everyone gels in a football sense. Friendship is good, but it's respect and trust that successful teams are built on. It's the sharing of common goals that glues team-mates together. It's why team sport is great training for life; it subtly teaches that being close friends with everyone you work with is simply unrealistic and learning to work effectively with all your team-mates is an acquired skill. Earning and giving respect from and to team-mates is the key to a healthy and constructive involvement in any group of people.

It would be easy to think that Hawthorn's Team of the Century on-ball brigade, who played side by side in a couple of premierships, had to be best buddies. Not so. While certainly not at loggerheads, and comfortable to catch up and say hello at any time, work colleagues is the best description for the relationship between Don Scott, Michael Tuck and me.

We played together for the first time in round eight of 1972 against Richmond at Waverley. A 24-year-old Scotty was playing his 101st game, I was playing my 52nd, and Tucky was on debut. We weren't the on-ball brigade that day, because Peter Crimmins was first rover; I was second rover changing out of the forward pocket. Tucky wasn't ruck rover just yet; he was a late developer who didn't exactly burst onto the scene and it took a couple of years for him to graduate into the senior team, let alone into the elite player that he became for an amazing 426 games.

Still, for about six years from the mid-1970s, the Scott/Tuck/ Matthews first ruck brigade was a permanent fixture.

There's an important lesson in all of this about human dynamics, and a very real difference between perception and reality. While I'm happy to deny the popular perception of the time that Scotty and I didn't get on at all, I can also confirm that we were never what you'd classify as best mates. We shared a passion and commitment to succeed and through our joint involvement at Hawthorn had common ambitions and goals. We didn't socialise outside club functions, but I would have been happy to have him alongside me in the trenches of the First World War. In a physical contact sport, his effort and competitive fire were great to have on our side.

Close friendships were even less important in the part-time era of last century. An occasional irritation wasn't an issue. It wasn't as if we spent five or six hours a day with each other at the club, as the fully professional players do nowadays, and as long as the respect and trust was there everything was fine.

It shouldn't have surprised anyone that Scotty, Tucky and I, who between us would captain Hawthorn for 16 consecutive years from 1976 to 1991, were more acquaintances than best mates, because we were very different people.

In the early 1970s I was a young man with a wife and a young family, when others of my age bracket were still out on the tear. We primarily socialised not with my team-mates but with people who lived near us at Dingley.

Scotty worked in the fashion industry and, in one of football's great ironies, he carried a man purse. Or a handbag. Or whatever you want to call it. It was part of an image that was in total contradiction to Don Scott the footballer.

From Box Hill in Melbourne's east, Scotty always reminded me of a wild young stallion who would charge around the paddock with bound-less energy and effervescence. Operating to the beat of his own drum, he was gruff and abrasive, volatile and unpredictable. And while his

SCOTT, TUCK AND MATTHEWS

volatility sometimes led to ill-discipline and an unnecessary free kick to the opposition, he was the sort of aggressive ruckman you loved to have in your side. He set a team benchmark in competitiveness and effort, and was the type of figure who was a huge asset to any side. Importantly, too, he was the type of aggressive ruckman against whom opposition sides didn't like to play – a bit like Jimmy Manson was in my coaching days at Collingwood, and Jamie Charman was at the Brisbane Lions.

Scotty was really dominant and had very little tact and sensitivity. He wasn't what you'd call warm and friendly, but he was a fantastic team-mate because he gave the team such effort, enthusiasm and competitiveness.

As much as I would have loved to be captain when Peter Crimmins was forced through illness to stand down at the end of 1975, there's no doubt that Scotty was the right choice. I'm not sure I had the strength of leadership character at the time that he had. Certainly, I felt I benefited from my five years as vice-captain under Scotty before stepping into the captaincy in 1981 when he stepped aside.

That was an interesting year. David Parkin, coach of the 1978 premiership side, had been pushed out at the end of 1980 after we'd finished seventh and eighth in his last two years at the helm, and Allan Jeans had taken over as coach. I was the new captain.

Without a hint of exaggeration, Scotty played the entire 1981 season without saying a word to anyone at the club beyond basic football requirements. He simply trained, played and went home. It took the great coaching sensitivity and tact of Jeans to convince him to postpone his retirement and play that final year – with the carrot of getting to 300 games and life membership of the league a significant incentive. After a very quiet and solitary year, where I almost forgot the sound of his voice, Scotty got to 302 games before slipping into permanent retirement at season's end.

Playing that last ultra-reclusive 12 months was not something most of us could do, but in a strange way was typical Scotty. He always did it his way.

Just as he'd done at three-quarter time in the 1971 grand final against St Kilda, when he helped to spark an extraordinary final-quarter fightback.

And just as he would do later in 1996 when Hawthorn's very existence was under threat. Indeed, loyal Hawthorn people have a lot for which to thank the man who wore the brown and gold number 23 jumper before Dermott Brereton. In fact, without him Hawthorn might not have survived in its own right beyond the near-thing merger with Melbourne, as the club battled dire financial troubles.

No doubt the club was in civil war. It was Scotty's group against the collective voice of reason at board level. I knew well and had a lot of respect for people on the Hawthorn board at the time, like chairman and club stalwart Brian Coleman and was a very close friend of another board member, Frank Buckle. The last thing any of them wanted was to see Hawthorn disappear as a stand-alone footy club. They were as loyal to the club as anyone; but the club was broke and the merger with Melbourne seemed like the only alternative. While distasteful to them all, the merger was preferable to extinction.

With a bit of help, Scotty mobilised the Hawthorn supporters in a public fight that would eventually save the club. While Ian Dicker, who later took over as president, was the driving force behind the scenes, Scotty's role as the public face of the rearguard action was absolutely critical. It took the accompanying smell of the club's potential death to jolt Hawks fans into action, but since then Hawthorn has developed into one of the real financial powers of the competition.

Tucky was almost the opposite of Scotty in a personality sense. A plumber from Berwick in Melbourne's south-east, where his parents ran a dairy farm, he was very shy and introverted. He'd come to training, do what he had to do, and go home.

Tucky had arrived at Hawthorn in 1971 and, although officially listed in AFL records at 188 centimetres and 76 kilograms, he was 66 kilograms dripping wet back then. And he hardly said a word. In fact, in the early days, he was known as 'Smiles' because that's all he did whenever anyone asked him a question.

In his first season at the club, when Hawthorn beat St Kilda in the 1971 grand final, Tuck played the entire year at full-forward in the reserves, kicking 60-odd goals. It wasn't the ideal position for a young up-and-comer, given that Peter Hudson was the full-forward in the seniors, and at the end of his first season he didn't even make the senior list for 1972. It was only after Huddo was injured that Tucky got his chance in round five. He kicked goals with each of his first three kicks against Richmond at Waverley, but had a poor one the following week and was subsequently dropped. He played a total of five games in 1972 and 11 in 1973.

Even in those early years, and right throughout his career, he was a fantastic running athlete. He never really extended himself at training, comfortable being unobtrusive around the middle of the bunch. His natural inclination was about blending in, not standing out from the group.

He was the sort of guy who might have made a top-level 400 metres runner if he'd chosen to. In fact, his running ability only became obvious when a pre-season promotion called the Footy Olympics, an athletic meet for VFL footballers, was held for a few years in the early 1970s. A few players in that era did some professional running over summer to get fit, because there was very little team training prior to Christmas; but in the 400 metres at the Footballers' Olympics, even though he didn't specifically train for it, Tucky would blitz them all and cruise to victory every year. He was a natural.

From 1974, he became a wonderfully skilful ruck rover. Not unlike emerging Fremantle star Nathan Fyfe, he was a tall midfielder who was ahead of his time in the mid-1970s.

It goes without saying that the 426-game AFL games record-holder had great durability. After taking a couple of years to consolidate his place in the senior team, he became a permanent fixture, and from 1974 to 1991 he had 17 years in which he played 20-plus games. In his 18th year in 1991, he played 19 games and captained the premiership team.

Tucky was appointed captain in 1986 because he was the most senior player. He was never going to be a really vocal, domineering leader, but he always set the right example and he was as reliable as they come. The club had plenty of on-field leadership during the late 1980s and it was perfectly logical that while he could still command a regular spot in the side he continued to fill the role of captain, until being retired as the reigning premiership captain after the Hawks won the flag in 1991. He never won a Hawthorn club championship, but he was runner-up seven times and his value to the side was immense.

When I think of the most important characteristics we want in a team-mate, the work-colleague-like relationship between Scotty, Tucky and me always comes to mind. While a close friendship with team-mates is admirable and nice, it is respect, trust and the determined commitment to achieving the team goals that are the most critically valuable. These latter qualities and the sharing of those incredible premiership moments provide the permanent bond that will bind Don Scott, Michael Tuck and myself forever.

11

A NEW ERA

It must have been a strange sight – one of the grand final teams
seemingly asleep on the dressing-room floor. So much for the
rev-up of the pre-game pep talk!

No-one knew it at the time, but the 1976 grand final was John Kennedy's swan song as Hawthorn coach. Four months later, in a shock announcement, John retired from coaching and his assistant in 1976, David Parkin, was immediately and unsurprisingly installed as the new coach of the reigning premiership team.

It was after a training session in late January that John told a stunned Parkin he was about to resign as senior coach and that his 1976 assistant would be endorsed by the club's board as his replacement. It was typical Kennedy: no fuss, no fanfare and no leaking out of his plans. John Kennedy had turned 48 shortly after Christmas and had coached Hawthorn for 14 years in two stints from 1960 to 1963 and 1967 to 1976, plus one game in 1957.

David had played 211 games for Hawthorn from 1961 to 1974, and had been captain of the 1971 premiership side. He'd actually retired in 1973 and had been appointed captain-coach of the reserves for 1974, but a string of injuries saw him back in the seniors for the second half of the season before hanging the boots up for a second time after the 1974 preliminary final loss to North.

In what was well before its time, when I look back I see there was very much a coaching partnership in play at Hawthorn in that 1976 premiership year. Unbeknown to most of us players, some troubling personal issues affecting his teenage son Bernard were causing John and his family a lot of time and stress. Consequently, assistant coach Parkin took a lot of the training in 1976, so when those family issues ultimately influenced John to retire, the senior coaching change-over was automatic and seamless.

Parko had moved to Perth in 1975 primarily to complete his Bachelor of Education, and while he was there the ever-combative back pocket player had been captain-coach of Subiaco in the WAFL. He returned to Hawthorn as assistant coach under John in 1976 and filled very much a hands-on role. Such was John's confidence in his offsider that he asked and in fact encouraged Parko to do a lot of the training and preparation work that was normally reserved for the senior coach. It was a perfect balance between the simple and proven methods of the established senior coach and the enthusiasm, imagination and variety of the younger up-and-comer.

Maybe this arrangement was the forerunner to the coaching partnership that Parko would have with Wayne Brittain at Carlton in 2000, before stepping aside to allow Brittain to take over in 2001. At the time, however, Parko insists there was no such succession plan in place at Glenferrie Oval. He was as surprised as everyone else when he inherited the senior coaching job at Hawthorn.

If John Kennedy was the authoritarian school principal coach, then Parko was more of the collaborative schoolteacher style. Very quickly he stamped his own mark on the coaching job as he revolutionised the role of the man in charge. And very rapidly the schoolteacher in him and his fanatical attention to detail came to the fore.

He was the first person to introduce a coach's room – even if it was really just an old storeroom adjacent to the offices at the opposite end to the players' locker room. It was chocolate brown, and was really dark and dingy, but that didn't worry Parko. He loved it. And he loved nothing more than his 'In Retrospect' review meetings, as he used to call them.

As a schoolteacher who became a college professor, he was a great writer. Each Tuesday night after a game, when we arrived at the club for training there would be a written report from him on the match from the Saturday before. On Thursday nights, we'd get a written summary of the team we'd face two days later, complete with strengths and weaknesses, and instructions for likely match-ups.

There wasn't a lot of extra individual coaching, but there was plenty of written feedback. He even introduced a mechanism whereby the players were invited to provide feedback of their own. By the late 1970s he'd introduced video highlights as a pre-game motivational tool. While it eventually became common practice, the implementation of the critically important planning, training, perform and review cycle was revolutionary and well before its time.

By this stage, I was a relatively experienced player and I immediately had a good relationship with the new man in charge. He was a lecturer at Burwood Teachers College at the time, and occasionally I'd drop in for a chat during the day. This was something I would never have contemplated under John Kennedy, but it was nothing more than a generational issue. Whereas I was 24 years younger than John, the gap was only 10 years between me and Parko. I was never comfortable talking one-on-one with John in my playing days, but I immediately found it much easier to do so with David.

Even when he first coached, Parko had a relaxed and collaborative communication style and was a great believer in structure and routine. He established and stuck rigidly to a four-stage plan. The schedule was regular training on Tuesday, Wednesday and Thursday nights, and every week, the process of performing, reviewing, training and planning was carried out.

(As my two daughters were five and six, I no longer asked to be excused from training as John Kennedy had agreed to earlier in the '70s. Being my own boss at my Brandon Park sports store allowed me to juggle work, football and family hours a little better, although getting home after 9 pm on Tuesdays and Thursdays was the normal routine.)

In what seems inconceivable in the modern era, there was virtually no weights work and no organised gym program. Up until the 1980s, if a player was skinny he stayed skinny; fortunately, I was naturally quite strong and bulky. Once organised weight work became normal, strength and bulk could be manufactured in the gym, so natural strength was not as great an asset. With my build and playing attitude, I think I played in the right era.

All the training was done out on the field, and under David some of it had the hallmark of the analytical teacher. Even though I was an experienced player, there were times when, after he'd introduced a new drill, I'd sneak to the back of the line so that someone else up the front could stuff it up.

The teacher in Parko was forever coming up with drills that were designed to make the players think more. For instance, during circle work, he'd introduce footballs of various colours that carried with them specific instructions. There would always be four or five balls going at once, and when you got a red footy you could only kick it. A yellow footy had to be handballed, and when you got a red footy with a stripe on it you had to run and bounce. At other times, he'd use his favourite witch's hats as instructional markers: run to witch's hat A, then bounce the ball to witch's hat B, then turn left at C and baulk D before kicking at E. It was complicated stuff back then, and I've got to admit half the time I was never quite sure what to do next.

During pre-season training we'd have competitive sessions with half a dozen groups of players competing for points in everything we did. This helped reduce the boredom that could come with extended repetition and fed the competitive juices of the players.

He also continued the old Hawthorn favourite of Catholics versus Protestants in a lot of games-related training. Whether it was soccer, volleyball or whatever we did, this was how the group was split up. It was Hawthorn's way of thumbing their nose at religious discrimination, which apparently had a bit of a foothold at some clubs in previous generations. I was a floater – a christened Protestant who had married a Catholic – so I always went to whichever side was a little light-on for numbers.

At Hawthorn going into 1977, there were big changes happening. Out was Kennedy and in were Parkin and Hudson.

The year heralded not only a change of senior coach but the return to VFL level of champion full-forward Peter Hudson. After the severe knee injury he suffered way back in the opening round of 1972 had prematurely ended his VFL career, and after heading back to Tassie to live, he'd started to play again for Glenorchy during 1975 and completed a full season in 1976.

Huddo succumbed to the lure of resuming in the big-time, having been encouraged and feted by the Hawks. It was no ordinary comeback, because, as I mentioned earlier, the successful Granada Tavern hotel he owned and ran meant he didn't stop living in Tasmania. There would have been only a handful of times that he even trained with the team that year, travelling to Melbourne on Friday and going back on Saturday night after the game. All six VFL games were played at 2.10 pm on Saturday in those days. Night footy for premiership points and indoor stadiums were still pipe dreams.

It was a mark of the Hudson magic that on this self-preparation regime he played 24 games and kicked 110 goals – an amazing effort from a player who so often made that description his own.

The Hawks posted a 17–5 home-and-away record that was good enough for second spot on the ladder. We thrashed third-placed North Melbourne by 38 points in the qualifying final, then the following week top-placed Collingwood beat us by two points in the second semi-final. They went straight to the grand final and we were back to a knockout preliminary final against the Kangaroos.

That hard-fought second semi was the infamous game where the Magpies' volatile match-winner Phil Carman inexplicably charged at Michael Tuck and hit him with a raised forearm to the head. The result was a two-week suspension that ruled him out of the grand final and which severely damaged Collingwood's aspirations of going from wooden-spooners the year before to premiers the following season. I know a bit about the rushes of blood that cloud clear thinking on the footy field, but this one by Carman at such a crucial time had dire consequences for the Magpies and is remembered by the Collingwood faithful to this very day.

For Hawthorn, the season ended abruptly the following week when we were badly beaten in the preliminary final by North. Personally, 1977 had been my best season, but in that knockout preliminary final my direct opponent, Barry Cable, was the outstanding player on the field, so the year for me ended on a particularly sour note.

This was the fourth year in a row that either Hawthorn or North had knocked the other out of the premiership race. North had got the better of us in the preliminary final in 1974 and the grand final in 1975, and we'd extracted our revenge in the 1976 grand final. But this year we'd lost by 67 points in what would be the biggest finals loss of my career until the very last game of all, which was still six years away.

Interestingly, of the 29 finals I would ultimately play, no fewer than 12 were against North. In fact, it was 12 of my first 21 in the decade from 1974 to 1983, explaining why there was such a fierce rivalry between the two clubs during that time.

At the end of the 1977 season, Huddo, having successfully faced the comeback challenge as a fly-in fly-out player, decided that his business in Tasmania had to take precedence and this time his retirement from the Hawks was permanent.

In 1978, after another good year, we again finished second at the end of the home-and-away season, this time on percentage behind North with a 16–6 record. We beat Collingwood by 56 points in the qualifying final, and then accounted for North by 14 points in the second semi.

There hadn't really been a clear-cut flag favourite until North struggled to overcome Collingwood in the preliminary final and in the process lost Brent Crosswell to injury. They'd already lost Peter Keenan to suspension after he had belted Don Scott in the previous week's semi-final. On grand final day, we were a clear-cut fancy as Norm Goss, who'd missed the two lead-up finals, and Robert DiPierdomenico, who'd missed the semi-final, came back into the side for Shane Murphy and David O'Halloran.

Prior to the grand final, I had my first taste of visualisation thanks to the ever-creative Parko. We were based in the old Melbourne change rooms at the MCG and he had all the players lie flat on their backs on the floor. He ensured everyone in the room was quiet and then asked the players to close their eyes and visualise what they were going to do in the game that was only a few minutes away.

It must have been a strange sight – one of the grand final teams seemingly asleep on the dressing-room floor. So much for the rev-up of the pre-game pep talk!

I found those few moments of silence and calm invaluable, and it confirmed my belief that the greatest trap for players on grand final day is to go out onto the field over-hyped. As I believed from that day on, the coach's job is to prevent excess hype, because the occasion itself will create enormous emotional stimulus. It was for this reason that when I found myself coaching Collingwood and later Brisbane in grand finals, I ensured there were no decorations or streamers in the rooms. I always wanted it to be as low-key as possible, because I believed that the prospect of running out onto the MCG in front of 100,000 people and playing for a premiership cup was stimulation enough.

In the 1978 grand final, our full forward, Mick Moncrieff, kicked two goals in the first two minutes, which allowed me to give a vicious spray to his opponent, Ross Glendinning. There would be no prisoners taken this day. We led by 19 points at quarter-time, but four goals from Phil Baker plus a screaming mark over Ian Paton in the second quarter saw North four points up at half-time. We kicked 7.6 to 3.4 in the third quarter, including six unanswered goals in a decisive 12-minute burst, and were never headed. Peter Knights, who had finished runner-up in the Brownlow Medal for the second time, was swung forward after he copped a heavy knock and kicked two important late goals.

Being 22 points up at three-quarter time, I was again able to adopt the 1976 final-quarter strategy of lead preservation by playing on-ball back rather than my normal on-ball forward style. It didn't work nearly as well this time, because North kicked five last-quarter goals, but we got four ourselves to win by 18 points.

It's rare for a first-year player from the suburbs to be an integral part of a premiership team, but that is what centreman Terry Wallace was in our 1978 victory. He played every game in his debut season in what was the start of a magnificent and I think underrated career. 'Plough', as he became known around Hawthorn, was a fantastic ball-winner with enormous stamina and courage who was the epitome of what is now called an inside midfielder – very much in the mould of greats like Greg Williams in the 1980–1990s and Simon Black of the 2000s. They're the type of player who does so much effective work in congested packs that you need to watch the replay tapes to fully appreciate their value.

I'd been 10 years at Hawthorn and had been lucky enough to share three different premierships with 42 different players. Only Alan Martello, Kelvin Moore and Don Scott had been a part of all three.

After a dominant few years and with a couple of premierships in our keeping, the future looked rosy. Little did we know at the time that it was in fact the end of an era – further proof for my growing belief that, in football, expectations and assumptions are a recipe for complacency and disappointment.

The future is always uncertain, as we found out when we slipped out of the finals in the following year. In 1980, we again failed to reach an even split in the win–loss column, with a 10–12 record, and slipped one spot further to eighth.

Nothing stays the same forever and the family club, as Hawthorn liked to market itself, was about to divorce one of its favourite sons. A coaching change was just around the corner. After captaining the 1971 flag-winning team and two years after guiding the club to the 1978 premiership as coach, David Parkin was moved on.

When a debate arose at board level about whether to reappoint David or to seek a new coach, Parko made the decision for them and immediately resigned. Hawthorn's loss was to prove Carlton's gain, as he coached them to the 1981 and 1982 flags.

Two of David's greatest supporters were chairman of selectors Ken Herbert and dual premiership captain Don Scott. Incensed with the club's treatment of Parkin, they both resigned in protest. In fact, at the Annual Meeting at the Hawthorn Town Hall a month or two later, Ken was slated to receive a life membership but instead of an acceptance speech he took to the microphone to knock back the award – on the basis that he did not want any part of a club that could treat David Parkin so badly. He then stormed out of the building, never to be seen around the club again.

Soon after Parko's departure and before a new coach had been appointed, I was called in to a meeting in the committee room with president Ron Cook and general manager Peter Becker.

While I was a strong supporter of David as coach, I also believed entirely in the board's right and responsibility to make decisions on coaching appointments. I never had any problems accepting the authority of the club's board to make hard decisions and personally I had accepted the change without issue. Going into the committee room, I was thinking that, as vice-captain and reigning club champion, the meeting would be something of a PR gesture to seek my support in a time when a fractious atmosphere was bubbling around the club.

At least, that was my thought when I arrived. As we chewed the fat, the discussion turned to coaching options and the fact that Alex Jesaulenko had been captain-coach of Carlton's premiership-winning team the year before, in 1979. Then the penny dropped. They were asking me if I was interested in becoming captain-coach of the Hawks.

I entertained the thought for a second or two, then dismissed it immediately.

To this day, I'm not sure what would have happened if I'd embraced the notion. It was almost as if the powers that be had felt an obligation at least to float the idea, just in case I was desperate for the job, and I'm sure they were relieved when I didn't pursue it.

Many people have asked me over the years whether I was ever offered the Hawthorn coaching job. The answer is no, except for that strange get-together in October 1980 when I reckon if I'd pushed the idea then the job could well have been mine.

What I did say at that meeting was that, as Scotty had retired, if the captaincy was up for grabs I wouldn't mind that. And so, even before the new coach was appointed, I was told I would be the next captain. (As I described in the previous chapter, Scotty actually played on for one final year in 1981.)

After a short search, Allan Jeans became Hawthorn's new coach and so began the most successful decade experienced by any VFL/AFL club during the last 50 years.

12

PERSONALITY PROFILING

I'm sure that if I'd known in my earlier days playing and then coaching at Collingwood what I learned at Brisbane, I might well have made some better decisions along the way.

For simplicity, I've mainly produced this autobiography in the chrono-logical order of my life, but a coaching and teamwork aid that popped up when I went to Brisbane is worth outlining here, because when I think back the personality profiling we did at the Lions reminds me of many of the people I played with at Hawthorn or coached at Collingwood.

There was a simple creed that underlined the mental approach to life at the Brisbane Lions for a decade. It said in short: 'We don't care what you think – we only care what you do.' It was a slightly more complicated way of saying 'actions speak louder than words', which wasn't exactly earth-shattering, but in implementing it we tried to understand in depth the personality tendencies of everyone involved in order fully to maximise individual performance.

The performance psychologist Dr Phil Jauncey was a consultant to the Lions when I arrived at the end of 1998. While I started afresh in most football support roles, he came well recommended and didn't carry any baggage from the previous era, so I was happy to keep him on. It was an important decision which would reap significant bene-fits right through my time at the Lions.

Phil was born in Adelaide but is an Aussie/American who speaks in an Aussie way with a real American twang you might find in the southern parts of the United States. It's not surprising, because he spent his first 16 years in the US. He came home to Australia to do degrees in Psychology and Human Growth and Development at the University of Queensland, went back to the US to do his masters and doctorate in Educational Psychology and Counselling at New Mexico State University.

Having spent a lot of time in the US, Phil was a basketball fan and his first involvement in the Brisbane sporting landscape was under Brian Kerle with the Brisbane Bullets in the mid-1980s. Later, he also worked as a consultant to the Bears/Lions in the AFL, the Brisbane Broncos rugby league team, Queensland Bulls cricket team and the Queensland Academy of Sport. From there, so highly was he regarded, he worked with the Queensland State of Origin rugby league team, the Australian cricket team, and the 1992, 2000 and 2004 Australian Olympic teams.

He came to one training session and to every game for my first two years in Brisbane. Phil never became a full-timer, basically because we couldn't afford to get him all week, but from 2001 we were able to upgrade him to a couple of days each week plus match days.

I never liked the 'sport psychologist' tag and, although qualified as one, neither did Phil; it somehow implied the mumbo-jumbo that players were being mentally rewired and programmed like flesh and blood robots at a Frankenstein experiment. All any psychologist can do is help players to help themselves.

Phil's official title was Mental Skills Coach. Just as we had conditioning coaches, strength coaches and football assistant coaches working on specific physical and football development, Phil's job was to help players and coaches with the mental side of the game. He had a great feel for the way individuals would react and how they should be treated, based on a personality profiling system he'd developed.

Essentially, he would have people complete a questionnaire of 40 multiple-choice questions in which they were asked to nominate the answer which they felt was closest to their views. It didn't have to be spot-on, and often wasn't, but the people completing the questionnaire had to pick the closest answer to their thinking of the four choices offered. From this, Phil would plot the answers on a piece of graph paper divided into four quadrants, and come up with a remarkably accurate picture of their personality profile.

Essentially, his system categorised people across four personality types – Mozzies, Enforcers, Thinkers and Feelers. We've all got a little of each characteristic, but are weighted heavily in some areas more than others. How much of each characteristic each individual had would help determine how they were likely to act and react.

His basic description of each personality quality was as follows:

Mozzies

Talk and activity are key flags. During battle, they need to be able to trust instincts. Thinking is a downer in game time. Mozzies learn via repetition rather than talk. They find it hard to process details and structured logic. They learn best by 'why' and general process logic. Self-discipline and organisation are major flaws for Mozzies. They require external guidelines. They want to please and thus respond to personal interaction more than group memos.

Enforcers

Being in control of their situation is the key to their success. This enables good talk and aggression. When feeling threatened, their natural instinct is anger and denial. Thus personal goal-setting and measurement are essential. Learning is dependent on them doing it for themselves, rather than merely impressing an authority figure. Once they understand the relevance of the learning, go to the 'what' detailed method of presentation. A great phrase for their stubbornness is 'Where do we go from here?' When they use excuses, believe them and follow them with 'So what you are telling me is that in future every time the "excuse" occurs, you will do the same thing?'

Thinkers

Knowing their structure is essential to success. They tend to worry about performance but often will not speak about their doubts. They need time to prepare themselves, thus they handle surprises badly. They learn by 'what' and details. If instructions are not clear, they will keep repeating them in their minds until they are clear. While doing that, they miss what is being said. They need to be able to identify their flags to get consistent performance, as they will continually be haunted by negative thoughts.

Feelers

This group finds it the hardest to succeed in professional sport because they want to withdraw when they feel others are not impressed with their efforts. They respond terribly to coaches getting angry and raised voices. They have to get up into their Mozzie mode (above confidence line). They learn via process and 'why'. Activity and repetition is useful. They need a lot of reassurance. They also badly need clear flags to deal with their mental demons.

I did Phil's test not long after arriving in Brisbane and was found to be 35 per cent Enforcer, 27.5 per cent Thinker, 20 per cent Mozzie and 17.5 per cent Feeler – or, as Phil described me, an Enforcer/ Thinker. This was based on my natural tendencies and, as he stressed relentlessly, your tendencies were not an excuse or a justification for acting on these impulses, but an explanation of sorts as to why we were likely under pressure to react a certain way.

Although I initially suspected personality profiles would change as we get older, Phil insisted otherwise. What changed, he said, was the manner in which people learned to manage each part of their personality characteristics – how experience teaches us to temper and control our natural reactions.

For me, this process underlined the basic definition of the word 'discipline', which is such a critical component in life let alone professional sport. Discipline to me meant 'doing what you should do – not what you feel like doing at the time'. And that is what we all tried to instil in our players in the most effective way possible.

Armed with this new-found knowledge, suddenly a few things started to make sense when I looked back on my playing days at Hawthorn. For instance, long-time ruckman Don Scott, who was as aggressive an on-field competitor as I have seen and who played such a key role in saving the club from a merger with Melbourne in 1996, exhibited all the characteristics of a heavy Enforcer. This meant that before a game Scotty and I would withdraw into ourselves to get ready for what we regarded as football war.

Conversely, Rodney Eade, who would later go on to be a successful senior coach at the Sydney Swans and the Western Bulldogs, had a lot of Mozzie in him. His pre-game routine for the last 60–90 minutes before battle was all about staying nice and relaxed, cracking jokes, and generally mucking around. I'm sure at the time Scotty and I used to think 'Rocket' wasn't ready to play, because he wasn't serious enough or focused enough, but having learned what I learned 30-odd years later I understood that what he was doing was simply what worked best for him. If he had, metaphorically, buried himself under a towel, it might not have worked for him, as it would have for Scotty and me.

If I could pick one personality from my days at Collingwood, I'd say Darren Millane was a massive Enforcer. That meant that to get the best out of him you had to make friends with him – ask for his assistance rather than give him a list of autocratic instructions.

The best coaches and managers have always been very good amateur psychologists, because technical skill aside, the coaching art is based on an accurate knowledge of what makes individuals and groups work best, both individually and collectively.

Phil's simple and easy-to-understand personality profiling was a great head start, and, in retrospect, this information had applications wherever I looked. I'm sure that if I'd known in my earlier days playing and then coaching at Collingwood what I learned at Brisbane, I might well have made some better decisions along the way.

I'd done countless personality profiling over the years, often with things that took five hours to complete and five hours to read. They were much too complicated. What I liked about Phil's system was that it was so simple. Every player and every staff member was profiled during my time in Brisbane, in an effort to help maximise their individual performance.

Most importantly, it was totally transparent. Everybody knew each other's personality type and percentage breakdown. There was no right or wrong, and no best or worst. And it most definitely was not an excuse for doing the wrong thing on or off the field. In no way was it a justification for doing something stupid or being reported. Moreover, we used the system to try to help players prone to that sort of thing to control their Enforcer tendencies. Similarly, we couldn't allow a Mozzie to disregard the team plans and team rules.

Really, it was a useful mechanism by which we could try to get the best out of ourselves and understand how best to treat people around us – a bit of a psychological head start, if you like.

The whole principle was mentioned regularly, and often in a light-hearted fashion. As Phil would say, 'You Mozzies go over there and buzz away together, and be sure not to interrupt the Enforcers, because you know they won't like it.'

All this was a wonderful coaching and management tool.

Brisbane games record-holder Marcus Ashcroft, for example, was a heavy Thinker. That meant whenever I had a task for him I'd always be sure he had a few days' notice. This was because he worked better knowing precisely what the task was, so he could plan the most effective strategy to fulfil it. This was especially important for 'Choppers' during the premiership era, when he played as a stopping defender and would usually have a specific close-checking one-on-one assignment.

Jonathan Brown was a Mozzie/Enforcer. He's very goal-orientated and task-driven, and doesn't especially like long planning meetings. Clearly, planning and meetings are an increasing part of the job in the modern era, so Browny had to learn to bypass his natural tendencies in this area, but I always knew if I was going too long because he'd start to get a bit fidgety and distracted.

The crazy thing about all this is that Phil himself is 60 per cent Mozzie. That's a massive dominance of one characteristic, and is exactly the opposite of what you'd expect for a person with his academic qualifications. While Mozzies will want to achieve, they will not normally be great students, but Phil has three or four tertiary degrees. As he explained to me, this only proves that his system identifies tendencies, not results.

Essentially, I learned how best to work with each character type. A Mozzie like Browny has to be encouraged not to think too much and to be more instinctive. If he was a first-gamer, for example, it was probably best to tell him of his selection as late as was practically possible rather than give him three or four days to stew over it. A Thinker like Choppers is the opposite. He's exactly what his tag implies – he needs time to plan and strategise.

An Enforcer doesn't especially like being told what to do. Someone like Justin Leppitsch had a stubborn streak in him and he performed best when you asked for his help and worked with him on a common level.

A Feeler will take criticism very badly, because they are always down on themselves anyway. Nigel Lappin, for example, could be a unanimous choice as best afield but he'd walk off the ground picking faults in his performance. Feelers think you are being heavily critical of them when you don't even realise it, and if you don't happen to talk to them one-on-one for any length of time they'll think you don't like them and are down on them for some reason.

There were a lot of players strong in a couple of personality sectors. Simon Black is a heavy Mozzie/Enforcer. He's at his best when he's up and aggressive, and not too structured. He needs to keep talking and will worry after a game. There's never a chance he'll be complacent, because he's always his own harshest critic.

Most leaders have a fair degree of Enforcer in them, and it won't surprise anyone to learn that Chris and Brad Scott were both heavy Enforcers. Michael Voss was too, although he wasn't as heavily weighted in that direction. He was an Enforcer/Thinker – more like me.

As much as anything, I learned via Phil's personality profile system how to work with myself, and my own strengths and weaknesses. For example, the Enforcer in me meant that whenever a player or an assistant coach came to me to discuss the possibility of altering something that we were already doing, I'd instinctively fight back in order to protect the existing system. This was the stubborn streak in me, as if altering something was a personal attack on me as a coach. Clearly this was totally illogical, because if all I ever did was push back, the players and assistant coaches would be reluctant to come and talk to me in the future with another idea for a better alternative, or a new plan.

I think in time I was able to fight my natural instincts, not that I always succeeded. I learned to bite my tongue most of the time and make myself listen. After all, the prime motivating force was to make the team better. Once I'd slipped back into Thinker mode and rationalised a new proposal, often I'd realise it was a good idea, so we'd implement it.

Looking back at all this, I think my Enforcer qualities were probably quite helpful and positive as a player. That was perfectly logical, because in a physical contact sport it was reasonable to have a fair mix of the two. I needed a strong physical presence in the contest, which was driven by the Enforcer in me, even if occasionally it went a little over the top and I was guilty of illegal aggression. But just as much I needed to be in Thinker mode, because when I was thinking well I was reading the play and knowing where to go to get the footy. As a coach, however, it was more important that I maximised my Thinker qualities because, essentially, that's what you've got to be as much as possible. After all, coaching is mainly about thinking.

I asked Phil once if there was any type of personality that reacted well to being yelled at and he answered 'No'. That was unfortunate because at the end of a game sometimes as a coach you drift unavoidably into anger, frustration and disappointment, and you just feel like yelling at someone. That's typical Enforcer. I learned as a coach I was much better off staying in Thinker mode where I could strategise and plan more effectively.

We even did a profiling evening with the wives and girlfriends one time. This enabled everyone to understand each other a little better and, to be football selfish, how to assist their playing partners to be better footballers.

We never went so far as to let personality profiling influence our team selection, but it was an influence in who we drafted. Logically, the right mix of different types is important. It's not clear-cut, and it's tempting to say that perhaps an even split of the four different types is ideal, but I'm more inclined to think that for a combative physical contact sport like football you'd be best off with 40 per cent Enforcer and an even 20 per cent of Mozzie, Thinker and Feeler.

Phil is a great believer that a coaching group needs a good spread of the different qualities. For instance, a group of heavy Enforcers working together is a volatile mix because their stubborn streak can often lead to friction and conflict.

There is never a substitute for pure football ability and all that goes with it, but in a game where we are forever looking for that minuscule edge, there is no doubt that Dr Phil's personality profiling was an extremely valuable part of the Lions' golden era.

13

THE COACH OF COACHES

Over 17 seasons at Hawthorn I only had three coaches –
John Kennedy, David Parkin and Allan Jeans. All multiple
premiership coaches, all icons of the coaching profession.
How lucky was I?

On 20 July 2011 the football world gathered, not only to pay their respects and to farewell Allan Jeans, but also to celebrate his life. His funeral, attended by a couple of thousand people, was held at the MCG, which for us footy nuts is the holy shrine of our game. It was a special place to give a special man the send-off he deserved.

This was someone who gave so much of himself to others, who provided guidance to so many people who had come under his influence. I had the good fortune to be one of this large and grateful group.

Another protégé was a Hawthorn team-mate and one of footy's really tough players, Dermott Brereton. Dermott said it for us all when he noted that the passing of Allan Jeans would stimulate more tears from grown men than anyone else he knew.

Many words were spoken about 'Jeansy', and many stories told, but a unique insight into his persona came in the eulogy – on behalf of all the players he coached – delivered by John Kennedy junior, a premiership team-mate of mine at Hawthorn and the son of my first coach, John Kennedy senior.

John told the story of how one night late in a season he'd bumped into a team-mate walking down the corridor of the dressing rooms at Glenferrie Oval. The player was looking rather downcast and John asked what was wrong. The team-mate explained he'd just been sacked by the club. When John expressed his sympathies for the team-mate's plight he was taken aback with the team-mate's reply that, while he was hurt and disappointed, he felt even worse that Jeansy had been forced to deliver such bad news.

The story was probably embellished just a little for effect but it said in a few words the gift that Allan Jeans had to get everyone on side. It's an unfortunate reality that coaches and managers are required to sack people quite regularly and the victim's normal reaction is to 'shoot the messenger'. While Jeansy always put the team first, he had the wisdom, sensitivity and caring manner to make the individual believe he cared about them too and that the bad news was as hurtful to him as it was to them. He always cared for his players as if they were his own sons. And, as my two previous coaches had done before him, he had a massive influence on my football philosophy, not so much in relation to playing but in my 20-year coaching career that followed. There has never been a better coach of coaches than the great Allan Jeans.

I've mentioned regularly throughout this book how uncontrollable good or bad fortune inexplicably enters our lives. Over 17 seasons at Hawthorn I only had three coaches – John Kennedy, David Parkin and Allan Jeans. All multiple premiership coaches, all icons of the coaching profession.

How lucky was I? Having these three men to learn from was the good fortune; being enough of a chameleon to adjust and thrive in the environment they created, to absorb the lessons they taught, that was up to me.

Even the order was perfect. Firstly, as an impressionable, individually driven, selfish youngster, the autocratic school-principal, team-first style of John Kennedy was critically important. Then, in the mid-20s prime of my playing career, came the extremely valuable innovative, collaborative teaching style of David Parkin.

Finally, when I reached the veteran stage of my playing days and retirement and maybe coaching was just over the horizon, came the enormous benefit of watching and experiencing the fantastic coaching/man-management skills of Allan Jeans.

Jeansy was a run-of-the-mill back pocket player with St Kilda, playing 77 games from 1955 to 1959, before taking over as coach in

1961 at the tender age of 27. In a remarkable 16-year reign he took the Saints to consecutive grand finals in 1965–66, including their only premiership in '66, and a further grand final in 1971. Later named coach of the St Kilda Team of the Century, he retired in 1976 due to what at the time was described as 'burnout', and it was something of a surprise to the football world when he replaced Parko as Hawthorn coach after the 1980 season. He'd had four years out of the VFL scene and had done some occasional coaching and development work in New South Wales and Queensland.

If John Kennedy was the authoritarian, school-principal coach and David Parkin the collaborative school-teacher coach, then Jeansy could be best described as a collaborative school-principal coach, or to be more accurate a collaborative police sergeant, which was his occupation outside footy.

His personal power and strength of character meant he was never a man with whom to take liberties. He commanded the necessary respect but his humble approachability allowed people to talk with him with a fair degree of comfort; not total comfort, though, because the coach is still the coach.

One of his favourite sayings was that while players might or might not like the coach, they must respect the position he holds. What he didn't say, but it was equally important to this concept, was that he never did anything to damage the respect for the position he held.

Jeansy was 47 when he joined Hawthorn as the senior coach, I was 28 and the newly appointed captain of the club, and we quickly established a good working relationship. I lived in the south-eastern suburb of Dingley and he was in nearby Cheltenham, so while I'd never been to the homes of my first two coaches, I was a regular visitor at the Jeans residence.

In the early 1980s I was slightly straining hamstrings quite often, which was limiting my training. Jeansy knew I was a keen tennis player and to top up my fitness would suggest coming over for a game of tennis on the court at his home.

The idea sounded good in principle but had a couple of major flaws. One, he was 20 years older than me and not terribly fit, and secondly he was not much of a tennis player. Just maybe the after-tennis catch-up to talk footy was his ulterior motive. Management lesson number one, find the common ground with every individual. Jeansy did this extremely well.

He generated a tremendous sense of loyalty among his players, and as the new captain and therefore a member of the selection committee, I tried to set the best possible example. That leadership need of being beyond reproach became clearer to me after Hawthorn were sent to Brisbane to play Essendon at the Gabba in round 14 in 1982. Back then, the Gabba had a pear-shaped playing surface which was surrounded by a greyhound track. It was hardly ideal for football, but the VFL saw some potential in the Queensland market and were delighted to pull more than 20,000 people on a Sunday afternoon to watch the Bombers beat us 22.19 (151) to 20.13 (133) on the back of seven goals from Simon Madden.

The important lesson for me wasn't during the match but the night before. One of my Hawthorn team-mates, Russell Greene, knew a couple of players at the local Windsor-Zillmere Football Club. So, rather than hang around the team hotel at Kangaroo Point the night before the game, a few of us went out to catch up with Greeny's mates who had played that afternoon. It was nothing more than something to do, and it wasn't as if we did the wrong thing and we were back at our hotel by 10 pm, but when we lost the game the following day there was talk around the club that some players might have had a less than ideal preparation the night before. Not much detail but some troubling innuendo.

When the issue was discussed by the match committee I felt terribly compromised. I wouldn't have played any differently if I'd spent the entire night before the game locked in my hotel room, but still I had a terrible feeling as captain of having done the wrong thing by the team. It was something that stuck with me, and from that moment on I became even more convinced that a prerequisite of good leadership is to be completely beyond reproach.

Jeansy was known as 'Yabby' to a lot of people after an incident in his early days in Finley in the Riverina district of New South Wales where he grew up. Apparently, he'd got so badly sunburnt as a kid one day that it was said he went as red as a yabby. The Yabby moniker stuck but I was never that into calling people by their nicknames, so to me he was more often than not simply 'Jeansy'.

Whatever I called him, he was a fantastic teacher for me during our shared time on the match committee, and the many lessons I learned during this period held me in good stead for the times that followed.

He was widely renowned for his simple three-phase philosophy of football: we've got it (the ball), they've got it, and it's in dispute. But there was a lot of depth to his tactical coaching, although his belief that footy is a combination of basics – what needs to be done every week – and tactics which might change from match to match, was the framework for his coaching style.

The Jeans philosophy was about getting the basics done well. That was the priority. The odd burst of tactical genius might win the occasional game but doing the basics well won premierships.

Jeansy was a magnificent orator. He had the ability to be calm and controlled and then, in an instant, could reach an ear-splitting volume that created total engagement with his audience.

Like most great communicators he could deliver a key message in a few simple concise words. Many of his sayings and parables are indelibly etched in my mind. That, in support of positive feedback, 'you catch more bees with honey than vinegar'. And to continually reinforce the need to keep trying and to never give up, that 'failure cannot cope with perseverance'.

In a similar vein, a clear message comes from his broken signpost story, which went something like this. A long time ago there was a man on a journey from a city called the Past to a faraway city called the Future. He came to a crossroads and discovered the signpost was broken and lying on the ground. Not knowing the way to his destination he was confused and uncertain. There was a stranger sitting on the side of the road who the traveller asked for directions to Future. The stranger replied that if you pick the signpost up and point the past back in the direction from which you have come, then the way to the future will be clear. The moral of this simple story is that remembering and learning from past experiences is critical to a successful future.

But the other key plank to his wonderful communication skills was his ability to listen, and to engage people in conversation. To get people talking he'd often just walk up to them and say, 'What do you reckon?' And then quite deliberately he'd be silent. He did it to me many times. The pregnant pause which followed his introductory remark always seemed like it was eternity but it was probably only ever a few seconds. I'd answer his question with a question of my own: 'Me or the team?' And in a flash he'd put me back on the spot again by saying 'Either'. And again he'd let the silence sit there.

Eventually you'd begin talking about whatever was front of mind, which was exactly what Jeansy wanted. It was his way of starting a genuinely two-way conversation. He wanted to know what was on your mind and this was his very simple method of drawing it out of his players.

He'd also do little things to elicit a particular response, or send a subtle message. As the ageing process set in I was always battling to keep my weight down to my optimum level, and when Jeansy wanted to remind me not to get too heavy, he'd pinch my belly as he walked past. This was long before skinfold tests, and although we used to get our weight recorded weekly, it was an effective method of reminding me to watch my weight.

Jeansy was a full-time police sergeant based in the force's Russell Street headquarters and he loved to work out in the police gym. One of his favourite activities after training was to invite players to wrestle him. Or 'rassle', as he'd call it. And even though he gave away a lot in years he was incredibly strong and it was nothing for him to get hold of a player – even some as big and as strong as Robert DiPierdomenico – and hold him down until his victim told him that Jeansy was the better man.

It wasn't exactly on even terms because the victim never knew the rassle was coming until Jeansy had jumped on them, usually when they were fatigued after a training session, and by the time they knew what was happening he had them pinned and from there they couldn't escape.

He tried to rassle me one day but I saw him coming, got in first and immediately grabbed him and slung him to the ground, grazing his forehead on the carpeted floor of the Hawthorn warm-up room on the way down. An extended wrestling session with the coach when the rules of combat were very grey just never appealed to me.

The two events were unconnected but he did successfully scare the life out of me on another occasion. One day I arrived at the club and was given a message from the front office advising that Jeansy wanted to see me. I walked down the corridor to his office adjacent to our changing rooms and when I opened the door I was quite taken aback to find him sitting with a gentleman in a formal police uniform. He introduced me to Senior Detective Doug Miller, who he said was investigating a complaint and he wanted to talk to me. My impulsive reaction was a 'what have I done?' panic. My footy life over the previous few matches flashed before my eyes.

I was mighty relieved when it turned out that the investigation was nothing to do with me, but was about a homemade product used by one of our club trainers and masseur, Bob Yeomans. Bob was a terrific fella who after Thursday night training doubled up as the cook in the traditional trainers' room fry-up that fed players, coaches and the assorted regulars who dropped in for a beer and a meal. It was a bit of a joke among the Hawthorn player group that the only thing that took big Bob Yeomans away from his cooking duties was when I was ready for my post-training calf massage. They reckon Bob was virtually my private trainer.

The concern was all to do with a concoction of eucalyptus oil mixed with a little liniment, which Bob used to give to the players to sniff before a game to help clear the nostrils and get everyone ready to go. There was nothing untoward going on but apparently someone at Essendon, our emerging rivals at the time, had observed our pre-game ritual and had questioned whether Hawthorn were doing anything shifty. It had somehow gone all the way to the Victoria Police Force and, on the basis that Jeansy was still working in the force, Senior Detective Miller had come down personally to see if there was anything worth investigating. The whole thing was quickly forgotten by most, but not Jeansy. He was a man who didn't have a lot of enemies but I suspect he thought it had come from Kevin Sheedy and he never had a lot of time for Sheeds thereafter.

Jeansy had taken over at something of an awkward time at Hawthorn. Whether he'd officially resigned or was pushed was immaterial – there was no doubting that Parko had been moved on, a mere two years after winning a premiership. Chairman of selectors Ken Herbert had walked out in protest, and Don Scott, captain during the David Parkin era and very much a Parkin man, had also retired in protest.

The saving grace for Jeansy was that he'd come in after Parko had gone. There was no suggestion of a link between the two, so the new coach was able to start with pretty much a clean slate. He was even able to convince Don Scott to play that one last year in 1981. As I've mentioned, even though Scotty didn't talk much to anyone he played a senior role as we had 13 wins and finished sixth, just missing the finals.

In 1982 the platform for the golden decade that was to follow was put in place. We finished second in the home-and-away season with 17 wins and ultimately came third overall. After losing to Carlton in the qualifying final, we then beat North Melbourne in the first semi-final but were defeated by the Blues again in the preliminary final.

At that time the games against Carlton were a personal struggle because I was picked up by Rod 'Curly' Austin and he got me every time.

It was in the semi-final against North at the MCG that an unknown 18-year-old kid from Frankston by the name of Dermott Brereton made his debut. He kicked five goals to serve notice of the wonderful career that was to follow, bringing the young Irish fire-brand five VFL/AFL premierships and a well-earned reputation as one of the toughest, bravest and best players of his era. As I reflect on this it takes me back once again to how fortunate Hawthorn was with the old VFL zoning system, even though most of the original Morn-ington Peninsula zone had been split up and allocated to Melbourne and St Kilda.

It happened that a small part of Frankston was still Hawthorn territory and from that tiny piece of real estate we plucked centre half-forward Brereton and premiership rover Richard Loveridge, who made his debut in round 1 of 1982 and immediately became a regular fixture in the senior team.

Dermott was a unique, powerful character and before long had become probably the first rock star footballer. The ginger-blond hair he started with quickly became a thick mop of bleached blond, there was a bevy of good-looking girlfriends, and he even swanned around in a red Ferrari at one stage. The Hawks' emerging star forward was massively flamboyant, while Allan Jeans was the ultra-conservative.

Yet, opposite as they were in personality, Dermott and Jeansy developed a fantastic relationship. Dermott accepted Jeansy as a great mentor and father figure who could help him fulfil his football potential, and Jeansy accepted Dermott as a natural talent who, if he was to maximise his football potential, needed to be cut a little slack when it came to the way in which he lived his life. It was never a question of how Dermott trained or how he played – he was always a guy you wanted on your side because, although he was not a big strong centre half-forward, he played with terrific skill, courage and inspiration.

Dermott's debut in the 1982 first semi-final was also memorable for the heaviest bump I ever delivered during my 17-year and 332-game career. As it happened the Kangaroos player on the receiving end has certainly gone on to bigger and better things. It was none other than the current CEO of the AFL, Andrew Demetriou.

It was all perfectly above board, at least it was in the '80s. At the time Andrew was a second-year player at North and was a 21-year-old playing his 20th senior game. He was chasing my team-mate Rodney Eade, who had the footy running towards goal, when I came from the opposite direction past 'Rocket' and delivered a top pace hip-and-shoulder shepherd. Back in those days it was a fair bump, although with the much tighter rules about physical contact nowadays, I'm not totally sure you'd get away with it in the modern era. The result was that Andrew was carried off on a stretcher, and as he has said on many occasions since, it was the first and last time his mother went to watch him play in a career that included 103 games at North from 1981 to 1987 and three at Hawthorn in 1988.

On reflection it was Jeansy's man-management skills that stood out so often. As a senior coach a generation or two older than his players, he knew it was critically important to have someone who he was close to, who was also really close to the players. In 1982 that was Norm Goss. He'd switched from South Melbourne in 1978 and had played 81 games with Hawthorn, including the '78 premiership. He hadn't played after round 5 in 1982, so Jeansy put him on as an assistant coach.

It would be going a little far to suggest he became Jeansy's spy, but he was definitely a pipeline of information from the playing group to the coach. Jeansy thought he needed just to be able to get a feel for any undercurrents going through the ranks. Gossy was very effective in this role because he was still really popular and so much one of the boys, but he was also very much an Allan Jeans disciple.

I pinched this principle many years later when injury forced Brisbane Lions midfielder Craig Lambert into retirement in 2000. Lamby and his wife, Melissa, had a great rapport with the players, especially the younger guys. He became an outstanding assistant who played a key role as the midfield coach, but also in the general karma of the playing group and helping us quell any spot fires before they became raging infernos. When Lamby suggested it would be a good idea to have a chat with an individual player, it was an invaluable heads-up that this player would benefit from a bit of TLC from the senior coach.

Season 1982 also saw me involved in a bizarre incident in which I broke a behind post out at Essendon's old Windy Hill ground. At the time I didn't even realise it had happened. The first I knew of the whole thing was in the rooms after the game when I was about to have a shower. I had a bit of swelling on my elbow so I went to see our head trainer, Ken Goddard. I showed him my swollen arm and he said straight away, 'You must have done it when you knocked the point post over.'

I had no recollection of doing any such thing. All I remembered was that in the last quarter I'd backed into a pack of players during a marking contest deep in the forward pocket. Or at least I thought it was a pack of players. It was only afterwards I learned that I'd crashed into the post, with the top section then disappearing into the crowd, it was terrific image-building stuff, which seemed to fit perfectly with my 'Lethal Leigh' nickname.

Channel Seven commentator Lou Richards, who as I mentioned had started the Lethal tag back in 1971, went into meltdown in his television commentary, raving about what a 'he-man' I was. From that day on, the broken-point-post incident became a popular talking point whenever football's famous moments were recalled.

In 2011 an unusual episode in footy folklore became even bigger when it became the subject of a TV advertisement as part of the Toyota AFL Legendary Moments campaign. It had been launched in 2004 with commercials to relive some of the more memorable incidents that footy has seen, and featured a cavalcade of household names, including Peter Daicos, Dermott Brereton, Alex Jesaulenko, Malcolm Blight and Tony Lockett. I was in exalted company.

Filming the advertisement was an interesting experience in itself. It was done near Junction Oval at Albert Park in Melbourne and was pretty much an all-day affair from 6 am. There was no script so I had no idea what was going to happen next. It was only when they set up the next scene that I was told what I had to do, and what I didn't realise was that a lot of people who were seemingly just inno-cent passers-by were, in fact, actors.

For example, there was a groundsman in a Parks and Gardens cura-tor's uniform hanging around, who approached a few times asking us to be careful not to break the point post and who was continually on the phone, seemingly checking with his superiors. Breaking the point post would have to be the obvious culmination of the shoot – which it was. It was only at the end of the day that the 'groundsman' introduced himself as an actor there to put a bit of uncertainty into my reactions.

Although the 1982 season didn't get us the ultimate premiership result, a decade-long dynasty had begun. As much as Jeansy had a reputation at St Kilda for being an overly defensive coach, he adopted a strong skill-first approach as soon as he arrived at Hawthorn. Accu-rate kicking was a selection priority as he made it a real focus to try to get more skilful players into the backline, because so much play could be set up from defence.

Play on and run hard from defence was the mantra and we were drilled week after week with a basic ball movement routine repeated almost every training session. Groups of three players would sweep the ball in a diamond movement from goal square to wing, then onto the other goal square, and rebound the ball out the opposite side. This was the basis for the Hawthorn fast-moving hard-running game that brought so much success in the decade to come.

Jeansy did what all the best coaches do – he maximised the value of the talent at his disposal. He converted Gary Ayres from a struggling forward to one of the best defenders in the game, and developed Russell Greene and Colin Robertson as attacking taggers.

As well, Chris Mew, a 1980 debutant, consolidated a permanent spot in 1982, while Peter Schwab had a taste of it through the same period. Gary Buckenara and Chris Langford debuted in the same year and at the end of that season Ken Judge was recruited from Western Australia.

Big changes were afoot at Hawthorn and big changes were happening in my own playing situation. While I'd won the club championship in '82 playing my normal rover/forward role, that was all about to end.

Jeansy had gradually concluded that, as an ageing on-baller who had just turned 30, the hard running required was now beyond my capabilities. For me the challenge was simple: survive as a permanent forward or perish from the team. I urgently needed the chameleon in me to adapt and thrive in this new environment.

For the previous decade 20-plus disposals and four-plus goals had been my personal break-even KPIs. Playing deep forward, that many possessions was unrealistic so adjusting to the reality of my new role was a massive emotional challenge which, till the day I retired three years later, I never quite successfully managed.

14

AN AMAZING TALENT

I often wondered whether, if Jeansy hadn't been a member
of the police force, Gary Ablett might have been persevered
with a little longer.

Also new to the AFL scene in 1982 was a 20-year-old from Hawthorn's Gippsland zone by the name of Gary Ablett, the younger
brother of my 1976 and 1978 premiership team-mate, Geoff.

Geoff was at Hawthorn from 1973 to 1982 and played almost all
of his 229 games on the wing before moving to Richmond for the
last three seasons of his VFL career. Another brother, Kevin, played
31 games for the Hawks between 1977 and 1980.

Kevin had ability but was largely an unfulfilled talent whose main
claim to fame came in a rather comical incident in a mid-week night
series game against Carlton, when he snatched the headband of great
Blues defender Bruce Doull and threw it away into the Waverley
Park mud.

Doully was balding rapidly on top so to compensate was growing
his hair very long on the back and sides; hence the wearing of his trademark headband to keep his greying locks out of his eyes. Usually totally
unemotional and unflappable, he wasn't going to take too kindly
to getting the headband pinched off his balding skull. I'm not sure
whether he was certain Kevin was the culprit, but the suspicion was
enough for Doully to blow his top for maybe the only time in his long
and illustrious career. Only the intervention of a jostling pack of players
and the urgent peacekeeping of the umpires stopped the Carlton half-
back from inflicting the violent retribution he was seeking.

It must be said that the parents of the Ablett brothers produced three terrific athletic specimens. They must have had an absolute abundance of speed genes, because all their boys were lightning quick.

Geoff was a talented, reliable, low-maintenance footballer who enjoyed a long and successful career. Kevin was equally talented but an unreliable and reluctant footballer, who never fulfilled his potential. Like Kevin, Gary, the youngest of the three, was unreliable and at times was a reluctant footballer, but he was so amazingly talented that he eventually defied sub-standard preparation and commitment issues to become the most naturally gifted player I've ever seen.

Great players can be measured by many criteria. What made Gary Ablett so special was that his career highlights tape would be longer and more spectacular than any player ever to have played the game. However, he was the exception to the normal rules, the physical freak who was to be envied but, importantly, never copied.

Gary is the classic example of the need to pick the right example to follow. Any other player trying to emulate his amazing ability to play football with a similar training and preparation effort would be destined to fail.

The great talent he became at Geelong was only in the embryonic stage as a 20-year-old at Hawthorn. Gary played six games in 1982 as a wing/half forward, picking up 23 disposals against Footscray in round 3 and kicking three goals from 18 possessions against St Kilda in round 22. We won the final home-and-away game by 88 points but he was squeezed out of the side for the start of the finals the following week, along with Andy Bennett and David O'Halloran, to accommodate the return of Peter Knights, Terry Wallace and Michael Byrne.

My memories of Gary in his one season at Hawthorn over 30 years later are rather vague. I was recently speaking to Rodney Eade, a Hawks team-mate at the time, and we agreed that our memories of the youngest of the Ablett brothers were fairly similar. That he played some exciting reserves team football and that the established senior players would avoid him in one-on-one match-play drills at training if they had a choice. His strength, balance and body use were very good for a mainly reserves-level performer.

Sometimes he turned up for training, many times he didn't, so dependability was sadly lacking, and overall there were only vague glimpses of the football genius that he became at Geelong. Gary was the football version of the small, half-forward moth at Hawthorn who developed into the bigger, stronger butterfly at Kardinia Park a couple of years later.

At Hawthorn he had some talent but absolutely no drive or commitment. During his time at Glenferrie he did nothing to maximise his natural gifts, was unreliable when it came to turning up to training, and he didn't have anything like the necessary personal discipline to be a regular senior player.

As is always the case with these kinds of freak characters who seem to break all the rules and can still play at a high level, it becomes an issue around the club. From a team-building perspective, the talented individual who isn't a team player becomes an irritation to the mere mortals who have to work hard and be strictly disciplined to achieve anything worthwhile.

The final home-and-away game of 1982 was the last time Gary wore the Hawthorn guernsey, and he was moved on when the club finally lost patience with his lack of commitment. Eventually it had become a question of whether the talented unreliable kid from Drouin was worth the trouble.

There were plenty of Gary Ablett misdemeanours during his short time at Glenferrie, but the one which broke the camel's back was when he lost his driver's licence. As it does for anyone in this situation, it presented a real problem in getting around. Gary solved this dilemma by ignoring the licence suspension and just keeping on driving.

One day when he was driving without a licence he was pulled over by the police. His response was to leave the car and do a runner. The police eventually discovered who he was, rang the Hawthorn Football Club and advised the club that if he didn't present himself to the local police station by 5 pm, they'd issue a warrant for his arrest. It became a delicate issue for Jeansy who, because he was a police officer, found it hard to deal with Gary's repeated indiscretions, especially when they'd reached the level where the police were becoming involved.

I often wondered whether, if Jeansy hadn't been a member of the police force, Gary Ablett might have been persevered with a little longer. Given the enormous success of the Hawks over the following decade it would seem the correct decision was made. On the subject of conflicting issues, I'm reminded of a regular Allan Jeans message to his playing group – not terribly politically correct, I admit – that 'If it helped us win games of footy I'd go and get the worst murderer from Pentridge prison.'

For Allan Jeans, personally liking or disliking players had absolutely no bearing on whether they stayed or went – it was totally about their value to the team effort.

Gary's unreliability, coupled with a growing list of brushes with the law, had eventually led to the Hawks removing him from the club after the 1982 season. What happened next, I find quite amazing. After disappearing from public view and playing country football with Myrtleford in 1983, Gary burst back into the VFL scene at the start of 1984, this time as a second-chance recruit at Geelong.

What was extraordinary was that, in a mere 12 months, the little kid from Drouin had become a completely different physical specimen. It was as if he'd been abducted by aliens and injected with some kind of magic growth potion. If it was aliens, they did a wonderful transformation job, because when we next saw him on a VFL field in round 1 of 1984, playing for Geelong against Fitzroy, he looked like a totally different athlete.

Whereas my recollection of Gary at Hawthorn was a player of about my size and build, he turned up in a Geelong jumper looking centimetres taller, and with an accompanying increase in body bulk and strength. AFL records list the Geelong champion at 187 centimetres. I am sure the 20-year-old at Hawthorn in 1982 was nowhere near that tall.

After that initial settling-in season, it was the following year when the star was really born. In 1985, in Tommy Hafey's third year as coach at Kardinia Park, Ablett kicked 82 goals in 20 games to finish third in the Coleman Medal behind Footscray's Simon Beasley (105) and Fitzroy's Bernie Quinlan (84). And the rest, as they say, is history.

The playing highlights were many. That fantastic nine-goal haul in the losing 1989 grand final, three consecutive 100-goal-plus seasons in 1993, '94 and '95, and all these elite performances on the back of a minimalist approach to his training.

What Gary produced on the field wasn't earned by a diligent off-field life. As I mentioned, he is a classic case of the high-performing individual who didn't live by the same standards expected of his team-mates. To be an effective team member requires, at a minimum, attendance and punctuality at group sessions, plus a shared commitment to achieving the team goals.

As far as excitement machines go he was the Lance Franklin of his time, but would he have reached the extraordinary heights that he did if he'd played in the 21st century? In the days of part-time football in the 1980s, when players only spent a few hours together during the week at two or three late-afternoon training sessions, it was a little easier for players who didn't always toe the team line to be accepted. Or at least tolerated, as long as their match-day output made some leniency worthwhile.

Back then the coach largely set the discipline standards and penalties. In the modern full-time era the current flavour of the month is for powerful player leadership groups to fill a key role in the disciplinary process, and they generally frown heavily on their peers who step out of line repeatedly.

From my experience coaches value playing ability more than team-mates are inclined to do, and are more determined to use the talent rather than discard it for non-football reasons. I suspect even the wonderfully gifted Ablett might have struggled to survive under the more stringent standards set by player leadership groups in the modern era.

The Gary Ablett dynasty appeared finished with his retirement at 34 years of age after the 1996 season, with 242 games and 1030 goals to his name, and to this day he remains my benchmark for having every skill a footballer could possibly hope to possess. Of course, it was not the end of a Gary Ablett dominating the competition.

In 2002, the Ablett senior tag became necessary when the son of the retired Geelong number five arrived at the Cats under the father-and-son rule. Gary Ablett junior went to Geelong for the bargain basement cost of 40th pick in the national draft.

A few things hit me about Ablett junior. Firstly, he is about the same size I remember his dad being as a youngster at Hawthorn. Obviously the 'aliens' never got hold of junior. Secondly, he has inherited his father's football brain. Both have a great ability to think their way around the field, they understand angles, the vagaries of the oval ball and read the play beautifully. Thirdly, Gary Ablett junior may well be an even more valuable player than his father.

The latter is a statement equivalent to the odds of winning lotto – the fact that the son of the most gifted player ever can be mentioned in the same breath as his illustrious father defies logic. It's like Don Bradman's son becoming a better cricketer or Rod Laver's son winning the tennis Grand Slam a couple of times.

Where the two Gary Abletts rank individually amongst the footy greats – Ablett senior is already a Hall of Famer and Ablett junior will be in the future – will be debated regularly over the years, but there is no doubt that they are the best father-and-son combination football is ever likely to see.

15

CROSSING THE FINE LINE

The message was simple: 'Remember, no matter how nervous you may be, this is what we're born to do.'

Somewhere early in my football life I developed a simple scoreboard formula I'd run through my mind late in games to assess my team's winning chances. If we were more goals in front than there were minutes to go, we'd probably win.

In fact, it was not so much about probably winning; it was more about when the possibility of losing no longer existed. Clearly this 'no-longer-can-lose' situation is rarely in play at three-quarter time – with 30 minutes left you need a 10-goal lead to be completely safe. Even with a 60-point margin at the final break, my mindset of never expecting and never assuming wouldn't have been totally comfortable that far out from the final siren.

As the Hawthorn players wandered over to the three-quarter-time huddle in the 1983 grand final, I experienced the most surreal moment of my entire football life. We led Essendon by 87 points, the Bombers needing to outscore us by 15 goals to deny us the premiership win we were so desperately chasing. Fifteen goals? As we gathered in front of the MCC members' stand I ran the number through my head over and over again – surely that margin put the result completely beyond doubt. Even the pessimist in me, who never accepted victory until it was absolutely certain, had to concede the wonderful reality that the flag was ours.

A quarter to go in a grand final and we couldn't lose. What a fantastic, euphoric feeling that was. I'd never experienced that emotion before at the final break – it was almost disbelief – and I'd never experience it again. Premierships being decided that far out just doesn't happen.

Allan Jeans addressed us as usual but I have absolutely no memory of what he said. As captain of the Hawks my mind had already progressed to the post-game when I'd have the enormous honour of walking to the presentation dais to receive the premiership cup on behalf of the winners. For a footballer, captaining a premiership team, receiving the cup and raising it to the cheering crowd is about as good as it gets. As vice-captain to Don Scott in our 1976 and 1978 victories, I had felt a bit envious when Scotty got this opportunity, and now this boyhood dream was so close I could almost touch it.

It always amazes me how the massive media coverage of football leads to premiership discussions flowing around the air waves from early in the season. Maybe the modern phenomenon of betting on the football with flag odds set and promoted every week has been the catalyst for the ever-growing footy results predictions industry. The fact is that premierships can certainly be lost early in the season, but can only be won late on grand final day.

The history books will show a then-record 83-point final margin and yet it was a premiership which could so easily have been snatched away from us. We'd finished second on the home-and-away ladder with a 15–7 win–loss record, a game behind North Melbourne and ahead of Fitzroy and Essendon on percentage.

In the qualifying final at the MCG, though, we fell in by only four points. Challenging us was a talent-laden Fitzroy side that included the likes of Bernie Quinlan, who kicked eight goals to almost single-handedly upset the start of our finals campaign, plus Paul Roos, Garry Wilson, Gary Pert, Richard Osborne, Matthew Rendell, Mick Conlan, Scott Clayton, Leon Harris, David McMahon and Garry Sidebottom. After leading by 21 points at three-quarter time, we were outscored 4.3 to 7.2 in the final quarter and just got home on the back of Peter Knights' six goals.

It only goes to show what a fine line it is, and how many little crossroads you need to encounter before you can even contemplate winning a premiership. There was no rhyme or reason as to why we'd come out three weeks later and obliterate Essendon in such an imposing fashion.

After the qualifying final nail-biter against Fitzroy we were never again threatened. We went on to beat minor premiers North by 40 points in the second semi at a wet and muddy Waverley Park. Mick McCarthy and I kicked nine of our 13 goals between us and Richard Loveridge had 34 possessions. We were in pretty good shape for the grand final against Essendon, who in a sudden-death ride to the premiership decider had beaten Carlton by 33 points, Fitzroy by 23 and North by 86 in the preliminary final to go in slight favourites.

At selection, David Polkinghorne missed out after playing in the two lead-up finals, making way for the return of Michael Byrne who was my deep forward partner. With me being a very short 178-centimetre full-forward, Mick provided the deep forward height and was the second ruck change with Ian Paton.

Significantly, in the era of 20-man teams, we'd only used 21 players in the entire finals series. It was the sort of good fortune you need if you're going to have a good September.

In the last address from the coach a few minutes before we ran out for the grand final, Jeansy took the time to offer instruction on a couple of things that weren't directly related to the game. In what was clearly a demonstration of his love of the game and his concern for its long-term welfare, he reminded the players to stand to attention during the national anthem as a mark of respect for the crowd at the MCG; especially all the young kids, and the millions watching on television around the world. Also, he reminded us that he'd promised the umpires the Hawthorn players wouldn't get involved in any meaningless pushing and shoving which invariably followed any major incidents.

We gathered nervously at the dressing-room exit waiting for the match-day official to release us and our pent-up energy onto the field. On grand-final day the two teams have specific times, a few minutes apart, to enter the ground and as captain I was waiting for the signal to lead the Hawks down the long race onto the ground.

The wait might only have been a minute or two but it was still unbearably long, and as the tension threatened to throw us over the emotional edge a few words from the captain seemed worthwhile. On impulse and with no premeditation I turned to our mingling impatient group with a few words I hoped would soothe the jangling nerves just a little – both theirs and mine.

It was a thought that always gave me comfort in accepting and relishing the ever-present pre-match anxiety. The message was simple: 'Remember, no matter how nervous you may be, this is what we're born to do.'

There was no answer – none was needed. Each of our players was in his own emotional space coping with the uncertainty of the contest to come and the frightening knowledge of the extreme feelings that would be coming their way at the final siren.

With that our time arrived as the match official released us from the cage our dressing-room had briefly become. Entering a packed MCG with the wall of noise growing as I walked down the race was a buzz I could never get enough of.

The cheer-squad banner was huge and as the players burst through and began the warm-up lap, the vast arena seemed like a postage stamp as the sound of the huge and excited 100,000-odd crowd seemed to invade the field.

We'd had the benefit of a week's rest going into the grand final but suffered an early blow when we lost Gary Buckenara with a snapped patella tendon in his knee halfway through the opening term. The big scoreboard at the stadium showed a shot of the shattered West Australian in hospital late in the game. Despite the early setback we led by 18 points at quarter-time, 57 points at the main break and 87 points at three-quarter time as the last-quarter utopia set in.

For me, it was just as well the game was decided a long way out. Throughout much of the season I was battling a sore groin, which had all the symptoms of what was to become known as osteitis pubis. Back then we just called it a sore groin. The longer the game went, the sorer it got and the slower I got. I'd been on a limited training regime for many weeks and the preliminary final week off was a godsend. Still, after the half-time break cool-down, the familiar soreness began to return.

During the third quarter I took a mark 30 metres out and copped a coat hanger from Roger Merrett, which cost him a two-week suspension. It earned me a 15-metre penalty which was probably just as well because, by that stage of the game, I didn't think I could kick 30 metres. It was my sixth goal for the day and the last time I touched the ball. It was all I could do to walk up to collect the cup, but it was the most glorious walk of my life.

My view that Allan Jeans was a great coach of coaches is borne out by the fact that of the Hawthorn 20 that clinched the club's fifth premiership in 1983, no fewer than eight went on to coach at AFL level, including the entire centre line. There was Peter Schwab, Terry Wallace, Rodney Eade, Gary Ayres, Gary Buckenara, Peter Knights, Ken Judge and myself.

The 1983 grand final was the beginning of an incredible rivalry between Essendon and the Hawks over the next few years, and 12 months later 17 of the 20 Hawthorn players who'd enjoyed such a wonderful victory in '83 were back again to take on the Bombers in the grand final. Peter Curran, Rod Lester-Smith and Peter Russo had replaced Bucky, Knightsy, who'd only played one and four games each that year due to injury, and John Kennedy, who went down after playing the first 21 games of the season.

If the final quarter of the 1983 grand final was football utopia, the corresponding final term in '84 was football hell. We'd led the Bombers by about four goals at each change, and were 23 points up at three-quarter time. It was 10.8 to 5.15. But Essendon ran right over the top of us with a nine-goal final term to win by 24 points.

In what was to be my second-last season, I'd played exclusively at full-forward. And there I stayed for the entire final quarter.

I can still visualise the scene. As the Essendon goal-scoring surge built and built and the premiership slipped from our grasp, here I was as captain, stuck in our forward line, a spectator with a growing sense of frustration and helplessness. And while I wasn't totally sure the old body was capable of doing anything too special, I was hanging out for Jeansy to give me a crack up on the ball and see if I could help arrest the Essendon revival.

The runner never came and we lost by four goals.

As the on-ball rover who was able to play loose man behind the ball to help protect our lead in the 1976 and '78 grand final victories, a very important lesson about on-field leadership became clear to me from these differing experiences. I realised it's impossible to exert any sort of positive leadership influence on your side if things are going badly when you're a captain who plays predominantly in the forward third of the ground. All you become is a spectator when your leadership is urgently required from centre back. From my experience, leadership on a football field can be exerted effectively from defence or from the midfield, but not as a permanent forward.

The contrast between the 1976 and 1978 grand finals, and my role in the final quarter of the loss in '84, was stark.

16

THE BRUNS INCIDENT

It had been an instinctive, thoughtless act of aggression on my part that tipped the game into chaos.

There was never a time when I didn't want to play top-level footy. I just always did.

As a youngster my earliest memories were about football, and wanting to grow up and play footy as an adult was always my driving ambition. Once I started at Hawthorn and I was living the dream the years quickly tumbled by. As my first coach, John Kennedy, often said, 'Gentlemen, it is later than you think.' At the end of 1984, all of a sudden I was 32 years of age and had been at the Hawks for 16 years. My playing days were rapidly coming to a close.

Allan Jeans would tell his players the tale of an ex-coach, comfortably in his middle age, who would claim that while his life was good and he had a few dollars in the bank, he would give anything to be 20 again. That story was once an interesting curiosity; now it applied to me, and I had total empathy as far as wanting to be young and starting off again.

Even before the 1985 season started, I knew deep down it would be my last year. As an aggressive ageing Enforcer the countdown to the end of my playing career – which had been the main focus of my identity to that point – was always going to test my composure and control.

My physical condition was degenerating quickly and my self-belief was sinking just as fast. I knew my playing days were rapidly coming to an end. What's more, Jeansy and the selection committee knew it too.

It was a lesson I tried to remember during my later coaching days. Veteran players coming to the end of their career become very insecure as their form wanes, and therefore need a lot of TLC from the coach to maximise their value during that inevitable downhill slide.

The inexperienced, insecure youngsters and the fading insecure former stars need the most attention from the coach. Players in their prime years and in good form are normally fairly self-sufficient.

It isn't only the physical ageing process that dogs the football veterans – like life and death, all you can do is delay the inevitable. The only question is when the battle will finally be lost. It was the resultant mental struggle that I found just as difficult.

As my body was failing, as my reflexes and balance were quickly deserting me, so was my calmness under pressure. It is a personal flaw of mine that when I feel out of control, my decision-making usually suffers. For an aggressive Enforcer footballer like me who was still trying to be a good captain and on-field leader, it was a volatile mix of emotions.

I've often joked over the years that I only played on for one last year in 1985 because I was captain and was on the selection committee, which would at least guarantee me getting a game each week. By the end of the season, that wasn't far from the truth.

In the modern era of full-time footy in which preparation protocols are more stringently applied, the natural ageing process can be fought off for longer. In terms of nutrition, my off-field preparation was never that good. I'm afraid my taste buds too often controlled my eating, and by the 1985 pre-season my fitness levels, while never great, were dropping me to the back of the group during any of our running drills. I'd become a short, slow, 178-centimetre full-forward surviving on my strength and footy smarts.

My playing style was about getting the footy and kicking goals. I was a poor chaser and wasn't good at locking the ball in the forward line, so this vulnerability had to be covered by being very good offensively. That meant in my final season as a fading veteran I needed to kick four goals a game to be a valuable and worthwhile member of the team; maybe three was break even.

When I became a coach I hated and discouraged players from thinking of kicking goals as the benchmark of their own performance.

One, it adds unwanted and sometimes harmful pressure on the individual player, and two, it can make him selfish and goal-hungry. Looking back, as a player I was probably guilty on both counts.

Still, unhealthy as it was, when playing permanent deep forward late in my career, goals were the main KPIs of my game, and on those criteria the first half of the 1985 season was reasonable.

Going into round 12 against Geelong at Princes Park, I'd kicked three-plus goals in six of the first 10 games for a total of 34 and the team's record was six wins, four losses and a draw. But my season, and in fact, my whole life, was about to take a dramatic turn for the worse.

Why? It's a nagging question I couldn't answer with any clarity either then or now. My guilty conscience would love to uncover a satisfactory excuse, but none exists that explains my lack of control. As a result of my blow to the jaw of Geelong's Neville Bruns, the mid-June game in 1985 between Hawthorn and the Cats at Princes Park was to become famous in football history for all the wrong reasons.

My part in the mayhem happened during a bizarre out-of-control last quarter, after Geelong's unpredictable full-forward Mark Jackson appeared to completely blow his top. Or he was certainly acting that way – with Jacko what was real and what was an act was so often hard to fathom.

Even after Jacko was reported a couple of times, his continuing theatrics deep in the Cats forward line continued to capture the attention of the crowd and even the players. It was a weird feeling, as the game seemed secondary to the provocative antics being played out deep in Geelong's attacking zone.

It was late in the match and the Hawks were four goals up, with the result largely decided. As an experienced captain my leadership role needed to be as a calming influence in a dangerous and volatile situation. At least that was the plan when I headed upfield from my position in the Hawthorn forward line to keep an eye on the events unfolding at the opposite end in the Geelong goal square.

The weather had become dull and overcast as the mid-winter late-afternoon light began to fade, and in keeping with the atmosphere becoming bleak, the game itself had turned eerily ugly. To my great regret, when control was desperately needed I totally failed the self-discipline challenge.

In an unforgivable moment of madness, I hit Cats rover Neville Bruns with a round-arm coat hanger as we crossed paths not far from the centre circle.

For every action there's a consequence and from that second onwards all hell broke loose. It had been an instinctive, thoughtless act of aggression on my part that tipped the game into chaos, my body having lashed out before my mind had the good sense to withdraw consent.

As soon as I struck the blow, my first thought was, 'Shit, what did I do that for?' My second was that Geelong payback would be coming. Then the lights went out. The payback came from my direct opponent, Steven Hocking, and he did a good job. He knocked me into next week and splattered my nose in the process.

After I got back to my feet and was assisted from the field to the interchange bench, even in my hazy semi-conscious state I remember asking the Hawthorn club doctor, Terry Gay, 'How's Brunsy?' His answer of 'not too good' only added further anguish to the physical pain I was feeling.

It was always like that with me. The Enforcer part of my personality profile, my dark side, which had sparked such a brutal act, was quickly replaced by the Thinker/Feeler quality. The Feeler part of me was concerned about the victim of my aggression and hoped the damage wasn't severe, while my Thinker part was already assessing what the consequence of my actions would be.

It's a moment I'd love to take back. In all seriousness if I'd suffered a broken jaw instead of Neville Bruns, it's a swap I would have gladly made. Broken bones heal, but to this day the guilt of my embarrassing and hurtful actions on that fateful afternoon during my 17th and final season with the Hawks have troubled me ever since and still do to this day.

Television footage had captured the hit and the publicity aftermath was massive. In fact, the incident became the catalyst for the introduction of reporting from video replays. It's hard to believe but prior to this time video evidence wasn't admissible in VFL Tribunal hearings.

With no report being made by any of the umpires, but with the offence obvious on the replays, a week or so later the VFL discovered Rule 10B, which allowed them to charge me with 'conduct unbecoming'.

What was even more disturbing was that a police investigation had been launched. The wild scenes at Princes Park on that cold dreary June afternoon became the reason – or maybe the excuse – for the authorities to interfere with football's traditional turf of controlling and disciplining its own game.

I'm sure the VFL's belated action in finding a rule that allowed them to charge me with an offence was in the hope that if they took action, the police would drop their interest. Unfortunately for me, that was to be a forlorn hope.

The charge of conduct unbecoming couldn't be heard by the VFL Tribunal, it had to go direct to the VFL Commission; hence I didn't receive a tribunal suspension. Instead the commission handed me a pre-ordained four-game deregistration. With a police investigation under way, I could have refused the commission hearing on legal grounds but decided that football should determine my playing fate.

A few weeks later, on the night of the commission hearing at the old VFL headquarters adjacent to the MCG in Jolimont Terrace, an unexpected meeting took place in the short lift ride up to the VFL offices. The Hawthorn party with me was a few team-mates who'd been summoned to appear as witnesses and my legal team – yes, my legal team. The law of the land and the law of the football jungle were suddenly intertwined. As we waited at ground level for the lift, the doors opened and there was the Geelong contingent on its way up from the basement car park.

As we entered the lift, in addition to the victim, Neville Bruns, there were a couple of Geelong administrators. Also standing among them was the young Cats defender Steven Hocking, who had avenged his injured team-mate by delivering instant and effective retribution.

On the Monday following the incident I'd sent a message to Bruns via Geelong coach Tom Hafey to apologise for inflicting his nasty injury, but this was the first time I'd seen him face to face, and after a quick acknowledgement I turned my attention to Hocking, who looked very, very nervous and decidedly sheepish. Given that I was his victim, he probably wasn't sure of my attitude to him.

I had been around the footy world for a long time, but appearing before the commission was still quite daunting. For Hocking, though, a raw 20-year-old in only his second season, it must have been positively overwhelming to be summoned to head office with media everywhere to face the same conduct-unbecoming charge that I'd received. That look of 'What the hell am I doing here and what's going to happen?' was written all over his face.

I genuinely had no issue with him for belting me in the heat of the game, and tried to ease his mind with the comment that he was only here for the show. There was no vision of his incident with me and, as I told him, no-one from Hawthorn was going to dob him in. I said he should relax because he was only here for the ride – tonight wasn't about penalising him.

The confidential advice from VFL CEO Jack Hamilton was that if I appeared before the commission a four-game penalty, which included the upcoming night competition grand final, would be the result, and after an unduly lengthy hearing that was what eventuated. One look at the vision proved me guilty of striking; I guess the extended hearing was for the commissioners to convince themselves that striking should come under the all-encompassing umbrella of 'conduct unbecoming'.

Even in the gravity of the situation there was one moment I found a bit amusing. One of the commissioners was Peter Scanlon, one of Australia's leading and best-known businessmen. As the vision was played over and over again, I have this image of Peter sitting on the floor to get a better view. Here was this distinguished middle-aged man of great status dressed in suit and tie and perched eagerly in front of the television, looking a lot like a little kid at home watching his favourite program.

When it came to Hocking's case, as was expected it was like a Mafia trial where all the witnesses said they saw nothing. So the Geelong player was found not guilty of his charge of conduct unbecoming.

In a quirky circumstance, for the month of my deregistration my VFL life membership meant I could park in the official car park and attend the VFL's official lunch on game day, but I wasn't allowed to go onto the field to play.

The football deregistration-cum-suspension of four weeks was a football penalty for a football crime. When I look back a few decades later, and taking into account the modern rules and regulations that govern the game, it was perfectly normal and understandable. However, at the time there was some personal aggro from my perspective, as there was I suspect with many others in the footy community, because this incident was the first time in football history that video evidence had been used to lay a charge.

I'm a great believer that normal is simply what happens most of the time. What is normal is constantly changing, though, and back in 1985 being suspended by video evidence was just not done. Now it happens most weeks and is completely normal.

The next step in the ongoing saga, however, was highly abnormal and still is. Police charges were laid for the first and only time in top-level football history. A couple of days after the commission deregistration, I received a summons from Victoria Police charging me with 'assault causing grievous bodily harm'. and informing me that the case would be heard in the Melbourne Magistrates' Court on 13 August.

In the lead-up to the court appearance I met with leading barrister Brian Bourke, who advised me that the maximum penalty for this offence was seven years' jail. These are not words you ever want to hear and while the possibility of jail was always extremely unlikely, my actions on the footy field had put me in a real-life minefield that was beyond my worst nightmares.

What happened next, we see regularly in police dramas. We plea-bargained. In return for a guilty plea the charges would be reduced to common assault, which at least ended the possibility that a gung-ho magistrate having a bad day might impose a jail sentence.

As there was vision of the offence, pleading not guilty seemed pointless. Fighting the charge would have entailed convincing the court that what happens on the football field is outside the laws of the land. That would have meant taking the legal battle into higher courts, with a lead time of many months or even years.

My legal advice was that a not guilty verdict would have more chance in front of a judge and jury, but the pressure of getting a quick resolution was riding me hard. Also, I felt ashamed of my actions and even I struggled with the philosophical argument of pleading not guilty just to win a court case. So, armed with the advice that the police prosecutor would be recommending a good behaviour bond, the decision was made to plead guilty and, hopefully, end the legalities there and then.

I still shudder when I remember the cold draughty corridors of the Melbourne Magistrates' Court and the nervous wait for my charges to be heard. If the tension hadn't been so palpable, though, I would have enjoyed sitting at the back of the court watching cases come and go as magistrate Mr Brian Clothier, SM, quickly dispensed his summary justice.

Getting a good behaviour bond seemed a lay-down misère after a case just before mine was quickly finalised. It too was a common assault offence with the added severity of the charge being for assaulting police while resisting arrest.

The guy who was up for the offence looked like he'd been through the system; this was obviously not an isolated, one-off appearance and he'd made no attempt to dress conservatively for the occasion. He was wearing a very loud multicoloured woollen jumper with matching gloves – no suit and tie for this bloke – and was representing himself.

His case for leniency was that he'd been through some bad police experiences earlier in his life and therefore reacted aggressively when the police tried to apprehend him. After a few seconds' deliberation from Magistrate Clothier, this simple defence was rewarded with a good behaviour bond for assaulting police. It seemed a certainty that I'd receive a similar punishment for an offence on a footy field.

Of course, the big difference was that the magistrate knew his decision in the case of the repeat offender in the colourful outfit was of nil public interest. No outside pressure on that one; just another in the conveyor belt of mostly trivial charges he'd hear day after day. The difference when my case was called was starkly evident to everyone in the court, including the man up the front with all the power.

In the wrong hands, or used without wisdom, judicial power can be a dangerous thing for the person facing a criminal charge. Sitting behind his large wooden bench, Magistrate Clothier was a stranger about to distribute his summary justice, but he must have felt the pressure of the occasion because, unlike the other myriad cases he would hear, the result of this case would be splashed across the front of the daily papers the next morning.

As my case was called, the interest level in the court immediately went through the roof. The large press contingent woke from their bored slumber and swamped the front benches to observe the details of the hearing that would be the following day's lead story.

When the guilty plea was tendered it was only a question of penalty, and as the prosecutor detailed the Crown's case I looked at the magistrate and wondered: why waste time? Unless he'd been on Mars for the last couple of months he already knew the case in intimate detail. The vision of the incident had been played endlessly on every television station for weeks.

The prosecutor agreed that a good behaviour bond was reasonable, there was some flattering character evidence and then the hearing was completed. It was judgment time.

The pressure was now loaded onto the magistrate because he was probably expecting a not-guilty plea, which would have shoved the case to the County Court and thankfully – from his point of view – out of his jurisdiction.

My guilty plea meant he was forced to accept the responsibility of deciding on a penalty; a decision which would be debated in the papers, on the radio and in the court of public opinion, where he had to live his life outside the Magistrates' Court.

Unlike the quick decisions in every other case heard that morning, Magistrate Clothier adjourned to consider his verdict. For my own curiosity I would have loved being a fly on the wall in his rooms: Who did he talk to? What were his considerations? What was going through his mind? Was there some counsel from his superiors?

After about 45 minutes he reappeared to deliver his verdict as a carefully worded statement, definitely his first for the morning I'd been in his court. After some pontificating about the many losers in the whole sordid affair, he refused the good behaviour bond option and imposed a conviction with a $1000 fine.

Nothing overly harsh in that ruling, you might think, except that the big penalty from this outcome was that little question asked on many forms: have you been convicted of a criminal offence? Unless the conviction was overturned, the answer for me would always be yes, and that could lead to all kinds of difficulties and explanations thereafter.

So unfortunately the legalities didn't end that day. They weren't over until the following April in the County Court when, on appeal, Judge Ravech overturned the conviction and granted me a 12-month good behaviour bond.

It's a long time ago now and the emotions have mellowed with the passing of time. As I look back, my attitude to the saga following what became known as the 'Bruns incident' can be summarised with a couple of thoughts.

Firstly, you do the crime, you do the time. I did the wrong thing so I can't really complain about the consequences of my actions. But even in retrospect the second is a lot more confusing. Why the police decided to pluck this one incident from the many potential assaults that have occurred on football fields over the decades is still a great mystery. That one charge from round 12 in June 1985 remains the one and only time in the entire history of the VFL/AFL that the police have taken action about an on-field incident.

Certainly, a select few individuals in the corridors of power must have known the answer to the 'Why this time?' question. I suspect that a couple of ministers in the Victorian Labor Government at the time, Sports Minister and ex-Geelong rover Neil Trezise and Police Minister Race Mathews knew the critical difference that sparked the police action, as did the incumbent Chief Commissioner of Police, Mick Miller. In fact, Mr Mathews was quoted in *The Sun* at the time as saying that the State Government had ordered an urgent police inquiry into the wild scenes at Princes Park. Later he was to say that an Inspector Phil Bennett had started the investigation independent of any government prompting.

These men are long removed from public life and the motivations that sparked the police action will never be uncovered. My curiosity, because that is all it is nearly 30 years later, will unfortunately remain unsated.

The bottom line is that these anonymous powerful decision makers proved that what happens on the football field is not above the law of the land and no-one can argue with that.

However, aside from the deregistration and police charges, the biggest impact of the Bruns incident and its aftermath was to make me question my whole competitive attitude. I feel fortunate that it occurred in my 17th and final year as a footballer because my whole playing philosophy had been that what happened on the field stayed on the field; that inside the white line was a place where normal civilities didn't apply and where the ends justified the means; that the footy field was a kind of war zone that I entered at the opening siren and left when the game finished. Noble and worthy concepts like sportsmanship, fair play and duty of care for opponents were secondary to winning and succeeding.

When my first coach, John Kennedy, used to speak of football as an impersonal game, he meant that it was not about the individuals, but simply about our team versus their team. The blokes in the opposition jumpers were after what we wanted and if we were to win they had to be forced to lose. Off the field they might be good blokes and some might become good friends, but during the two hours of hand-to-hand combat that a game of football was, they were obstacles to be overcome.

In the cold light of day, particularly as a middle-aged grandfather looking back, this mindset is difficult to reconcile with the fairly passive person I've always been off the footy field. The civilian me was a stark contrast to the tough man 'Lethal Leigh' playing persona, where bending the accepted rules and codes of physical contact to win was part of the deal.

As youngsters, in moments of sarcasm if they couldn't get their own way, my daughters, Tracey and Fiona, would occasionally chide me, saying, 'Dad, you're not that tough.' My standard reply was they could tell whoever they liked because no-one would believe them!

On the same theme, there was a standing joke at Hawthorn that when we did drills on the punching bag, the bag would beat me on points.

Yet on the field my competitive instinct was ruthless, callous and very physical. While this dark aggressive side bubbled over occasionally and got me into trouble, it also sparked the ability to use my body as a battering ram, which was the base from which my playing success was built.

Also, looking back now from the higher moral ground of modern attitudes to rough play, and given the stricter contact interpretations that have evolved in the intervening decades, those rules I once bent would be smashed to smithereens under the vastly more stringent player protection regulations that are now in force.

The soul search I did back in 1985, and which I've done since, about my on-field playing style wasn't – and isn't – terribly pleasant. While I prided myself on my chameleon quality of changing to survive, after that regrettable incident against Geelong, moving on and continuing to play as the ultra-aggressive competitor I needed to be to play at my best was likely to have been an insurmountable challenge.

17

THE END IS NEAR

My body was ageing and my confidence was shot – the rot
was setting in fast.

Going into that fateful game against Geelong in round 12 of 1985, my season so far could best have been described as a struggle. While my fear that I wouldn't be an automatic selection in the Hawthorn team hadn't yet materialised, that was all about to change.

The Hawks beat Geelong by four goals that day to go to a reasonable 7–4 win–loss ratio, so the team was travelling quite well. I wasn't sharing the team's good fortune, having ended the game with concussion, a smashed nose and, even worse, a bruised and battered self-esteem.

Twenty-four hours after that nasty last-quarter incident with Neville Bruns, my initial thought was that I should never play again. If a football match environment could provoke such an angry, violent act, maybe it was time to call it a day.

Allan Jeans visited me that Sunday afternoon, which I really appreciated, giving me the benefit of his counsel, as well as an important message to consider. Jeansy took the typically commonsense view that the incident the day before shouldn't be my last playing memory, and that I should reconsider my retirement plans. After a day or two I took the coach's advice to see out the year. However, I completely eradicated from my thinking any remaining ideas of playing on beyond the end of the season.

The mood was lightened a little when my daughter Tracey arrived home from school the following Tuesday with the statement that

'Dad, what's all the publicity about? You footballers hit each other all the time, don't you?' Ah, from the mouths of babes.

Concussion was the reason I missed the following match but the urge to play was missing anyway. I took the field the week later in round 14 against the dominant Essendon at Waverley Park – we lost badly and I played an absolute shocker. After the game, bad had turned to worse when VFL football manager Alan Schwab delivered the letter advising me of the conduct unbecoming charge to be heard by the VFL Commission in 10 days' time.

It was a slight stay of execution. Clearly, the Swans game the following weekend was going to be my last before the deregistration holiday and at least I finished with a bang, getting a bit of the footy, kicking six goals and having a good match as the Hawks recorded a 73-point victory.

While the expectation was that the commission would hand out a three- or four-week penalty, going into that match against the Swans there was also the faint possibility that I could get deregistered for the rest of the season; so, unlikely as it seemed, this could have been my last game ever. As it eventuated the penalty was to miss rounds 16, 17, 18 and the mid-week night series grand final against the Bombers.

They say never to give a sucker an even break, but that is exactly what my suspension inadvertently did. During my enforced absence from the Hawthorn full-forward position, a star was born in the form of my replacement, a porky kid from Queensland who in his first year had only played five games leading into round 16 of 1985, against Richmond at the MCG. While that inexperienced kid was never the greatest athlete or preparer, he took the opportunity with both hands. That youngster was the great Jason Dunstall. My forced absence gave him the chance to show Allan Jeans and his fellow selectors what he could do as the Hawks full-forward target, without my experience and status drawing the ball to me most of the time.

Hawthorn won all three regular season games during my period of deregistration, and scored 66 goals in the process; playing in the full-forward position without me getting in the way, Jason chipped in with 14 of his own. It was the birth of a magnificent career that produced 1254 goals from 269 games, with the added value of him being undoubtedly the best chasing and tackling full-forward who has ever played the game.

Dunstall came from Coorparoo in Brisbane and would play 16 games for a moderate 36 goals in year one of what turned out to be a phenomenal career. I'd met him the day after the 1984 grand final, when the club was trying to recruit him in the face of strong interest from Fitzroy. He'd had a fairly tough introduction to the VFL, playing as the second forward target to yours truly. It was never going to be easy for Jason given that when Hawthorn players won the ball through the middle of the ground, my status as a player meant I was the main target. Even if my designated position was forward pocket, a young full-forward yet to earn his stripes was always going to be the secondary target.

It's a fact that very often the experience and standing of a player pressures team-mates to give him the footy, and when performance no longer justifies that faith, the team has a problem. That was the situation Hawthorn faced in 1985 when my ability to be an effective target forward was declining rapidly. It was during my deregistration absence that Jeansy concluded the only way to overcome this problem was to move me away from the full-forward area to allow Dunstall to be the main man.

Jason was always a very powerful aerobic athlete but endurance was never his strength. He was always at the back of the pack in the running drills and I remember the *Sun* journalist and ex-Collingwood captain Lou Richards posing the question at the time, 'How will Hawthorn ever be any good with two slow blokes like that in the forward line?' He was right about me, but, as would become patently obvious, Jason was anything but slow, and over the years he used his speed off the mark to become not only one of the great leading forwards but arguably the best defensive forward the game has ever seen. Indeed, as much as Peter Hudson was a freakish goal-kicker, if I had to pick one person to play at full-forward in an all-star team I'd go with Jason because of his defensive capabilities.

By late 1985 the way forward was clear for all to see. As a full-forward, Jason was the future and I was the past. During my period of deregistration some terrific performances by the team and the new full-forward meant that for the remaining games I was to become a back-up bit-part player.

As the team's captain who had always led from the front it was a challenging situation. Even though I'd committed to playing out the season I was starting to question whether I was even worth my place in the side, and while they weren't saying it out loud in match committee I'm sure Jeansy and his fellow selectors were thinking along similar lines.

We all knew my gig as an automatic selection was up when we played North Melbourne in round 22. Although we won by 64 points to finish third on the home-and-away ladder with 15 wins and a draw – a great launching pad for the team's premiership campaign – it was terrible for me personally because I had a shocker. I only had 11 possessions and went goalless in a team total of 23 goals. My body was ageing and my confidence was shot – the rot was setting in fast.

It had been my custom not to attend the Tuesday night selection meeting just in case my place in the team needed to be discussed. That obviously happened in the week leading into the Sunday qualifying final against Footscray – now the Western Bulldogs – because the phone rang Wednesday morning and the familiar voice on the line was our chairman of selectors, Brian Coleman.

In an apologetic tone, he said, 'We thought maybe it would be an idea to start you on the bench on Sunday.' Brian was a good friend and great supporter of mine and I had no beef with him or the other selectors, because the team interest coming first was ingrained into everyone at Hawthorn.

My downhill slide was a fact of life and I was always treated with great respect by Jeansy and everyone at the club. However, the die was cast – for the few remaining games, if I was in the team I'd be seeing plenty of the interchange bench. And back in the '80s the spells on the bench were lengthy; it wasn't the revolving door it is in current footy.

During Thursday night training I felt the fittest and freshest I'd been for many weeks and prior to the Friday session I wandered over to the coach and declared myself ready to start. As captain I wanted to lead from the front, and late the day before the qualifying final Jeans rang me to say I'd be starting on the ground and in the centre square. Now the pressure was on for me to fulfil my part of the bargain.

Fortunately, I had quite a good game; not in the best couple of hundred that I played, but at least serviceable. We jumped out of the blocks, got the early break and went on to beat the Bulldogs by 93 points.

Unfortunately, we then lost to the dominant Essendon by 40 points in the second semi-final and I spent most of the second half on the bench. The season, and my career, had reached knockout territory: one loss and it was all over.

This was assuming, of course, that I got a game, which was no certainty. I now had the challenge of focusing on the match and its needs, when each time I played a game it might be my last. It was quite a battle and not one I handled very well.

My definition of concentration is the ability to focus on the task at hand and to be impervious to all peripheral issues. This is something I've always done very well. My family are amazed – and frustrated, I might add – that even when I'm watching sport on TV, or anything else interesting for that matter, my concentration is so locked in that when they talk to me, I simply don't hear them. Yelling at me sometimes does the trick!

In this situation, though, while my body was ageing and slowing down, my performance was also being badly affected by my inability to block out the peripheral issues of impending retirement and my waning automatic selection status. This late-career experience further convinced me that players need security in the team to produce their best. It is a myth that playing for his spot in the team will keep a player on his toes and performing better. Mostly, it just makes a player tentative and scared of making mistakes; never a great base for optimum performance.

The preliminary final was a rematch with Footscray and we were playing for a spot in our third consecutive grand final. Personally, I was also playing for my spot in the team, even if we got through.

I started in the forward pocket, opposed to the 1985 Brownlow medallist, Brad Hardie. Players don't win Brownlows as dour stopping defenders. I liked playing on Brad because he was an attacking backman who didn't play close body to body, but instead backed his judgement to beat his opponents to the footy. His ball-winning ability could cut you up, but because he didn't play tight he always gave you a chance if you were good enough to take it.

The first quarter was his. Every time he got the ball early in the game he seemed to charge out of the back pocket and set something up downfield. The coach's faith in me was already at a low ebb, and with me unable to get the footy or to pressure Brad as he charged up the ground, Jeansy's patience ran out quickly. At quarter-time I was sent to have a spell on the bench, and I spent much of the game there alongside another 33-year-old, veteran Hawthorn Team of the Century centre half-back Peter Knights.

It was quite ironic that we were sharing this unwanted interchange experience, because our time at Hawthorn had been a shared journey since we'd both arrived at Glenferrie Oval as 17-year-olds way back in 1969. We even played in the same schoolboys trial game at Glenferrie in 1968; we represented Victoria in Perth as teenagers in 1971 and many times thereafter; we shared three premierships, and would have shared a fourth in 1971 if Knightsy hadn't injured his knee in the second semi, and we were both born in March 1952.

Also, in a bizarre coincidence 10 years later, at the end of 1995 we were both sacked from our senior coaching positions – Knightsy from Hawthorn and me from Collingwood. I have always hoped Peter is keeping good health!

Yet in physiques and image we were complete opposites. Knightsy was tall, blond and athletic; I was short, dark and squat. He was a much loved and admired ball player, while in the eyes of most footy fans I was more like the big bad wolf.

What Knightsy didn't have was luck with injuries, although if you leapt as high as he did, landing badly and getting injured was almost an occupational hazard. Peter was a wonderful, wonderful player and an automatic selection for his entire career, but as we spent this unwanted time on the interchange bench I was playing my 331st game, while he was only playing his 262nd, almost 70 less. In fact, the injury interruptions that had dogged his footy had kept him out of the team for the five weeks since round 19.

We'd shared so many football highs, been centre stage so often, and now we were sharing the embarrassment and frustration of maybe finishing our careers stuck on the bench as the struggle with the Bulldogs ebbed and flowed.

We led by one point at the last change. I'd like to say that as captain I was a bundle of encouraging enthusiasm as we emerged from the anonymity of the concrete dugout and walked to the three-quarter time huddle, but I wasn't. My competitive flame was barely flickering, and after watching the match as a spectator for over an hour I had emotionally withdrawn from the contest and was very dispirited.

Being off the ground for a half of football was a new and unpleasant experience for me and it had created a massive emotional downer that I wasn't handling very well. In personality profiling terminology, I had degenerated into my Feeler mode and virtually moped out to my team-mates as they gathered to regroup for the final charge to another grand final or a preliminary final elimination.

Nothing was said until it was time for the players to resume their positions. Seemingly almost as an afterthought, Jeansy turned to our first rover, Richard Loveridge, and said, 'Scholar, I want you to have a break. Leigh will go forward and Felix [Peter Russo] will go back on the ball.'

His personal message to me was as blunt as it was simple. 'Come on, Barn, we need you to do something.'

As the teams resumed our positions, my early game nemesis Brad Hardie again became my defensive match-up. Fortunately, unlike the first quarter, now the breaks came my way and instead of me chasing him I started to find the footy and he had to chase me.

At the first centre bounce I reacted sharply to a scrubby kick out of the centre square congestion and got to the fall of the ball first to mark around centre half-forward. On autopilot instinct I got away from the mark as quickly as possible and saw Jason Dunstall ready to lead into vacant space towards the forward pocket. I was able to weight my kick into his path and he slid into a low chest mark.

He slotted his set shot, we got the vital goal and I got a boost of much-needed adrenalin, the body's natural energy upper. Having 'rested' on the bench for the previous two quarters while the other players had spent most of their energy in three quarters of frantic finals footy, I had a competitive advantage to balance the negative of the ageing body.

It was the late-game effect that the modern sub can occasionally produce. Armed with a burst of energy that had been missing for many weeks I had a really good quarter, kicked a couple of goals, helped in another few and got the ball seven or eight times.

We got a few goals clear and, despite a late Bulldogs surge, held on to win by 10 points. It was refreshingly like the good old times to feel important again and to have performed a significant role in earning the victory. We were into our third consecutive grand final against Essendon. After a good finish to the game it appeared my position in the team was assured.

18

THE FINAL CURTAIN

In a few short hours at the MCG on Saturday, 28 September
1985, the primary focus of my life had moved from
current to past.

Former Australian cricket captain Allan Border once said that for a competitive sports person, when you walk off the playing field for the last time, part of you dies. After my final game of 1985 I can totally empathise with that comment.

So, while there's no perfect way to move into the past player category, finishing on grand final day as the premiership captain would have to be as good as any. What stood between me achieving that personal dream, as well as the Hawks winning the flag, was a very imposing Essendon team.

After we'd thrashed them by 83 points in 1983 they'd improved considerably to overrun us late in the 1984 decider. And in 1985, they'd beaten us comfortably in our three meetings prior to the grand final.

Under the coaching of Kevin Sheedy, they'd also had a tactical victory that exploited the rules in order to slow down the quick-moving running game that Allan Jeans had implemented so successfully. Back then, the time-wasting penalty was only 15 metres. Against Essendon in 1985 every time a Hawthorn player took a mark in the back half he was held up and often thrown to the ground. The resultant 15-metre penalty was deemed by Sheeds to be a more than worthwhile sacrifice to halt our ability to play the ball on quickly and to change direction into open field, where we could use our superior running game.

The critically important AFL Laws of the Game Committee system, which is now in place to monitor and recommend rules adjustments if coaches start exploiting the existing ones and begin wrecking the look of the game in the process, didn't exist in the '80s.

Wheels turned quite slowly back then but by the start of 1988 a change was made to introduce the 50-metre penalty. Anyone who, like me, thinks the 50-metre penalty is often too severe for minor offences can blame Sheeds, because his team's overt time-wasting tactics in the mid-'80s were the catalyst for its introduction.

Since we'd beaten them in 1983 the Bombers had developed into a powerful unit with a particularly imposing group of talls. Their ruckman Simon Madden was the best follower/resting forward of his generation, and when you added Paul Salmon, Roger Merrett, Paul Vander Haar and captain Terry Daniher, the result was an aerial dominance which was difficult to match. They'd only lost three games for the season and were red hot favourites to go back to back.

Again, I didn't attend Tuesday night selection when the non-playing selectors thrashed out the first draft of the likely line-up, and by the final after-training meeting on the Thursday the key decisions had been made. While my last quarter in the preliminary final gave me a selection reprieve, sadly Peter Knights wasn't so lucky. His late-season injury interruption and a poor game against the Bulldogs led Knightsy to be left out, along with Rodney Eade. They made way for Michael Tuck, who hadn't played in the senior team since the final round of the home-and-away season because of a shoulder injury, and David O'Halloran, who was one of the biggest grand final selection gambles of all time. 'Rubber', as we called him, hadn't played a senior game since the 1984 grand final. Our main specialist ruckman, Michael Byrne, had a dicey ankle and was not selected.

That meant there were four changes from the 1984 grand final side, with Byrne, Peter Curran, Ian Paton and Colin Robertson out for Jason Dunstall, Robert Handley, Chris Langford and Russell Morris. Thirteen players were lining up for their third consecutive grand final – Gary Ayres, Dermott Brereton, Robert DiPierdomenico, Russell Greene, Ken Judge, Richard Loveridge, Mick McCarthy,

Chris Mew, David O'Halloran, Peter Schwab, Michael Tuck, Terry Wallace and myself.

The official grand final team line-up lists Langford as the Hawthorn first ruck. Langers eventually became a terrific full-back but compared to the great Bombers ruckman Simon Madden, it was like an apprentice versus a master.

One of Allan Jeans' favourite themes was that 'loose lips sink ships', and even in the final match committee there was a secret not known to all. As the meeting finished I was selected to start the game in the forward pocket, but Jeansy asked me to stay back for a chat, in which he confided that, in fact, I was going to start in the centre square at the opening bounce.

Hawks CEO John Lauritz attended Thursday night selection and I think Jeansy feared he might talk about the team line-up to a few insiders at the post-training drinks over at the social club. Hence the subterfuge, even in the inner sanctum of the match committee. As Jeansy always said when advising players not to tell even wives or girlfriends about the team plans, 'Your wife will tell the butcher, he'll tell the greengrocer, he'll tell a few friends and pretty soon the whole world will know.'

Throughout our lives we're learning, and in retrospect the experience of the week leading into my last grand final was a major lesson in what is required to optimise playing performance. In a nutshell, the challenge is to minimise the hype, not to build it up. Ensuring fever-pitch motivation isn't the issue, remaining calm and emotionally composed is what's required. Neither myself, nor the Hawthorn team, managed this very well in the lead-up to the 1985 grand final.

Firstly, I allowed my impending retirement to be a distraction for me and probably for the other players. I did far too much media during that last week, too much talking about the big picture of career and retirement and not enough concentrating on the specifics of the game that Saturday. When I coached it was a lesson I tried to convey to the teams I was managing leading into grand finals. Control the controllable and don't get distracted by peripheral issues. That includes the result which, even by the opening bounce, is still a long-term three hours away.

The couple of hours at the MCG before the game are when the nerves and gut-wrenching tension can really bite and overwhelm the emotions. Individuals cope as best they can but if the atmosphere gets too stimulating, players' arousal levels can go over the top. Preventing this is the grand final day goal that we didn't achieve before the 1985 premiership decider.

Our reserves team was in the curtain-raiser grand final and included many experienced big names, including Knightsy, Rocket Eade, Gary Buckenara, Michael Byrne, Colin Robertson, Steve Malaxos, Greg Dear and Peter Curran. During their lap of honour after winning their match, the euphoric group with their premiership cup in hand came into our dressing rooms to wish us luck and to share their joy.

I'm sure they had the best of intentions but the burst of frenzied activity, on top of our building arousal level, certainly tipped me over the top and any sense of control quickly evaporated. As the emotions of the moment and the season-defining game to come hit my senses, unwanted tears welled in my eyes. Crying tears of joy or sadness post-game on grand final day is quite normal; crying pre-game is to be majorly avoided. The whole event with the reserves was an adrenalin boost that wasted valuable emotional energy long before it was needed, and if I was affected that way then I'm sure my team-mates must have been as well.

To say we were hyped up running onto the field 20 minutes later would be a massive understatement. The Hawks players were ready to engage in football war.

We knew Essendon had been the dominant side all year but we built ourselves up to think we could win and were determined to attack the game and to be the more aggressive team. At the first bounce, Simon Madden jumped high and thumped the ball towards goal. I intercepted it and a long kick forward found Dermott Brereton, who kicked the first of his eight goals. But that was about the end of the optimism.

We threw everything we had into that opening term but at quarter-time Essendon still led by nine points. Halfway through the first quarter a wild brawl had broken out on the wing in front of the Southern Stand. The pre-game message from the coach was that if there were fireworks it was to be: one in, all in.

As I saw it, our centreman Terry Wallace seemed to trigger the explosion when he was third man into a fairly innocuous push and shove going on between the Hawks' Mick McCarthy and Terry's opponent, Leon Baker. Then it was on. Players charged in from all directions. I charged in too but wasn't exactly sure what I was trying to do.

Flying the flag was the main objective and once I was intertwined among the wrestling throng of players, it quickly became a quite harmless pack of mauling bodies. Gradually it petered out. After a few seconds' frenzy, the pent-up aggression was exhausted and the players did little more than act tough until the umpires restored order. Then we all got back to playing footy.

Unfortunately, the emotionally sapping pre-game over-arousal, combined with the first quarter of energy-sapping exertion, came back to haunt us later in the game. At three-quarter time the deficit to Essendon was only 30 points, but we were gone a long way out and the Bombers kicked 11.3 to 3.3 in the last term to win by a whopping 78 points.

Late in the match the last mark I was ever to take, and the last time I'd handle a footy during a game, came at a nasty price. A wild spoiling swipe from my Essendon opponent, Steven Carey, missed the ball and hit me flush on the side of my face. I asked the umpire for the 15-metre penalty but he declined my request. It would have been nice because the set shot from around 40 metres was now beyond my range.

The blow didn't hurt me, but tentatively touching to feel any wound or blood was my instinctive reaction. Boy, had that happened a lot over the previous 20 years – get a knock to the face and feel for the tell-tale red moisture. If the fingers discovered blood, the next step was to get off the field to a mirror to properly assess the damage. Like the regular jarring of fingers that has made my dexterity later in life quite poor, the beautiful well-earned stiff tired body the morning after a match and the burning determination in the pit of my stomach as I drove to a game, all these familiar feelings were about to end.

Then the siren sounded. It was a welcome end to a forgettable last quarter as Essendon surged away, the margin increasing the longer the game went.

After wanting to play football for as long as I can remember, it was now over – the inevitable had suddenly arrived. In a few short hours at the MCG on Saturday, 28 September 1985, the primary focus of my life had moved from current to past.

There are two prevailing emotions post-grand final: one, the unbelievably contrasting feelings that the result stimulates – exhilaration if you win or a mourning kind of sadness if you lose; and two, the initial and comforting release of competitive pressure – that, either good or bad, the unknown has at least become the known.

In the 1985 grand final, the sharpness of losing was blunted by the game being decided a long way out, but after this match walking off the field for the final time was a strange, once-in-a-lifetime experience for me.

The situation also made it a little different for my team-mates. A few had some words of comfort and regret that we'd performed so badly. Dermott Brereton, who was a magnificent lone hand in a miserable day, came up and said, 'I wish we could have won it for you.' Dermott had tears welling in his eyes and all I could say to him was that he'd done more than anyone could possibly expect and he'd stood up when it counted. Surviving and thriving on the biggest stage became a Brereton specialty in the dominant Hawthorn era that was to follow.

After the task of congratulating the winners was completed it was time to leave the arena – for the final time. It was a very emotional moment as the forlorn, beaten Hawthorn team left the field, and as we approached the race leading into our dressing rooms, a voice yelled, 'Let's carry Barney off.'

As soon as I was raised onto the shoulders of Russell Greene and Terry Wallace, an incredible sadness hit me and the waterworks that I'd held back in that pre-game excitement began to flow freely. The newspaper photos showed the situation quite graphically. A group of footballers in the prime of their careers carrying a greying veteran, who was losing forever that which he'd so valued for so long.

They say a drowning person sees their life flash past; for me, the football career I'd aspired to as a boy and treasured as an adult would finish in the next few seconds.

After a few minutes alone in the coach's room to compose myself, I had a massive mood swing. All of a sudden the weight of the competitive struggle disappeared. It was a relief – almost elation – to know that the pressure of team success and living up to my own expectations was now in the past. In football terms I was an old bloke who no longer had to fight off the younger challengers. The unwinnable fight was finally and mercifully over.

Strangely, as much as it hurt to see such a one-sided scoreboard, it probably helped me to move on fairly quickly after the game. It wasn't as if we'd lost a nail-biter, which, if it happens in a grand final, can really haunt you – blowing a three-quarter-time lead the year before still eats away at me nearly three decades later. This one was gone a long way out, and in the rooms afterwards I sat pretty quietly with my dad, who came to every game I ever played at club level, and elder brother, Russell. As I've mentioned, my mother, Lorna, stopped going to the footy when I began to play for the Hawthorn senior team – the tension and the crowds were too much for her. The dressing rooms were strictly men-only back then, even after grand finals, and my wife, Maureen, and Tracey and Fiona were waiting outside until I'd showered and changed.

As the night wore on my cheekbone started to cave in, and I discovered I had a depressed fracture from that late-game blow. On the Tuesday following, I had surgery to repair the damage. While I was in there I asked the doctor if he'd straighten my nose – or at least do the best job he could. It had been smashed for the first time by an accidental elbow from team-mate Ian Bremner in a practice match back in 1970. After I'd had it fixed at the end of that season it was broken again early the following year, so I'd decided to put off any future repair until the end of my career. Now that time had come: I was now an ex-player.

I hung around the Hawthorn playing group for a bit longer than I would normally do over the next few days, clinging as long as I could to being part of the team. It was a melancholy time. I had grown up at Hawthorn and the club had been my footy home – from my arrival as a 17-year-old until my retirement as a married 33-year-old adult with teenage children of my own. My future was uncertain after grand final day 1985, because there was no constructive role for me at Glenferrie Oval. So, as scary as it is when we close a door behind us, in a footy sense it was time for me to leave home.

19

HEADING TO VICTORIA PARK

The rich and powerful club that Collingwood seemed to be
when I was offered a job late the previous season was actually
in a fight for its very survival.

When the telephone rings early in the morning, it is rarely good news. As the phone next to my bed woke me from my slumber about 7.30 am on Sunday, 13 April 1986, there was the normal foreboding that accompanies those wake-up calls.

I tried to quickly gather my senses with a tentative hello and heard a familiar voice on the line. As the first-year assistant coach at Collingwood, it was my boss, Magpies senior coach and club legend Bob Rose. In a solemn voice he said, 'Leigh, I think it might be time for you to take over.' In a matter of seconds the sequence of events that elevated me from assistant to man in charge was in motion. The final appointment was ratified by the Collingwood board the following morning.

Now, at 34, six months ahead of schedule after a whirlwind 'transition period' that barely qualified as a transition period, I was coach of the most famous football club in Australia.

A few months earlier, after the 1985 grand final, there hadn't been many firm future options in place. But fortunately, as one door closed, others began to open.

During my final few years at Hawthorn, I'd worked in the club's marketing department and CEO John Lauritz had offered me the opportunity to continue in that role with the add-on of also becoming an assistant coach to Allan Jeans. However, once I put my mind to the future, I realised that after 17 years at Glenferrie Oval it was time to go elsewhere if the opportunity arose.

The thought of taking on a senior coach role straight away had no appeal – I was mentally worn out and wanted a break. But when Collingwood, with Bob's knowledge and encouragement, approached me with the chance to spend a year as his full-time assistant (remarkably on more money than I was getting during my last year as a player), then take over at the end of the 1986 season, I was definitely interested.

It had all started with a surprise phone call from football identity Oberan Pirak in August, who asked if we could catch up for a coffee. I'd met Oberan before, but didn't know at the time of his association with the Magpies. A few days later we met at a coffee shop in Glenferrie Road, where he outlined the succession plan that would culminate in me becoming senior coach of Collingwood after one season as an assistant.

It was flattering, but I can only ever serve one master at a time and advised him that my final few games as a player with the Hawks needed every bit of my concentration. Thinking about the future beyond was a distraction that I couldn't afford, although I said that I'd love to take the interest further when my playing commitments were finished.

At the end of the season, I also received a tentative approach from high-rolling Sydney Swans owner Dr Geoffrey Edelsten. Having bought the club in 1985, he wasn't happy with their 6–16 win–loss record in his first year at the helm, and was on the lookout for a replacement for coach John Northey.

I had begun writing a book about my playing career, eventually titled *Lethal*, with long-time football commentator Mike Sheahan. I'd had the surgery to repair the fractured cheekbone I'd suffered in the grand final, as well as finally getting my badly bent and flattened nose straightened. A few days after the surgery we were working on the book at Mike's home when I had a nose bleed that wouldn't stop. The only solution was a trip to hospital, where they gave me a pethidine shot to sedate me for the afternoon. As I lay in my hospital bed in a warm, mellow, drug-induced state of semi-consciousness, I can still recall day-dreaming that maybe living in the Harbour City as coach of the Swans mightn't be too bad.

I met with Dr Edelsten a couple of days later and, unfortunately, my still leaky nose bled all over his boardroom table. While the two things are probably unrelated, the next we heard was that he'd appointed veteran Richmond, Collingwood and Geelong coach Tom Hafey – although there was still interest from the Swans about me going there as an assistant.

Collingwood also made follow-up contact soon after the 1985 grand final. At a meeting with Magpies president Ranald Macdonald, board member Allan McAlister, board member and chairman of selectors Ron Richards and coach Bob Rose, the succession plan was put on the table. At a time when many senior coaches, including Bob, were still working jobs outside football, I was offered the chance to become the first full-time assistant in the VFL. The Collingwood offer was $80,000 per year when I'd only received $50,000 in my final year as captain of Hawthorn. It was ridiculous, really, when you think about it – no wonder the finances at the club were heading for disaster.

It was maybe the first-ever coaching succession plan at VFL level. As it happened it was a forerunner – 25 years in advance – of a very different Collingwood succession plan. When Mick Malthouse was convinced to coach in 2010 and 2011 with full knowledge that new assistant coach Nathan Buckley would replace him in 2012, it seemed to create a fair bit of tension, because Mick's part in the arrangement wasn't completely voluntary. There's no doubt that when the time came for the handover he wasn't a willing participant.

The big difference in our 1986 arrangement was that Bob was genuinely committed to standing aside, just as Paul Roos willingly embraced the Sydney Swans' 12-month coaching succession plan that culminated in John Longmire's appointment as coach in 2011. In general, coaching succession plans are asking for trouble unless the incumbent coach fully supports the idea, and even then the timeline shouldn't be any longer than one season.

I was thrilled to accept the job at Collingwood and pleased to move on to a new chapter in my life. However, working at Victoria Park was quite a surreal experience at first. Going there to play in an opposition jumper had always been a positively scary experience, such was the crowd fervour at the parochial Magpies home ground. It took me a few weeks to drive into the car park without breaking into a cold sweat.

Settling in wasn't hard, though. Behind the scenes football clubs are all very similar – a group of people who come together and are linked by the common goal of living out their personal ambitions through the team cause. I have always thought that loyalty is easily transferable from club to club because it comes from within. While clubs have to work to create an environment that encourages loyalty from every team member, the quality comes mainly from the values that the individual lives by.

My loyalty is to the cause that I serve, and while for many club die-hards I was probably always the bloke from Hawthorn, for me Collingwood quickly replaced the Hawks as the centre of my football life, and as I had done with the Hawks I quickly fell in 'love' with my new club.

The small footy offices that were to be my weekday home for the next 10 years were adjacent to the dressing rooms under the dilapidated Ryder Stand; I suspect neither had altered much for many decades. Not much space was needed because there were few full-timers. There was football manager John Birt, secretary/receptionist Tine Kingdon, and now a third, me, as the new assistant coach. The only other full-timers were property steward Bill Cook, recruiter Bill O'Keefe and conditioning coach Ray Giles. These days the football department at any AFL club would be 30-odd full-time employees to service the 45 players on its training list. Player numbers are the same but the full-time era of the last 15 years has spawned a gigantic increase in coaching and support staff.

It was common practice at the time, as it still is, for clubs to try to recruit people from the best-performing teams. Hawthorn had played in the last three grand finals and the Collingwood power-brokers reasoned that there was merit in trying to tap into the Hawks' system through its retiring captain. On the same theme the Magpies also recruited Peter Power from reigning premiers Essendon to be the head conditioning coach.

Back then, there was a widespread train of thought that successful players would automatically make successful coaches, even though to me it was illogical, because the two roles are totally unrelated. The best analogy I can think of is in horse racing. For players and coaches, substitute jockeys and trainers – both in the same industry, but the two jobs are completely different. Sometimes a jockey will become a successful trainer, mostly they won't. Sometimes champion players will become successful coaches; again, mostly they won't. Great ability as a player is certainly no hindrance, but apart from an initial credibility with the players you're coaching, it isn't of any great help either. Coaching is mainly about man management; playing is about individual physical performance.

What is still fashionable is to appoint the next generation of coaches from the current top teams. The reflected glory from being involved with one of the trendsetters remains a prerequisite – no club looking for a new coach is considering assistant coaches from teams outside the top four.

The trap for the champion player, who is usually driven by a dominant personality and healthy self-belief, is to control the egotistical view that he will personally find new ways to win games of footy. It's only when he actually starts doing the job of a coach that he'll realise 90 per cent of the job is, in fact, about getting the basics right. And that he can't, and shouldn't, try to reinvent the coaching art.

Another challenge for the great player turned coach is to willingly move from the spotlight of centre stage to a largely invisible support role. Although being out there and marketing the club is part of the brief of the modern coach, I have no doubt the coaches most appreciated by their players are the ones who maintain a low-key public profile. Allan Jeans, Tom Hafey and Mick Malthouse are good examples; the great NRL coach Wayne Bennett fits under the same umbrella. They shun media attention, and while the media might find them hard work, their players love them.

It was a challenging time to join the Magpies. Since their record-breaking 15th premiership in 1958, they'd played in nine grand finals without winning one, which had spawned the unflattering 'Colliwobbles' tag. The upside was that Collingwood was a perennial finalist – if the club dropped out of the finals it would quickly bounce back. But the jinx of bombing out in grand finals was like a dark cloud hanging over Victoria Park.

It seemed to pervade the enormous fan base, best illustrated by the many letters from supporters to the senior coach pleading for a grand final win before they died. Winning games and playing finals seemed to be a given, while the elusive next premiership was a distraction to the essential needs of here and now. My firm belief – and the philosophy I pushed as soon as I became Collingwood coach – was that living in the moment, being realistic and avoiding exaggeration was how premierships were won. The natural hype generated externally from the fans, and the consequent media attention, couldn't be allowed to seep into the collective psyche of the team. That was a coaching challenge that constantly needed to be won.

Senior coach Bob Rose was an absolute legend of the club, and is widely regarded as the best player ever to have worn the black-and-white stripes. He played 152 games from 1946 to 1955, won the club Best and Fairest in 1951, 1953, 1954 and 1955, and in the 1953 premiership side topped the club goal-kicking list, was runner-up in the Brownlow Medal, and won All-Australian selection. He was an inaugural inductee into the AFL Hall of Fame in 1996.

He'd coached Collingwood from 1964 to 1971, taking them to three grand finals, two preliminary finals and seven finals series in eight years. The Magpies didn't win a premiership during his coaching tenure, but grand final losses by four points to Melbourne in 1964, one point to St Kilda in 1966 and 10 points to Carlton in 1970 prove his coaching credentials. Why any game of footy is won or lost by less than a kick defies logical reasoning; mostly it depends on which team has the footy gods on their side. I experienced most things during my footy career but fortunately losing a grand final by a few points wasn't one of them. The 'what ifs' must eat at you for the rest of your life, and for Bob, who'd suffered this excruciating fate three times as a coach, it was a tough cross to bear.

After John Cahill's exit as coach at the end of 1984, Bob had answered the call from the boardroom and returned to the senior job in 1985, and the Magpies then finished seventh with a 10–12 record.

It was highly unusual for the senior coach also to be on the club's board of directors. On the odd occasion during that first summer, I'd supervise training on the ground while Bob attended to his director's duties in the stately mahogany Victoria Park boardroom made famous in scenes from the movie loosely based on Collingwood, *The Club*.

The season didn't start well. A 55-point loss at home to defending premiers Essendon in the opening round was followed by a 34-point defeat at the SCG to the new-look Hafey-coached Sydney Swans. The next week was worse. After leading North Melbourne by 22 points at half-time, we were outscored 12 goals to one in the second half and suffered a humiliating loss. Three rounds into the season we were winless and second last on the ladder, with only Geelong below us because of a slightly inferior percentage.

The catalyst for the changes that followed was the club's dire financial position, but the poor on-field performance was certainly a factor. Hence the necessity to embark on a big shake-up at board and management level and to back it up with a new senior coach. We were scheduled to play the struggling Cats at Victoria Park in the next match – a key reason, I believe, in Bob Rose handing me the senior role that week. The timing gave me the best chance to kick off with a win.

From my point of view, it had been a fairly unproductive and unstimulating six months as a full-time assistant coach, during this era when players were still part-time, still working day jobs outside footy and training late afternoons. I was now eager to take on the responsibility of the senior job. It was a sign of my healthy assistant coach wage that, when I moved up from assistant to senior coach, the payment stayed the same.

Losing the opening three games was an on-field blow but that was insignificant compared to the club's financial problems. It's hard to comprehend that the powerhouse that Collingwood has become in the current Eddie McGuire-led era is the same club that was virtually bankrupt 25 years ago.

The changes implemented back then to keep the banks from closing the doors were massive. The main roles in the running of a footy club all changed on that tumultuous weekend. There was a new CEO, Rob Petrie, a new football manager, Graeme Allan, and the fresh-start symbolism of a new senior coach. Allan McAlister had succeeded Ranald Macdonald as president during the previous off-season. We had the enthusiasm of a new beginning, but experience on the job was in very short supply.

The rich and powerful club that Collingwood seemed to be when I was offered a job late the previous season was actually in a fight for its very survival.

My first act as the incoming senior coach was to go to Frankston Oval on the Sunday afternoon to watch a young full-forward called Jamie Shaw play for Preston against Frankston. He was a big goal-kicker in the VFA at the time and I was keen to assess his VFL potential. But sitting in the back of the stand that day by myself, I found it a little hard to concentrate on my talent-spotting duties. The big picture of where to start in my new senior coaching role was dominating my thoughts. I was able to contemplate in peace what lay ahead because news of my senior appointment wasn't to be announced until the following day.

Was I ready to be a senior coach? Probably not, but then nobody ever is because everyone learns on the job. What I had was a terrific background at Hawthorn with the great benefit of playing under three of the all-time great coaches in John Kennedy, David Parkin and Allan Jeans. In terms of experience it might have been like a kid starting at school, but I was eager to accept the coaching challenge.

Resisting the temptation to let my ego run rampant, I simply followed the successful Hawthorn model – with a little help from the great 'Yabby' Jeans. He was a magnificent coach of coaches and in my first year at the Collingwood helm he was a great mentor – even though he was still coach at Hawthorn. He was happy to help me against anyone except the Hawks, and I talked to him every month or so. It was some time before the young fella would get a win over the old master anyway; in fact, I suspect the Collingwood people thought I was a Hawthorn double agent, because in our first five meetings the Hawks prevailed by an average of 64 points.

When I rang Yabby during my first week as a senior coach he gave me two simple pieces of valuable advice. One was to ring the club president the morning after selection to discuss the team. It's a basic of human relationship building to get the boss onside by keeping him in the loop in terms of your thinking and strategies. It's a more than worthwhile investment of time.

Two was to 'get them chasing and tackling'. As a player, this was only a secondary consideration for me – I always joked that it was impossible to tackle with the ball in your hands – but in the 20-odd years I coached, getting my teams chasing and tackling was 90 per cent of my coaching focus. A team that tackles well is usually competitive.

In the three basic footy phases – winning the contest, maintaining possession, or chasing and tackling to get the ball back off the opposition – the latter is the hardest and most unnatural. Whether it's the chicken or the egg, or whether it's the motivation that comes from getting the hardest part of any task done first, if this part of a player's job gets done well, the team is likely to perform at its optimum level. Tackling effectively and attacking the contest fiercely would be the basis of my coaching philosophy – it was then all about totally committing to the job and learning as you go.

The longer I coached, the more I realised the value of balancing my naturally serious, intense personality with support staff who had a more easy-going demeanour. We didn't have a specialist ruck coach, and a chance meeting with livewire former North Melbourne premiership ruckman Peter 'Crackers' Keenan at the *World of Sport* Sunday morning sports show resulted in Crackers coming on board and staying for the entire decade I coached the Magpies.

His relaxed and casual manner off the field camouflaged a very competitive, aggressive attitude to football – exactly what we needed to develop in our young ruckmen Damian Monkhorst and James Manson. Crackers was a terrific ruck coach with the added benefit of generating a good karma around the player group, because of his light-hearted fun-loving style.

It was quite refreshing that my personal-performance ego could be put aside, because the task as a coach was now totally a 'we' thing. There is very little measure of a coach's individual contribution beyond the performance of the team; ultimately you succeed or fail by your team's performance.

The flip side, of course, is that come match day your emotional state will be determined by the actions of others, so the stimulating nervousness I had as a player was replaced by an uncomfortable anguish and tension, as control of my emotions was passed into the hands of my players.

While I would have loved to have the sensitivity and diplomacy of Allan Jeans, or the collaborative-teacher style of David Parkin, when I look back at my coaching persona when I started out it was more akin to the autocratic-principal approach of John Kennedy.

In political terms I coached as a benevolent dictator. Everything we did was for the good of the team, but I tried to direct and control anything that might affect on-field performance, and basically the Enforcer in my personality was the basis for my coaching style. It was 'my way or the highway'. The essential art of compromise was something I needed to learn through experience in the job.

As time went on I realised that the immature Enforcer in me had to be tempered, because my best coaching was done in my controlled Thinker mode. I have to say that occasionally regressing into the angry aggressive Enforcer mode was one of my coaching flaws; this personality trait helped me as a player but was to be a hindrance as a coach.

One of the beliefs that I took in my transition from playing to coaching was that if my players couldn't thrive under a tough uncompromising coach, then they wouldn't thrive and succeed in the tough uncompromising pressure of game day. When I began coaching in 1986, my approach in the team setting was to be intense, harsh and abrasive. The more friendly individual discussions were mainly via a five-minute Friday night phone call to each of the players in that week's senior team to clarify their role and what we expected of them the following day. I'm sure some players enjoyed the regular night-before chat, while for others it was probably a chore. In this era before cell phones, at least the players knew they needed to be settled in at home by mid-evening or I'd keep ringing until I eventually made contact.

Initially my success as a player egotistically influenced me to think that all the Collingwood players should be a clone of me. *Think like me, play like me.* Bad mistake. Everyone is a bit different and needs to be coached accordingly. Some team needs are not negotiable but within that basic framework individuals need to be treated in whatever manner stimulates their best performance. One size does not fit all; this was my first coaching lesson.

But as I settled into the job, and as much as I learnt I had to be myself and couldn't be an Allan Jeans clone, from a football point of view I still worked on the basic philosophy of taking the Collingwood playing group and trying to get them to play the successful Hawthorn game style.

Part of the ongoing coaching challenge is to moderate and blend short-term, medium-term and long-term objectives. From my experience a coach who has been in the job for an extended period will be tempted to focus primarily on short-term outcomes, whereas a coach new to the position, as I was at Collingwood, is more likely to think medium and long term. This encourages a new coach to make base-building and cultural decisions that might mean short-term pain for long-term gain.

My management philosophy was clear. If the crunch comes, the club interest must come before the team and the team must come before the individual. We're always searching for win/wins for all, but the club interest must always take precedence.

Given the financial plight there was one critical thing that Collingwood had to do – we had to try to balance the books. In this regard we were all in it together. My time working in the Hawthorn marketing department was to prove invaluable in understanding and accepting the financial reality that revenue is hard to generate and therefore costs had to be controlled.

Soon after my appointment as coach, there was a tense and difficult meeting with the player group in which club president Allan McAlister dropped a savage cost-cutting bombshell – all players would be required to accept a 20 per cent pay cut. It was an unstable volatile environment with big changes in motion, many of which only became clear to me a few days after that fateful phone call from Bob Rose.

I felt morally bound to take the pay cut as well, but for the playing group it wasn't voluntary – it was mandatory. And it came at a price. Two very good players in Geoff Raines and Mike Richardson, each in his fourth year at Collingwood, weren't prepared to accept the situation. They were given an open clearance to the club of their choice and were transferred to Essendon.

There wasn't one player happy with the pay cut but it probably had a strangely bonding effect on the large majority who accepted the bitter financial medicine to keep the club afloat. It was a sign that sometimes shared adversity can bind a group together, because after the turmoil that erupted at Victoria Park after losing the first three games, we went on to win 12 of the last 19 to narrowly miss the finals on percentage.

Off the field the club also regrouped, and the new president, the new football manager, Graeme 'Gubby' Allan, and myself, the new coach, began a working triumvirate that would run for the next decade. Not only that but history records that I coached VFL/AFL for 20 seasons – 10 at Collingwood and 10 at the Brisbane Lions – and Gubby was football manager for every single one. It was to be an enduring partnership that started as a random, forced relationship during the massive changes at Collingwood in early 1986.

Gubby's transition into the football manager's role was in keeping with the strange workings in place at the time, because he played in the round three loss to North and retired immediately to take on his new administration role.

When we started, neither of us had any experience in our new positions, so it was a great show of faith from the club to hand us the reins and let us take over. Gubby and I were paid employees but, as still occurs in the modern full-time era, the president is an honorary job. This didn't stop Allan McAlister spending countless hours on club affairs, and he and Gubby formed a fantastic off-field team with big-target recruiting their specialty.

At every game they sat inside the fence near the interchange bench, which provided a powerful symbolism to the players that they were part of the on-field team. The visibility of the president was enhanced further by Allan and Gubby walking laps of the oval during training, usually accompanied by Ron Richards, the long-serving chairman of selectors – another honorary job – and 1953 premiership player. They weren't just suits who wandered down from the boardroom on match days.

As an inexperienced first-time coach I count myself very fortunate to have had the support and counsel of these men. Coaching is often a very lonely job and what any coach needs the most is the confidence and trust of the key people at the club. Importantly, they encouraged and allowed me to back my judgement in the coaching of the team.

A regular theme from Allan still sticks in my mind. If he said it once, he said it 100 times: 'Leigh, assess all the facts but keep doing what you think is right.' What more could anyone ask of their boss? The important follow-up, of course, was that anything Gubby and I wanted to do, he'd do his best – usually successfully – to get it approved and done.

After Thursday night selection I'd give Ronnie Richards a lift home. It was a great opportunity to enjoy his football wisdom, which had come from spending a lifetime around the Collingwood footy club. From player to reserves coach to chairman of selectors to board member, he had done it all. Some of his thoughts and sayings still resonate.

Like 'Old blokes to the back line', illustrated by him suggesting late in Denis Banks' career that Banksy convert from being a goal-kicking half-forward to an attacking defender. Ronnie believed that ageing forwards could often finish their careers as good defenders. Banksy proved this theory correct in the 1990 premiership campaign.

Like 'Fumblers to the shithouse', as his colourful description that if a player continually fumbles, he is of no value.

Like 'Don't keep them around if you know they're not good enough', as a reminder that if you decide a player isn't up to it at senior level, get rid of him, because if he keeps playing well in the reserves the temptation will be to give him a senior game, when that position should be going to an untried youngster who might turn out to be very good. In other words, Ronnie believed in playing the kids.

Like 'He'll die in your arms', as a vivid description of any player he believed would crumble under intense competitive pressure. I can't think of a player he tagged with this characteristic who survived very long. Ronnie knew what it took and was a great judge of which players would continually let the team down.

Another of his beliefs was that during a match you should never swap a player winning his position with a player losing his position, because you might end up with two losers. Instead, swap two players who are both losing – there is little to lose and you might end up with a couple of winners.

I thought of Ronnie's theory about never swapping a player winning his position when watching the round 16 2012 clash between North Melbourne and Carlton. Kangaroos full-forward Drew Petrie started well against Blues full-back Michael Jamieson and had a few goals on the board early in the match. At the other end, Carlton's starting full-forward, Lachie Henderson, had led into a few marks and was looking dangerous, but nevertheless was shifted back onto Petrie who continued to dominate. The end result for the Blues was that one winner and one loser now became two losers. The old Ronnie Richards theory was borne out once again. In footy, while many things change, many things stay the same.

The old-style honorary experienced chairman of selectors was an enormous help to the senior coach over the decades, but disappeared when the full-time era began around the late '90s. These days, the convention is for clubs to appoint an inexperienced senior coach and then spend a few hundred thousand to buy some experience in the form of an ex-senior coach, such as Essendon did employing Mark Thompson to assist James Hird, as did Collingwood with Rodney Eade to help Nathan Buckley. What Ronnie Richards did for nothing is now getting paid very handsomely indeed.

Graeme Allan tells me he knew of the changes about to happen at Collingwood before he played his final game early in 1986. This says a lot about Gub, who I have got to know very well and who has become a close friend in the years since. He's an extraordinary networker who always seems to know what's going on before it becomes public.

'Mates' is only a term, I guess, but while I reckon I've got a few close mates, Gub has hundreds. His mobile phone never stops ringing, and he is a fantastic relationship builder, which made us a pretty good partnership. We were quite opposite personalities who seemed to complement each other. I was a nuts-and-bolts micro-coach/manager with no great natural empathy for people I didn't know well, while Gub was a terrific people's person who everyone liked.

His stubborn perseverance where he never took no for an answer, his ability to instantly befriend, and his knack of finding the solution to any obstacle made him a fantastic recruiter. And if there was a problem to be fixed, there was no better man.

One Monday morning in the late '80s Gubby informed me that Darren Millane had got into a fight over the weekend with one of Alphonse's mates and, our star wingman having broken the other bloke's jaw, Alphonse was after him. Now I'd heard Alphonse's name so I knew this was not good news. However, after watching the *Underbelly* series about the Melbourne underworld on television a few years ago, I realised how serious that threat had actually been, because Alphonse was the now-deceased Alphonse Gangitano. Unless the waters were smoothed quickly, Darren didn't have a healthy future.

Gubby did what he does so well. He found someone who knew someone who knew someone, and eventually the threat ceased to exist. As always the details were sketchy, but as always the job got done.

Both at Collingwood and then at Brisbane, his relaxed friendliness and natural optimism were a terrific foil for my normally autocratic and often pessimistic coaching demeanour. Gub thought in terms of the big picture, while I concentrated on getting today and tomorrow right. For me, after each match the world as I knew it changed and there was a fresh beginning from which to move forward. My attitude on match day was to expect the worst and hopefully be pleasantly surprised. Ambitions should always be high but should never be accompanied by grandiose expectations and assumptions.

The massive changes and the resultant turmoil at Collingwood going into round four of 1986 might have been absolutely necessary, but once those changes had been made they needed to be followed by perseverance. The balancing of when to change and when to persevere is a constant coaching/management quandary, and while gradual change is normal and healthy, when big changes are made, patience and perseverance must follow to allow the changes to have the intended effect. And the upheaval at Collingwood in early 1986 was the start of much change to flow through over the next 12 months.

My first game as coach went well. As I mentioned, I believe Bob Rose had chosen his time specifically to give me a soft introduction to coaching against a side at the bottom of the ladder. All went according to plan as we beat Geelong by 45 points.

The team that day had only five players – Mick Gayfer, Shane Morwood, Darren Millane, Tony Shaw and Jamie Turner – who would be part of the drought-breaking premiership team of 1990, just five seasons later.

In 1988, we won 15 games with one draw to finish second at the end of the home-and-away rounds, and I'd love to boast that the journey to the top four was the result of a detailed plan. However, there was a roller-coaster ride in between which was going to test those essential elements of patience and perseverance.

In the VFL in 1986, each club's playing list was largely made up of players from their metropolitan and country zone areas.

Each club had a reserves team that played as a curtain-raiser to the seniors and an under-19s team that played away at the visiting opponent's home ground. Lee Adamson was the reserves coach and Keith Burns coached our under-19s. Our under-age team was going well and we made a strategic decision late in the season to keep the group together, rather than elevate the best youngsters up into the reserves, as was the practice at the time. We figured there was something to be gained about them learning to win together.

The Collingwood under-19s team eventually won the flag that season and included a bunch of unknown youngsters who'd become household names in the years ahead. Gavin Brown, Gavin Crosisca, Damian Monkhorst and Mick McGuane were still developing at under-age level under Burnsy's astute coaching, but were all destined for senior level premiership honours.

My original position as assistant coach wasn't filled and I didn't even need to change offices. In fact, the small space I occupied when I arrived was my work area until the day I was sacked after the 1995 season. The football offices under the old Ryder Stand were so badly run down they should have been condemned and the players' changing area was only a bigger version of those I'd left behind at Chelsea in the late '60s. It was one large room with lockers around the edge – Chelsea only had hanging hooks – which doubled as the pre-game warm-up area and as the venue for the coach's pep talk. There was no private coach's room for just players and coaches and there was always a crowd to hear the coach's address. Legendary coach Jock McHale had probably worked his magic in these largely unchanged rooms, but that had been many decades ago.

Talking to the players on game day, where it was just them and the coach, was a priority for me, so in the corner of the gym adjacent to the big dressing room we removed the sauna and constructed out of plywood a small room with tiered seating for the players. It was very basic but served its purpose as a private coach's room on match days. It must have been lightweight, though, because after a close loss to the Swans during that first year I blew up a bit, and in response our burly full-forward stormed out, slamming the door behind him as the whole room threatened to fall down around our ears. That same volatile ex-player is now my Channel Seven and 3AW colleague Brian Taylor. These days he's generally tagged 'BT', but at the Magpies he was always 'Barge'; no-one at a football club avoids a nickname.

Three defeats in four weeks, including a 45-point loss to Hawthorn at Waverley, followed my first-up win over Geelong, but an encouraging 9–1 streak broken only by a one-point loss to Sydney had us fourth on the ladder at round 17.

As I've mentioned, my philosophy was 90 per cent about getting the basics done well; the other 10 per cent was the tactical approach. Basics are what you need to do every week against every opponent, while tactics are the variations in your game plan from match to match. And even a basics coach like myself can occasionally try a bit of tactical surprise.

In the modern era of large coaching panels, in which vision of every game is available from many different camera angles, anything a team does is quickly scouted and uncovered – innovative tactics don't remain a secret very long.

Back in the late '80s, though, there were no games live on television and only a couple of matches a week were covered by the cameras that provided the Saturday night replay content. Effective tactics from team to team were sussed out quite slowly.

The most memorable match during that 9–1 streak was against

Fitzroy in round 11 at Victoria Park. Under the coaching of Robert Walls, around the 1984–85 seasons the Lions had developed a very successful kick-in strategy. Up until this time defending was largely done by covering your direct opponent, which Fitzroy exploited by gathering in a tight bunch around centre half-back. After some subtle blocking inevitably a Lions player would lead unopposed to the vacant outside space, their full-back, Gary Pert, would deliver the easy pass and they were away. As this tactic gradually became known, the initial opposition response was to position a couple of outriders to block that outside space, but this set-up still failed to stop the Lions' attacking surges. Simply, there was too much space for a couple of outriders to adequately cover.

Our round 11 match would be my first experience of coaching against Fitzroy and their innovative kick-in drills. Blunting the effectiveness of their kick-ins was a high priority. The thought arose of keeping our six defenders on their direct opponents, but using the other 12 to set up a defensive zone in our forward line. The question was whether 12 players could cover the space within a kick of our goal well enough to not allow an easy free target.

With the help of our property steward, Bill Cook, and armed with a dozen large orange marker cones, prior to our Thursday training session we experimented with the positioning of the cones as make-believe players. We positioned the cones with three spread across the ground about 20 metres from the goal square, four spread across the half-forward line from flank to flank about 40 metres out, and five spread across the ground from wing to wing about 60 metres out.

The final touch to the positioning was me going up into the elevated coach's box in the old Ryder Stand and yelling out to Billy – this was before cell phones – to move the cones into what was basically a 3/4/5 formation of markers for our players when we trained later that afternoon. We explained the concept to them prior to training, and then, using the cones as marker points, went out to practise defending the Fitzroy bunching kick-in system that had given them a terrific competitive edge for a couple of seasons. It's no use having plans unless they're backed up with practice.

The dangerous space was over the back of our 12 zoning players, so the plan was that if the ball was kicked long, they should punch it back into the Collingwood forward line, where our zoning forwards were positioned unopposed within a kick of our goals.

It wasn't long into the game before we scored our first behind to the social club end of Victoria Park, and I'll never forget the surprised look on the face of Gary Pert as he confronted the mass of black-and-white jumpers covering the space into which his team-mates would normally lead.

With no easy target the Lions full-back kicked long to the back flank just as we hoped he would. Our big ruckman Wes Fellowes did his job and thumped the ball back into our forward line to our waiting unmanned zone players, and we kicked an easy goal. We booted 10 goals in that first quarter and had a 44-point win.

Because many teams were emulating the Fitzroy method, our 12-man zone approach to defend the opposition kick-in scored us a lot of goals during that 1986 season. It proved to this young coach that finding a competitive edge that your players believe in is an incredibly valuable coaching tool.

Coaches are basically sellers of hope, and proving to your players that if they do what the coach asks then success will come is the very reason they will commit to following instructions. That small win with our defensive zone tactic was a vital starting point in my coaching journey.

Three consecutive defeats from round 18 to 20 sent us sliding to eighth, but heading into the final round we were still in the mix. To play finals we had to beat bottom side St Kilda at VFL Park and second-placed Sydney had to beat fifth-placed Fitzroy at Victoria Park – the Lions' home ground at the time.

Barge, who would win the 1986 Coleman Medal as the competition's leading goal-kicker from Sydney's Warwick Capper and Footscray's Simon Beasley, went into the final home-and-away round on 98 goals. He got one in the first quarter but strained his groin muscle and looked to be gone for the day. At quarter-time he pleaded with me to give him 10 minutes to see if he could continue, as he was sore without being crippled. Limping around for those next 10 minutes, Barge eventually took a mark on the lead and kicked his

100th goal. He then hobbled from the field with his strained groin now completely torn.

It was a rare moment of compassion when I put the interests of an individual before the team. While we won, Fitzroy did also, so our season was over. If the Lions had lost, we would have gone into a finals campaign without our century-kicking full-forward, who I'd allowed to aggravate his injury in a quest for a personal honour. While the fact that Collingwood didn't make the finals meant no harm was done and I was pleased that Barge got the elusive 100, it was many years before I again fell for the trap of not putting the team unequivocally first.

So my first coaching year was over, I'd learnt many lessons on the job and the Magpies had had a promising year. After a poor start we'd played some good footy and we had a seemingly bright future ahead. However, it turned out to be a false dawn. There were dark days ahead that would challenge our ability to set a course and then persevere through the rough weather to come.

20

A CLUB IN TRANSITION

Unfortunately, things didn't get a lot better.

Competition of any sort continually throws up unpredictable curve balls; just when everything seems to be tracking well, the unexpected comes calling. Never expect, never assume.

Shortly after the end of a 1986 season in which Collingwood's fortunes on and off the field had improved from diabolical to reasonable, we were put back on our heels with the exodus of a couple of key players. Our centre half-back, Greg Phillips, and attacking back flanker, Bruce Abernathy, both decided to return to Adelaide. Maybe it was a predictable aftermath of the 20 per cent pay cut that had been forced on all our players as the club struggled to stay afloat earlier in the season, or maybe it was just their urge to return home, but we couldn't change their minds and a significant chunk of experienced talent left the club.

Then an even bigger management problem reared its head. The Magpies captain for the last four seasons had been Mark Williams. He was in protracted and very public contract negotiations with the club at the end of the season and was entertaining an offer from the newly formed Brisbane Bears. It was unhealthy for our player group to have their leader equivocating about whether he was staying or leaving, and we were very concerned about the message it was sending to the rest of our players. That our captain – of all people – was playing financial hardball and wasn't prepared to commit to the club couldn't be tolerated much longer, so we decided to give Mark an ultimatum.

We told him one Friday late in October that by the following

Monday he either had to accept the Collingwood offer or it would be withdrawn. It was time for the tail to stop wagging the dog.

Mark might have thought it was simply a negotiating tactic but we were a club determined to set a culture of individual subservience to the team cause, and sometimes that meant risking short-term pain for long-term gain. While I'm sure Mark was aggrieved at the time, and quite possibly carried that ill-feeling forward, we felt that this principle needed to be enforced. The deadline came and went and so did our captain.

After Mark's successful premiership-winning coaching stint at Port Power, I suspect he'd now fully understand and probably agree with the stance we took back in October 1986. As history would show, Mark became the first signing with the fledgling Brisbane Bears, who would join the expanding national competition with the West Coast Eagles in 1987. Coincidentally, he'd be joined by a couple of ex-Collingwood team-mates, Geoff Raines and Mike Richardson, who also headed north after their short time at Essendon.

The bottom line was that since the turmoil only six months earlier, for various reasons five talented and experienced players had left the club. As one was our existing captain, we needed a new leader. It may have been a complete coincidence but none of the five players who'd left had grown up at Collingwood; all had been recruited from outside Victoria or from other VFL clubs. This fact was clearly in our thinking when we met to choose our new captain. With an 'outsider' like me as coach we needed a big dose of grassroots Collingwood to rebuild the battered Magpies spirit, and the appointment of our new captain had to fulfil this crucial aim.

Our vice-captain in 1986 was centre half-forward David Cloke, and rover Tony Shaw was the deputy vice-captain. Both were good candidates – hard workers, brave competitors and good role models. It would have been a risk-free decision to automatically elevate Clokey into the captaincy, but after playing 176 games for Richmond and being part of the Tigers' 1974 and 1980 premiership teams, he'd only been at Victoria Park for four seasons. He was already 31 and, because he hadn't grown up at Collingwood, it troubled me a bit as to whether he was the right fit for the rebuild ahead of us.

The big forward and effective back-up ruckman had been part of the recruiting spree initiated by the previous Magpies regime, which had swept into power in 1982 after a few heartbreaking near misses that had further perpetuated the Colliwobbles myth of grand final failure. In the five seasons from 1977 to 1981, the Magpies had finished second, third, second, second and second.

John Cahill was recruited from Port Adelaide as coach in 1983. Also new to the Magpies that year were Phillips, Raines and Richardson. Abernathy came across from North Melbourne the following year. They were all now gone. I was new to Victoria Park so it seemed to me that the new Collingwood captain needed to be black and white through and through. Preferably, in the situation as it was at the time, we needed to find a home-grown product and Clokey didn't fit the bill.

A visit to his liquor shop in Kew to personally deliver the news and its rationale was a necessary task, but one I dreaded. It's great fun delivering good news, but doing the opposite is like pulling out a sore tooth; the sooner you get it done, the quicker the pain subsides. I would have loved to let Gubby or Allan do the job for me, because generally speaking the messenger gets shot, and I wasn't looking forward to telling David of the decision to overlook him for the captaincy.

I knew he'd be bitterly disappointed, which he was. However, he took the news without any histrionics and, in fact, had the class to at least pretend to understand our thinking. David always had a serious, gruff exterior and never appeared flustered or upset, so his calm reaction was in keeping with his general demeanour. I drove back to the club with a weight off my shoulders, because an unpleasant task is always a load until it's completed.

When I started coaching, I didn't have great empathy for individual feelings. It's only with the benefit of reflection that I realise the damaging subliminal message that was sent to David Cloke by our decision to appoint a 'Collingwood person' as captain. Effectively we were telling David that while we still wanted him to play for the Magpies, his age and background at another club meant we were demoting him down the player priority order. It would have been a terrible blow to his pride and status.

The aftermath was a gradual decline in Clokey's form, and he left Collingwood as a 34-year-old at the end of 1989 to play a final couple of seasons back at Richmond.

Often we learn slowly. The gradual lesson for me was that veteran players, like very inexperienced youngsters, need plenty of TLC from the coach. Players in their prime are usually pretty self-sufficient. Looking back, I never gave Clokey enough individual attention after the captaincy decision was made. In coaching or management, delivering bad news goes with the territory but it can be done bluntly or with sensitivity. Hopefully as time went on I learnt this lesson and gradually got better at communicating with the tried and true Allan Jeans method of honesty tempered with diplomacy. The team always comes first but caring for the individual is also important.

This bitter experience in his last few years at Collingwood and what it did to his football philosophy was something I pondered when David was in the news as part of his son Travis' very public contract negotiation with the Magpies in 2012. While the general theme was that Travis had received a good offer from Collingwood and should re-sign, it isn't hard to imagine that his father's footy journey had reinforced the fact that clubs will do what is best for them and that every player eventually outlives his usefulness, so why shouldn't the individual do what's best for himself? The seemingly stubborn approach by the Cloke camp to get the best possible deal for Travis may have had some foundation in father David's personal experience a few decades before.

I might have been an inexperienced coach back in 1986 but I needed no convincing that a winning team desperately needs good on-field leadership. Preferably, that would be spread across a lot of players, which is the basic logic behind the modern leadership group approach adopted by all clubs in recent years. The theory is that player empowerment leads to ownership, accountability, hopefully a healthier club environment, and ultimately a better team performance. The leadership group system in place these days may be helpful, but it's useless and even self-defeating without the player character and intellect to make good decisions.

Fortunately, we had a player with the leadership ability and, importantly, the entrenched Collingwood background – our 26-year-old deputy vice-captain Tony Shaw. While he would probably rank fairly low in modern draft standards for speed and athleticism, he was as good as you'd find for courage, heart, self-belief and mental toughness. Short in stature, our new captain proved to be one great competitor.

Back in the part-time footy of the 1980s, the captain's responsibilities were largely about on-field leadership and being a good role model, and through 170 games over nine years at Collingwood since his debut in 1978 Shawy had exhibited all the qualities we needed in our captain. And importantly, he was Collingwood through and through. I was very fortunate as coach to have a captain of Shawy's stature work alongside me and lead the player group for the next seven years.

The end of my first year as a VFL coach also marked the first year of the national draft. And while we didn't pick up anyone too memorable with four of the club's five picks – Grant Fielke (West Adelaide), Dave Robertson (North Adelaide), Brendan Hogan (Assumption College, Kilmore) and Wayne Tanner (Norwood) – our third-round selection was a winner. Craig Kelly, also from Norwood, was selection number 36 overall and would prove to be a really important addition, although he took a lot of convincing over a couple of years before he eventually made the move over the border to Melbourne.

We also secured two players from Western Australia via the interstate recruiting system. Michael Christian was a 191-centimetre, 23-year-old defender and Craig Starcevich a 193-centimetre, 19-year-old centre half-forward. But we only got 'Starce' after a real battle with Essendon. We'd identified him as a likely type throughout the year and thought it was pretty much a done deal, so we were a little taken aback to learn he'd accepted an invitation to attend the grand final as a guest of Essendon. All of a sudden we were on the back foot and sensed that we had to find a counter to any obligation he might feel to the Bombers. We decided to invite Craig's parents, Flo and John, to the grand final as guests of Collingwood.

While Hawthorn won the senior grand final that year (it was terrible for my ego to see the team improve after I retired!), importantly our under-19s also won the grand final. The Starcevichs had a great day at the footy and then joined the jubilant celebrations back at the Collingwood Social Club. Eventually their son signed with us. Happily, all worked out in the end but there was certainly a lesson there about going the extra yard with that sort of thing, and never taking anything for granted.

This recruiting experience popped into my mind 25 years later in late 2011 when Gubby Allan, now football director at the Greater Western Sydney Giants, recruited Melbourne midfielder Tom Scully as their marquee signing going into the Giants' inaugural season. In a modern version of the 'Starcevich recruiting method', it transpired that while Tom joined the club as a player, his father, Phil, was also coming on board as a full-timer in their recruiting department. The fact that the AFL made the Giants include Phil Scully's wages in the club's salary cap was proof that they believed his employment was part of Tom's total remuneration package. Gubby learned long ago that, particularly with young players, keeping the family happy is worth the investment. Maybe what worked with the Starcevichs back in 1986 was where this philosophy began.

The confidence and belief that was built during my first honeymoon season, in which a new coach generated the enthusiasm of a fresh beginning, disappeared very early in 1987. We started the season with a 91-point Victoria Park loss to Sydney. Getting thrashed at home is an enormous blow. Where we were as a team was starkly evident when champion Swans centreman Greg Williams collected 32 possessions and two Brownlow Medal votes opposed to Collingwood teenage debutant Neil Brindley, a graduate from the previous year's under-19 team. It was to be Neil's only senior game. Basically, we'd thrown him to the wolves by setting him a task beyond his abilities at the time.

Unfortunately, things didn't get a lot better. We finished 12th of 14 teams with a 7–15 record and didn't beat a side in the top six. If you don't play finals you need something positive going into the summer, so a five-point win over ninth-placed Essendon at the MCG in the last game at least gave us something to hang our hat on.

The only pleasing thing was the development of some of the younger players. Christian (19 games) and Starcevich (13 games) slotted into VFL football nicely, while under-19 graduates Brown

(16 games), Crosisca (seven), McKeown (four) and McGuane (three) also had their first taste of senior football.

So, in my first two years as Collingwood coach we'd finished sixth and 12th. History shows that if a coach doesn't get a few credits in the bank by the end of his third year, he rarely gets a fourth.

Another year of the Magpies losing more than we won and my coaching career would be over. Somehow, between the end of 1987 and round one of the following season, a much better way needed to be found. Our playing group discovering a massive inspiration and uncovering an unknown inner strength in the Gippsland bush was a summer training bonus that was beyond our wildest dreams.

21

REBUILDING

We were in the ballpark but didn't get it done when the
September crunch time arrived.

Following a very poor 1987 season, the search immediately began for a vehicle to lift the self-esteem of a Collingwood playing group which had endured a disappointing and confidence-sapping year.

We simply couldn't afford to wait and hope that the new season would miraculously bring success. Somewhere in the summer training program we desperately needed to inject a large dose of self-belief. The conditioning program to build fitness, strength and skill had to be a mere starting point.

The performance of any difficult athletic task requires not only the physical capability but also the mental strength to push through the pain barrier, and the emotional durability to overcome the inevitable discouragement along the way. It isn't only training the body; the mind must be trained as well.

Collectively for Collingwood post-1987, it was about building trust and respect among the team. A really tough training camp as a culmination of the pre-Christmas training period seemed a worthwhile initiative to help in that process. Tough we wanted, but an even more valuable life-threatening experience happened by accident.

Over the years, footy teams going away together have taken many different forms. Originally, it was the post-season holiday or even the pre-season trip away with a bit of training thrown in, such as the Hawthorn week in Sydney that I attended as a rookie 16-year-old back in 1969.

The bonding value of the old-style, post-season holiday trip, which may have engendered greater friendship through partying together but very little in terms of what is really important, has become largely redundant now that players are full-time and around the club day after day for 10 months of the year. Clubs hardly need to push their players together in the off-season as a getting to know each other exercise. Some player groups still run supporter functions to pay for their holiday trips. This is quite bizarre when you think about it, given the relatively high earnings of footballers these days compared to the average fan.

Recently the financial benchmark for the training camp concept has risen considerably – from the high-altitude training camps in the United States made fashionable by the modern cashed-up Collingwood to trekking the Kokoda Track in Papua New Guinea pioneered by Hawthorn. Taking 50 to 60 players, coaches and staff overseas is a multi-hundred-thousand-dollar investment.

It was still the same Collingwood back in 1987 but nothing as grandiose as an overseas jaunt was even remotely on the radar back then. However, as I've said, we urgently needed to do something during the pre-season to give our players a sense of pride in themselves and a greater respect and trust for their team-mates.

This was the clear objective, this was the 'why'. As always the challenge was also to solve the question of 'what', 'how' and 'when'. These four words became a regular coaching checklist for me. Answering, explaining and selling all four of these principles needs to be done to get any group of people committed to a common task: what we want to do, why we need to do it, how we're going to do it, and when.

What we wanted at that time was an inexpensive, out-of-comfort-zone, survival camp that would provide bonding through shared adversity, resourcefulness through forced self-sufficiency, and hopefully a sense of achievement and pride from surviving a difficult experience.

The concept we eventually came up with was to finish our pre-Christmas training with a mid-December week-long training camp, which would culminate in a four-day, three-night trek through the McAllister Ranges in the Alpine National Park near the small Gippsland town of Licola.

This idea came from our conditioning coach, Mark McKeon, who was doing some consultancy work with Laurie Hayden and Associates, a corporate training company. Through the Hayden group we were introduced to a couple of ex-Army trainers, Tony 'Shep' Roydan and Mal Girdwood, who were engaged to organise and run the camp.

At the time, Shep was a partner in the All-Fit Training Camp situated at the old Lion Park in Bacchus Marsh and had previously headed up the phys-ed training department at the SAS training base in Perth. Mal had taken schoolkids trekking through this part of Victoria and arranged the use of the nearby Peninsula Grammar Outdoor Centre, where the team was based for a few days prior to the trek.

Shep ran the in-camp adventure activities, high ropes course, abseiling, flying fox and then supplemented the fun stuff with some really tough circuit training, as well as introducing the players to milling. This entailed putting boxing gloves on, kneeling chest to chest facing your designated opponent and punching underhand into each other for a 30-second burst. No-one got hurt but enhancing aggression through milling became a regular drill at Collingwood over the next few years.

While I joined the players at the live-in camp as an observer, Shep was running the program. He had the great knack of grabbing a group of men, who would immediately accept his control and authority. One of the first things he did was to introduce a ban on calling team-mates 'mate'. His idea was that it was both respectful and disciplined to call each other by Christian names or even nicknames, and not the lazy 'call-everybody-mate' habit. The penalty was 20 push-ups on the spot.

While it was up at dawn and early to bed, night-time was punctuated by the intermittent sighting in the shadows around the camp of the local 'yowie', who looked amazingly similar in size and shape to our resident practical joker Darren Millane. Walking around a dark corner and getting scared witless by the hairy ape-man was too much for Gavin Brown, who grabbed a carving knife from the kitchen and went hunting the monster. Browny never did find the yowie, which was a stroke of good fortune for our other champion wingman.

Planning the route of the hike along the many fire-break tracks criss-crossing the national park was Mal's baby. It was to be total self-sufficiency, apart from water being replenished in the creeks along the way. All food and supplies for the few days needed to be carried – there were no drop-off supply points.

I joined the players for the few days at the Outdoor Centre but went home before the trek began. The decision had been made that the trek was only going to be for those who performed inside the white line. Mark McKeon was also the match-day runner so he had the dubious honour of being the only non-player invited to go.

Apart from having Mal to guide them, it was largely an exercise in survival through player empowerment without a designated leadership hierarchy, and in fact it was largely a next-generation playing group. Injury issues prevented the experienced Peter Daicos, David Cloke, Brian Taylor and Denis Banks from taking part, while Tony Shaw's wife, Deb, was pregnant and due any day, so Shawy was also excused.

When I drove out of the Outdoor Centre on the Monday afternoon, it had been a worthwhile few days. While working hard together, the players were also undergoing a valuable bonding experience by being stuck in the middle of nowhere with no television and no communication with the outside world. They weren't developing friendship through getting on the booze together; more importantly, they were being forced out of their comfort zone by sharing some scary moments. If, like me, you don't like heights, activities such as the high ropes courses 20 metres up in the treetops and abseiling over the edge of a 30-metre cliff do tend to get the heart pumping. Peer group pressure, though, overcomes any individual misgivings – everyone does it and everyone survives.

But while the camp's dormitory-type accommodation was pretty basic, this was planned to be the easy part. It would be five-star luxury compared to the next four days trekking up and down the Gippsland mountains, carrying and preparing their own food and sleeping rough under the stars; or rain, if the weather turned bad.

While I headed back to suburbia, the players got themselves organised to head off into the bush the following morning, expecting to be trekking for a few days and back in Melbourne by Friday evening. With mobile phones not yet widely available, communication with the outside world was non-existent – they were on their own. In a symbolic sense, the strong would survive and the weak would perish.

The next time I was with the players was at the club's annual Christmas party at Parade College in Bundoora the following Sunday. For some unknown reason, when I arrived at the function you could almost cut the tension in the air with a knife. It was only then that I became aware of the reason for the angst among the players – the trek had turned into a disaster and they were blaming me and Gubby for allowing the debacle to happen. According to the more cynical players, we'd not only allowed but, in fact, had planned the whole thing to take place.

As it turned out, the players got lost a couple of days into the trek and had to back-track to try to find their way out, eventually emerging from the Alpine National Park starving and tired a day and a half overdue. They'd been forced way beyond any level of fatigue they'd ever experienced, and found that with no alternative but to either lie down and die or to keep going, they found the strength and will to continue. Some did it a little easier than others, but under extreme duress those who best handled the physical and mental stress earned the respect and trust of their team-mates.

A prime example was a little-known youngster by the name of Shane Kerrison, who was mainly playing in the reserves. Kerro's strength of mind and body to fight his way through adversity really came to the fore during the ill-fated Gippsland trek, and his status amongst the group was greatly enhanced from that point onwards.

Events and circumstances that seemingly become catalysts for vastly improved performance are rarely apparent at the time. Like trying to nominate a premiership dynasty in advance, these things need a retrospective view.

What history tells me is that the extreme test of mind, body and soul that this trek into the Gippsland Alpine National Park provided was a significant stimulus in the Collingwood team – which had finished the 1987 season as an also-ran – improving sufficiently over the summer break to start the following year playing like a top team. It was a truly amazing transformation; boys seemed to become men almost overnight.

We leveraged the experience in every possible way. A football that the players had carried on the trek was mounted and displayed in the dressing rooms as a constant subliminal reminder. We employed Shep Roydan as a match-day motivator cum trainer/water boy. Like the mounted footy, he was a link to the trek and its hard-learned lessons, and for the next year or so whenever a game was close at three-quarter time, a mention of pushing through the pain and fatigue barrier 'like you did on the camp' always got a positive response.

Developing and maintaining an elite football team is like putting together an ever-changing jigsaw puzzle. I firmly believe that once the players had survived that disastrous hike – which got the nucleus of the next generation Collingwood players lost and way out of their comfort zone, and turned the intended very difficult experience into something unplanned and almost life-threatening – it became a gigantic piece of the puzzle that saw the battling Magpies of 1987 transformed into a top-four team the following season.

The next step, though, was always going to be the hardest. Going from the bottom to mid-list is difficult and going from mid-list to the top bunch is even harder, but to finish as premiers is basically beyond planning control. We'd made the leap from being an also-ran to being competitive with the competition frontrunners, but unfortunately both the 1988 and 1989 seasons would finish badly, as we bombed out without a finals win in both years.

You can plan to be good and to get everything controllable done perfectly, but the performance pyramid becomes very narrow at its peak and to end up sitting alone on the top requires plenty of good fortune to accompany the necessary good management. That reality is the bottom line but inside the football club we had to act on the underlying belief that every decision, every initiative, might well be the difference between success and failure. Talented players need to be recruited, they need to be conditioned, coached and developed well, and the indefinable club environment (or 'culture', in current terminology) must be conducive to optimal performance. But the latter isn't a science – it's an art based on feel and judgement.

If there is one indispensable principle that underpins elite sport, it's that the desperate urge to find a better way must be never-ending.

The search to develop a competitive edge that gives a team a physical advantage, or at least a boost to the belief that we're doing things better than our opponents, is an extremely valuable commodity.

Now that full-time footy has fully evolved over recent years, millions of dollars are now being spent on the 'arms race' to find that elusive thousandth of a per cent, because every little bit helps in the quest to be the best.

As an example of this trend, around the turn of the century Collingwood and North Melbourne were devoting roughly the same amount to their football departments. By 2010, though, as I mentioned earlier, the Magpies were spending about five million more than the Kangaroos. Courtesy of the salary cap, the two clubs' player payments would be similar, so the increase and massive gap came in the non-player expenditure sector. Unless Collingwood are very wasteful, they must be gaining a competitive edge through their financial power; likewise the West Coast Eagles, who seem to operate on an unlimited budget.

While the outgoings at Collingwood 25 years ago were much less, we were equally determined to find a competitive edge. Our conditioning coach, Mark McKeon, was challenged to seek out new and better ways to prepare our players. In conjunction with the club's nutritionist, Lorna Garden, we introduced skinfold measuring of players to encourage lower body fat through better nutrition, and started a vitamin supplementation program to enhance energy levels.

As a recovery and injury prevention initiative, Mark also introduced a 15-minute supervised post-training and post-game stretching routine. All these things are now a normal part of being an elite AFL player, but back then they were quite cutting edge.

Player recruitment is always critical and the Collingwood recruiting team, headed by Gubby, introduced some terrific talent in the late '80s. The newcomers came from near and far. From the under-19s came Gavin Crosisca, Gavin Brown, Damian Monkhorst and Mick McGuane. From other states came Michael Christian, Tony Francis, Craig Kelly, Graham Wright, Scott Russell and Craig Starcevich. Doug Barwick was recruited from Fitzroy.

We drafted Craig 'Ned' Kelly from Norwood in South Australia in the 1986 draft but, as I've mentioned, he was very reluctant to leave

Adelaide. Eventually he came across in 1989 after we took him on the club's trip to Miami and Toronto after the 1988 season for 'world championship' games against Geelong and Hawthorn respectively.

An October game on the other side of the world as part of a post-season exhibition should have little significance as far as future prospects are concerned, but this one did. For starters, Ned played well at centre half-back on the great Dermott Brereton, and in a marking collision splattered gun full-forward Jason Dunstall's nose all over his face. In an instant, he'd earned the respect of his new team-mates as a tough, committed competitor who was scared of nobody, no matter how big their reputation. Ned was a player you wanted on your side.

He was very smart as well, and later had great business success with his sports marketing company, Elite Sports Properties, but he also had enough white-line fever to make him a brutal on-field performer. Ned was a core part of the Collingwood 1990 premiership team and was always a pleasure to coach.

While the fortnight overseas was very much an end-of-season trip with a couple of games and a bit of training thrown in, the chance to get a win over the Hawks was worth the effort. For one thing, they were the champion team of the time; also, we hadn't beaten them since I'd been appointed Collingwood coach.

The game in Toronto against Hawthorn, who'd won the premiership by a whopping 96 points a couple of weeks earlier, was played at the University of Toronto on a narrow rectangle-shaped gridiron field. Our pre-match meeting was held in an unusual place, up in the back row of the grandstand, where the narrowness of the ground was clearly visible. We decided that, because attacking in a straight line to goal would mean having to negotiate a heavily congested area crowded with players, the best option was to kick the ball across field to the opposite side of the ground and then use the space to run the footy forward.

The Collingwood players bought into the plan, the method worked a treat and we won quite comfortably. Although our opponents were in real holiday mode and the win took place in a seemingly insignificant post-season exhibition match on the other side of the world, it was still a victory over our invincible nemesis and was a valuable step in the team's development.

In round one the following season we beat Hawthorn by 10 points at Waverley Park. Just maybe the Toronto game played its part.

The successful ploy that day in Canada of switching play across field also had a more practical benefit. It encouraged us to bring the idea back and into our normal game plan. We had great success over the next year or two of kicking the ball – whenever possible –across from the wing into the centre square, and then quickly playing on and surging quickly into our forward line from the centre corridor. This became part of our successful attacking method thereafter.

Another benefit from our frequent trips to Adelaide chasing Craig Kelly was reacquainting Gubby and myself with the 33-year-old Norwood veteran, former Collingwood defender Michael Taylor, who'd returned home to finish his career at the Redlegs after playing 92 games for the Magpies in the early '80s. We convinced Mick to come back to Victoria as an assistant and to captain/coach the Collingwood reserves team.

As works so well in suburban footy, I've always been a great believer in the value of having a playing coach with young teams, and with so much youth in our reserves, having the universally respected former Magpie out on the field to lead and coach our youngsters gave us great development value in 1988 and 1989.

The senior team had a vast improvement from seven wins in 1987 to 15 wins and a draw in 1988 and then 13 wins in 1989. But, as I've said, in both years we suffered winless finals series – we were in the ballpark but didn't get it done when the September crunch time arrived.

The good news was that the freakishly talented Peter Daicos, who had the most sublime ball skills, had played most of these two seasons after a foot tendon injury had kept him off the field for much of the 1987 season. Primarily playing as a midfielder, Daics, who could be a goal-kicking genius, had only kicked 20 goals in 1989. We had to get better in this critical aspect of his game. The other big plus was a breakout year for Gavin Brown. In only his third season, he had emerged as an All-Australian wingman.

When I think about Browny, what I first saw and what he became were polar opposites. During his early days at Collingwood as a shy teenager, by my judgement he was a timid footballer. But as he matured and gained confidence he became an unbelievably brave and desperate competitor.

The lesson is to be careful about judging youngsters too early. Lack of confidence and lack of character dominance often make young players appear timid at the contest. A year or two in the system and feeling secure in the team often leads to the nervous uncertainty gradually disappearing, to be replaced by increasing assertiveness and visible determination.

When Melbourne ended our finals campaign for the second consecutive year in 1989, no-one, including me, could possibly have predicted that Gavin and Daics would lead our deep forward attack in 1990 with a combined total of 146 goals. Daics would kick an amazing 97 and Browny – seconded more and more from his favoured midfield role by team needs to a medium-sized, fast-leading full-forward – added a further 49.

My last memory of the disappointing 1989 season was a late-night phone call following our finals bomb-out from a tired and emotional Magpies captain Tony Shaw. In the dressing rooms after the loss to the Demons, I'd basically cracked it with the team and during my outburst had said that 'even Shawy didn't attack the footy hard enough'. Now even in the middle of a red mist coaching rage, I'd never accuse Tony Shaw of lacking courage. No braver or committed footballer has ever played the game.

What had stuck in my mind during my frustrated spray was an isolated incident during the game when our captain got stuck in between going for the footy and thinking about going for the footy. By the time he went, he was half a step late and was beaten to the ball.

These few words floated away quickly from my memory, but not Shawy's. His competitive pride had been pricked; to him, being accused of not attacking the footy hard enough was akin to chopping off his arm.

When the phone rang in the early hours of the following morning, a tired and emotional coach took the call from an even more tired and emotional captain, who was majorly aggrieved and hurt by his coach's careless post-game words that Shawy took as a criticism of his hardness at the ball.

I willingly apologised for saying anything that could be interpreted that way, although I must say my alcohol-induced croaky voice wasn't working all that well and Shawy had been stewing for many hours and was clearly very hurt by my comments. I could hear and feel the pain in his voice.

While I was already a Tony Shaw fan, if I ever needed further evidence about his pride, immense drive and raging competitive spirit I got it that night. If he had inadvertently and probably for the first time in his life not instinctively charged flat out head first at the footy, it would never happen again.

If there was a man with the mental strength to lead the Magpies through the myth of the Colliwobbles, it was him.

22

THE LAUNCHING PAD

That grimace as he walked into the medical room after the
match against North will live with me forever.

It was about 30 minutes after the final home-and-away game of the 1990 season when Darren Millane walked slowly from the players' area into the medical room at the now-defunct VFL Park. Anyone within close proximity could almost feel the pain that went with his every tentative step. As the local anaesthetic wore off, he gently cradled his damaged hand like he was carrying a bomb which might explode at the tiniest vibration.

Waiting for him was club doctor Shane Conway and a plaster cast to immobilise his broken thumb. It was a potential season-ending injury that could have been a crushing blow for our 1990 finals campaign, but on the contrary became an extraordinary inspiration.

Darren had just had a team-high 30 possessions in Collingwood's 89-point win over North Melbourne. It was a win that had cemented second spot on the ladder and provided a wonderful launching pad for a finals campaign the Magpie faithful hoped would finally see the end of the dreaded Colliwobbles, as well as a 32-year premiership drought.

But it was more. Much more. It was a fitness test to determine whether a player pivotal to Collingwood's hopes could play for five weeks in a row with a broken thumb. And despite the agony that had engulfed him as the painkillers wore off, the man we called 'Pants' – a nickname that had stuck from him wearing bright yellow trousers in his early years at the Magpies – was overjoyed. He'd passed with flying colours.

Courage comes in many different forms, and with adrenalin flowing through his veins during a game of footy, a player can do amazing things. For instance, when a flesh wound needs urgent repairing during the heat of battle, it's quite normal for a few stitches to be inserted without local anesthetic. But can you imagine if you cut yourself in the backyard at home? Would you go to a doctor and get a few stitches into the wound without painkillers? Not likely. It's just not something you'd contemplate.

Knowing in advance that pain is coming and being prepared to endure the agony anyway, and for a number of weeks – now that is extreme courage. Yet during the 1990 finals series that was exactly what Darren Millane was prepared to do. For as many weeks as the Magpies stayed alive, he was prepared to put up with the excruciating pain of playing football at the top level with a broken thumb.

All had been going well at Victoria Park through the first 18 rounds of the season. We had 14 wins and were equal first on the ladder, although second behind Essendon on percentage. A six-point loss to the Bombers in round 19 was hardly terminal, but an 83-point defeat by Hawthorn in round 20 could have been – especially after Darren had collided front on with Jason Dunstall in a marking contest and was reported for striking.

It looked like a two-week suspension was inevitable, but almost as if the footy gods were on our side, he escaped penalty after a bizarre couple of days and a few ill-chosen words from a breakfast radio announcer. Trying to be funny, the announcer had said on air, 'Darren Millane is a thug.' This provided the critical opening for the club to threaten legal action, because of the defamation directed at our champion wingman by the radio station and the announcer. We'll never know if the legal intrusion had any bearing on the tribunal outcome, but Pants was surprisingly found not guilty of the charge.

It was a lucky break that looked to have been wasted when a few days later Darren walked off Victoria Park during the round 21 clash with Fitzroy with a smashed thumb. That we'd beaten the Lions by 86 points to get things back on track was secondary. The doctor put his thumb in plaster straight after the game and ordinarily it was a six-week injury. It was season over for a player who, in many ways, helped provide the essential heartbeat of the Collingwood team. It was doom and gloom everywhere you looked. Or was it?

On the following Tuesday Darren walked into my office. He told me he'd seen the club's orthopaedic surgeon, John Bartlett, and there was a chance he might be able to play. It'd mean wearing a plaster cast throughout the week, getting it removed before the game and replaced immediately afterwards. Having it heavily strapped and with a decent dose of painkilling local anaesthetic was a given. However, it just wouldn't be possible for him to have anything like normal feeling in the damaged hand – not a great asset when you're playing top-level footy!

If this sort of injury had happened earlier in the season, you wouldn't even consider this option. But Darren wanted to at least have a crack at it. So, on the basis that there was no alternative, and after we received medical advice that he wasn't going to do any long-term damage with this rather radical step, we agreed to give it a go.

Clearly, that was only step one. In a very tight season where the top four teams all finished within a win of each other, our top-two hopes had been on the line against North in the final round, so we had to know before the game whether our strategy with Darren was going to be remotely possible. So for training on the Thursday night we had his thumb heavily strapped but without the aid of painkillers. That was to be the final match-day aid.

Back in that era before full-time staff, I was still running the fitness tests. I always remembered John Kennedy saying that any injury above the shoulders didn't count, because it didn't affect your movement or ball-handling (although in the modern era I suspect John might reassess things when it comes to concussion). My attitude towards the Millane situation was similar. I figured that, because he could still run, provided he had some reasonable ability to handle the footy with his damaged hand, maybe he could get through and be of value. I believed – or at least I'd convinced myself – that the power-house wingman with one half-bung hand would be better value than his fully fit replacement.

I've got to admit that privately I'd decided pretty much straight after Darren told me he wanted to try to play that I'd let the round

22 game against North be the decider. The fitness test I gave him was the softest I'd given anyone. It was the right thumb that was broken so while I kicked the footy at him as hard as I could, it was directed slightly to his left. It was more just to see if he had any chance of carrying his injury into a game, and he did what little I asked of him without any trouble.

In reality, the challenge for the medical staff of making the thumb pain-free, while still allowing some feeling and movement so that Darren could handle the footy, was impossible. They could minimise and delay the pain during the game but they could do nothing for him during the period after the painkillers wore off and before his thumb could be put back into plaster. That grimace as he walked into the medical room after the match against North will live with me forever. Such was the agony as he pushed his hand through the sleeve, he'd barely been able to get his shirt on. It was a massive challenge, but there was one thing I knew for sure – if anyone could handle this cycle of pain for a few weeks, he could.

Pants Millane was an enigma in many ways, but underlining it all was that he was a young man with enormous mental toughness. He lived life like he played football – as if there was no tomorrow. He partied hard but also trained hard. He was a bull of a man with a big, extroverted personality who was always the life of the party. During the communal spa sessions at training on Monday nights, he'd keep the rest of the playing group entertained with stories of his off-field exploits, and none involved having a quiet night at home. He was everything most young footballers aspire to be – a charismatic confident fun-loving personality, who had great success with the girls and was a terrific player. In the testosterone-fuelled atmosphere around a footy club, these qualities tend to be much admired among the playing group.

However, Pants had never left home. He lived in a garage converted into a flat at the back of his parents' house in Noble Park, and, as I lived in the neighboring suburb of Dingley, I'd occasionally pick him up on the way to Sunday morning training. Most of these times there was a female – usually a different one – who we dropped off somewhere on the way into Victoria Park.

While he regularly burned the candle at both ends, his influence around the players and around the club was just so powerful. Leadership strength is often a natural quality. Pants was a born leader.

Any coach or manager must learn quickly to get his peer-group leaders onside. In a football team the on-field leaders must be an extension of the off-field coach, if the desired outcome of every player pulling in the same direction is to be achieved. My job was to find the ways and means to make Pants' undoubted influence a positive one, at least around the club. When I think back, in personality profile terms he was a 'heavy Enforcer', which meant he reacted well to friendship and badly to blunt instruction. He was also basically anti-authoritarian, so being his friend was a better option than being the authoritarian coach.

The challenge was to harness the leadership and composure under extreme pressure that he'd shown during that ill-fated trek through the Gippsland mountains, when he'd helped lead the playing group out of a potentially life-threatening situation. He had the capacity to have a strong influence on the playing group – good and bad. He was second in influence among the players only to skipper Tony Shaw, and in a lot of ways he headed the social activities of the players. While I had no doubt that Shawy's influence around the club would be nothing but positive, the task for me as a coach was to ensure Darren also helped lead our group in the right way. I knew I didn't want him as an enemy. I wanted him onside – in fact, I needed him onside.

A few years earlier, Darren had been identified by Sydney and St Kilda as a likely prospect before Hawthorn looked set to sign him. He trained with the Hawks at Glenferrie but according to football folklore he didn't like the atmosphere and went back to captain Dandenong in the VFA under-18s. Collingwood swooped and signed him, and he debuted as a 19-year-old in 1984. He won the Best and Fairest in 1987 and quickly became a favourite, not just with the players but with the Magpie faithful.

I'm sure I never managed to get Darren to temper his social life too much, but around the club he became a believer in what we were trying to do and what the team was about. That was crucial, because I knew that if on match days he was repeating and reinforcing the coach's match-day themes, other players were more likely to follow, and he'd be a very powerful and positive influence out on the ground.

Until his injury Darren had had an outstanding 1990 season, as would be shown later in the end-of-season awards. He'd win the AFL Players Association Most Valuable Player Award, was chosen in the All-Australian team with Magpie team-mates Shaw, Graham Wright, Peter Daicos, Scott Russell and Mick McGuane, and he was runner-up to Shawy in the Copeland Trophy.

Because of his importance to the side, we were prepared to take a risk with his broken thumb. It was a defining moment in the season. If the patch-up job had failed or Darren was unable to cope with the pain, it might have tipped our campaign over. But we were desperately hoping he'd get through – I knew if he did, it would be an enormous boost to the group.

So could he do it in that game against North? Twenty-two kicks, five marks and eight handballs later, we had our answer. In an era when 20-man teams used to average 200 kicks and 100 handballs a game – or 10 kicks and five handballs per player if we want to be specific – he'd more than vindicated the faith we'd shown in his mental toughness and his will to compete, by giving him a chance to continue living his football dream.

More importantly, the fact that he was prepared to endure such pain week after week, knowing precisely what it was going to be like, was a huge inspiration to his team-mates. It made anything that anyone else might have been going through seem trivial. Through the courage and commitment of one player under extreme adversity, a potentially massive negative turned into an equally massive positive in our quest to win the 1990 premiership.

Over the previous summer we'd recruited two key additions to our midfield, South Australians Tony Francis and Scott Russell. Both had been drafted in 1988 – Scott from Sturt at number 30 and Tony from Norwood at number 95 – and neither had moved to Melbourne for the 1989 season. We'd made it a priority in the lead-up to the 1990 campaign that both would be wearing the black-and-white stripes.

Scottie had agreed to move and was released by Sturt, but Norwood were blocking the way for Francis. We believed the young Redlegs rover would be a key addition to our side, so at the time of a local airline strike Gubby Allan and Allan McAlister caught an international flight to Adelaide for meetings with the player, his parents and Norwood officials. But no luck. Norwood simply refused to release the 19-year-old.

After a long day, without any way of flying home, the Collingwood recruiting pair decided to drive back to Melbourne. As the El Supremo told the story, Gubby did his best Formula One impersonation and had them home in six and a half hours. The following morning they came into the club to deliver the bad news. After much debate it was decided that we wouldn't give up, and that Gubby would return to Adelaide. So, for the second day in a row, he caught an international flight to the City of Churches. Again, he visited the Francis home and again he met with Norwood officials, but this time he took with him a little incentive.

Although it was strictly against the rules at the time, he offered Norwood $100,000 to release the player rated arguably the best untried talent outside the AFL. That did the trick, but when he got back to Melbourne he still had to convince the board to back the initiative. After much discussion the board ticked off on it on the proviso that the 'investment' be camouflaged, so as not to flout the rules so blatantly. So, Collingwood found a $50,000 sponsor for Norwood for the next two years.

Pre-season expectations were optimistic but after we'd failed badly in the previous two finals series, even I was wondering whether the myth of the dreaded Colliwobbles was an insurmountable curse. Even before I'd got to Victoria Park I was only too familiar with this frequently discussed phenomenon. The numbers didn't lie. In 31 years since the club's last premiership in 1958 the Magpies had been to the finals 21 times. They'd finished minor premiers five times and had played in nine grand finals (including the replay in 1977). And they'd come up empty every time.

There had been some close calls, headed by the draw against North Melbourne 13 years earlier, when they'd led by 27 points at three-quarter time. It was four points against Melbourne in 1964 and one point against St Kilda in 1966, after they'd led both matches at half-time. In 1970 they lost the unlosable game to Carlton after being in front 10.13 to 4.5 at the main break. And in 1979 against the Blues they kicked the first four goals of the game before going down by five points.

It was an imposing history of failing at the final step, but more relevant to me were the events of the previous two years. In 1988 we'd finished second on the home-and-away ladder only to go out in straight sets via losses to Carlton (38 points) and Melbourne (15 points). And in 1989, after sneaking into fifth spot, we were put out in the first week, again by Melbourne (23 points).

Only half a dozen members of our 1990 playing list had ever won an AFL final – Denis Banks, Peter Daicos, Ron McKeown, Darren Millane, Tony Shaw and Jamie Turner. And the club hadn't won a final in six years. Whenever a finals campaign beckoned, media attention turned to the dreaded hoodoo, and although I was firmly of the view that nothing mattered until we actually got to the finals – and more specifically to the grand final – clearly it was an issue and there were scars that had to be healed.

As a playing group our aim was to be tougher and harder than our opposition and to be the best tackling team in the competition. If you try to establish a fundamental concept, you have to sell its importance. So, as a reward for the tackling effort and to reinforce to the players the importance of putting this facet of the game high on the priority list, we introduced a special tackling award. Through a club contact, we'd secured a holiday at Great Keppel Island, off the Queensland coast, for the player who laid the most effective tackles. At the time the resort's marketing theme was 'Get Wrecked on Great Keppel Island', so our tackling award became known internally as the Wrecker Award.

However, we didn't win a practice match, and the season proper didn't exactly start well either. We lost to West Coast in Perth by 46 points, and Tony Francis, one of our boom recruits, was reported for kicking an Eagles opponent in the bum and suspended for six weeks.

We won the next four, though, but lost to Essendon and Hawthorn in rounds six and seven. The following game against Fitzroy was a real turning point. At three-quarter time we trailed 7.14 to 9.19 but we blitzed the Lions 10 goals to nil in the final term. That one dominant quarter of football was the catalyst for a nine-game winning streak.

For five weeks in a row from round 11 we were second on the ladder behind Essendon on percentage, and after we beat Sydney at the SCG and Melbourne knocked off the Bombers at Windy Hill in round 16, we sat alone on top. It was to be the only time we held this position. A loss to Footscray the following week snapped our winning run and pushed us back to second. And there we'd stay.

In round 19 we lost by six points to Essendon at VFL Park. It wasn't a major setback but the game the following week was, when we were smashed by Hawthorn at the same venue, by 83 points after Jason Dunstall had kicked 11 goals. At the time I wondered what else could go wrong. I got my answer the following week when in the first quarter against Fitzroy at Victoria Park, Darren Millane suffered his seemingly season-ending broken thumb. The 86-point win over the Lions was quickly forgotten.

For several days one of our key players was gone for the year, until an unexpected ray of hope emerged. In a few short days, the expected damaging loss of Pants Millane for the duration of the season turned into the slim chance that he'd get through the ultimate fitness test of playing the final home-and-away game.

In a campaign that was full of sliding-door moments, this was the biggest. We beat North by 89 points, with Peter Daicos kicking six, Gavin Brown five and Craig Starcevich four. But just as importantly, our number 42 got through unscathed and played really well. Although his pain was excruciating in that post-game period, he'd proved to himself and us that he could do it. Now, it was just a matter of how long he'd need to do it for.

23

THE JIGSAW PIECES BEGIN TO CLICK

The Collingwood team of early September 1990 wasn't perfect,
but then again, neither were any of our finals opponents.

Sliding-door moments – random events that have huge consequences for what happens thereafter – have been a common occurrence during my decades around the world of elite football. During the opening match of the 1990 finals series, one such moment intervened to have a massive impact on the weeks to come. For all the plotting, all the planning, whether we like it or not, sometimes unpredictable good or bad fortune comes along either to help or hinder.

As Collingwood coach, with the benefit of hindsight there was one moment of on-field chaos that turned out to be of great assistance in our ultimately successful premiership campaign. As a close, hard-fought qualifying final at Waverley Park between Collingwood and the West Coast Eagles was a minute or so from the final siren, we were desperately clinging to a one-point lead. The football was deep in the Eagles' forward line being forced around the boundary line by Darren Millane. With every step the ball was getting further from goal, when West Coast runner Robert Wiley inexplicably got in the way of the players pursuing the footy and knocked the ball out of bounds.

Under the current rules it would have been an automatic free kick against the runner for interfering with the play. Back then it was the umpires' call and Wiley and the Eagles were given the benefit of the doubt that his interference was accidental. This decision had vital repercussions.

A free to Collingwood would have wasted up to 20 seconds, and after the set kick the footy would have landed up on the wing with only a few seconds to go. It would have led to a probable Magpies victory and immediate progression to the second semi-final against Essendon the following week. Instead, a boundary throw-in about 50 metres from the West Coast goal resulted.

The Eagles won the footy from this clearance contest and a quick kick forward was marked by their full-forward Peter Sumich, on a difficult angle but well within goal-scoring range. Along with every Collingwood person at the stadium, my heart sank. In the coaches' box we knew this would be the last kick of the game. The result was now completely out of our control.

While we still led by one point, once Sumich had taken that diving chest mark the agony and embarrassment of suffering our fourth consecutive finals loss was staring us in the face. If there was one thing that irked me about coaching compared to playing, it was the lack of control over what happened on the field. This agonising moment waiting for Sumich to take his shot epitomised this uncomfortable time, that terrible reality when you know you're completely in the lap of the gods, or in this case the Eagles full-forward's left boot.

He was only about 15 metres from goal but on a fairly acute angle with his favoured left side to the boundary. For a left footer like him, whose natural kicking action was to markedly hook his kick from left to right, it was a difficult angle. I reckoned he was a 50-50 chance to kick the goal, although missing altogether was very unlikely. So at best it would be a draw, at worst a five-point loss.

Strangely, my mind drifted briefly to the time at a very wet and boggy Arden Street way back in the '70s when Hawthorn were playing North Melbourne, and the Kangaroos star forward Malcolm Blight had a shot after the siren with exactly the same scenario in place. With us leading by a solitary point Blighty slewed the slippery ball off the side of his foot, putting it out on the full to give the Hawks an unlikely win. In bone-dry conditions here at Waverley, lightning like that striking again was a forlorn hope.

Everyone in the stadium was on their feet, including the two coaches' boxes. The short time that expired as Sumich got himself settled seemed to last forever. With our players providing as much distraction as the rules allowed and the crowd at fever pitch, he took his kick. When the goal umpire ran sharply to his right and paused under the goal post, we all held our collective breath. Hallelujah, it was a point! Almost instantaneously the siren sounded and the match was a draw. With no extra time in finals back then, the game would have to be replayed seven days later.

While we hadn't won, importantly we hadn't lost, and our opponents would have to make the return trip to Perth in between – a distinct disadvantage to them and a big advantage to us. Maybe the footy gods were with us after all. There were many twists and turns in the month ahead, but I firmly believe that taking two weekends of footy to eventually beat the Eagles, and consequently giving Essendon two weekends off, was to be of great benefit to our premiership campaign. That key moment when the Eagles runner inadvertently changed the flow of play, and probably the end result of the first qualifying final, was a critical factor.

My basic attitude to a football season has always been about staying alive and in contention. In terms of our aspirations that September, at the end of that first drawn final we were in exactly the same position as we'd been at the start of the match – still in contention with a double chance.

Premierships are only won on grand-final day, so until the two combatants are finalised, winning the flag is just a pipe dream. The long-drawn-out six months of home-and-away football eventually ends and the non-finalists are eliminated. In 1990 there was a final five that went forward to start the September campaign. What had happened prior to that stage was largely irrelevant and soon forgotten.

To emphasise the fresh starting point, it was our custom at Collingwood to hold an in-club dinner for players, coaches, support staff and board members on the Monday night before the first final. It was a subtle reminder that the minor-round season was over and a new finals season had arrived.

An outside guest speaker was worthwhile if we could find someone suitable. Through Collingwood board member Brad Cooper, later to become vice-president, we were able to get former Australian

Wallabies rugby union coach and prominent Sydney radio personality Alan Jones to come to Melbourne to address the dinner.

I was never big on getting outsiders to talk to the players, but Jones, although he knew little about AFL football, was renowned as a magnificent orator. I figured it couldn't do any harm, and as it turned out he was first-rate. Aside from his eloquence, his message couldn't have been better if I'd written it myself. He spoke to the players about time and space – particularly about the team working to give each team-mate as much time and space as possible to make good, effective on-field decisions. And conversely, to work as hard as possible to deny time and space to the opposition, and thereby force them into rushed decisions and errors.

The Jones message fitted hand in glove with my fundamental coaching theme, which was 90 per cent about tackling, chasing and working to minimise the opposition's time and space with the football.

It was interesting to reflect on this philosophy and in doing so I realised that as a coach you often coach the things you didn't do yourself as a player. And that certainly applied to me. As a player I always thought the process was primarily about getting the footy and using it. If an opponent was alongside me I'd lay a tackle, but chasing to tackle wasn't something I focused on or did. As a coach, though, finding ways and means to sell the defensive need for chasing, tackling and pressuring was probably my main coaching theme right through from my time at Collingwood to my time in Brisbane.

Essendon had finished top of the ladder with 17 wins, and Collingwood, with 16 wins and a percentage of 130.2, claimed second spot ahead of West Coast (16 wins, 118.4 per cent) and Melbourne (16 wins, 113.2 per cent). Hawthorn, with 14 wins, made up the final five. Inevitably, all the media talk in week one of September was about the Colliwobbles and how we'd go about defying its negative influence. Externally, it was the proverbial elephant in the room as we prepared to take on West Coast at VFL Park.

It wasn't discussed internally and for me it wasn't an issue at all. Going into that first final of 1990 our own two-year-old mini-history of finals failure was the uncomfortable nag in the back of all our minds. That was our unspoken emotional hurdle to confront and overcome. Alan Jones' words about denying the opposition time and space was a theme our players embraced. The best way to quell the nervous tension is to concentrate on a handful of controllable aims. Winning the footy and winning the game means having to beat the opposition. This can never be totally controllable but chasing and tackling when the opposition has the footy is a simple matter of individual choice, intent and commitment. While all of this is sound thinking, there were a lot of nervous players that day because negative thoughts and fear of failure are normal, if unwelcome, companions when you enter the field of battle.

I have a vivid memory of Tony Shaw approaching the coin toss with that cold determined look of a man ready to go to football war. Such was his take-no-prisoners attitude that normal niceties like shaking hands with Eagles captain Steve Malaxos were not on his agenda that day. Not great sportsmanship, admittedly, but more importantly to me it was a clear indication that Shawy was setting himself for no-holds-barred, hand-to-hand combat. In the pursuit of victory he'd do whatever it took. Leadership has many facets. Small in stature but gigantic in bravery and competitive spirit, our captain was ready to lead from the front; his uncompromising will to win would relentlessly drive his team to follow his example.

The game began well enough except for that most critical of factors – our conversion was terrible. A wasteful 3.6 meant a good performance had only earned us a narrow five-point lead at quarter-time, and another inaccurate 4.5 second quarter followed. Eighteen scoring shots to the Eagles' 11 but only a 12-point break was the position at half-time. We were going okay on the scoreboard but had failed to capitalise on our early dominance and midfielder Mick McGuane, who'd been terrific to that point, had tweaked a groin which was tightening up. He was done for the day and spent the second half on the bench.

The Eagles had the better of the third term and while we still led by two points at the last break, we had the look of a team which had lost its run and energy, and its confidence. Both the occasion and the pressure applied by the opposition were grabbing us by the throat.

Our situation became even more dire after West Coast scored the first two goals of the final term, the second from the boot of classy Eagle Chris Lewis, who was killing us every time he touched the footy. We were in trouble and desperately needed some individual inspiration. Ironically, this would be provided by a player coming off the interchange bench to play his last 15 minutes of AFL football.

Brian Taylor had joined Collingwood in 1985 after five years, 43 games and 156 goals at Richmond. He'd topped the Magpies goal-kicking in his first five years at Victoria Park, and had topped the ton to win the Coleman Medal in 1986. He was a very good player at his best. A confident, powerful character in mind and body, he led hard at the ball, had strong hands and had that quality unique to the big one-position full-forward; he demanded the footy whenever the ball came into his area. He was the typical dominant marking target with that type of player's usual vulnerability – if he didn't get the footy in the air he was in trouble. For the bulky power forwards like BT, their poor ground-level chase and second effort meant that individually kicking four to five goals was the offensive break-even point.

Even at his best, BT was of this ilk, and a chronic knee problem had reduced his mobility and effectiveness enormously. As the finals approached he'd only played in rounds one, two and seven, although he was recalled for round 21 against Fitzroy. He contributed nicely with four goals but only got one against North in round 22.

Going into the finals it was debatable whether an injury-affected BT was in our best line-up. Our season had been set up with nine consecutive victories from rounds eight to 16 and our big full-forward hadn't been part of any of those wins. His position in the team was shaky but we went with him for that first final.

BT did his part early, generating five shots at goal; however, he missed them all and then faded out of the game. As we searched for more run out of our team our burly forward was sent to interchange for most of the second half. Probably out of desperation more than optimism, we sent him back out midway through the final quarter and he immediately had an impact. A strong diving chest mark, an accurate conversion and then a free in the next marking contest; another goal and we were back in front.

The next goal we got – and the final Collingwood score in that tension-packed final quarter – was possibly the most spectacular and memorable display of magical ball skill I've ever seen.

I can still visualise Darren Millane winning possession hemmed on the boundary line at half-forward, left of the main Waverley grandstand, and giving a pressured handball with his broken right hand over his left shoulder to a waiting Peter Daicos. The goal-kicking genius was in a near-impossible position tight on the boundary, with his left side hemmed against the line and Eagles defenders coming hard from his right side. His options were seemingly nil, but somehow he fashioned a 20-metre kick off the outside of his right foot, which had to go at a right angle to the direction he was facing. The degree of difficulty was off the scale.

An all-round strong team – and not depending on individual brilliance – is the aim of every coach. It's a forlorn hope. Whether it's the Wayne Careys, Gary Abletts, or the modern versions like Jonathan Brown or Lance Franklin, individual brilliance is so often the difference between winning and losing.

I've seen Daics kick the impossible goal on so many occasions that the intervention of luck can be dismissed. You can only be lucky so often.

This one at such a crucial moment was breathtaking. In a split second he deduced that to score a goal the footy had to land on the goal line at the feet of the goal umpire or the bounce of the ball would veer it off course. His kick was never more than a metre off the ground and the footy did exactly as he intended. It landed on the line at the umpire's feet and continued through before the awkward bounce of the oval ball could take effect. A freakish goal set up by an equally freakish finisher.

Spectacular goals were a Daics trademark, particularly the controlled grubber. His ability to know how the ball would bounce and change direction was an art he mastered a generation ahead of his fellow players.

With a few minutes to play we were now eight points in front, but a quick goal to Eagles centre half-forward Karl Langdon and then a rushed behind pushed the game to the epic finish controversially involving the Eagles runner and the Peter Sumich point as the siren sounded.

Nobody was really emotionally prepared for the draw but the one thing I knew was that we had to move on very quickly. The key thrust of my address to the players in the rooms shortly after the final siren was that we hadn't been defeated. Given that we'd lost our three previous finals, this was a better result. And we were going home to our own beds, while the Eagles had to jump on a plane and endure a four-hour flight home to Perth, and then come back to Melbourne again a few days later. Whatever our situation, we had to be better off preparation-wise than our opposition would be when we met again the following Saturday.

At least, that was the thought that we emphasised post-game and during the week. The mindset that you'll be able to play a game out more strongly than your opposition is one of the more powerful motivations that a team can have. Whether it's a physical fact or merely an ingrained belief, thinking that you're fitter leads to a determination to work harder than your opponents because they'll tire more quickly.

There was an unlikely side benefit to this unexpected result. It meant that minor premiers Essendon, who'd enjoyed a week off to start the finals, would now have two weeks off. And while a chance to freshen up sore bodies at the end of a long season was understandably greeted with open arms, a double break was anything but good. It was the last time this would happen, because shortly afterwards the AFL legislated to ensure that all finals except the grand final would be played to conclusion via extra time. This is fine in principle, and while there's a certain financial and romantic appeal about a grand final replay, it'll only take a grand final draw involving a non-Victorian side for that rule to be changed to playing extra time.

The following day, another piece of the Collingwood puzzle fell into place beautifully when the side we feared most, Hawthorn, was eliminated by Melbourne at the MCG. I watched the game with Gubby Allan and his young son Marcus from the back row of the old Southern Stand – where the roof had already been removed ahead of the redevelopment – and we walked away with a really positive vibe and the realisation that sometimes a loss by another team can be a win for yours. The Hawks had beaten us twice during the home-and-away season, including the 83-point hiding three weeks earlier. Could we beat them? Optimistically, maybe. Frankly, I was happy we wouldn't have to find out.

I was always quite a conservative coach in terms of tactical innovation. My belief was that doing the basics well won more games, and more premierships, than tactical innovation. It was my view that players have only so much mental energy and changing too much from week to week, from opponent to opponent, can distract them from the core function of getting the basics done better than the opposition. There is no absolute right or wrong, though – successful coaches such as Kevin Sheedy, Rodney Eade, Terry Wallace and Michael Malthouse have done well with a greater slant towards specific match-day tactics than was my coaching style.

Former Brisbane Lion Brad Scott went from playing under my coaching to being an assistant with Mick Malthouse at Collingwood. We've spoken about the difference and Brad has rated me a 90-per-cent basics/10-per-cent tactics coach, whereas Mick is more 70/30 – quite different in emphasis but both of us are multiple premiership coaches.

Drilling and practising the basics was always my priority, but rarely do you play the same opponents in consecutive weeks, so we had the opportunity to learn from fresh memories of the drawn game. It meant we could go into the replay against the Eagles with a greater focus than we'd had the week before on blunting a few of their strengths, as well as making a surprise positional switch or two of our own.

Our first challenge in preparation was to look at our side, and this meant some tough decisions to rebalance our team to make it quicker. With the Eagles looking faster and running stronger in the second half, we decided to load up with as much speed and run as we could muster.

A perfect football team is fantastic at winning contests, fantastic with ball in hand and fantastic at pressuring the opposition. The Collingwood team of early September 1990 wasn't perfect, but then again neither were any of our finals opponents.

We'd won 16 of our 22 home-and-away games, so we were a very good team. What we concluded and acted on after the drawn qualifying final was that our best chance to go all the way was to become a fantastic chasing and tackling team. Excelling in all areas was the obvious aim, but maximising our defensive pressure was most within our capabilities.

To chase requires intent and the energy to run, but to tackle requires the speed to catch. So our selections and positioning had to favour the qualities of speed and run. The commitment and intent part of the equation needed to be a coaching sell as a necessary KPI to win – to put it in modern terminology.

It has an element of the chicken or the egg, but it's my coaching experience that if teams are of similar ability, the one that tackles more effectively usually wins. In footy, working hard to pressure and tackle the opposition needs the most prompting by a coach. You never see kids in the park tackling each other; instead, they're marking, kicking and handballing. The commitment to chasing and tackling also has its psychological value. The greatest motivation for getting any task done is getting the hardest part out of the way first, and in footy chasing and tackling is the hardest, most unappealing part. So, applying good defensive pressure usually leads to playing well in all areas. That was my consistent coaching sell, but for the replay against the Eagles it was ramped up even further.

Despite his critical last-quarter contribution in the first qualifying final we decided that the inflexibility created by a full-forward struggling with a crook knee meant leaving Brian Taylor out of the team. Ultimately this was the end of his career. At 28, after kicking 527 goals in 140 games, he never played another match. While he remained available, the more agile forward group that we put onto the field in the replayed qualifying final clicked and stayed in place for the duration of our finals campaign.

This Brian Taylor is, of course, the very same person who has become one of the leading AFL callers and commentators on TV with Seven and on radio with 3AW. We're now colleagues and friends, but it wasn't that way in September 1990. Back then, after he was left out of our finals line-up, our relationship became quite frosty.

This was my first experience with a player who was actively pursuing a media career while still playing. I had another very public and much more damaging example many years later at the Brisbane Lions, but that's for later in the book.

Knowing that his playing days were numbered, as the season progressed BT began seeking out media opportunities and also decided to write a book on the inner workings at Collingwood. Behind the scenes, football clubs become a very closed shop, almost a secret society of sorts, and the thought that these inner workings and relationships would be exposed by an insider created some angst that bubbled around most of the season. Nothing terribly controversial was likely to emerge, but it did create a question of loyalty and trust as to which master was being served first – the team or the budding media career.

I suspect from his comments over the years that BT believed these issues were the reason for his omission from the team for the replayed final. If so, he's totally wrong. It was simply a judgement call we made on what would give us our best chance of winning.

We didn't have another big forward who was any better than BT with a bung knee, but we did have the goal-kicking wizardry of Peter Daicos. And while he was by no means a pack-marking forward, he had been a wonderfully consistent avenue to goal all season. To be honest, Daics applied no more chasing pressure than BT, but he could be part of a forward group without needing to be the dominant marking target, and he could play anywhere in the attacking half. So we put our faith in the 'Macedonian Marvel', and then to maximise the chase and pressure inside our forward half, we went for the wonderfully talented Gavin Brown as a medium-size full-forward. Browny was a terrific winger but we needed his great ball-winning and second-effort chasing and tackling to anchor our forward group. We turned to Gavin Crosisca, who'd played much of the year at half-back, as a hard-working, hard-tackling, if undersized, centre half-forward.

Denis Banks, who'd missed the previous five matches through injury, returned to replace Crosisca in defence. Our tallest defender, Michael Christian, who'd been out of the side since round 21, came back to fill a very specific function. Craig Starcevich was ruled unfit. So for the replay the 'ins' were Banks and Christian and the 'outs' were Taylor and Starcevich.

We reasoned that the Eagles' classiest players and best ball users were their half-forward Brett Heady and midfielder Chris Lewis, who had been brilliant the previous week. These players needed to be denied time and space.

The Heady role was given to our most disciplined shut-down medium-sized defender, Michael Gayfer. Gayf was a prime example of a player who had very little offensive talent or ball skills; in fact, we would have been happy if he never touched the footy, but he became a very valuable contributor anyway. What he did have was the determination to manufacture his mind and body to be the best they could possibly be, to embrace the non-glamorous tagging roles and to play within his limitations. In the still part-time era around 1990, he prepared like a full-time professional of the present day. He worked hard on the fixable, becoming a clean ball handler and diligently building his endurance and strength, and eventually became a premiership player because he had the discipline, concentration and competitiveness to regularly shut down the opposition guns.

When Michael Gayfer walked over at the start of the game to physically engage Heady with hands-on, touching, close-checking defence – and, truth be known, probably holding off the play as well – the Eagles forward knew he'd have no time and space and would be in for a very tough day at the office. As a forward I would have hated playing on Gayf. Any forward expects a defender alongside them, but it's no fun when they hold, push and lean on you all day.

Over the years, not many defenders have had the courage to take the 'pain' of this type of close-contact defending, because before the current era of a million television cameras, a well-placed backhander was a final resort to stop the holding. Gayf accepted the occasional whack from frustrated opponents and just kept on annoying them. For him, a belt across the face was a badge of honour.

For the Lewis match-up, we went the opposite route; we turned to one of our very best attacking midfielders, Michael McGuane, to take this crucial assignment. This was decided at our Sunday recovery session after the drawn final. The proviso was that Mick had to get over the groin strain that had kept him off the field for the second half the previous day.

Over the course of his career, Mick's preparation effort was a bit erratic. He was not a great natural athlete and had to work extremely hard to get himself in shape. When he got himself fit he was a fantastic player; when he let himself go, he dropped off his elite level quite a bit.

I'm a great believer in the value of players who become quasi-on-field coaches. In this regard Mick was as good as I have coached. His dad, Brian, had coached for many years up around Ballarat and coaching was in his son's blood, so Mick understood and was interested in the intricacies of the game. He became a litmus test for me when I was giving instructions. If Mick didn't understand what I was trying to get across, I could be sure the other players would have no idea. When I looked at the players in the coaches' room and saw Mick subconsciously nodding his head as he had a habit of doing, it always gave me a sense of comfort that my words were getting through.

Having Tony Shaw and a fit Mick McGuane around the stoppages gave us two on-field coaches. They could follow and enforce instructions, they could think for themselves, and, if necessary, could think for others as well.

Once Mick volunteered to take the Lewis match-up, he embarked on a three times a day injury treatment program to get himself fit to play. The Eagles playmaker was a terrific player but never looked like a great endurance athlete, and I think Mick fancied his chances that, even if his groin was a little sore, he could still handle the opponent-control role he'd been eager to play. The focus was stopping first, with counter-punching attack the second option, and Mick embraced this function. He was eventually passed fit to play late in the week.

The other big change for the replay was how we decided to use the ruck position. Strange as it may seem, varying types of ruckman can have a big influence on their team's overall speed and run. During the '70s my Hawthorn ruck team-mate Don Scott's aggressive, energetic, bouncing style help the Hawks win so many games. When he lined up at the centre bounces, pawing the ground like a crazed animal, looking like he was ready to charge straight through his opponent, it was an upper for us and a definite downer for the opposition. In general play, his great athletic ability around the ground compared to the average lumbering ruckman made us quicker as a team. In the modern translation, Scotty gave us a lot of what Nic Naitanui gives the West Coast Eagles. The young Eagle has even more talent and agility but will probably never develop the wild aggression of my ex-captain. It will be a scary sight if he ever does.

The Don Scott playing persona was a one-off, but we had a version of the 'manic' ruckman in the Collingwood line-up in the guise of ex-Tasmanian James Manson. Only 194 centimetres, somewhere between a big forward and a relief ruckman, James wasn't highly skilled but he was a player who would commit every fibre of his being to the team cause. He was a real Jekyll and Hyde. A mild-mannered, softly spoken gentleman off the field but with a serious case of white-line fever on it. In fact, our ruck coach, Peter 'Crackers' Keenan, also had a fair bit of the mad ruckman about him as a player, so James had a willing mentor to bring out his wild side.

Our usual opening ruck was Damian Monkhorst, a conventional big man, 202 centimetres and bulky, aggressive and competitive, but as you'd expect quite slow. In order to begin the match with the quickest and liveliest team possible, we decided to start 'Monkie' on the bench and use Jimmy as our one big forward, although he'd be in the centre square to do all the centre bounce ruckwork. We'd use Michael Christian floating as a spare defender to do the back-half follower duties. 'Chrisso' had the height to compete in the air at the around-ground ruck contests but had greater agility than most ruckmen.

So the plan was simple enough: hope that Jimmy could give us some Don Scott-like aggression and kickstart us in the centre square, and maybe sneak forward and kick a goal, while Chrisso would give us height and creative run out of defence.

This starting big man duo was an enormous contrast in personality. While they both wore the Collingwood jumper, in most other ways they were complete opposites. It takes many types to make a football team. Melding different personalities, different characters and different abilities into a cohesive successful unit is one of the many coaching challenges.

These two team-mates were very different people with very different interests. Footy was their common bond. Jimmy was a musician who played in a band and did a bit of part-time house painting; Chrisso was a stockbroker who went to work in suit and tie.

Chrisso was a thinker and planner, Jimmy was impulsive and always seemed to be living by the seat of his pants. Things just happened to him. For instance, if my memory serves me correctly he had his car stolen more than once during his few years at the Magpies. As a young footballer he lived his life from minute to minute. Post-football he now runs a successful graphic arts business.

Pre-game, Jimmy turned into an aggressive competitive beast whose enthusiasm for the contest to come would often bubble over into physically manhandling team-mates as his way of getting them as aroused as he was.

Chrisso was much more calm and controlled. One day at Victoria Park, as the team was about to enter the arena, there was a great commotion on the edge of the Collingwood dressing rooms as the two team-mates came to blows. On this occasion, Jimmy's habit of belting into his colleagues wasn't well received by the victim, as the normally unflustered Chrisso decided to belt him back. Team-mates quickly broke them up but, as they say, in a heated environment strange things can happen.

Nevertheless, while cold, controlled vigour must be the aim, having the raw aggression in the first place is the starting point. Jimmy Manson had an admirable wild streak we loved having in the team, but he was always volatile and unpredictable. Consistency was not the big fella's forte, so we really weren't sure what we'd get against the Eagles that day. What we got was much, much more than we could have realistically expected.

Sometimes the jigsaw puzzle you put in place just clicks. This was one such opening stanza. We jumped out of the blocks brilliantly, kicking eight goals to two in the first quarter. Big Jimmy did a magnificent job getting us going from the centre square, took four clunking pack marks and converted two of them for goals. After 20 minutes we introduced Monkie into the action, and as Jimmy came to the bench I rang down to congratulate him, and thank him, for his inspirational first-up burst. There was still a long way to go but as I spoke to him I choked up as the emotion got the better of me.

Simply put, a coach invests his faith in his players once the game begins and under the immense pressure of the occasion, Jimmy had rewarded that faith with the best quarter he'd ever played in the black-and-white jumper. If I could have hugged him, I probably would have. The uncertainty of seven days earlier when the tension of the occasion turned nine first-quarter scoring shots into only three goals was, all of a sudden, a distant memory. Nine scoring shots for eight goals was the flying start we desperately needed. You never think that far ahead at the time but we were well on our way to winning our first final.

We led by 36 points at the first change and 49 at half-time, and although the Eagles surged a little in the third quarter there was no way back. After kicking five goals to nil in the final quarter, we won by 63 points.

Offensively we were very good; 19 goals will win most games comfortably and our goal-kicking list had a good spread with 10 individual scorers. Daicos (4), Brown (4), Crosisca (2), Francis (2) and Manson (2) were the multiple goal-kickers.

Our attack on the footy was very good as well and our tackling pressure was great. The chasing has to be led by the speed in the team and our quickest players – Doug Barwick, Tony Francis, Darren Millane, Scott Russell and Graham Wright – were all terrific in this area.

Our new forward Gavin Crosisca got his couple of goals, competed hard and laid five effective tackles. In an era when 40 tackles for a team in an entire game was a very high total, to get five from a forward was terribly valuable. Gavin Brown's forward fifty work was also outstanding. His brand of desperate contest-winning not only got him four goals but 20 possessions as well.

Remember that this was before the modern era of many junk stats, in which players under pressure will handpass the footy like a hot potato before someone finally gets a creative disposal; the result is usually disposal numbers over 400. Around the 1990s, though, the average was more like 200 kicks and 100 handballs. Back then, a midfielder getting 20 was good, so a forward kicking four goals and getting 20 possessions was exceptional.

After winning 19 goals to nine we still headed the effective tackle count 36 to 30, a stat we could home in on during our post-game review and build on in the games to come.

Both our tagging roles were wins for us. Gayfer kept Heady goalless and even with a sore groin McGuane did the job on the dangerous Lewis. At the time, on-field sledging and physical hassling had very lax boundaries compared to the modern era of footy field 'work-place' political correctness, and I'm sure the verbal and physical battering that Mick and his willing offsider, Tony Shaw, gave Lewis that day smashed even the more liberal norms of 20 years ago. They weren't just playing footy, they were engaging in footy war, and they had won.

While our ruck trio lost the raw hit-out stats, as so often happens it didn't equate to winning the all-important clearances. Into the bargain, Chrisso had 24 possessions which gave us an extra attacking defender.

The players' performance made all our pre-game plans effective.

I have no doubt that we were physically and mentally in much better shape after the replay than we would have been if we had salvaged a fading win the previous week. I firmly believe that taking two weekends to finally get over the Eagles – courtesy of a couple of unknowing allies, Eagles runner Robert Wiley and the errant left foot of their full-forward, Peter Sumich – turned out to be a distinct competitive advantage. While it's true that the harder you work the luckier you get, it was further evidence that a bit of random, uncontrollable good fortune is often the difference between success and failure.

We'd got through the replayed qualifying final game unscathed injury-wise, we were running strongly at the end and this Collingwood group's finals drought had been comprehensively broken.

As we looked forward to a second semi-final against Essendon and the chance to reach a grand final, our players had found that vital but elusive competitive edge to believe in and build on; the hard-contesting, hard-chasing, hard-running game style that had enabled them to thrash the Eagles was no longer a theory.

The coach's words now only needed to be a focusing reminder. Their outstanding performance on 15 September 1990 at Waverley Park proved to them they had the capabilities to go all the way.

A premiership was now within their grasp as long as they could handle not only the pressure of equally determined opposition, but the often suffocating hopes, expectations and adulation of the hungry Magpie army of supporters. What our players needed to play at their best was realism, short-term focus and a healthy fear of failure. The last thing they needed was to get caught up in the overinflated hype of looking too far ahead.

For the duration of our campaign, as much as humanly possible our footy department and players had to divorce ourselves from the rest of the club.

24

A TOUGH DECISION

My words to Ronnie were short and to the point: 'Sorry, mate,
we can't find an opponent for you and we're going to have to
pull you out of the team.'

The Allan Jeans quote that 'success is where opportunity meets preparation' is often relevant in football. It is particularly apt when it comes
to winning premierships.

It's a blunt reality that to win a premiership a team first has to get
into the grand final. Since 1994 that has meant winning one of the
two preliminary finals. However, back in 1990 the system in place at
the time meant the winner of the second semi went straight into the
premiership decider.

After 10 long months of preparation, qualifying for the grand final
and the opportunity to play for a premiership came down to a mere two
hours of football. Yet what happened inside the white line that memorable Sunday afternoon at the MCG, when Collingwood took on
Essendon, is not what has stayed with me the most over the years. My
most vivid memories of the day have little to do with the on-field action.

Few of the 56 finals I've been involved in over the years as either
player or coach have gone so smoothly. A 12-point half-time lead blew
out to a comfortable 63-point win. We kept Essendon to only seven
goals and, as we did to West Coast the week before, again kept our
opponents goalless in the final quarter.

That Sunday at the MCG ended extremely well, which was in
stark contrast to the way it began; at least for me personally, and
unfortunately also for our regular full-back, Ron McKeown.

It was only a couple of hours before game time – as I prepared for our final planning meeting with the players – that we realised we'd made an error of judgement in selection. It led to one of the cruellest loads I ever had to lob on an unsuspecting player when the last-minute decision was made to withdraw Ronnie from our selected team.

I can only chronicle as best I can remember what transpired in the lead-up to that moment. We'd left VFL Park the previous week after beating the Eagles with confidence high and no injury concerns. The week on the track was nothing out of the ordinary. We made sure all our ball movement drills were done under the pressure of having a team-mate hassling and chasing, which was a normal philosophy I employed during finals training.

This was still the era of late-afternoon training, normally Tuesday and Thursday with the occasional Wednesday as a top-up. After training on the Thursday evening, the players would head home and the match committee would sit down to select the team. There were no injuries to concern us and the only freshly available regular senior player was Craig Starcevich, who'd been out injured for the qualifying final replay the weekend before.

Our task this Thursday was to pick an 18-man team plus two interchange and three emergencies. There were only two players on interchange back in 1990 and they were likely to spend much of the day warming their heels on the bench. In current-day footy the interchange is a revolving door of action as players are constantly rotated on and off the field; no player spends more than a few minutes on the bench and rarely does a player spend more than 90 per cent of the game on the field. Twenty years ago it was more about picking a starting 18-man team with a couple of interchange for emergencies, including at least one spare defender to balance the starting back six.

As the week before had gone so well, we decided to stick to the same team that had thrashed the Eagles, with Starce coming in as one of the emergencies. If form warranted it, naming an unchanged team was something I loved to do as a coach, because it gave the players a sense of stability and confidence. This was a policy easy to put into practice in the week leading into our second semi-final assignment.

It was my usual custom in finals to tell the emergencies to be at the ground with their gear and to prepare as if they were playing, because last-minute changes for any reason would be our prerogative – and I meant it. When I look back I was a very hard-arse coach back then, because having set the policy of being open to a late change if necessary – or if we thought it would benefit the team – I then put considerations for the feelings of individual players very much to the back of my mind. Our team goal was to win the match and individuals had to submit to the team cause.

As it turned out, in the 27 finals I coached at Collingwood and the Brisbane Lions, this was to be the one occasion when the last-minute voluntary judgement option was exercised.

While we made the late change, it wasn't because of the situation that was causing us the most concern. Peter Daicos couldn't train on the Friday with a sore calf muscle. He was still unable to sprint flat out on the Saturday and we were close to ruling him out. We decided to give him another 24 hours, which meant it would be game day before the final decision was made.

As a coach it's always a judgement call on the individual player as to whether you leave his availability to the last minute. Daics had kicked 92 goals to that point of the season, and his immense value warranted us waiting. However, great capabilities also create pressure on the individual player; sometimes a sore spot is a nice excuse just in case you have a bad day. I had a suspicion that this fear-of-failure psychology was floating around in Daics' subconscious state as he battled his calf soreness. These factors led us to delay the decision until the morning of the match, when hopefully the competitive adrenalin, the body's wonderful natural upper, would kick in to get him over the line.

Regardless of his physical state a player must declare himself right to play. A fitness test might rule him out, but to play he has to put himself on the line, remove any injury alibis and be ready to go. This only happened definitively on the Sunday morning of the game.

I'm not sure Daics was certain he was okay but he declared himself ready to play, and with the medical team believing his calf was tight, not strained, we took the calculated gamble. If he broke down during the game, we were in big trouble as we didn't have another forward on interchange. However, sometimes we look back at our own experiences, and mine told me a sore calf could be manageable, particularly for someone who played close to goal and didn't depend on breakneck speed. Daics and I did have a little in common athletically.

In the few days prior to the game there had been much deliberation about who'd be the replacement if our champion goal-kicker couldn't play. If Daics was out, Craig Starcevich would come into the team as his replacement. It wasn't a like for like. In fact, Daics' unique skill-set made him something of a one-off, but Starce was a hard-running, tall (193 centimetres) half-forward flanker; not a great contested mark for his size but a tough match-up for any defender. Few opponents with his height had the running power to stay with him as fatigue set in later in games.

While it should be no excuse, I think the Daicos doubts and the fact that Starce was the next forward in the team had a great bearing on my last-minute change of heart about Ronnie McKeown. When I got to the coach's room to prepare for our match-day planning meeting, I put the Collingwood defenders' name tags up against the Essendon forwards. Why it had taken me so long I'll never know, but I had the sudden terrible realisation that I had simply not factored in – until agonisingly close to game time – the significant difference between what we needed in defence for the Bombers, compared to the West Coast Eagles.

While I'd shared my concerns at match committee during the week about maybe having one tall defender too many, and again with Gubby Allan at the MCG as we sat together watching the second semi-final curtain-raiser, I didn't take action to rectify the selected team until way too close to the game.

Back in 1990, when players still had jobs outside football, the main planning meeting was usually held on match day a couple of hours prior to the game. In the modern era this detailed planning meeting is held the day before the match, so the selection error that hit me like a ton of bricks in the coach's room at the MCG as the Collingwood players gathered outside would now never happen. It should never have happened back then either, but it did.

The Essendon forwards' name tags were up on the whiteboard in the coach's room in their normal formation. Paul Vander Haar would play at centre half-forward and the gigantic 205 centimetre,

112 kilogram Paul Salmon would play deep around the Bombers goal square. Essendon's veteran ruckman, the great Simon Madden, would change into the forward line and be relieved in the ruck by Salmon. These two man-mountains gave the Bombers a couple of talented, very tall targets close to goal who were also very good ruckmen, Madden probably the best of his era.

Salmon was no longer the freakish goal-kicking prodigy of his second season in 1984, when he kicked an amazing 63 goals in the 13 games he played, before suffering a season-ending knee injury. Back in that incredible half-season, the big fish was defying the laws of nature; players of his height and bulk cannot average five goals a game. For a short time before that injury, he was the exception to the rule.

I can also well remember his six goals in the 1985 decider when Essendon creamed Hawthorn. Salmon made our medium-sized full-back David O'Halloran look like a midget.

Our usual centre half-back, Craig Kelly, looked fine on Vander Haar, but for the mainly Salmon/occasional Madden match-up I thought we needed our biggest defender, so Michael Christian's name tag went next to Salmon's. As our regular full-back, Ron McKeown was our best defender on the fast-leading, regular-sized full-forward type but at only 188 centimetres he was a bit small for the Essendon giants, so he'd have to take the Bombers' third tall. Any thought of using Chrisso as a mobile back-half ruckman – as had been so successful against West Coast the week before – was out of the question: the Essendon ruck duo were too big and too good in the hit-outs for a fill-in part-time ruckman. Our normal followers, Damian Monkhorst and James Manson, would have to resume their ruck partnership and play at their very best to handle the Madden/Salmon challenge.

Essendon having two big spine players as the anchor points of their forward set-up was totally predictable; however, it was the support cast that suddenly sent a chill up my spine. There wasn't a key position player among them.

Of the other likely Bombers forwards, there were only smalls, or agile, medium-sized runners. I put the name tags up on the white-board. Mark Harvey, Peter Cransberg and Andrew Manning seemed the next tallest behind Salmon and Vander Haar, and none of them were deep forward targets.

We had Shane Morwood, Denis Banks, Michael Gayfer and our starting interchange Jamie Turner who were well suited to these types of subsidiary medium-sized half-forwards, and if needed regular half-back Gavin Crosisca could be summoned from his assigned forward-line duties. Then I immediately searched for a suitable opponent for Ronnie McKeown and I couldn't find one, except as a back-up if Michael Christian couldn't control Salmon.

Ronnie was a talented footballer, but a poor endurance athlete. He never developed the fitness to play away from the full-back line and his lack of run rightly pigeonholed him as an extremities player. He was capable deep back or even deep forward; however, he struggled in the midfield space.

I stared at the whiteboard in front of me for a moment or two, trying to digest what my logic was now telling me. The team looked more flexible and better balanced with a running forward, Craig Starcevich, being in the 20 instead of Ronnie. The nagging doubt about Peter Daicos' sore calf only added to my belief that the late change would increase our chances of winning.

My harsh and uncompromising coaching mantra of team first and individual second made rectifying our selection stuff-up an absolute must. If it's humanly possible, never let the embarrassment of making an error prevent you from accepting the mistake and doing your best to ensure that the one mistake doesn't become two through your failure to remedy it.

My next step was to bounce my thinking off someone whose judgement I trusted. Chairman of selectors Ron Richards was close by and, as happened so often, he became my sounding board. He was fully supportive of making the late change, so, as the time for our planning meeting was rapidly approaching, it was time to act. I walked out into the dressing rooms to tell Ronnie McKeown of our last-minute decision to leave him out of the team.

Many of the Collingwood players were still in their civvies. Not Ronnie. He was already dressed in his jumper and shorts, which rubbed a bit more salt into the wound. At the time I think Ron Richards and

I both wished he was like Mick McGuane, who wouldn't put his match uniform on until a few minutes prior to the warm-up.

I can't imagine anyone enjoys delivering bad news, and as cold and calculating as I was in my younger days, I was no different. My words to Ronnie were short and to the point: 'Sorry, mate, we can't find an opponent for you and we're going to have to pull you out of the team.'

It didn't seem the time for a drawn-out conversation or explanation, as the hard-arse coach in me was immediately back in team-preparation mode. My only concession to being a caring coach was to ask Gubby to look after Ronnie when our planning meeting broke up, and even that had something to do with not allowing his disappointment to become a negative influence around the dressing room.

With the benefit of hindsight, and out of respect for Ronnie McKeown's feelings, one, I should have made the decision much earlier, and two, I should have spent some time with him after the other players left the coach's room, explaining in greater detail our reasoning and making him aware that I felt his pain. While my conscience was clear that the decision needed to be made, I should have been more compassionate about the obvious anguish of a very disappointed player.

As I became a more experienced coach, hopefully I developed a more caring attitude to the players. In fact, once we reached full-time footy around 15 years ago, fire and brimstone coaching became redundant. In the current era of needy generation-Y players who are full-time professionals, are around the club all week and who all employ managers to maximise the value of their careers, coaches caring about their players as individuals has become a mandatory part of the coaching art. In personality profile terminology, while my stubborn team-oriented Enforcer streak was never far away, as a more experienced coach I do believe my Thinker/Feeler caring side came into play a bit more often. It very rarely did in my decade at Victoria Park.

A more practical matter was how the late alteration to our 20 would affect the rest of the team. As a player all I wanted from the selectors was to pick a team that gave us the best chance of beating the opposition. Under the same circumstances back in my playing days at Hawthorn, I would have wanted the coach to make a late change if he thought it would help us win. Then again, not every player was as cold and calculating about victory as I was, and into the bargain I'd never been the unfortunate victim of being left out at the last minute.

My early coaching attitude was to be very mindful of what it felt like to be a player. This is one advantage of the young coach. On this basis my belief was that while his team-mates would feel for Ronnie McKeown, overall this last-minute change in the team was proof that, as we needed the players to do on the field, as coaches we would do whatever it took to win. Any potentially disruptive effect was minimised by Ronnie, who kept his feelings to himself and didn't create a scene. I wouldn't have been surprised if his cat got a good kicking that night, but he kept his composure around his team-mates. There are a few players I coached over the years who I suspect would have reacted with a lot less dignity under the same duress.

As a coach, the end of the detailed planning meeting was the point where I handed control over to the players. One of the things I've always loved about AFL footy is that, compared to sports with a small rectangular field, offside rules, lines of scrimmage etc., it is more a player's game than a coach's game. At least it was. Up until the advent of full-time footy, the impact of coaches was quite minimal. We put the players out there and let them play. Over the last decade, though, coaching intervention has increased massively. These days, there are almost as many coaches as players, detailed positional structures are pre-planned, and the game is analysed to within an inch of its life.

Back in 1990, the Collingwood players knew my coaching attitude that once they walked out of the pre-game planning meeting the result of the game was totally in their hands. On this day, they knew there was a grand final berth up for grabs and they totally accepted the challenge.

From the time the players left the coach's room meeting, the rest of the day worked out perfectly. Of course that's a retrospective view; at half-time, when we were only a couple of goals up, the game was still in the balance. As I headed to the dressing-rooms at the break, I said to myself that this had to be treated like any normal game. I reminded myself that a coach can't play the game for his players; all he can do is help navigate the course, and they must drive the car.

There were all the familiar feelings, the typical tension in your gut, that terrible fear of failure and the uncertainty of what lay ahead.

Even in a second semi-final the half-time atmosphere in the rooms doesn't change that much – it is nearly always quiet as most players drift into their own little world. Frankly, most look like zombies, staring blankly into space as they assess what the first half has presented. Their main thoughts are largely about their individual performances, rather than the scoreboard.

After 10 minutes or so of mental and physical rest, they're summoned into the coach's room where part of the task is to get players' mindset back into where the team effort is at and what needs to be prioritised in the third quarter. This is where the coach may need to be the opposite of the rest of the world. It's the experience of every coach of a team behind at half-time to hear loud advice from supporters over the fence, often along the lines of 'Come on, Matthews, get into them!' As if yelling at our players will solve the problem of the opposition playing better. If only it was that simple. Really, this is just disappointed and frustrated fans wanting the coach to abuse the players on their behalf.

In a coaching role – or any management position, for that matter – being the opposite of the rest of the world often means being supportive and morale-boosting when confidence has plummeted and the team is playing badly. Conversely, when your team is dominating you often need to find a few things to criticise, in order to bring your team back to a more neutral emotional point for the restart of play. To a struggling team, you have to sell a plan to get back in the game; to a dominating team you need to bring them back to reality. Successfully doing this is part of the coaching art.

Having a 12-point lead at half-time of the 1990 second semi didn't put us in any significantly different position than we'd been an hour before at the start of the game. No major positional changes seemed warranted – the game plan hadn't altered, so all that was needed was a reinforcement of the basics: in hard and low at the footy, attack long and direct, and chase, pressure and tackle. Deny the opposition time and space. I also had to keep emphasising and nurturing the belief that we'd run the game out better than the ageing Essendon.

The basic message was the same at three-quarter time, when the lead had increased to 28 points – keep working, keep chasing, keep forcing the ball forward and ignore the scoreboard. Play the game minute by minute, keep the pressure up and the opposition would fade. That was the theme as we headed into the quarter that could earn us a grand-final berth.

Then the floodgates opened. We dominated the quarter, kicking 5.7 to the Bombers' measly two behinds. The longer the game went the stronger we looked. We ended up kicking a healthy 17 goals, and our tackling pressure was great all over the field – the stat favouring us 47 to 29.

Peter Daicos got through the game, not only getting his three goals but joining the tackling party, leading the team tally with five. Daics averaged four goals a game in 1990 so his three goals was nothing unusual, but tackling was never his forte – he averaged only one or two per game. Like I said, Daics and I had a bit in common as players. However, even our main attacking weapon had bought into the team theme of desperate chasing and tackling to lock the ball in our forward line. This was a great fillip and encouragement to our entire playing group.

The competitive edge that came from being an outstanding defensive team, which had begun against the Eagles the week before, had been repeated against Essendon. In consecutive weeks against the first and third-placed clubs, our work rate and pressure had eventually overwhelmed the two teams who'd be playing off in the preliminary final the following Saturday.

The only downer from the game was that our back-pocket player Alan Richardson had cracked his collarbone and would therefore miss the grand final, which, because of the qualifying final draw and replay, was scheduled to be played 13 days later on the first Saturday in October. Grand finals on the last Saturday in September hadn't been kind to Collingwood over the decades, and while I'm not overly superstitious, I also don't like to tempt fate, so playing our grand final in October was of some strange illogical comfort. It was as if this might just break the spell of bad luck that had plagued the club during its losing run of grand finals since the last premiership in 1958. Maybe this was finally to be the Magpies' year.

25

ON THE CUSP OF HISTORY

*With every eye in the room on him, the skipper stood in front of his team-mates and declared emphatically, 'I've played in two ****ing losing grand finals and I'm not playing in a third.'*

As I've mentioned, for me there was a gigantic difference between playing and coaching. One of the many differences was that as a player the post-game was a time to reflect on that day's contest. After a win and a good performance, it was a chance to smell the roses – to belt out the club theme song, arm in arm with your team-mates, and share the emotion of the victory; sometimes exhilaration, sometimes just a warm sense of satisfaction but always an extreme feeling I have rarely got outside competitive sport. Sometimes it might be akin to getting off a roller coaster and having the adrenalin rush of knowing you've survived the fear; even if, in sport, it's the fear of failure rather than the fear of being harmed.

However, as a coach, once the siren sounded to end one game, I was immediately thinking of the next. The walk to the dressing-rooms was a few minutes to plan what to say to the players and how to react. I never planned to be too expansive in the post-game wind-down because, like most coaches, the game usually put me in a fairly heightened emotional state that wasn't necessarily conducive to being ready for accurate and constructive feedback. That would happen a day or two later when the game-day emotions had subsided.

Of course, this is the retrospective view of a retired 20-year coach. Many times as a young coach at Collingwood and occasionally at the Brisbane Lions later in my career, my emotions overwhelmed my good sense and I reacted badly under the post-game heat. However, when the siren sounded to end the 1990 second semi-final, I was in a very controlled and calculating frame of mind.

As I headed off on the 100-metre walk along the boundary line from the coach's box in the MCG Members' Stand to the Richmond rooms, our dressing room for the day, even from my position on the arena the excitement and expectations of the Collingwood fans was palpable. Their team had made it into the grand final. It was the club's first in nearly a decade, and also the first since I'd become coach, so it was clearly not an average winning day at the footy. Yet my role amongst the inevitable celebrations was to swim against the tide of feel-good emotions to start the process of getting ready for the premiership-deciding game a fortnight later.

The fantastic euphoric feeling that was bubbling around the Collingwood rooms that post-game is the best reward the players and staff can get for accepting the competitive challenge, for thriving under the pressure and surviving to win. They deserved the 10 minutes to enjoy one of those rare moments; then it was time to call them into the coach's room to wind up the day and to start the build-up to the grand final.

The last player into the room was Tony Shaw. It was then we all noticed he was hobbling a bit and looked in pain. Pulling off his boot, he revealed a sock with the white foot section soaked red with blood from a huge blister that, unbeknown to anyone, had developed during the game. A blister is never listed in the injury report but anyone who's tried to run with badly blistered feet knows there is a pain barrier to be overcome. While not as totally debilitating as a damaged joint or broken bone may be, a bad blister is bloody sore. For it to have worn through enough layers of skin to be bleeding freely, the pain must have been excruciating.

Shawy's mental ability to conquer physical discomfort – whether it was fatigue or pain – was already well known to his team-mates. This was just another example of his fantastic leadership quality of never asking someone to do anything he wouldn't do himself, and that if he set his mind to do something he usually delivered. This was a man you would happily follow into any battle.

As a kid, I had the boyhood dream to be the best footballer there ever was. Here I am in my North Melbourne jumper, ready to go to the footy with my family to watch Langwarrin in action. *Craig Borrow/Newspix*

My first Victorian jumper after being selected in the under-14 schoolboy team to play in Canberra in 1964. Fortunately, I got a few more when I grew up. *News Ltd/Newspix*

With my first wife, Maureen, and elder daughter, Tracey, who was about four months old at the time. The photo was published in *The Sun* newspaper to celebrate my selection in the Victorian team in 1971 at the age of 19. *News Ltd/Newspix*

The typical posed action shot at training popular in earlier football eras. Always loved the thud of the footy hitting my chest.
News Ltd/Newspix

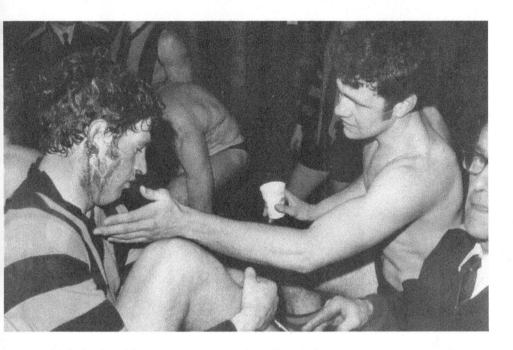

You wouldn't think we'd just won a premiership! Here I share a quiet moment with Hawthorn's freakishly talented full-forward Peter Hudson after the 1971 grand final. Following a heavy hit from St Kilda's Kevin 'Cowboy' Neale, 'Huddo' badly split his earlobe. A few missed shots later in the game prevented him from breaking the all-time VFL goal-kicking record of 150. *Fairfax Photos*

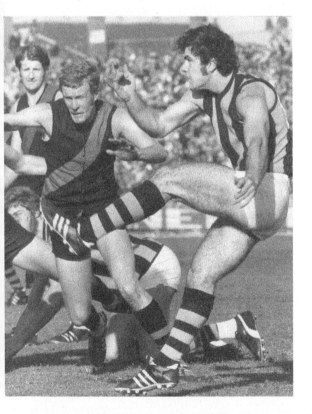

A left-foot snap at goal against Essendon at their Windy Hill home ground in 1972. Attempting to smother is Ken Fletcher, father of the Bombers' great full-back, Dustin. *News Ltd/Newspix*

Hawthorn has just won the grand final, but September 1976 was also a sad and sobering time. Our team-mate Peter Crimmins would pass away just a few days after the game, after a long battle with cancer. *Courtesy of Hawks Museum*

It was fantastic playing for Victoria with my brother Kelvin, as well as being team-mates in Hawthorn's 1976 premiership victory. It was a far cry from the battleground of our backyard footy games in Langwarrin and Chelsea!

Don Scott and I couldn't have been much more different in personality, but with Michael Tuck we made a pretty good on-ball division. All three of us were selected in Hawthorn's Team of the Century. *News Ltd/Newspix*

David Parkin had huge shoes to fill after John Kennedy's departure as coach, but he did an amazing job. He played a major role in our 1978 premiership, including an unusual but highly effective pre-game visualisation exercise. *Courtesy of Hawks Museum*

A typical muddy day at the Hawks' home ground at the time, Princes Park, in the early 1980s, and my 'dangerous' tongue-out playing habit. Lucky I didn't bite it off! The suburban venues of the old VFL days were very often far from the pristine well-drained surfaces of the modern AFL competition. *AFL Photos*

For a footballer, captaining a premiership team, receiving the cup and raising it to a cheering crowd is about as good as it gets. I had that honour in 1983 when we beat Essendon by a record 83 points. *AFL Photos*

In a moment of madness in round 12, 1985, I broke Geelong rover Neville Bruns' jaw with a round-arm coat hanger. Not in my worst nightmares, though, did I imagine I'd end up facing criminal charges over the incident. Here I am heading into Melbourne Magistrates' Court with CEO John Lauritz and former Hawks coach John Kennedy.

BELOW LEFT: It wasn't a great way to end my playing career, bowing out after our loss to the Bombers in the 1985 grand final. Part of me died that day when I left the playing field for the last time. *News Ltd/Newspix*

BELOW RIGHT: Early days as Collingwood coach in 1987. My first couple of years in the job were challenging, with the club facing financial difficulties and struggling on the field. *AFL Photos*

ABOVE: Half-time during the 1990 grand final against Essendon, and in the heat of the moment I crossed the line by abusing an opposition player. I wrongly threw a few choice words in the direction of the Bombers' Terry Daniher after his KO of our full-forward, Gavin Brown, during that game's infamous quarter-time brawl. *Craig Borrow/Newspix*

BELOW: Celebrating the Magpies' first premiership in 32 years with club president Allan McAlister. The 'Colliwobbles' had finally been buried. *AFL Photos*

With Tony Shaw in the rooms after the grand final. 'Shawy' was an inspiration during the 1990 finals series, and throughout his time as Magpies captain. *AFL Photos*

I'm looking a bit tense here during the first Anzac Day match between Collingwood and Essendon in round 4, 1995. It was an unforgettable game and it was great to be there when the tradition began. *AFL Photos*

ABOVE: I had a wonderful time during my stint as Victorian coach in 1997 and 1998. It's very different to the week after week, month after month routine of club coaching. *Getty Images*

BELOW LEFT: A day in late 1999 of completely contrasting emotions. In the afternoon, I was photographed with Mum to commemorate me being named AFL Player of the Century. Later in the day, though, Dad, who'd been in poor health, had a heart attack and passed away.

BELOW RIGHT: My dad – my incredibly valuable first coach and lifelong supporter.

ABOVE: It's almost impossible to explain what your emotions are like the instant the final siren sounds after winning a grand final. This photo shows the moment of unadulterated exhilaration when the Lions were victorious against Essendon in 2001. *Allsport Australia/ALLSPORT*

BELOW: On the dais with Michael Voss. 'Vossy' was a wonderful competitor and magnificent captain. *AFL Photos*

ABOVE LEFT: My great friend and long-time colleague Graeme 'Gubby' Allan, then the football manager of the Lions, was alongside me for all my premiership victories as a coach. I probably wouldn't have accepted the offer to coach in Brisbane if he hadn't agreed to take the job. *Sean Garnsworthy/Getty Images*

ABOVE RIGHT: Enjoying the post-match rendition of the club song with Vossy and Jonathan Brown after the 2002 grand final. I have to admit, though, I didn't appreciate victory that day as much as I should have. *AFL Photos*

BELOW: Vossy and I and a few thousand fans at the Brunswick Street Oval the day after the game. It was great to be able to celebrate with the Lions supporters in Melbourne. *AFL Photos*

ABOVE: We defied the footballing gods to make it three premierships in a row in 2003. It was a medical marvel that we got a side good enough to win on the paddock. After our 50-point victory against Collingwood, I celebrated with my wife, Deb, and her children, Clint and Abbey.

BELOW LEFT: The 2004 premiership was the one that got away. Port Adelaide were worthy premiers – here I am with Port coach Mark Williams after the siren – but the scheduling of the preliminary finals did the Lions no favours. *Mark Dadswell/Getty Images*

BELOW RIGHT: The media conference in 2008 to announce my resignation as Lions coach. If I look relieved, it's probably because I was. There is always a sense of relief after making a hard decision. *Peter Wallis/Newspix*

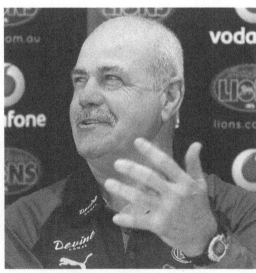

Running a leg of the torch relay for the Sydney 2000 Olympics was a great experience. My leg of the journey was through the suburbs of Ipswich.

I've always said the MCG is my favourite place in Melbourne. Having my statue among the great names in the ground's Parade of Champions is the single greatest honour I've ever received. *Robert Cianflone/Getty Images*

ABOVE: My most treasured memento. A montage commemorating premierships with three clubs, with personal messages from Allan Jeans, Tony Shaw and Michael Voss. It was such a privilege working with all three of these men.

BELOW LEFT: Another great honour was winning the AFL Players Association Most Valuable Player Award in 1982. It was an even bigger thrill when the annual award was named after me in the early 2000s. *Ron Lockens*

BELOW RIGHT: A photo of me with my valued mentor and first coach at Hawthorn, John Kennedy, when we were announced as the inaugural legends in the Hawthorn FC Hall of Fame.

ABOVE LEFT: A Father's Day photo published on the front page of *The Sun* in 1975 with my daughters, Tracey and Fiona.

ABOVE RIGHT: With my granddaughter, Amber, who accompanied me in the 2003 grand final parade.

BELOW: In 2007, looking through Mum's scrapbook of my career with my grandchildren (from the left), Bella, Ky and Amber. *Craig Borrow/Newspix*

With every eye in the room on him, the skipper stood in front of his team-mates and declared emphatically, 'I've played in two ****ing losing grand finals and I'm not playing in a third.'

Shawy had twice experienced the terrible downer of losing a grand final, having been in Tom Hafey's Collingwood team that had been runners-up in 1980 and 1981. His graphic statement of intent was inspirational stuff from an inspirational leader. His words, straight from the heart, were delivered with a conviction and strength of purpose that the rest of the team knew would be followed through. Anyone can say the words, but Shawy's team-mates knew their captain would deliver.

Anything I was going to say now paled into insignificance. My usual speech – 'Look after yourselves tonight and see you at tomorrow morning's training session' – was all that was needed to end the day's formalities. I knew they'd all be at recovery but the look-after-yourselves edict would likely fall on mostly deaf ears.

The no-alcohol-consumption bandwagon, which had started a month earlier as a response to the debacle against Hawthorn back in round 20, hadn't gained many permanent passengers. This was still the era of players having a big night out after a game and most of the Collingwood players – usually led by Darren Millane – were willing participants, normally at the infamous Tunnel nightspot in the King Street precinct of the CBD. Minimising the drinking was the best we could hope for.

This was only the fifth of the 20 years I coached. When I finished at the Brisbane Lions at the end of 2008, compared to the part-time players of a couple of decades earlier the players prepared their bodies much, much better. It certainly varies from individual to individual but as a general rule the modern player has much greater discipline in nutrition, diet and after-hours socialising, and has a vastly improved training and preparation lifestyle.

Actually, a good comparison to illustrate the difference between then and now is current Brisbane captain Jonathan Brown, who has many personality traits similar to Tony Shaw. Both are powerful charismatic characters, and both are born leaders who love a chat and a beer. Browny would have loved to have played a decade or two earlier, back when a big drink post-game was completely normal.

Shawy was able to indulge his penchant for a few drinks after a game and at the Shaw family's regular Sunday get-together, because it was the norm for most players back then. Nowadays it isn't, so Browny and his modern-day contemporaries who like a beer have to exercise the discipline to curb their natural desires. The modern player is certainly not a complete teetotaller, but even post-game the majority are unlikely to have more than a couple of drinks. With the match-day adrenalin still flowing through their systems it's very difficult for players to find healthy ways to relax and unwind after games; even more so those played at night.

Modern players are undoubtedly much better athletes and much better footballers, but with the unfortunate accompanying by-product of being under greater pressure and scrutiny. As young men working at their well-paid but short-term livelihoods, and under rigidly imposed discipline, many become highly strung and emotionally as tight as a drum. Like the nervy racehorse which might sweat up in the mounting yard, waste energy and have run its race before it even steps onto the track, being well prepared emotionally and mentally is just as important for a footballer as being physically fit.

Back in the 1990s and earlier the preparation disciplines were not as rigid and the post-game drink was a valuable emotional relaxant in the week-to-week playing cycle. As I've said, the players were not nearly as well conditioned but I believe this cycle of letting off some steam after the match helped to lessen the build-up of pressure and stress. However, when September arrived and knockout finals were on the agenda, the danger of players 'sweating up' like a nervy highly strung thoroughbred racehorse, wasting energy and failing to produce under finals pressure, was ever-present. It seemed to me that our Collingwood team of 1988 and 1989 had suffered from this affliction.

So having made the grand final and with the history of the Colliwobbles sure to be the prevailing theme with the media and our fans, the biggest coaching challenge was to set up a two-week preparation phase that would best ensure the players ran onto the field in the optimum emotional state to perform at their best. Unless our players went on an unlikely bender during that fortnight, fitness levels wouldn't alter very much. It was their emotional state that might vary the most.

All sportspeople search for that 'in-the-zone' feeling where you become totally immersed in the game and are so in tune and comfortable on the field of play that, when the contest ends, you look back on it as a type of out-of-body experience. It's almost as if the on-field competitor in the heat of the battle is just not the same person as the off-field civilian. I'd entered that state of mind many, many times as a player, but hadn't got there so often in the seven grand finals I played.

When I look back on my own grand final performances I think I suffered a fair bit of damaging performance anxiety. Learning from my own experiences, my plan with the Collingwood players was to do everything we could as a football department to reduce anxiety as much as possible. To use a personality-profiling description, as a player I mainly operated in my heavily goal-oriented Enforcer mode. Although winning the 1990 flag at any cost was my personal aim, in my role as coach I needed to get into my Thinker mode and to plot and plan a strategy that would give us the best chance of getting our players in the zone to perform at their best on grand final day.

As coach and manager of the group my own behaviour and demeanour had to be the starting point. If I appeared stressed or flustered that would be a bad example and could rub off on our players and staff. Fortunately, I was born with a naturally cold, unemotional exterior that never seemed to show my inner turmoils, so appearing calm and in control was not so hard.

If I even mentioned winning or losing to the players or to the media, the players might have got ahead of themselves, as they say. Winning chances are always enhanced by focusing on individual roles and specifics rather than the result or, worse, the vastly different emotions that come from victory or failure.

Living minute by minute, concentrating on what to do today and tomorrow, was the way I lived my football life, so staying in the moment was easy for me. 'Never expect, never assume, never look too far ahead' had been ingrained in my football psyche seemingly forever.

As a player I'd been involved in seven grand finals and in six of those we qualified in the second semi, so having to wait for the preliminary final result before we knew our exact opponent was also quite familiar territory.

The first week of our fortnight to the grand final needed to be stress-free. Get any grand final administration stuff done in advance, like getting tickets for family and friends organised, tend to injury or sore spots, and as coach don't get fussed when training is mundane and unenthusiastic. That in-between week isn't conducive to sparkling track sessions, because with the actual opponents still unknown, players' minds aren't yet focused on the game – and as coach you don't want them to be.

Our only injury problem was Alan Richardson's broken collarbone. I had already written him off but there was some talk he might come up. However, recovering from this type of injury in a fortnight was defying nature. It was simply not possible.

We already knew that Shane Kerrison would be Richo's replacement as the next-in-line small defender. Kerro hadn't played since round 20 but was a tough competitor and a desperate chaser and tackler, who'd enhance us even further in that department. Richo was in good touch and would have held his spot, but Kerro was a more than adequate replacement, so there'd be no wait till the last minute decision as we'd had with Peter Daicos in the second semi. This was also not a Darren Millane situation of playing with a damaged thumb. Richo needed to be in perfect condition to keep his spot. But there was no urgency; the decision could be made late in grand final week.

In an emotional sense the grand final build-up really only starts once the preliminary final winner is known. Actually, these are very strange games to watch when your team has already qualified. As I watched and waited to find out who our grand final opponent would be, I always found myself willing both teams to lose. Obviously a forlorn hope. It's also quite natural to barrack for injuries and suspension. Forget the rubbish about wanting to beat your opponents at their best; playing either team with a few of their stars injured or suspended would be great. When the siren sounds to end the preliminary final, all of a sudden it's back to a two-horse race and a 50-50 chance. There is an emotional gulp that is almost physical.

In keeping with the aim of reducing anxiety and hype, we planned a Saturday night away for coaches and players, accompanied by wives and girlfriends. Functions are normally a bit more festive when the girls are there as well. Player-only get-togethers tend to be either boring or involve heavy drinking, and I wasn't planning an unhealthy night on the booze. We figured having a weekend together after the preliminary final might be a nice relaxing start to what would be, by its very nature, an extremely stressful week to come.

The players and coaches would go as a group to the game out at VFL Park and have a good look at our potential opponents, before heading down to meet the girls at the Peninsula Golf and Country Club situated near the southern bayside suburb of Frankston. We'd have a few drinks, have a meal together, stay the night, and on the Sunday morning those who wanted could play golf or bowls and then head back home.

Our barracking for injuries and suspensions in the preliminary final was quickly centred on Essendon, who got in front early and just kept going to eventually win comfortably by 63 points. The bad news for us was no injuries and no reports, and Simon Madden had been fantastic in the ruck. He was late in his stellar career – approaching 33 years of age – but after his performance against the Eagles I'm sure our ruckmen, James Manson and Damian Monkhorst, would have been a fair bit more concerned than they were prior to arriving at VFL Park.

Big Monkie had been struggling to find his best form late in the season, and as our 200-centimetre ruckman his performance against Madden would be critical. I made a mental note that building his confidence during the week needed to be a priority. Someone had already suggested putting together a season highlights video of his good play as a method to build his belief and morale. That tape was already being prepared.

Essendon were good but West Coast had a shocker, which should have been no surprise as the preliminary final was the sixth consecutive week they'd played away from Perth. This was after they'd finished third on the ladder. In the year the competition name changed from the Victorian Football League to the Australian Football League, the unfairness of the Eagles being denied a home elimination final against Melbourne when they'd qualified higher on the ladder than the Demons was laughable, but personally, as a born-and-bred Victorian who thought we owned the game, it wasn't an issue that provoked much sympathy from me at the time.

It's fair to say my views have changed a little in the decades that have followed and that, grand final aside – and even that's debatable – it should be a simple right to have a home final if you finish higher on the home-and-away ladder than your opponents. After being dragged kicking and screaming, the Melbourne-centric AFL administration eventually got to this point, but it took them some 15 years after 1990 to get there.

(The Eagles got their own form of revenge. The improvement they made during the summer of 1990/91 was remarkable; whatever they did in their training that pre-season was good enough to be bottled. They won the opening 13 rounds in 1991 and were transformed from a very good team to a super team. If a week is a long time in footy, I guess eight months is an eternity. The Eagles team that put Collingwood to the sword at the WACA in round 17 that season was the quickest, strongest, most athletic group of supermen footballers I had ever coached against.)

However, as we left Waverley Park to make our way down to the Peninsula Golf Club, the Eagles and their situation had no place in our thoughts. Essendon was the external opposition, and our internal challenge was to be at our optimum level physically and emotionally in seven days' time.

We were fit and hard, and importantly the Collingwood players *believed* they were fit and hard. I had no concern that further motivation or incentive was needed. Any player who glides onto the MCG on grand final day to be hit by the explosion of noise and emotion generated by the 100,000 crowd is guaranteed to be excited and motivated. As I've mentioned, being overhyped and overanxious is potentially the most dangerous by-product; hence the Saturday away to at least start the week with a relaxing low-key night. It was the first small step in the challenge to best manage the emotional rigours of the big week to come.

What happened down at Peninsula comes under the umbrella of 'Gee, it was different back then.' The night started quietly enough but after the girls got into the cocktails and the players' planned 'one or two drinks' began to exceed more than a few, the function was quickly becoming quite raucous, and it continued well into the night. Jimmy Manson got his guitar out and a good time was had by all.

I have to admit to mixed feelings at the time – with the premiership-deciding game less than a week away, a New Year's Eve type party was certainly not part of the plan. However, if we wanted a relaxing fun evening at the beginning of a stressful week, well, we certainly got one.

Despite my misgivings, I look back at that night down at the Peninsula Golf Club as a terrific way to start the week; not physically ideal, I admit, but in the big-picture campaign to reduce the damaging pressure of grand final week it more than served its purpose. Maybe if we'd lost the following week my views might be different, because success tends to justify whatever we do, while failure makes us question everything.

It was only many years later that I became aware that a small contingent of the younger bucks in our team didn't want the party to end and, anxious for some female company, snuck out and headed to a local nightspot. As usual, Darren Millane headed the escapees. I'm so glad he was such a positive powerful influence around training and on the field, because he was a terribly negative lifestyle role model. Can you imagine that little episode remaining a secret in the modern era when social media and every cell phone doubles as a camera?

Nowadays it would likely be public in time to be splashed across the Sunday papers. Even during that era, it would have been an embarrassing headline. I can see it now: 'Collingwood party into grand final'. Like I said, the expectation was different and the discipline much more lenient 20 years ago. Anyway, given what was standard practice back then, I suspect the Essendon players would have had a decent post-game drink themselves.

The concept of making grand final week as normal as possible is perfectly valid in principle, because familiarity in routine and surroundings is a great aid in maximising composure. In practice, it is a few days unlike any other on the football calendar. Brownlow Medal dinner on the Monday night, a match-day-sized crowd at Thursday night training, the Friday grand final parade through the city, saturation media coverage heaped on only two teams – and, of course, the huge difference that comes from winning or losing.

The only thing the same is the game itself. Same duration, same rules, but with the ultimate prize we aim at all season hanging on the result. Clearly, a 'normal week' is impossible. Just as clearly, the team whose players best survive the enormous hype of the week and get onto the field physically and mentally in the best shape wins the premiership. Not easy, but that's the grand final week challenge before you even get to the opposition team.

In order to manage the unusual build-up, my advice to the players was this: symbolically separate your off-field self from the on-field player. Take your body where you're required to be during the week, but try to imagine the player part of you as being inside a transparent glass bubble that sees what's happening around you, but doesn't allow anything inside that can adversely affect the competitor part of you that has to perform inside the white line on match day. My advice was also never to forget that while the media and the fans can hype it up as much as they like, your week and your job is to get ready to play a game of footy. Enjoy the excitement because it's a special fun time in a footballer's life, but don't allow yourself to get overwhelmed by it and distracted from your core role.

It sounds like you're playing mind games with yourself, but to a large degree that's exactly what needs to be done. On the practical front, turn the phone off and the answering machine on: a hundred well-wishers ringing to wish you luck is nice but a similar conversation repeated over and over becomes a chore. Players can't hide from the world so it's wise to have a pre-prepared line – even for family and friends – when they ask the standard line of 'How do you think you'll go?' I tried to convince the players it wasn't rude to have a one-line answer to this standard question, something simple like 'I think we'll go alright.' Not entering into a detailed discussion about the game every five minutes is good policy.

Another initiative under the keep-it-normal theme was to deliberately not decorate either our dressing rooms at Victoria Park or at the MCG on match day with club colours. Attempting to treat the match as a normal game of footy is blown right out the window if balloons, streamers and crepe paper adorn the dressing room walls just because it's a grand final. Actions always speak louder than words.

As a coach, whenever you're preparing for any game – let alone a grand final – you're always on the lookout for a focus point or two. I'm a great believer in homing in on specifics rather than vague generalities, as well as always endeavouring to simplify the message. When stakes are high it's easy to get fazed and stressed by the consequences of the result. Over-coaching and overcomplicating is to be avoided.

My method to help keep a clear and focused mind was to encourage the players to concentrate on their individual roles and to buy into a couple of bonding team themes. Anything to prevent them thinking too much about the awful and scary difference between winning and losing.

I had one of my periodic conversations with my mentor and former coach Allan Jeans early in the week. As Hawthorn had been eliminated by Melbourne in the first week of the finals, he'd generously offered to assist if he could. I was talking to him about my search for a coaching theme to focus the team's concentration on a specific point or two. As a former sergeant in the Victoria Police, he mentioned that when the police plan an operation, first they give it a name; then they work out what needs to be done to achieve the initial aim of the exercise. No idea is completely new – it is usually someone else's that we package to suit our own purposes. I was never too proud to pinch an idea from someone else, so from that conversation 'Operation Tackle' became the object of our grand final week planning. That was the heading on the pre-game handout for the players and on the whiteboard in our planning meeting.

The themes were few but hopefully well-chosen:

'Operation Tackle '
First 10 minutes, set the scene.
Get numbers to the contest.
Long and quick into the forward line.
Force the ball forward.
Aggressive and disciplined pressure.

We never spoke about winning or losing – that was so far in the future it was irrelevant – and the start of the game was our sole focus.

Our big-picture goal was to out-pressure Essendon, particularly when they had the footy – we would be on automatic pilot with contest winning and our ball use. The coaching sell was that if we denied the Bombers time and space by chasing and holding the tackle, we'd give ourselves the best chance to win. That was our competitive edge that had blossomed through that memorable September. Our opponents might beat us in some contests for the footy, but they couldn't stop us chasing and tackling. Operation Tackle was totally in our control. The coaching theme was to focus on the performance of these specific match objectives and let the rest of the game take care of itself.

We'd won the second semi against the Bombers comfortably, so, as we were playing the same opposition and were coming off a couple of 10-goal finals wins, it wasn't a time for change. We would have loved to have named a stability-enhancing unchanged team. The one unfortunate forced change would be Alan Richardson out with his cracked collarbone; in would be an ideal replacement in our tough backpocket/tagger Shane Kerrison. At least that was my expectation until Richo came to our Thursday night training session eager to prove his fitness.

Over the previous few days he'd recovered his normal range of movement in his shoulder and wanted to give it a go. No-one could blame him: what player would voluntarily miss a grand final?

All players are a mix of on-field ability and let's call it 'teams-manship', to give a name to the combination of qualities that each player brings to his team above his playing talents. Richo had limited on-field talent but was well-respected and well-liked by his team-mates and coaches, and was a fantastic contributor to team spirit. Like everyone else at the footy club, I held him in high regard. Yet despite my personal feelings, without a glimmer of hesitation my role as coach that Thursday training session was to deny him his boyhood dream of playing in a grand final.

Fully recovering from a cracked collarbone in a fortnight was simply not physically possible. My task that afternoon was to prove this cruel reality to Alan Richardson by breaking him down. We couldn't afford for him to get through training and then break down during the match, which would leave us a man short.

I was expecting the ball-movement drills to find him out, but he got through them okay. Then I thought the tackling-technique work would end his chances, but he got through that intact as well. Unfortunately, the final step had to be a heavy-contact fitness test. As a 38-year-old it was only five years since my retirement, so I usually did these tests myself.

However, there was nothing usual about this fitness test. With group training over, the 15,000 Collingwood fans who had thronged into Victoria Park for the last training session before the big game were engrossed in the physical workout the coach was trying to give his injured player and they were willing the player to survive. There was no doubt they were barracking for player over coach. Richo's team-mates were doing their own thing before leaving the ground and, like the fans, were undoubtedly hoping that he'd get through.

I tackled Richo to the ground, I bumped him full bore, and still his wonky collarbone was unaffected. If he was in pain, he certainly wasn't showing it. Every time we tackled or bumped the crowd roared. I wasn't enjoying this very public fitness test one little bit and said to Richo that we'd call it a day and have a look at him on Friday after the grand final parade.

To my amazement, the training session and fitness test hadn't broken him down, but the one last thing I wanted to do before we left the field was to crunch into him when he wasn't expecting or bracing for the contact – as would happen many times during a game. As we were walking off together I suddenly drove my shoulder into his chest, then grabbed him and dumped him forcefully into the ground with my weight on top of him. Still he didn't flinch. There was the Friday test to come, but when we finalised the grand final team that night, A. Richardson was named in the back pocket and Shane Kerrison as an emergency. From assuming for a couple of weeks that Kerrison in and Richardson out would be the team change from the second semi line-up, I drove home that night thinking that it was now an even-money bet and, more importantly, contemplating what we could do in the Friday fitness test to be sure one way or the other.

We gathered at Victoria Park mid-morning the next day to get a bus into the grand final parade, and when I asked Richo how he'd pulled up from his training session the previous night, his response made the decision for us. He knew he wasn't right and had decided to pull out of the side.

In keeping with the theme of reducing stress, I decided not to tell Kerro he was definitely in the team until match-day at the ground. His likely match-ups would be the Bombers Alan Ezard and Darren Bewick, who he'd played on many times before, so I took the view that it was better for him to worry about whether he was actually playing, rather than having his inclusion lobbed on him a day in advance. Kerro was a tough little bugger – remember he thrived at that late-1987 survival camp in the Gippsland bush – and would relish getting the last-minute chance to play. Just maybe, one brief hour of pre-game tension might be better than a long 24 hours with a possibly sleepless Friday night in between. At least that was my theory, and after the Ron McKeown late-omission debacle before the second semi, I was also happy to keep our options open in case Essendon coach Kevin Sheedy tossed in a last-minute change of his own.

As always the grand final parade through the Melbourne CBD was great to be part of. Mick McGuane and – if I can remember correctly, Peter Daicos – decided not to take part, as an attempt to stick to their normal pre-game routine. There was no absolute right or wrong in their decision, however waving to the massive crowd lining the route from the back of a vehicle is no chore, and, in fact, is one of the more memorable aspects of the whole grand final experience.

After years of mirth and derision at the Magpies' history of grand final failure, during the parade I sensed for probably the first time ever that the non-Essendon supporters were leaning their support towards Collingwood. Even footy fans who'd grown up as passionate Collingwood haters seemed to be of the mind that it was time to finally bury the Colliwobbles myth. These were strange times indeed.

Because our team gathered at Victoria Park and returned there after the parade, we decided to have a bit of exercise on the field and then hold the detailed planning meeting we usually had at the ground on match day.

During my last three years at Hawthorn, the team travelled to the grand final parade together and then went back to Glenferrie Oval for a planning meeting. I decided to follow that lead but threw in the short unstructured training run as another step in our campaign to avoid wasting nervous energy. There's no doubt in my mind that exercise is a great reliever of pressure and anxiety.

We had our light run around, had our planning meeting where Operation Tackle was the focus, and by mid-afternoon the group commitments were completed. My final message to the players before they headed off was simple enough: from that point onwards, the grand final distractions were over and it was now just a game of footy. As an attempt to manage their naturally growing anxiety and the inevitable fear of failure, this was a reminder from the coach that the sun would come up Sunday morning no matter what the result. It was also meant as a confidence builder, encouragement to back their match-day instincts and not to get caught up in 'analysis paralysis'. Finally, I told them that over the next 24 hours they should trust the familiarity of their favoured preparation cycle from then until game time. With the Saturday night party at the Peninsula Golf Club in the back of my mind, my only rider was not to do anything between now and the game that their team-mates could even remotely construe as contrary to being fully prepared.

I drove away from Victoria Park much more relaxed than I'd been prior to that final planning meeting. As a player, the final day and night leading into any game was quite nerve-racking; when it was the premiership decider, the normal tension could explode off the scale. This was my first grand final as coach, and while my desire to be on the winning side was as strong as any time I'd been inside the white line in a Hawthorn jumper, I fully realised my role was to assist the players to get ready to perform at their optimum, and then sit in the coach's box and hope like hell they did.

It is a constant in coaching that your aims and emotions are invested in the performance of your players. I was confident the team was physically ready to perform at their peak. I'd tried to learn from my own experience in order to best manage the environment and process to get our players onto the field mentally fit as well. There was one final step yet to come, when, as I've mentioned, the players would walk into the dressing rooms at the MCG usually used by

Richmond to find only the permanent Tigers paraphernalia up on the walls. There wouldn't be a black-and-white streamer in sight. The look would be identical to the second semi-final a fortnight before.

The longer I coached, the more the final planning meeting became the symbolic handover of control to the players. My belief has always been that whatever a coach contributes on match day, it's insignificant compared to what happens in the days, weeks and months leading up to the actual games. So I was quite buoyant with relief as I headed towards my home in the south-east suburb of Dingley. For me, the die was largely cast and my job as coach was 95 per cent done. The off-field team had done its best in the preparation phase; from now on it was up to the players.

I couldn't say I was confident, but then again I simply never thought of a game of football in terms of confidence or pessimism. For me, the most predictable thing about the sport is its unpredictability. We could win if we did our best and the footy gods smiled on us – that was about where my attitude stood. Whether you're a player, a coach or a passionate fan, when you go into a grand final the unknown aspects of what might transpire, and the difference these unknowns make to the emotional consequence, are positively scary, but also unbelievably exciting and stimulating. The General George S. Patton quote which had been sent to me a few weeks earlier said it all: 'Accept the challenge without reservation or doubt and risk the depression of losing, so you may experience the exhilaration of victory.'

These few words describe the emotional challenge of grand final day in a nutshell. The only certainty was that at the end of the day we'd experience one of these extreme and totally contrasting feelings. Knowing this confronting reality and handling the pressure it creates is why players who perform on the big day are so universally feted.

26

THE AGONY IS OVER

We'd won the premiership and that realisation and acceptance
was the sweetest moment of them all.

I slept remarkably well the Friday night before the 1990 grand final; much better than I ever had in the seven I played in with Hawthorn. The whole experience as a non-playing coach was so very different. Playing at my best required me to summon up every fibre of my being, and for an average football athlete like me it took a total commitment of mind, body and soul. This meant finding the aggression to thrive in the battle zone of a heavy physical contact sport.

Coaching had no physical price to pay, so my performance anxiety going into the 1990 premiership-deciding game didn't lead to the night of restless tossing and turning that I remember from my playing days. However, once I was up and about the normal game-day coaching demons started to nag. Had I said enough? Had I said too much? What needed to be said in the pre-game? In all of the 461 games I coached, and even more so in the five grand finals, how I wished I could have checked in with a supreme coaching god to get an answer to these perplexing questions. Obviously – and unfortunately – no definitive answer exists. Over the years I gradually concluded that even on the biggest days I needed to resist the temptation to over-coach and that I should never alter game plans on match day. As 1990 was only my fifth year as a coach I was still coaching by instinct rather than vast experience, but these two basic coaching principles were already entrenched in my thinking.

So when the team gathered in the coach's room in the bowels of the old Northern Stand about 90 minutes before the game, there were no last-minute surprises or fresh instructions. Kerrison in and Richardson being out injured were finally confirmed to the whole team, followed by a reinforcement of the Operation Tackle game plan that we'd detailed the day before. Then it was out into the bigger locker-room area for players to complete individual preparations: getting their ankles bandaged, having a massage, and, in Darren Millane's case, it was time for Dr Shane Conway to inject a vial or two of novocaine local anaesthetic into his broken thumb before the heavy strapping was applied.

At this point of the match day, I could always feel the tension of the rapidly approaching contest growing uncontrollably within me, so, conscious of not wanting to be a stress carrier, it was my habit to head out of the rooms and watch the reserves curtain-raiser from the players' race down near the ground. I'd only come back into the dressing rooms when the pre-game warm-up was about to begin.

The club's conditioning coach and match-day runner, Mark McKeon, called the players in to begin the 10 or so minutes of group stretches and ball-handling drills. On grand final day the dressing-room warm-up is still maybe 30 minutes before the opening bounce, so the objective for the players is to keep emotional control and not get too hyped too early. I still remembered fighting back the tears five years earlier when the premiership-winning Hawthorn reserves swarmed into the dressing rooms of the senior team preparing to confront Essendon.

My final words to the players before they entered the field of battle were from the heart as much as the head. After the finals failures of the previous two seasons, this group of players had persisted, competed and earned their way into the grand final. I felt proud of their efforts and told them so, adding that, 'Win, lose or draw, I'll still be proud of every one of you.'

It's part of the coaching art to pick the right word or two at an opportune time that might help your players – sometimes to inspire them, sometimes to plant a bonding thought. That day, the words of pride were an attempt to soothe the gnawing performance anxiety that needed to be kept at bay. Maybe these few words about what they'd already achieved would ease the feeling that the next two hours would totally determine their worth.

As I've mentioned, on big occasions like grand finals the biggest trap is players becoming overhyped. The result is the wasting of vital nervous energy, trying too hard to win the game from your own efforts, and consequently losing self-control and concentration on the task at hand. Keeping our players as calm as possible was my coaching objective.

It was interesting, and I only noticed this after watching a replay of the game, that the Collingwood players didn't charge onto the arena like hyped-up crazed animals but walked down the players' race as a calm, controlled unit led by their determined, steely faced captain Tony Shaw. He was clearly a man on a mission and so were the players he led.

I was a fan of players exhibiting a cold, calculated demeanour, rather than appearing hot and angry. Maybe our off-field strategy over the previous fortnight to encourage a controlled relaxed atmosphere had achieved a measure of success.

However, there was one position where I highly valued a good dose of hot and angry white-line fever and that was in our ruckmen. I'd observed how my Hawthorn premiership team-mate Don Scott had so successfully used the crazy ruckman approach to unsettle 'saner' opponents. We had our own version in James Manson, who had a similar wild-eyed manic on-field persona. Our other ruckman, Damian Monkhorst, was one big tough unit, but not in the same extroverted manner that Jimmy was.

Prior to the opening bounce the starting ruckman from each team faces his opposite number across the centre circle. The last thing you want at this point is cold and calculating; this is where a hot, angry, crazy ruckman wanting to kill his opponent is a godsend, as far as setting the tone for his smaller team-mates. Jimmy would be our starting ruckman and, sooled on by our ruck coach 'Crackers' Keenan, had the licence to let out every ounce of his natural aggression. Facing him across the centre circle would be Simon Madden, who, while a wonderful player, was by comparison – and I say this with the greatest respect – an intellectual ruckman. On the field, Simon was the exact opposite of the unpredictable and volatile Jimmy Manson.

On this day our plan A of throwing the extroverted energetic Manson at the Essendon rucks didn't work to our advantage. As the game unfolded, the 'thinking' Bombers ruckman Madden got on top of our 'crazy' one. Fortunately, we had a back-up option, and when we put Monkie into the ruck in the second quarter, the tide turned our way and he went on to play a fantastic game.

When the match got under way, our effort was great but our execution was sloppy. The pre-game look of calm and control had disappeared in a nervy haze of rushed uncertainty. We were wasting opportunities and deep in the Essendon forward line the 206-centimetre Paul Salmon was looking like a man mountain. He took two strong marks on Michael Christian and I immediately made a change by shifting our centre half-back, Craig 'Ned' Kelly, onto the big full-forward. But in the next one-on-one contest, Ned was hope-lessly outmuscled and out-marked.

Realising that I'd panicked with the original positional switch, and not wanting to let one mistake become two, we reverted to our pre-match plan. I sent Mark McKeon out to Chrisso with a simple message. It went something like: 'He's your size and shape – you're our best match-up, he's your man for the day, and keep playing in front.' And I didn't think about moving him again.

Many games, let alone grand finals, are won or lost by scoring accuracy. Just to name a couple recently, Geelong lost the 2008 decider and Hawthorn blew their chance in 2012 through inaccurate conversion. This same disease was afflicting Collingwood badly for most of the first quarter. Suddenly, though, at the Punt Road end in front of the soon to be demolished Southern Stand, Daics released the growing pressure with a classic drop-punt goal from a really tight angle with his right side hemmed against the boundary in the right forward pocket. Yet again he'd made the impossible possible. As the legendary Jack Dyer might have said, the angle was so acute it was a wonder the ball didn't get stuck between the goalposts!

But that was Daics. Some players – like, say, Tony Shaw – killed the opposition with death by a thousand cuts, while Daics did it more with quality than quantity. His first of only five kicks that day pro-duced the magic goal that gave a badly needed boost to both the scoreboard and the team's morale. Then Gavin Brown capitalised on an Essendon turnover to get our second goal, which gave us a three-point lead when the quarter-time siren sounded.

It was at that point that the 100,000 people in the stadium witnessed the most chaotic scene you'd ever see on a football field. As I made my way down from the coach's box to the interchange area, suddenly all hell broke loose in the forward pocket on the opposite side of the field near the goals at the Jolimont end. An almighty brawl involving every player in the vicinity broke out and every other player on the field sprinted towards the growing melee. It was after the siren, so the umpires restarting play to distract players from the fight wasn't an option. Like an out-of-control bushfire it would have to burn itself out.

When I got down onto the arena big Damian Monkhorst, who had finished the quarter on interchange, was standing near the boundary line and was just another spectator until I strongly suggested he 'go over and see if you can help out'. In all the chaos I still get a laugh from the image of our big ruckman being momentarily undecided whether to discard the old-style dressing gown that was worn by the interchange players back then. I can visualise the big fella looking a lot like an oversized praying mantis sprinting towards the brawl and, as he went, peeling off the gown like he was Clark Kent turning into Superman.

For the minute or two that followed, I was just another incredulous spectator waiting to see what the outcome might be. If there were 100,000 people in the stands, it seemed as if half of them were on the field – it was just amazing. Forty-odd players were fighting the main event on the other side of the field, when all of a sudden to my right a group of officials decided to have a go as well.

Caught in the middle of this mauling group of bodies dressed in the red, black and white of the two clubs was Channel Seven boundary rider Bernie Quinlan. He was attempting the peacemaker role with little success. It was hard to tell who wanted to be involved and who was trying to break it up. Collingwood team manager Eddie Hillgrove was caught up in the grappling melee, as was our runner Mark McKeon. The Essendon participants I recognised were their coach Kevin Sheedy and runner Peter Power. The next thing I noticed was our football manager Gubby Allan a few metres from the pack of officials giving a very good impression of a boxer shadow-sparring fresh air. I must have missed Gub's brief bout, because when common sense prevailed and he eventually joined the Collingwood huddle, it was with a bloodied hand that turned out to be broken. Sheeds must have a very hard head.

I yelled at Gub, 'What do you think you're doing – get back over here!' because while doing anything to win was my footy morality, even for me fighting opposition officials was going a bit too far. Sheeds and I had the odd push and shove as opponents back in our playing days, but having a punch-up with him as the opposing coach was not even vaguely on my radar.

The dust finally settled on the player brawl and the one real victim was Gavin Brown, who lay motionless on the ground surrounded by Collingwood doctor Shane Conway and a group of worried trainers. Apparently, Browny had been thumped by his opponent, Terry Daniher, as they raced into the melee and was clearly badly dazed. He was gone for a while, if not the entire game.

When peace was finally restored and all our players came together in our quarter-time huddle, I was reminded of horses really hyped up in the mounting yard after a race, with eyes flared and nostrils snorting. Our players, or at least the majority of them, had that wild-eyed look. I don't know if it's physically possible, but to this day I'm sure Craig Kelly's eyeballs were rolling a bit.

The bottom line was that extremely high levels of adrenalin were surging through every player on the field. Calmness and control was our objective, so we needed to make sure the players' minds got back on to Operation Tackle and playing football. The players would often refer to Gavin Brown as my love child because I so highly valued the bravery and ability he gave our team, so when I tried to convince them that exacting revenge for Browny would be counterproductive, the high regard I had for their wounded team-mate might have added some weight to the message.

Usually at breaks in play when the coach addresses his players, they're only half-listening. They're distracted by what's happened in the match so far and what might happen in the next phase of the game. After the mayhem of the preceding few minutes, though, this was one message we couldn't afford to fall on deaf ears. It had to really sink in. I demanded that every eye in the huddle was looking straight into mine. As forcefully and as loudly as I could, I implored them to make the footy their object – not the Essendon players. I told them that the umpires would be looking to re-establish their control. They'd go over the top in rewarding the player who went at the footy, and show no mercy for anyone over-enthusiastic in their attack on the man. Get in first for the footy and you'll be rewarded – that was the message I tried to sell.

I looked around the group for any subtle feedback. Shawy looked under control. He knew footy was an impersonal game, so he'd lead the attack on the footy rather than look for revenge. Mick McGuane was a smart footballer and would understand what was required. But my greatest comfort came when Denis Banks started to repeat my message about being first to the footy with controlled aggression. Darren Millane jumped on board encouraging the same theme, which was just as gratifying, because these two were the most likely and able to deliver some physical payback. Fortunately, our two big aggressive ruckmen also looked calm enough, and while Craig Kelly's eyes may not have stopped rolling, at least they were doing so more slowly. But the ultimate feedback would only come when the game resumed.

After the wild scenes of a few minutes earlier, a heated expectation buzzed around the stadium as the two teams resumed their positions for the start of the second quarter. History tells us there were no further on-field fireworks but in the attack on the footy and con-trolled-aggression battle the Magpies players did it better. Most games of footy are won by the team having a period of play that creates the winning gap. Collingwood won the 1990 premiership by establishing a 34-point half-time lead. Five goals in the first nine minutes of the second quarter was the crucial period.

We outscored the Bombers six goals to one in the second term. Three of them came after undisciplined 50-metre penalties against Essendon that turned possible goals into certain six-pointers. This was a critical factor in the end result. There is nothing more morale-boosting for a team than being advanced to the goal square after a 50-metre penalty. In a split second the pressure of a nerve-jangling shot a fair way out from goal is replaced by the soothing comfort of a close-in gimme. Conversely, the award of the penalty frustrates and deflates the opposition enormously.

When the siren sounded for the half-time break I made a decision I'd like to take back. It seemed unlikely that Gavin Brown would be able to return to the field so the thought occurred to me to use him to try to unsettle Terry Daniher. The Essendon veteran is one of the really good blokes in football and no way would he have meant to KO Browny. Like most players he could get a little white-line fever at times and his aggression could bubble over, but I suspected it might not be sitting too well with his conscience that he'd knocked out a well-respected ball player. Anyway, that was my theory.

I was out of the coach's box early, collecting Browny from interchange and asking our team manager Eddie Hillgrove to ride shotgun as we quickly walked to the top of the Collingwood race. We were using the old Richmond rooms which, of course, were adjacent to the old Melbourne rooms that were being used by Essendon. A high cyclone wire fence divided the two races and I was waiting on the edge of the arena as Terry got to the Bombers race. I grabbed Browny firmly with my left hand and as TD approached yelled at him that 'Browny would be back to get him'.

Without waiting for a reply I then dragged our still groggy full-forward up into the Collingwood race walking adjacent to Terry, who, fortunately, headed into the Bombers race. Terry's reply, 'It's all part of the game, mate,' was delivered in his usual laconic laidback manner. No harm was done but I still get a shudder when I think what could have happened if TD or anyone else in the Essendon team had taken physical exception to my words. It had the potential to reignite the quarter-time chaos.

I was wrong to engage in any sort of conversation with an opposition player. It just shows that on grand final day, when everything is on the line, sometimes you do things you shouldn't. My silly stunt was a case of act now and think later. It's why the AFL introduced double suspensions for grand final indiscretions, and why they later moved to have the two teams enter the arena from different parts of the field.

My ill-advised mind games had no effect on Terry's aggression because during the third quarter he knocked out Craig Starcevich after our half-forward had taken a mark near the wing. It was a bad loss for us because Starce had been a very good player, but I couldn't have been happier with the resultant 50-metre penalty, never mind the kick eventually being taken from about 35 metres by Mick McGuane. He was as straight a kick as I'd seen and split the middle with his shot. Daics then kicked another spectacular goal off the outside of his right foot from near the behind post to extend the lead to 46 points.

I was checking every 10 minutes or so with club doctor Shane Conway on the health of Gavin Brown, and about halfway through the third quarter he cleared him to return to the field. Browny only had four kicks for the game but after Essendon had pegged a couple back, he kicked the last goal of the term. It was a massive boost to the team and sent us to three-quarter time 40 points up.

Given Collingwood's history of falling short at the final hurdle, I don't think anyone in the ground was any more confident than the basic 'they should win from here'. As I've said, I was never comfortable unless we were more goals in front than there were minutes left to play, so as far as I was concerned we were nowhere near over the line. I certainly wasn't taking anything for granted, but I was comforted by the fact that in the previous two finals against West Coast and Essendon we hadn't conceded a goal in the final quarter. I knew this was a really tough, committed unit who, during that September, had become a fantastic defensive team. They were in the zone and wouldn't surrender without a huge fight.

As it turned out, we again held the Bombers goalless in the final term. They had plenty of the ball early in the quarter but managed only behinds. Simon Madden hit the post from only 20 metres out straight in front, and I remember thinking that after all the grand final misfortune Collingwood had suffered over the decades, the footy gods were finally with us.

Our players had earned their lead through clearly winning the Operation Tackle mini-battle. Their attack on the contest was super – no Magpie player took a short step all day – and the competitive edge they gained by being the best chasing and tackling team that footy had seen to that point in time was illustrated by them laying 52 effective tackles to Essendon's measly 27.

After 20 minutes of torrid bunfight footy, Doug Barwick posted the first goal of the final term with a snap from 25 metres. Then the victory moment came.

About 28 minutes into the final quarter, Tony Shaw gathered the footy on the half-forward flank in front of the Collingwood coach's box in the old Melbourne Cricket Club stand. Our gallant skipper turned calmly inside onto his trusty left foot and delivered his 32nd possession for the day into the waiting arms of Damian Monkhorst who marked unopposed about 40 metres out. The big fella took his time and slotted the goal.

It was only his third for the whole season but for me it was the goal and the moment in time that I'll remember forever. We were now eight goals in front with only a minute or two to go. After living that game second by second – never expecting and never assuming – in that precious second or two when Monky's kick sailed through, I accepted that we were going to win. And just as importantly, with me being a natural pessimist, the possibility of losing no longer existed. We'd won the premiership, and that realisation and acceptance was the sweetest moment of them all.

The thought of enjoying the boundary line atmosphere grabbed me so I walked down from the box. As I headed towards the inter-change area, my first unconscious action was a celebratory overhead fist pump in the direction of where I thought my wife, Maureen, was seated. Then I saw our football manager, Gubby Allan, coming towards me. It had become the custom for Gub, along with President Allan McAlister, to be perched on small fold-up stools next to the Collingwood interchange area. Gub had been my main coaching/management partner since we'd started together back in 1986. We'd spent nearly five years overseeing the Collingwood footy department and had become very good friends. This was a time to savour.

I looked around to see the majority of the off-field group who had shared the journey. Our chairman of selectors, Ron Richards, and coaches and selectors Michael Taylor and Lee Adamson had followed me down onto the ground. The excitement bubbled over into embraces all round. It's funny what a grand final win does to you. Maybe I'm a bit homophobic, but I'm not usually a hugger of other men – except after I've won a premiership. Then I'm hugging everyone in sight.

I took a seat between Jimmy Manson and Craig Starcevich, our two interchange players for the last few minutes. With an arm around each of the only two players within touching distance, this was a surreal minute or two. It isn't an exaggeration to say that at this point, as a coach, you love the players who have given you this incredible feeling. I've got to say those few moments waiting for the final siren were as good as it gets.

However, when the blast of noise finally ended the game I found my reactions quite confused. I wanted to throw off my serious game-day face and join the excited hugging throng around the Collingwood interchange area, but instead I jogged out onto the arena with no particular destination in mind. How to celebrate a premiership victory as a coach was a new experience which threw me a little for the initial few minutes after the siren.

Late in the game the tens of thousands of Magpies fans had joined the celebration, with the haunting slow chant of 'Collingwood, Collingwood, Collingwood' echoing around the great stadium. This was the moment when the emotions of the club's gigantic supporter base became reunited with its football team. Now we had the common goal of enjoying a premiership.

Particularly back in the part-time era, my attitude as a coach was largely to do my best to divorce the team from the often unrealistic thinking of its collective fans. I tend to agree with rugby league coaching legend Wayne Bennett who has been quoted as saying, 'Once you start listening to the fans, very soon you'll be sitting with them.'

However, after a grand final victory when the need to concentrate on our match-day roles can be put aside for a short time, sharing the joy and adulation with the wider supporter base is just fantastic. Once the siren goes and the flag is won, everyone who cares for the club can join the celebrations. After the 1990 victory the whole Collingwood community embarked on a premiership party that was like no other, either before or since.

I also learnt that day the answer to a question I've been continually asked ever since: did I enjoy winning a grand final more as a player or coach? Basically I only ever coached because I got too old to keep playing, and on match days I never enjoyed coaching like I did being an on-field performer. But coaching the 1990 premiership team proved to me that coaching a premiership is even more enjoyable than playing in one.

While not necessarily an accurate measure – because the depth of player talent at the coach's disposal is the indefinable prerequisite – team success is the only way you can realistically judge yourself as a coach. Therefore all your endeavours are directed towards maximising team performance. In coaching, your whole emotional state is on the line via the efforts of your players, and when we won the grand final it was the most magnificent, exhilarating feeling.

It was mayhem in the Collingwood rooms after the match as everyone celebrated the end of the 32-year premiership drought. It was wall-to-wall people. Later, we had the official dinner at the Southern Cross Hotel in the city with the club's inner sanctum and the well-heeled supporters who could afford to be there.

One of the absolute highlights followed, when the team piled onto the bus to go to Victoria Park to meet the fans. It was only a few kilometres away but the traffic was chaotic. Eventually we got there about 10 pm and I'll never forget the look of utter joy on the faces of so many people who'd been disappointed so many times before. A stage was set up in the middle of the ground facing the old Collingwood Social Club. When the players were introduced, the crowd, who were packed like sardines onto the oval, must have been swaying four or five metres left to right. It was like a rock concert without the music. It was actually quite terrifying, and if anyone had fallen over they would have been trampled. Thankfully, though, nothing untoward happened.

This was the same part of the Victoria Park playing surface where, a month or so later, a small white coffin containing the 'Colliwobbles' was ceremonially buried by Magpies 1953 premiership captain Lou Richards. His hosting of the fun proceedings was under his guise from latter years as football's original funny man. This event didn't draw the 30,000-odd Collingwood supporters of grand final night, but about 10,000 Magpies fans turned up to have a laugh and to share the enjoyment of winning the elusive flag. Premierships are won and celebrated every year; the Collingwood party was going to be bigger and go much longer than most. Coming down from that mountain was going to test us all.

After our rock-star-type appearance at Victoria Park, for safety reasons the hit-and-run mission was cut short and the bus took us back to the Southern Cross. Then, for the first time in my Collingwood days, I accompanied the playing group to the infamous Tunnel nightclub, down in the King Street precinct. While the Tunnel name conjured up images of the social excesses of many of our players, I figured it was as good a time as any to sample it with the group. As none of us was in a fit state to drive, a bunch of us piled into a horse-drawn buggy we hired outside the hotel. It was sprinkling with rain, but no-one cared. Saturday night after a grand final win is a time you feel no pain.

27

A SPECIAL BUNCH

*Sustained excellence is what we all aspire to, but finding your
best under the often-debilitating pressure of knockout games late
in a final series is an achievement to savour.*

While symbolically and practically premierships can only be won on
grand final day, getting into contention is a very long-term process.
To me, success always takes the pyramid shape – a big strong base and
small at the very tip.

I've been to Egypt and seen the great pyramids outside Cairo. You
can't help but be amazed at the sheer size of these monstrous mono-
liths built nearly 5000 years ago. The romantic in me immediately
looked to the tip of this gigantic stone block structure and thought
about how great it would have been to place the final stone on the
top. But then the practical Thinker in me turned my gaze to the base,
which is maybe 100 × 100 metres. Without successfully building
from the bottom up, there was no chance of finishing the pyramid
and getting to that end point of the tiny tip at the top.

The same analogy applies to sporting success. The Collingwood
premiership was won on 6 October 1990, but in fact getting in the
position to win had been many years in the making. There is never
a definitive starting point; building to ultimate success comes from
many historical factors.

Maybe even the Collingwood grand final losses way back in 1980
and 1981 had an influence. Tony Shaw and Peter Daicos suffered the
disappointment of those years and were desperate to experience the
winning feeling. Likewise the 1984 losing preliminary final team that

included these two, plus Denis Banks, Darren Millane and Shane Morwood. Also, Doug Barwick was in the Fitzroy team that lost to Hawthorn in the 1986 preliminary final. An experienced senior group who had got close without going all the way was a helpful building block.

The sacrifice of accepting the forced pay cuts during the club's near financial bankruptcy of early 1986 may have had the subliminal effect, on the players who stayed, of putting the cause of the team and the club before their individual finances. I have a feeling this may have been an unplanned but healthy by-product of a difficult time for all involved. From my experience, whenever individuals put the team interest before their own, it generally makes them feel much better about themselves. Their investment in the team is always a big motivational factor.

The player bonding that resulted from the team's ill-fated trek through the Gippsland National Park in late 1987 was also significant. That adventure was certainly a turning point. From a poor performance in 1987 that resulted in only seven wins, the team improved remarkably to be near the top in 1988 with fifteen wins plus a draw. The group grew together and strengthened enormously after the shared adversity of that experience.

However, in any football club success is impossible without recruiting the right players. In a nutshell, the right players must collectively have both the required physical competence and competitive character. To me, that is still 90 per cent of the successful team recipe. Then comes the football coaching, physical and mental conditioning, and the culture or environment that is created around the club to get the best result from the raw player resources. Whether the most valuable players are born or made is always a contentious point. The answer is a combination of both, which can vary from player to player.

The 1980s was a period of great change in the footy world. The VFL Commission was formed (later to become the AFL Commission) and the expansion into the national competition began, with South Melbourne going to Sydney and the West Coast Eagles and the Brisbane Bears being formed in 1987.

As the decade progressed, recruiting sources also changed. The initial form of the current draft system began at the end of 1986, but at the same time the Victorian country and metropolitan zones that had been allocated to the VFL clubs 20 years before in the mid-'60s were still in place, as they were gradually phased out during the late '90s.

The 20-man Collingwood premiership team was recruited from all of these categories, while Shane Morwood and Doug Barwick had come from other VFL clubs. The majority were from the zones. These come under the category of 'good fortune'; they're virtually born on your doorstep.

The judgement selections were the draftees Graham Wright (pick number three), Craig Kelly (34), Scott Russell (39) and Tony Francis (95), and, before the draft system was introduced, the interstaters Gavin Crosisca (Queensland), Michael Christian (Western Australia), Craig Starcevich (also WA) and James Manson (Tasmania). The club got great value from selecting this group from outside Victoria.

When you have the good fortune to coach a good team, it's easy to overrate your personal contribution. The longer I coached the more I realised that no-one can turn poor talent into a successful team. Ultimately, all you can do is get the best from what you've got, and all coaches eventually learn that achieving the team's goals and ambitions is dependent on the performance of his players. This is an uncomfortable reality of being a non-playing coach.

We all want to win premierships but a great consolation prize is the belief that you have got the maximum from the talent at your disposal. And while I'm so thankful that the Collingwood team of September 1990 played well enough to win the flag, the fact that we never reached that elite level again has troubled me ever since. Did I fail in my part or did the players fall off the mark? It was probably a mixture of both. We were all in it together.

Maybe it's simply an issue of sustained excellence, that a group of players strikes a purple patch during a short period of time but can't collectively sustain the level of performance into the next season and beyond. In 1990, almost every Magpies player had a career-best year.

All-Australian selection is a good guide to any season's very best performers. In our premiership year, six of the 22 were from Colling-wood: midfielders Tony Shaw, Darren Millane, Graham Wright,

Mick McGuane and Scott Russell, while Peter Daicos was selected on a half-forward flank. None made the team the following season, and of those chosen in 1990 only McGuane ever made All-Australian again.

Judged over the players' entire careers, Collingwood in 1990 was not a great team of individual champions. What they became over the final few games of that season was a champion team with a solid but unspectacular defence and a hard-tackling, if makeshift, forward group. The midfield was the team's great strength, while our key position players would never give the All-Australian selectors any cause to consider them for selection in the season's best. Our talls were the most vulnerable part of the team.

Some of our vital building blocks, particularly in the finals campaign, were fantastic on-field leadership, some inspirational example setting, a few great individual performances, a couple of superb finals cameos and a large group of players who played key roles within the overall team structure.

Player leadership groups weren't even on the radar 20 years ago. Tony Shaw was captain, Peter Daicos vice-captain and Gavin Crosisca deputy vice-captain. If the Magpies had a formal leadership team in addition to that, it would have included Darren Millane, Mick McGuane, Gavin Brown, and maybe one or two of Craig Kelly, Denis Banks and Shane Morwood.

In terms of ability and influence, this group was made up of the core leaders of the team, and they would drive the team performance. In some ways, I coached them and they coached the others.

In my later coaching stint at the Brisbane Lions I refined this concept and would talk to our coaches and senior players about the subject of core players and consultant players. In business, companies often employ outside consultants to provide expertise that they don't have within their full-time staff. Consultants undoubtedly assist the group effort but aren't the heart and soul of the organisation. I believe sporting teams are similar.

Because of the combination of their experience, competitive character, on- and off-field personality and playing ability, certain players become the fabric of the team. These are the core players, while, in business speak, many players are better described as consultants. To use the modern buzzword, this core group creates most of the team culture. Every coach learns quickly that getting the team's core players onside is simply crucial. If your core players become obstructionist and disgruntled, coaching successfully is impossible.

While any team would love to have 22 core players, it is just not possible. Inexperienced youngsters, for instance, are just trying to survive, so usually they can't give much to the team fabric. Players who aren't automatic selections are in the same boat. If you have half a team of core players, you're in good shape. Collingwood had developed a strong leadership core going into the 1990 finals series.

Back then it was mostly example setting on the training track and on the field during matches. Nowadays, players are asked to sit in judgement on the behaviour of their team-mates. Different times, different codes, different expectations obviously apply, but it's interesting to ponder how this group at Collingwood would have handled the few of its members who enjoyed quite an active social life. Would this peer-group scrutiny have quelled these tendencies or would it have created conflict? I think probably the latter.

However, in contrast to the modern era of elected leadership groups spreading the load and responsibility, this was still the time when the appointed captain fulfilled the vast majority of the functions of player leadership, while the coach was the primary group manager and disciplinarian.

Tony Shaw was a fantastic captain who was both respected and liked by his team-mates. As a competitor he was brave, determined and well prepared. It was fitting that he delivered on his statement of intent after the second semi-final by being the unanimous best on ground in the grand final and winning the Norm Smith Medal – the first captain to do so. Not bad for a boy from Reservoir, in the northern suburbs of Melbourne, who for the first half of his career was just the short, slow kid brother of former Magpies captain and Copeland Trophy winner Ray.

No player I coached – or, for that matter, that I've seen – has exceeded Shawy's hugely competitive nature, and no player has got more out of his natural ability. He was a man with incredible mental toughness and composure under pressure, and he never looked flustered, which rubbed off on his team-mates and made him a terrific leader.

To pinch a line from the great Ron Barassi, you should have no pride in your natural ability, because that came from your parents, but you can be extremely proud of making the most of the talent you're born with. Shawy made the most of his natural gifts. We were so fortunate to have him as our captain; his contribution to the premiership was massive.

It was somehow fitting that when the siren sounded, Darren Millane had the footy. The memory endures in my mind of him throwing the ball in the air with absolute joy at having met the challenge. He was now part of a premiership team, yet I suspect he was equally celebrating having survived his own personal challenge of breaking the pain barrier with his broken thumb. And not only did he make it onto the ground, he played very well. For five matches, he'd had to cope with the weekly cycle of taking the plaster off pregame, getting the pain-deadening injection and applying the support strapping; then, after the match, he had to deal with the extreme discomfort before the plaster was reapplied. He not only provided great inspiration, his commitment to the cause subtly convinced his team-mates that we were playing for a prize that was worth the pain and sacrifice.

The other unexpected benefit of the injury was that it forced Darren to play a little more within his limitations. Unless he was a great actor I don't think he was driven by the fear of failure that plagues most of us. His enormous confidence and bravado often overflowed into thinking he was bulletproof and therefore confusing his ambitions with his capabilities. Knowing he had limited use of his broken thumb appeared to quell his temptation to try the low-percentage play and this influenced him to play in a more controlled and more predictable manner. Crazy as it sounds, I really think that during September 1990 his broken thumb didn't detract at all from his on-field performance – it may even have helped. His performance during that finals series will remain the stuff of legend.

As usual, he also led the partying and after a sleepless night was still going strong the next day in the rooms at Victoria Park. About midway through the afternoon he summoned all the players and coaches – plus President Allan McAlister – into the vacant video-editing room under the Ryder Stand, where he proceeded to impersonate everyone there. Allan told me that being invited into this inner-sanctum gathering was a highlight of the whole weekend. No-one in the room will forget Pants hamming up his impersonations and, as he loved to do, enjoying being the centre of attention and entertaining his mates.

It was a tragedy when roughly 12 months later he was killed in a car accident on Queens Road, St Kilda, in the early morning of 7 October 1991. With a blood alcohol level of .322 he was clearly well over the limit and had made a terrible decision to drive. He paid the ultimate price when he drove into the back of a truck, and a young life was cut wastefully short.

Early morning wake-up calls are rarely good news. When the phone rang that day it was a distraught Gubby Allan who, with Allan McAlister, had performed the awful task of identifying the body. When he said the words 'Pants has been killed', for some reason my first thought was that he'd been murdered. The publicity aftermath was huge. I always get a bit miffed by the way the media tends to hijack the passing of public figures. It is family and friends who suffer the long-term loss of a loved one, not the masses who only know the person by acquaintance or reputation and quickly move on.

When our enormously popular Hawthorn team-mate Peter Crimmins died of cancer shortly after the 1976 season, at least it was illness that gradually claimed his life. The sudden accidental death of the indestructible alpha male Darren Millane in his prime – just 26 years of age – was a huge shock. Obviously football was very much a secondary issue, but for our team it was like cutting its heart out.

Pants had many of the traits to be the next Collingwood captain after Tony Shaw. However, while perhaps he would have matured sufficiently into his late 20s to be appointed to the leadership role, I honestly doubt it. A key quality of a captain is to set the example and be beyond reproach, which would have required an extreme and unlikely transformation.

In some ways he reminded me of a couple of former premiership team-mates at Hawthorn, Ian Bremner and Dermott Brereton. They were terrific players to have on your side, strong dominant characters who were always core players in the team. They were never serious contenders for the captaincy, though, because they also had the boyish Peter Pan quality of not really wanting to grow up and seemingly always being on the lookout for a bit of fun. They were great to be around but the necessary conservatism that goes with leadership wasn't their forte and neither was it with Darren Millane.

The whole Millane episode played out over the last weeks of the 1990 season was a one-off, and it was impossible to repeat, as was the incredible tally of 97 goals that Peter Daicos kicked during his fantastic season. Daics was 184 centimetres, and a mainly opportunist, half-forward crumber who played anywhere forward of centre, and he certainly wasn't anchored close to goal as the team's primary avenue of attack. For him to get within a few goals of the century has to be one of the more outstanding exhibitions of goal-scoring in the history of the game.

I would go so far as to say that Daics averaging nearly four goals a game as a non-target forward was of greater value to Collingwood's season in 1990 than the great Hawthorn full-forward Peter Hudson was when averaging over six a game when he kicked his VFL-record-equalling 150 in the Hawks' 1971 premiership year.

The key stat for me was that Daics' 97 goals was 24 per cent of the Magpies' total of 404 for the season, while Huddo's 150 was a massive 40 per cent of Hawthorn's 379 goals that year. Collingwood didn't have the unhealthy dependence on Daics that Hawthorn did with Huddo. This example highlights what I call the conundrum of the gun full-forward – absolute icons of the game like Hudson, Tony Lockett and Jason Dunstall who can only play the spearhead role deep in attack. These stars have been some of the game's biggest names and drawcards. Fans idolise them, the media drools over them and every club would love to have one, but this type of player also totally dominates his team's forward 50 area and the power of his presence seems to force team-mates to look for him every time. My belief, formed over the years as a player, coach and commentator, is that it's unhealthy to have one player kicking more than 30 per cent of your team's goals, and that premierships are almost impossible to win if this figure creeps up to around 40 per cent.

It comes down to every player having a goal-scoring 'break-even'. Of the players mentioned, I would think that Huddo's and Lockett's break-even was five, while Dunstall's was maybe four, because he was a terrific chaser and tackler. He was undoubtedly the best defensive full-forward I've ever seen.

Unlike the big target forwards, Daics could play anywhere around the forward half and didn't dominate the avenue to goal, so his break-even was more like a couple a game. Averaging double this over the season was an absolutely outstanding effort. However, the value of not being overly dependent on our leading goal-kicker was shown in our big wins in the second semi and grand final, when the team scored a total of 30 goals, despite Daics only kicking five. Back in the late 1960s and early 1970s, if Huddo didn't get his five plus for Hawthorn, we'd probably lose.

Daics mightn't have been able to kick the same quantity of goals as Huddo, but his ability to manufacture goals from half chances, on either his left or right foot, was often breathtaking. He wasn't blessed with great speed or stamina but was a footballer with ball skills to die for. Every little kid in a Collingwood jumper dreamt of being able to make the ball talk like the number 35 they flocked to see. His contribution in getting the team up into second place going into the finals was critical, and the handful of cameo goals he kicked at pivotal moments during the finals campaign was invaluable.

The mind races when I think of Daics' many goal-scoring specials, but the match on the Gold Coast at Carrara in round 20 in 1991 against the Brisbane Bears sits firmly at the top. That night, he slotted 13 in just about every possible way a goal can be kicked. The one he scored from next to the behind post at the southern end when he somehow fashioned a bouncing top spinner while being tackled to the ground by his Bears opponent John Gastev was as good as a goal can possibly get.

While Daics kicked 75 goals from 19 games that year, he was playing mostly close to goal as a medium-sized full-forward, so, as far as I was concerned, his break-even was now up around four a game. Repeating his amazing 1990 effort of 97 goals as a floating forward proved to be impossible. It was just too hard; it would have been like winning the lotto in consecutive weeks.

Another performance that was difficult to repeat was Gavin Brown's cameo late in the season as our target full-forward. Browny debuted in 1987 and got into the All-Australian team in 1989 as a wingman. He was flanker size at only 184 centimetres, but in the team's time of need in 1990 he was summoned away from the position that was making him a star into the lower possession role deep in attack. On my break-even goal-scoring criteria Gavin's strong marking for his height, fanatical attack on the footy and terrific second efforts at ground level meant a couple of goals per game were enough to pay his way, even when playing deep forward.

The big bonus was that his fantastic one-on-one competitiveness, speed and strong tackling fitted perfectly with our September team strategy of becoming the best defensive team the game had seen. Over the two finals that earned us a grand final berth, he took 19 marks and kicked nine goals – a mighty effort. As he was knocked unconscious in the quarter-time grand final brawl, we can forgive him for only getting his two-goal break-even that day.

After his arrival at the club, Gavin's nickname quickly became 'Rowdy' because as a personality he was very quiet, and as a player he was much more a doer than a talker. We probably cost him another All-Australian selection in 1990 by pushing him from wing to full-forward, but I'm sure his premiership medallion was more than adequate compensation.

Another important cameo was Gavin Crosisca's performance at centre half-forward during the last three finals. He was never going to be a power forward in the Wayne Carey / Jonathan Brown mould, but while, at 188 centimetres, he was at least approaching key position size, it was his ground-level second effort and tackling pressure that convinced us late in the year to shift him from his normal half-back flank position into the half-forward line to balance the qualities of our other forwards and to help us lock the ball in.

Only a real football nut would be able to name Gavin Crosisca and Gavin Brown (184 centimetres) as the key forwards in the 1990 premiership team. Again, it's hard to think that two players of this height could be more than a stop-gap set-up.

As it transpired, Graham Wright not only moved upfield and took over Browny's wing position, but grabbed his All-Australian spot as well and was runner-up to Tony Liberatore in the 1990 Brownlow Medal by one vote.

Wrighty gave the team speed, run and class. He loved to run and bounce the footy, which made his play extremely penetrating. Run 30 or 40 and kick it 50 was his game style.

The speed of our player group was improved enormously over the pre-season by the arrival of South Australian first-year recruits Scott Russell and Tony Francis. Scott was a terrific runner, ball carrier and ball user, who made such an immediate impact that he became one of the rare players to make an All-Australian team in his first year. Tony had great speed and bored in to the ground-level contest with an urgent aggression. Sometimes this made him rush his decisions – composure under pressure wasn't his strength but he was certainly competitive and determined and used his acceleration speed to chase hard, as well as being a strong and committed tackler. Both players used their core strengths in fantastic grand final performances. Scott was our best link-man, running hard to get the footy and deliver a game-high 25 kicks. Tony won the footy well with 24 disposals and led our match-winning 53 team tackles count with a terrific personal contribution of eight.

The addition of these three speedsters to our midfield group in 1990 was critical in complementing the close-in ball-winning and toughness of Tony Shaw, the creativity of Mick McGuane and the strength and size of Darren Millane.

We also got some great value out of our defensive role players. Craig 'Ned' Kelly was in only his second year with us after being recruited from Norwood, but had quickly become a strong anchor point at centre half-back. He was tough, brave and smart, although a year or two later I must say we had our doubts about his smarts. Ned had a patch playing deeper in defence at full-back where he decided that subtly pinching his opponents around their midriffs would be an annoying tactic worth trying. He got through unscathed doing it to Jason Dunstall and Gary Ablett, but when we discovered that he was intending to employ this tactic against the fearsome Tony Lockett, we seriously advised him that it would be counterproductive. Plugger was one player you didn't want to get angry unless you were certain big Damian Monkhorst was at your shoulder. Ned took our advice and lived to fight another day.

Off the field he has blown everyone out of the water. In the mid-1990s, when Ricky Nixon's Flying Start group was pioneering player management and had formed the Club 10 brand to market a group of the game's biggest stars, the AFL was concerned about where this new world might lead and wanted to support a rival that was more onside with footy's head office. Through Collingwood contacts, and with Gubby Allan's help, this was the opportunity for Craig – who was nearing the end of his playing career – to launch the very successful management, promotion and marketing company Elite Sports Properties. As I've mentioned, he was drafted in 1986 but didn't come to Collingwood until the 1989 season. I always remind him that his now multi-millionaire status could have come earlier if not for those few years of indecision.

Shane Morwood and Gavin Crosisca (for most of the season) were our attacking defenders – mostly our defence was a shut-down-your-opponent type bunch. Mick Gayfer was the ultimate human blanket, and while we seriously didn't want the ball in his hands, he had the great ability to quell the influence of top-line opponents such as Tim Watson and Brett Heady.

Shane Kerrison, Alan Richardson and Jamie Turner were tough, aggressive, no-frills defenders who could be relied on to give no peace to their usually quicker and more highly skilled opponents. Michael Christian gave us defensive height and could run and create if used in that type of role; Ron McKeown was our best full-back against the hard leading spearheads and Denis Banks was the 30-plus veteran who gave the back group stability and confidence.

As I've said, Denis played most of his career as a forward but on the suggestion of our chairman of selectors, Ron Richards, was pushed back into defence to finish his footy. He was a footballer you were happy to have on your side: one, because he was a tough and reliable on-field competitor, and two, because Banksy could handle himself in the boxing ring and had the well-earned reputation of being someone not to be messed with around the night-spots as well.

Darren Millane and big Damian Monkhorst had the same

reputation, which was certainly helpful on the footy field battle-ground when threats of violence to opponents might be considered more than bluff. While I can't remember Darren – or Monkie for that matter – ever hurting anyone on the field, one match against bitter rivals Carlton at the MCG in the late '80s proved to me that there was no bluff with Banksy.

In a hectic passage of play during the third quarter the Blues' David Rhys-Jones split Banksy's eyebrow with a flying elbow. There was no immediate remonstration, but later in the quarter, just in front of our coaching box in the MCC Members area, as Rhys bent to pick up a ground-level ball, Banksy came in from the side and hit him with a perfectly timed round-arm right cross. It was lights out for the Carlton winger and a two-week suspension for our half-back. One of our conditioning coaches, Ray Giles, used to get heavyweight boxer Dave Russell in to spar with any of the players game enough to stand opposite him in the ring. Dave would only ever give his sparring match-up a short sharp jab to the ribs if they got cheeky, but the threat of the damage he could do was always there. Banksy was always one of the first in the ring, and both Dave and Ray formed the view that he could have been a very good fighter if he'd wanted to give it a go. I'm sure David Rhys-Jones would strongly agree.

For the last month of the 1990 season, our forward-line height came from one of our ruckmen playing deep forward and from Craig Starcevich playing as a tall half-forward flanker. Craig was 193 centi-metres but wasn't a strong-marking power forward. What he had was enormous stamina which was hard for the opposition to match with an opponent of similar height.

Apart from Peter Daicos, our other medium half-forward was Doug Barwick. He came across from Fitzroy in 1988 and was the typical half-forward flanker of that era. Dangerous anywhere forward of centre, he could score from long range and kicked a valuable 36 goals for the season.

While the 1990 Collingwood premiership team had a few house-hold names who will stand the test of time as AFL Hall of Famers, ultimately the flag was won because when the crunch came, all the players performed their assigned roles, tackled like maniacs, and for those final few weeks they found that elusive physical and mental zone from which optimum performance can flow.

Sustained excellence is what we all aspire to, but finding your best under the often-debilitating pressure of knockout games late in a final series is an achievement to savour. The latter was the challenge that the Collingwood playing group successfully mastered in 1990.

28

HANGOVER

A premiership hangover that leads to overconfidence and
complacency will do it every time.

Every September, a team wins the flag and the following year that
same club embarks on the challenge of repeating the feat. Over the
decades this has proved to be beyond most teams, or more particularly
clubs, because inevitably the same 22 players never contest consecutive grand finals.

For a whole lot of reasons, during the four decades since I played
my first game in 1969 back-to-back premierships have been extremely
rare. Only Richmond in 1973–1974, Carlton 1981–1982, Essendon
1984–1985, Hawthorn 1988–1989 and Adelaide 1997–1998 have
been able to back up and win again. The Brisbane Lions in 2001,
2002 and 2003 is the only 'three-peat' since Melbourne in the late
1950s, so winning consecutive premierships is clearly no simple task.

However, failure to even make the finals the year after holding up
the premiership cup is the ultimate fall from grace. That was the extent
of the Magpies' demise in the 12 months following the 1990 triumph.

There are a multitude of reasons why back-to-back premierships
are as rare as hen's teeth. Sometimes it's simply that fitting every
finicky piece of the premiership jigsaw puzzle perfectly together
doesn't happen two years in a row. To name a couple of examples,
great teams like North Melbourne of the 1970s and Geelong of recent
years haven't been able to go back to back. North played in five consecutive grand finals from 1974 to 1978, won in 1975 and 1977, but
couldn't win two in a row, while Geelong's absolute dominance from

2007 to 2009 could easily have netted them three consecutive flags. Instead, the wins in 2007 and 2009 were sandwiched around a blown opportunity in 2008, when the Cats' terrible inaccuracy (11.23), combined with Hawthorn's fantastic conversion (18.7), cost them the elusive three in a row.

Sometimes it's just that a club finds a patch of elite form at the right time. Essendon's win in 1993 came from a late-season surge when, of the Bombers' 13 home-and-away wins that got them to the top of the ladder, eight came from the final 10 rounds. They didn't get close the year before or after.

Alternatively, sometimes a team has one outstanding season. Carlton won the premiership easily in 1995, losing only two games, but, like Essendon, didn't make the grand final in the preceding year or the one after.

Occasionally, a rare burst of elite-level September form can win a premiership. That was what Collingwood achieved in 1990. During my time at the club, we never got into the last four again.

When a team fails to back up after winning the flag, the old chestnut of the dreaded premiership hangover is readily trotted out as the reason why. While premiership success can blunt a team's hunger and diminish its work ethic, mostly the reasons are much more practical and physical – such as injuries, drop in form of individual players and other clubs improving more quickly. Anyway, it's a false assumption that the best team of the year goes on to win the flag. Hawthorn in 2012, Collingwood 2011 and St Kilda 2009 were the best teams of those years, but failed at the crucial final step.

However, I must admit that the hangover certainly bit Collingwood hard after 1990. Breaking the club's 32-year premiership drought – and the euphoria that created – made us self-satisfied and soft: in preparation, discipline and competitive drive. I'd played in seven grand finals for four premierships with Hawthorn, but was ill-prepared to manage the aftermath well enough to get the team back in the emotional and physical neutral starting point that was essential if we were going to begin the new campaign successfully.

Maybe it was beyond human intervention. The hype around Victoria Park after the 1990 victory was so over the top it was ridiculous.

Talk flowed freely of the players being regarded as immortals, because they'd conquered the Colliwobbles; there was similar talk that the coach had the job forever.

Yes, in the euphoric atmosphere after the Magpies won the 1990 flag, Allan McAlister pronounced me coach for life. Five years later I got the sack. I guess all this means is that, for murder, life is 20 years, while in footy coaching it's five ...

It was further evidence that there should be an amnesty on anything said in the 24 hours following a grand final. For both winners and losers the exaggerated emotions can lead to statements that in the clear light of day are best unsaid.

That my coach-for-life status was gradually voided during the five years after 1990 was indicative that very little September success was forthcoming at Collingwood after the drought-breaking victory. While we were a very competitive team for the five years from 1988 to 1992, every year apart from 1990 our finals performances were failures.

The five home-and-away seasons were all pretty good. Of the 110 minor-round games during this time, we won 72 with two draws, and, leading into the finals series finished respectively second, fifth, second, seventh and third, but only in 1990 did we manage to win a final.

Consequently, history has judged this team as one of the worst flag winners of recent decades. Obviously long-term greatness requires longevity of excellence and this key aspect didn't follow, but in the final three games of 1990 the Collingwood team was a very worthy premiership-standard unit that demolished its opponents in a manner which has rarely been achieved before or since.

A 59-point victory in the qualifying final replay, 63 points in the second semi and 48 in the grand final, in the process outscoring our three opponents 49 goals to 21 – these winning margins are testament to an extremely dominant team. The Collingwood players were not 'lucky' to win the premiership; in fact, they were as clearly superior to their opposition late in the 1990 finals campaign – the first under the AFL banner – as any team since.

The best defensive team wins the majority of premierships but an over-the-top intense defensive effort is hard to replicate season after season. Collingwood's success in 1990 was so heavily reliant on outstanding defensive pressure that when our tackling level dropped, so did the team performance. Also, we were dependent on two medium-sized forwards, Peter Daicos and Gavin Brown, to lead our attack, and the 150-goal tally they kicked between them in the premiership year was unlikely to be repeated – unfortunately that's how it turned out.

Collingwood was not necessarily the best team of 1990, although six Magpies players made the All-Australian team. A lot of our players had career-best years, which is a common denominator for teams that have one outstanding season. This proves yet again that individual and team performance go hand in hand. Most footballers eventually realise that it's much easier to play well in a good team. Therefore if they invest in making the team better, it will be easier for each player to perform his individual role. This is a great life lesson from elite team sport.

This is what coaches sell to the individual to commit himself to the team cause. Individuals will invest in the group goals once they believe they'll receive the benefit from being part of a success-ful team. Achieving the status of a premiership player is a powerful individual reward.

That is the coaching sell in the build-up phase to a new season. However, once you've reached the pinnacle, if you don't quickly dismiss the comfortable post-premiership feeling, it can lead to com-placency in preparation or a waning competitive drive. It's hard to argue that in both these key areas we dropped a few notches after the 1990 premiership.

Certainly, the skinfold callipers measuring body fat got a big workout when pre-season training resumed in 1991. The scales were no better. Many players reported in for pre-season training in very poor condition. One measurement that sticks in my mind was James Manson weighing in a whopping 11 kilograms above his normal weight. He wasn't alone – Craig Kelly reported back to pre-season a troubling 6 kilos over. Many of the Collingwood players suffered from a poor fitness base at the start of the pre-season, which was a good indicator of the team's collective lack of hunger. As coach I failed to get the players as committed or driven as they needed to be, and the fanatical pressure footy they played to win the premiership had been left behind in the post-match celebrations.

Because of this experience I became further convinced about what I call the 'tip of the iceberg' theory. When we see an iceberg only the tip is visible above the water but we know there's a gigantic chunk of ice below the waterline. Attitude and behavioural issues have a similar dynamic. If you observe symptoms or signs of a problem, you can be pretty certain a bigger version lurks unseen beneath the surface.

From a low base at the start of the pre-season, our conditioning coach, Mark McKeon, had worked hard to get the players in shape. Supervised training went well enough and then in early February came our first game against another club. We journeyed north for a Sunday pre-season fixture against the lowly Brisbane Bears, who'd finished bottom the previous year, winning only four games.

We were physically ready to compete but I'm afraid to say we were nowhere near ready emotionally to embrace a contest. After the heady atmosphere of the previous premiership-winning game of the season before, travelling to play in the early afternoon of a hot, extremely humid Brisbane day was more a chore than a chance to hone our game for the upcoming season. For all of us – including me, I have to say – there seemed little to gain. The lazy attitude that plagued us for the next six months was taking hold.

Our dressing area was in the small Gabba cricketers' rooms in the old Northern Stand, with the grass greyhound track still circling the pear-shaped cricket oval. Victoria Park or the MCG it was not. This was well before the redevelopment that gradually took place in the decade after the Bears shifted to Brisbane from the Gold Coast in 1994. The conditions and surrounds were certainly not conducive to getting the Collingwood players turned on to play, and our level of competitiveness was nowhere near sufficient.

Fitness can easily be tested and measured; attitude cannot. Winning ways have to become a permanent habit – they aren't some-thing you can pick and choose on a whim. The first on-field indicator of the team's competitive attitude in the new season pointed to the misguided belief that top form could be turned on like a tap. As we waited to play this mundane pre-season game I can remember looking around the small rooms and the grassed area out the front and seeing a few of the players lounging around reading the Sunday papers. They seemed so nonchalant that I should have instantly recognised this tip-of-the-iceberg moment. It was the one and only time I've ever seen newspapers being read pre-game in an AFL dressing room. Picking through the *Footy Record* is commonplace during the waiting down-time; that's very different, though, because at least it's footy-related. Reading the gossip pages or the financial news isn't a good way to focus on the heavy contact contest that any game against another club will provide.

The game was a disaster and the Bears totally stitched us up. The contest certainly wasn't a chore for the home team and beating the reigning premiers was a challenge they were very much up for. Ability is never enough if effort is lacking – this was the moral of the day and these were my angry words at the time. Later that season we again went north to play the Bears – this time on a Saturday night at the Gold Coast – and won by over 100 points. That was a bit more indicative of the talent difference between the two teams in 1991.

While I did plenty of bad-cop yelling and cajoling over the next few months, it largely fell on deaf ears. The comfortable warm and fuzzy feelings of October 1990 had depleted the team's determination and drive, both in terms of preparing and competing. Everyone, including the players, thought we were trying our hardest, but really we were subconsciously just going through the motions.

What I do firmly believe is that when a team possesses a competitive edge over their opposition, the placebo effect of belief and hope is just as powerful as the physical benefit. But a competitive edge is an elusive and slippery commodity that can easily be lost, as opponents catch up and then surpass previous best practice. A premiership hangover that leads to overconfidence and complacency will do it every time.

In the desperate search for a new competitive edge and the need to find a better way, recruiting improved talent is always part of the process. We thought we got a good break immediately after the 1990 season when one of our fringe youngsters, Terry Keays, was recruited by Richmond in exchange for pick four in the national draft. We were delighted that Jason McCartney, a boom teenager from Nhill in western Victoria who'd dominated at under-18 level as a strong marking centre half-forward, was still available at pick four. We knew Jason was a keen Essendon supporter, so the day after the draft some of the Collingwood hierarchy decided to pay him due respect by hiring a plane to Nhill to visit the McCartney family and welcome them to the Magpies. The travel party was Gubby Allan, Allan McAlister, our recruiting manager, Gerard Sholly, and yours truly. None of us were that keen on jumping on the light plane, but it seemed a better option than a very lengthy six-hour road trip. We were comforted that our single pilot transport had twin propeller engines. In this circumstance two engines seemed much better than one.

Our nerves were calmed further after we arrived safely and were enjoying the warm hospitality at the McCartneys'. Then, a monstrous thunderstorm swept through the town – strong winds, heavy rain, claps of thunder, lightning bolts, the whole deal. The storm blew over before we headed to the small airport for the flight home, and as we boarded the light plane, the pilot informed us that the bad weather was now between us and Melbourne. So began one of the scariest hours of my entire life.

The pilot had to continually alter course to avoid the worst of the storm. It's one thing to be on the ground when a bad storm hits, but being in the air in the middle of the darkness with lightning flashing all around us was no fun at all. It was a very quiet, thoughtful and terrified little group huddled in the small aircraft, hoping like hell the pilot knew what he was doing. It also crossed my mind more than once that Jason would have to turn out to be another Dermott Brereton or Stephen Kernahan to justify us going through the anguish we were experiencing. When the clouds disappeared and we saw clear skies through to the bright lights of Melbourne, the relief and joy was almost like winning another premiership.

Jason never became the champion power forward we hoped he would be and never justified his extremely high junior ranking. Maybe it was part of the karma balance. If the September footy gods shone on us in 1990 they seemed to desert us thereafter. Maybe they too were suffering from the premiership hangover that afflicted the Magpies the following year.

Over the summer break after the 1990 season, both grand finalists – us and Essendon – slipped behind the competition pace-setters. The West Coast Eagles of 1991 were vastly improved and finished on top, winning 19 games with a percentage of 162 – an outstanding season. Hawthorn regained the mojo that had got them to seven consecutive grand finals from 1983 to 1989 and won 16 games to finish second. Geelong was the other big improver, finishing third, also with 16 wins.

After starting the new season reasonably well and having three wins and a draw after five rounds, we then lost our next six games before regrouping to win nine of our next ten. Still in contention leading into round 22, we travelled to Kardinia Park needing to beat the third-placed Cats to make the finals, but we were beaten by 41 points. The memorable and well-celebrated premiership win of 1990 was now only a distant memory.

If you're not improving compared to the opposition, you're going backwards. That was Collingwood's fate after our premiership win in 1990.

Living in the moment was something we failed to do. Being either overly buoyed or overly dejected by past events is a big distraction when you need to be totally focused on the tasks at hand. It was a learning experience for us all. If I ever coached another premiership team, I hoped I'd be better prepared to manage the aftermath and prevent the symptoms of the dreaded premiership hangover infiltrating the ensuing seasons.

29

THE WINDOW IS CLOSING

I'm not really superstitious, but our 1993 season, which started
so well, finished very badly and some strange things happened
along the way.

The 1991 season was terrible for Collingwood. On-field it was disappointing. We started as reigning premiers and dropped out of
contention to finish seventh, two points out of the finals. Then in
early October came the tragic death of Darren Millane. On the field
the group had fallen from the top of the tree and then suffered the
shock loss of a popular and talented team-mate. It was a crossroads for
the Collingwood Football Club.

Competitive sport teaches resilience. In the world of the AFL,
losing at least every third week is about as good as it gets, which
means disappointment and failure is part of playing footy. Football
has helped train me to cope with this inevitable emotional roller-
coaster of elation some days and, quite often, despair on others. The
fresh starting point of the week-to-week and then season-to-season
cycle gives us the hope that no matter how drab the present is, the
future can be better.

However, it isn't normal for a team-mate and friend to be acciden-
tally and suddenly killed in the prime of his life. Fortunately, it's an
extremely rare occurrence but it also means there's no precedent in
terms of coping with the tragedy and its repercussions. The club permanently retired the Millane number 42 Collingwood jumper. That
was the easy and respectful thing to do. How we handled the situation around the team – firstly, when the players resumed training a

month or two after his death, and eventually when the season started the following year – was partly my responsibility.

My view was that the human side, the loss of the son, brother and friend, was by far the biggest issue. Collingwood losing the talents of a key player was insignificant in comparison. So I concluded that there was very little to be done or said. Short and long term, we dismissed any thought of using the passing of Darren Millane as a kind of perverse 'motivation'. To do that would have entailed the tackiness of confusing footy with life and death, which should always be avoided.

I doubt I ever mentioned Darren's name to the team as a whole at any time after his death. Footy clubs back in the 1990s didn't have player welfare people to care for the well-being of their players, but I'm sure football manager Gubby Allan provided his usual sympathetic ear to anyone who needed somebody to share their thoughts with.

One player who reacted in a positive manner was Mick McGuane. The death of his much-admired team-mate and friend stimulated Mick to dedicate the 1992 season to Darren, and he embarked on a torturous pre-season fitness campaign. He was not a naturally gifted athlete, but with a career-best condition base added to his terrific talents as a footballer, the result was a fantastic season. He won the Copeland Trophy as club champion and made the All-Australian team.

We were able to recruit a top-notch full-back when Gary Pert moved across from Fitzroy, and the future Collingwood CEO had a very good season, finishing second to Mick in the club championship.

1992 was a very tight year. Under the final-six system in place at the time, Carlton missed the finals by percentage behind sixth-placed St Kilda despite winning 14 games. There wasn't much between the top bunch that year.

We lost one of our core players midway through the season against the Eagles in Perth when Craig Kelly went down with a bad knee injury which ended his year. By most measurements the team had a very good season, winning 16 games and coming third, only finishing behind top-placed Geelong on percentage. We'd won the same number of home-and-away matches in 1990.

The bad news was that despite only missing top spot on percentage, we weren't guaranteed a double chance. Under this finals system, which only lasted three years from 1991 to 1993, as we'd finished third we'd play St Kilda, who finished sixth.

So our assignment was a knockout elimination final against the Saints at Waverley Park. The match took place on a beautiful sunny spring day perfect for the marking prowess of high-quality power forwards, and we were confronted by two of the very best – Tony Lockett and Stewart Loewe. Ron McKeown did well to boot five for us as we managed only 12 goals and went down by eight points.

We were dominated by the St Kilda big forward duo. Between Lockett and Loewe they took 18 marks. 'Plugger' kicked five goals, which I guess was only average for him, and Loewe got two. The great Robert Harvey also ran amok, which gave the two power forwards plenty of supply.

All the good big marking forwards cause a lot of angst for coaches. It's the conundrum of the gun full-forward. As I've said, if you have one in your team you're concerned about being too dependent on him; however, if one is on the other team you worry, plot and plan how to stop him.

Tony Lockett caused me more heartache than most. Apart from his efforts in the 1992 elimination final, three years later with the Sydney Swans his last quarter in the final home-and-away game cost us eighth spot on the ladder. In between, at the end of 1994 we almost recruited Plugger into the Magpies jumper, a footy department initiative that was vetoed at the last minute by the Collingwood board.

While overall our 1992 season was quite good, in the big picture we were an average offensive team and had lost the fanatical tackling pressure that won us the premiership two years before. On grand final day in 1990 the team laid 52 effective tackles – an incredibly high total for that era – but in the elimination final loss to the Saints we laid only 18. Our competitive edge in out-pressuring our opponents had disappeared. As well, our magical goal-kicking strike weapon Peter Daicos had reached the veteran stage and was nearing the end. Replacing his unique talents was going to be an impossible task.

The reason premiership windows close is because champions are extremely rare; therefore continually replacing retiring champions with players as good is very difficult. In fact, the draft system is designed to help the bottom teams, who get the early picks, and to disadvantage those up the top, who, all things being equal, get the less talented later selections.

Of course, this equalisation mechanism only works if the selected order of talent on draft day remains the same as the teenage draftees grow into mature footballers. History clearly tells us that it does not, so drafting remains a judgemental art rather than a precise science. In any case, replacing champions with champions is rarely possible. Hawthorn in the 1980s was an exception, which partly explains the club's decade of dominance. As an example close to my heart, Peter Knights and I retired at the end of 1985 and the following year Jason Dunstall and John Platten emerged as great players.

At the end of 1992, with the afterglow of our premiership still recent, the football department was making all the footy decisions – in contrast to the Plugger situation in 1994. Gubby and myself, and always supported by Allan McAlister, almost had carte blanche. During 1992 a very drawn-out recruiting operation had been launched, a complicated series of events that would eventually get Nathan Buckley into a Collingwood jumper.

It took another 12 months for Collingwood to finally secure his services after a saga that saw him spend the intervening season with the Brisbane Bears. That he went on to become such a wonderful player was no surprise to me after I'd seen him play for Port Adelaide in the SANFL finals in 1992. It was no secret because Port coach John Cahill, a former coach of Collingwood, had already declared Buckley to be the best young player he'd ever coached. With this extravagant wrap from the very experienced Cahill, seeing Buckley play live just once was enough to convince me he was a rare talent. All I said to Gub was, 'Get him if you can.' From then on Gub was like a dog with a bone and the chase was on.

Gubby was a terrific recruiter. Like me, he had a goal-oriented Enforcer personality type and would stubbornly persevere through the obstacles and find ways and means and people to get the result he was after. If he didn't succeed in a recruiting chase, he treated it as a personal affront.

We worked well together for many years, partly because we shared the view that the end justified the means. Having now finished my footy club involvement, I have to admit that this mentality of succeeding at any cost, the callous ruthless attitude of the younger me, does play on my conscience a bit when I reflect back.

Coaches and club management went into the 1993 season with the firm belief that Buckley would play that season with the Brisbane Bears, the club he was zoned to, and would then somehow come to Collingwood the following year. How that would happen was only known by a select few and I was happy not being in on all the fine detail.

Going into the 1993 season, we were still a very good team and started like one, winning our first three. This included a victory at Victoria Park by 10 points over Geelong – who'd been runners-up the year before. That was a game to remember: two great forwards in a goal-scoring shoot-out. Gary Ablett kicked seven for the Cats and Peter Daicos got eight for Collingwood. Actually, Daics' first opponent on the day was Steve Hocking, who happened to be the player who spread my nose all over my face in retaliation after the infamous Bruns incident. Seeing my assailant getting the run-around was a bit of a bonus.

It was also some coincidence that these two freakish talents had a day out together to thrill the crowd. Gee, they were fantastic to watch when they were on song, but they also had the similarity of being highly skilled naturals who didn't eagerly embrace the intense conditioning work necessary for most mere mortals.

This match was also the last time Daics produced his goalscoring magic. We knew his career was nearing the end but after watching his exhibition that day no-one at the ground, including me, could have foreseen that he'd only play three more games that season, which would turn out to be his last. A bad knee injury to an ageing body ruined what would be his final campaign.

Round four, against St Kilda, also at Victoria Park, was memorable for very different reasons. This was the day the Saints' indigenous star Nicky Winmar reacted angrily to being abused about his colour and race by leaving the oval with his jumper pulled up, pointing proudly at his exposed dark skin. I think the majority of the taunts were from spectators over the fence, but quite feasibly they could have come from opponents as well. It wouldn't have been that abnormal back then.

This incident was a catalyst for a few things. For me, it meant a rethink about my belief at the time that what happened on the field should stay on the field. And that on the footy field battleground, verbal abuse was open slather. 'Normal' is simply what happens all the time. In my playing days, there were no rules or moral issues governing what was said on the field. I wasn't an unprovoked sledger myself and never heard much racial abuse in my time. I admit to once calling North Melbourne's indigenous rover Jim Krakouer a little black so and so, although that was only after Jimmy threatened to punch me in the nose in protection of his less aggressive brother Phil.

Gradually, over the ensuing years, an AFL racial and religious vilification code was put in place and enforced with heavy sanctions. It took me a while to embrace the need, but we all have to learn to change with the times to be more inclusive of minorities. In the process we've learnt to choose our words very carefully so as not to offend. The term 'aboriginal' has been replaced by 'indigenous', and nowadays any use of the abbreviated term 'abo' is totally repugnant. We've also learnt that we should be very careful about ever saying 'they' about anything remotely racially based, and that you don't have to be a racist to make an embarrassing racist comment.

The graphic photo of Winmar's act of proud defiance against the Collingwood crowd went straight to the front page of the daily news-papers and it became football's main talking point the following week. Enter Allan McAlister. Now Allan was a terrific support to me when I coached under his presidency, but he did relish his media profile and basically I don't think he could pronounce the words 'no comment'. He was always available to give his views on almost any subject.

When asked in a press interview the following week about his views on the Winmar/Aborigines-in-football issue, Allan replied with words to the effect that everything would be okay if they acted like white people. It was an off-the-cuff, badly worded remark. While Allan never showed any sign of having a racist attitude, his unfortunate throwaway line started a firestorm that had many repercussions.

Firstly, it started a massive public relations campaign to repair the damage to both Allan's and Collingwood's reputation. A big part of that effort was our agreement to play a reconciliation game against an indigenous All-Stars team in Darwin during the following pre-season. It took place at 1 pm on a hot, humid, sunny February afternoon. The conditions were oppressive in the shaded coach's area. Out on the field in the boiling sun it was stifling and our players were up against the enthusiastically supported and highly motivated All-Stars team. They must have felt a bit like the Washington Generals being the bunnies for the Harlem Globetrotters. For us, winning was secondary to surviving the debilitating conditions, and hopefully our involvement would help weaken any suggestion that Collingwood was a racist club.

At half-time I walked into the shower area to find our Tasmanian-born winger Graham Wright sitting almost semi-conscious on the floor. He had cold water pouring down onto his head in an unsuccessful attempt to revive himself from his exhausted state. If we'd put him back on the field in the second half, I seriously think we might have killed him. All things considered, as former prime minister and part-time Collingwood supporter Paul Keating might have said, this was a loss we had to have. We did our duty, we played, we survived, and got home to Melbourne otherwise unscathed.

A more immediate consequence of the Winmar incident and Allan's inflammatory comments was the reaction of a Darwin indigenous entertainer by the name of John Kelly. He performed the indigenous ritual of 'pointing the bone' at the Collingwood Football Club, which he said would suffer from the curse. When Allan quickly apologised for his remarks, Kelly removed the jinx. However, events that followed would indicate that his application technique was much better than his removal methods.

I'm not really superstitious, but our 1993 season, which started so well, finished very badly and some strange things happened along the way. One such thing was a nasty, completely untrue rumour that I was having an affair with our centre half-back Michael Christian's wife, Clare. While the Christians were separated, to the best of my knowledge Clare was living back in Perth, and although there wasn't a skerrick of truth to the innuendo, it ran rampant as juicy gossip normally does. It persisted all season and from the comments over the fence at odd Collingwood games in recent years it still does. Eventually, I even had a word to Chrisso to make absolutely sure he knew the rumours had no substance. We had a laugh about how something so untrue could spread, but it was no laughing matter. I could imagine how often our players were asked about this subject and what was going on with their coach. It was an unnecessary distraction.

The most notable change in our team fortunes came in round 10 against North Melbourne at Victoria Park. We went into the match travelling well and up near the top of the ladder with a 7–2 win–loss record. By the final siren we'd had the stuffing completely knocked out of us. Getting thrashed on your home territory by 83 points can have a disastrous effect, and if you want to apportion some blame to the John Kelly 'pointing-the-bone' jinx, there happened to be an indigenous Kangaroos player who destroyed us that day.

Adrian McAdam was his name and he was a real shooting star. It was his debut season and the 22-year-old from central Australia had kicked 29 goals in his first five games to take the game by storm. His opening salvo was up there with the best ever. Coming into the match we knew he was dangerous, and after he'd kicked nine goals and stitched up our reliable shut-down defender Michael Gayfer and a few other Collingwood backmen along the way, we now knew from first-hand experience how talented he was. After his bag against us he'd kicked an incredible 38 goals in his first six games. We were a bit unlucky, because like a shooting star that shoots across the sky before disappearing, McAdam was dazzling for half of his first season and then burnt out very quickly. He was gone from North after three seasons and only 36 games.

Another 22-year-old joined the Kangaroos' picnic that day but this was merely an entrée for the most valuable footballer I have ever seen – the dynamic and wonderfully talented Wayne Carey. His rare combination of raw power, aggression, agility and ball skills was going to dominate footy for the rest of the decade. Wayne had the perfect build for the hard-running power-forward role. At 192 centimetres, he had the height, but importantly the distribution was ideal for a footballer: long body and relatively short legs. That helped create the waddling gait that spawned his 'Duck' nickname but it also gave him a low centre of gravity and a fantastic balance that complemented his immense strength.

It has been said for a long time, and I agree, that centre half-forward is the hardest position in footy, and if you have a gun one, it provides enormous impetus for a team. There are plenty of examples during my time in football: Richmond with Royce Hart across half-forward in the late 1960s and early 1970s, Hawthorn with Dermott Brereton in the 1980s, Carlton with Stephen Kernahan around the same period, and the Brisbane Lions with Jonathan Brown in the early 2000s.

An average day at the footy for Carey was 20 disposals, 10 marks and three goals; he was a match-winning colossus. In my time in footy no player has won his team as many games as Wayne did for the Kangaroos. I think 1993 was his breakout season and this round 10 fixture at Victoria Park – when he made our tall defenders look like boys on a man's job – was, as an opposition coach, frightening to watch. It was also embarrassing for his opponents, who were made to look totally second-rate.

In coming months and years, Carey overwhelming the opposition would become quite normal, but watching it happen on our own turf at Victoria Park, on top of the McAdam goal-scoring exhibition and the overall thrashing that North had handed out, sparked an angry reaction on my part. The helpful principle of the coach acting the opposite of the rest of the world was thrown out the door during the following days.

The team left the field to the abuse of the shattered Collingwood faithful, and as the players slowly trudged into the dressing rooms, confidence and morale was rock bottom. All this after an isolated poor couple of hours of bad form – remember our record was still a more than creditable seven wins, three losses for the season. This was what I should have emphasised to the forlorn players sitting in front of me. Instead, I made the mistake of sharing the anger of the disappointed Magpie supporters, vented my spleen and gave them an almighty spray. The players left my post-match tirade even more dejected than they'd been as they walked off the oval.

We then followed up with a week of punishment-type training. The next week we went to the MCG to face Melbourne, with the added purpose of redeeming ourselves from the North debacle. The mental doubts were nagging away: was the week before a one-off or had we lost our top-team mojo? The Demons had won only three of their nine games so they weren't in the cream of the competition, but our worst fears were realised when they blitzed us from the very beginning with a seven goal to three first quarter. They increased the lead to six goals at half-time and then finally to eight at the final siren. It was another huge blow to the team's self-belief, which had taken such a big hit the week before.

Actually, we were a bit unlucky – another pointing the bone consequence? – because another shooting star got us that day when Allen Jakovich matched Adrian McAdam's nine goals the week before. Jakovich only played 54 games before fading from the scene, but he was very good on his day and unfortunately for us this was one of them.

It was a terrible day all round. In a case of very bad timing, I allowed myself to be miked up in the coach's box for a documentary being produced on my footy career. As part of the project a long-distance camera was trained on me to record my reactions. What transpired on that disappointing day at the MCG, coming on top of the North belting, happened to make it one of the more stressful matches I've coached. It was embarrassing to view the footage when a bad day in the coach's box was there to be watched and heard. Talk about your frailties being there for all to see.

After two games and two big losses, the mood in the Collingwood dressing rooms would be even bleaker than seven days before. What to do, what to say? That's always the quandary when the final siren sounds. As I started the long walk down to the rooms, with a few minutes to get my thoughts together my mind was buzzing overtime. I can't say that I'd formulated any clear strategy, but at least I had the good sense to buy some time and not let the angst and frustration I was feeling lead to another outburst. What I said, however, was not much better. On the spur of the moment, I announced, 'I'll see you all at Victoria Park at six o'clock tomorrow morning.'

There is no logical reason to call an early morning training session the day after a game. Clearly, it was punishment for playing poorly the previous two weeks. It was also confirmation to the players that their performance had become sub-standard. While this might have delivered a fightback from the team, it also had the potential to sap their confidence and self-esteem even further. The Colling-wood players had had two very poor weeks and so had their coach. In a 20-round season, we'd left the MCG after the Melbourne defeat with a still reasonable record of six wins, four losses at the midpoint of the year. Thereafter, though, we went 5–5 to miss the finals by one win. We were able to beat the poor teams but became uncom-petitive against the competition pace-setters Essendon, Carlton and North Melbourne.

That fortnight turned out to be a turning point for the status of the team. In 1992 and early 1993 we were of top-four standard, which put us in premiership contention. However, after this couple of down weeks we never reached that elite level again. We were still competi-tive but stuck around the middle of the ladder. We'd reached the peak of Mount Everest in 1990 and now we were struggling even to reach base camp.

There are many reasons for Collingwood's demise during this period, but the best way of learning from your experiences is firstly to analyse your own individual role. I now look back on the way I handled the aftermath of rounds 10 and 11 of 1993 with much regret. It was not good management. What players want and need from the coach is a plan to be better, not just abuse and punishment when they play badly. I allowed the Enforcer in my personality profile to overwhelm the Thinker, and that only served to inflame an already difficult situation.

In the Dr Jauncey personality profiling terminology, I was heavy in both the Enforcer mode and the Thinker mode. The Enforcer part made me egotistical, success-driven, goal-oriented, stubborn, in need of feeling in control, and meant I had a tendency to get angry when threatened. The Thinker part was the plotter and planner that acted on well-reasoned logic, not on the emotion of the moment.

I was in my eighth season at the Magpies in 1993 and consequently felt total ownership and responsibility for the team performance. When 'my' team bombed out badly, my Enforcer mode took over. I got angry and blamed the players for 'letting me down'.

What I should have done was not react to the post-match dis-appointment, but instead go to my Thinker mode and realise that team morale was badly wounded and that empathy with the players' feelings would have been more beneficial. Sometimes an isolated really bad performance needs to be quickly dismissed and left behind, so the panic of being badly beaten doesn't become infectious. A principle I came to firmly believe in was not saying much to the players straight after the match, but then a day or two later giving calm, honest feedback, and then quickly shifting to future plans and training aims. Of course, principle is always easier than practice.

I was a younger, more aggressive coach at Collingwood than I was in my later job at the Lions, but the internal conflict between my Enforcer and Thinker tendencies was a constant battle throughout my coaching years. My Enforcer qualities got on top of my Thinker ones more often towards the end of both of my coaching stints, which has led me to believe that five or six years – maybe seven at the most – was my optimum length of term as an AFL coach.

30

BUCKLEY IN, SHAW OUT

I wasn't totally convinced he was going to become the all-time
great he turned out to be.

I'm not sure that any one person knows all the details and machina-
tions of how Nathan Buckley got to Collingwood, including Bucks
himself. It came out of an era in which draft practices and salary cap
guidelines weren't anything like as strictly regimented as they were to
become in football's rapidly approaching new world of professionalism.

Late in 2012, the Adelaide Crows and now Sydney Swans forward
Kurt Tippett got 11 weeks suspension for his part in breaking the
AFL rules concerning draft tampering and salary cap rorting. Adelaide got fined and lost draft choices, while Crows officials Steven
Trigg and Phil Harper got six months and two months respectively.
Tippett's manager, Peter Blucher, had his player agent accreditation
suspended for 12 months. How the player and manager got a greater
penalty than the officials who set the deal up is beyond me, but that's
another story. Suffice to say that over the years the AFL boys' club has
always tended to look after its own.

Judged against the relatively innocuous Adelaide/Tippett situation, from what I do know of the Buckley arrangement, if Tippett got
an 11-week suspension, Buckley's illustrious career at Collingwood
might never have been allowed to begin, and the officials of various
clubs – including Gubby Allan and then Bears and now Sydney
Swans CEO Andrew Ireland – would have suffered heavy sanctions.
The Tippett affair was like shoplifting, whereas the long drawn-out
Buckley recruitment saga was more like a vicious armed robbery.

I don't know many of the intricate details of the deal. In late 1992, all Gubby told me was that despite Buckley playing for the Brisbane Bears in 1993 he would be at Collingwood the following season. It's fair to say that even the less stringent player clearance rules of the early 1990s were smashed to bits by a complicated strategy that entailed Collingwood using Brisbane as a holding pen for a year in order to eventually snare the talented youngster. The long-term recruiting coup came to fruition when the Bears cleared Bucks to Collingwood after his one season in Brisbane.

I've got to admit that in Buckley's first season at Collingwood in 1994, as much as he had an extraordinary skill level and an equal appetite for the game, I wasn't totally convinced he was going to become the all-time great he turned out to be. In the two seasons I coached him he wasn't strong enough over the footy and I was concerned about whether he had enough competitive grunt. I was also concerned that his enormous desire was a heavy millstone around his neck and he hadn't yet grasped the mechanics of being a good team player. And he was so keen to show the power of his kicking that he'd drill the ball so low and flat that turnovers were too often the result, because he lost control and team-mates couldn't always handle the footy being rocketed at them. We continually pushed and prodded to convince him that the best disposals make it easier for the target to take possession and therefore that he needed to soften his short to medium length kicking.

He was undoubtedly a very good player but my initial impression of the young Bucks wasn't that he was a gun match winner – which was the status needed to justify the big price we paid for his services. Maybe my expectations at the time were just too high. Again, never expect, never assume. He was still an inexperienced player in his second and third seasons in the AFL and I was hoping he could be the saviour of an ageing team.

My doubts about his potential greatness were proven to be very wrong. Certainly, his contribution to the Magpies over 14 seasons – including nine as captain and winning six Copeland Trophies – was an outstanding effort. Equally important, he has grown into a really impressive, driven young man.

We worked together on Channel Seven's Friday night footy coverage in 2009 and I really enjoyed his company. Having coached Bucks as a youngster way back in the mid-'90s but having had only limited contact since those years, it was interesting to observe the changes in him. Even away from the football environment it was obvious he'd matured from a youngster who was a little too self-absorbed with his own performance into a young adult who had fully grasped the mechanics of working effectively within a team environment. Everyone at Seven loved his desire to do the best possible job, but also respected his willingness to follow direction and perform whatever role was asked of him. He had learnt how teams work and was now a terrific team player. Understanding the basics of group mechanics is the necessary starting point for any successful coach or manager.

It seemed to me that Nathan Buckley had all the credentials and the necessary character to be an outstanding coach. Eddie McGuire and the Collingwood hierarchy obviously shared that view, which was why the plan for him to succeed Mick Malthouse didn't take a U-turn despite a premiership and a runners-up finish in the two seasons before the handover at the end of 2011.

Getting Bucks into a Collingwood jumper back in 1994 was a great coup and I was totally on-board with making it happen. However, when I consider the complicated swings and roundabouts and the high price required in getting him to Victoria Park, I wonder whether we sold a bit of our soul and damaged the group culture in the process.

There are lies, damn lies, and then there are statistics. The numbers tell us that in the six years of the 1990s that Bucks was at Collingwood – 1994 to 1999 – the club won only 50 of the 132 games played, got into the finals only once – in his first season in 1994 – and then dropped into the bottom half thereafter before finishing last in 1999. I'm certainly not blaming Bucks for this decline – a poor period of drafting was the main culprit and the decline may have been even worse without him. But there were a few unhealthy by-products that accompanied his recruitment.

Playing talent is critically important but so is a strong team fabric of unity, trust and respect that flows between players, coaches and club management. A particularly unpleasant part of the deal hatched with the Bears was that we'd agree to trade in return for Bucks any two players outside a 10-man list of selected untouchables. It was like putting the rest of our list up for sale. Depending on which way you looked at it, the Bears were able to tell every player outside this nominated 10 that Collingwood was prepared to let them go and that therefore we didn't value their services that highly. The Bears have said they had this conversation with about 20 of our players. This had to be a real downer for team morale.

It didn't end there. The Bears were chasing Craig Starcevich and when he was reluctant to go, Gubby strongly advised that if I wanted Bucks then I needed to convince Starce that his future at Collingwood was bleak. I put my principles aside and did exactly as I was asked. Armed with my negativity about his future at Victoria Park, Starce eventually agreed to move north. It is a mark of his outstanding character that before he left he came into my office, shook my hand and thanked me for all I'd done for him in his time at Collingwood.

It was also a good lesson to never burn your bridges. When I was appointed coach of Brisbane later in the decade, Starce had retired and was the Bears conditioning coach. The dignified manner in which he handled his forced departure from Collingwood stuck in my mind and I was more than happy for him to continue in the role under my coaching. Good or bad, you reap what you sow and so often what goes around, comes around.

While Bucks came into the club for the 1994 season, Peter Daicos was forced out, although practically the two issues were not closely related. Here was another of our premiership heroes being shown the door. I wonder whether our players thought this was a by-product of Nathan coming in.

Sharing premiership success creates an enormous bond among all those involved, and in Collingwood's case it was said that the players who delivered the flag in 1990 would be set for life. This is mere emotional rhetoric but if it's repeated often enough players start to believe it to be true. Surprisingly to them, the players received no great financial gain from their grand final win and in the years to follow discovered the harsh reality that when they outlived their usefulness they'd be discarded. An all-time great, Peter Daicos, was the first of the icons to go when he was retired against his wishes, but many other team-mates who'd shared the flag-winning experience had been either sacked, traded or eased into retirement during the intervening three years.

After the 1991 season, it was Denis Banks and Doug Barwick; after 1992, James Manson; now, after 1993, it was Peter Daicos, Craig Starcevich, Michael Gayfer, Shane Morwood and Jamie Turner.

Players coming and going is – and always will be – a fact of elite-level footy. However, with the talent eligible to be drafted being a little thin in the early 1990s as zones were phased out and new clubs joined the AFL competition, Collingwood got very little vibrant young talent out of our early decade drafting. Consequently, we developed a bit of a top-up mentality in an attempt to remain in premiership contention, and recruited a large number of players from other AFL clubs. The better known names included Gary Pert (from Fitzroy), Tony Woods (Fitzroy), Brad Hardie (Brisbane), Brad Rowe (Brisbane) and Ian McMullin (Essendon) before the 1992 season, Barry Mitchell (Sydney) before 1993, and Brenton Sanderson (Adelaide), Brad Plain (Essendon), Jon Ballantyne (Western Bulldogs) and Buckley before the 1994 campaign.

Bucks was still young with a long career ahead, but his recruitment was the reason that Starce and promising youngster Troy Lehmann went north to the Bears. The revolving door of outsiders coming in and respected team-mates leaving didn't help in creating a united, harmonious environment within the player group. We did what we thought was best at the time, but I'm not so sure we handled very well that slippery set of attitudes and actions that constitute the development and maintenance of an elite team.

Gubby and I both had a firm view that while a good group culture is valuable and needs to be directed and nurtured at all times by coaches and management, this indefinable quality mainly resides in the collective contribution of the player ranks. While the level of competence and competitive character within the player group has always been the primary driver of an effective team culture and ultimately its on-field performance, our management decisions may not have helped this aim.

Faced with an ageing team, we introduced many players from other clubs in the post-premiership years and, in the process, risked damaging the fabric of the existing group. Our team performance graph would indicate that the mass recruiting of players from other clubs was unsuccessful.

Actually, for a player who read the play so well on the field, Daics didn't read his situation very well at the end of his injury-ravaged five-game 1993 season. He should have seen the signs and retired. Because he didn't, the club had to make the running on his future.

Partly due to the salary cap, partly to injuries and partly due to their age, we'd made the decision that only one of Daics and Tony Shaw – our veterans aged 30-plus – would remain on our list for the 1994 season. Shawy had already handed the captaincy to Gavin Brown and we'd made both Daics and Shawy aware that the final decision would be made after a couple of pre-season games, which was something you could do back then. We came to believe that Shawy's body was likely to get him on the field more often than Daics, and eventually he got the nod and went on to play his 17th and final season.

After the decision to delist Daics was made in February, I walked straight out of the meeting to make one of those trips you dread. I was going to visit him at his pub in Carlton to tell him the bad news. Difficult tasks need to be carried out as soon as possible, because they eat at you until they're done.

Gubby was about to join me when I said that maybe it'd be better if I went alone – he was back in his office before I'd even finished the words. As I've said, delivering good news is terrific enjoyment; ending the career of a great player who wanted to play on was the exact opposite. It is a furphy that experienced players always know when their time is up: most need to be pushed, particularly in the well-paid modern era. Daics thought he could continue but on receiving the bad news he took it as he should, with dignity. I always tried to prepare players, and myself for that matter, for that inevitable finishing date by continually pushing the reality that one day it would end for us all – the only thing we didn't know was how or when. If it was decided by others, accepting it and going with respect and dignity would enhance the legacy you left.

Times were changing at Victoria Park and the high price and highly publicised recruitment of Nathan Buckley made many in the playing group that little bit more on edge, concerned about who might go next. That was the initial downside bubbling beneath the surface after his arrival.

It didn't affect the heavy Enforcer personalities like Tony Shaw, Craig Kelly and Gavin Brown. They just wanted to make the team better, no matter what. However, the heavy Feeler/Thinkers like Mick McGuane, Graham Wright, Tony Francis and Scott Russell were probably a bit uncomfortable with the direction of the club's recruiting symbolised by the big-ticket arrival of the golden boy from Brisbane. I'm not so sure we gave enough consideration at the time to the under-standable sensitivities of the existing players. The lesson is that bringing in a high-priced recruit does come with baggage, particularly if the team has an existing nucleus of recent premiership players.

The latest under this category is Kurt Tippett going to the reign-ing premiers the Sydney Swans after the 2012 season. This reeked of top-up recruiting. Tippett, who has never got close to All-Australian selection standard, joined the Swans as their highest-paid player, which must have rankled many of the existing flag-winning team, as well as their managers. This will be a challenge to the much-admired Bloods culture that has given Sydney such a strong team fabric.

These issues can always be lessened by the new player's attitude and work ethic. From the very beginning, Bucks was an exemplary trainer and preparer. I suspect his healthy confidence, enormous drive and sometimes broody intensity unsettled a few of his team-mates, who might have felt uncommitted in comparison to the brash young newcomer.

Whatever concerns were felt by some players, it didn't seem to visibly affect the opening of the 1994 season. The team bounced into the year with three straight wins, followed by two close losses, and Bucks' form was justifying the high price of his recruitment.

One of our early wins was against Carlton at the MCG in round two. It was apparent from the time I arrived at Collingwood that beating Carlton was critically important. In the Melbourne footy scene, all other rivalries come and go over time; for example, the annual Anzac Day clash against Essendon has assumed gigantic status, but in 1994 that was yet to come. The Magpies versus the Blues has been *the* rivalry over many decades and always gets both clubs' huge supporter bases really buzzing.

Personally, I most admire goals that are crafted and thought out, rather than the freaky instinctive ones, and this was the game that Mick McGuane kicked maybe the goal of the century. I can still picture it. After a centre bounce, he took possession around the wing side of the centre circle, then turned towards the half-forward flank on the MCC Members' side. He took off towards the Punt Road end, having bounce after bounce as he evaded the Carlton tacklers. With some great shepherding protection by his Magpies team-mate Mark Fraser, Mick crossed the 50-metre line. All of a sudden, a goal was a possibility. With that thought he kept running, had another bounce, sold an exquisite dummy to evade another tackler, steadied and split the middle of the goals from point-blank range. It was beautiful to watch the way he weaved and thought his way through the traffic. It was done with guile rather than speed – a fantastic memory for every Magpies supporter at the ground.

The 1994 season was when the MCG became Collingwood's main home ground. We only played three games at Victoria Park that year and, of course, none after 1999. Going to the big crowd-pulling venue was smart and essential marketing, as the cost of running an AFL club was rising rapidly. Footy was entering the period where increasing revenue was becoming the main priority. In the modern professional era, this aim has taken over completely.

However, going to the MCG to play home games was not so good for the team's chances of winning games of footy, which was my primary concern as coach. As an opposition player at Hawthorn, I would have loved playing against Collingwood at the MCG, rather than the dreaded task of surviving the afternoon at Victoria Park. It was scary walking in, not much fun on the field and very nasty walking back to your car after the game, particularly if you happened to win. All opposition players took very long showers after games there, because giving the home crowd time to disperse was a very good policy.

I only got knocked unconscious a handful of times playing footy, and once was at Victoria Park in the mid-'70s. Right in front of the part of the ground with the most passionate, rabid supporters – the Social Club up the railway line end – a blow to my head from the knee of Collingwood defender Phil Manassa knocked me into next week and off the field for the duration of the game. That day a deliberate long shower wasn't necessary. A couple of hours after the match, when the club doctor finally decided I was conscious enough to go home, the crowd had well and truly dispersed.

The Victoria Park home ground advantage was massive for Colling-wood over the whole of the last century. The stats show it clearly. Since 1897, the club won 75 per cent of its Victoria Park games and about 50 per cent of its matches at the MCG. In 1994 we were three from three at our home base and seven wins from 13 at the MCG. In our premiership year we were seven from seven at Victoria Park and three from five at the MCG.

Moving home games to the MCG had another unfortunate by-product. As part of a program to encourage supporters to travel the few kilometres from the MCG back to Victoria Park after games, a question-and-answer session with the senior coach was put in place. About 6.30 pm, after just enough time for the supporters' post-match alcohol to sink in, and usually with Brian Taylor as MC, it was a standing-room-only, open-slather questioning of the team perfor-mance and my coaching. It was a bit of a chore if we won; if we lost, it was really hard work.

We were very competitive all year and won 12 of our 22 games to finish eighth, only one win and percentage behind North Melbourne who went into the finals third with just 13 victories. A few more games at Victoria Park might well have got us the couple more wins to finish top four.

This was the first year of the final-eight system, and at this time eighth played first, which meant our task was a four-hour flight west to take on the West Coast Eagles. We were given little hope. At the time, the Eagles in Perth was the competition's horror assignment, but we'd beaten them by six goals at the MCG during the season, so I thought we had a sneaky chance.

There aren't that many players who have kicked six goals in an AFL game, but a tough trivia question would be: who did it for Collingwood against the Eagles in round 13, 1994? The player was the little-known Andrew Tranquilli, who, in a career total of 12 games, kicked only 20 goals. As had happened earlier in the year against West Coast at the MCG, in our elimination final in Perth we needed a player or two to do something special. We also had to stop the brick-wall-type dominance of the Eagles' half-back line, made up of three gun weapons: their inspirational captain, John Worsfold, the man mountain, Glen Jakovich, and the extremely creative Guy McKenna. We'd played Nathan Buckley across half-forward a lot in his first season and decided to use Gavin Brown forward as well. We hoped these two could exploit the Eagles' defensive tendency to zone off their direct opponents.

We were now in knockout territory, where, if we lost, the season was finished. The enormously respected Tony Shaw had read the play well and had already announced that 1994 would be his last year. After 17 seasons and 313 games, this might well have been his final appearance in the black-and-white jumper he'd worn with such distinction. With a big final to prepare for, Shawy's situation was not exactly at the forefront of my thinking. That changed after a bizarre Friday night training mishap.

As it was to be a Sunday final, the team travelled to Perth on the Friday and had a light training session at the match venue, the WACA, late in the afternoon. During that run Shawy pulled up with a strained calf. It looked as if he wouldn't be fit to take his place in the side, which would mean his career was over without him again getting onto the field of play.

Tony always believed in the healing power of a masseur with 'magic' hands, so that was the cure that he sought out. In my mind, I had already ruled him out of contention. I was in my hotel room late in the evening when a knock on the door revealed Shawy with club doctor Shane Conway in tow. He excitedly informed me that after spending a couple of painful hours under the hands of the 'best masseur in Perth', he was now cured, and his calf was 100 per cent.

He then proceeded to sprint up and down the corridor to prove his fitness. It was silly really, but I had such regard for his always positive attitude and amazing mental strength that I wanted to believe he was fit to play. The decision was made to assess his situation over the next couple of days.

My philosophy on fitness tests was always to try to break the player down. I figured that was better than it happening during the game, which would leave us a man short. On this occasion my overwhelming respect for my ex-captain, a man who was so influential in our premiership win and who had given me and his club so much to be grateful for during his long career, influenced me to back his judgement. Shawy's fitness test was soft at best. We allowed him to make the final call on the Sunday morning without putting him through a vigorous match-type fitness session. It was a mistake because he broke down in the first 10 minutes and spent the rest of the game on the bench.

It was the last time in my coaching career I allowed a player to declare his own fitness without a severe workout to make doubly sure, although a situation with many similarities would again test my judgement many years later on grand final day, 2003.

The Eagles had lost only once in Perth all year but the Collingwood team really served it up to the locals, and we almost pinched a win in the seemingly mission impossible. After trailing by four goals at three-quarter time, we kicked six goals to two in the final quarter to pull within two points. In the final seconds a long kick forward landed within the grasp of Mick McGuane well inside the 50-metre arc, but he couldn't hold a falling chest mark. Given that Mick was such a consistently accurate kick, and one of a handful of players I'd want with ball in hand for a clutch shot on goal, it was one of those moments that got away. The Eagles won, and weren't troubled thereafter, winning both the preliminary and grand finals by huge margins.

It was the end of our season, but for most of the players there'd be other games to come. Not for Shawy – his playing days and, ultimately, his youth were now ended. I knew what he was going through, and I felt his pain, as did his team-mates. There was more than a close elimination final defeat with which to cope.

Post-match the visible dejection hung in the air. A close loss was certainly no consolation at this point, particularly when we'd had our chance to win. The losing feeling is bad at the best of times; that day, its exaggerated version became a form of shocked mourning.

This was one of these moments when your body aches with grief. In the cold light of day it's only a game, but that rationale comes later – much later. I looked around the locker area at the grieving players who were sitting heads bowed, staring at the floor. The support staff were also standing around the room in a silent state of shock. No-one made eye contact as everyone struggled to regain their composure. As coach, I knew it was my job to say a few soothing words to begin the healing process and to move forward. I spent a minute or two in the vacant shower area to gather my thoughts and then returned to the players.

I began speaking, but such was the emotion of the occasion I had to stop. I had tears welling up in my eyes and, looking around the room, it was a pretty common state of affairs. After a few words I began to choke up, so I wasn't able to deliver what the situation demanded. What I wanted to say to the team about their efforts and about Tony Shaw's career unfortunately remained unsaid.

When I look back, maybe the exaggerated emotions in the Colling-wood rooms, and my own failure to be composed under pressure, were not only about that day's events. It was a period when my private life was going through significant change. I had separated from my wife, Maureen, and, having gone straight from living with my parents into married life back in 1970, I was living alone for the first time in my life. I read once that regardless of the circumstances a marriage break-up is one of life's more stressful experiences, and I'd agree with that. It's hard to dispute that a stable home life is helpful to an effec-tive work life, and conversely, being unsettled in your personal life can't help in terms of being focused and effective professionally.

While I think the art of putting your existence into compartments and not allowing one to affect the others has been a lifetime strength of mine, later in my Collingwood coaching career I suspect the com-partments were seeping into each other, which adversely affected the clarity of my thinking. I fear that I was not at the top of my game in my final years at Collingwood.

Strangely, with the passing of time I look back on how we handled Tony Shaw's last game with no regret. Sure, the decision to play Shawy was based on our hope that a great competitor could defy the odds stacked against him, and, critically, because I knew how important he was to our team. If we were going to have any chance of beating the Eagles in a cut-throat final in front of their hostile crowd, we needed every bit of our former captain's mental strength and fighting spirit. Although the punt failed and logic tells me that we should have given him a more thorough fitness test, in retrospect I'm not sure I wouldn't make the same decision again.

Sometimes as a coach/manager you have to back certain individuals and be prepared to take the good with the occasional bad. Picking well who you put your faith in is a critical part of the coaching art.

31

MY TIME IS UP

This rebuttal of my coaching authority by the board should have been the signal for me to resign.

My contract to coach the Collingwood football team was terminated a few days after the end of the 1995 season. It had actually been signalled emphatically about 12 months earlier.

Particularly back in the part-time era, I always believed that the senior coach should have the final say on all matters that relate directly to team performance. And throughout my time at Collingwood that was the case – until late 1994.

The football grapevine suggested that Plugger Lockett might be on the move from St Kilda, and Collingwood football manager Graeme Allan was on to it. After all, it had been all of 12 months since the high-profile Nathan Buckley pick-up and Gubby loved nothing better than orchestrating a recruiting coup, and has proven over the years to be very good at it.

Gubby came to me one day and said he thought Plugger was gettable. What did I think?

Lockett was 28 but still physically sound, and while we had 20-year-old Saverio Rocca, who was a promising young full-forward, it was an irresistible temptation to grab a proven gun. It was also indicative of the prevailing Collingwood mentality of topping up talent from other clubs. Equally, on reflection, it was a sign that my coaching outlook had become very short-term. Sometimes your subconscious takes over your thinking without you really knowing.

Plugger was a volatile character and would come with a little baggage, but there was no question about his football worth. He was one of the great full-forwards in the game's history, and, in the end, I agreed to get him if we could. It seemed an opportunity too good to knock back.

Collingwood president Allan McAlister was on board and supported the idea, so Gubby went to work. The deal was done. Lockett was all set to join the club for the 1995 season. The only stumbling block was the sign-off from the Collingwood board. For nine years this had been pretty much automatic. What Gubby and I wanted – assuming we could afford it – we generally got.

Not this time. The board overruled the football department, and Lockett subsequently went to Sydney and played a further five full seasons with the Swans. Maybe it all turned out for the best. I suspect the publicity-shy Plugger enjoyed the lack of notoriety in the harbour city, and the Collingwood media spotlight might well have worn him down. As it turned out, Sav Rocca kicked 93 goals in 1995 and won the Copeland Trophy, so the board appeared to have made a good decision. It was also further evidence to support the club's growing belief that they could no longer trust my judgement.

The fact that the board went against its coach, football manager and president on a recruiting decision was indicative of the crumbling chain of command that was developing at Victoria Park. It was the beginning of the end for me as Collingwood coach – within four years, my symbolic 1990 coach-for-life status had evaporated. It was also a sign that Allan's authority as president was in decline, and he moved on not long after me.

This rebuttal of my coaching authority by the board should have been the signal for me to resign. My whole relationship with the boards of the two clubs I coached for a total of 20 seasons was based on the simple principle of them trusting me to run the footy side of the club. That was what I demanded. The Enforcer qualities in my personality meant I needed to feel in control to work at my best. Therefore, if that total trust and faith was no longer forthcoming, I would happily be sacked without angst. That was always the deal. But at the time, I put this principle aside and accepted their verdict about Plugger without fuss.

Maybe it was simply a professional decision because I still had two years of a coaching contract to run, or perhaps it was indicative of my drive and need for total control waning. It was a strange reality that later in both my coaching stints I began to deliberately delegate more, and both times the teams seemed to get worse. Anyway, the net result was that the end of my coaching usefulness at Victoria Park had probably come.

The problem was that I had fallen in love with the Collingwood footy club and, as it was now home, I didn't consider falling on my sword. Over a 40-year period I ended up being a well-paid employee at three football clubs. That would indicate that my loyalty was transferable, which it was. However, once I'd settled into each of these three clubs I couldn't imagine voluntarily leaving. Despite the Collingwood board giving me the hint that they no longer trusted my judgement, I felt no compulsion to call it quits at the end of 1994.

I made another short-sighted decision when Tony Shaw was offered an assistant-coaching role at Carlton in 1995. It had been obvious from the time Tony captained the premiership team that he was likely to succeed me as coach. As an outsider who had originated at another club, I would never be part of the Magpies' historic inner-sanctum, and when I finished my stint it would be time to go back to the club's black-and-white roots. Shawy fitted the bill perfectly.

So, not wanting to risk losing my coaching successor, the club, with my full support, convinced him to knock back the Carlton offer and accept a coaching development role with us. It was not a formal succession arrangement that I knew about; maybe I was simply not in on the plans. I'm sure there were a few wheels turning behind the scenes in 1995 that I wasn't aware of – namely that, unless there was drastic improvement, Shawy would take over at the end of the season. I suspect even the players had an inkling of this likely progression. All in all, when players sense the incumbent coach may not be there long term, it isn't a healthy environment. The senior coach knows deep down he is on borrowed time and becomes increasingly grumpy, while the likely successor is waiting in the wings and trying to be supportive, but not wanting to be aligned too closely with the existing coach if the wheels begin to fall off. And fall off they did, as we failed to win a game until round seven.

It was difficult for Tony as well. At one point later in the year we were playing top-placed Carlton at the MCG and he suggested that, rather than watch the game from the coach's box with me, he'd go to the other side of the ground to get a different perspective. Not a bad idea when you think about it. But when they thrashed us it also meant he didn't have to do the long walk with us back to the rooms in front of the unhappy Collingwood fans. It's human nature not to want to hang around with a leper because you might get leprosy.

If we'd thought long-term we would have encouraged him to move away from his Collingwood home to a new football club environment. Clubs can become a bit inbred and I firmly believe that experiencing life outside the team you played for is a terrific grounding for eventually coaching.

In hindsight, Shawy would have been better off going to Carlton as an assistant to David Parkin and experiencing a different club to the one he'd grown up in and known for so long. He might still have been the man to replace me, but even 12 months living away from home would have been invaluable.

Shawy was respected by his team-mates, but it was a friendly respect, rather than fearful. This meant they could have a bit of fun at his expense, which was highlighted by an unusual incident that occurred that summer. Looking for a challenge after retiring from playing, he decided to enter the gruelling 42-kilometre Melbourne Marathon. Late in the event as extreme fatigue set in, he became disoriented, drifted off the course and ran into a tree. After being heavily dazed, but mainly due to dehydration and exhaustion, he spent a few hours in hospital. The following week he arrived home to find a pile of sawdust on his front lawn, courtesy of a couple of Magpie team-mates, with a sign saying, 'Shawy, we got the bastard for you.'

With our ageing champion retiring, we punted on bringing another one into the club, namely my 1983 Hawthorn premiership team-mate Dermott Brereton. Talk about falling for short-term thinking. Dermott was a 30-year-old football cripple who had got on the field only 13 times in the three seasons since playing in the Hawks' 1991 flag win. He would cost us nothing in draft picks and little in dollars and when our sprint coach, Bob Newton, gave his running action the all clear after a secretive training session on the cricket ground behind the Malvern Town Hall, we selected him in the pre-season draft.

While his body was wounded and failing, I had enormous respect for Dermott's competitive character and football knowledge. With the Lockett recruitment idea terminated, we thought maybe he could kick us a few goals around the forward pocket and become an on-field coach to get the best out of Saverio Rocca.

This was a punt that Dermott made work, despite a recurrence of a strained calf in a March practice game at Victoria Park. Predictably, this injury derailed his level of fitness, which had been quite good until then.

I would love to have coached him when we were both in our prime. His ability to impact games with aggression, enormous bravado and great skill made him a terrific player, and his influence on those around him went well beyond his own performance. He also thought his way around the field better than most.

Dermott's great feel for the intricacies of the game comes out in his incisive commentary on TV and radio, although he can theorise a bit at times when he tries to read players' minds and confuses instinctive actions with thought-out strategy. He's always an enthusiastic story-teller and, like all good raconteurs, doesn't let the truth stand in the way of embellishing a good story. At Collingwood, we knew his extroverted personality would be good for the team, so we happily gave him a chance to continue playing.

While we were only hoping he could perform a worthwhile on-field role, we were confident he could assist Sav Rocca to be a better player. In 1995 the two of them were exact opposites: Sav was young, had the physical talents but not the footy smarts, and Dermott had the smarts with a worn-out body.

Dermott got onto the field 15 times for 30 goals, which was a reasonable return for a low-cost recruit, but the bonus was the enormous influence he had on Sav kicking a career-high 93 for the year. Nine of these came in round four at the MCG against Essendon, the first of the now traditional Anzac Day blockbusters.

What an incredibly memorable match. It's extremely rare for players or coaches to appreciate the spectacle the fans may be seeing.

You're concentrating so hard on what you're doing that the aesthetics of the contest completely pass you by. Of the 800-odd games I've been directly involved in, only two have hit me this way.

The first was as a player in the 1984 second semi-final between Hawthorn and Essendon. In the final few minutes of a close game – particularly a knockout final with a big crowd going berserk – the action moves to a level of frantic intensity that makes the ground feel the size of a phone booth. Everything is pressured and rushed as the space seems to shrink. This match was like that from start to finish, and even as a participant I could sense the incredible contest being fought out this day.

We all have our likes. Mine is the tension of close scores plus the excitement of 30-odd goals being kicked. The 1984 second semi qualified on both counts.

The other was as a coach, this Anzac Day clash of 1995. It was a very different game well before the opening bounce. As a big crowd was expected, we decided that the Collingwood team should meet at Victoria Park and hire a bus to take us the few kilometres in to the MCG. We arrived at the ground a couple of hours before the scheduled start to discover a massive crowd overflowing onto and blocking traffic in the adjacent Brunton Avenue, and the police had to escort the bus to our dressing rooms in the Southern Stand.

My initial thought was that the gates had not yet opened to let the crowd enter. Then when I walked through the dressing rooms and onto the ground, we were greeted by an amazing sight. The stands were already full, with no curtain-raiser and no entertainment, and the game still a couple of hours away. No-one could leave their seat because the modern pre-selling of reserved seats was in its infancy; at this point it was first in, best dressed. A big crowd was still outside because they couldn't get in.

A sea of the two clubs' combined colours of black, white and red packed the arena, the crowd filling in the time by reading newspapers or the *Football Record* or chatting to those around them. There was a strange low hum in the background as nearly 100,000 footy fans congregated with nothing much to do, but satisfied that they had their seat when many others didn't.

Unlike the grand final, when there is half a stadium of unbiased theatre goers, the ground was full of two armies of supporters waiting patiently for the contest to start, all mixed in together. I love that about AFL crowds. Fans of the two clubs often go to the game together, barrack hard for their respective teams, and then when the match ends go home together. It's great that no segregation is required – long may it last.

The modern Collingwood/Essendon Anzac Day occasion was launched with a bang before the game even got under way. Sometimes the sizzle can be better than the sausage. Fortunately, this match lived up to its hype.

This game had it all. A nerve-racking draw was the result at the end of an incredible, high-scoring, free-flowing spectacle with 33 goals kicked, in front of a stadium full of screaming fans which created an atmosphere I vividly remember to this day. Even concentrating on my job in the coach's box couldn't shield me totally from the excitement flowing around the vast arena.

Like that 1984 second semi, this game had close scores, high scoring and a sense of excitement enhanced by sharing the experience with 95,000 people. Human beings really are herd animals when you think about it. Most of us are drawn to being part of a big crowd at events like the Melbourne Cup week racing or the footy finals. We even tend to pick restaurants by going to the full ones and avoiding those with few patrons.

A six-goal-apiece opening quarter got the fans into the game straight away. Then, after Essendon got 16 points clear at the long break, we had a seven-goal third quarter to go into the final term with a 14-point break. Then the Bombers came at us hard. The last quarter was pressure footy at its best as the lead swung back and forth.

Late in the quarter, Sav Rocca took his 10th mark and his ninth goal resulted. Collingwood by six points. There was no countdown clock in the coach's box back in 1995 – that coaching aid wasn't introduced until 2004 – so the exact time to go was uncertain. I did a quick calculation. There'd been eight goals kicked in that final quarter and it was over 30 minutes on the time clock. The siren could be any second, or there could still be a few minutes to play.

I reckon there turned out to be about a minute to go, and in modern footy, armed with the exact time to play, we would order a flood back to congest the Bombers' forward line. This game, we didn't. Then, damn it, from the centre bounce Essendon immediately swept the ball forward, and from the forward pocket the exquisite skills and economy of movement that came to typify James Hird came to the fore, as he waltzed through the congested pack of players and, almost in slow motion, snapped the equalising goal over his left shoulder. It was a vision I can still easily recall, both with admiration for Hirdy's composure under pressure and with dismay that an outright win had been pinched from our hands.

After the ensuing centre bounce, though, and in the game's final passage of play, a win became a possibility again as Nathan Buckley – who was wonderful all day – took possession around the middle of the ground and charged forward. The great MCG stadium couldn't possibly have ever heard a louder noise than at that moment, as the huge crowd let out a collective roar of anticipation. In the coach's box we held our breath; the time to intervene in the game had long gone. We were now merely spectators as well.

At this critical moment, Bucks was confronted by the conundrum of the gun full-forward, which Sav Rocca had been in this particular match. The huge frame of big Sav, who'd already dominated with nine goals, imposed himself on Bucks' vision and that was where the long pass went. Maybe Bucks could have got to 60 metres and had a long bomb, maybe another forward was free, but ultimately the gun full-forward acting as a very powerful ball magnet forced the kick in Sav's direction. The mark was spoilt and the siren sounded a few seconds later to end an enthralling contest.

It's great to be there when a tradition begins. I feel fortunate to have seen the first derby in Perth between the Eagles and Fremantle only a few weeks later, and I was also there for the inaugural Adelaide versus Port Power showdown in 1997.

The Anzac Day blockbusters have become the biggest home-and-away game on the football calendar, as well as great money-spinners and image-builders for both Collingwood and Essendon. Every season the logical debate arises about the fairness of this great occasion being confined to only two clubs. While the tradition built up since 1995 is partly to do with having the same two heavily supported Melbourne teams each and every year, it is equally because the whole observance of Anzac Day by the football world, and probably the wider community, has grown significantly over recent decades. April 25 has unofficially assumed the status of Australia's national day. To most of us, Australia Day on 26 January is simply a public holiday; Anzac Day has become our day of remembrance and commemoration. It is the Anzac spirit that provides the real magic at the MCG during the emotional pre-game ceremony. Once the ball is bounced, it's just another game of footy.

I subscribe to the view that it isn't fair that only two clubs get to share the fruits of playing at the MCG on Anzac Day. The right should be earned, not inherited. On balance of all the considerations, I would award the honour to the two top-finishing Victorian teams of the previous season. It's all a bit hypothetical really, because the revenue-producing priorities of modern footy mean that the proven cash cow won't be risked, even in the interests of greater fairness to all. So in the balance of political power the status quo is likely to remain, particularly while Eddie McGuire is Collingwood president. Eddie is one bloke you don't want to have on the opposite side of a debate, as I was to find out in the next phase of my football life.

The excitement of the memorable Anzac Day clash didn't last long. Hawthorn stitched us up by 10 goals the following week at Waverley Park. Jason Dunstall got his customary six goals against us and Sav Rocca slid down from nine to nil in seven days. Richmond beat us the following week back at the MCG, and with a draw against the Bombers all we had to show from our opening six games, our season was in tatters. As a coach going into his 10th year and whose tenure was seen to be in doubt, it was a disastrous situation for the whole club.

Living in the moment and leaning on the week-to-week cycle that keeps you sane is always the aim, regardless of the win–loss ratio, but when I look back probably the whole football world – including the media and, unfortunately, the players as well – knew I was a dead man walking. I knew too, not that deep down; in fact, even before the season kicked off, my subconscious pushed me into looking further ahead than I normally would.

My good friend Mike Sheahan was chief football writer at the *Herald Sun*, and with his encouragement during the pre-season the paper offered me the opportunity to write a paid weekly column. When I agreed, it was an indication that I was preparing for life after coaching.

I must say that after the Anzac Day game the season is a bit of a blur. After our very poor winless first six games, we recovered reasonably well to win the majority of our matches thereafter, so we were still in finals contention when we travelled to Sydney for the last round of the season. We'd only won eight games, plus two draws, so we were a long way from a winning season, but 10 wins – or 40 premiership points – would eventually be enough for the final spot that was occupied, going into the final round, by Melbourne with 36 points. The Demons were rolled by the Brisbane Bears at the Gabba on the Friday night, so the Bears, having won their 10th game, replaced Melbourne in eighth spot. Our assignment the following Sunday against the Swans was crystal clear: win and we'd play finals.

The Swans had only won seven games, but with a total of just seven victories collectively in the preceding two seasons, they were on the up. You certainly wouldn't have predicted they'd claim a berth in the grand final berth 12 months later, but with the recruitment of that man Tony Lockett, they'd improved from hopeless to competitive.

Lockett hadn't played earlier in the season when we comfortably beat Sydney at Victoria Park in round seven. This was to be his first appearance against the Magpies since the club had turned its back on his recruitment a year earlier. To this day, I wonder whether that last-minute rebuttal had any effect on his psyche in this match – just maybe he had one big point to prove. Plugger was certainly in form. The big fella had kicked 29 in the previous three matches and had reached his hundred for the season the week before.

At least we had a couple of good experienced defenders in Gary Pert and Craig Kelly to be Plugger's direct match-up. Keeping him to four goals would be a big win for us, but I knew that on his day he could kick 10. We had Sav Rocca, who had the ability to kick big bags, but nowhere near the consistency.

How I wished the game was in Melbourne. Against the Eagles in Perth 12 months earlier under the pressure of a knockout game, we'd travelled well and were competitive. However, on that day we'd been rank outsiders. This time we were the favourites, and the comfort of playing at home in front of the parochial Collingwood army of supporters would have been a welcome advantage.

We started well enough and led by 25 points at half-time – then the Swans surged. We still led by two goals at three-quarter time but were starting to fade. As the players trudged into the huddle for that last regrouping before the final term which would decide, in football terms, whether we'd live or die, I looked for signs of fight and energy, but what I saw was a pretty lacklustre, tired group of players. I can never recall the exact words I've used at breaks in play. Whatever I said had no positive effect.

Cheered on by the Sydney crowd, the Swans ran right over the top of us, as we played a terrible last quarter. We were outscored eight goals to two and, even worse, cracked under the pressure and accepted the defeat long before the final siren. And that man Lockett again became my nightmare as he dominated the quarter with four goals, to take his tally to 7.4. If he had a point to prove, well, he certainly proved it. In the battle of the power forwards, Plugger, the established star, won the points easily over the young up-and-comer, Sav Rocca, who had a quiet match, only kicking a couple.

The siren sounded to end the misery of our capitulation, and as I headed down to our rooms – which were very small and pokey; in fact, the same ones still used to this day by the Australian cricket teams – my mood was dark. Not angry – more like sad and melancholy. Because the rooms were so small, and with no coach's room to address the players in private, I decided not to say anything at all. Frankly, I was also lost for words. What I said post-match was usually in preparation for the following week or the following season – but for me, there would be no following season. If I hadn't been contracted for another year, I might have announced my retirement then and there, because the die was cast. I would never coach a Collingwood team again. The short stand-off would begin, and in order to get the last year of my contract paid out, the practical part of me would wait to be pushed.

Regrettably, I allowed the sense of loss – not only that day's match, but the loss of my club and the loss of a big phase of my life – to control my thinking and actions. Instead of at least respecting the players by saying a few words to wind up the day, I withdrew into myself as my mechanism of coping with the strange mix of emotions I was feeling. The rooms were like a morgue as the usual mourning of a bad loss creates a speechless few minutes until the shock passes and life moves on.

Coaching was always a lonely profession on occasions like this. I always blamed myself when we lost and when you glanced around the room it was easy to think everyone else was blaming you as well, which only exaggerated the emotional downer. So, as the support staff packed up the gear and the players gradually showered and changed, I quickly made my way to the team bus for a bit of solitude.

There was no-one else on board as I took my normal seat at the very front on the right-hand side, immediately behind the driver. Shortly afterwards, Eddie Hillgrove, Collingwood's team manager during the decade I coached, entered and sat down next to me. Eddie had become a very good friend who'd seen my losing mood many times, but I think he sensed that this was something different. The subject of my coaching tenure had never been discussed with me, but Gubby had made me aware of the board's thinking. While I thought everybody around the club knew the lie of the land, Eddie was visibly shocked when I volunteered my thinking that today would be the last time I coached Collingwood. He was the only Magpies person I spoke to about that subject during that weekend, and no-one else raised the topic in my presence. I gather that the wheels were turning behind the scenes.

Strangely for Collingwood, there was no discussion in the media about whether I'd be replaced, and nothing happened in the next day or two. The following Tuesday I had an end-of-season lunch with Gubby and the other full-timers in our football department at Rob-era's restaurant in Fitzroy. At the same time the Collingwood board was meeting and I was under no illusions as to what was going to happen. I had a year to run on my contract but I knew it was time for a change – and so did they.

After a nice meal and more than a few wines, we returned to the club and I was told of the board decision. I was offered the chance to resign but, given my contractual situation, I'd already decided I'd rather be sacked. And it'd be best to do it quickly. A press conference was scheduled for 5 pm. There was already a fair media crew gathering outside the club as the inevitable grapevine went to work. Feeling the effects of the wine, I went for a walk around the streets of Collingwood in an attempt to clear my head.

There was no bitterness or bad vibes. President Allan McAlister and his board had been an incredible support to me during my 10 years in the job, but when your time is up it's up. I was pretty relaxed as I fronted the media for the last time as a Collingwood person; maybe having a bit of wine on board helped.

My decade at the Magpies ended amicably and I'm so thankful for the opportunity they gave me. Being involved in such a big and massively supported club provided an excitement I'll always remember with great fondness. I had a fantastic playing career at Hawthorn that I would never swap, and was later to coach for 10 years at the Brisbane Lions, which was an extraordinary period, but if I was a young footballer choosing a club, I reckon Collingwood would top my list.

Over the next few days, Frank Buckle, my friend and unpaid manager when I needed his help, negotiated a settlement on the last year of my Collingwood contract. By that stage I was earning about $200,000 per season and, from memory, received about half that as a lump sum payout.

I was able to say my formal goodbyes at the Copeland Trophy night shortly after, but from the time I cleared out my office and walked out the door, it was like walking off a cliff. In a short day or two, the role that had been the centre of my existence for the previous decade was reduced to nil.

Elite-level football clubs have a cult-like character. When you're there the involvement and commitment is total, and when you leave the lockout is also total. As a coach, the moment your successor is appointed is the moment you become a stranger in your own house. The king is dead, long live the king.

32

JUMPING THE FENCE

*Without a club role, there were no big sporting wins to provide
these highly emotional moments. When the next one came,
it was nowhere near an AFL field and there wasn't a
footy in sight.*

When my coaching decade at Collingwood finished in early September 1995, I was 43 years old. For the previous 31 of these, every winter weekend my life had revolved around the cycle of heading off from home to be involved in a game of footy. Whether it was my hobby as a boy, or my paid passion as an adult, this meant accepting the competitive challenge, because for me what happened in these couple of hours would have a huge bearing on my emotional state. It was a stimulation that I loved and hated at the same time. For the first time in almost my entire life this routine would be broken.

Later in the month I was at a preliminary final breakfast with Kevin Sheedy, who'd just completed his 15th season as Essendon coach, and we were discussing my future plans. I asked Sheeds what he'd do in my position, and he replied that he'd seek out another coaching job straight away. I've often heard coaches talk of themselves as career coaches, but anyone who thinks they'll coach for a lifetime is kidding themselves. It takes a rare breed to coach for decades. One, you need to be successful to hold the position; and two, you can't let the pressures of the job totally dominate your existence. I think Sheeds qualified on both counts. Conversely, I never thought of myself as a career coach. For me, coaching was just what I did for a certain period of my life.

When the Collingwood job ended, my initial feelings were of a release of pressure, and a big weight lifted from my shoulders. I had absolutely no desire to continue coaching elsewhere the following season. I was worn out. I was also sick of that terrible losing feeling that is an inevitable part of the process – even if you eventually succeed – and was keen for a break to recharge. I probably thought I'd coach again but certainly not in the next year or two.

Of course, I was also addicted to the adrenalin rush and challenge of the football contest, so removing that required weaning myself off the habit like a junkie would his drugs. While the euphoric emotional highs I got at a game of football were extremely rare, they were also the most exhilarating moments I had ever experienced. I'd miss the stimulation of competing and I'd *really* miss the overwhelming joy of an exciting win.

Without a club role, there were no big sporting wins to provide these highly emotional moments. When the next one came, it was nowhere near an AFL field and there wasn't a footy in sight. It came in October 1998 when I was standing 17,000 kilometres from home on the sidelines at Croke Park in Dublin, Ireland, as the siren sounded to end the International Rules contest between Ireland and Australia. I was coach of the Australian team, we'd won by one point, and for the next hour or so the excitement was equal to anything I ever felt in my entire football life.

The journey to this career highlight began with a meeting I had with AFL Football Operations Manager Ian Collins in the middle of the year. He told me that the International Rules competition was being relaunched and asked if I'd take on the role of Australian coach. It didn't take much time for me to accept.

There is no escaping the fact that working in the media doesn't give me anything like the sense of belonging that comes with a day-after-day team involvement and the emotional roller coaster that inevitably comes with winning and losing. You still enjoy it, and there's always that certain amount of performance adrenalin, but generally whatever you feel on a Friday as a media commentator, you'll invariably feel on the following Monday, because what happens over the weekend doesn't carry the same emotional consequence.

So, without really knowing what to expect, my appointment as Australian coach was something very special. Just having the Australian coat of arms on our uniform was a big buzz in itself. The International Rules game is nothing like AFL: with a round ball, and a rectangular field with soccer nets for goals, basically it's Gaelic football with tackling. The part-time Irish against the professional Australians is supposed to be the big evener-up.

The game was completely foreign to us all, apart from our ring-in Irishman turned Australian, the Melbourne ruckman and 1991 Brownlow medallist, Jim Stynes. The 1998 series was obviously not played under 'country of origin' rules, as it is now. Of course, Jimmy was a young Irish Gaelic footballer who migrated down under to make a great success of his new sport.

With only a short time to prepare for a game very different to AFL footy, in the few training sessions we had we prioritised learning to handle and kick the round ball, and leaned heavily on using our patriotism as the main motivator.

However, there was nothing artificial about our national pride when we lined up before the game with the coat of arms on our chest, and proudly belted out the Australian national anthem ahead of the rebirth of the International Rules series. It was fantastic that AFL players, who were generally confined to club colours, had the chance to represent their country.

It was a strange feeling. I was coach of an Australian team that was about to play Ireland in the first of two Test matches, but my knowledge of the sport was virtually nil, how to best play the game was a mystery and we knew none of the opposition players. I had never played International Rules and had virtually no idea of the technicalities of this new sport. And because International Rules is as much like AFL as badminton is like tennis, it was very much a case of the blind leading the blind.

Back in this period the AFL All-Australian team, as selected on performances during the AFL season, formed the nucleus of the squad that would take on Ireland. It wasn't necessarily the best method of selection, as the football world would soon understand when players better suited to the nuances of the hybrid game were chosen in later years. However, it was a rare and special honour for devotees of the Australian game – just getting fitted out with my Australian uniform was a special thrill.

North Melbourne premiership captain Wayne Carey had been selected as All-Australian skipper and AFL officials had invested a lot of time and effort into convincing the Kangaroos champion to make the trip. It's fair to say that part of the deal was to completely relax the usual disciplines associated with professional football. To enhance the status of the contest, it was critical that the All-Australian captain – and football's biggest name – made himself available. This was despite his particular football strengths not being a great help in the International Rules game; neither was the fact that he joined the team in Ireland direct from the hard drinking of the North players' post-season holiday in Thailand.

The trip to Ireland fell in the weeks immediately after the end of the 1998 AFL season, so to get the majority of the All-Australian side to forgo their annual break, it had to be a bit special and it had to be a very good time. As the Irish Gaelic footballers were amateurs, for the sake of fairness the Australian players had to play for free as well, aside from a living allowance. Probably the most influential thing I did as coach was to convinced the AFL management that the players, and me, should at least fly business class on the long flight to Ireland.

The final 23-man squad that included 12 members of the official All-Australian side took off on a joint mission of football and fun. A key non-playing member of the travel party was my old Hawthorn team-mate Robert DiPierdomenico. The infectiously enthusiastic 'Dipper' was in charge of team bonding and morale. Always the life of the party, he had a fantastic ability to bring people together. As odd as it might sound, on a tour like this it was a critical role.

Another section of our travel party determined to make the most of the trip were the AFL head office management staff. If there was a key AFL official back in Australia, that person would have been very lonely. They were all there to support 'their' team and to join the party. One drawback of being an independent official of our game is the need for impartiality. If you work for the AFL, you are basically denied – at least outwardly – the ups and downs that come with barracking for a particular club. Not in Ireland. This was the one time the people from headquarters were able and keen to show their true colours, and I suspect the enjoyment they got out of the whole exercise was an additional motivating factor in keeping the International Rules concept going in the years that followed.

This was never more evident than on our first morning in Dublin. Having arrived on Thursday ahead of the first Test on the Sunday, Russell Greene – our conditioning coach and another Hawthorn premiership team-mate – decided to find a park near the team hotel for a bit of a loosen-up jog. We had a rough idea where we were going, but as we walked through the city streets AFL chief executive Wayne Jackson, decked out in his training gear, quickly volunteered to run ahead to the next corner to see whether our next turn should be right or left. It wasn't the sort of behaviour you usually associated with the league boss, but it reflected beautifully the enthusiasm Wayne and his offsiders had for the tour.

It wasn't exactly a complete vacation, but if you were comparing the strict disciplines of a normal AFL preparation with the players' usual end-of-season holiday, it was closer to a footy trip. Carey, the typical alpha male, not only captained the team on the field but led the party off the field.

After the games some of the Irish players would come back to our function at the team hotel. They were big names in Ireland but got nothing for playing Gaelic football and were a bit shocked by the earnings of their Australian opponents. When told that Wayne was getting almost a million dollars to play footy, his defensive opponent that day responded with a very funny and succinct comment. With half the gathering within earshot, and with a few jars of Guinness on board, the incredulous young bloke from county Cork told his audience, 'I can't believe it – he's getting a million dollars, and tomorrow morning I've got to go home and milk the f---ing cows.'

As a coach, given my limited exposure to the hybrid game I was hardly likely to pull off any tactical masterstrokes, so I saw my role as primarily being that of a motivator. I really wanted to emphasise to the players the whole idea of national pride and the honour associated with representing our country. We proudly displayed an

Australian flag as our team emblem for the pre-game address, and I made sure everyone not only knew the words to the national anthem but pumped them out proudly when the team lined up before the start of the match.

In the first Test we were behind pretty much from the outset, but not so far back as to be out of it. With a couple of minutes to go we were still eight points behind, when a long ball came into the Australian forward line and, as was the primary scoring objective, David Neitz knocked it into the back of the net for a six-pointer to get us within two points.

Moments later Scott Camporeale kicked an 'over', which got us three points and we were suddenly in front by a solitary point. It seemed like an eternity between then and when the Irish time-keeper sounded the final siren, but I can honestly say that the excitement I felt when the siren went was one of the great moments of my sporting life. We were leaping around like idiots as our exhilaration overflowed.

To win in such a way so far from home was a tremendously euphoric experience – the type of feeling you dream of, but on the other side of the world from where those dreams might usually come to fruition. In the rooms afterwards we gathered in a giant huddle, a room full of people who are normally opponents warmly embracing each other as Australian brothers in arms. We belted out 'Advance Australia Fair' with a passion and ferocity that I'd never done before and have never done since. It was an amazing few minutes at a most unlikely venue. I'm not stretching things to say that it was right up there with winning a grand final.

That was only the beginning of our 12 days in Ireland, and our next match wasn't until the following Sunday. In keeping with our clearly defined intention to ensure the players enjoyed themselves, the party went on all week. Not all of the players were out getting totally sloshed every night, but the more social animals – led by their captain – made up for the few of their team-mates who were trying to take care of themselves. The one firm rule was that we all met in the hotel foyer at eight o'clock each morning for a team walk, mainly to make sure they'd all survived the previous night's socialising. Our other expectation – or, more accurately, hope – was that there'd be no booze the night before we played.

It was wet in Dublin for the second Test, and not only had we enjoyed the festivities for the previous week, with a slippery ball I knew the locals' soccer skills would give them an advantage. I was right on both counts, and while it was the hardened professionals of Australia (although off a week-long party) taking on the amateurs of Ireland, we lost by 11 points. And such was the downward spiral of our preparation that if there had been a third Test another week later, we probably would have lost by 50 points.

We were going downhill fast, but that was the relaxed attitude to kick off the new venture. It was a price the AFL was prepared to pay to get the big footy names involved. While my job was more co-ordination than actual coaching, it was a great honour to be coach of a touring team representing our country. I'm really pleased Ian Collins made the call to offer me the role.

Actually, I got a few pleasant calls from 'Collo' in the few years after I finished at Collingwood. The centenary year of the VFL was celebrated in 1996 and as part of the celebrations a match between two teams of ex-players was scheduled as a curtain-raiser to a Melbourne v. Geelong game at the MCG. Ian asked me to captain-coach one of the teams, with Ron Barassi coaching the other. Both teams wore the type of outfits that our forefathers had used a century before, including the long-sleeved woollen jumpers, long shorts and felt peaked cap.

It was a fun exhibition, and also, undoubtedly, my worst-ever coaching performance – even worse than my babysitting of the Australian team in Ireland a couple of years later. The tone of the game was obviously lighthearted, and even my one responsibility of putting our on-field 18 in positions was completely ignored by the players. By the end of the 30-minute game, both squads of 25 players were all on the field together. In fact, this made it a real throwback to the distant past, because I think this was the way footy was played in the late 1800s.

Another memorable call from Ian Collins was to advise me that I'd been selected in the AFL Team of the Century; although it was more accurately the VFL Team of the Century, because every member had played in the Victorian league. An even bigger thrill was that

I'd be announced as an inaugural legend in the about-to-be-formed AFL Hall of Fame. When you start off as a little kid just wanting to play footy, then wanting to play in the big league, then when established wanting to play for Victoria, and finally extending your aims to wanting to be the best, this was all your dreams coming true.

I was furthered honoured when I was asked to speak on behalf of the inducted legends at the Hall of Fame function held at Melbourne Park, the home of the tennis centre, which hosts the Australian Open every January.

It was quite a nerve-racking experience. There were over 1500 people in the room, including the 136 inductees. This included coaches, umpires, administrators, media and the 120 Hall of Fame player members, many of whom had been my childhood heroes. The 12 legends were announced one at a time, and the five of us present at the event were introduced onto the stage. The term 'living legend' is a wonderful tag, and whenever it's used as an introduction I can't help thinking that, while the legend part is great, the living part is even better.

Then it was time for me to say a few words on behalf of the inaugural inductees. I could feel my heart pounding as I stepped forward. Onstage with me were Ron Barassi, Graeme 'Polly' Farmer, John Nicholls and Bob Skilton. Fellow inductees Jack Dyer and Dick Reynolds were still alive, but I'm pretty sure weren't at the function, and the remaining legends had already passed away. I wasn't game to look at the many famous faces in the audience. I'd thought about what I would say, but when I started talking I could feel my voice quivering – the whole thing was a bit overwhelming. At moments like this, all you can do is to speak from the heart and make it short and sharp.

My overriding thought was how much I loved the sport of football. The game had been so good to us all and given us so much – the Hall of Fame selection just topped it off. We were so very fortunate to have found a sport that enabled us to live out our dreams and ambitions, and while tonight the game was acknowledging our contribution, we owed the game much more than we could ever repay. Getting fame and a little fortune from our hobby made us very fortunate men. These were the sentiments I tried to convey.

The whole Hall of Fame concept is an incredibly humbling experience. On the night it seemed to transcend individual club loyalties, as inductees were warmly welcomed into the game's official royal family.

Another call from Ian Collins in early 1997 offered the opportunity to coach the Victorian State of Origin team against South Australia in Adelaide. I immediately accepted. Playing for the Big V used to be a dream for any youngster growing up in Victoria. However, as the VFL spread its boundaries and morphed into the AFL in 1990, state-versus-state football became difficult to fit into the football calendar. The days of players being excused from club duties to play for their state disappeared during the 1970s, and by the end of the decade player selection became based on state of origin.

By the late '70s, State of Origin games were played for a few years on the weekend after the VFL grand final. I refused to make myself available for this post-season time slot, and almost got suspended for doing so.

Now, as coach of the Victorian team, I felt that trying to force players to play representative football lowered the status of the whole event and was counterproductive to the honour of playing for your state or country. When the selected squad arrived at the MCG for a training session, this thought was uppermost in my mind. I taped a Victorian jumper onto the whiteboard, got the large squad of players into the meeting room, and said simply, 'If you're available, we'll see you back here in 30 minutes. If you're injured and can't play, or if you just don't want to play, we'll find players who do.'

We reconvened our pre-training meeting half an hour later. The dropouts had headed home with no questions asked, while those remaining became the nucleus of the Victorian team to take on South Australia.

Compared to club-level football, coaching a representative team is just great fun. You're given a group of talented players from an almost unlimited pool and you only have them for a short period of time – weeks or even days. It's nothing like the week after week, month after month, year after year drawn-out routine of club coaching. It's a bit like being a grandparent. You get all the good times with the grandkids, but none of the full-time grind of parenthood.

I only coached Victoria twice. We defeated South Australia that year, and the following year we beat the Allies team at the Gabba. The issue of state versus state football pops up annually, usually around the time of rugby league's very successful State of Origin games between New South Wales and Queensland. These games work firstly because the two states only play each other – no other state could field a competitive team – and secondly, the matches are a greater priority than the club competition, as shown by players missing club games the weekend before.

In the AFL system of an established national competition with players originating from many states and territories, regular State of Origin games aren't going to happen. However, selecting teams each year and giving those players picked a state jumper could and should be done.

I wore the once-famous Big V jumper 14 times. Most of my Hawthorn guernseys have gone to charity auctions and the like, but I still have my Victorian jumpers and will never part with them. Players get picked in the All-Australian team without playing a game. There's no reason why the various state bodies can't do the same. The modern players born in Victoria – the Jonathan Browns, Gary Abletts and Dane Swans – should, like me, have a wardrobe full of Big V jumpers.

After I left Collingwood, the other big change was jumping the fence and joining the media. My football breeding was to regard the media as the enemy, but as they say, if you can't beat them, join them. Instead of the weekly routine of training and playing, my work life would revolve around television commentary for Channel Seven, a weekly newspaper column with the *Herald Sun* and some radio work for 3AW and later with Triple M.

Immediately, the difference was stark. I was still going to the footy but had no real emotional involvement in the result of the game. That was initially quite refreshing. The other realisation was that what is automatic and normal in team sport is not so in the outside world.

In the sports team environment, there were collective goals, as well as individual roles within the team. After each match, players received easily measured feedback via things like the scoreboard, the premiership ladder and some fairly basic statistics, plus some individual feedback from the coach and the ever-enthusiastic offerings from family and close friends.

As a competitor I craved feedback to help measure and improve my performance. But when I moved from the playing ranks into the media, I quickly realised it didn't happen. When I asked how I was going, I was told simply, 'Don't worry – you'll hear about it if you're not doing a good job.' It was a world in which ratings and sales provided the ultimate collective feedback for management, and while I learned to live with that I realised as I prepared to coach again the importance of good, consistent feedback. Right there and then, I made it an absolute priority.

A few frustrations aside, I really enjoyed my time in the media, and I learned to appreciate things from the other side of the football fence. But one constant that never varied was the fact that, no matter what you are doing, preparation is paramount. If you want to perform at your best, you need to ensure you're properly prepared.

Bruce McAvaney, the on-air anchorman of Channel Seven's AFL coverage, was the common denominator between my initial media stint after coaching Collingwood and my more recent venture back at Seven after my Brisbane Lions days. He is a perfect example of something that never changed. Regardless of whether it was football, racing, tennis, track and field or whatever, Macca was always immaculately prepared.

Each Monday he'd meticulously journal all the results and statistics from the previous weekend, together with any interesting pieces of information he thought could possibly be useful somewhere down the track. For every quirky fact he squeezed into his commentary, he would store away dozens of others.

The McAvaney professionalism is well known to all who work with him, but it was never more evident than when he was preparing to host the 2012 Brownlow Medal coverage. His primary function on the night was to keep things moving, to ensure the formalities were properly conducted and to keep the vote count together.

His one big live involvement was to be an extended interview with the winner at the end of the night. It was never going to be a challenging situation, given the euphoria that the player would be feeling, but

Bruce wasn't going to do just another interview. Ever the professional, he wanted it to be special. So, in the weeks leading up to the Brownlow Medal dinner, he made an appointment to see a dozen of the most likely winners and spent an hour with each of them to ensure he was properly equipped.

The other thing that strikes me about Bruce is that he's a very good team player. He has a great ability to make his co-commentators look good by leading them into their areas of expertise. Whether it's at the Australian Open tennis with Jim Courier and Lleyton Hewitt, the spring racing with Richard Freedman and Francesca Cumani, or the football with Tom Harley or myself, he never lets his own ego get in the way of what's best for the coverage.

Denis Cometti, the other half of Seven's Friday night commentary team, is always similarly well prepared. Don't think for a moment that all those one-liners he comes up with are off the cuff. If you walk into the area where Denis is calling, you'll see Post-it notes stuck up everywhere to serve as a reminder of something he has thought of in the days leading up to his call.

Off camera, Denis is exactly as you see him on screen. He's cool, calm and collected, and very witty. I always get a laugh out of his occasional reference to 'The Beast', who is in fact his son, a professional wrestler in the United States who uses that name. But if I can divulge a little secret about the man from Perth with the booming voice, he doesn't like the wind. Or, more particularly, his hair doesn't like the wind. If he's asked to host a segment from the open-air third level at the MCG, he'll do just about anything to get out of it, and to ensure he stays in the still confines of the inside studio.

My television and radio commitments offer a totally contrasting insight into the question of preparation. Television is pictures with words to top it up, and by its very nature is heavily pre-planned and organised. It has to be, especially on free-to-air television where the target audience is as much the general public as it is the hardened football fanatic. It needs to incorporate not just football intricacies but information of a broad and general human interest.

Channel Seven management likes a busy coverage with short sharp segments and many on-air voices. This has become even more so in my more recent second stint. In the lead-up to a Friday night game, our producer, Glenn Postill, will make contact to discuss topic options for the pre-game show. I'll often ask how much time he wants to devote to a topic, and the answer is usually around 30 seconds – maybe 40, if it's really worthwhile.

The production that goes into every segment of television is extraordinary, and is in total contrast to the ad-lib world of sporting radio. Using my recent experiences as an example, if we're on air with 3AW from noon until 6 pm on a Saturday, I'm expected to be at the ground by 11.30 am. Then we'll discuss the topics that we'll be working through during the two-hour pre-game. Maybe two or three brief interviews are locked in, but aside from that, and a couple of notes that our host Brian Taylor may have scribbled down, it's largely ad lib from then on, with BT driving the agenda.

I love radio because I love talking football. That's what radio is. From noon on a Saturday with 3AW, I'll spend two hours chatting with other guys who also love the footy – Mike Sheahan, Matthew Richardson, Matthew Lloyd, Dr Peter Larkins and BT. The match coverage is pretty straightforward, and then we've got the post-match talk-fest, generally hosted by Tim Lane, who joins the coverage when the match begins. Again, the role of the host is crucial because he's got to think on the go to lead the direction of the discussion and maybe find an interesting talkback topic or two. I only try to fight one bias: when supporters of the losing team queue up to blame the coach, my instinct is to defend him because on almost all occasions players lose games, not coaches.

From my experience of the three mediums, writing is the hardest. There is no producer – you have to do the whole job from start to finish. By far the most difficult part is thinking up an interesting topic in the first place. For the non-journalists like me, it's a slow process after that to get my thoughts into words.

I admire the entertaining wordsmiths. Patrick Smith's articles in *The Australian* are my current must-read. His turn of phrase is always enjoyable, as long as you or yours are not the target of his cynicism. Patrick does confuse his opinion with cold hard fact, but that's a failing he shares with many others in the media.

The news-breaker specialists have it really hard. If they take the time to check the total accuracy of an exclusive, someone else will likely beat them to the story, so going off with innuendo and opinion rather than cold hard facts is a well-worn path to getting the highly valued scoop.

Maybe journalists too are just victims of the modern media age. Former British Prime Minister Tony Blair wrote an interesting article about the UK political commentators after finishing his term at Downing Street. The tenor of his comments was that because the media had grown so quickly this generation – with the advent of websites, social media, etc. – the need to fight for space in this very crowded domain meant that opinion was increasingly being dressed up as fact, and hard-hitting sensationalism and controversy was a necessary element to survive. He could easily have been talking about the evolution of the AFL media.

What did happen in my few years around the press box was that it changed my view of the media as the enemy. Over the last couple of decades football has become part of the sports entertainment industry, and the media provides the critical conduit between the consumers – the fans – and the product providers – the AFL and the clubs. Because of the game's huge popularity and fan base, anyone who works in footy, particularly at club level, is very well paid. The free publicity that the footy media generates is a big factor in this and an integral part of the professional full-time era. The media is neither friend nor enemy to the players and clubs, and, like the umpires, is an indispensable part of modern football.

Another thing that hit me during my post-Collingwood period in the media had an application to teams or groups of any type. Channel Nine had launched *The Footy Show* in prime time, 9.30 on Thursday nights. People like Eddie McGuire, Sam Newman, Doug Hawkins and Jason Dunstall became overnight celebrities. With the rights to cover the matches, Channel Seven was the football station at the time, but Channel Nine seemed to be where all the big stars worked, the network was great at self-promotion and it had a much bigger profile and following. It was the glamorous alternative, and at the time I couldn't help but think that if I had a choice about where to work, I would have chosen the pace-setters at Nine.

From this example I became further convinced that all coaches/ managers need to generate pride in team, club or organisation. It's extremely unhealthy if any of your staff has an inclination to move to one of your competitors. I believe that coaches and managers have to be aware of this dynamic as part of the overall challenge of making their team the preferred work destination in their industry.

If I ever coached again, this was a principle that would be at the top of my list of priorities.

33

TOO GOOD TO REFUSE

*What he said was stunning: 'Brisbane wants you to coach them
and they're prepared to pay you $500,000 to do it.'*

I guess all our lives are punctuated by random, sliding-door moments that change the course of our destiny. Mine certainly has been, but never more so than a phone call I received at the MCG on Sunday, 9 August 1998.

Richmond was playing Collingwood and I was there for the *Herald Sun* to do a piece on the game when, just before half-time, my mobile phone rang. On the other end of the line was my solicitor, Jeff Browne, who said he had something important and confidential to tell me. As I was seated in the crowded press box, I told him to hold on as I walked up the stairs to a quiet area on the concourse behind the stand. After a few words of greeting, he got to the purpose of his call. What he said was stunning: 'Brisbane wants you to coach them and they're prepared to pay you $500,000 to do it.'

Apart from running his successful law firm Browne and Co., Jeff was the AFL's main legal advisor and I knew he was a close friend of Brisbane Lions CEO Andrew Ireland, so he was well connected – this was a genuine offer. My first thought was pretty basic: *Gee, that's a lot of money.* I was receiving about $200,000 a year when I left Collingwood and was earning a similar amount from my combined media work, so just the simple maths of an extra $300,000 annually was quite a carrot.

Despite the great offer, my initial interest was lukewarm at best. Firstly, my addiction to coaching was cured and going back to that all-encompassing lifestyle had little appeal. Also I was a conservative Melbourne boy who'd grown up and had always lived in the city's southern bayside suburbs. After living in Langwarrin as a child, a few shifts in between had got me to my current townhouse in Brighton. At 46 years of age, I'd shifted a total of about 20 kilometres in my entire life. Making the big move to another state seemed like shifting to the other side of the world. I'd happily go north to the Gold Coast for holidays, but moving permanently away from Victoria was just not on my radar.

When I'd finished at Collingwood nearly three seasons earlier, I thought that after a year off I'd want to coach again. But one year led to two, and then two to three, and the urge got less, not more. A couple of clubs had made tentative approaches but I was enjoying my media jobs and was comfortable not having the stress of my team winning or losing to worry about.

At least, that was my conscious attitude. There must have been a part of me still open to coaching, though, because my response to Jeff was to let me think about it and I'd give him a call back the following day.

A few weeks earlier, I'd been approached by the Fremantle Dockers to see if I might be interested in their coaching job and, again, it was not a blanket 'no' but an agreement to meet with a couple of their officials. The meeting took place but I contacted them the next day with a firm 'not interested' and I never heard from them again.

After hanging up from Jeff, my mind was spinning. I went back to the press box and, although I was distracted, watched the second half and quickly completed my newspaper copy. My next call was to Graeme Allan.

Gubby had remained at Victoria Park after I left, but for the previous year or two had shifted from the football department over to the Magpies' marketing area. He had remained a friend and confidant, so with the Lions offer buzzing through my mind I rang my old mate and asked if he was free to catch up that evening. He said he was about to head out with his family for a pizza near their home in Warrandyte, but when I told him I had something I wanted to discuss he sensed it was important, cancelled the family dinner and agreed to meet me in a little Italian restaurant in Doncaster. After talking about the Brisbane approach, my lukewarm interest warmed up a bit when, off the cuff, he announced that if I was interested he'd be happy to come along and give me a hand. Whether his wife, Anne, and sons, Marcus and Patrick, would share his interest was obviously still to be determined.

Now this was an unexpected turn of events. Gubby still had first-hand knowledge of the inner workings of an AFL football department and our partnership had worked well at Collingwood. The possibility of having my trusted lieutenant go north with me was a positive development. After leaving Gub, I drove to the Parkdale home of my partner, now wife, Deb to share the news of the day's events. I wouldn't have gone to Brisbane without her coming with me, and her response to a potential move was positive. So, although I was still a reluctant passenger, the train was moving forward rather than stalling. I rang Jeff Browne the following morning with a willingness to at least do the courtesy of meeting with the key Brisbane officials.

That meeting took place the next Friday morning in the board room of Browne & Co. solicitors. Jeff did the formalities of the introductions, then left us to it. Representing the Lions was their chairman, Alan Piper, deputy chairman, Graeme Downie, and Andrew Ireland. I'd never met Alan or Graeme but knew Andrew quite well through our involvement in footy over the years. He'd played 110 games for Collingwood in the late 1970s before moving to Brisbane, where he eventually became CEO of AFL Queensland, and then general manager of the Lions.

We talked for an hour or so and I was right up-front. Alan asked straight out if I'd be interested in the job and I told him I was 90 per cent sure it would be a no. After the meeting, Andrew and I chatted for another 15 minutes on the footpath, and if nothing else his persistence was enough to get me thinking. I was 46 and I was going to be a long time in the media if I didn't coach again.

The media was satisfying but not terrible stimulating compared to playing and coaching. I always think it's a bit like being a eunuch in an Arabian harem: you get to watch but never participate. However, while coaching was incredibly challenging and stimulating it took over every part of my being and totally dominated my life. Also, during the last period of my Collingwood tenure I hadn't enjoyed my coaching persona – too often I regressed into a grumpy Enforcer – and because the Magpies had dropped to mid-list before I finished, my confidence had taken a jolt as well.

Like a chameleon that changes colour to fit into its environment, in football I tended to become what I needed to be, when I needed to be it. In other words, both as player and coach I wore this competitive cloak, and being able to take it off over the previous three years had been refreshing, if a little mundane. Whatever my personality was during this period it was the real me, although, looking back, my life was a bit in limbo – both personally after my marriage break-up and professionally without the automatic goal-setting and aspirations of club-level footy.

Another practical reason for my initial reticence about taking the Brisbane job was my Melbourne-based family. While Mum and Dad still lived in the Chelsea home that my brothers, Russell and Kelvin, and I had grown up in, they were both heading into their 80s and becoming quite frail. There were also my daughters, Tracey and Fiona. Both were now in their mid-20s, but your kids are always your kids no matter their age. And I was about to become a grandfather, as Fiona was pregnant and due in a few months' time. On 15 December my granddaughter Amber was born – her age will always signify how many years ago I moved to Brisbane. At the time, though, her impending arrival was just one of many reasons either to remain in Melbourne or to stay in my comfort zone and not to coach again.

After the meeting at Jeff Browne's office, a busy week followed. I caught up with Gubby a couple of times as the idea started to gain momentum, while the Lions people met with AFL boss Wayne Jackson to discuss the financial implications of what they were looking to do. Although they were told the league wasn't in the business of under-writing coaching contracts, Jackson indicated to the club that they'd support the initiative and try to help out in other ways, if they could. I got a phone call from Wayne, who encouraged me to take the job, and another from Channel Seven boss Kerry Stokes, who indicated that they'd release me from my contract and would support my move north. Apparently, Channel Seven in Brisbane took out a $50,000 sponsorship with the Lions. For all the rumours over the years, that was the net AFL involvement in me taking the Lions job.

Persistence is a great quality and, despite my early negativity, Andrew Ireland kept making contact on behalf of the Lions. He suggested I ring Craig Starcevich, who was in his first year as Brisbane conditioning coach. Of course, Craig had played in the 1990 Collingwood premiership team and in 1994 had reluctantly gone north as part of the Nathan Buckley deal. He gave me a good understanding of the lie of the land around the Lions and was very encouraging about the need for my style of coaching/management. Starce said there were many conflicting voices interfering in areas outside their specialty. From his comments, it sounded like the club's whole chain of command had fallen apart. Individuals in any successful team need to accept authority and to know, accept and perform their roles, and have trust in others to do the same. According to Starce, this stopped happening at Brisbane during their spiral down the ladder in 1998 – no wonder they'd had a disastrous season.

I tossed all the pros and cons back and forward, until gradually, over a couple of weeks, the appeal of the job began to outweigh my initial reluctance. The Allans were in, Deb was keen, and, truth be known, the financial deal was just too good to knock back.

If there was a moment my 'maybe' became a definite 'yes', it was at the 50th birthday party of Channel 7 colleague Drew Morphett at La Bruschetta restaurant in Malvern. Drew and I went back a long way. Many years earlier, in my final couple of years as a player, we'd worked together with Ron Barassi and Doug Heywood on the ABC footy panel TV show. By this time the talk of me coaching the Lions was in the public domain. The conversation all evening included the usual references to sunscreen, sunhats and golf clubs – the type of things you'd associate with a holiday in sunny Queensland.

I remember thinking at the party that I could feel myself symbolically sliding down a well into coaching again. That night, I decided to accept the Brisbane job.

The next weekend was the final home-and-away round and, as it happened, I was scheduled to be at the Saturday night game at the Gabba between the Lions and St Kilda as part of the Seven commentary team.

After many phone conversations it was an opportune time to meet again in person with Alan Piper and Andrew Ireland. On the Saturday afternoon we met at Alan's luxurious townhouse overlooking the Brisbane River in the Dockside complex at Kangaroo Point, only a kilometre or so from the Gabba. I reiterated my requirements to become Brisbane coach and we finalised a three-year deal. A five-year deal was on the table, but I had no interest in a commitment of that length.

I'd identified three issues that were pivotal to my agreement. One, I'd oversee the whole football operation. Two, I wanted Gubby to be appointed football manager. And three, I wanted to know if the club would be able to fund the footy operation we wanted to put in place.

My conviction that Gubby coming with me was non-negotiable tested the resolve of the club, because the popular Scott Clayton was the incumbent football manager. Andrew knew Gubby quite well, so his qualifications for the job weren't questioned, but I'm sure the Lions didn't think that replacing Scott was part of the deal when I was first approached. I was aware enough that the club didn't think of me as a coaching genius – more a big footy name who had coached a premiership win, which was of great PR value given that they were overlooking fan favourite Roger Merrett. All the ramifications of bringing in a coaching/administrative pairing must have caused much discussion behind the scenes.

I had barely looked at the Lions list. That would come if I was appointed. The first building block was very basic: it was all about both me and the club knowing how our arrangement would work, and from that starting point building the necessary infrastructure to support the players' efforts to perform at their best. Gubby and I would manage the footy department, while all I wanted from Alan and Andrew was confirmation that the club would give us our head and that they could fund our plans. For instance, we wanted to introduce deep-tissue massage twice a week for every player – an $80,000 to $90,000 annual cost.

As soon as these basic needs were agreed to, the deal was done. We shook hands and I left that meeting as the new but yet to be announced Brisbane Lions coach. It made my night in the Seven commentary box quite surreal, because even my co-commentators were unaware of the afternoon's developments. What made it even stranger was that I desperately wanted the Lions to lose.

It's fair to say I viewed the game a little differently that night because what happened actually mattered to the next phase of my life. I didn't yet have any emotional attachment to the Lions, so, as I watched the game unfold, my mind was on the future. The reason I wanted Brisbane to lose was because, if they did, 'we' would get an extra priority pick in the upcoming national draft. Bottom position and first pick was already confirmed, but another loss would get second pick as well. As the new coach, I was happy to swap the potential impetus of a last-round win for the second-best draftee in the country.

If for some reason I'd been coaching the Lions that night, the controversial concept of tanking this match would have been a serious consideration. Club-level football people who fight tooth and nail to build a premiership team understand the need to sometimes sacrifice the here and now to gain future rewards.

After starting the season with high expectations, the Lions had endured the year from hell. John Northey had taken the Brisbane Bears to the preliminary final in his first season at the club in 1996, and following what was generally accepted as a hiccup in 1997 after the merger with Fitzroy – when the new-look Brisbane Lions side had been lucky to fall into the finals – they were tipped to be a force in 1998.

It didn't work out that way. Captain Michael Voss had suffered a badly broken leg in a 71-point loss to Fremantle at Subiaco in round 11, which left the Lions at the bottom of the ladder with a 2–9 record. The club was in turmoil. There seemed to be bickering at all levels and Northey was sacked several days later.

Roger Merrett, former captain and favourite son, was installed as caretaker coach for the rest of the season. As so often happens, he started with a honeymoon period – a draw in his first game, followed by consecutive wins, which temporarily saw the Lions climb two spots up the ladder. It didn't last. They lost the next seven by an average of almost 10 goals, and, heading into round 22, they had the wooden spoon already locked up.

Under Stan Alves, St Kilda had a lot to play for. They were equal third on the ladder with Sydney and Melbourne – just behind the Swans on percentage and just ahead of the Demons. All three spots could change in the final round, with Sydney to meet 14th-placed Collingwood at the SCG on the Sunday, and Melbourne to meet ninth-placed Richmond at the MCG at the same time.

Andrew Bews, a former Geelong captain who had chosen to finish his career in Brisbane, was playing his last game at the Gabba. He was enormously popular with the Lions players, as he had been at Geelong, and coach Merrett had called on his troops to find something special for him.

All of a sudden, I found myself emotionally involved in what turned out to be a fluctuating contest. The Lions were 20 points down in the second quarter and 21 points up inside the last six minutes, before surviving a stirring St Kilda comeback to win by a solitary point.

The Lions got home by a split second, with Saints captain Stewart Loewe kicking a close-in goal just after the siren. When the umpires ruled that the last score didn't count, the Gabba erupted, at least most did – except for me and the handful of Saints fans. The Lions had restored a little lost pride to a club which had been ridiculed for much of the year, but in the process had blown the valuable priority draft pick.

As I watched the close win unfold I thought to myself, *Damn, that loss is going to cost us a very good player.* As it turned out, Brisbane took Des Headland with first pick in the draft, and Fremantle opted for Justin Longmuir with the pick that would have been Brisbane's had they lost that last game.

As far as long-term benefit was concerned, the result had gone the wrong way for the Lions, but I was excited and stimulated by the fact that I was again emotionally involved in a game of football. The familiar emotions that had been dormant for a few years, that restless tension at the footy, was a welcome feeling.

It was time to accept the challenge again.

34

BUILDING THE BASE

*It was becoming increasingly obvious that me and my sport
barely registered on the city's sporting radar.*

On Tuesday 7 September 1998, I got an early morning flight from
my home city of Melbourne to my new home city of Brisbane. I had
two important tasks: a press conference to announce my coaching
appointment and my first meeting with the Lions players. When I
arrived in Brisbane, I grabbed a copy of *The Courier-Mail*, Queensland's daily paper, from the news-stand and, as I was waiting to
be collected, began browsing for the AFL news that was filling the
Melbourne *Herald Sun*.

As most of us sports nuts do, I started from the back, and quickly
discovered the essential difference between the AFL heartland of
the southern states and the frontier north of the Murray River.
With the AFL finals about to begin, I was 12 pages in before I
found a half page of AFL. In profile terms – as determined by *The
Courier-Mail* – AFL in Brisbane was like an army outpost in the
Wild West cowboy movies, surrounded and overwhelmed by the
superior forces of the Indians of the other football codes – mainly
rugby league and, to a lesser extent, rugby union. Making the Brisbane Lions the preferred destination for AFL players was clearly
going to take some doing.

Nearly 15 years later, and even with the Lions' great success in the
early 2000s, little has changed: AFL coverage in *The Courier-Mail* is
still usually a dozen pages from the back. I'm used to that now but it
was quite a shock to the system when I first came to Brisbane.

Club property steward Graeme Smart arrived to pick me up in his 'Bearmobile', the nickname given to his small equipment van decorated with Lions colours and signage. You only get one chance to make a good first impression and this was not it. Having a first look at Brisbane and the Lions from the front seat of the Bearmobile was a second-rate experience, not in keeping with the top-notch elite club we aspired to be. Every little bit is important and I made a mental note that never again would the Bearmobile be the airport pick-up vehicle.

The press conference was important because I'd come to Brisbane with the clear intention of marketing both the Lions and the sport of AFL the best I could by being open and accessible. Hopefully my first contact with the local media would get that objective off on the right foot.

However, my main task that day was to address the Brisbane players and set the scene for what lay ahead. I guess in the modern era of in-depth coaching interviews my plans and expectations would have already been locked in and detailed in a PowerPoint presentation. There was no such detail at this point, because Gubby and I wanted to meet with a lot of people around the club before big decisions were made and implemented. When I'd started at Collingwood many years before, I coached by the seat of my pants within the successful framework of what I'd seen at Hawthorn and from my various coaches. After a decade of coaching, followed by three years of watching two or three games live every round, I'd be beginning afresh but this time from an experienced base.

My starting point was not so much about playing footy but establishing what we now call 'group culture'. Actually I hate that buzzword – lately it's become football's version of secret men's business. It isn't that secretive or complicated. Culture is simply the group's dos and don'ts. It has been accurately described as what you do when no-one is there to tell you what to do. Truth be known, every club aspires to a very similar group culture. The statements of specifics and intent are the easy part. The big difference is the quality of the team's leadership and personnel. Culture changes as people come and go.

Based on my past experiences and early knowledge of the Lions' situation at the time, I went to Brisbane with a few overriding principles in my mind to build a strong culture base from which to develop an elite football team.

MY INITIAL PRIORITIES
1. Establish a clear chain of command;
2. Recruit the best possible coaching and support staff and sell that belief to the players;
3. Use positive reinforcement whenever possible.

ATTITUDES TO INSTIL
1. PRIDE – Promote pride in your team and pride in yourself;
2. RESPECT – Be respectful to others and earn respect yourself;
3. TRUST – Give trust to those around you and earn the trust of others.

ACTIONS TO LIVE BY
1. BE COURTEOUS – Be courteous and helpful to others as they perform their individual roles;
2. ACT WITH COMMONSENSE – Ask yourself when contemplating an action: if everyone in the team did this, will we be better or worse? Whether you should or shouldn't is normally clear if that question is answered honestly;
3. BE PUNCTUAL – The one absolute rule. If one person is late, the whole team is held up.

These were all only words, but I believed that if all our endeavours supported these few simple aims we'd have a good framework on which to build healthy team harmony.

The bowels underneath the old Lions Social Club at the Gabba served as the dressing-room area with adjacent offices. That day, staff and players were milling around waiting for direction. As the existing club coaches, Roger Merrett and Rod O'Riley, were also there, and their future was still unclear, I decided that the initial meeting should be just the players and their new coach.

I was in the meeting room as the players entered. As you'd expect with a new unknown boss, the atmosphere was quiet and unsure, not loud and raucous. It was quite a big area with a large whiteboard on one wall; facing opposite were three levels of bench seats that ran the length of the room. A set of double doors next to the whiteboard was the one entrance.

The first thing that hit me was the number of players who looked injured. The front row was almost full of players either with plaster on a part of their body or crutches to help them walk. It was a wounded group hard hit by injury; no wonder their season had been a shocker.

I made the point of not starting until the clock on the wall hit the appointed meeting time of 11 am and then closed and locked the meeting-room doors. I started to address the players when a knock on the door interrupted me. The latecomer was Lions youngster Steven Lawrence, coincidentally the son of one of my toughest opponents, Barry, who'd played for St Kilda.

There was a fair chance someone would be a minute or two late for the meeting, which I knew would allow me the opportunity to push the need for punctuality by refusing him entry. There's no use having principles if they're not supported by actions. I told Steven that he was late and I'd catch up with him after the meeting was finished. I'm confident the whole player group got the message loud and clear.

My intention was for the meeting only to be a short scene-setter, not long and drawn-out. There were only two subjects I wanted to discuss. First was that the chain of command around the club seemed to have fallen apart and needed to be re-established. The simple principle to achieve this was that, from this point forward, players would play, coaches would coach and management would manage. We would assist and have trust in others to perform their roles and wouldn't step over the line of interfering in others' assigned jobs.

After the conflict and turmoil of the previous campaign, selling this theme to the players was like leading a thirsty horse to water. For example, as the 1998 season went off the rails, some Lions board members had bypassed management and coaches to seek the views of individual players about how they were being coached. The playing group had first-hand experience of the dangers of players being asked to critique their coaches, so being firm on sticking to the established chain of command was a policy I was confident they were ready to embrace.

I tried to sell the same theme to the club's voluntary board and full-time administration. Like the players, they were also ready and eager to oblige after the previous season's debacle.

My second issue was to be a seller of hope by guaranteeing the players that we'd put together a support staff that would be the best in the competition. How we'd prove this was a good question. However, under my principle of positive reinforcement – and even before we had made specific appointments – I'd already committed myself to constantly telling the players how lucky they were to have the coaching, medical and conditioning group they had. It would be another small step towards the critically important aim of making them proud of their team and club.

I was still doing my weekend media work until the season ended and had the commitment in place to coach the Australian International Rules team in October in Ireland. The Lions rented a two-bedroom apartment at Dockside in Kangaroo Point for me and Gubby to share when we were in Brisbane. Deb and her son, Clint, and daughter, Abbey, would come up permanently after Christmas, as would the Allan family.

We spent most of our mid-weeks in Brisbane working through meetings with a lot of our more experienced players and the club's off-field personnel. This was mainly a fact-finding mission to hear all their views and we were in constant discussions with Andrew Ireland to bounce things off him as well.

I firmly believe that any group benefits from regularly developing a new starting point. This requires an accurate assessment of where the group is 'today'. The outside view is helpful because there is no ownership of what has happened in the past, but digging beneath the surface from within is also critically important. Gubby and I needed to embark on this investigation before we planned in detail for the future. What and who to keep and what to change had to be answered eventually, but taking the time to find out the current situation was our initial aim.

There had obviously been a fair bit of politicking and conflict behind the scenes the year before and we soon decided that we didn't have the luxury of working out who was worth keeping and who we should move on, so it was largely a blanket sacking and then starting again. In terms of our support staff, we wanted to use the value of fresh people and a new beginning.

Of the club's existing full-time football department staff, we retained Craig Starcevich as conditioning coach, Shane Johnson as player welfare manager, Nicole Duncan as football secretary and Kinnear Beatson as our Melbourne-based recruiting manager. Every other position would be changed. It was unfortunate for those replaced but the winds of change needed to happen.

I love going into a club and looking at everything with fresh eyes. After a while you assume ownership of what is in place and it's certainly harder to critique your own work. At the beginning of a coaching tenure the fresh look provokes a lot of new ideas and an unfettered willingness to make changes. During this process, avoiding throwing out the baby with the bathwater becomes a big challenge.

One thing that never changes is the value to a senior coach of an assistant who is still one of the players in spirit and who knows what's going on within the player group. When we broached this with Andrew he suggested Michael McLean, who had retired at the end of 1987 after 95 games with Footscray and 88 with the Brisbane Bears/Lions. 'Mag' – short for 'Magic', as he was known – was from the Northern Territory and had been a trailblazer for indigenous players travelling to Melbourne to have a crack at the big league. He'd overcome many obstacles to become a very good player and, in the process, had earned a reputation as a first-class football citizen. We made contact, he came back to Brisbane from Darwin for an interview, and he accepted the role as our forwards coach. Mag had great empathy for people, was a terrific listener, and, according to Phil Jauncey's personality profile, was a Feeler/Thinker, which would be a good balance for my heavy Enforcer tendencies.

Three seasons earlier, when I'd left Collingwood, we trained late afternoon on the assumption that most players still had a job outside the game. When I went to the Lions the evolution to full-time footy was complete. Few players had a job apart from football, so we were now a full-time club training during the day. And with full-time players, we needed mainly full-time staff.

We decided we needed three assistant coaches, a senior conditioning coach, a specialist strength coach, a video/stats operator and a property manager. Add me as senior coach, Gubby as football manager, Nicole Duncan as football secretary and Shane Johnson as player welfare manager, and that would be our full-time football department.

In a 2013 AFL club you could multiply that number by about four. Player list numbers are the same at around 45, but a 400 per cent increase in other football department staff is a fair indication of the off-field arms race that is plaguing the competition. At the turn of the century, a club's footy department could meet around a boardroom table and everyone could comfortably have their say – now it would be impossible to find a table big enough. The result is that the off-field group is now many small teams working within one big organisation. I read once that the maximum number of people who can work cohesively as a team is five to seven. From my experience this is an accurate assessment.

One of the survivors in the transition period was strength and conditioning coach and 1990 Collingwood premiership player Craig Starcevich. As I've mentioned, his strength of character when he was virtually pushed to the Bears as part of the Nathan Buckley trade really stuck in my mind, so when I got to Brisbane I knew enough of him to want to continue with his services. Andrew also supported retaining Craig, so he was recontracted.

As a coach who was now a generation away from playing, I was keen on players who had recently retired to fill the assistant coach roles. Apart from Michael McLean, I immediately approached ex-Essendon captain Gary O'Donnell, who had just retired. I had been a great fan of the way Gary played his footy but was even more impressed with the classy way he conducted himself off the field. We offered him the defensive portfolio and he accepted.

Our final appointment was ex-Fitzroy and North Melbourne player Matthew Armstrong, who had retired at the end of the 1996 season. He had a Lions connection, having played with the Fitzroy part of the merged club that became the Brisbane Lions, but it was his background at the Kangaroos that really interested me. I was a great fan of North coach Denis Pagan's game plan and was keen to get one of his ex-players onto our coaching panel. We spoke to Mattie and he agreed to join us as our midfield coach.

To top up our new off-field team we appointed Scott Murphy, a well-regarded power sports specialist with a rugby background, as our strength coach.

The other important part of the puzzle was to put together a top-class medical team. Recognising that the player list was unhealthily injury-prone, the previous football manager, Scott Clayton, had already started discussions with a couple of new physiotherapists – we merely completed the process.

By the start of the 1999 pre-season we had an entirely new medical operation, headed by physio Peter Stanton. He'd spent 10 years at the Australian Institute of Sport in Canberra and, among other postings, had worked extensively with the Australian track and field team. It was a medical group that also included fellow AIS and Olympic phys-iotherapist Victor Popov, sports doctors Paul McConnell and Andrew Smith, and nutritionist Michelle Cort. These people weren't totally full-time, but they were at the club a lot and attended all group sessions and games. Supplementing them was orthopaedic surgeon Jim Fardou-lys and a specialist podiatrist, massage co-ordinator and a stretching specialist. Our whole off-field team was encouraged to push the enve-lope to find us a competitive advantage in the use of the various sports sciences. This aim was more than met in the years that followed.

Ex-Geelong captain and Brisbane ruckman Damian Bourke became part-time ruck coach and Bob Newton, my old running coach at Collingwood, who specialised in speed development and running technique training, also came to our training sessions. As well, for the first time we employed a full-time video and statistics operator in Cameron Woodrow, and a full-time property manager in David Brooks.

Former Hawthorn premiership player and 1991 Brisbane Bears reserves premiership captain Peter Curran became our Melbourne-based man on the ground who scouted the opposition games for us. Two other key people were also retained: Barry Lowe, our honor-ary team manager, and our consultant performance psychologist, Dr Phil Jauncey.

In the modern professional club almost the entire staff is full-time or well-paid part time, but Barry, like Eddie Hillgrove, my team manager at Collingwood, did it because he loved the involvement and loved the club. These people epitomised what pre-professional sport teams were about, an era when representing your community with many unpaid individuals digging in to give the team a hand was how clubs were run. The way my two team managers performed the difficult task of organising the often prickly players – and coaches – with care, composure and diplomacy was first class. Eddie was there for my 10 years at the Magpies, while Barry was there for my first game as Lions coach and was still there for my last a decade later. Both were terrific people who were more important to the team karma than they were ever given credit for.

I hoped our new football department was ahead of its time and that it would become the best ever established by an AFL club. Ultimately, it was up to the players to perform but we wanted to give them every possible support to play to the very best of their ability. The added placebo effect of players believing that their coaching, conditioning and medical team was cutting edge was initially enhanced by me telling them so as often as possible. During the first couple of seasons before we achieved the ultimate team success, we needed to use every possible means of making the players proud of their team and club.

We got our off-field team together and at the same time the annual football cycle turned to the players. The same principle applied: who to keep, who to recruit and, finally, who to reposition. Again, a fresh look at our existing list was helpful – without the accumulated baggage that came from previous close contact – but my basic philosophy was to assess our players over the following season. Our recruiting philosophy was to top-up rather than to make wholesale changes.

As we were putting in place the building blocks to get the best out of our existing players, the opportunity to get a young talent from outside the draft presented itself. We thought it was worthwhile at the time. History tells us it was a critical component in the development of a premiership team.

I hadn't even been a week in the job before a meeting that would have huge ramifications down the track. On 12 September 1998,

Gubby, Kinnear Beatson and I went to Waverley to watch the Geelong Falcons play in a TAC Cup under-18s semi-final – and, more particularly, to watch a big lad named Brown. Jonathan Brown.

The Brown family lived in the western Victorian town of Warrnambool and Jonathan was the son of ex-Fitzroy player Brian Brown, who just happened to be a long-time close friend of my right-hand man. In fact, the relationship between Brian and Gubby went much further than just friends – they'd been team-mates at Fitzroy and taught together at Parade College, Bundoora, in Melbourne's northern suburbs. Gubby had even met young Jonathan on the day he was born when he joined the proud new father for a few celebratory beers. Now we were hoping their friendship would help clinch a prime recruiting coup for the Lions.

Young Jonathan was eligible to join the Lions under the AFL's father/son rule, because Brian had played more than 50 games for Fitzroy – 51, in fact. Plus two games for Essendon. But with this huge opportunity came a problem. At the time, each club could only draft one 17-year-old and the long-time Fitzroy supporter was only 17. With first pick in the upcoming national draft courtesy of our wooden spoon, we'd already identified Des Headland as our preferred choice, so we couldn't take them both.

Hoping to convince Jonathan not to nominate for the 1999 national draft so that we could take him 12 months later, we met him and Brian and his mum, Mary, for dinner at the Jells Park Hotel, a pub very close to the Brandon Park Shopping Centre where I had my sports store in the late-'70s. We also brought along the Lions' new sprint coach, Bob Newton, who was a friend of the Browns from their joint involvement at Fitzroy many years earlier.

As I would learn later, Jonathan was eager to get into the AFL via the upcoming draft rather than wait 12 months for us to take him. Both Port Adelaide and Hawthorn had shown a bit of interest in him being their one 17-year-old pick but were not offering a guarantee that he would definitely be drafted. Apparently, on the day that draft nominations closed, Jonathan spent two hours with his father, who was a teacher at Emmanuel College, Warrnambool, contemplating his decision. The deadline was 2 pm and it was only just before then that he finally decided not to nominate and instead wait a year and join the Lions for the 2000 season. At the time I was pleased: if I'd had a crystal ball to read the future, I would have been ecstatic.

Jonathan had played senior football with South Warrnambool at 15 and was also a handy first-grade fast bowler with Wesley CBC in the Warrnambool district cricket competition – he'd once been invited to join the Victorian under-17 squad. As a boy, he split his time between his two sporting loves, but thankfully, when it came time to choose, football got the nod. He spent a few weeks up in Brisbane that summer and, after watching him train with the Lions, I knew very early on he was going to be a special player. Big, powerful, aggressive and a good endurance runner with good skills, he looked a fantastic prospect.

I suspect Hawthorn and Port Adelaide have long regretted their decision not to pursue Jonathan more vigorously, because if either had committed to take him with their first draft pick he says he would have nominated and been drafted. It was one of those sliding-door moments that was extremely costly for those two clubs and a gigantic bonus for the Lions, who, because of the father/son connection, got a gun centre half-forward for the relatively small investment of pick 30 in the 1999 draft.

Maybe the 'evener-up karma' hit us in late 2005 when Marc Murphy, son of Fitzroy champion John, decided to knock back an automatic father/son eligibility move to Brisbane when Carlton guaranteed to take him pick one in that year's draft . We feted him and his family the best we could, but for Marc, not having to leave his home state became the overriding and unsolvable issue. At least the Blues paid a decent price for the terrific player Marc has become; we would have got him for the bargain basement price of pick 41. What a difference getting his services would have made to Brisbane's future! It's an unavoidable fact that Jonathan Brown is the last All-Australian the Lions have drafted. Having no All-Australian players coming into a club during the course of a decade will automatically lead to a mediocre team performance.

The AFL and the fans love the tradition of the father/son rule but getting a youngster as a third-round pick, regardless of his ability, was always unfair. Geelong picking up Gary Ablett at pick 40 and Matthew Scarlett at pick 45 because their fathers played for the Cats was like winning lotto. Travis Cloke to Collingwood for pick 39 was similarly a huge win for the Magpies. In 2001 the AFL changed the father/son rule from the father playing 50 games to needing to play 100 games, meaning that if Jonathan had been born two years later Brisbane would have had no hold over him.

In recent years, the AFL has introduced a bidding system to give a draft value to any young players who are eligible under the father/son criteria. Other clubs can nominate what draft number they would devote to the player. The club to which he is eligible then has to use its next pick after that nominated bid. The bidding system is much fairer because, while still a bonus, it is not a huge windfall, as Jonathan Brown was for the Lions when we got him in return for the bargain price of pick 30. With this fairness value measure in place, I think it's valid to reduce the father/son eligibility criterion back to a much lower games figure. The even 50 that applied a decade ago seems sufficient to me. I hope the AFL makes the change when it next considers this peripheral, but tradition-building issue.

With Jonathan Brown warehoused for 12 months, we topped up mainly with draftees, and we drafted quite well that year. Our recruiting manager Kinnear Beatson's three selections – Des Headland, Craig Bolton and Aaron Shattock – all became premiership players. Unfortunately, Craig's was at Sydney. He was recruited by the Swans after the 2002 season when he was unable to get a permanent spot in the Lions team in the premiership years of 2001 and 2002.

We suffered in later years from losing his services, but at the time both Darryl White and Justin Leppitsch were well in front of him for selection. He was enormously well liked but, as a youngster with us, he was a nervous stress-carrier. When he went to Sydney with the centre half-back position given to him to lose, Bolts blossomed and became a really valuable player. Despite the Lions losing him before he'd peaked with us, everyone at the club enjoyed his success because he is an outstanding and extremely well liked young man.

We traded for the enigmatic Adam Heuskes. Now he was a talent. As we were to discover, he also had a very short concentration span and level of commitment. Drafted by Sydney as pick five in 1993, he'd played some terrific football for the Swans but then went to the newly formed Port Power as an uncontracted pick-up and had a great season, winning All-Australian selection as a half-back. At 190 centimetres he had good height and was a good mover. In my opinion, when he could play loose man in defence he played this role as well as anyone in the competition. That he was the Power's first All-Australian in 1997 and that they were happy to swap him 12 months later says a lot about the decline in how he was regarded in Adelaide. Still, he was a player whose talents I rated highly, so, with not enough due diligence about his off-field character, we did the deal. It's part of a coach's ego that he thinks he can make a leopard change his spots.

Adam's behaviour would eventually revert to that which got him kicked out of the Power, but initially he was a revelation. He was a charismatic, extroverted character who bounced into the club like he owned it, and his influence was so profound that he was voted by the players into their leadership group after only a few months. He looked to be a terrific investment.

Significantly, on a playing list that was coming off the 1998 wooden spoon, there were 20 players who'd share in the premiership success that was just around the corner: Jason Akermanis, Marcus Ashcroft, Simon Black, Daniel Bradshaw, Shaun Hart, Des Headland, Chris Johnson, Clark Keating, Nigel Lappin, Justin Leppitsch, Alastair Lynch, Beau McDonald, Craig McRae, Tim Notting, Luke Power, Brad Scott, Chris Scott, Aaron Shattock, Michael Voss and Darryl White.

I thought that the bottom placing wasn't indicative of where the team stood in the AFL competition rankings, but it didn't take long to work out where it stood in the Brisbane sporting market. My daily reading of the *Courier-Mail* gave me a fair idea and a McDonald's-sponsored charity lunch just prior to the Christmas break made it completely clear.

The lunch was held in the large function room in the since-redeveloped stand on the Stanley Street side of the Gabba ground. Seated next to me was legendary Brisbane Broncos coach Wayne Bennett, who had already coached a number of NRL premierships.

I knew the name and the reputation. His public persona made John Kennedy and Allan Jeans look like media tarts. They were at least courteous – Wayne's attitude to the press was downright prickly and unco-operative. His players loved him, though, because away from the media spotlight he was caring and a good listener who, like Allan Jeans, became a valued mentor to many of the people he coached.

I was first up on stage to be interviewed by the MC, former rugby league great Gary Belcher. It was a sold-out event with tables placed in every nook and cranny to seat everyone in the overflowing room. As often happens at very large functions, the microphone wasn't controlling the attention of the audience. During my interview the noise hardly stopped – people were talking, cutlery was clinking. It was plough through and get off. When I returned to the table, I said to my fellow coach, 'Gee, Wayne, hard audience this one.' Then he was brought to the stage. And for the whole duration of his 20-minute interview the room was so quiet you could have heard a pin drop!

In Melbourne, where AFL footy is the city's sporting religion, I was a fairly well-known name and face. After only a few months up north in my adopted new world in Brisbane, it was becoming increasingly obvious that me and my sport – and in Queensland, it isn't 'footy' it's 'AFL' – barely registered on the city's sporting radar.

If we were to succeed in growing the pride in our club that was essential for us to prevent our players wanting to run back home to the comfort of the southern states, this was a situation we had to change. The obvious starting point of winning games and playing finals would be crucial, but marketing the club well enough to increase our popularity in Brisbane would also be critical. This was a very difficult challenge that we needed to win.

35

THE HONEYMOON BEGINS

The painful reality was that we'd missed a wonderful opportunity. You never knew when, or if, that opportunity would present itself again.

After we got our off-field staff in place for the 1999 season, and the top-up recruiting was completed, it was time to focus our attention on the squad of players we'd inherited. Rehabilitation was the first priority. Many players were coming off injury-ravaged years and we needed to get them healthy again. A lot of injuries and a good year on the field are just not compatible. It's like 'lamb ambassador' Sam Kekovich becoming a vegetarian – the two things don't go together. But getting and keeping the players fit was largely the domain of our new-look conditioning and medical team. My job was to take a fresh look at the playing list with a view to repositioning a few players in order to get an improved team performance.

We'd already acted on a view I'd formed as an external observer by trading two players, Tristan Lynch and Scott Bamford. To me, this pair just looked too light to play heavy, physical-contact football. Whenever I'd seen them in action for the Lions I thought their lack of bulk made the team look small and weak. A frail-looking team will never hack it in the AFL, and being strong in the contest had to be a non-negotiable in the way we needed to play. Going in lower and harder than the opposition by getting head and shoulders close to the footy was to be a constant coaching theme of mine. Like any performance aim, the recognition and acknowledgement of those who do also has to be supported by not playing those who don't.

Omission from the team is the ultimate statement but the use of game vision in the review process is a terrific aid. My intention was to use positive reinforcement vision 80 per cent of the time and never use negative examples more than 20 per cent – and even then not to embarrass the individual but to utilise the vision as a learning tool for the rest of the group. And it was always about improvement of technique, rather than an intent issue, such as being brave or scared, for instance.

Sometimes it's worth exaggerating the truth a little and I did that as we got close to the playing season. A year or two earlier, I'd heard my Hawthorn premiership team-mate Terry Wallace comment that he thought the Western Bulldogs team he was coaching were the fittest they'd ever been. I loved the confidence that must have given his players. Always happy to pinch a good idea, I decided to use the positive reinforcement theme on the Lions players. The Wallace example was taken a fraction further at a late-February training session when I told the players they were the fittest team I'd ever seen. There was no evidence to support such an extravagant claim but I've long thought that belief and confidence in your fitness is just as valuable as the physical value of actually being fit.

There were a couple of positioning issues I intended to act on. First was to strengthen the defensive group. One initial thought was that veteran full-back Richard Champion was a bit too attacking and therefore a bit too loose for my liking. This key defensive role must provide stability and surety to give confidence to team-mates up-field, so I wanted to try other options.

A few potential candidates would come from a bunch of full-forward types the club seemed to have – namely Justin Leppitsch, Alastair Lynch, Daniel Bradshaw and Jarrod Molloy. I had been at a Lions game in round 17 the previous year when caretaker coach Roger Merrett had given Justin the job on Tony Lockett. Plugger had still kicked seven goals but I'd been in the Channel Seven commentary box that day and thought that for an inexperienced defender Leppa looked competitive against one of the game's very best; particularly when the Lions defence was under siege the whole match. So I spoke to him over the summer about the move to full-back and, while I don't think he was thrilled, he agreed to give it his best shot.

Justin was an interesting personality for a defender because he was a heavy Enforcer with the usual tendency to be stubborn, goal-oriented and wanting to feel in control. I'm not sure exactly how I presented the possibility of him moving into defence, but as I developed a greater understanding of how to best manage the various personality types I should have asked for his help. I should have said that for the team to improve we needed to find a new full-back and we believed he was the best man for the job. Heavy Enforcers – and, as I've mentioned, I am one myself – react well when asked to help and badly when told bluntly what to do.

The shift was great for the Lions and great for Leppa, who was selected in the All-Australian team for the first time in his debut year at full-back. He grew up playing forward but in my opinion his natural flair and adventure made him an unreliable and unpredictable forward. However, the forced discipline of playing close to the opposition goals and against their best marking target helped him to play more within his limitations and improved his game immeasurably.

It turned out be a win/win swap because 'Champs' went the other way and gave us a terrific season across half-forward. When he strained a quad muscle against Port Adelaide in round 18, it was a severe blow to the team, which was on the verge of an unprecedented rebound from wooden spoon to premiership threat.

With the retirement of Andrew Bews, we needed a small defender to play on the opposition goal-sneaks, such as Melbourne's Jeff Farmer, Geelong's Ronnie Burns and Phil Matera of the West Coast Eagles. It was a role that required a close-checking starting point to stop the opponent, but also the courage and ability to attack on the defensive rebound. Jason Akermanis was a talented youngster who had grown up in Brisbane, and in his four years at the club had shown glimpses of his ability, mainly as a goal-kicking half-forward flanker. We decided to give him first crack at the back pocket role, alongside new full-back Justin Leppitsch. Building our team from the back was a critical aim. Teams without forward flair can still be competitive, but a poor defence will always lead to a struggling team.

The Akermanis experiment didn't start well. We played Hawthorn at Waverley Park in a February practice game and he was outbodied and outmarked a few times by the Hawks' Tony Woods. 'Aker' just looked lost in his new role, when, like many inexperienced defenders, he was trapped in indecision between going for the ball and defending his direct opponent – and eventually did neither. The first look wasn't encouraging and I wondered if it was such a good idea.

In fact, the whole thing could have been over before it really got started. With Aker not selected, the senior side played interstate again the following weekend and the non-travellers had a Sunday morning training session at the University of Queensland. Aker turned up visibly affected from a big night out, which prompted some earnest discussion about his future at the club. As a new coaching group determined to establish some firm ground rules and principles about behaviour and preparation, we gave serious consideration to using the unproven youngster as a sacrificial lamb by sacking him – it would have been the ultimate example to the rest of the team. In the end we decided that the issue could be managed with some stern words to Aker in front of all the other Lions players. That we took the softer option of lecturing rather than sacking was partly because I had yet to form a view on his playing talents.

Ability on the field will always be a huge factor in how different players will be managed. Each player has strengths he gives to the team and weaknesses that deduct from his overall value. Part of the leadership art is to keep accurately judging each player's 'net score' after adding and subtracting the pluses and minuses. The coaching/managing role is about trying to increase the positives and reduce the negatives. If, for whatever reason, a player gets stuck in negative territory, he has to be removed from the team. Aker's preparation issues were never questioned again, but as his career developed – and despite his wonderful talent – the judgement call on whether his net value to the team was positive became a hot topic that took up more of my time than any other top-line player I ever coached.

Any experienced coach/manager knows that you end up spending 90 per cent of your time on 10 per cent of your people. From the time Aker won the Brownlow in 2001, he became a prime example of this management principle. As the decade wore on he took far too much of our management time – and eventually his senior team-mates' time as well. While we want all our players to be problem-free, I consoled myself with the view that if everyone was perfect my job would become redundant. Confronting difficult issues is what we were there for. It took a lot of managing, a lot of massaging and a lot of tolerance from his senior team-mates, but the ultimate benefit to the team, the club and the promotion of the sport by the enigma that was Jason Akermanis was invaluable.

Going into 1999, however, Aker was just another young Lion trying to get a game. After those initial on- and off-field hiccups it was full steam ahead, and when given another opportunity, he slotted so well into that small defender role that, like Leppa, he was selected in the All-Australian team. The pair of first-year defenders also shared the 1999 Lions club championship.

Michael Voss had a limited summer training program as he gradually recovered from his broken leg of the year before, and after missing round one he played most of the season, and he too made the All-Australian side. You'll only have three players in the All-Australian team if your club has a very good year – and, in the case of our season, that was an understatement. Compared to the dispirited group of the disastrous five-win, bottom-placed 1998 campaign, we had a fantastic year. Except for the footy gods frowning on us late in the season when we were hit by a few untimely injuries, this reborn and reinvigorated group of players was within a smidgin of going all the way. We'd been hopeful the new regime in place around the football department would spark a honeymoon year, but what happened was quite remarkable.

After rocking the boat with massive changes in off-field staff since the previous season, we decided to maintain the player-leadership status quo, which was a joint captaincy of the young turk Michael Voss and the 30-plus veteran Alastair Lynch.

Michael was coming off a broken leg and Alastair was getting into his twilight years and was still struggling with the after-effects of a severe case of chronic fatigue syndrome that had – as Lynchy would often joke – put him to sleep for most of 1995. History tells us that a badly broken leg like Vossy had suffered is probably more career-threatening than a knee reconstruction. The bottom line was that both our captains had gigantic question marks over their futures, and neither was available when we got to the opening match of 1999 against St Kilda at the Gabba.

There was no great expectation from Lions supporters because our pre-season hadn't produced anything special, but the fans must have wanted a look at the team under the new regime and a good Gabba crowd of 20,000-odd was in attendance. When playing at Hawthorn or coaching Collingwood, the size of the crowd was of absolutely no concern to me; however, in Brisbane the attendances at our games were one measure of how well we were doing in marketing the club, something I regarded as an important adjunct to my core role of coaching winning teams. The last three games of the season built up to crowds in the mid-20,000s, which was close to stadium capacity at that stage of the ground's development – it was an encouraging growth in support.

The whole coaching role was very different to my decade at Collingwood. From my first week at the Lions I became part of the club's senior management team, which met at 8 am every Wednesday. These meetings helped me develop a really good working relationship with chief executive Andrew Ireland, marketing manager Judy Kilby and media manager Peter Blucher. My involvement in this group – as well as attending the monthly board meeting – gave me a valuable overview of the club's affairs.

Gubby, Andrew and I also met club chairman Alan Piper most weeks for a breakfast catch-up. The benefit of this regular communication was that it galvanised the concept that we were all in it together and that the football area was part of the whole club, that they weren't just the highly publicised rock stars who earned the big bucks.

After the internal conflicts that seemed to have rocked the previous season, every indication was that the club was united again, making it a challenging but stable environment in which to work and play football. That situation would undoubtedly be enhanced or diminished by the team performance once the games started, so that first match against St Kilda was more important than just the four points for a win.

Life can be so fickle and football is no different. It was a great game for us, and we recorded a monstrous 89-point win over the

Saints under new coach Tim Watson. Tim and I had been colleagues in the Channel Seven commentary box on grand final day only six months before. The big win gave us valuable momentum and the thrashing was the worst possible start for a new coach.

With both joint captains unavailable, ex-Fitzroy skipper Brad Boyd, who had come to Brisbane in 1997 when the two clubs merged, was captain for the night. Brad had an absolute blinder, and 30-odd possessions as a midfielder, topped off with four goals, made him the unanimous best on ground. After an injury-plagued couple of years with Brisbane – he'd only played one game up until late 1998 – his future looked bright. But you never really know what the future holds. He played the opening eight games until a chronic back problem that refused to be cured flared again. Brad missed round nine and, after months of frustration, his injured back prevented him from ever playing again. His career was cut short way too early.

The euphoric atmosphere that a 15-goal lead would normally create was halted completely during the last few minutes of play when a near-tragedy took place. I had come down to the boundary line from the coach's box with my 'marketing cap' on, wanting to make sure the players properly acknowledged the fans after the game. As I walked out of the players' race onto the ground there was a frenzy of activity near our interchange area as both Lions and St Kilda doctors huddled over a motionless body. The game of footy was quickly forgotten during this obvious medical emergency. The patient was Lions head trainer Murray Johnson, who almost died then and there.

Murray had been with the club since the Carrara days and had taken over as head trainer the previous summer. Twice his heart stopped beating as he lay motionless on the ground after collapsing late in the final quarter. Medical staff worked for 30 minutes to save his life after what was thought to be a heart attack, but which turned out to be a heart arrest, something that occurs when oxygen isn't getting to the brain. First on the scene was former Hawthorn and Brisbane player Robert Dickson, who was the Lions' match-day runner. It was just as well because he was trained in first-aid procedure and performed mouth to mouth before doctors and ambulance officers took over. After a very tense time, Murray was revived and he eventually made a complete recovery. He remained head trainer for the Lions for most of my decade at the club.

I had my own dose of how fickle life can be on Thursday 15 July 1999, in the week leading into our return clash against St Kilda in round 16, which was scheduled to be played at VFL Park the following Saturday afternoon. My father, Ray, had been in Frankston Hospital for a couple of weeks, suffering from pneumonia. I'd spoken to him most days on the phone from Brisbane and he was gradually recovering.

Coincidentally, during this same period the *Herald Sun* was counting down to picking their player of the 20th century. When I got a call from the newspaper on the Wednesday advising me that, two days later, I would be announced as the *Herald Sun* Player of the Century it was the biggest honour I had ever received. It was an enormous thrill and, fortunately, I'd already had more than my share along the way. I happily agreed to their request to take a photo with my parents the next day at the Chelsea Football Club – where, of course, my playing career had begun. I was coming down to Melbourne a bit earlier than the team to visit Dad in hospital that night anyway. Unfortunately, Dad couldn't be involved in the photo session, but he was recovering well and would be ready to come home in a day or two. My mother, who was about as introverted as anyone could be, was reluctant, but agreed to participate.

The Lions usually travelled to Melbourne about lunchtime the day before a match, but I was there on the Thursday and drove to Chelsea to pick up Mum – we'd have the photo taken and then head to Frankston to visit Dad. We'd be joined at the hospital by my elder brother, Russell, to discuss potential rehab facilities for Dad between his time in hospital and coming home. My other brother, Kelvin, lived a few hours away in Paynesville, near Bairnsdale, in East Gippsland, so we'd touch base with him by phone.

The first part of the day went according to plan – the photos with Mum were taken at the Chelsea footy club and then we headed to the hospital. When we walked past the nurse's station in Dad's ward, we were told he'd just eaten his dinner and was looking forward to our visit. Even in his prime Dad was not very tall, but as he aged and suffered the pain of bad arthritis, he seemed to shrink by the year. As he got to his early 80s, his quality of life had fallen away quite badly.

From the doorway of his hospital room, he looked like a little old man dozing off in a chair next to his bed. Nothing unusual about that – as Dad got older he could drop off to sleep anywhere, anytime. As we walked over to wake him from his slumber, though, what we found was incredibly disturbing and a vision that I'll never forget.

When we said hello he lifted his head and mumbled a few incoherent words that made him sound like a semi-comatose drunk. His face was jaundiced and his eyes were a terrible yellow. This wasn't what we were expecting; we thought he was almost ready to go home. We called the nurses, who ushered us out of the room. Soon afterwards, they told us that in the few minutes before we arrived for our visit, Dad had suffered a massive heart attack. He never regained consciousness. The nursing staff put him in a private room on a respirator where Mum, Russell and I could be with him as he slowly faded away. We knew he was dying but when a nurse came in around 8 pm, took his pulse and said, 'I'm sorry but he is gone now,' it was still a shock.

On 15 July 1999, I was given the 'player of the century' moniker and my father suddenly passed away. As I said, how fickle life can be. Both my parents enthusiastically shared the ups and downs of their sons' lives and part of the hospital visit was to tell him face to face the good news about the *Herald Sun* award. I never got the chance. He would have enjoyed the honour as much as Mum and I did. Dad was a regular church-goer with a strong religious faith, so maybe somehow he got to know.

I hope so because it was Dad who started my interest in footy. My earliest football memory is of him drilling stab kicks to me with the almost-round, blown-up, faded, sandy-coloured footy in the backyard at Langwarrin, with me feeling the thud on my chest as I marked it. He saw almost every game I played – from my first, aged 12, for Chelsea to my last at 33 with Hawthorn. He was supportive without being pushy and was a terrific football father. Even more importantly, I can confidently say that my father was a very nice man.

We will always miss our parents when they're gone but my father's poor health and fading quality of life made it something of a relief he was no longer in pain. It is a little easier to accept the loss and quickly get on with life, so there was never any thought of me not joining the team for training when they arrived in Melbourne the following afternoon.

We beat St Kilda comfortably to be 10 wins, six losses and proceeded to win the final six matches. In some irony for me, this included the round 22 clash against Collingwood at Victoria Park, which was scheduled to be the final game ever played at the famous venue. We were desperate to win as we were fighting for the highest possible finals berth while the Magpies were confined to wooden spoon territory.

For the home club the whole day became a celebration of the great tradition that the club had built from its base in the middle of the inner Melbourne suburb of Collingwood. I was there as coach of the Brisbane team but the venue had a special place in my heart as well. I must say I never experienced those warm feelings for Victoria Park during my playing days. The tiny visitors' change rooms nestled next to the parochial Social Club stand – which was where the Brisbane players were getting prepared for the game – were the same rooms where I had many nervous pre-games as a player in the brown and gold of Hawthorn, feeling as if I was about to become a Christian thrown to the lions in the Coliseum.

This last game of 1999, though, was quite different. It was a cold rainy Melbourne day and the surface was wet and muddy. It wasn't a great day for footy but the stadium was packed. The passionate but also usually feral Magpies faithful were there in their droves for a nostalgic trip back into the club's history and to farewell their spiritual home. The result of the game that day was largely irrelevant to the historical celebration.

While the Lions players got ready, I stood inside the boundary line outside our rooms watching the pre-game parade of club greats, including a few I had spent so much time with: Bob Rose, Wayne Richardson and Ron Richards. The atmosphere created by the fans in the ground wasn't feral – it was thankful and happy, as it should be. Collingwood supporters had enjoyed a fantastic journey during the club's proud history.

I had a pleasant surprise as I walked across the oval to the visitors' coaching box situated up the very back of the outer stand, when the crowd gave me a really nice warm round of applause. For an opposition coach to be applauded at Victoria Park must have been a first. It proves that the day had nothing normal about it and that at least some of the Collingwood fans had accepted that the little bloke from Hawthorn had been, at least temporarily, one of their own.

The Lions won the game comfortably and finished third on the ladder with 16 wins and a competition-high percentage of 145. Essendon finished on top with 18 wins and even their percentage was only 126. The Kangaroos were second with 17 wins and a percentage of 115.

The last part of the season was spectacular. A 10-goal first quarter against the Eagles in round 17 was outstanding but paled against a 21-goal first half against Fremantle at the Gabba in round 20. Being 113 points in front at half-time in front of a rapturous home crowd was something you'd usually only dream about. Even a born pessimist like me had to concede we couldn't possibly lose from there.

We had 10 or 12 goal-kickers each week, our midfield led by Michael Voss was dominant and our defence – built around Justin Leppitsch, Matthew Kennedy at centre half-back, Chris Scott across half-back and our new defender, Adam Heuskes – was outstanding. Michael seemed to have recovered well from his broken leg and we were getting better at understanding the training loads that Alastair Lynch could handle as he battled the aftermath of his severe chronic fatigue of a few years earlier.

It was the fifth year of the final-eight system and at that time it was 1 v 8, 2 v 7, 3 v 6 and 4 v 5, with the two highest-placed winners going into the preliminary final and the two lowest-placed losers eliminated. The current system of the top four playing each other for a preliminary final berth and the bottom four playing each other for survival was introduced the following year.

We went into the finals in really good form and were a serious contender but, as I've said, that is all any team can be heading into the finals. In the modern AFL system we take 22 rounds to eliminate half the competition and then four weeks to eliminate the other seven, until one survives to be premiers. It's a long-drawn-out process. What would happen in the few weeks of September would make or break our year. The season had been a vast improvement on 1998 but I never got any sense that the players were satisfied with a big climb up the ladder. On the contrary they'd found that elusive zone and were playing at the upper level of their ability. Positive momentum is a great asset and when September arrived we were flying. Unfortunately, only a short time into our first final the footy gods gave us a major injury to our most indispensable player. The variation in good or bad fortune experienced by finals contenders has decided many premierships over the decades. In 1999 bad luck intervened to majorly hinder our chances of going all the way from bottom to top in one 12-month period.

Carlton finished sixth, so they came to Brisbane for a Saturday night qualifying final at the Gabba. We continued our blistering form and won every quarter to win by 12 goals. However, a first-quarter incident on the wing in front of the Northern Stand severely dented our campaign.

Michael Voss launched himself at an overhead mark and his ankle buckled as he landed. It looked pretty innocuous but the aftermath was dire – it was season over for our co-captain. He was the worst possible loss, because Michael was the heart of our midfield and an outstanding leader and on-field organiser.

If we could win again the following week at the Gabba against the Western Bulldogs, we'd face North Melbourne at the MCG in a Friday night preliminary final. When you're away from the emotional comfort of your home environment, particularly in interstate knockout finals, the importance of being mentally strong is magnified many times. I'd punted on Tony Shaw against the Eagles in 1994 because we needed his incredible mental toughness to rub off on his team-mates. Michael Voss had that same quality and effect on the Brisbane Lions.

I can't say that playing North Melbourne was occupying one skerrick of my thinking after the Carlton game because in the week-to-week cycle of football, looking too far ahead will usually mean disaster. And the way I look at it, too far is any more than a day or two. All our thoughts were on how to beat the Bulldogs the next Saturday night, which we did by a comfortable 53 points.

After a 10-game winning streak, in which we'd won in each football city, we were now into the final four. Our average margin of 60 points was easily the biggest by any side in the VFL/AFL that had won 10 straight, while in the last eight games of the home-and-away season we'd receive every Brownlow Medal vote on offer. The team was in fantastic form but the obstacles were mounting.

From the Bulldogs game Chris Scott and Craig McRae were both reported. At the Monday night tribunal hearing leading into the Friday night match against North Melbourne, both players received suspensions. As is so often the case, it's not so much about what goes wrong but when it goes wrong. In the space of a couple of weeks, we'd lost the services of our co-captain Voss, Chris Scott, our club champion of 1998, and Craig McRae, who gave us speed and run.

Chris had been rubbed out for a late bump on the Dogs' Stephen Powell, who was one of his best mates. It was something he'd done in the schoolyard many times over, but although we didn't think there was much in it – as there wasn't with the McRae striking charge – on this occasion, the ramifications were dire.

We decided to roll the dice and took both cases to the AFL Appeals Board, which was convened on the Thursday night, only 24 hours before the Kangaroos game and after our final planning meeting. The timing was less than ideal but we really thought both players had been harshly treated. When they lost their appeals, we had lost twice. We were still without their services, and we'd also been forced into the uncertainty of too many ifs and buts in our planning meeting.

Not knowing our exact team until late on the Thursday evening didn't help, but the most important fact was that we were without three valuable players. When Simon Black went down with a fractured eye socket early in the game against the Kangaroos, courtesy of a coat-hanger from North full-back Mick Martyn, it was the beginning of the end. We did well to lead by four points at half-time but eventually the Kangaroos were too good and ran over us in the second half, so the chance to go from bottom to first was now gone.

The AFL had taken the Brownlow Medal count to Sydney and I bumped into North coach Denis Pagan in the foyer of Fox Studios next to the SCG on the way into the function. He was understandably anxious about our attitude in relation to Mick Martyn. There was no report and no clear vision, but there was talk of an AFL investigation into the incident. Denis probably doesn't know how close he came to reversing our initial thoughts that whatever happens on the field stays on the field.

When he enquired about the situation, it was with the clear message that he was expecting us to 'look after' his player. That was always our intention but when Denis seemed to consider it an obligation rather than a favour, we had serious second thoughts. Still smarting from losing the chance to reach the grand final, and with the Black family happy to nail the player who had inflicted a very nasty injury on their son, we were tempted basically to tell Denis to go and get stuffed. Eventually we stuck with the policy of trying to help and did our best to convince Simon that we might need a favour from the Kangaroos one day. He agreed with the logic of assisting rather than sinking an opposition player.

He was spoken to by AFL investigations officer Rick Lewis and, in fact, was shown some vision that was very incriminating for Martyn. Simon told me later that for a while he thought he might be in trouble for giving false evidence. The underlying player fraternity philosophy of the 'hittee' wanting to help the 'hitter' is the reason why the victim is no longer called to tribunal hearings. The reality is that the vision will give a more realistic account of the incident than the victim. In the end I think we did the right thing, but I'm not so sure Simon's parents, Ray and Fran Black, were as convinced.

It was a time of mixed emotions. While we had every right to feel proud about the improvement from 1998, the painful reality was that we'd missed a wonderful opportunity. You never knew when, or if, that opportunity would present itself again. It didn't help, either, that in the grand final North beat Carlton, the side we'd hammered by 73 points three weeks earlier. I'd suggested to our playing list that they might want to go to Melbourne and watch the match to see what they'd missed out on, and, to their credit, many of them did. I hoped it had whetted their appetite for the year ahead. In a football sense the challenge was only just beginning. I always believed that after a change of coach there will be an inevitable honeymoon period, but that there was no guarantee it would continue. And it didn't.

The previous year had been largely positive; however, our 2000 campaign would encounter a gigantic problem before it had officially begun. For the next 12 months a series of negative issues, a couple of bad management decisions and some simple bad luck would end the coaching honeymoon I'd enjoyed during my first year in Brisbane.

Only a few days after the 1999 season ended, Gubby Allan and I had a very disturbing meeting with Lions CEO Andrew Ireland. He shared the bombshell that, if no action was taken, the club would be $500,000 over the salary cap the next season. As the salary cap at the time was a little under five million dollars, this meant that to be compliant for the 2000 season we needed to reduce our player payments by roughly 10 per cent.

To say we were shocked was an understatement. As Andrew negotiated player contracts and managed the salary cap, the obvious question to him was how the club could possibly be paying its combined player list 10 per cent more than the rest of the competition. His answer introduced me to the concept of Brisbane players needing to be paid more than their southern state counterparts as compensation for not submitting to the go-home mentality of returning to the AFL heartlands of Victoria, South Australia and Western Australia.

When we went through the salary cap player by player, it was obvious to Gubby, who could remember the Collingwood payment scale, that the Lions players were being very well paid to remain in Brisbane. As Andrew explained, and as I was to find out first hand during the years that followed, the northern states players frequently become prime recruiting targets for, in particular, the proliferation of Melbourne-based clubs.

Gubby had poached Anthony Rocca from the Sydney Swans to join Collingwood a few years earlier, so he needed no convincing about the northern clubs' problems as far as retaining their players against the marauders from the AFL heartlands. The player managers emphasised the 'go-home' factor very well in negotiations, which meant that a 10 per cent premium to stay tended to be the going rate. As a result, going into the 2000 season our salary cap was a mess. We desperately needed an additional player retention allowance of about 10 per cent on top of the standard salary cap if we were to be any more than a breeding ground for the clubs down south. So we obviously had some selling to do at AFL head office.

Andrew, Gubby and I were able to arrange a meeting with AFL CEO Wayne Jackson and football operations manager Ian Collins. There, we explained the situation and mounted our case that we should be given a 10 per cent retention allowance on top of the standard salary cap of $4.75 million.

At the time of the Brisbane–Fitzroy merger at the end of 1997, the club had been allocated an extra salary cap allowance of $300,000 to cover relocation costs. It was reduced to $200,000 in 1998 and $100,000 in 1999. Armed with the ability to confidentially compare our player payments to other clubs, the AFL officials sent us away while they did their due diligence. Eventually they agreed with the logic of our argument and agreed to an extra retention allowance of a flat $400,000 per year. As a club, we had to fund it ourselves, so that was a big problem for our marketing and finance people. Overall, at the time we saw it as a significant win. Little did we know what a political minefield this retention allowance would eventually become.

This concession from the AFL was designed to help us balance our salary cap, but, as they knew, we still had to do our bit and shed a player or two to get it fully under control. We reluctantly traded our talented and popular ruckman Matthew Clarke to the Adelaide Crows. In return for Mattie, we got selection number six in the national draft, ultimately using this pick on South African-born forward Damien Cupido. Unfortunately, Damien didn't have sufficient competitive character or preparation discipline and became one of football's many wasted talents.

With Matthew Clarke gone, we decided to draft some height in the form of Sydney Swans forward/ruckman Stefan Carey. This turned out to be quite possibly the worst recruiting decision I ever made. We were encouraged to recruit him from the Swans by his good friend Adam Heuskes, who had given us such a fantastic first season after crossing from Port Adelaide at the end of 1998. The mistake was a double banger. Stefan was not much value as a player and he became a willing social playmate for Adam, who obviously needed little encouragement to burn the candle at both ends.

In any group, people with similar interests tend to find each other. Having one loose cannon can sometimes be worthwhile; having two normally leads to trouble. That was emphasised by this pairing. It might have happened anyway, but during the one year Stefan was at the Lions, Adam gradually degenerated from a very valuable player to a constant problem.

Actually, even before Carey was recruited Adam was a central figure in an incident that occurred in London on the players' end-of-season trip. The aftermath was a sexual assault allegation that caused a police investigation to be launched. No charges were ever laid but police from Scotland Yard came to Australia a couple of times during the 2000 season to conduct interviews with all the players who'd been on the trip. It was a worrying and distracting issue that hung over the player group for most of the year.

The reality of the go-home factor really hit home when a week or two after the season one of our talented youngsters Shane O'Bree announced he wanted to go home to Victoria. He had been a first-round draft pick from North Ballarat Rebels in 1997. Captain of his club's TAC Cup premiership side and the Lions' second pick at number 10 overall, he was chosen between Luke Power (number six) and Simon Black (number 31) and had played 19 games with the Lions in 1998–99. He was certainly considered part of the club's future, but after indicating to the club that he was keen to sign a contract extension he did an about-face and decided he wanted to go back to Victoria. Not so much Ballarat but Melbourne, and, more particularly, Collingwood. He was one that got away. We got no compensation at all – although that was partly our choice because we refused to trade him.

We did our best to convince Shane not to leave and even a trip by Gubby and me to his parents' home in Ballarat for a face-to-face was of no value. He had no issues with the Lions or even living in Brisbane; he simply wanted to go home. If that meant leaving the club that had finished third to join the Magpies who had finished last, so be it. No one could really blame him for his stance but for the future of the Lions this wasn't a situation we could take lying down. Any players walking out on us had to be met with stubborn resistance and even scorn. As a not-so-subtle lesson to our many players who'd come from other states, we refused to deal with the Magpies and forced them to take Shane in the pre-season uncontracted players draft. Then I deliberately labelled him a traitor for leaving. 'Traitor' was a harsh and inflammatory word but we needed to be very damning of players going home. All our players needed to value the strength of their team-mates who persevered and stayed, and to look down on the weakness of those who bailed out. The future of the club depended on this attitude to prevail.

We had another issue that would affect the early season games. I'd played at the Gabba for Hawthorn against Essendon back in 1981 on a pear-shaped surface surrounded by a greyhound track. Obviously, it had changed a bit since then, but now it was to be further redeveloped for the Sydney Olympic Games. The well-known home of AFL and cricket in Brisbane was to host some Olympic soccer. This was fantastic news for the Lions because it meant that not only would the playing surface be upgraded and the public seating and amenities improved, but we'd be able to move from very basic player facilities under the old social club into new rooms at the opposite end of the ground.

It was one of those indefinable benefits. There is the practical effect of better facilities but there is also the placebo effect. If you feel good about your workplace it helps you feel proud of your club, which contributes to performing well on the field. I liked the idea that our players would have a new and improved home base.

But it did come at a bit of a price at the time. Our first four games were scheduled away from Brisbane due to the Gabba playing surface being redeveloped. It meant we'd play six of our first seven games interstate. When you throw in pre-season trips to Cairns, Hobart and Melbourne, it meant that by the end of April we'd travelled the equivalent of Brisbane to London return, and no doubt it took a toll.

Our busy schedule did bring us a role in a moment in football history. With the Olympics scheduled for September the season was brought forward a few weeks, and in round two in Melbourne on Sunday 19 March 2000 we took on the Western Bulldogs in what turned out to be the first AFL game played without the intervention of the elements at the $450 million Colonial Stadium. It was the third game overall at the new ground, but with rain in the area, for the first time the massive roof was closed.

It was an amazing and surreal experience to look up and see a roof covering a full-sized football ground. Both as player and coach there was always some worry and uncertainty about what the playing conditions would be on the day. No more. When we went to Colonial Stadium (since renamed Etihad Stadium) at the Docklands in Melbourne, it would always be still and dry. It was a world away from the Glenferrie Oval mud-heaps of my early playing days.

We won the match comfortably but in the aftermath there was plenty of feeling in the Brisbane camp. The Bulldogs were a side that were very bullish in the way they went about their football. The terrible trio of Tony Liberatore, Jose Romero and Paul Dimattina seemed to be the ringleaders of a ploy that was causing quite a bit of angst around the competition. The AFL had introduced the blood rule whereby a player seen to be bleeding had to leave the field, and there was a belief that a couple of the Dogs players were deliberately scratching their opponents to force them off the ground for treatment.

Our players were talking about this annoying tactic at a Sunday morning recovery session at Melbourne Aquatic Centre after Simon Black – not for the first time – had been subjected to exactly this treatment the night before, as Craig McRae and others had been previously. As we gathered on the bus before heading to Melbourne Airport I specifically addressed the issue. I told the players that if we wanted the Bulldogs to stop using that ploy, maybe we needed to take a stance. I believed that if we didn't want to keep being the victim, we had to take the initiative.

In what I took as a sign that we were not a bunch of little kids who would put up with being bullied, the playing group endorsed the idea of making it public. It was impossible for umpires to see what was happening, so the following day we lodged a formal complaint with the AFL against Romero, alleging that he had deliberately scratched Simon Black. Romero was subsequently suspended for two matches and the Dogs ceased this annoying practice.

That round two game against the Bulldogs was our only win in the first month of the season. Having started the year with a 1–3 record,

Jonathan Brown played his first game in round five against Adelaide at the Gabba. In cricketing parlance, which was so familiar to him, he didn't bother the scorers. His statistics in a 30-point win read: one tackle, one free-kick for and one free against. Team-mate Jarrod Molloy had played on from the Brown free-kick, and by the end of the day he'd exerted a lot of energy without registering an effective disposal. It would never happen again. Fortunately he got a second chance the following week against St Kilda in Melbourne, and while he didn't exactly burst onto the scene Jonathan's 13 games in his first year were a great launching pad for his second and breakout season in 2001.

The St Kilda match was worth more than the four points. After a long battle with cancer, Brisbane Lions chairman Alan Piper passed away during the week prior to the game. The team decided to make this match our Alan Piper memorial game. If we won, the team line-up would be printed on a wooden plaque which would be hung on the wall of the players' room for posterity. We had a good win and the board was proudly put on the wall a few weeks later. Maybe five or six times in my decade as Lions coach, we declared that there'd be a special 'board' memento if we won. It couldn't be done too often because the effect would have been lost, but I reckon we won most of the matches that were given this pre-game status. Anything that concentrates team focus is extremely helpful.

Both games against St Kilda during the 2000 season were significant in the history of the Brisbane Football Club but the one at the Gabba in round 21 became memorable for quite a bizarre reason. Whenever you think you've seen it all, something occurs that makes you scratch your head in amazement and say to yourself, 'I can't believe that just happened.'

Such as when Peter Hudson played for Hawthorn against Collingwood in round 21 of 1973 – having not played since the opening round in 1972 – and off a few weeks' solo training he came over from Tasmania on the Saturday morning. Huddo was no fitter than half the fans at VFL Park that day but he still kicked eight goals against the mesmerised Magpies defence. It's still hard to believe this could have happened, but it did.

Such as when I arrived at Waverley Park in round nine of 1980 to play North Melbourne and parked next to young Russell Greene who'd played for St Kilda the week before. My first thought was that one of us was at the wrong ground until Russell told me he'd been cleared from the Saints to Hawthorn the previous evening and was playing with the Hawks today. It was hard to believe that that unlikely scenario could take place, but again it did.

Such as the quarter-time brawl in the 1990 grand final when the whole ground – not just the players – seemed to be fighting, or like the 2003 grand final when, with the opening bounce only 45 minutes away, I still didn't know whether the injured Nigel Lappin could take his place in the team. Football continually throws up the unexpected and the hard-to-believe-it-happened. The aftermath of the round 21 game against St Kilda at the Gabba was another of these times.

Adam Heuskes had been going backwards for most of his second season with the Lions. His tell-all skinfold measurements were stamping statistically that his condition and fitness were not good enough, his form was poor and he was eventually omitted from the senior team. He was recalled for the round 21 game and played quite well in our comfortable 90-point win. I have never seen or spoken to him since. Now that is an unlikely first.

Adam didn't turn up the next day for Sunday morning training and was absent again on the Monday, so, as was our procedure, Gubby's job was to track him down. None of Adam's team-mates seemed to know his whereabouts and he wasn't answering his phone. It was all a bit of a mystery.

I was having lunch with Gubby and a couple of our assistant coaches at one of our regular café haunts near the Gabba on the Monday afternoon when Gubby's mobile rang – it was Adam. It was a short conversation. He was in his home town of Adelaide, he wasn't coming back, and at only 24 years of age was retiring from top-level footy. No ifs, buts or maybes – that was his firm decision.

I immediately phoned Adam, but my call went to his voicemail where I left the message for him to please return my call. There was no response that afternoon so I tried again the following morning. He never called back. So, end result: I coached a player whom I haven't seen or spoken to since the post-match of the last match he played.

Adam's decision to retire immediately, even before the season had ended – and in particular to forgo the final year of his contract – took us by surprise, but the ramifications turned out to have a very positive influence on the club's future success. Without ever having spoken to Adam, I can only speculate about his motives, but I've concluded that what he did was quite a noble act. He could have stayed and received his contracted payment for the 2001 season; however, I believe he knew that he couldn't live the lifestyle required to be part of an elite football team, and rather than mess us around any further, he decided to hit the road without any fuss or fanfare. This also saved us the hassle of trying to trade him out to another club with a year still to go on his contract, which would have been necessary but probably difficult to achieve.

At least he was honest with himself, a loose cannon distraction was removed from the group, and the salary cap saving would be extremely valuable for future recruiting. A win/win situation resulted from Adam's bizarre and sudden exit.

We won our final four games comfortably to finish in sixth spot with a 12–10 win–loss ratio, and then beat the Bulldogs in an elimination final at the Gabba. The team was in good form but the win took us to Melbourne to take on Carlton, who had become a bit of a nemesis after thrashing us twice during the season. And the day started badly, well before the team bus departed the Parkview Hotel for the MCG.

About 6.30 am the phone in my hotel room rang. I was still asleep and, as I've mentioned a few times in this book, from my experience early morning calls are usually bad news – this one certainly was, at least in terms of our team's winning chances that afternoon. The voice on the phone was Lions player welfare manager Shane Johnson, telling me that our young forward Daniel Bradshaw wouldn't be available to take his place in the team.

Daniel's girlfriend, Ange, later to become his wife, was pregnant and had been staying with her parents in Wodonga. With her boyfriend in Melbourne, she decided to travel down to watch the game, and although staying elsewhere, which was the team rule, she dropped into the hotel to say hello. She left about 10 pm but, soon after, her waters broke as she went into labour. Shortly afterwards, our number two goal-kicker headed off to the Royal Women's Hospital where Ange had been admitted.

With the birth unlikely in the next few hours, at about 1 am Daniel returned to the hotel where he had a restless night weighing up what he should do the following day. Play football in a knockout final or be there for the birth of his first child? – that was his dilemma. When I spoke to him, as the team coach I wanted him to play, but as they say in parliament it had to be a conscience vote. I advised him of exactly that and by then his mind was already made up so there was no sense in trying to talk him out of it. After a bad night's sleep and the birth of his child imminent he wasn't really in any fit state to play football anyway.

In personality profile, Daniel was a heavy Thinker, and the worry and stress of playing good football while his wife was in labour was something he couldn't have successfully managed. Frankly, I'm not sure many could. A few rare people can put their lives into compartments and not let one affect the others: maybe Tony Shaw, Michael Voss or Jonathan Brown. Daniel isn't like that. Playing football was out of the question. He returned to the hospital and Jake Bradshaw was born at 3.40 pm at about half-time in the game at the MCG.

By then, we were six goals down and eventually lost to Carlton by 82 points. After my two seasons at the Lions, we were in the ballpark but after the first-year honeymoon, the second season had flattened out quite a bit. We looked a mile from a premiership and needed significant improvement. While the base of our success pyramid was in place, we had yet to find the tools to complete the journey to the small tip at the very top. That was the challenge as we left 2000 behind and started planning for what was to become an amazing 2001 season.

36

THE SORDID SEARCH FOR A
COMPETITIVE EDGE

I wasn't sure whether to be proud or sad.

When the Australian Crime Commission (ACC) released a damning report in early February 2013 that linked sport, drugs, organised crime and match-fixing, it was sure to create huge headlines. Whether the findings and conclusions were as big on specifics as they were on rhetoric remained to be seen. Overall, I think it's worthwhile bringing these issues into the public domain. It may be acting on the iceberg theory that if you can see the small tip above the water you just know there is a lot more hidden from view. I've found this iceberg logic to be an accurate assumption in the area of human behaviour.

The vulnerability of sport being infiltrated by criminal elements is a cause for great vigilance by sports bodies and law enforcement agencies. That is the biggest issue from the ACC report but the 'sexy' part is that drugs are the criminal world's link to the players. Illicit drugs are supplied illegally, so, by definition, criminal figures are the suppliers. Unfortunately, I think we must accept that illicit drug use some time during the calendar year by some players at most elite footy clubs is more a probability than a possibility. Illicit drug use is a gigantic problem in our society and footballers aren't immune from the outside world.

The AFL illicit drug policy is welfare-based. If a player is found to have taken an illicit substance, the first two positive tests are treated like an illness to be treated rather than an offence to be penalised. The time is rapidly approaching when the image of the game and what it will accept from its players will force a tightening of the regulations.

One strike with treatment rather than penalty seems fair enough, but a second positive test should have some kind of sanction. It doesn't have to be draconian – a four or six match suspension to push the point that the game won't accept this behaviour from its players would be sufficient. A third positive test is where a severe two-year suspension becomes valid.

The area of performance-enhancing drugs is much more black and white. If a player is proven to have taken a banned substance, they receive a two-year suspension. The contention in the ACC report was that banned substances that don't show up in current testing are being used. This allegation regarding non-detectable performance-enhancing drugs became the specific issue to be investigated by the Australian Sports Anti-Doping Authority.

When the ACC report hit the airwaves I hadn't been involved at club level for four years, but I still think I understand the basic competitive attitude and motivations of elite individuals and elite teams in any sport. The risks for a team to deliberately use banned substances are just too great, so I don't buy that big groups are involved; however, the odd individual searching for an advantage is quite possible. In my view, the will to win for the desperate competitor has few moral boundaries. The same necessary trait of taking risks on the field will usually lead to pushing the preparation boundaries off it. To the modern footballer, supplements have become as normal as wearing football boots, and to dabble in a grey-area substance that might be banned, but is undetectable in a drug test anyway, is a massive temptation. The administrators must set the rules and regulations for their sport and the competitors must be forced to comply. If any athlete doesn't, then 'if you do the crime, you do the time' must apply.

Naturally, everyone wants to be an honourable winner, but if the choice is between being a squeaky-clean loser and a rule-bending winner, I think the latter would hold sway with the successful teams and competitors I have observed. It might be as simple as staging for a free-kick, using every means possible to poach your opposition's best player, or to be ahead of the game in what is popularly called the sports science area. Fierce competitors will always look to bend the rules – not necessarily break them but at least twist them to their advantage – and the extension of that attitude is that the search for a better way is a never-ending battle. Every team is trying to find a competitive edge and every individual has the same challenge. In the AFL world during the last few years it has become an obsession, and preparing the perfect athlete has gone beyond the quest for the best training techniques and good nutrition into the use of performance-enhancing supplements to speed up the process.

Now that I'm no longer involved in this constant challenge of finding that competitive advantage over an opponent, I find myself regarding this quite normal quest as a little sordid. We seem to be approaching the stage where God-given physical abilities are being moulded by increasingly artificial means.

Football's evolution over the last 40 years has gone in this direction. When I went to Hawthorn in 1969 players got fit by ball work and running. There was no organised weight work and little focus on good nutrition. That continued into the '70s when, if you were born to be skinny, like champion Melbourne wingman Robert Flower, that's how you played. If you were born to be bulky like me, then that's how you played. Body sculpting was for the next generation of footballers.

In the '80s weight programs came into prominence and bulging well-defined muscles were developed. I wouldn't be surprised if the odd player in those days popped a few steroids as a means of getting the desired body shape. Of course this was all quite legal; it was well before footy banned any substances. During my time at Collingwood I even had a discussion with club doctor Shane Conway about putting a young skinny defender, Jason Croall, onto a course of steroids, because weight training alone wasn't getting him strong enough. Nothing eventuated but according to the rules of the day it could have been done.

In the '90s the body-shape-changing regime at AFL clubs continued to thrive. Thanks to club-organised gym programs, along with better nutrition leading to lower body fat readings. the average footballer was getting stronger and bulkier while carrying less body fat.

Then, in the late '90s full-time footy arrived. With players now not working jobs outside football, the next step was training during the day. The accompanying progression was the need for full-time coaches and full-time support staff whose total focus was on improving the capabilities of the playing personnel.

This was the state of the game's evolution when I became Brisbane coach at the end of 1998. It was also about the time when the benefits of better and more individual training programs, as well as increasing education on what to eat and what to avoid, was still not enough in the search for the competitive advantage. In the first decade of the 21st century, the next progression became finding and using a large variety of supplements to top up the value of best practice training and nutrition. As time has gone by, in both a physical and moral sense, the fine line between legal supplements and substances that are in the grey area of being allowable at the time, but maybe banned next year, can become quite blurred. Strictly within the drug-taking codes, the popping of pills, taking supplement powder or even getting the odd injection is now quite common and normal.

In my decade at the Lions it was constantly emphasised that the club doctor had to tick off any non-food substance that a player consumed, even something as innocuous as cough medicine or a headache tablet. Whether that happened 100 per cent of the time is impossible to know for sure, because in the insatiable search for that edge, individual players may have occasionally bypassed getting the doctor's all-clear. Some players used the internet to do their own supplement research but were constantly advised by the club doctors and conditioning staff that anything imported directly was a big no-no, because the ingredient mix listed was often not accurate.

Compared to the size of the off-field support staff at a modern AFL club, we were positively skeletal when I came to Brisbane for the 1999 season. But what we lacked in quantity we made up for in quality. My first undertaking to the Lions players was that we'd get them the best off-field support team in the competition. With the great benefit of hindsight I'm convinced we did just that. The conditioning and medical team that gave us a terrific competitive advantage at the time was an excellent sports science unit as well. The term 'sports scientist' was not really much in use back in the late '90s and we had no one with that title on our staff, but the creative environment that was encouraged sparked some very cutting-edge innovation.

When the 2013 Crime Commission report was released and suddenly the sports scientists were painted as the bad guys, I pondered whether the premiership success of the Lions in the early 2000s – coupled with the highly publicised innovation of the club's conditioning and medical support team – was the trendsetter for the modern incarnation that has exploded in numbers, expenditure and emphasis a decade later. I wasn't sure whether to be proud or sad.

The compact group that came together over the summer of 1998/99 was head conditioning coach Craig Starcevich, strength coach Scott Murphy, physiotherapists Peter Stanton and Victor Popov, doctors Paul McConnell and Andrew Smith, and nutritionist Michelle Cort. They all had their specialties but worked really well together – as a good team does – by concentrating on performing their own jobs first and foremost, but helping others with their roles as well and always being on the lookout for new ideas.

Craig was the only one of the group with an AFL background and his understanding of the sport as a player with Collingwood and Brisbane proved to be very helpful. He was also extremely fit himself and would do most of the endurance work with the players, which, in the time well before the use of GPS technology, gave him a good feel for the difficulty of the assigned running drills.

My attitude to the initiatives recommended by our conditioning and medical staff was that if it might help, if we could afford it, if it was legal, and if it had no harmful side-effects, then we should do it. 'Every little bit helps' was our motto.

Some of the things we did were quite basic, such as players having the choice of their own hotel room when we travelled. Previously, everyone had shared with a team-mate, and although this was cheaper, it wasn't conducive to a good night's sleep. A bloke snoring in the other bed is not much fun. Slightly more unusual was the suggestion that in an air-conditioned hotel room, filling the waste paper bin with water might help minimise any dehydrating effect of the dry air. It couldn't do any harm and it might just have helped, so even a non-playing coach like me gave it a go.

It was the lot of the Lions that we lived and trained in the hot and sweaty Brisbane climate and we travelled every second week.

Therefore much of the thinking, planning and innovation to improve performance was to reduce the potentially damaging effects of dehydration and travel.

It seemed logical and became normal for our nutritionist to travel with the team to make sure the hotel buffet meals were suitable for the best athletic performance, so that was easily introduced, but when club doctor Paul McConnell wanted to take some small bottles of oxygen on board for a long trip to Perth, the pilots took a lot of convincing that it was safe. The plane was delayed while discussions took place, although eventually we were given the okay.

The other passengers on the flight must have wondered what was going on as the Lions players had stints on the oxygen masks for half-hour periods during the five-hour flight. The theory was that a pressurised plane at 30,000 feet had a lower oxygen content than normal air; hence the desire to put the players on pure oxygen to minimise any negative effects. Again, it couldn't do any harm, it might help, so give it a go.

The next step in reducing the potential negative effects of flying would have been to have our own plane that could be flown at a lower altitude, but that was obviously cost-prohibitive. What we were able to do was the next best thing – get a co-operative pilot.

Craig Starcevich came to me one day with the news that he'd been speaking to a Qantas pilot by the name of Don Lehmann who lived near him in Coorparoo, who'd volunteered to pilot our flights. Our physios Peter Stanton and Victor Popov were particularly keen on the benefits of flying at a lower altitude than the usual commercial flights, and when we met with Don he said that if he could be scheduled on our flights, he could do just that. Getting him assigned to us was the challenge, but Don gave me the scheduling contact at Qantas head office in Sydney, and after a few phone calls they agreed to put him on our flights.

With Don at the controls, our plane – weather permitting – would usually cruise along at around 18,000 feet, with greater oxygen content in the passenger cabin than if we'd been at normal commercial altitudes. The physios were confident that our players, particularly after a game, benefited from this lower altitude flying. Once again, every little bit helped.

Another method by which we attempted to reduce the damaging effects of dehydration in the Brisbane humidity was that, under my coaching regime, our on-field ball-work sessions were always late afternoon to avoid the sun and heat in the middle of the day. That was an easy initiative, as was a simple thing we did during day games at the Gabba. The interchange bench was a very hot area under the direct afternoon sun, so, as players waited to go on the field, we seated them in the shaded area in the Lions players' race about 50 metres away. Of course, this was in the early 2000s before the interchange bench became the revolving door it is today.

The next anti-dehydration initiative was much more radical. The practical issue of becoming dehydrated by sweating liquid out quicker than it can be digested through the stomach is the big problem when it comes to staying properly hydrated. To bypass the slow digestion process, our doctors trialled and began to use extensively an intravenous drip to get saline solution quickly into a player's bloodstream.

This became a normal treatment for Lions players cramping during a game, as well as for selected players at half-time and – depending on body weight loss – for many players post-game. I must admit that, at half-time as I addressed the players, it was very strange that the coach's room looked a lot like a hospital ward, with IV drips attached to players' arms hanging from the wall. Our conditioning and medical team, and importantly our players, were convinced that this practice was a terrific competitive advantage that aided second-half performance and helped with post-match recovery.

The use of IV drips during games was outlawed after the qualifying final at the Gabba in 2001 against Port Adelaide when a Port complaint was investigated by the AFL. Once the practice was made public, the image of the game became the issue and it was banned during the following week. I go into more detail about the controversy with the IV drips later in the book.

We played at the Gabba a couple of weeks later in the preliminary final against Richmond. Without the IV drip method of hydrating players at our disposal, our off-field team went to plan B. The cool room in the players' lounge was cleared of beverages and filled with players.

At half-time, those who might have benefited from an IV drip to rehydrate quickly were ushered into the 'big fridge' with the thought that the extremely cold air would cool their skin and help them sweat less. Less sweating leads to reduced dehydration.

During the early 2000s we introduced many innovations. Our medical team was able to get the permanent rental of a hyperbaric chamber to aid injury recovery. We also purchased a hypoxicator machine, which basically produced low-oxygen air. Players would put a mask on to breathe the modified air which simulated a high altitude environment. A few players took this concept further by setting up their bedrooms as an altitude room in order to sleep in low-oxygen air.

Of course, most new initiatives come at a cost. Along with the need to find improvement in all areas, I tried to balance initiative with financial responsibility by encouraging our support team to at least sometimes look to drop something to fund a new idea. As the club's board and finance people would attest, this attitude to the balancing of the books was totally unsuccessful. Every year the football department wanted to spend more money. Nothing has changed in recent years. 'More is better' is the competition-wide mantra.

We all search for that high-performance environment where creative ideas are encouraged and elite performance can flourish. When I look back, in the early 2000s the Brisbane Lions found this elusive state – both on and off the field. As people come and go, nothing lasts forever, but for this short period of time the players received the physical benefit and the emotional comfort of a cutting-edge support staff that gave them great pride in their club. Rather than be concerned that they were stuck outside the football heartland of the southern states, I think the players firmly believed that at the Lions they had the chance to be the best they could possibly be.

This was a critically important building block in terms of getting into a position to go all the way and win a premiership.

37

THE PREMIERSHIP TURNING POINT

*Only a spendthrift with a good sense of humour would have
backed us to win the premiership four months later.*

Thirty minutes had expired on the clock on the scoreboard at the
Jolimont end of the MCG during the final term of the 2001 grand
final, when Brad Scott drove a long kick down the boundary line to
the wing in front of the Southern Stand. We were 26 points in front
of Essendon as the kick lobbed on top of a pack of players, where the
immense power and strength of our veteran full-forward, Alastair
Lynch, enabled him to stand tall and take the mark. Then the siren
sounded. We'd won the premiership.

It is so rare to reach the tip of the success pyramid, and when you
do it's just such an overpowering place to be. Without a countdown
clock to anticipate the end of the game, the siren was the magical
moment when the incredible mix of exhilaration, euphoria and
ecstasy hits you like a lightning bolt and completely overwhelms your
senses. I could never get enough of that feeling. The incredible buzz
coming from these premiership-winning moments would probably
total no more than a few hours in the four decades I was involved
in top-level football, and unfortunately this fantastic feeling subsides
into just another pleasant memory very quickly.

There is never a definitive starting point in the journey to a
premiership. Crossroads and turning points are never terribly evident
at the time. It is only with the great benefit of hindsight that we come
to these conclusions.

When the Brisbane players trudged off Carlton's Optus Oval

home ground on 19 May 2001 after the Blues had inflicted a 74-point thrashing, only a spendthrift with a good sense of humour would have backed us to win the premiership four months later. Yet as unlikely as it seemed at the time, this uninspiring loss would serve as a springboard for an incredible burst of winning form that was about to explode from the ashes of this demoralising defeat.

As the devastated players gathered in the small, pokey player rooms at Optus Oval, I sensed this was not the time for an in-depth review of the game, but my heart took over and I felt compelled to deliver a few strong home truths to the playing group. As they had done in the MCG semi-final the year before, Carlton had stitched us up badly, and Anthony Koutoufides had destroyed us yet again. For the few seasons around the turn of the century, Kouta was a key position sized player who played some irrepressible footy as a monster-sized ruck/rover, and the Lions seemed to be his bunnies at this point of time.

Seventh on the ladder with a 4–4 win–loss record, we were going nowhere fast. It wasn't so much the magnitude of the loss that spelled trouble but the nature of the defeat. It was a big day for the club. The recently named Fitzroy Team of the Century was paraded on the ground prior to the game and a lot of Melbourne-based fans had turned out for the occasion. And yet, after kicking the first two goals, we hardly fired a shot against opponents who completely overwhelmed us – our defence leaking like a sieve as we conceded 21 goals. What happened in the match review process back at the Gabba on the following Tuesday was to become something of a light-bulb moment, which provided the stimulus for how the season panned out thereafter.

The bus trip back to the airport was predictably quiet. Reflective introspection is a footballer's usual travelling companion after a bad loss, as he digests the day's events. I was in my normal seat in the front row on the right-hand side behind our regular driver, Bill, as I entered the emotional dark cave that was always my miserable sanctuary for a few hours before I'd emerge and start planning ahead.

I hated that losing feeling but had been there enough times to know that the downer would pass. The reality was that, although our season wasn't dead, we were badly wounded and seemed to be back where we'd been after Carlton had humiliated and eliminated us the previous September. Already much had changed in the intervening months but almost halfway through the 2001 season the changes didn't seem to have made us any better.

The on-field changes had started when Adam Heuskes walked away from the club late the season before, and then when Jarrod Molloy, Steven Lawrence and Brett Voss decided to head to Melbourne, we had the salary cap room for some selective top-up recruiting. We'd be strengthened by the inclusion of Clark Keating and Brad Scott, who hadn't played a game in 2000 due to injury, and in the lead-up to the new season we made a couple of critical recruiting decisions. One was a calculated gamble, the other was made possible by Adam Heuskes' sudden late-season departure.

I'd always had an enormous amount of time for Martin Pike as a footballer. He'd played 141 games for Melbourne (1993–94), Fitzroy (1995–96) and North Melbourne (1997–2000). A top 10 draft pick by Melbourne and a member of North's 1999 premiership side, at 27 he still had plenty of decent football in him, but he had a well-earned reputation as being a bit of a social nightmare. It was that old 'temptation of talent' question again. Should we take a punt on his undoubted talents? Or should we go with the conservative line? With the departure of a loose cannon named Heuskes, should we replace him with a loose cannon named Pike? My view was that one loose cannon was manageable, so with Adam gone the recruitment of a player who had been sacked for off-field issues by both Melbourne and the Kangaroos shouldn't be totally ruled out. Talent is hard to resist.

The Brisbane Lions had had the chance to recruit Pikey via the merger between the Bears and Fitzroy at the end of 1996 but had chosen against it, despite the fact that he'd won Fitzroy's very last B & F that season. My understanding was that with a pretty young playing group at the time the new entity decided they didn't need someone of his personality. Instead, they'd taken captain Brad Boyd, Chris Johnson, Jarrod Molloy, John Barker, Simon Hawking, Scott Bamford, Shane Clayton and Nick Carter. By the end of 2000, after Molloy had chosen to return home with a year still to run on his contract, only Johnson was still with the club.

When Pikey was delisted by North at the end of the 2000 season after one alcohol-related misdemeanour too many, a spark went off in the back of my mind. I wasn't prepared to pass him over without some investigation. By chance I bumped into North champion Glenn Archer one day and asked him specifically about his ex-team-mate. Glenn told me that Pikey was well liked and well respected by his team-mates as an on-field performer, and that it was only an occasional off-field incident that had led to his exit from Arden Street.

Tempted by his unquestioned talent, I asked Gubby to arrange for us to have a chat with him at the Parkview Hotel on St Kilda Road. It was a 3 pm appointment. On the day, it got to 3.05, then 3.10 and 3.15 – no Pikey. I thought to myself that this only underlined what a lot of people had been saying. He was too unreliable.

But at 3.20 pm he charged in through the doors of the hotel wearing a suit and tie and covered in sweat. He'd been at the Carlton Crest Hotel around the corner on Queens Road, and when Gubby had rung his mobile to confirm the venue he'd sprinted the 400 metres to the Parkview.

I was impressed that he'd gone to the trouble of getting dressed up. He didn't often wear a suit and it showed it meant something to him – that he wanted to make a good impression. He did. We had a good, honest, forthright chat before we parted company. We made him no promises but privately we were committed to exploring the option further.

What swung his recruitment from 'maybe' to 'yes' in my mind was his family situation. Pikey's partner, Amanda, was about to have their first baby. The responsibility of fatherhood is usually a calming influence and he knew this was his last opportunity to make a good living as an elite-level footballer. Those two factors were critical in us deciding to give him another chance. I had little doubt that Martin Pike's on-field talents could help us. He could play a variety of roles and had been part of a successful team at North. His body was fit and strong and, after discussing his potential recruitment with Michael Voss and a few of our senior players, we decided to draft him if he didn't get picked too early.

When it came to the 2000 national draft we took West Australian youngsters Ash McGrath (number 13) and Richard Hadley (number

22) with our first two picks. Our third pick (number 29) was allocated to Queenslander Jamie Charman, who joined the club as a zone selection after the AFL had road-blocked a rule which could have seen Gold Coaster Nick Riewoldt join the Lions. Nick was ruled to live outside the Lions' metropolitan recruiting zone, which was 50 kilometres from the Brisbane CBD, and went to St Kilda as the number one pick in the draft.

In the trade period we'd received pick 33 for 81-game local Steven Lawrence, who went to his father Barry's former club, St Kilda.

I was never a great delegator to my assistant coaches, but was happy to defer to the specialists in areas outside my expertise. Selecting the untried teenagers was one such area, so generally I was little more than an observer on draft day. I always figured the recruiting staff spent their entire year assessing the potential talent and that I had to trust their judgement. You couldn't make an informed decision watching a couple of highlights tapes, anyway. Occasionally, I might intervene if there was someone who had played at AFL level, such as Martin Pike. We'd taken three untried teenagers with our first three picks, and on draft day when the 30s come around proven players come into focus, so when our turn came to use pick 33 it was time to move. I leant over to Lions recruiting manager Kinnear Beatson and said, 'Let's take Pikey now.' It turned out to be a fantastic selection.

We hoped to get a year or two of good service but we got four and a bit when he played 97 of a possible 100 games from 2001 to 2004, before he tailed off and finished at the end of 2005. Because he had little bargaining power and because we were constantly under salary cap pressure, Pikey never got paid what his playing talents deserved. It was one-year contracts only and he really just got whatever was left when the other key players had been contracted. This inequity was his constant gripe but I guess you reap what you sow.

Pikey was a tough and versatile medium-tall with underrated ball skills. He was also a sledger extraordinaire who was more than happy to verbalise and intimidate his opponents. He was only a moderate preparer but was a very determined on-field competitor who gave us some terrific football.

Pikey was to be the second of our experienced pick-ups heading into the 2001 season. Earlier, we'd traded Jarrod Molloy to Collingwood in exchange for Queenslander Mal Michael.

Molloy was 24 and had played 61 games for Brisbane from 1997 to 2000, on top of 59 games for Fitzroy from 1994 to 1996. He'd played some quite good football as a bullocking forward and had even spent a bit of time down back in 2000. But with Alastair Lynch and Daniel Bradshaw clearly ahead of him as tall forwards, and with a young Jonathan Brown on the horizon, Molloy had reasoned that his opportunities might be limited. He asked to be traded back to his home town in Melbourne to play for the Magpies.

About the same time the football grapevine was telling us that Collingwood weren't altogether opposed to the idea of letting Mal Michael go. Born in Papua New Guinea but a Queenslander in football terms, he was still only 23 and had played 61 games with the Magpies from 1997 to 2000. He was close friends with a young and emerging Chris Tarrant, and the mail we were getting was that the Pies thought Mal was a bad influence on Tarrant, so were happy to let him go.

Mal was holidaying in Thailand at the end of the 2000 season and had been frustrated because he couldn't find an Australian newspaper with any football news. A phone call from his manager, Ron Joseph, had alerted him to the fact that something was on and that a move to Brisbane was possible, so Gubby and I went to Melbourne to meet him face to face. When Mal returned home from holidays he found a note from Ron under his door, telling him to meet us at midday at his manager's office.

While Mal's football had been nothing special to that point, we were hopeful – more than confident – that he could hold down the full-back position. If he could, it would allow us to shift Justin Leppitsch out to attack from the half-back line. After the meeting we decided to proceed and an hour later he'd made up his mind to come back to Brisbane, where he'd spent his teenage years, and join the Lions. All that had to be done was the trade.

Collingwood wanted a direct swap – a contracted Molloy for an out-of-contract Michael. But we figured we had the upper hand because Molloy was contracted, so we pushed to get a second-round draft selection thrown into the trade. The Magpies eventually agreed and it would prove very handy. It was the pick with which we would get Richard Hadley, while that third selection under 30 gave us the confidence to take the 27-year-old Martin Pike as our fourth pick.

We really didn't know just how well we had done. For the next four seasons the Lions' goal-to-goal line from full-back was Mal Michael, Justin Leppitsch, Michael Voss, Jonathan Brown and Alastair Lynch. I defy anyone to name a team with a better spine at any time in VFL/ AFL history.

We thought at the time it had been a pretty good trade and draft period, but we didn't realise that the five newcomers – McGrath, Hadley, Charman, Pike and Michael – would play such an important role in the years ahead. In one summer we'd picked up five premiership players.

There was one significant piece of good fortune associated with the whole exercise. We wouldn't have had the opportunity to pursue Pikey had Adam Heuskes not walked out on the club late in the previous season. Adam's sudden departure and retirement was another of those unplanned moments that stimulated quite a few very positive outcomes.

As well, the retirement of Craig Lambert – due to chronic calf muscle problems – led to an important addition to our coaching group. Craig stepped into a vacancy created by the voluntary departure of Matthew Armstrong and Michael McLean and joined Gary O'Donnell and Scott McIvor as full-time assistant coaches.

Apart from his normal functions as an assistant coach, Craig was of great value to my coaching at Brisbane in the manner that Norm Goss was to Allan Jeans at Hawthorn, when Gossy retired from playing and became Jeansy's assistant. As a recently retired player at Collingwood who then became football manager, Gubby Allan fulfilled a similar role for me when I started coaching the Magpies.

Effective leadership is a lot about rectifying a problem before it becomes a disaster. Having a confidant who is close to and knows what the player group is thinking and feeling, and is aware of the karma and irritations bubbling around in the group, is an enormous advantage to any coach. Many times, Lambie would alert me to an issue around the player group that needed addressing or to an individual player who he felt would benefit from some TLC from the senior coach. He developed a great rapport with all the very different characters in this group, from the heavy Thinker/Enforcer Michael Voss to the extreme Feeler/Thinker Nigel Lappin to the Mozzie/Enforcer Simon Black. The friendship and respect that developed between players and coaches came in no small way from the personality and caring nature, not only of Lambie, but the whole Lambert family.

The first reality that hit me when I went to Brisbane was that the large majority of the Lions players were recruited from the southern states. There was good and bad in this. It was helpful that because the players were away from their hometown friends they socialised together as well as playing together. Living the lifestyle required of a disciplined athlete is easier if you're surrounded by friends of like mind. The downside was that they were teenagers who were removed from the love and care of their families, so homesickness was always a threat. In a practical sense, this made them logical recruiting targets for clubs from the AFL heartland in the southern states. The influence of the Lambert family helped enormously in keeping the marauders at bay.

Even when Lambie was still playing, I'd noticed that he and his wife, Melissa, daughter, Brylee, and sons, Billie and Bailey, seemed to be a surrogate family for many of the Lions youngsters who'd mostly been drafted from outside Queensland. A third son, Bodie, was born in 2002. Youngsters who wanted to share a family atmosphere were always welcome at the Lambert household. When Lambie retired from playing, we jumped at the chance to get him onto our coaching ranks to look after our midfield group. It proved to be a very good decision.

Over the summer leading into the 2001 season, there was a significant change in the team leadership. Alastair Lynch, who had shared the captaincy with Michael Voss for four years, decided it was time to step aside. Vossy, now in his mid-20s, became the sole captain.

With the evolution over the last decade of formal leadership groups of six to eight players, the role of the captain has been diluted from what it was back when football headed into the new century.

It is still an important function but a little less than it was historically. Up until the group leadership approach became fashionable, the partnership between off-field coach and on-field captain was a critical relationship.

At Collingwood I was blessed to have Tony Shaw as captain for the majority of my coaching tenure. They say lightning never strikes twice, but it did – and with even greater force – during my time at Brisbane, Michael Voss being our captain for most of the decade I spent there.

Michael was Tony Shaw in a bigger, more powerful, more skilful body. Shawy had the inspirational attitude of a human battering ram, but not the strength or bulk to be one. Vossy had the combination. I can't recall him ever going outside the rules, but his attack on the footy or an opponent with the footy was brutal. I can still picture a game against Essendon at Etihad Stadium when, on the boundary line in front of the coach's box at the northern end, Vossy sprinted 20 metres to bury his shoulder into a top speed tackle on the Bombers' Damien Peverall. The speed and power he generated in the attack on this contest was indicative of the way he played his footy.

Above and beyond his leadership and skill, it is Michael Voss the battering ram that made him a once-in-a-generation player. And I believe that the aftermath of the badly broken leg he suffered in 1998 prevented him from reaching his optimum level. He was a wonderful player who battled chronic injury issues for the entire time I coached him, so while he was great, with a sounder body he could have been even better.

Like Tony Shaw, Vossy was an inspirational captain who was above reproach both on and off the field and was both respected and liked by his team-mates. He was an enormous help to me in my role as coach and our weekly one-on-one catch-up to chat about what was happening around the team and what needed addressing was both valuable and enjoyable.

The club went into the 2001 season having made the usual few changes in players and coaches. Every organisation is always balancing the conflicting needs of perseverance and change. Time never stands still and in any football team change is happening whether we plan it or not. What every club wants is to generate better performance from whatever change takes place. A noble aim, but always easier said than done.

Human performance will always fluctuate to some degree, and even more pointedly with regard to the athletic and football capabilities of the player group. From year to year some players might improve, some might stay the same and some might go backwards through form, injury or ageing. One common denominator of the best AFL teams is a proliferation of players spread from their early to late 20s. These are usually the peak performance years and as we entered the new season the age and experience profile of our core player group was in good shape. Whether this would translate into us progressing into being a premiership threat was the question to be answered.

The two players outside this peak age window happened to be our 19-year-old centre half-forward, Jonathan Brown, and our veteran full-forward, Alastair Lynch, who was about to turn 33.

Jonathan was the most mature teenager I ever coached. John Kennedy often said that a player can be a man at 20 or a boy at 30. Browny fitted this theory perfectly. He was a man well before the official age of 21. A dominant teenage key position forward is as rare as hen's teeth. In that conflict between change and perseverance, we went into the season committed to persevering with Browny through his development ups and downs. When he took Geelong apart at the Gabba in round six with a 19-disposal, seven-goal performance, his enormous value was clear for all to see. A big man with great skill, enormous courage and midfielder standard endurance, he was a player package who could excel at centre half-forward, the hardest position on the field, in a manner only rivalled by the great Wayne Carey. If a chronic groin injury hadn't struck Browny down around his mid-20s prime, he might have even surpassed the legendary Kangaroo, whom I rate as the most valuable player I have ever seen.

At the other end of the Lions' age scale going into 2001 was Alastair Lynch. The value he gave us during our grand final sequence when he was aged 33–36 was quite extraordinary. Earlier in his career he probably had many of the same athletic gifts as Jonathan Brown, but the symptoms he suffered in the aftermath of his battle with chronic fatigue illness were a constant problem until the day he retired. Combined with the natural ageing process, this had left him with a very poor endurance base, although fortunately for us he still had very good speed and power.

However, the only position he could now play was deep forward around the attacking goal square. Again fortunately for the Lions he was able to play this anchor role, which was so critical to the successful implementation of our game plan, in a manner that became one of the team's great strengths. What Lynchie gave us in his mid-30s – when most players were comfortably retired – was nothing short of superb.

I never prepared the team to be at its peak in February, so winning the pre-season competition wasn't our focus. Nonetheless, after a disappointing end to the 2000 campaign, and with a fairly healthy list, we figured that, after getting within striking distance the previous couple of years, it would be good for us to build momentum and try to win some silverware – even if it wasn't the real thing.

After beating Adelaide in Wellington, New Zealand, we lost to the Western Bulldogs in a very wet cyclone-hit Cairns. We then beat Carlton at the Gabba to qualify for a semi-final against Hawthorn that we expected would be played in Brisbane. It wasn't. If we'd known that, we mightn't have been so committed to the challenge, because it meant another interstate trip. While it wasn't something we planned for, the hard-fought victory over the Hawks in Melbourne in a pressure game was still good experience. Learning to win on the road is so important for the non-Victorian teams who have to travel every second week, especially given that the one certainty in footy is that the holy grail of the premiership will be decided at the MCG.

We faced Port Adelaide in the Ansett Cup grand final at Football Park on Saturday night, 17 March. We were embarrassed 3.8 (26) to 17.9 (111) in front of 35,304 people, but still we'd gained some experience. None more so than Robert Copeland, a 19-year-old from Kilcoy, in the Sunshine Coast hinterland, who had never played a game of AFL football at any level. Not even a practice match. He was on the rookie list but when Michael Voss was ruled out at the last minute with concussion, he got a call-up to begin a fairytale debut season that would end in even more extraordinary circumstances six months later.

The pre-season changes had little positive effect early in the year. We looked similar to the year before; competitive but losing as many as we were winning. Outwardly, things weren't too bad – we'd lost three of our first four and then won three in a row heading into the Carlton game in round eight. But still something was missing. And after a diabolical performance against the Blues, we were at the proverbial crossroads.

We always did the formal match review two or three days after a game, because I wanted the emotional consequences of the contest to subside. If both the players and I could have an unemotional look at the game, I believed we'd have a better learning experience before we moved on to the next week's match. The purpose was to learn from the previous weekend's experience, not to embarrass or humiliate anyone. My theme of pushing the positives 80 per cent of the time continued, but after a big loss there are always many negatives that might attract scrutiny. Rather than dwell on our flaws, though, after the Carlton game I decided to focus on what the opposition had done well as an example for us to follow.

A couple of key messages resonated from the Blues' performance, and these were based not around their stars such as Anthony Koutoufides, Craig Bradley and Brett Ratten, but around the roles of a few of Carlton's lesser lights, like Anthony Franchina, Darren Hulme and Scott Freeborn. They were the taggers: the blockers and the tacklers who did the hack work that enabled their more skilled team-mates to display the full array of their offensive talents. The contributions of this unheralded Blues trio seemed to vividly illustrate the concept of each individual playing his role, and that not every role is going to be particularly glamorous. This wasn't a new coaching theme but after the Carlton thrashing it seemed as if the light bulb went on within our players' minds.

The theme that emerged was about players being prepared and willing to perform their assigned match-day role. My job was to ensure that those who didn't get the external recognition received the plaudits internally within our group. Reward and recognition is a powerful motivator and not everyone can be the big goal-kicker or high possession-getter. The players' acceptance of this concept as a means of becoming a more successful team was born out of the beating by the Blues at Optus Oval, and it grew as the wins mounted over the following months.

The mantra that became part of the language at the Lions was: know your role, accept your role, train for your role, perform your role and be recognised for your role. It was about defenders appreciating the defensive efforts of the forwards; about midfielders who were prepared to chase, tackle hard and to push back to help out in defence; and about the goal-kicking forwards appreciating the defenders' efforts and those of the taggers who shut down their direct opponents, even if it meant not getting a lot of the ball.

We introduced a weekly role-appreciation award for which players would nominate the team-mate who'd best performed his assigned tasks in the previous match. The other weekly award was the player who led the tackling stats. Craig Lambert looked after this crucial area, along with our tackling coach, Ian Mellor. They went through the match video and Ian worked with the players on their technique at training and Lambie produced the stats feedback where the costly missed tackles were deducted from the effective ones.

Eventually we benchmarked that for the team to play at its best, we needed about 60 effective and no more than 10 missed. The rewards for doing well in these two basic areas of role playing and tackling were – importantly –acknowledgement within the peer group, plus the player with the most votes got a dinner for two or the match ball signed by the senior team from the previous game.

While the theme of playing your role was eventually embraced by the whole playing group, I felt it was led by Alastair Lynch, Craig McRae, Marcus Ashcroft, Brad Scott and Shaun Hart.

Our game plan was that when a player was under pressure and had no obvious better option, he should bomb the ball to the top of the attacking goal square. We could only succeed doing this with a big strong man wrestling the likely pack under these high balls. That was Lynchy's job. It was frustrating work because it wasn't easy to mark the ball in these heavily contested situations, but if the ball came to ground it was 15 metres out in front of our goal and 150 metres from the opposition's. As much as Alastair marked a few, his main job was to make sure the opposition didn't. His immense strength to make a good contest in front of our attacking goal square – usually when he was outnumbered by defenders or the opposition ruckman dropping back – was the reason this tactic worked really well. It was this exact play that generated the chance for Jason Akermanis to crumb the final goal of the tight 2002 grand final.

While it was Aker that day, it was predominantly the role of our small quick forward Craig McRae to get to the front of the deep forward aerial contest. Crumb the footy if he could, but, if not, use his speed to chase and tackle to lock the ball in our forward line. This meant resisting the temptation to chase easy kicks so he could be in position to work off Lynchy's contest. 'Fly', which was Craig's nickname, never got many external plaudits so it was important he was continually recognised and thanked for his work during our match reviews. The way Fly accepted, valued and performed his forward worker-bee role was a great example to the rest of the team.

Marcus 'Choppers' Ashcroft had been a high possession-gathering midfielder for his entire 12-season career, which had begun with the Brisbane Bears back in 1989. As we looked to improve our team we felt we needed a disciplined small/medium defender who had the shutdown focus of my old Collingwood favourite Micky Gayfer, but with the ball skills, talent and run to attack when the opportunity arose. Marcus was called on to perform this function, which was required partly to balance the attacking flair of Chris Johnson. Johnno was a terrific attacking back pocket, but pretty loose if his opponent dragged him up-field. Choppers was the coverer in these situations and, having previously forged a successful career as an attacking midfielder, his willingness to accept and embrace the shift to the close-checking defensive role was also a great example to his team-mates.

For the Lions, Brad Scott and Shaun Hart became more talented versions of what Franchina, Freeborn and Hulme were for Carlton. No wonder both are coaching at AFL level – Brad the senior coach at North Melbourne and Shaun an assistant with the Gold Coast Suns.

They were often given specific tagging roles on the opposition stars, which they accepted willingly, and both had the courage to leave their opponents to attack when the time was right. What they were asked to do took discipline, determination, great endurance and the nous to develop an effective strategy against their assigned opponent. Pretty good qualities on which to build a coaching career. Brad was the more forceful Enforcer of the pair, so this may partly explain his quick progression to senior coaching.

Shaun sticks in my mind whenever I mention my belief that individuals will invest in the team cause, but will sacrifice only very rarely – perhaps for their country in time of war, or for their family, if necessary, but not for their footy team. In this context, 'invest' means that you give and hope to get a return; 'sacrifice' means giving and expecting nothing in return. Hartie is one of the few people I've met who might defy this convention. It might be explained by his strong religious faith but Shaun was such a natural giver that I became convinced he did it simply because of the great care he felt for those around him. He was hardworking, humble and just a fantastic person to have in our team.

Although one result of the Carlton debacle was a greater group focus on individuals playing their roles, it didn't get us a win against the Adelaide Crows the following week at the Gabba. A five-point defeat left us with a troubling 4–5 record going into round 10. Every season I played or coached, the initial goal was to get the wins in credit over the losses. In a 22-round season, that would get a team 12 wins and, usually, a finals berth. As we headed into round 10, the basic maths told me that even to get to that benchmark we now needed to win eight of our remaining 13 games. Lose again and it was eight of 12, so the noose was tightening.

We had the benefit of again playing at home but the bad news was that our opponents happened to be Essendon, which had been wearing the crown as the competition's undisputed juggernaut for a couple of seasons. The Bombers were reigning premiers, and heading into their trip to Brisbane they'd only lost twice in their previous 34 games. They were as close to an unbeatable force as flesh and blood can be. But the reality that the Essendon players were exactly that

– flesh and blood human beings – was a coaching theme we stumbled on and used as a focus point in the pre-game build-up.

We desperately needed the win but our lead-in form didn't give us much chance, so we confronted one almighty physical and mental challenge to get the job done. We'd need to do something special. This was a game where doing the footy basics well would not be enough. To win we needed to find a special strategy, both to bond our team effort and to narrow the players' concentration onto what we were doing, rather than being fazed by the seemingly unbeatable supermen in the red and black jumpers.

The Carlton game taught us some valuable lessons. The Essendon game would make us believe we could beat the best.

38

2001: REACHING THE TIP OF
THE PYRAMID

For the first time a premiership flag was heading to the
AFL frontier in the north.

My early-week coaching preparation for our round 10 game in 2001 at the Gabba against pace-setters Essendon was a little out of the ordinary. On the way back from Sunday morning training I drove around the south-eastern suburbs between the Lions' base in Woolloongabba and my Carindale home, visiting the various video rental stores in that part of Brisbane. I was trying to rent or buy a copy of the movie *Predator*.

After a few failures I finally found a store in Cannon Hill that had a copy to rent. Rather than just show match vision as part of the build-up to what was to be a season-defining game against the rampant Bombers, I planned to take our players to the movies or, more particularly, to show them a scene in *Predator*. Starring Arnold Schwarzenegger, the film was set in the South American jungle, with Arnie leading a small commando unit being hunted by an alien monster who had the technology to become invisible. The unit was being picked off one by one when, after another costly skirmish, some random fire – in the direction of where the commandos thought the alien was – left some green liquid staining the undergrowth. This was when big Arnie muttered the line about the alien that seemed to apply equally well to our required mindset against the dominant Essendon. In that unique Schwarzenegger accent, after seeing the green liquid he said, 'If it bleeds, we can kill it.' I just loved that line. So at our Tuesday review meeting I showed our players these few minutes of *Predator*.

My intention was simple. Sure, the Bombers were a very good team with a fantastic recent record but, like us, they were still only flesh and blood. Simple analogies often resonate with players; my hope was that this reference to the seemingly unbeatable alien who was found to bleed and was eventually killed had connotations regarding our next opponents, who'd been equally invincible.

All coaches search for a theme that might bond the group, and occasionally they become public. A good example was the 2008 grand final, when Hawthorn coach Alastair Clarkson used the analogy that the Hawks' opponents, Geelong, were like a shark which would die if it couldn't constantly swim forward, so his team needed to slow the free-flowing Cats down at every opportunity. I'm not so sure the shark analogy had any real impact on the Hawthorn players, just as I don't really know whether the alien comparison with Essendon was of any value to the Lions. It all comes under the every-little-bit-helps category.

I've never believed that being confident of victory helps all that much; however, believing you can't win is certainly disastrous. What I wanted was for the players to think they had a good chance of winning, provided they did A, B, C and D. And, frankly, when my players entered the arena I only wanted two or three key match needs to be occupying their thoughts. Over-coaching that leads to complication and confusion is always counterproductive.

While that simplifying principle was always part of my coaching philosophy, we needed to find a specific game plan designed to beat Essendon. All coaches need to follow the golden rules of coaching. Explain and clarify the method, sell its value, and then do the physical habit-making drills on the field at training.

The specific tactics against the Bombers were not terribly complicated. Essendon had a great ability to block up the opposition forward line, so rather than kick to their defensive numbers we decided we'd attempt never to kick over the mark and, whenever possible, we'd bring the ball across field and then play on to alter the angle of our forward thrusts. Bringing the football from wing back into the centre square from set kicks was our preferred option. This was partly to blunt an opposition strength, but it was equally to give the group a specific team plan to execute. No tactic was going to make the winning difference – doing the basics better than the Bombers would be needed to win us the game. Observable tactics become a sexy discussion point for commentators, but, to use an Allan Jeans-ism, the team that plays the best basic three-phase football – winning the contested footy, effective use of the footy and pressuring the opposition into error – will usually win.

At the time the bookies had Bombers a hot $1.65 favourite to complete back-to-back flags, and we were on the seventh line of betting at $26. Not one tipster selected the Lions to win the game. Essendon had beaten us at the Gabba the previous season by over 10 goals and the general consensus was that a repeat was on the cards. We were given a boost, though, when Essendon's main ruckman, John Barnes, was a late withdrawal.

On a beautiful balmy Brisbane Saturday night, a capable Lions team graduated into a real giant-killer. Jonathan Brown, still only 19 and in only his 23rd AFL game, set the scene early. At the first bounce he charged in from centre half-forward like a snorting bull and immediately afterwards ran head-first at oncoming traffic to intercept a floating handpass. Then, running with the flight of the ball, he pulled in a diving chest mark. He'd set a tone that was matched by another youngster entering his prime, the 22-year-old Simon Black, who was best afield in his 46th game. Everyone else followed. We held Essendon to two goals in the first half and won by 28 points in front of a sell-out, record Gabba crowd of 36,149. It was a fantastic night at the footy as the Lions killed the alien monster.

My main post-match satisfaction came from the fact that we'd stabilised our season by getting our wins level with our losses. In hindsight, though, the win over the reigning premiers gave the players confidence and belief that if everyone committed to their individual roles, the team would be able to play at its best. As they say the proof was in the pudding. The role-playing mantra that emerged after the Carlton thrashing had borne fruit against the very best opposition.

When a team produces an extremely high level of performance, the next challenge is to do it consistently. Living in the moment and focusing on only the next few days is the key, and the Lions players did this extremely well in the weeks, months and years ahead. This is how I lived my whole football life, so hopefully my natural attitude of taking it one week at a time rubbed off a little on the team.

After the match against the Bombers, the challenge was to follow up with another top-notch effort against the West Coast Eagles in Perth. The Essendon game, like every match, was reviewed, lessons learnt and then it was consigned to history as we concentrated totally on the week's preparation and the next opponent. We diligently repeated that process week after week, and lo and behold, after round 17 we'd won 12 games, which was always my benchmark number to grab a finals berth. From that first mini-achievement of finals qualification, we then continued the winning streak to get to 17 wins at the end of the home-and-away season.

This put us in second position, behind Essendon on percentage. Port Adelaide finished a game behind us in third spot. In the few seasons that followed, the emergence of the Power as a competition pacesetter – they would finish the home-and-away season on top in 2002, 2003 and 2004 – would have enormous ramifications for our next three finals campaigns. The Power were to be our opponents in the second qualifying final at the Gabba on the Saturday night, with the prize a home preliminary final.

On the Monday night leading into a finals campaign, it was my tradition to get the players and the club's inner sanctum together as a subtle signal that the short, season-defining finals month was about to begin. We'd won our last 13 games but that only qualified us for what lay ahead. I invited my 1990 Collingwood premiership captain Tony Shaw to Brisbane to address the team at our pre-finals function. Guest speakers weren't a regular event under my coaching, but so highly did I regard Shawy's competitive spirit and determined attitude that I was keen for him to share his views with our whole club, let alone our players.

On a wet and slippery night at the Gabba we started nervously against Port and were terribly inaccurate early, while they made the most of every scoring chance. However, down 3.9 to the Power's 7.1

at half-time, the team maintained its composure to dominate the second half and win comfortably by 32 points. This gave us a week off and took us to the highly valued home preliminary final. The tip of the success pyramid was now within view.

The only negative was Alastair Lynch being reported by a goal umpire for allegedly striking Port Adelaide's Darryl Wakelin in the opening minute. Video evidence captured by chance by an AFL film crew sent to the ground to film marketing footage showed Lynchy pushing Wakelin in the face with an open hand, and Wakelin going to ground.

At the hearing on the Tuesday night the tribunal noted that Lynch, never before suspended for striking in 14 years and 248 AFL games, seemed to be the retaliator in the incident and that his actions were 'reckless' and 'off the ball'. After a 90-minute hearing they took into account all this, plus a glowing character reference from ex-Brisbane coach Robert Walls, in imposing a one-match penalty. So the veteran full-forward walked from the tribunal comfortable in the fact that if the Lions could survive through the preliminary final, he could play in the grand final. It was not an ideal situation, but better than it could have been.

Later that evening, any concerns over our football fortunes disappeared for a few days. I was watching the Channel Ten late news when host Sandra Sully announced that, in a breaking story, one of the World Trade Center skyscrapers in New York was on fire. The graphic viewing that followed into the early hours of the following morning as the free world was plunged into horror by the September 11 terrorist attacks was unbelievably disturbing. What we were seeing in vivid colour on our TV screens as the two giant buildings collapsed was impossible to comprehend. I went to bed that night glad we didn't have to play the following weekend. Football seemed very, very insignificant that week.

We found ourselves in the middle of our own furore when I'd confirmed at my regular Monday morning media conference that during and after the qualifying final win we'd used IV fluid replacement as a means of treating player dehydration. I'd done so in response to a story which had run on Adelaide radio earlier in the day and I was staggered by the media uproar.

It was nothing new. We'd been doing it regularly for almost two seasons to help combat the heat and humidity in which we played in Queensland. It was the brainchild of our ever-diligent medical and conditioning staff, and was based on the fact that it was the best way for players to rehydrate. They could only drink so much liquid and an IV drip was a much more effective means of achieving the desired outcome.

I was surprised I had to defend and explain the use of saline fluid administered intravenously in the treatment of high-performance athletes exposed on a regular basis to high humidity and repeated travel. To me it was simply medical experts at the top of their field utilising a perfectly legal technique for the betterment of the players – specifically, to prevent injury, aid recovery and prolong careers. Or from a strictly medical viewpoint, fulfilling an obligation to do their utmost for their patients. But apparently Port Adelaide officials who had driven the story weren't happy.

Some of the media reports were outrageous, such as those which suggested that players had a plastic shunt put in their arm before games to allow the drip to be immediately inserted at half-time. That players might be playing a game with a shunt in their arm was a malicious and inaccurate insult to our medical professionals.

The AFL quickly agreed with the Port Power concerns, and later on the Monday the Lions accepted an AFL directive to terminate the use of IV fluid replacement as a match-day treatment for player dehydration. I was reluctant to stop a practice which was totally within the rules and of significant benefit to the players, but head office is there to regulate the sport and maintain the image of the game, so any further opposition was pointless.

The aftermath was that in February 2002 the AFL announced that it would fine clubs $100,000 and strip them of premiership points if they were found using intravenous drips inappropriately during games. The revised legislation allowed for the use of intravenous fluid replacement only if a player was considered so severely affected that he needed the treatment, and in that case he wouldn't be allowed back onto the field for the duration of the match.

There was no legislation that prohibited the use of this technique after matches, so on occasions we continued to use it to aid post-game recovery. The AFL regularly sent spies to visit our rooms to check on our half-time activities.

It was all about perception. The AFL didn't like the image of a dressing room with IV drips everywhere and I accepted that. In retrospect I can fully understand and agree with the AFL's decision, because players on IV drips at the local footy would not be a great look. It was only a small part of our medical protocols and, while I was worried that a competitive advantage had been lost, it was time to put the issue behind us. However, I was glad we weren't playing the following week because it was a topic that had dominated week two of the finals and was an unhealthy distraction.

By the week leading into the preliminary final we'd moved on, and the banned IV drips were replaced with a new method of player rehydration. We emptied the drinks out of the large cold room in the after-match function area. This giant refrigerator was where the players most prone to becoming dehydrated would spend most of the half–time break. It was partly a placebo effect but the theory was that cooling the body in a cold temperature would minimise sweating a little and therefore help to reduce dehydration. Having talked up the competitive advantage of our IV drip system to our players, once it was banned we did a U-turn and tried to convince them that the half-time 10 minutes in the cold room would have a similar effect.

Sometimes things happen that are totally out of your control that either help or hinder. After Carlton had destroyed us the last time we'd played them back in round eight, I was more than happy not to have to confront the Blues again when Richmond eliminated them in week two of the finals. This left the Tigers as our preliminary final opponent.

If there is such a thing as a low-stress preliminary final, this was it. I was always a bit toey confronting Richmond because, on his good days, their star forward Matthew Richardson was capable of winning them the game. Fortunately, Justin Leppitsch kept Richo under control and we beat Richmond by 70 points after leading all night, and going further in front the longer the game went.

It was a terrific night at the footy. We'd got through without injury and Alastair Lynch was available to return for the grand final after his one-week suspension. The team was in really good shape and the footy gods had been shining on us for most of the season. Could we get it done for another week? This time it would be away from the comforts of our home base at the Gabba, down in Melbourne at the MCG, where we'd take on the might of Essendon, who had beaten Hawthorn in the Saturday afternoon preliminary final.

As I walked down from the coach's box to the ground I bumped into Richmond coach Danny Frawley. He extended his congratulations and said, 'You can win it.' It was the first time I'd really thought a premiership was more than a long-term dream. We were so locked into our week-to-week routine and mindset that it was only after qualifying for the grand final and hearing Danny's words that winning the flag entered my conscious thoughts. My job, however, was to maintain the focus on one day at a time. Thinking too much about a premiership and its aftermath and consequences during that last frenetic week of September is a distraction that can easily cause a debilitating emotional and physical fatigue. What I'd be pushing was that we had to concentrate on a few game-needs that would give us our best chance of beating Essendon, as opposed to thinking about winning a grand final.

This was an internal challenge for each individual to confront during the seven days leading up to the game and my main role as coach/manager was to create a process and environment to best facilitate this crucial aim. That had to start with my post-match address after the victory over Richmond, so finding the right words was the issue occupying my thoughts as I headed for the rooms. There was no sense of achievement or satisfaction – qualifying for the grand final had to be merely a stepping stone and the players needed to share that view. They sang the club song with gusto but then it was into the coach's room where the week's attitudinal programming would begin. At that point, the celebration of that night's victory had to finish.

I didn't give a long, drawn-out address; instead, it was a short, concise planting of the beliefs I had formed from my previous grand final involvements. My advice was simple – think of your emotions as being inside a clear glass bubble. I told the players they'd need to physically live in the outside world but not allow the external hype to invade their mental state. The challenge was to get through the very different routine of grand final week and reach the opening siren ready to perform at their best. Enjoy the moment but don't let it penetrate your mindset. Don't get caught up in it and don't get distracted or excited. Relax, take it all in, and remember it's just another game of football once the ball is bounced.

It was good to be back in that last week in September for the first time in 11 years, but I was conscious that it was going to be a new experience for the bulk of our group. Among the players, only Martin Pike had played in a grand final. What was a first was being part of a non-Melbourne club. That fact made a gigantic difference to the logistics and difficulties involved. For normal games outside Brisbane, our travel party was 40-odd people, including the players. For the grand final the extras of wives, girlfriends, staff, administration, board and inner-sanctum supporters more than tripled the standard travel numbers. The additions were welcome but we didn't want them staying together at the team hotel or travelling on the same flight as players, coaches and match-day staff. We had a firm travel policy that in a symbolic sense the match-day team was going off to war for a couple of days and anyone outside this group should be kept at arm's length.

Our football secretary, Nicole Duncan, looked after the logistics of our team travel which, because of her great competence, usually ran like clockwork. With a day or two's notice Nicole had to organise flights, accommodation and other transport for the usual match-day 40, which was fairly routine, but also the extra 100-odd who needed to be flown and accommodated separately.

While in a football sense it was just another game, because of all the peripheral issues it certainly wasn't. So, on the Sunday morning after the recovery session we got all the wives, girlfriends and administrative staff into the club for a briefing on operational matters: flights, accommodation, buses, tickets and functions. They were little things which can take on a big significance in grand final week if not handled properly.

Players were advised to turn their mobile phones off because responding to the many ticket requests, or even answering the many good luck calls, becomes quite tedious after a while. All the players and the senior coach received four reserved seats to be purchased at face value. Our instruction was: allocate them early in the week and tell everyone else you can't get anymore. I suspect CEO Andrew Ireland and football manager Gubby Allan had an emergency ticket stash for urgent requests if players, such as the Brown clan, needed more than the standard four to get their whole family to the big game.

A major part of grand final week is managing the media interest. A mass of journalists had flown to Brisbane to be on the spot. So, Monday was media day. In what was to become a tradition in grand final week, we opened the doors to as many members of the senior squad as possible who felt comfortable doing press, radio and television interviews. It was a steal from the American Super Bowl designed to satisfy the demands of the media and minimise the intrusions later in the week.

Coaches playing deliberate mind games are largely a media fabrication. You get asked a question and you give an answer. However, in my normal Monday press conference I had a few comments that I planned to pop out. Essendon coach Kevin Sheedy, a consistent rival during my whole career as player and coach, was trying to encourage all Victorian supporters to barrack for the home-town team. I wasn't worried about that – there was no way the fanatical fans of Collingwood, Carlton or any of the other Melbourne teams would be supporting the Bombers. If I was any judge, the attitude of the nonaligned supporters would be that if their team couldn't win the flag, then send it interstate where it would be largely out of sight and out of mind.

When the press asked about the Essendon coach's comments, I laughed off his urgings as ridiculous and dropped the line that the left side of his brain often didn't know what the right side was thinking. I guess it was a bit cheeky, but Sheeds has always had a thick skin and doesn't get sensitive about a bit of byplay. Mainly my intention was to emphasise the eccentric side of his personality and to make a subtle statement to our players that we weren't frightened and, in fact, were quite prepared to have a go at the big boys. When I made comments to the media I was always conscious that our players would learn what I said, so I regarded them as my main audience. My 'mind games' with Sheeds were my way of telling our players that, while we were from outside the football heartland, we needed to think of ourselves as powerful invaders not timid intruders.

Much to the AFL's disappointment, we elected not to fly our invited players to Melbourne on the Monday night for the Brownlow Medal dinner despite a threat from the league of hefty fines. Our stance was perfectly sensible – we simply didn't need our senior players making an extra trip to Melbourne. The usual Friday grand final parade meant we would already have to fly down on the Thursday, instead of our standard Friday at lunchtime. The AFL's attitude only proved that its Melbourne-centric head office had little idea of the practicalities of life for its non-Victorian clubs.

The AFL's official airline was Ansett and there was a major hiccup when they collapsed into bankruptcy over the preliminary final weekend. This had disastrous ramifications for many thousands of people but, as it turned out, provided an unexpected bonus in terms of our quest to make the whole week as stress-free as possible. On the Monday before grand final day we suddenly had no way of getting to Melbourne. The solution that we eventually found was to have an enormously positive effect on maintaining our planned approach to minimise stress in the days leading into the game.

The worst-case scenario for the AFL occurred – or just maybe they'd had some inside knowledge – when our midfield star Jason Akermanis won the coveted award. We were all rapt for Aker and I was even more pleased we'd adopted the stance of keeping our players in Brisbane. It must have been the most low-key Brownlow celebration in history. After Aker's video link interview from our club function at the Gabba with MC Bruce McAvaney at the main Brownlow event in Melbourne, a small group of us headed downstairs to the football offices. There was Aker and his wife, Megan, Gubby and Anne Allan, our media manager, Peter Blucher, player welfare manager, Shane Johnson, and my wife Deb and I. Over a drink no stronger than a cup of tea, we had an enjoyable chat about the night's exciting conclusion and what it might mean for the following days. Aker was able to do a brief media conference about 11 pm and another all-in media call on the Tuesday, but at least he'd slept in his own bed and wasn't caught up too much in all the hype that often comes with winning the game's highest individual honour.

In the big-picture swings and roundabouts, Aker winning the Brownlow in 2001 was a pivotal event in the rocky relationship that would develop over the following years between our flamboyant midfielder and most of the leadership of the whole Brisbane Lions football club.

While everyone at the Lions was genuinely thrilled when Aker won his Brownlow, this achievement unfortunately became the platform for his eager campaign of self-promotion which caused much of the conflict that developed over the next five years between me as his coach and many of his senior team-mates.

The situation that developed in the ensuing seasons highlights the subtle and unstated reality of the relationship that exists between an individual and his footy club. Players work together on the team goals – winning games, etc. – but to a large degree compete against their team-mates to achieve many of their individual aspirations – things like senior selection, profile-building, endorsement income, club championship finishing order and the percentage of the salary cap they receive.

In a team sport, though, this contest needs to be kept out of sight, or at least handled with diplomacy. Most players accept this restraint as a fundamental investment in the development of a strong team culture, but over the years Aker quite often crossed the fine line of visibly putting his personal interests before the team's. Any coach/ manager wanting to successfully blend individual needs with those of the team needs to be alert and ready for the high performer who is not a good team player.

Armed with the status of being the reigning Brownlow medallist, on top of a naturally extroverted personality, Aker was able to leverage his new-found status to seek out opportunities to work in the media and to build his own profile. The search was very successful and he was soon doing gigs in print, radio and television. And did he give them their money's worth.

Believing, quite logically when you think about it, that a successful media career would last far longer than his playing days, the problem was that he tried too hard to be a very good media performer. Aker seemed to also enjoy the notoriety and was more than willing to create headlines and controversy to build his image. As the years passed, the angst between him and our team leadership gradually increased, as his eagerness to provide good value to his media employers was seen around the club as a higher priority than his commitment to do the right thing by his football team.

It was a gradual process that culminated in our senior players and coaches losing trust in their blond-headed team-mate and deciding they wanted him out of the club. Until the murky end point in 2006, quelling this bubbling discontent that started soon after Aker's Brownlow win became one of my biggest management challenges. From that time onwards, individual irritations among his team-mates needed to be massaged regularly to maintain team harmony. With this critical element under control, we could get the best value out of Aker's on-field talents, which undoubtedly helped our group aim to win games of footy.

The task would not be mine alone. Our captain, Michael Voss, and our core players accepted the reality that Aker helped our winning efforts, and while his self-promotion would create discontent and some embarrassment at times, it was an issue we could successfully manage. I think we did it very well for a few years and he was a key contributor to our premiership success without our team fabric being eroded. I guess the dam wall was always going to eventually break.

However, this regrettable future scenario was not even a glimmer on my radar after Aker won the 2001 medal. My only concern was whether it would affect him or the team the following weekend.

Sticking as close as possible to our normal routine had to be our comfort blanket. On Tuesday morning the players did their usual weights and stretching before our weekly review meeting, and a short skills session. The main training session of the week on Wednesday afternoon was transferred to our summer training base at Coorparoo, a kilometre or two from the Gabba, the official headquarters of AFL Queensland and one-time junior club of my ex-Hawthorn team-mate Jason Dunstall. We deliberately chose this venue because the open ground with no grandstands could be a little windy, which was good preparation for the often swirly and difficult conditions at the MCG. As I'd done at Collingwood a decade before, I planned to have a congested last training session to prepare for the inevitable frenetic opening in a grand final. I also thought that getting away from the elite environment and very firm surface at the Gabba might create a more relaxing atmosphere.

After one last weights session on Thursday morning it was off to the airport. Because of the Ansett collapse, our normal routine needed to change. There were no domestic flights available, so the club had chartered two 91-seat Flight West jets. I'd usually frown on breaking routine like this, and having players travelling with wives, girlfriends, children, directors, administration staff and a few selected sponsors. But it turned out really well. We had the plane to ourselves and it was so relaxed it helped to fend off the onset of unwanted grand final nerves.

With photographers and cameramen everywhere, Daniel Bradshaw was first off the plane. Ordinarily, the whole thing might have been a daunting experience for the publicity-shy forward, but carrying his 13-month-old son, Jake, it was like a trip to the shops. Having the partners, and particularly the children, on our own flight helped to create a less stressful travelling atmosphere, which wouldn't have been the case if Ansett hadn't stopped flying. It was a lesson we heeded. Thereafter, for our run of four consecutive grand finals we travelled as a large group on our own flight.

From the airport the official travel party boarded one bus bound for the Parkview Hotel on St Kilda Road, and the families group boarded another bus for the Holiday Inn in the Melbourne CBD. Again, Nicole Duncan had done the majority of the logistics planning and had organised a separate itinerary for the families and close friends, as well as being tour leader. At the Lions we were always very conscious of the 'happy wife, happy life' logic, and if the players were confident their families were being looked after, they had one less issue to worry about.

Most players took part in the traditional grand final parade on the Friday morning, but not Chris and Brad Scott. They played golf. I was happy with that. Whatever they felt was best for their preparation was fine by me. For me the grand final parade is just great fun. It has nothing to do with playing the game but it's a terrific experience that provides great memories which I'll always cherish.

We expected Essendon to have an overwhelming advantage in terms of public support, but I was pleasantly surprised as we made our way through the streets of the Melbourne CBD. There was plenty of red and black, but there was just as much maroon, blue and gold – if not more. The numerous supporters from Brisbane who had come south, many by a long bus trip, were at the parade in big numbers, while there was also a strong ex-Fitzroy presence. The dream of the first Lions premiership since 1944 was within reach, emphasising the benefit of being a two-state club.

But it extended further. As I thought they would, the Melbourne non-Essendon footy public had shunned Kevin Sheedy's urgings, and it seemed anyone who didn't barrack for the Bombers had jumped on the Lions bandwagon. When Essendon captain James Hird was introduced at the end of the procession he was loudly booed, which I reckon shook the Essendon captain a bit and buoyed our players, who appreciated the support of the large contingent of Lions fans. All of a sudden they felt more at home.

Later on Friday afternoon about 3000 Lions fans packed Albert Oval, opposite the team hotel, for the last training session of the year. It was a quick and incident-free closure to a faultless preparation. From the time we walked back across the street to the Parkview Hotel for our final planning meeting, the comfort of a normal routine in the last 24 hours before match time could now be put in place.

We had 26 players in the travel party, but with no major injury concerns selection was pretty straightforward. Alastair Lynch, who had missed the preliminary final through suspension, would return at the expense of Matthew 'Max' Kennedy. Max had been an enormously well respected stalwart of the Bears/Lions after going to the Bears back in 1990, and was forced to endure being close to a grand final berth but just missing out. He would retire at the end of the season.

Des Headland and Aaron Shattock joined him as emergencies, with Craig Bolton and Dylan McLaren also on standby. Unfortunately, grand final teams always have players who might be one selection away from being in the team and consequently they're only a smidgin away from a premiership medallion. It is a cruel reality of team sport which highlights yet again that success or failure is so often a matter of seconds and inches, and being in the right place at the right time. The difference between winning and losing can be scarily small. At least Des, Aaron and Craig later became AFL premiership players.

The footy gods seemed to be with us. We'd been terribly fortunate to have pretty much our best side available right through September. And when we got through the lead-up finals against Port and Richmond without injury, our selection meetings were very short. Through its form, the team was picking itself.

Fearing the potential impact of the great James Hird, we asked Brad Scott to accept the role of curbing his brilliance. Hirdy may have been struggling with a groin injury but Brad did the job really well, displaying the discipline, concentration and determination that became his hallmark.

We altered our recent team a little to best control the Bombers' two dominant key forwards, Matthew Lloyd and Scott Lucas. Maybe because I was yet to have total faith in our first-year full-back Mal Michael, we decided to start him on interchange and push Justin Leppitsch back to the crucial role on Lloyd. Although he was 192 centimetres tall, Lucas was mainly a hard-running, leading type centre half-forward, so we decided to start Chris Scott as his opponent. Chris would concede him 10 centimetres but we thought that as Lucas was not really a pack mark, matching his run was more important than matching his height.

Apart from those couple of adjustments we went with the usual positioning structure that had won us the previous 15 games in a row. In the balance between change and perseverance, sticking to our successful formula was a no-brainer. We always tried to find a group focus to verbally and physically annoy a player or two in the opposition, and we decided that two of the Bombers' potential hot heads, Mark Johnson and Damian Hardwick, would be our grand final targets. We found out that, because of his large calf muscles, Hardwick was nicknamed 'Astro Boy' at the Bombers and apparently didn't like it, so that name was going to be shoved down his throat all match.

Our players had the valuable belief, which was emphasised by the coaches, that they were fitter than Essendon, and that, with the forecast warm weather, if the game was made tough and hard we'd finish the stronger. We ended the meeting by watching our usual pre-game tape of player highlights with a music backing. This was a weekly production by our video/stats man Daniel Knocke. A different tape was produced each week and I'd asked Daniel to find plenty of desperate tackling efforts, because pressuring the opposition is always a key emphasis from coaches. Get the hard things done and the easier things will instinctively follow. The grand final version was one of Daniel's best and the musical backing was the John Farnham rendition of 'Dare to Dream'. It was exactly what I wanted. Bright and upbeat, where pictures painted a thousand words and the positive reinforcement was extremely strong. Before a game, you never really knew, but the vibe was good – relaxed but determined.

After the half-hour planning meeting finished, I got a pleasant surprise when I returned to my hotel room to see the TV news vision of Essendon's final training session. Their much-admired veterans Michael Long and Dean Wallis, who weren't in their selected team, had announced their retirements and had been clapped onto the ground through a players' guard of honour. It looked a very emotional time at Windy Hill, and I immediately thought, 'You beauty.' Every little bit helps. The retirements would be a distraction, not a motivation, and high emotion the day before a grand final is the last thing you need.

Our usual policy the night before a game was that players could do whatever best suited their individual preparations. The only proviso was that it could not be construed by their team-mates as being counterproductive to performing at their best. We always tried to treat our players like men and the commonsense rule of asking yourself whether the team would be better or worse if everyone did what you were doing usually gave the right answer.

My normal Friday night in Melbourne was to visit my daughter Fiona and three-year-old granddaughter Amber at their East Brighton townhouse. So, as a stickler for routine and loving my time with them anyway, that was where I spent the evening before the game.

I woke Saturday morning to a bright sunny day that was forecast to be in the high 20s. That was good news: a last-man-standing war of attrition was going to suit us fine. The footy gods were still smiling on us.

We all did our own thing to fill in the morning. Craig Lambert, Gubby Allan and I went for a walk around the Tan Track at the Botanical Gardens and stopped off at the café next to the Botanical Hotel in South Yarra for a cappuccino caffeine hit. Some players went for a stroll. When we played in Melbourne, Luke Power, Shaun Hart and a few other Lions players were regulars with footy in hand, heading to the cricket ground over the road from the Parkview for a loosen-up jog.

As the time to depart for the MCG slowly approached, my tension levels started to build. Whatever control I had over our week's preparation would end shortly. As I sat in my hotel room waiting for the time to go down to the bus, how I wanted to check in with some kind of supreme coaching god. Had I said too much? Was there more or better instruction to be given? What should I say at our pre-game gathering?

These match-day doubts and uncertainties are the normal coach's lament, but as I sat in my room at the Parkview for the first time before a grand final, the extreme and completely contrasting emotions that were waiting in a few hours' time at the conclusion of the match were a fearsome prospect.

For some comfort I ran my competitive mantra through my mind: accept the challenge without reservation or doubt; risk the depression of losing so you may experience the exhilaration of victory. It didn't help. My gut was churning and I wanted it to be five o'clock and the result decided. The nervous anticipation, and the control that ceased when the game was handed to the players, was an unpleasant experience that I never overcame in the 20 seasons I coached. The awful feeling that hit me late that 2001 grand final morning at the Parkview became a ritual for the next four years.

When the grand-final sequence ended, so did this anguish. Yet I remember 2005 grand final day when, for the first time since 2000,

I was only an uninvolved spectator. I recall looking at my watch about 11.30 am and wishing I was at the Parkview with my guts churning, waiting to go to the MCG to put my emotions on the line. Funny how what you hate about something is what you love about it as well. It might be nerve-racking heading into a grand final as a coach, but I have never felt more alive than at those times.

I headed down to the bus, hoping my naturally cold exterior wouldn't betray my internal turmoil. A coach who looks like a nervous wreck is the last thing your players need. At noon the Lions team bus, with our usual Melbourne driver Billie Elms at the wheel, pulled away from our team hotel. A police escort accompanied it on an extra-quick trip to the stadium. One policeman on a motorcycle rode ahead of the bus, with one behind as well, as we travelled down the tram lines of inner-city Melbourne up St Kilda Road towards Flinders Street Station, then right into Flinders Street and on to the MCG. Police escort is the way to travel; a 20-minute trip was done in five. So much for keeping things normal!

I sat in the front seat behind the driver and was first out of the bus and straight into our dressing rooms, which were the old Melbourne rooms in the Northern Stand. Apart from the support staff in their maroon, blue and gold polo tops, the rooms remained undecorated with Lions colours – as I'd done when coaching Collingwood back in the 1990 grand final. Our task of making a very abnormal day seem like a normal football match wouldn't be hampered by our rooms looking any different to a standard home-and-away game.

The grand final day pre-game warm-up schedule is different because of the pre-match entertainment. The players had an early walk on the ground, which helped settle their nerves, before we convened the final 10-minute planning reinforcement meeting. This would be the last time before the quarter-time break that I'd address the players as a group. As usual at Brisbane there would be no pre-game pep talk – that particular tradition was left behind when I finished at Collingwood. Again, as usual, we started the meeting with the same five-minute video we had shown the previous evening. Then it was a short reminder about our match plans and objectives.

My key messages had been delivered and reinforced before match day, but they were repeated on the whiteboard in the coach's room:

- Controlled aggression of mind and body
- Pound in at the ball – in lower and harder
- Attack the hips when second to the ball – dump them
- Forward under pressure / Use free team-mate if time and space allows
- Attack the goal front – space
- Play your role – know/accept/perform
- Disciplined and thoughtful starting points at stoppages
- Total involvement football

From this point, my main aim was not to be a stress-carrier, so I headed down the race while the Lions players completed their preparations. Then the time came. As our team gathered waiting for the call to enter the arena, my few last words were simply about the pride of the journey we had shared and my confidence that they were as ready as they could possibly be. Emphasise the simple basics: attack the footy low and hard, kick long early, and chase, tackle and pressure.

As I've mentioned, Martin Pike aside, this was a first-time experience for them all. How our players would handle having the spotlight of the whole football world upon them was the imminent challenge as Michael Voss led his team-mates down into the great coliseum. This is where they'd be hit by the great wall of noise that characterises the grand final occasion for the on-field performers.

The rest of us headed for our seats in the stands. Even as coach I now felt little more than a glorified spectator. My usual final comment to the players after the match-day reinforcement meeting was that the game was now theirs. That's the stark reality when the ball is bounced to start the match. My emotions and those of anyone else with a Lions interest were in our players' hands.

My attempts at minimising the players' stress in the build-up had no positive effect early as we nervously wasted scoring opportunities with a 3.7 opening term. We led by five points at quarter-time, but 32 minutes into the second term we trailed by 20. In the last decisive play before the long break, Simon Black turned inside on his non-preferred right foot and delivered the ball perfectly to a leading Alastair Lynch. From about 40 metres out our veteran full-forward held his nerve and kicked his second goal. This cut the margin to 14 points. We were close enough if we were good enough.

As was forecast, Melbourne had turned on a hot day for the grand final and our medical and conditioning crew were ready. Without the IV drips that had been employed for much of the season, they left nothing to chance. Unable to gain vehicular access for a cold room they might otherwise have hired, they converted an existing sauna in our dressing rooms into a cold room. There the players spent much of the half-time break to lower their core body temperature and prepare for the second-half onslaught.

The valuable belief that we'd be able to finish stronger than the Bombers was a key half-time reinforcement. We'd altered our backline during the second quarter by shifting Mal Michael to full-back onto Matthew Lloyd, which allowed Justin Leppitsch to move up-field to centre half-back on Scott Lucas. Away from his deep in defence role, we were hoping Leppa could assist our defensive run. Chris Scott moved across to the back flank and we got Tim Notting onto the field off interchange into his customary wing role. It's hard to believe but the interchange was used quite rarely back in 2001 – only about 20 per game per team. We'd picked the starting line-up with the hope that a fresh Tim Notting could be introduced to the game when others were beginning to tire, and that with a freshness advantage he could have a big impact.

As the game started to open up in the second half, our fitness and running power, which was a real strength of the team, came to the fore. From the 32-minute mark of the second quarter until the 23-minute mark of the fourth quarter, we kicked 11.8 to Essendon's 2.4. We led by 16 points at the final change, although Essendon pulled to within 10 points eight minutes into the final quarter, before Tim Notting, his fresh legs crucial, goaled on the run. Then, 16 minutes into the final stanza, Beau McDonald took the ball from a boundary throw-in, twisted past two opponents and gave a deft handpass to Michael Voss. Vossy ran to the boundary line inside 50 metres and somehow squeezed a floating, inside-out torpedo between the big sticks. We were up by 26 points.

Vossy's reaction was a great example of perfect concentration in action. After kicking the goal he allowed himself to celebrate the moment and delivered a one-fingered salute to the cheering crowd before quickly switching back on, his facial expression turning in an instant from joy to cold determination as he charged back for the next centre bounce. This was a small example of why Vossy was such a wonderful competitor and captain. His team-mates followed his lead, and the important ability to know when concentration can be switched off and when it needs to be fully turned on became a great strength of the Lions team of the early 2000s.

The floodgates were opening as we forged 38 points clear getting towards time-on. Everyone in the stadium thought the game and the premiership was ours, and I drifted towards that thinking myself, but then from the next two centre bounces Essendon kicked a couple of quick goals. *Damn.* In my head space where the result is in the balance until the possibility of defeat no longer exists, the game was still alive.

But a few minutes later, without another score for the day, and with the footy in the hands of Alastair Lynch, the siren sounded, and I got that delicious exhilaration of victory that comes from accepting the challenge and winning. Today it was the other team who would feel the flipside, the depression of losing. When I went to Brisbane as coach in the lead-up to the 1999 season, my main hope was that we could be competitive, but a fantastic group of players supported by a terrific off-field team had achieved a significant milestone. For the first time a premiership flag was heading to the AFL frontier in the north.

We'd won our 16th game in a row – equal sixth on an all-time list of winning streaks headed by Geelong's 23-game effort in 1952–53. It was a run which had started and ended with 2000 premiers Essendon, and included 10 wins at the Gabba.

We couldn't have been happier when Shaun Hart won the Norm Smith Medal as best afield. In all my time in football, I don't think I have ever met a more selfless person. One by one, the players were presented with their premiership medallions, then I received the Jock McHale coach's medal, before Michael Voss and I were presented with the premiership cup.

Raising the cup to the crowd is such a great moment; however, as the players mobbed the stage I withdrew to join the off-field group. As much as we share the joy, it's the players who have done it. To succeed they need to commit mind, body and soul to the contest and it's only the on-field performers who rightly get to carry the cup over to the delirious supporters on the other side of the fence.

As a coach, I always felt envious of the players in these moments. I knew what they were feeling because I'd been fortunate to be in their shoes a few times. That hour or so spent on the ground after a grand final win is such a very special time for a player. After the club theme song is played over and over during the victory lap, it has become traditional to end the day with the song by Queen, 'We Are the Champions'. I've got a terrible voice but when that song comes on I feel like singing along, because it exactly explains how you feel as part of the champion team.

After the players completed a slow walking lap of the ground, sharing the moment with family, friends and the thousands of supporters, they headed into the packed dressing-rooms, which were excitedly chaotic. Before the moment had gone I wanted to briefly wind up the match part of the day and, at Martin Pike's instigation, we shared a special moment whereby each player and coach was asked to share what he loved about the person next to him. Having been a member of North Melbourne's 1999 premiership team, Pikey said this was a time to savour with your team-mates and coaches, and that we shouldn't cut it short before eventually joining the throng outside the inner sanctum of the coach's room.

After an hour or two in the dressing-rooms and then a team stroll to the centre of the MCG for a photo with the premiership cup, it was off to the Melbourne Tennis Centre, where 10,000 people were waiting patiently for the team's arrival. From there, we went on to Crown Casino, where 1600 people attended the official premiership dinner. On the way to the airport on the Sunday morning for the flight back to Brisbane, we stopped in at the old Brunswick Street

Oval, spiritual home of Fitzroy. There, about 8000 fans enjoyed the first Lions flag for nearly 60 years.

When we arrived back in Brisbane around mid-afternoon, a similar crowd awaited the team at the Gabba. With the Lions having a supporter base in both Melbourne and Brisbane, it was so different from my previous premiership experience at Hawthorn and Collingwood. The unexpected bonus of being in a one-team town was accentuated on the Tuesday after the grand final, when I enjoyed one of my very special football experiences as an estimated 10,000 people packed the inner-city streets of Brisbane for a giant tickertape parade.

But as the season ended so well on the field, a major problem became apparent off it. At the meeting of the club's board in late October it was announced that, despite the premiership win, the club would post a financial loss of $845,000. As this came as a surprise to the directors, long-serving CEO Andrew Ireland decided to fall on his sword and resigned effective immediately.

Andrew knew his footy, was a terrific administrator in his time at the Lions and was a great support to me in my coaching role. His departure was to have costly ramifications for the club's relationship with the AFL. The AFL world has always had an element of a private boys' club, where admission as a fully-fledged member requires a long and respectful waiting period. Having a chief executive with these networking connections is an enormous advantage, particularly for a team based outside the southern states heartland.

Andrew was well connected to the Melbourne head office; his replacement, Brisbane lawyer Michael Bowers, was not. He was completely new to AFL football. Michael had a fair bit of dominant Enforcer in him and while the Lions thrived with him as their CEO, the supportive relationship the club enjoyed with headquarters was gradually eroded. He seemed to get AFL chief executive Andrew Demetriou offside, which could never be a good thing. A series of conflicts between the Lions and 'City Hall' over the next few years would create a rising level of angst that would become very apparent a couple of seasons down the track in late 2004.

During Michael's management term, the Lions had a few years at the top of the tree on the field and with this on-field success a very strong financial base was built. By the late 2000s the Lions' $800,000 loss in 2001 had been turned into having nearly 10 million dollars in the bank.

The financial loss, despite winning the premiership, was an issue the board had to confront. They made a calculated decision to work to generate greater revenue rather than cut costs in the football department. If the club had accepted AFL financial assistance it would have come with a few strings attached. This calculated gamble to go it alone didn't endear the club to the AFL at the time, but it helped our future prospects because it avoided the cost-cutting that would have been quid pro quo for their support.

When I met with the board post-season to be advised of this position, it was an opportune time to discuss with them whether every resource would be put into the short term and winning another premiership. Chairman Graeme Downie had the view that consistently finishing no lower than mid-ladder was critical for the club's financial viability. However, it was agreed around the table that, while our premiership window was open, such longer-term thinking would be put on hold to give us the best chance of going back to back.

This strategy that the whole club adopted had repercussions such as doing everything we could to keep all our players. Fortunately, this post-season conversation and agreement with the board was repeated for the next three years. In a practical sense, this period of sustained success made it very difficult to balance the salary cap. Thinking short term was the catalyst for heavily back-ending player payments to keep the team intact and under the salary cap. This concept entailed a player getting, say, $900,000 over a three-year contract, accepting maybe $200,000 in the first year and $350,000 in the final two years. Recontract them now and worry about next year when it came. Gubby was our salary cap manager who negotiated all the player contracts, and the always practical Gub would often say that back-ending contracts only became a problem if the club went out of business.

Around the football department, as one successful season ended in September another would begin a few days later. The only difference was that we were reigning premiers with the chance to achieve the elusive back-to-back flags.

Gubby set the challenge for our coaching/management partnership by pointing out our failure to prevent the Collingwood premiership hangover after 1990. Hopefully, that experience would help us better manage the Lions' new campaign. One challenge ends and another begins. As they say, 'Success is a journey, not a destination.'

39

2002: A GAME OF SECONDS AND INCHES

In the wet slippery conditions, the game was going to come down
to a bit of random chance or some individual brilliance.

After winning the last 16 games straight to win the flag in 2001, the premiership hangover in 2002 never eventuated. There was very little change in personnel, either on or off the field, and the philosophy of living in the moment and continually searching for improvement in everything we did was the attitude that drove the whole football department.

Importantly, the team culture was never to think like defending premiers. From the beginning of the pre-season, our task was to start again from scratch with the full knowledge and belief that winning the previous year would have no effect – either good or bad – on the season to come. The problem of fitting all our premiership players into the salary cap would be a growing issue, but the consistency of attitude and application driven by our core players became a great strength of the group. There was always a healthy fear of failure.

Apart from Alastair Lynch, who was defying the ageing process by being an outstanding forward target despite approaching his mid-30s, the core of the team were in the prime of their careers. With the premiership win came not complacency but confidence in the team's capabilities, without any feeling of expectations or assumptions. Of the three premiership years, the middle one in 2002 was when the team was at its peak.

After winning the opening four games, our unbeaten streak had extended to 20. When the very best any player does over a long career is win two out of three, it had been an amazing run. Even a close game was rare, with 18 points being the closest margin in that fantastic sequence. It ended in round five against the Eagles in Perth, when the home side overran us with an 11 goal to five second half. The team was mortal again and I sensed that, late in the final quarter, our players gave up a little, as if they felt they had to lose eventually so let's get it over and done with. The routine was to get back to business, learn the lessons and prepare for Geelong at the Gabba the following week.

Coming off a loss was an unusual experience but the rebound was good with a big win over the Cats. The season flowed smoothly thereafter with only three close losses, and we got to the final round in first position on the ladder, but with the tough assignment of playing Port Adelaide in Adelaide for the vital top spot going into the finals.

If two Melbourne clubs finish one and two on the ladder, there's no advantage for the top team; however, back then for non-Melbourne clubs the advantage was gigantic. While the national competition became official when the name was changed from the Victorian Football League to the Australian Football League in 1990, over a decade later it was still administered as a Victorian competition with a few teams from outside Melbourne.

That philosophy from the Melbourne-based head office was emphasised by the agreement with the Melbourne Cricket Ground that regardless of who earned the right to a home preliminary final, at least one had to be played at the MCG. The thought that two non-Melbourne clubs might earn the right in the same year was ignored. In 2002 three non-Melbourne clubs – Port Adelaide, Brisbane and Adelaide – finished in the top three positions, so the warning was spelled out quite clearly.

I've heard it said that leadership is fixing a problem before it becomes a disaster. In 2002 and 2003, the AFL decision-makers were able to dodge the bullet of two clubs from outside Victoria earning the right to host a preliminary final. It should have been no surprise when their failure to act in the early 2000s embarrassingly hit the integrity of the competition straight between the eyes in 2004. Unfortunately the Brisbane Lions would get the pain from the wound. Whether the failure to act when the warning bells started ringing was incompetent or deliberate, only a few people very high up in the corridors of power at AFL House know for sure.

For some strange reason I had the misguided belief in 2002 that if both Port and the Lions won our qualifying finals, the AFL would find a way to give us both the home preliminary final we'd earned. Maybe the higher prioritising of integrity and fairness that was the catchcry after the Australian Crime Commission report of early 2013 was not so important a decade before.

This unresolved issue and being able to control our destiny made the prize from this final game of 2002 absolutely critical for both teams. In a titanic struggle the Power beat us by six points to take top spot and relegate us to second position. They now had the box seat. However, regardless of that loaded gun around potential home preliminary final venues, I went down to the dressing-rooms needing to be positive. My attitude to our players and at the post-match press conference was that the result didn't matter that much, because whether first or second the task ahead was the same. They were my words; I knew the reality was quite different.

The first qualifying final between Port and fourth-placed Colling-wood was in Adelaide on the Friday night. With 18 wins, Port had finished five games in front of the Magpies. The home team was the heavy favourite but they were playing for the same valuable prize, a home preliminary final. The game wasn't on television in Brisbane so my only way to keep tabs on the scores was on the National Indi-genous Radio Service coverage.

Collingwood were a goal or two in front for most of the match but I thought Port would pick them up eventually. When the minutes ticked by and the Magpies were holding on to a slender lead I started to really get interested. As they reached the 30-minute mark of the final term, Collingwood got a goal – from Leon Davis, I think – to go 13 points up. They looked home, and when the siren went without further score I let out a loud whoop that caused my wife, Deb, to run into the lounge room thinking something had gone wrong. On the contrary, the result of this game a few thousand kilometres away in Adelaide was a huge boost for us. As far as a home preliminary final was concerned, our destiny was back in our own hands.

The hurdle was the Adelaide Crows at the Gabba the following night. I never mentioned the home preliminary final carrot – it was all about the methods we'd use to beat the Crows. I'm sure our players were fully aware of Port's defeat and, maybe buoyed with that unexpected bonus, they blitzed Adelaide from start to finish.

Players have their bunnies and during this period the Crows were Alastair Lynch's. He would often get Nathan Bassett as his full-back opponent and he'd throw him around like a rag doll. Our 34-year-old veteran spearhead totally dominated with 12 marks and seven goals to set up our big win. His younger Lions team-mate, 21-year-old Des Headland, was nearly as good as he racked up 33 disposals and three goals.

Des was a player approaching his peak years but he'd go back to Perth at the end of the season. His partner, Chantelle, was about to give birth to their second child and she returned to Western Australia with their young daughter, Madison, so Des wanting to go home to reunite his family was understandable. However, the move to Perth and the influence of his childhood mates was a disaster, as far as trying to get the most out of his great talents. Des never played a better game of football than he did against Adelaide in the qualifying final of 2002.

Port Adelaide beat Essendon in one semi-final to stay in contention. But the harsh cost to Port of losing to Collingwood in the first week of the play-offs was that, rather than a home preliminary final, they had to travel to Brisbane for a Saturday night game against us. The home state venue was a massive boost for our chances.

I watched the television coverage with a detached sort of interest as Collingwood defeated the Crows during the afternoon match. The Magpies were into the grand final, but unless we could beat Port it would have no relevance to us, so reversing our loss to the Power in round 22 was the only thing occupying my thoughts.

Our preliminary final against Port was no walkover, but after getting clear in the second quarter it became a comfortable nine-goal win. We were in the grand final for the second consecutive season, with the chance to go back to back. The whole club had a practised preparation routine to follow, and when Simon Black won the Brownlow, as Aker had the year before, even the omens were good.

We had our best team available – all fit and well – so we couldn't have got to this point of the season better placed. The footy gods, combined with the fantastic efforts of our players and staff, had got us into an ideal position. Everything had gone so well until I looked at the body language of the Collingwood players at the grand final parade. Mick Malthouse displayed his usual air of readiness for any challenge that might come his way and his composure had rubbed off on his players. They looked relaxed and in control, when I wanted them to be tense and uptight. And their captain, Nathan Buckley, looked scarily focused. With terrible – almost end-of-the-earth – conditions forecast for the big day, they looked ready for the bun-fight the game was likely to become.

The forecast was accurate and when I awoke on grand final morning my first eager look out the window of my room on the sixth floor of the Parkview Hotel revealed a cold wet windy Melbourne day. Not that our team were duffers in the wet at all, but the miserable conditions were going to even things up. The wet wasn't the problem; it was the freezing conditions that were my greatest concern. The boys from the sunny state would be shoved right out of their comfort zone. The likely slog would suit the Magpies – I reckon that while I was concerned about the wet weather Mick would have been rapt.

We were raging hot favourites, which is always a concern. Players can be influenced by external views and therefore complacency can creep in. My forebodings were accurate when, after a goalless first quarter, in which fortunately Collingwood only kicked one, we totally butchered our second-quarter dominance with a wasteful 4.8, to lead 4.12 to 4.4 – only an eight-point margin despite having eight more scoring shots.

Then, when Collingwood surged clear during the third quarter, we were in real trouble. We'd lost our second ruckman, Beau McDonald, with a dislocated shoulder early in the game, which meant we had to use Daryl White as the relief back-up to Clark Keating.

Whenever the Magpies threw Anthony Rocca into the ruck I got particularly nervous. He was too mobile for our ruckman when he pushed into the Magpies forward line after the centre bounces, so our plan was to play Mal Michael as a spare defender to take Rocca when he drifted forward.

I had allowed Fox Footy to put a recorder into the coach's box to tape my comments, with me having the right post-game to veto anything I didn't want to go to air. They titled it 'The Lips of Lethal'. My outburst when Rocca took a mark 40 metres out with Mal nowhere in sight was definitely deleted. Making plans and players not sticking to them is a coaching frustration at the best of times. Mal losing concentration and conceding an uncontested mark and a resultant goal in a low-scoring grand final caused this angry coach to briefly blow his top and question the intelligence of our full-back. It was a spur-of-the-moment comment which I thought was best left in the sanctity of the coach's box.

The last couple of minutes of the third quarter were critical. A long set-shot goal from the boundary line in front of the Southern Stand by Jonathan Brown showed terrific composure under pressure. Some players would shrink from the responsibility; Browny loved the pressure and wanted to take the shot. Then, in almost the last play of the quarter as the sun finally broke through the heavy clouds, Jason Akermanis won the footy under pressure and fed a handball to Michael Voss, who slotted an inspirational long goal from outside the 50-metre line to give us a four-point lead at the final break. It was no coincidence that Browny and Vossy got, and used, half-chances to kick critical goals. They're a couple of a rare breed who simply will themselves into the action.

The weather closed in again and in a torrid last quarter only three goals were kicked. In a game in which a total of only 19 goals were scored, it's the scoring opportunities taken or missed that stick in my memory the most.

From our coach's box in the Southern Stand, we were positioned maybe 50 metres behind Rocca as he lined up his infamous last-quarter set-shot, the goals probably 100 metres from our position. The VIP area, where Collingwood president Eddie McGuire was seated, was a level above the coach's box, looking at the same angle from the same distance. In flight it looked disturbingly on line, and although the footy was well above goalpost height, from my view it appeared to have squeezed inside the goals. When the goal umpire signalled a behind it was a fantastic result that came as a very pleasant surprise, after my initial thought that we'd conceded a vital goal.

Our kick-in specialist Chris Johnson had already grabbed the footy. Johnno later told me that he was also under the line of the goal-post next to the goal umpire and knew immediately that it went over the post and would be a behind. Premierships are won by seconds and inches; this was one that went our way.

Collingwood got their only goal of the quarter to hit the lead, and with the rain pelting down scoring was becoming impossible. In the coach's box there was a feeling of helplessness. In the wet slippery conditions, the game was going to come down to a bit of random chance or some individual brilliance. The two goals that won us the match came from our basic game plan when under pressure of bombing the ball to the top of the goal square, where Alastair Lynch would make the contest 10 to 15 metres out in front of our goal. In one of these plays his opponent, Shane Wakelin, turned away from the footy to grapple with Lynchy and the umpire awarded our full forward a contentious free-kick. He goaled from point-blank range to put us a couple of points in front.

The sealer came from Jason Akermanis a few minutes later. Because of the close checking of Paul Licuria and a sore groin that was limiting him to kicking only with his left foot, Aker had been used exclusively as a small crumbing forward in the second half. He was tending to run to the back of the pack rather than staying to the front, as our assistant coach Gary O'Donnell accurately observed. With Gary's prompting, the message was sent out with our runner Craig Starcevich to tell Aker to crumb in the front of the pack.

Under pressure on the forward flank in front of the MCC Members' side of the ground, Brad Scott grabbed a hot possession and did as he was drilled: a long kick to the front of the goal square, where Lynchy made his usual strong attack on the football. The wet ball was impossible to mark in a contest but it was forced to the front of the pack where Aker, one of the game's best finishers, pounced on the footy. He had a moment to balance, turned onto his trusty left foot and kicked a beautiful goal over his right shoulder to put us nine points in front.

Countdown clocks in the coach's box were introduced the following season. As it turned out, there were still about five minutes to go. My most vivid memory of the epic scoreless last few minutes was a Michael

Voss special that epitomised his enormous will and competitiveness. On the wing in front of the Southern Stand, there was a one-on-one marking contest between Vossy and another tough nut, Collingwood's Scott Burns. The footy lobbed on their heads from a wild kick out of our forward line and the Magpies' runners surged out after it. The numbers streaming to the contest were all in black and white, and if they won the footy our defence was hopelessly exposed. From our coach's box I can tell you my heart sank, but Vossy held his ground and took the goal-saving contested mark. I could have kissed him.

The crowd noise was deafening as we hung on to the nine-point lead and I never heard the siren. For me, that magnificent moment of exhilaration that accompanies victory came with the play on the Members' wing on the opposite side of the ground from our coach's box. Like a giant Mexican wave, the crowd on that side of the field suddenly rose as one as they heard the siren sound. We'd achieved back-to-back premierships, a feat that had eluded many great teams over the years.

While, as always, the post-game hours at the ground were fantastic, as the evening progressed I found myself becoming increasingly grumpy. The Lions function that night was held in the middle of the Docklands oval with the same set-up as there had been for the Brownlow a few days earlier. The atmosphere was cold and lifeless and at about 11 o'clock I said to Deb, 'Let's go back to the hotel.'

I couldn't get into the celebration spirit at all, but the venue wasn't the real issue. The following morning I realised I'd fallen into the terrible trap of expecting and assuming. While this was completely foreign to my competitive philosophy, I'd allowed myself to assume deep down that we'd win comfortably. Because the grand final went down to the wire with a heap of nervous anxiety suffered along the way, it hadn't met those expectations and I'd stupidly drifted into being miserable after winning a grand final.

The night after winning a premiership is so rare and should be so special. I wasted this opportunity after the 2002 victory. My mental note to myself was to make sure it would never happen again. At least my personal motivation to be in this position the following year was stronger than ever.

40

2003: DEFYING THE FOOTBALL GODS

*What they did under extraordinary duress over the last five
quarters of the 2003 season was remarkable.*

It was Tuesday morning of the 2003 AFL grand final week when I saw Nigel Lappin get out of a car in the carpark outside the Lions' Gabba headquarters. He was like a 90-year-old cripple. Even taking one slow, small step at a time, he could barely walk. Nursing a broken rib, he was in so much pain that the thought of him playing football five days later seemed totally implausible. Yet in one of the most amazing displays of courage, Nigel not only took his place in the side but was a valuable contributor to a Lions team that completed a magnificent premiership hat-trick.

The quiet, understated member of the Lions midfield group known as the 'Fab Four', Nigel had been injured in the closing stages of the preliminary final win over the Sydney Swans at ANZ Stadium the previous Saturday night. He was a victim of friendly fire, taken out by an accidental knee from fellow Lion Shaun Hart as he backed into a marking contest. Nigel was as sore as anyone I've ever seen, yet over the next seven days – and even longer – we saw a remarkable show of courage and character that headlined a team performance of similar quality.

Playing interstate for the fourth time in five weeks, the Lions defied the footy gods to beat Collingwood in the grand final by 50 points and in VFL/AFL history emulate the feat of the great Melbourne sides of 1955, 1956 and 1957. Only the 1927–30 Collingwood premiership teams had enjoyed a longer reign. And that was more than 70 years earlier.

It had been a challenging year. As late as round 20, two weeks out from the finals, we were sixth on the ladder. After eight wins and a draw in our first 10 matches, we'd gone 2–5 and then 4–6 to sit three games behind runaway leaders Port Adelaide and half a game behind Adelaide, Collingwood, Sydney and Fremantle.

Wins over Geelong at home and the Western Bulldogs away saw us finish third behind Port and Collingwood, but it was to be a much more challenging finals campaign than the relatively smooth and incident-free finals month of 2001 and 2002.

The Lions 'three-peat' campaign looked decidedly sick after the first quarter of the qualifying final against Collingwood at the MCG when Michael Voss jarred his knee. The skipper had undergone mid-season surgery for the second year in a row and had carried a bad knee for the last 10 weeks of the home-and-away season. This incident made a chronic problem unmanageable. He spent the final quarter on the bench as we lost a low-scoring game by 15 points, and as we walked out of the MCG that night I was convinced the 2003 All-Australian captain was done for the year. Another grand final seemed a long way off.

Privately the medical staff feared Vossy was cooked too, but Gubby wasn't about to give up. Dr David Young, one of the premier orthopaedic surgeons in the AFL, might just be the answer, he thought. So, knowing that our assistant coach Craig Lambert had a long and close relationship with Dr Young, Gubby asked Lambie to call the surgeon late on the Saturday night as we licked our wounds back at the team hotel. In consultation with Lions surgeon Dr Jim Fardoulys, they devised a course of action that would at least give Vossy a chance.

On the Sunday morning, when the rest of the team returned to Brisbane, our captain stayed in Melbourne for an MRI scan. On the Monday he visited Dr Fardoulys with the scans. The good news was that there was no further structural damage and no long-term risk. The pain was a problem but they reasoned that if they could deaden the knee maybe the discomfort would go. The doctor injected some local anaesthetic into Vossy's knee so he could have a light run Monday afternoon. With the pain deadened he could run freely, and after repeating the procedure he was able to train once during the week and appeared ready to play. This process would be repeated right through September.

Already we were in unfamiliar territory. Having enjoyed a 'straight sets' September journey in 2001–02 and enjoying a weekend off before a home preliminary final both years, we found ourselves playing in week two of the finals for the first time. But it proved an important turning point. Coming off our lowest score of the season in the qualifying final against Collingwood, we regained lost form against Adelaide in a Gabba elimination final on the Friday night.

The Voss issue was a big worry. We were unhealthily dependent on our captain for his on-field leadership and organisation around the midfield stoppages, and now, as much as the signs were positive, we weren't even certain he'd last the match – let alone be a significant contributor.

So I made a decision to start Vossy on the bench in the knock-out final against Adelaide. It was a symbolic gesture to the team that they had to regard him as the cream on the cake. They had to be prepared to do it without him. As the ball was bounced, Vossy sat riding an exercise bike adjacent to the interchange area just to keep his knee warm.

Things fell into place perfectly. Alastair Lynch kicked six goals and Nigel Lappin was superb through the midfield as we booted 7.4 to 2.3 in an emphatic final quarter to win by 42 points. Vossy's solid effort was a bonus. More important was a general lift in our overall form. We were starting to look as if maybe we could be a contender.

For the second consecutive season Port Adelaide had finished on top, but had again squandered the right to get a home preliminary final when, this time, the Power dropped its home qualifying final to the Sydney Swans. On the footy politics front, the AFL had dodged another bullet. If we'd managed to beat Collingwood in the first qualifying final there would have been no Melbourne team eligible to host a preliminary final. The issue of one preliminary final being automatically at the MCG was a quickly brewing problem, but it would only be solved after a potential disaster became a reality.

After beating the Crows it was off to Sydney to play the Swans at the Homebush stadium in our first final outside Brisbane or

Melbourne. It was our first-ever game at the venue that had hosted the Sydney Olympics three years earlier.

We were able to get accommodation at the Crown Plaza in Parramatta only a short distance from the ground, which was better than staying in the Sydney CBD and then taking the long bus trip out to Homebush. The Saturday afternoon preliminary final at the MCG was again casual viewing as we prepared for the Swans, but my interest did spark up when Anthony Rocca got reported. If the dangerous Collingwood power forward was suspended, it would be a huge blow for the Magpies, who went on to eliminate Port Adelaide and reach their second consecutive grand final. As with the previous two seasons, until we won our preliminary final the team that had already qualified was totally irrelevant to us.

The crowd was huge, with over 70,000 people turning up to create a great atmosphere, but an extremely hostile environment for the visiting team and great emotional nourishment for the Swans. After a good first half we led by 15 points at the long break, but as the third quarter progressed we started to fade. We still led by three points at thee-quarter time but Sydney had kicked the last four goals and were powering home. The Swans had come off a week's break, which at the end of a long season is enormously valuable, and we were looking tired and emotionally spent.

I suspect every Lions supporter in Australia thought the losing die was cast. Fortunately, our players didn't share that pessimistic view. As I finished my address and headed to the coach's box I looked back at the huddle and saw that Michael Voss was urging his team-mates to keep the faith. This group of players had a collective drive and will to win that often pleasantly surprised even me. What they did under extraordinary duress over the last five quarters of the 2003 season was remarkable.

As our players headed to their positions, something special was needed and that's exactly what they produced. Martin Pike seemed to be the ringleader but the whole team joined the party. From looking gone at the end of the third quarter, they jumped into the final term from the opening bounce with an energy and run that came seemingly from nowhere. We grabbed the game back with an outstanding

30 minutes as we totally dominated the Swans with a 6.6 to 0.1 final quarter to get home by 44 points and qualify for our third consecutive grand final.

But an incident late in the game tempered my enjoyment of the post-game atmosphere. Amid the excited players in the rooms was one very sore Nigel Lappin, who'd received an accidental knee in the ribs from Shaun Hart. X-rays later confirmed a broken rib, plus severe bruising and soft tissue damage. My old Hawthorn team-mate Robert DiPierdomenico had bravely played on with a punctured lung in the 1989 grand final after a heavy early clash, but this was different. Nigel had the injury before the match would get under way.

We'd all but given up hope that he could play in the decider. When we went to the Parramatta pool for a recovery session the following Sunday morning before flying back to Brisbane, we told Nige to stay in the bus. I kept him company for a while and I'm sure no player in history has ever been in more pain six days before playing in a grand final. As the injury occurred very late in the game and hadn't been reported in the media, we decided to keep it to ourselves. On the off chance Nige got onto the field, we were keen that Collingwood didn't know the extent of his injuries.

Any chance of keeping the extent of the injury under wraps was blown out of the water when Jason Akermanis revealed the news of Nigel's broken rib in one of his regular media gigs. Yes, as hard as it is to believe, this was someone who happened to be one of Nige's team-mates. When Aker exposed the true extent of the injury in the press, I was flabbergasted and very, very angry. I couldn't believe a player could betray the best interests of his team or a team-mate, as Aker had done. As they say, with friends like that who needs enemies? After the season ended, Aker said that everyone knew about Nigel's injury anyway, so he thought he might as well provide the scoop.

Grand final week is the time for unity, not conflict, so I decided not to broach the issue either with Aker or the other players. I was seething but the team interest seemed to be best served by both privately and publicly leaving it alone. This approach was shared by our player leadership core. I admit to spending most of the week thinking that, if the match went badly, Aker would be playing his last game for the Lions. Either his team-mates would have killed him during what would have been a grumpy Mad Monday, or the club would have lost patience with him putting his own interests so blatantly before the team's and put him up for trade.

With Aker's help, Nigel's injury had become public knowledge but many other problems remained in-house. Vossy had his bad knee – that was fairly well known. Not so the fact that Alastair Lynch had a bad thigh, Jonathan Brown a cracked bone in his hand, and Clark Keating, Chris Johnson and Justin Leppitsch each had sore shoulders. Or that Martin Pike had an iffy hamstring and Darryl White bruised ribs, and that Craig McRae was struggling with a bad wrist. Lappin aside, we were confident all would play, but still there was a lingering concern about the team's general fitness and energy levels.

Unlike the previous two seasons, our 2003 build-up had encountered many hiccups. Without the benefit of a home preliminary final, the routine was very different and much more difficult. After needing to travel to Sydney to qualify for our third consecutive grand final, not returning to Brisbane until mid-afternoon Sunday, and then flying again on the Thursday to Melbourne, the scheduling was a significant challenge to overcome.

When you travel a lot, as all the non-Melbourne clubs have to do, you soon learn that travelling in consecutive weeks usually has a residual tiredness effect in the second game. The group appeared a bit wounded going into the premiership decider, and the supreme confidence in the team's fitness compared to the opposition wasn't there this year. It was going to be a battle to be mentally and physically ready.

One advantage was that after the loss to Collingwood in the first week of the finals we'd learnt a lot. We'd beaten them comfortably at the MCG back in round 19, while Anthony Rocca had been suspended and would miss the grand final. Only their captain, Nathan Buckley, would have been a bigger loss and we had some specific plans to minimise his impact. Being better prepared for them this time was a coaching theme we started to sell to the players immediately after they'd beaten the Swans.

On the Monday night, at the Lions' Brownlow function at the Gabba, Nigel Lappin had led the count after 12 rounds but he was nowhere to be seen. He was home in bed desperately trying to catch up on what had been virtually two sleepless nights. He wasn't going to win because he'd missed rounds 13 to 17 with a strained thigh and he would eventually finish 12th with 17 votes – five behind a three-way tie between Nathan Buckley, Adelaide's Mark Ricciuto and Sydney's Adam Goodes.

On the Tuesday our medical team called on the advice of noted Brisbane pain management specialist Dr Brendan Moore to determine if it was even remotely possible for Lappin to play. Under X-ray at the nearby Mater Hospital, he administered an experimental intercostal block. The idea was to see if we could deaden the pain sufficiently for him to play. This treatment worked well but Nigel, who suffered from a lot of allergies, had a few side-effects and had become quite disorientated.

At Wednesday's team training at the Gabba he was a spectator, doing some slow handball drills on the sideline with Craig Lambert. He could barely move. Whenever the ball hit the ground he kicked it to Lambie rather than bend over. But how he was on the Wednesday wasn't the issue, because we'd give him until Friday night to prove his fitness. We'd already decided there would be no match morning test for Nige. From my own experience I knew the pain from rib damage could improve enormously over the few days between weekends, but both for Nigel's mental state and for team stability we all needed to know his availability at the Friday planning meeting.

On the Thursday afternoon Nige joined the team flight to Melbourne and later that night he was named in a side in which Tim Notting was left out to make way for Marcus Ashcroft's return from injury. Richard Hadley, who had played just his second AFL game in the elimination final against Adelaide, retained his spot for what would be just his fourth game. Tim had suffered the same heartbreaking fate as Matthew Kennedy in 2011, when he made way for Alastair Lynch, and as Robbie Copeland had in 2002, when Chris Scott returned from injury.

Chris, who hadn't played since the qualifying final due to a chronic groin injury, was among the emergencies, with Notting and Aaron Shattock. As always, all 25 players in the travel party were told to prepare as if they were playing.

We had to assume that Nigel would take his place in the team and prepared accordingly. If he was right to go, he'd benefit from a protective guard, so on the Friday morning he and Lions medico Dr Andrew Smith visited the Orthotic & Prosthetic Centre in Port Melbourne. This was the company which had made a special comeback head-guard for Essendon captain James Hird after he'd suffered horrific head and facial injuries in 2002.

There they met Mark Randall, a clinical orthotist and prosthetist and a keen Essendon fan. A specialist in the design of protective devices, he'd heard media suggestions that Lappin might wear the same guard that Dermott Brereton wore to protect a broken rib in the 1989 grand final. Mark had contacted the club and discussed the possibility of designing a protective guard more specific to Nigel's particular rib problem. The hope was that it would maximise the impact protection and minimise the restriction of movement. It consisted of two centimetres of high-density foam, with a three millimetre hard thermo-plastic covering, a three millimetre soft neoprene cover, and a five millimetre rubber strap attached to some Velcro that would hold it in place. Moulded to the shape of Nigel's ribcage, the cost all-up was only $240.

On the Friday afternoon Nige again had the intercostal block applied before a light team training session at the oval opposite the Parkview Hotel. He did the skill drills without a problem, but we still had to prove to him and us that he could take heavy contact. Aaron Shattock was the crash test dummy and I told him specifically not to hold anything back. First, Nigel had to lay a couple of solid tackles on Shatts. Then it was his turn to be tackled. Then he took a couple of overhead marks while hit hard through the body. Miraculously, he was passing the test.

In cold overcast conditions with a rain storm imminent, the standard 3000 Lions fans looked on at the final training session – as they were now doing for the third consecutive season – with great interest and, I'm sure, admiration. Even more importantly the Lions players were observing the courage and willpower of their much admired team-mate. Nigel Lappin and Darren Millane, whom I coached when he carried a broken thumb through the 1990 finals for Collingwood, were almost polar opposites in personality. Darren was a confident extroverted dominant Enforcer and Nigel was an insecure introverted Thinker/Feeler. Despite these huge differences, they were both loved and respected by their team-mates, and history will record they share the distinction of very visibly breaking the pain barrier to provide enormous inspiration for a couple of premiership victories.

As the rain storm hit Albert Park we sprinted back over to the hotel, with Nigel having proved his fitness to take his place in the team. He had a long chat that evening with Lions mental skills coach Dr Phil Jauncey to help combat the mental demons inside his head, but seemed comfortable enough with what had transpired. We thought the test was over and passed, but we were wrong. What we didn't realise was that, sometime during the fitness test, Nigel had suffered a slightly punctured lung. Or at least that was the assumption from the medical staff after a visit to hospital on the morning after the grand final. The discomfort that troubled Nige on the Friday night and pre-game Saturday was more in keeping with a punctured lung than a broken rib. As of Friday night at our planning meeting, however, he was ready to play.

On standby if Nige was a last-minute withdrawal was Chris Scott. Ironically, they were best mates. They'd lived together in their early years in Brisbane and Chris had been groomsman when Nigel married his wife, Claire, the year before. As the planning meeting broke up, I sensed the disappointment in Scotty's body language. It was understandable. He was a former club champion and a key member of the 2001–02 premiership sides. Except for a bad run with chronic groin injuries which hindered his agility, he would have been an automatic selection.

I was concerned about the possible impact his visibly downcast mood could have on the rest of the group, so an hour or so later I visited Chris in his room. I was sympathetic to his feelings and could understand what he was going through, but I stressed the importance of not making it obvious around the rest of the team. I didn't need to be convinced one iota of the quality of Chris Scott as a person, but I've got to say that, if it was possible, my admiration for him increased even more afterwards because he carried himself impeccably from that moment on. Discipline is doing what you should do, rather than what you feel like doing at the time.

I was to find out later that Nigel had a terrible night's sleep. He dropped off alright but woke about midnight. He was still very sore and was having trouble breathing. He reluctantly called the doctor's room and, after a couple of sleeping tablets, grabbed a little more sleep, before waking again at 4 am. There would be no more sleep as he turned to the television for company. He had an early breakfast and rang his pregnant wife, Claire, who was staying with the other players' wives and girlfriends at the Holiday Inn in the city. As unselfish as any player I've known, he confided to Claire that he wasn't 100 per cent confident and was worried he'd let the team down.

Most of these overnight issues were news to me and the plan to get Nigel ready to play pushed on. Forty-five minutes ahead of our scheduled departure, he, Doc Smith and Dr Brendan Moore took a quick taxi ride to the hospital where, for the third time in six days, Dr Moore administered the intercostal block. We had a car on standby in case there was any delay, but they made it back to the hotel in time to catch the team bus.

The countdown entered its final stages. Nigel got through the on-ground warm-up without any difficulty as Chris Scott was stripped, strapped and even with his sore groins needled as if he would play. Back inside the rooms, Nige revealed that he was struggling to take a deep breath. I hoped it was just last-minute anxiety. Nigel had a massive call to make – the medical team had done all they could do, but in the end it had to be his decision.

Physiotherapist Peter Stanton, a close Lappin confidant, expressed the view that there was no way we should try to talk Nigel into it: purely for his mental state, Nige had to declare himself able to play. So a pregnant pause began with the clock ticking. I vividly remember thinking that here we were, 60 seconds from the deadline to lodge the final team-sheet for a game that could win us a premiership, and we still didn't know who was playing. This was crazy.

Team manager Barry Lowe waited anxiously on the side. He'd crossed out emergencies Shattock and Notting on the team-sheet but still we had 23 names. Nigel didn't exactly inspire confidence – the anguish of not being sure which way to go was killing him and he looked physically worn out. A couple of times I got close to saying, 'Bugger it – he's out.' Then finally, Nige said, 'I'm right.' Barry put a line through Chris Scott's name on the sheet and I walked out of the room. I didn't want to give him time to change his mind.

Off the field, insecurity and uncertainty could have been Nigel's middle names, but when he ran over the white line he became a desperate and driven competitor. It was his on-field strength of character that we were banking on to get him through. It was a risk I would have taken with very few players. The other reason for taking a bit of a punt was that the power of the mind on grand final day has enabled players to defy logic and great physical discomfort by willing themselves through.

Suddenly, all the indecision was forgotten. Nigel was just another player. Once he was cleared to play, there was never any thought that Nigel wouldn't start on the ground. It wasn't like the Voss situation of the first final. Sitting on the bench would have done his head in. He had to be in amongst it from the outset. My only concession was to switch the champion midfielder to half-back where he might be tackled a little less often. It was hardly a concession – he'd been named at half-back in the 2003 All-Australian side.

It was common policy at the time for Vossy and Nathan Buckley to go head-to-head whenever we met, but with Vossy's bad knee I was concerned Bucks could perhaps exploit his limited running power, especially if he pushed forward after the stoppages. So I decided to use Vossy in at the centre bounces but otherwise play him as a half-forward pushing up to the stoppages. After Robbie Copeland started at half-forward at the centre bounces, he then went to the Collingwood captain as a shut-down tagger.

It was a day of typically mixed Melbourne weather. A bright dawn had given way to a heavy and prolonged storm and we were to get intermittent showers, wind, a little hail, and even occasional sunshine. It was the hot of 2001 and the cold and wet of 2002 all rolled into one for our crack at an historic AFL hat-trick.

And it was a medical marvel that we got a side good enough to win on the paddock. I joked afterwards that we almost needed one bus for the medical staff and another for the players, but Dr Jim Fardoulys,

Dr Brendan Moore, Dr Andrew Smith and Dr Paul McConnell had done a wonderful job. Likewise, physiotherapists Victor Popov, Peter Stanton and all their associated helpers and consultants.

Ordinarily, the medics might have used two vials of Marcaine, a standard painkilling injection formula. Prior to this occasion, I think the most they'd ever used in one game was four. On grand final day 2003 they used 18. I suspect Lappin and Voss had most of that between them.

It would be the fourth meeting of the year for two sides who had become fierce rivals. We'd won by 14 points at the Gabba in round four after being comfortably clear, and by 39 points at the MCG in round 19, when we kicked eight goals in the first term. But the Pies, a more complete outfit than that which we'd beaten in the 2002 grand final, had got over the line by 15 points just three weeks earlier at the start of the finals. The bookmakers couldn't split a bruised and battered Brisbane and a Collingwood side which had enjoyed a much smoother preparation but for the suspension of Rocca.

On the bench for the start of what would be his last game was Marcus Ashcroft. It was a remarkable feat that he was even fit. The 32-year-old had suffered a four-week knee injury just two weeks earlier, but such was the durability of one of the game's most resilient players that he wasn't even considered one of our large group under an injury cloud. Alongside Ashcroft sat Blake Caracella, a 2000 premiership team member at Essendon, and grand final rookies Jamie Charman and Richard Hadley.

After a week that had brought so much uncertainty, the match was to go remarkably smoothly. Seconds after the start Jonathan Brown was felled with a heavy bump from Collingwood's Scott Burns, but he slowly got to his feet and waved the trainers away. He was badly shaken but it was going to take more than that to put the 21-year-old playing his third grand final out of business.

With Clark Keating dominating the hit-outs and Simon Black superb at ground level, after leading by 14 points at quarter-time we added 6.2 to 1.4 in the second quarter and were ahead by 42 points at the main break. Collingwood rallied in the third but still we were 35 points up at the final change.

Lynch's fourth goal at the 15-minute mark of the final term had the commentators saying it was beyond doubt, but it became more comfortable as goals followed to Brown, Akermanis, Hart and Brown again.

It got out to 69 points but when Collingwood kicked the next three goals my fear-of-failure instincts kicked in. I had this panicked thought, 'What if they get another quick clearance?' We just needed to slow them down. And who do you think threw themself head-first on the ball to create a restart? None other than Nigel Lappin. Realistically the outcome wasn't in jeopardy at that stage, but Nige sensed the same illogical fear I did, and put his damaged body on the line, as he'd done the entire match.

Vossy had spent a bit of time on the bench in the second half and my last message for the day was to get him onto the ground for the final siren. He deserved it. And he deserved the massive ovation he received as he pulled off his tracksuit and walked to the boundary line to go back onto the field. To get through the finals and captain his third consecutive premiership team after looking gone three weeks earlier was a marvellous effort.

This was the first season of a countdown clock in the coach's box, so with about 30 seconds to go I decided to head down to ground level. I was at the top of the aisle around the famous Bay 13 area when the siren sounded. There is no better noise than the blare of sound that ends a grand final with your team in front. Hearing this beautiful noise three years in a row is a magnificent and cherished memory.

There was no question about who would receive the Norm Smith Medal. Simon Black had 16 kicks and 23 handballs for 39 possessions – the most on the last day in September since records had been kept. Plus 23 gathers, nine clearances, seven inside 50s, nine effective tackles and a goal, in arguably the most dominant individual grand final performance by a midfielder I have ever seen. He had 34 possessions after quarter-time. Of my best 50 games, none were in the seven grand finals I played in, so I have enormous admiration for anyone who plays career-best football on the most high pressure day on the football calendar. Simon has produced some terrific footy over a long period of time but I reckon his best-ever performance was in the 2003 premiership decider.

Blacky polled 15 votes from a possible 15 to win the medal from Keating (seven), Akermanis (six) and Michael (two), joining James Hird and Greg Williams as just the third player in history to win a Brownlow Medal, a Norm Smith Medal and a premiership medal.

His performance was above and beyond. He got his hands on the ball enough for two players. It was as if he had his own ball out there. It was a monster performance, and on reflection I'm not sure why we only rated him 4.5 and not a perfect five in the club championship voting. Gee, we were hard markers.

Aker played a beauty, kicking five classy goals. Our anger over his lack of loyalty the week before seemed an eternity ago. The purpose of our existence, to be the best team we could be, was enhanced by Aker's on-field talents, so in the post-premiership feel-good moments, we moved on. I reminded myself that if all our players were perfect, I was out of a job. Managing the imperfections in individuals so as not to impact too negatively on the team was a key coaching function. Playing talent is rare and should only be discarded as a last resort. I think we all knew we'd get to that point eventually, but this was not the time.

One by one, the players received their premiership medallions. For Martin Pike it was his fourth premiership medal. He celebrated with a four-fingered salute. For 15 others it was their third. For Copeland, Bradshaw and Caracella their second. And for Charman, McGrath and Hadley a first-time moment they would never forget.

As it had in 2001 and 2002, the lap of honour lasted almost an hour. For Marcus Ashcroft it was his last on-field act as an AFL player. After 318 games he was done. A chronic hip problem would prevent him playing on, but what a way to go out. Having waited a record 268 games to win his first flag, he'd gone out with three in a row.

Browny, who'd played all but two minutes of the entire finals series with his damaged hand, had become the game's sixth-youngest triple premiership player and the youngest in 46 years. He was 32 days short of his 22nd birthday.

Vossy, later to win his fifth club championship by a vote from Blacky and Luke Power, had become just the sixth triple premiership captain. In his acceptance speech he made special mention of the players' wives and girlfriends. This came as a follow-up to a special request I'd made of the same group 10 weeks out from the finals. Things weren't exactly going perfectly, and I asked the players' partners to be even more understanding and considerate, that we were all in it together and that we needed their help if we were to go all the way.

Lynchy, the oldest player in the AFL in 2003 at 35 years of age, had become the fourth-oldest person to win a premiership. Blake Caracella had become the 21st player to share premiership wins with two clubs, and Richard Hadley, who had played in the Lions' 2001 Ansett Cup grand final loss to Port Adelaide aged 17, had tasted the ultimate football glory in just his fourth game at the highest level.

Personally it was a dominant victory that defied my deliberately humble pre-game expectations and assumptions after the lessons reinforced from the year before. After wasting the rare joy by allowing myself to be disappointed with only a 'close win' in 2002, I was up for a bit of partying after this one. As I've got older I drink less because I hate the following morning's hangover, but this night would be a rare exception. This meant I was into the Crown Lagers straight after the game, and when the team finally got to the post-grand final function at the Convention Centre, the party was in full swing.

On the way up to the function, in a lift crowded with players who'd taken the club to three consecutive premierships, the fun-loving Justin Leppitsch – at least he was this night – cheekily asked me, 'Where would you be without us?' My equally cheeky reply, with my inhibitions loosened considerably by the booze and the post-premiership euphoria, was, 'Leppa, I guess all I'd be without you guys would be the player of the century.' This was a rare occasion when a story from football mythology was actually true.

As I was determined to do, the party I missed after 2002 was more than made up for a year later. I still look back on the third grand final victory in 2003 as one of the few times the footy gods were defied. So many things have to fall into place to win a premiership but, despite so much going wrong during the campaign, the Lions players won without good fortune on their side.

A few days later, when the dust had settled, I was asked to say a few words at a function hosted by Queensland Premier Peter Beattie at the Tattersall's Club in Brisbane. What I said that Wednesday after winning the third consecutive flag, I still firmly believe to this day.

As I stand here today, with the premiership only a few days old, I think of when I came to Queensland five years ago. I'd never lived outside the southern suburbs of Melbourne. It was a great adventure to be asked and to go to another part of Australia. I've always believed in pride, respect and trust as qualities that are really important in a group environment, and so one of the things I did initially was that every time I went out into the public domain to speak or appear at a function, I made a commitment to always wear our club uniform.

Sometimes you've got to exhibit the pride even before you feel it, I guess, and it's nice to stand here five years later and for all of us to feel genuine pride in our Brisbane Lions team and the uniform we wear. It's about this time you say to yourself, 'Success is a journey – not a destination.' It's been a short 12 months since I stood here this time last year. And what we've had for 24 months now is the pressure of being premiers. That pressure is something we put on ourselves. It's not something that can be put on from outside.

External pressure on football teams and football clubs is the most overrated thing. It's almost a media fabrication. The pressure comes from your own expectations, your own self-esteem, your own standards that you expect from each other. And what happens when you win a premiership is that you commit yourself again, that the only way you can be satisfied at the end of the following 12 months is to win it again ... and that's bloody hard to do. The ability of this team for 24 months to handle the pressure of being premiers and not to allow that to affect the way it went about its job is one of the most remarkable and memorable factors of this particular group of people.

And when we say a group of people, we also include the ones that exist to put our football team on the field. It also includes the environment that is created from within the football club from the board and the CEO and the finance and the marketing and all the areas of the club, before we even get to the football department, which is the medical staff, conditioning staff, the coaching staff, and all the people who are more hands-on with the players. Unless all the areas of that football club are operating efficiently, then the whole deck of cards tends to fall over. So the way this club has thrived off the field has been something that is a cause for great pride for us all. It has created the environment for the football and playing part of our club to have the consistency of attitude, preparation and performance.

Why did we win? We won because this group of players was able to focus in on what they had to do and produce a pleasant surprise for us all. I guess 'surprised' is probably the wrong word because this group of people have surprised me quite regularly. But I've got to say in the previous couple of years they were like robots – you wind them up and put them out on the ground and they went and played. But this year a few issues hit us. The footy gods didn't seem to be smiling on us the last two months. We had a lot of issues and it was the perseverance of the medical staff and people around the club to keep exploring means and methods to get players on the field ready to perform, and to not just accept that problems may be unsolvable. Then there was the courage of a lot of players to put themselves on the line when they were not certain about their physical condition. It was quite remarkable. Very rarely do you defy the footy gods, but this group has done exactly that.

However, even after a premiership win, one season ends and the feel-goods quickly fade. The goal that was open to us in 2004 was huge. Ambition knows no bounds, and racking up three in a row gave us the chance to do something thought unfathomable in the AFL national competition – to do a 'four-peat'.

41

YOU CAN'T BEAT CITY HALL

This was one very big catch that had got away.

There is always a cruel equilibrium in the emotional response of the two teams as they gather on the MCG turf after a grand final. The extreme joy of the winning group is always balanced by the utter despair of the losers. As this annual scenario presented itself after the 2004 premiership decider, it was Port Adelaide who were savouring the exhilaration of victory, and after the three previous seasons as winners, it was our turn to experience the bitterness of the loser.

As the Lions group gathered to lick our wounds and waited to pay due respect to Port before leaving the field, I happened to come across AFL chief executive Andrew Demetriou and football operations manager Adrian Anderson. They went to shake hands and offer their condolences, but my prickly mood was not into conciliation, it was into shooting the messenger. In my mind the AFL had denied us our best chance at winning a historic fourth consecutive premiership and here were the league's two main office bearers and decision makers having the temerity to act friendly when clearly they'd been the enemy.

I was in no mood for diplomacy, frankly I felt more like punching them on the nose, and muttered to them, 'You blokes have got to be kidding,' before turning my back and walking away. Given what later became obvious about who was actually responsible for the AFL actions, or non-actions, I realised that it was Andrew, not Adrian, who was probably the main culprit.

My angst at the time – which I must admit has grown over the intervening years – is not meant to take anything away from the victors. Port had undoubtedly done their time and thoroughly earned their win. On the day they were far too good for us. After finishing on top for the third consecutive season, the Power had finally won in the first week of the finals to claim the advantage of the home preliminary final, which they'd used effectively to reach the premiership decider. As the second-ranked qualifier behind Port, we'd also earned the right to play at home. However, due to the agreement between the AFL and the MCC that the Melbourne venue had to host at least one preliminary final, we were forced to play Geelong at the MCG.

Like a heat-seeking missile searching for a victim, this potential competition inequity had eventually found an unfortunate target, which to my regret happened to be the Brisbane Lions. History tells us the AFL negotiated a new deal after the scheduling debacle of 2004, and the MCG relinquished its right to at least one preliminary final. It was a year too late for the Lions.

The AFL's handling of this festering issue was at best incompetent, or maybe the Lions were being told in no uncertain terms not to get City Hall offside.

The obvious prerequisite of winning four premierships in a row is winning the first three. Having achieved that and then getting so close, but eventually blowing our chances, is not a great memory. However, it's the feeling that external intervention played a part that riles me the most. I always feel quite sick whenever I think about the culmination of the 2004 season. What transpired late in that September was like a veteran game fisherman hooking a world-record-sized marlin, only to have it slip the line as it got close to the boat. This was one very big catch that had got away. Maybe the fish was just too strong, because Port Adelaide was a hungry and talented opponent, but the thought that someone might have deliberately frayed the line is particularly galling.

The finals scheduling that transpired in September 2004 seemed to be telling us that the footy gods, who the team had defied to win in 2003, were getting even. After finishing second at the end of the home-and-away series, we'd beaten St Kilda by 80 points in the Friday night qualifying final at the Gabba and the finals system said we had therefore earned the right to a home preliminary final. We were fully aware of the agreement in place that one preliminary final had to be played at the MCG.

When the top-placed Port Adelaide won its Sunday qualifying final, as the second-ranked qualifier we'd be the travelling team, if the MCG arrangement was enforced. I was greatly concerned about the increased difficulties this would create for us, but now that the crunch had come, I hoped the AFL would, as per normal, negotiate its way to a fairer outcome. I was mistaken. Or did they really try? I'm told on good authority that the deal the MCC wanted at this time in order to relinquish the rights was the same deal agreed to a few months later.

We were hoping against hope that a satisfactory resolution would be found to give us our hard-earned home preliminary final, but that ended in the middle of the following week. When the full scheduling of the rest of the finals was made public, my blood really started to boil. Gubby Allan walked into my office late that Wednesday morning. He had a glum look on his face, so I knew it wasn't going to be good news. And it wasn't. Not only had the AFL ruled that our upcoming preliminary final would be in Melbourne, it was scheduled as the Saturday night game.

It was a cruel blow to our unashamed quest for a fourth consecutive premiership. I guess the failure of the AFL to find a way to renegotiate the MCC agreement was predictable given the strained relationship between the Lions and head office. But the killer blow was the timing of a night final instead of the usual Saturday afternoon. Even if we got to the grand final, we'd be coming off a major preparation handicap.

For some reason the AFL had scheduled the two preliminary finals as night games. The three previous seasons both had been on the Saturday – one in the afternoon and one at night – to give the grand final combatants a similar lead-in.

As the AFL had set it up, Port would play a preliminary final at home on the Friday night of the penultimate weekend of the season. It would be against either St Kilda or Sydney, who were to meet in the semi-final the previous weekend. We'd play at the MCG on the Saturday night of preliminary final weekend against the winner of Geelong versus Essendon.

There were suggestions that the sudden change from the status quo was a decision taken at the insistence of the match broadcaster, Channel Ten, but Andrew Demetriou vigorously denied this. 'The AFL controls its own scheduling, make no mistake – we initiated when the games would be played,' he said at the time. All my information supports his comments that the AFL chose the scheduling, which proves that City Hall had its own agenda, including giving Port an earned final at home in Adelaide on the Friday and the Lions an unearned Saturday night final interstate. There was no logic in this unfathomable combination of scheduling, except to make our task more difficult.

The AFL chief said that even as late as the Tuesday afternoon of preliminary final week they'd tried to convince the MCC to allow our preliminary final to be played at the Gabba, but the MCC continued to enforce the agreement. I remain suspicious of just how hard they tried.

Once the die was cast, it was time for me to bite my tongue and treat the scheduling as neither here nor there. I knew I couldn't say what I really felt publicly because it would send a bad message to the players. I wanted the matter closed, so my public comment was: 'We know our opponent, we know our venue, we know the date, we know the time ... we know the prize. That's all that matters.'

As I tried to reinforce with the players that if we were good enough we could still win it, I was cynical and suspicious enough to privately wonder why the AFL had chosen this scheduling path. I didn't need to say any more because senior football writer Caroline Wilson did it for me in *The Age*. She wrote that the decision to hold Friday and Saturday night preliminary finals for the first time in the history of the AFL was 'the worst decision the AFL chief executive has made as he nears his first anniversary in the top job. Already embarrassed by the 1989 AFL–MCG agreement binding the league to a Melbourne preliminary final, Demetriou has further compromised the grand final by allowing one team a full 24 hours less to prepare.'

I suspect Caroline was aware from her contacts at the AFL of the strained personal dealings between Andrew and Lions CEO Michael Bowers, who were both stubborn Enforcers who frequently seemed to butt heads. I doubt she had considered the many issues that had occurred over the previous couple of years that had eroded the previous harmonious relationship between Brisbane and the AFL's Melbourne head office that had existed during my initial year or two at the club. The AFL's encouragement for me to take the job in late 1998 and the acceptance of a salary cap retention allowance at the end of 1999 indicated they wanted to help if they could. Wayne Jackson and Ian Collins were now gone and by the end of 2004 the new management regime had developed a very different attitude to the Lions cause.

It was only when I was putting this book together that I fully realised the large number of occasions in the early 2000s when the AFL and the Lions ended up at the opposite ends of an issue. The result was that our former 'favourite son' status gradually became more like the naughty kid at the back of the classroom who wouldn't do what he was told. Maybe the angst from City Hall towards their Queensland club started with the IV drip controversy in 2001 and the ongoing issue of players not flying to Melbourne to attend the AFL Brownlow Medal functions if we reached the grand final.

In 2002, the league had steadfastly rejected our dogged campaign for draft concessions to encourage more talented young Queenslanders to play AFL without leaving home, and in 2003 the Lions management had significant run-ins with the AFL hierarchy. They weren't happy when we refused to abandon a long-term relationship with the Parkview Hotel to move to the official AFL hotel in the CBD, or when the club signed a sizeable sponsorship with the Queensland-based Golden Circle group. Even though AFL CEO Wayne Jackson had flown to Brisbane to help announce the deal, the league was upset because of a supposed conflict with AFL major sponsors Coca-Cola.

Then during the season we also seemed to be the main complainers about the extreme hardness and patchy grass cover at the Docklands stadium and many of our players made their concerns public. Andrew Demetriou was the AFL's football operations manager at the time and the consequent controversy initiated by the Lions players was a hassle for all involved, because there was no obvious solution. There was even talk that the Docklands games should be transferred to the

MCG. The AFL was not happy. It was yet another reason for the AFL chiefs at City Hall to look down on the upstarts up north.

Journalist Caroline Wilson always knows what's going on at headquarters and wrote in *The Age* on 14 June: 'Both parties remained furious at the manner in which Brisbane has dealt with the issue this week in making public a complaint to the AFL before the league had received the Lions official letter. Football operations chief Andrew Demetriou is believed to have angrily reprimanded Brisbane's chief executive officer Michael Bowers three days ago.'

The big stick came out in 2004. In April the AFL fined the Lions $260,000 for administrative breaches. According to headquarters, the club had breached AFL rules on lodgement of documentation concerning player payments and additional services agreements. 'The Brisbane Lions Football Club has been sanctioned for 26 breaches of the AFL Player Rules involving failure to lodge documents within the required time frames,' AFL football operations boss Adrian Anderson told a media conference at AFL House.

The rules required the lodgement of various information such as additional services agreements, variations to contracts, changes to contracts when players reach milestones, requests for information about changes to contracts, and other payments related to signing fees and such promotions. Each breach carried a $10,000 fine.

I couldn't help myself. At the regular Friday media call I weighed into the situation with a swipe at the league's all-encompassing powers. 'It reminds me of one of my old school-day lessons, about the philosophy of power corrupts and absolute power corrupts absolutely,' I said. 'You could say it's only money if you wanted to be flippant. It'd almost be laughable if it wasn't so much money. It's a bit like being transported for stealing a loaf of bread. You think that went out with the British Empire but obviously it hasn't.' Maybe I should have kept my mouth shut.

The club had further ruffled the AFL's feathers when we sold the Gabba ground pourage rights to Cadbury-Schweppes, rather than to the AFL's sponsor Coca-Cola. The AFL invoked its last resort option. The Lions were charged with bringing the game into disrepute and the Commission imposed a $500,000 fine. There were no legal grounds for the ruling but the club decided to accept the fine and move on.

I'm sure there was an element at AFL House who thought Brisbane were off doing their own thing and wouldn't do what we were told. It was as if we'd become too big for our britches – and maybe we had.

Certainly, the AFL's hierarchy didn't like the fact that we'd won three premierships in a row. One had been terrific for the development of the game, and two was probably acceptable, but three had really stretched things. It was embarrassing for the league's equalisation policies because it wasn't meant to happen. And now that we'd got to within two wins of a fourth flag, we were not exactly the AFL's pin-up boys.

The scheduling of the preliminary finals was a crunch moment in our season, and being forced to play our final at the MCG on a Saturday night was a big blow to our premiership prospects. The AFL had had a choice between a day game and a night game. And as the team most directly affected, for us it was about much more than a 2.30 pm start versus a 7.30 pm start.

If we'd been drawn to play on the Saturday afternoon we would have been able to catch an evening flight home and the players would have got a good night's rest back in their own beds. Preparation for the grand final would have started on the Sunday morning and things would have been much more normal. But because we were drawn to play at night, we wouldn't get back to Brisbane until mid-afternoon on the Sunday and the recovery process was virtually put back a day. Further impacting this situation was the fact that if Port Adelaide were to win their home preliminary final on the Friday night, they'd be almost two days ahead of us in recovery.

Did Andrew Demetriou really try to provide the fairest preliminary final scheduling? It's something I'll wonder about until the day I die – especially after the league found a way the following year to vary the long-standing MCC contract and provide a mechanism for two interstate preliminary finals if two clubs from outside Victoria earned that right.

The AFL head office intervention in September 2004 that handicapped our prospects was, and still is, a major annoyance, but as we all should do, I also look back and critique the things that were in my control. There are a few of my decisions that season that I'd like to alter if I could.

For much of the year the campaign went really well. Our win–loss ratio was good enough to keep us near the top all year, despite injuries and suspensions being a constant problem.

At our first pre-season training session, I decided on a slight tweaking of our 'living in the moment' philosophy. For the players, the 2004 campaign had begun with a meeting at the Gabba on 19 November 2003. I'd arrived carrying a picture frame with photographs of the Lions' 2001, 2002 and 2003 premiership sides celebrating at the MCG. At the right-hand end of the frame was a blank space, with room for a fourth photo. Written across the top of the frame were seven words: 'I want to be part of four.' They were my words. And across the bottom were eight more words: 'Do you want to be part of four?'

One by one, in alphabetical order, the Lions players took the framed photo montage home. I wanted them to really connect with the opportunity we had within our grasp.

The game had changed immeasurably in the 74 years since Collingwood had won four premierships in a row between 1927 and 1930, evolving from a 12-team competition played exclusively on Saturday afternoons at suburban grounds in Victoria to a 16-team national competition. Comparing the AFL in the 2000s to the VFL in the 1920s was like comparing an F-18 fighter to a Tiger Moth.

I made a decision over the off-season to use our unique opportunity to win a fourth premiership as part of our motivation in 2004. I thought dangling this carrot in the face of the players might just add a little extra stimulation, even if only to enhance their commitment to summer training. At a club function shortly afterwards, the 2001–03 premiership cups were on display, and sitting next to them was an empty trophy base.

One of the great strengths of the Brisbane playing group through the premiership years was their ability to live in the moment. They were able to block out the external issues and pressures, to put the past behind them, and worry only about the present – to dissociate themselves from that which didn't really concern them and focus only on the things they could control. But this was one of those times when thinking of the long-term goal seemed worthwhile.

The salary cap squeeze increased with each premiership and, as we were back-ended up to our eyeballs, with the support of the playing group we instituted a scheme to offer compensation for high performers. We abandoned individual player incentives and instead implemented a High Performance Reward Scheme funded by five per cent of the salary cap ($300,000).

It would be split on a votes-per-game basis among the top 11 place-getters in the club championship. Initially we'd proposed that 10 per cent of the cap be devoted to the scheme, but the players – and, more particularly, their managers – felt that that percentage was too high. Still, as the HPRS recipients wouldn't be decided until the club championship night held at the end of the season, this mechanism allowed us to push $300,000 from the 2004 salary cap into the 2005 payments. It would exacerbate future problems, but with the continuing agreement of the club's board we were focusing on the short-term and doing everything possible to continue our premiership-winning sequence.

Again, because of this strong focus on the present, it was a largely unchanged playing group. But we'd carried a heavy toll from the 2003 flag. Michael Voss (knee), Justin Leppitsch (shoulder/wrist), Simon Black (knee), Alastair Lynch (achilles), Beau McDonald (knee), Brad Scott (broken leg), Chris Scott (groin) and Craig McRae (wrist) were unable to complete much of the pre-season training, and before we were too far down the track Jonathan Brown (knee) and Blake Caracella (ankle) had joined the casualty list.

Happily, our disrupted preparation didn't translate into too many on-field woes. We finished second on the ladder with a 16–6 record and went 12–1 at home, losing only to West Coast. It had been a remarkable run at the Gabba. We'd gone 52 wins, six losses from July 2000 until September 2004.

We knew there was a bit of a risk with an ageing core group. Alastair Lynch was the oldest player in the competition at 35 and he almost retired at the end of 2003, but we were able to convince him to play one last year. From many players in their prime years back in

2001 when we won our first flag, we were now starting to get a battle-worn look about the group.

Above and beyond the accumulated wear and tear of a number of successive 25-game seasons, we were getting a worrying number of players around the 30-year-old mark. By March 2004, Shaun Hart (32), Martin Pike (31), Craig McRae and Darryl White (30) joined Lynchie in the over-30s. We were now an ageing team and we hadn't been able to draft youngsters who could adequately replace this group. Our margin for error was getting very slim. Our conditioning and medical team was really earning its money patching the team up as a myriad of physical issues started to pile up.

The one area we were improving was in the ruck. Jamie Charman was still only 22 but was quickly developing into a real weapon. Our other premiership ruckmen, though, were very injury-prone. Beau McDonald had chronic knee issues that would end his career and Clark Keating only ever got on the field about every second week. I loved having a lively ultra-aggressive ruckman in my teams. Don Scott was that for Hawthorn during our 1970s premierships and James Manson and Damian Monkhorst were likewise for Colling-wood in September of 1990 when the Magpies won the flag. Charmo was becoming that kind of player for the Lions.

He was a young vibrant next-generation ruckman who was becoming a real force within the team and the competition. That all changed in round 17 when we beat Adelaide at the Gabba by 141 points. Ten minutes into the final quarter we were 94 points up when Charmo was involved in a bit of a push and shove with his Adelaide counterpart Matthew Clarke. My alarm bells started to ring. Even at his most docile, our big ruckman was a pretty combative type and he looked very angry and hot under the collar. I was worried he might do something silly and get reported, and when after a minute or so he still looked agitated I thought it would be a good idea to get him off and give him a few minutes to cool down.

Premierships are won and lost by seconds and inches, and this time a few seconds of tardiness on my part resulted in a gigantic cost. Between me sending the message down to the interchange bench and the runner delivering it, we'd kicked another goal and Charmo was back waiting for the centre bounce. There was no centre circle back then, and he was coming in from what seemed around centre half-back. You could see it in his eyes – he was going to run flat out and launch into Clarke with all he had. He jumped knee first but somehow his knee caught Clarke's hip and he fell awkwardly. He'd damaged the posterior cruciate ligament in his knee. Season over.

We'd picked up enough of a percentage boost to jump to the top of the ladder, ahead of St Kilda, Port Adelaide and Melbourne, but we'd paid a huge price. It was one of those sliding-door events, a cross-roads moment that went badly. How I wish I'd acted quicker. Getting Charmo off before he injured himself might have won us that fourth flag. The combined strength and size of the Port Adelaide ruck pair Dean Brogan and Brendon Lade overwhelmed us in the grand final; I reckon a fit Jamie Charman would have made a huge difference.

There were another couple of similarly costly moments in the final home-and-away game against North Melbourne at the Gabba. It happened to be the universally respected Anthony Stevens' last game for the Kangaroos. We'd led by 27 points at half-time and fitness coach Craig Starcevich made a specific point during the break of reminding me that Alastair Lynch had had a limited preparation through injury. He'd only played four of the first 13 games due to a thigh problem, and we agreed that if we had the game in control we'd give him a shortened match. I'm sure that if Starce had had his choice, he would have kept Lynchie off after half-time.

We kicked nine goals to one in the third quarter on our way to what would be a 113-point win. About 10 minutes into the third term, with our conditioning coach's views in mind, I sent the message down to bring our veteran full-forward off. But again, like the Charman situation a few weeks before, there was a few seconds' delay in getting the message to Lynchy and, as the runner headed in his direction, he took off on a long, searching lead from the goal square. He took a diving chest mark, got up and threw the ball into the ground. He didn't even take his kick because he'd strained his hamstring. He missed two weeks and although our physios got him back on the paddock for the preliminary final, he was never anywhere near 100 per cent again that season.

The terrible doubt of 'what if' still nags me. What if I'd listened to Starce at half-time or what if I'd got Lynchy off earlier before he hurt himself? Like I've said many times in this book, the footy gods of good or bad fortune have an enormous impact on the end result.

The cost from the aftermath of the Kangaroos match was increased by a late-game injury suffered by Clark Keating. He was a walking injury waiting to happen at the best of times, and consequently, with a badly disrupted preparation and with the game well under control, he was safely parked on the bench alongside Michael Voss, who we often got off a bit early if we could afford to.

With about five minutes to go we had to interchange a player off via the blood rule. The replacement had to be Voss or Keating, and I decided to send Clark back on with the express instruction to go deep in the forward line and keep out of trouble. In the last few moments of the game he 'ignored' my instructions and went for the footy around our attacking goal square, straining his calf muscle. He'd miss the first final.

Our third-string key position sized ruckman, Dylan McLaren, carried the ruck division magnificently in the first final win over St Kilda, and 'Crackers' Keating got back on the field for the prelim final win over Geelong. However, his calf injury had a big negative impact on his last couple of games. As with the Adelaide match where we lost Charmo for the year, a 100-point win had costly injury repercussions.

We had a number of core players who missed plenty of football that season and Jonathan Brown was another to miss eight weeks, although with him we couldn't blame injury. He missed rounds one and two, nine and 10 and 16 to 19 through three separate suspensions. Browny was playing '80s-style heavy contact footy under the stricter rules of the early 2000s. There was some scuttlebutt that he undertook anger management courses, but that was rubbish.

The suspension interruptions that afflicted his footy for a season or two disappeared when the big fella learnt the hard lesson that to go high at an opponent would cost him games. His early career reports weren't from hot uncontrolled anger, but a failure to play to the rules of the day. As he matured, Browny eventually managed the right balance of attacking the footy rather than his opponents. In a way, his reports were because of a Baby Huey-type quality of just not knowing his own strength. This flaw almost cost him a controversial suspension after the first final of 2004.

In a melee after the quarter-time siren he was reported for putting a headlock on the Saints' Jason Blake as he vigorously wrestled the St Kilda defender to the ground. No damage was done to Blake, but umpire Steve McBurney, never afraid to make a contentious decision, laid a charge of unduly rough play. A melee charge or even a wrestling charge, which carried fines as sanctions, would have been reasonable. A charge of unduly rough play was major overkill. The offence wasn't serious enough to warrant a suspension, the automatic penalty for being found guilty of rough play.

I spoke to umpires boss Jeff Gieschen about whether umpire McBurney might be prepared to downgrade the charge to wrestling, but that request was refused. So, for the first time in my coaching career at Brisbane, I headed to Melbourne with Browny and Gubby to join our advocate Sean Carroll and plan our approach.

We were always going to vigorously defend the rough play charge but in the end the case wasn't even heard. It was tossed out on a technicality after the tribunal accepted the submission from Sean that, as the incident occurred after the quarter-time siren, 'play' had ended so rough play was impossible. This commonsense argument had been noted by a couple of observers, including Anne Allan, Gubby's wife.

Despite protests from the AFL's prosecutor, Rick Lewis, and claims the wording of the charge should be able to be changed, the tribunal agreed with our advocate's argument and Browny walked out, clear to play in the preliminary final without having to utter a word. I don't believe the tribunal throwing the case out on a technicality would have been accepted had the offence been more significant or caused some harm to Blake.

Having viewed the incident many times before making their decision, they were fully aware that rough play was quite an exaggeration of what had actually happened. Allowing the technicality was a simpler shortcut to justice being done. As we left the tribunal hearing at the *Herald Sun* building in Southbank, we could hardly hide our delight. With Browny's bad suspension record over the previous year, a guilty finding might have resulted in our gun centre half-forward missing any remaining finals. This threat being removed was a massive boost for our 'four-peat' aspirations.

However, the outcome at the tribunal did add to our trouble-maker reputation at City Hall. Andrew Demetriou admitted that we'd acted responsibly in utilising all fair means to clear our player, but he'd wanted the case to be allowed to run its course. He suggested Lewis could, and should, have altered the wording of the charge during the course of the hearing. In what turned out to be his last case, Lewis quit amid claims he'd been victimised by the AFL CEO.

For the fourth year in a row the Lions topped the club representation in the All-Australian side with five. Nigel Lappin picked up his fourth selection, Simon Black and Jason Akermanis their third, Chris Johnson his second, and Luke Power was included for the first time. In the four-year period from 2001 to 2004 the Lions had won 17 All-Australian jumpers. Next best was Port Adelaide with 11. As I'd said to the players at my first meeting back in September 1998, team and individual success are indelibly linked. Great teams are made up of great players, and having many All-Australian standard performers in the group is a prerequisite for sustained success. During their premiership era of the early 2000s, the Lions are proof of this reality.

The following fortnight passed without incident and we headed south for the preliminary final on the Friday on the 11 am plane, with our regular Qantas pilot Don Lehmann at the controls. As usual we travelled at the lowest altitude that Don could safely fly. Then it was straight to the Parkview, where we solved a mystery that had bugged us since the 2003 grand final morning when Darren Cartwright, The *Courier-Mail*'s AFL writer, had reported very accurately some of the key messages from our final team meeting on the Friday night. He was so accurate that I was convinced someone had leaked confidential information.

Happily, it wasn't the case. And we proved as much when we were told by the hotel reception that when Darren booked his accommodation for the preliminary final he'd specifically asked for room 304. Suddenly, the penny dropped. Room 304 was next door to the Lions' meeting room. He'd heard it all through the wall. From that moment, room 304 was always allocated to a Lions staffer.

I spent my usual night before a game in Melbourne visiting my daughter Fiona and granddaughter Amber, where I watched Port fall in against St Kilda at AAMI Stadium with a six-point win, having appeared to suffer no injuries. They were into their first grand final.

Lynch and Keating returned from injury for our preliminary final against an emerging Geelong, who had lost their first final to Port in Adelaide by 55 points, before beating Essendon at the MCG by 10 points. It was the first and last time a non-Victorian side would be forced to play at the MCG in a preliminary final after having earned the home ground advantage, and it was as tough a game as you'll see. Even Jonathan Brown said as much at the time.

The good fortune of Browny being cleared at the tribunal looked to be wasted when, after a heavy collision during the opening term, he went down holding his right knee. The night and the season looked to be over as he hobbled to the interchange bench. He got back on the field, but the knee damage he suffered would severely restrict his movement.

We trailed by two points at quarter-time and led by two and four at the next two breaks. There were never more than two straight kicks in it as the last quarter went goal for goal. Tim Notting bounced one through from inside the centre square, Aker snapped truly and Blake Caracella calmly put through the sealer. We had nothing left as we hung on to win by nine points. It had been a gruelling last-man-standing type of game that left the players totally spent. A historic four consecutive flags was now only one win away.

It was a happy and festive Lions rooms after the game but I got no feeling that the players were anything but focused on what lay ahead. Their mental state wasn't a concern. However, getting them sufficiently recovered physically to be at their best a week later – again back in Melbourne – now that was a big challenge.

It was our second interstate preliminary final win in as many years and a magnificent effort. But as we drove away from the MCG that night, I wondered how much it had taken out of the players. I think history will record that travelling interstate to win a preliminary final and then again to win a grand final will be a very rare event. For us, achieving this feat two years in a row would be thoroughly testing.

The AFL had a slice of history on their hands – it would be the first grand final between non-Victorian clubs. We were installed as favourites against the newest club in the competition, who had never played in an AFL grand final and never won a final at the MCG. And I found myself coaching against Mark Williams, the former Collingwood captain who I'd effectively moved on 18 years earlier.

We'd considered staying in Melbourne for the whole week if we won the preliminary final, but all things considered we didn't think that was our best option. Given that we failed in the grand final, it's impossible not to ponder whether we made the right choice. Just as I wonder whether we should have refused to come down on the Thursday to participate in the Friday grand final parade. At least making the threat privately to the AFL when they were considering the preliminary final scheduling may have given us some leverage to at least get a Saturday afternoon timeslot.

In retrospect, one controllable factor I would have changed would be to cancel the normal pre-grand final week Sunday meeting with players and partners. After arriving back from Melbourne it was late afternoon before the players headed home. Every little bit counts and I wish we'd sent the players straight home from the airport, instead of hanging around the Gabba waiting for everyone to arrive. This was a time when a change of routine may have been helpful.

Even before a full medical post-mortem, I knew we'd be one player down in the grand final. Midway through the second quarter of the preliminary final Shaun Hart had run with the flight of the ball into the Brisbane forward line and crashed face first into the kneecap of his team-mate Daniel Bradshaw coming flat out the other way. The collision was sickening. The 2001 Norm Smith Medallist was assisted from the field with a broken nose, a double cheekbone fracture and four jaw fractures. Doctors described his injuries as not unlike those of a road accident victim who hadn't been wearing a seatbelt. They inserted four plates that would stay with Shaun for the rest of his life and untold wires that would keep his jaw locked together for six weeks.

This example of extreme courage would be his last act as an AFL footballer. A selfless team player, Harty deserved a better exit from the game. A few of us coaches visited him in the Epworth Hospital after the match and his face was a mess. He spent grand final week in hospital, while the club flew his wife, Linda, and their sons, Jessy and Ricky, to Melbourne and put the family up at a serviced apartment in nearby Kew. On the Thursday night Shaun visited the players for dinner at the team hotel. He wanted to offer his support and, typically, he said how pleased he was that someone else would have the opportunity to enjoy the same satisfaction he'd experienced for the three previous years.

But Harty wasn't our only injury worry. Jonathan Brown pulled up very badly from the injured knee he'd suffered in the first quarter collision with Geelong's Darren Milburn. The media were told it was bruised but it was much worse. It was same knee on which Browny had undergone surgery seven months earlier. He'd heard it crack, and although he got through the game, he knew he was in trouble.

It was to be a big week for the still only 22-year-old power forward. On the Saturday night after we beat the Cats, he sat up all night with assistant coach Craig Brittain icing his knee. An hour on, an hour off. There was more of the same on Sunday, when he could barely walk because of heavy swelling and internal bleeding. On the Monday, scans confirmed cartilage damage, chronic bleeding and bruising of the bone. Still, surgeon Dr Jim Fardoulys was confident he'd get him up.

The successful Voss treatment the previous September, which had entailed deadening the knee joint, would be the probable solution as far as getting Browny on the field. The painkiller would help, and you could add to that the last-match mind-over-matter attitude that has enabled players to survive amazing discomfort on grand final day. All of this might just get him over the line. The fact that Browny regarded himself as physically invincible was a bonus. If he could run, he would think he could play.

There was a further unexpected complication which we managed to keep secret. Browny had woken up in a lather of sweat on the Sunday night with a badly infected elbow. He had no idea where it had come from, because there was no broken skin. But the pain was horrendous and he knew that if he didn't get his elbow under control, it wouldn't matter about his knee.

He spent much of his week in the club's hyperbaric chamber, staying away from the media on Tuesday and not stepping outside for training on Wednesday. He flew south with the team on Thursday afternoon and was named in the side, but missed the grand final parade on Friday morning on medical advice.

We knew we had to be sure Browny could run, twist and turn before we confirmed that he'd play, so we needed to do a fitness test. We decided to do it in private. So, as the team bus left for the parade, Browny stayed at the hotel and shortly afterwards headed down to the hotel's underground car park with physio Peter Stanton and Doctor Paul McConnell. He sat low across the back seat of the car, trying in vain to be unobtrusive. There was no hiding under a blanket, as was reported in the press, but two newspaper photographers were on to him. They'd noticed he hadn't got on the bus so they checked out any car leaving the hotel. They got him. At least we managed to avoid the television cameras.

With two photographers for company, Browny went through his paces at Wesley College, about 500 metres up St Kilda Road from the hotel. The first 10 minutes didn't give anyone much hope. He could barely jog. They had no option but to resort to painkillers. Slowly he started to warm up. And by the time Alastair Lynch arrived after the parade to lend support, Browny was starting to run without discomfort.

By the end of a 45-minute session in which he kicked, ran and did some body-on-body work with assistant coach John Blakey, he'd done enough to get the all-clear. If we'd had a crystal ball, we would have scrubbed the Friday test, because in proving he was fit to play he further inflamed an already swollen joint. Without the fitness test he would have got onto the field fitter and moving more freely than he eventually did come match day.

Four hours after his test, Browny was given a movie star's welcome when he arrived for our final training session at Albert Oval. With the knee hidden under a tracksuit, he didn't train. He'd done enough to prove his fitness. Barring unforeseen problems overnight he was right to play. So, we made just one change to the preliminary final side, with Darryl White returning for Shaun Hart.

Browny barely slept that Friday night. The pain was relentless and again he resorted to ice and physiotherapy, but he didn't think of not playing. He missed the on-ground warm-up because medical staff didn't want him to exert his knee any more than necessary. At about 1.45 pm, 45 minutes before game time, he went through the same painkilling protocol and again at half-time. He estimated later he was maybe 60 or 70 per cent fit. I think he was being extremely optimistic. Browny underwent surgery on his knee shortly after to repair a cartilage that had split in half. He was six weeks on crutches and three months in a brace. To actually play in the grand final was a miraculous achievement.

The Power kicked the first three goals to lead by 19 points, but late in the second quarter we got four quick ones to get seven points up. It might have been more. Jason Akermanis got a holding free-kick about 30 metres from goal straight in front, a soda shot for a player with his finishing skills. Port's primary aggravator, Damian Hardwick, got in his face trying to draw a reversed free-kick. Aker took the bait and reacted with a slightly high shove back.

If there was one principle I coached consistently, it was to never do anything even remotely aggressive if we had a free. My regular line to my players was that they could hit you with an axe and you still shouldn't react. Damian went down as if shot, with the full-on knee-buckle backflip to the ground. It was a 50-50 call and the umpire rewarded the acting and reversed the free. From the Hardwick rebound play, Port goaled. It was a 12-point turnaround and although we led by a solitary point at half-time, much of the momentum was gone. A tight scoreboard at the main break was always going to suit Port. As we were against Essendon back in 2001, they would have been confident they'd run the game out stronger than their opponents, while we had unspoken concerns about fading late in the match. A great mindset for Port and a terrible one for us.

Port kicked the last four goals of the third quarter to lead by 17 points at the last change. We'd need the type of desperate last-quarter fightback that we'd summoned from nowhere in the 2003 preliminary final in Sydney. Being a year older and a year tireder against a hungry and talented Port Adelaide, we were out of miracles. When they added the first two of the final term we were physically and mentally gone. As they say, fatigue makes cowards of us all, and with tired legs the fight evaporated as well. In the end they finished with nine of the last 10 goals to win 17.11 (113) to 10.13 (73).

The golden era had ended. At the time I had little comprehension of what a big fall was to come in the years that followed. We stayed on the ground to watch Port receive their premiership medallions before one last meeting in the coach's room inside. I told the players how proud I was of their effort, but reminded them that they'd missed an opportunity. It was a painful reality that we'd have to live with from that day on.

Still, I felt very fortunate to have coached a playing group that had physically, mentally and emotionally put themselves on the line every week to get to four grand finals in a row and to bag three premierships. While having finally lost one was disappointing, it was tempered with a melancholy type of resignation that you can't win them all.

I was in the middle of my address to the players and staff gathered in the coach's meeting room when Alastair Lynch jumped to his feet and asked if he could talk to the team. He was very emotional and a bit teary as he announced his retirement. It was choke-up time for us all and any thought of me saying anything further was forgotten. It had been a sad way for a champion to go out. In the end his ageing body had let him down in his 17th season. The strained hamstring in round 22 had tipped his physical condition beyond the manageable. From early in the grand final when he pinged a quad, only a series of painkilling injections kept him on the field.

The frustration and emotion of being basically useless got the better of Lynchy during the third quarter when he lashed out at Power fullback Darryl Wakelin. It was an incident totally out of character. After the final siren Lynchy walked to the edge of the Port Adelaide huddle and apologised to Wakelin before he left the field. Later, he repeated his apology publicly. It wasn't the way football should be played, he said, admitting his actions had been born out of the frustration of being unable to contribute on grand final day.

Charged six times by the AFL on video evidence, he faced the tribunal via video link from Brisbane and pleaded guilty to attempting to strike, but not striking. After all, he'd made no contact. He was fined $15,000 and suspended for 10 matches. The 36-year-old did not get one disposal in the grand final and, when combined with the suspensions, it added up to a miserable way to end a decorated career. He became an inspiration to the many chronic fatigue sufferers by playing footy into his 30s after being bedridden for a year with the illness in 1995. The regrettable end to his playing days should be only one bad memory amongst a host of very good ones.

Lynchy wasn't our only retiree. Craig McRae had announced prior to the finals that the 2004 season would be his last. Shaun Hart made it three. The mass exodus of premiership players had begun in earnest.

On reflection, to win a fourth consecutive grand final would have been to defy the footy gods two years in a row. We'd done exactly that in 2003, but weren't able to do it in 2004. We'd come up against an opposition that was in very good form, very good physical condition, they were hard and hungry, and on the day we weren't good enough to overcome them.

However, I would have loved to play the preliminary final in Brisbane, because with an ageing team it was an advantage we had earned, and we desperately needed to be at our best on grand final day. Port was tough enough opposition anyway, but the effect of the AFL scheduling decision was a handicap that might have been the final straw that broke the camel's back. Three premierships in a row was great – four would have been even better.

As we learn painfully from time to time, you can't beat City Hall!

42

KNOWING YOUR TIME IS UP

After 20 seasons, and at 56 years of age, tonight would be the last game I would ever coach.

In my previous coaching stint at Collingwood, the club terminated my tenure at the completion of my 10th year in 1995, with one season to run on my contract. The Magpies told me my time was up. I didn't have to make the difficult decision to finish myself.

When the 2008 season came to an end, I was finishing my 10th year as coach of the Brisbane Lions, and again I was contracted for one more season. The big difference at the Lions was that I was still getting total support from the club's board and administration. We were playing the Swans in Sydney in the final home-and-away game. As I sat in my room at the InterContinental hotel on the afternoon of the match, I suddenly made the big decision to sack myself and to retire from coaching. This time it was me who decided my time was up.

When travelling interstate, the afternoon before a night match was always a tense time for me. The match planning had been completed and it was largely private waiting and thinking time, until the team left for the match venue. This particular afternoon my normal introspective soul search became about me and my future. One second I was planning for the Lions' future with me as coach, when suddenly it became obvious to me that the inevitable time to finish my coaching career had arrived. The timing was sudden but the concept was not. Over the previous couple of years the question of when and how my time at the Lions would end had popped in and out of my mind all too often.

It had been a bad week leading into the Sydney game, because our 2008 finals aspirations had ended the previous weekend with a terribly disappointing loss at home against Carlton. After leading by 32 points at the last break, we were embarrassingly overrun as we failed to goal in the last quarter and went down by six points. As coach you always take ownership of the team performance, and as defeats go, this one was about as bad as they get. We'd basically thrown the game away, and with it went any chance of playing finals. This demoralising defeat meant we'd miss the finals for the fourth consecutive season.

At my Monday morning press conference I was asked about my future and responded with my standard line that I'd continue until either I decided to stop or the club terminated my contract. Off the back of my comments, the *Courier-Mail*'s AFL writer, Andrew Hamilton, contacted Lions chairman Tony Kelly to ascertain the club's position on my future. Tony, who had become a close friend, gave his full support, but the fact that he was even asked the question was something I noted with some concern. The club and I had shared a fantastic relationship, and hanging around after outliving my usefulness was something to be avoided at all cost. Better to go a year early than a year late. That was my underlying attitude in all the years I coached, but as the season reached its final week on the field, it was full steam ahead into the last game and the planning for the following year.

We were already planning a major change, with one of our ex-physios, Peter Stanton, returning to the club as full-time high performance manager, overseeing and coordinating our conditioning and medical operation.

On the Friday prior to the Swans game I travelled to Sydney first thing in the morning with Jonathan Brown to attend a Vodafone promotion, and we spent a few hours talking about our operation and what we could do to improve the team. There was no thought at all in my mind that I wouldn't be the 2009 coach.

Browny had been playing hard-ball with the club all season about a long-term contract extension, and he had yet to recommit to the Lions. While I never thought he'd leave, because by nature he is a stayer not a leaver, there was a gigantic offer on the table from Collingwood. We were told the money was around $1,000,000 per season in the salary cap and guaranteed 'work' earnings of another $500,000 in off-field third-party deals. With this kind of option available, he was going to hold out to push the Lions to the absolute upper level of what the club could offer. Nothing wrong with that – a professional footballer getting the best possible contract is fair enough. As I suspect Travis Cloke did at Collingwood in 2012, Browny got a better offer from the Lions late in the year by holding out. He eventually got the fourth year he wanted but the money was still only about two-thirds of the Magpies' total offer.

In one of the many little things that add to an end result, I got a phone call from Gubby on the Saturday morning telling me that Browny had agreed on terms to stay. This was terrific news; he was our marquee player and the symbolism of him leaving would have been terrible for the club. Apart from losing his playing talents, the instability created by his departure would have been very damaging. If Browny had left the Lions, I wouldn't have felt able to resign.

The tipping point came after a conversation with friend and confidant Bruce McAvaney. Since working with him at Channel Seven in the late '90s, I spoke to Bruce regularly about all things football and sport and always valued his counsel. I rang him on the afternoon of the round 22 game from my Sydney hotel room just to chew the fat about our usual sports-related topics. We started talking about knowing when your time is up, and for some reason I asked him how it would sound if I announced that 2009 would be my last year. His reply was that it would sound as if I'd already half-retired.

I hung up the phone and a few minutes later the divide had been crossed. It was now final. After 20 seasons, and at 56 years of age, tonight would be the last game I would ever coach.

While the final decision was made in one moment of clarity, when I think back it had been coming for a while. There had been difficult times after the end of our grand final run from 2001 to 2004. After reaching the summit of the mountain for four consecutive grand finals, the aftermath, when the team suffered a huge fall off the cliff, was hard to stomach for all of us – including me as coach.

Whatever we did in the future would never match our extraordinary recent past. Midway through 2005, Channel Nine commentator

Dermott Brereton summarised our rapid decline in one sentence. He said during one of his calls, 'It's so sad seeing them play; it's like watching the fall of the Roman Empire.' The fall from grace in 12 months was massive.

The transition to the post-premiership era was going to test the whole club, and we weren't up to the challenge. The pruning of the list began as soon as the consecutive premiership run was broken. Aaron Shattock, a 2002 premiership team member restricted by injury to seven senior games in 2004, was traded to Port Adelaide after the Lions were unable to offer him a contract for salary cap reasons. Blake Caracella, a dual premiership player with Essendon (2000) and Brisbane (2003), also felt the salary cap squeeze when he was de-listed. He would later be claimed by Collingwood in the pre-season draft. It was the start of a huge player exodus to come. Of the 2004 grand final team, only 11 players would remain at the club two years later.

The football wheel never stands still and the game's in-built equalisation measures are hard to fight off, unless club recruiters are absolute geniuses or are very lucky. In the last few years, Geelong has been the latest dynasty to fight this ultimately unwinnable battle. Their recruiting operation, headed by Stephen Wells, has done a brilliant job since the turn of the century to recruit a group of players that has kept the Cats up at the very top since 2007; to stay there permanently, his genius will need to continue. Otherwise, the AFL's equalisation policies will eventually bite.

Equalisation has been a valuable plank in the growth of the national competition since the late 1980s, when the AFL Commission adopted the American NFL model of a draft and salary cap to stop the rich and powerful dominating the game. For the modern player, there's also a different type of equalisation, because the fame and fortune has a price: the not so desirable intense public scrutiny and forced lifestyle discipline. Of course, at the elite level there are around 800 players on AFL lists. All receive the scrutiny and forced discipline, while only a small percentage actually get the fame and fortune.

The equalisation process is working to pull the top teams down and to help the bottom teams up. After the Lions had reached four consecutive grand finals, we went into 2005 and beyond with the gigantic challenge of resisting the competition's natural order, which for us was an eventual decline. Football has changed plenty over the years, but one basic stat remains constant. Over a long period of time, winning two out of every three games is the very best that can be achieved. Of those who have coached over 150 games, the highest winning percentage is Tom Hafey with only 64 per cent. At the end of 2004, over the previous four seasons the Lions had won 75 per cent of their matches. The price for that level of sustained success would be an inevitable downturn somewhere in the future.

I think I sensed that our premiership window was being slammed shut when I addressed a post-2004 grand final supporters' function at the Brunswick Street Oval the morning after the game, as my off-the-cuff words expressed what I was feeling. I urged the fans to enjoy what we'd shared over the previous few years, because it might never happen again. At the time, my thoughts were more of realism than pessimism, but my subconscious antenna was accurate, because the next 12 months was a gradual decline that saw us plummet from grand finalists to the worst team in the competition by season's end. We started quite well, but the final three matches were horrible.

The aftermath of the grand final loss was a five-game suspension for Jonathan Brown and three games for Simon Black. As the late-20s and early-30s veterans were starting to fade, we'd desperately need to find an even greater contribution from our younger stars. Added to the retirement of Alastair Lynch, Craig McRae and Shaun Hart, the absence of the pair for the early part of the season was a big hurdle to overcome.

The reservoir of confidence built over the previous few seasons held us in good stead early in the year. A win over St Kilda in round one was followed by narrow losses to Port Adelaide and the Sydney Swans. The difference between winning and losing close games isn't huge in terms of practical on-field performance, but it's gigantic in terms of what it does to the team psyche. Then when we were thrashed by Hawthorn and the West Coast Eagles, after five rounds we were struggling with a 1–4 win–loss ratio.

We needed something to change the flow of the season and we got it when Jonathan Brown returned from suspension in round six against Essendon in Melbourne. There was no rustiness as he played quite possibly his career-best game with a totally dominant 14 contested marks and eight goals. And that was with him spending most of the last quarter on the interchange bench.

Being his first game for the season, I was concerned about not over-fatiguing and injuring him, so with the result decided we took him off. I rang down to the bench to congratulate Jonathan on an outstanding effort and to tell him that we thought it best to give him a short game. The big fella was not happy. He could see a 10-goal game coming and wanted to 'fill his boots', as Allan Jeans would say.

Browny was at the peak of his powers, a 23-year-old in his fifth season with the football world at his feet, a hard-running strong courageous power forward who could dominate matches as few before him. He had the natural endurance of the good midfielders and would join the elite runners in the training drills – and as a great competitor he'd try to beat them. He was also a giant of a man of over 100 kilograms, and keeping up with the lightly built medium-sizers came at a great cost. About halfway through 2005 the dreaded symptoms of groin soreness that became clinically known as osteitis pubis struck him down. The effect of this complaint is not so crippling that you can't play, but it severely limits your ability to train and you get sorer and sorer as matches progress.

We'd become terribly reliant on our young centre half-forward and even used him as an emergency centre square player if the team needed a lift. At the Gabba, this meant putting him into the hard centre cricket pitch area. Despite ground curator Kevin Mitchell's best endeavours, the wicket block was either muddy or extremely hard. No wonder the Lions' ruck brigade had careers shortened through injury.

I'm sure that Browny throwing his big body around in the very hard centre of the Gabba wasn't ideal. Whatever we did or didn't do, the end result was that, in the middle of his prime years, he had a losing battle with injury. He got on the field 14 times in 2005 but was severely limited in the second half of the year. In round 21 our finals chances ended and so did Browny's season. The soreness had become too bad to continue playing.

Then in 2006, after he played the first 10 games, a back fracture ended his year before halfway. Our performances during 2005 and

2006 became unhealthily linked to Browny's fitness and both fell away badly.

Our decline during 2005 can best be illustrated by the contrast between what happened in round one and round 22, both games against St Kilda. Our last home-and-away round of the season against the Saints was at the Docklands stadium on the Saturday night. That day had started really well. I was at a midday ceremony at the MCG where a life-size statue of me in my playing days was unveiled outside gate 8 on the concourse behind the Great Southern Stand. When MCC chief executive Stephen Gough phoned me earlier in the year to tell me I was the next recipient of a statue outside the great stadium, it was an enormous thrill. I've always said the MCG is my favourite place in Melbourne and it has been the venue for so many special times in my football life. Having my statue among the great names in the ground's Parade of Champions is the single greatest honour I've ever received.

That part of the day was a career highlight; the Saturday night was a disaster. In the opening game of 2005 we beat St Kilda by 23 points, while 22 weeks later they creamed us by 139 points. A hundred and sixty-two points is one gigantic turnaround. It was an embarrassing evening at the footy as the Saints kicked 21 goals after quarter-time. After being similarly thrashed by 84 points by the Swans in round 20, we'd degenerated into a rabble. We had 13 premiership players in the team so we had the proven names, but the physical capabilities had disappeared and so had the energy and fight. The unwanted but not uncommon human cycle of lack of hope leading to lack of physical energy had hit us hard. The post-premiership era was going to be ugly. However, just how ugly – now that would take us all by surprise.

Personally it was a mixed year. My mother, Lorna, passed away on the afternoon before our round 18 fixture against the Western Bulldogs in Melbourne on 30 July. It was the only game I never actually coached in my 20 years as a senior coach. Mum took ill late in the week, was hospitalised on the Thursday, and was in a bad way when I visited her at the Mornington Hospital on the Friday.

I completed the Friday pre-game planning with the team, but when I went to the hospital on the Saturday morning she'd lapsed into a coma. It was obvious she was passing away, so I rang Gubby to advise him that it would be better if one of the assistants took over the match-day coaching. Surrounded by her three sons and seven grand-children, who she loved dearly, Mum died about 4 pm. My partner, Deb, had flown to Melbourne from Brisbane during the afternoon. I met her back at the Parkview Hotel, where I had the surreal experience of monitoring the game of the team I coached on the radio. It was not good listening when the Bulldogs won by 28 points.

On a brighter note, Deb and I got married at the end of the season. She had planned the wedding while I was preoccupied with my coaching. At the wedding reception I only half-joked that we should have swapped roles, because the reception went much better than the Lions' football season.

It was at the end of 2005 I first asked myself whether my coaching was part of the solution at the Brisbane Lions, or part of the problem. I was still getting total support from the club, but after finishing at Collingwood I'd concluded that, in principle, six to eight years was about my optimum coaching tenure. By this time, I'd completed seven seasons as the Lions' coach. While I gave no real consideration to finishing my tenure, maybe I should have. The 2006 campaign was an even worse year on the field than 2005 and diabolical off it.

This was the year we endured the agonising, drawn-out process that resulted in Jason Akermanis being sacked from the club. Every second Lions-supporting kid had Aker's number 12 on their back, so forcing out one of our most popular players with the fans was a terrible last resort.

There was no one starting point in 2006 that led to the final decision late in the season. As I've mentioned, if anything the difficulties with Aker began after he won the Brownlow Medal in 2001. Going into 2006, there was no real sign of the imminent disaster to come. Aker had won the 2005 club championship and, for this reason if no other, I decided we should bring him into our player leadership group. He was now one of our more experienced players and I thought he was better in the tent than looking on enviously from outside. I spoke to a few of the Lions' core leaders about my thinking – Michael Voss, Justin Leppitsch, Chris Scott and Jonathan Brown – and while they had plenty of reservations the decision to elevate him into the leadership group was agreed to.

That was all fairly positive but from the beginning of the season his natural individualism, combined with his outspoken media comments, grew the occasional irritation into an almost-weekly charade. As the 2006 season developed, the manageable became unmanageable. Why that happened, and what I could have done to stop it, has been a bit of a bugbear ever since.

I could never work out whether the series of conflicts that arose with Aker were just random or cleverly planned. He was already contracted for the 2007 season, but I think he saw himself as the next Sam Newman and just maybe wanted to get to Melbourne to pursue the greater AFL media opportunities down south. Perhaps getting out of his contract was part of the plan. He was certainly giving his media employers great bang for their buck and me plenty of headaches. It seemed like I was spending more time on Aker issues than the rest of the team combined. The media loved the 'coach in conflict with star player' story, but my relationship with Aker wasn't why he got sacked.

The first point of no return came after we got beaten in round seven at the Gabba by the Sydney Swans. We'd won only one of our five games, so we were really struggling. As I finished my post-match address, Michael Voss got to his feet and implored the players to stick together and be careful about their public comments, so as not to inflame our situation. Aker didn't heed his captain's request and was his usual vocal self during his following week's media work. Now the you-know-what really hit the fan. It was one thing for Aker to make life difficult for his coach, but defying his captain's authority couldn't be tolerated, so the match committee decided to omit him from the team to play Hawthorn on the Gold Coast the following Saturday night.

Michael and I spoke to Aker before Thursday training to advise him of what we were doing and why. He sat there quite passively but with no hint of apology. I'm sure he thought that we had to change, not him. Vossy was concerned that the press were building up the coach/player conflict, so he suggested that as captain he should speak to the media before training to announce our decision. I agreed.

That was a bad decision. I should have spoken to the press instead of Michael, or maybe not have made it such a big deal by giving the press notice of Aker's omission. I guess we knew that once he was told, his press contacts would know soon after.

Naturally, Aker being dropped for disciplinary reasons was big news, which smothered another emotional omission, that of our triple premiership centre half-back, Justin Leppitsch. I've often spoken of all players being positioned somewhere in the spectrum from core at one end to consultant at the other. By my terminology, core players are the heart and soul of the group and they represent and shape the team culture. They *are* the team.

'Consultant' is my description of players who provide their individual talents without giving much back to the group. They can still be extremely valuable in the winning effort, but do not contribute a whole lot to the team fabric. As an example at the modern Collingwood, Nick Maxwell and Scott Pendlebury appear to be definite core players, while from the outside Dane Swan looks more like a consultant. Swan's talents undoubtedly help the Magpies on the field, but he doesn't appear to be a great influence on the team culture, and I suspect is a management challenge for coach Nathan Buckley.

During the Lions' premiership era no player was more core to the team than Leppa, so leaving him out was quite a wrench for us all. While he wasn't in pain, the aftermath of a crushed disc in his back that had ended his 2005 season after 14 games was crushing the nerve to his calf muscle. The result was a subconscious hobble that badly affected his speed and his ability to play at high tempo – only he didn't know it. After he really struggled in the Swans match we discussed his future, but he was determined to keep going. Purely from a playing value perspective, we couldn't justify his position in the senior team. With Aker dropped to our reserves to play against Southport in the curtain-raiser to the seniors playing the Hawks, Leppa felt compelled to take his place in the team, so as not to appear too 'big' to play in the reserves. After that one last game it was obvious his injury wasn't going to get any better and the following week he formally retired at only 30 years of age. I had no hesitation in inviting him onto our coaching panel the following year.

There was a fair irony that Jason Akermanis and Justin Leppitsch were relegated to the Lions reserves in the same week, although for very different reasons. After Aker won the Brownlow in 2001 he went on a post-season speaking tour, and in search of content he used a series of 'dumb' jokes as part of his routine. It got back to the club that, for some insane reason, he was using Leppa as the butt of the jokes as the dumb bloke. As you can imagine, Leppa and many other people around the club were angry and bewildered as to how Aker could be so disrespectful to a team-mate. If there was a starting point to the tension between Aker and many of our core players, this was probably it.

Yet despite this personal slight, Leppa was able to put his feelings secondary to the team's best interests by having the core-player attitude that we should use Aker's on-field ability to help us win more games of footy. The Lions senior players thinking of their outspoken team-mate as a consultant who was there to assist the core of the team helped with this aim.

Regardless of what some people who have never managed anybody might think, a coach's job is to be the guardian of the group's best interests. We only took the stand of omitting Aker from the team because we believed our core players wanted us to. However, for me personally, having accepted the ultimate responsibility for the decision and after observing the subsequent media and fan reaction, this was no ordinary game. Like it or not, fair or unfair, how the team performed against Hawthorn would be the ultimate evidence that our fans would judge us on. On that basis it must have been a good decision, because a really spirited performance led to a seven-goal win.

As we moved forward there were only three choices: sack Aker completely, give him another week or two penance in the reserves or bring him back into the fold quickly. I pushed to bring him straight back into the team. I figured that if we were ever going to get him back in sync with our core players, it had to be done immediately. That might have been a mistake, because in terms of rehabilitation the one-week suspension had no long-term effect.

The die had been cast and the media interest and commentary was like the third party in a marriage break-up – it made reconciliation almost impossible. The relationship between player and club spluttered along for a couple of months. Aker believed he was right and everyone else was wrong. The end finally came after round 18. Around lunchtime at a café near the Gabba on the Thursday before our round 19 clash against Hawthorn at the MCG, an agitated club captain Michael Voss walked up to me and asked whether I'd seen the *Herald Sun*. Aker had done an extensive double page question and answer interview with journalist Damian Barrett, and as Vossy put it in blunt terms, 'Mate, he's pissing in our faces.' The content of the article was nothing that untoward, but it finally tipped everything over the edge. A bubbling volcano of discontent surrounding Aker and all the key people around the club was about to erupt.

We decided to convene a meeting of the player leadership group, along with all of our coaches, to thrash out what we would do. There were six players and six coaches, including myself. The coach with the responsibility of being Aker's mentor in 2006 was Daryn Cresswell, who wasn't totally sold on the idea, but everyone else was firm that it was time to remove him permanently from the group and therefore from the club. I spoke to Lions CEO Mike Bowers and chairman Tony Kelly about what had transpired, and they were fully supportive of the action we were proposing. The whole Aker circus had involved the club's senior management for much of the season. It's hard to think that one player could exasperate to utter frustration the key people in a whole club, but, with the help of his media cronies, that is exactly what he did to the Brisbane Lions in 2006.

Finally, I made the phone call to tell Aker of the decision that we wouldn't be picking him for the rest of the year, and that we would trade him at year's end. Aker thought it was my idea, that I was the driver of his departure, and if I wanted I could get him reinstated. I usually subscribe to the belief that effective management is convincing others to make the decision you would have made yourself. However, truth be known, on this one I followed rather than led. Aker had worn me down and I knew I was too negatively biased to make an informed judgement. So when the footy area's management group made a unanimous decision to end the association, I was happy to concur.

It was probably always destined to end badly, but, given Aker's rocky relationship with many of our influential players, getting the most out of his playing abilities was one of my proudest management achievements. With my coaxing, our core players – led by the team-first attitude of Michael Voss and Justin Leppitsch – convinced themselves that our noble purpose was to be the best football team we could be. That was what we existed for.

They knew Aker's on-field talents helped us win games of footy, so putting up with his individualism and loyalties to his media gigs was a worthwhile price to pay. They waited patiently in the shadows without complaint while he did his trademark post-win handstand in the centre-circle spotlight, a routine the fans absolutely loved. As a marketing tool for the Lions and the sport, he was fantastic.

My part of the deal was to manage the occasions when he crossed the line into embarrassing his team-mates or the club. Initially, when issues regularly arose, he was apologetic or claimed to have been misquoted, but by 2006 he was now in his late 20s and not prepared to be managed. Ultimately, the 'TEAM' motto of Together Everyone Achieves More applies very well to the fact that we use the people around us to help achieve our aspirations, and the partnership between Jason Akermanis and the Brisbane Lions was, despite the many potholes along the journey, very good for both parties. Whatever Aker had to give as a footballer, I'm convinced the Lions got by far the best of him. I would love to have managed the partnership to a more convivial end, but that was a challenge too big for me.

After the final Aker episode, we again beat Hawthorn, but then the team fell apart with five consecutive losses to leave us fourth-last with only seven wins for the season. In the final match against St Kilda at the Gabba, they creamed us by nine goals. It was this game that convinced me that our great captain, Michael Voss, was nearing the end – and that was with him being close enough to our best player on the night.

As usual, Vossy tried his guts out and got plenty of the footy, but it was all on heart and will. To my eye his speed, acceleration and reflexes were on a rapid slide. Every disposal was under pressure and another year would only make him slower. He was already contracted for 2007, but as such a wonderful warrior and competitor, I was concerned about how his Thinker/Enforcer type personality would handle the inevitable decline. Champion players with a dominant streak, such as Vossy, have a very frustrating time shifting from centre stage to the support cast. The mental strain is very difficult to handle. Maybe I was judging Vossy's situation from my own late-career experience, but I was already sensing a growing grumpiness in his normally cheerful demeanour.

About a week after the season ended we caught up over a coffee at his house in Mount Gravatt to talk about the future, both for him and the team. He was quite forthright in his views about the team's coaching and preparation systems and that personally he didn't feel fully prepared when he ran onto the field. It sounded to me like an ageing champion blaming his frustrations on others. That was not the Michael Voss I knew. After thinking about our conversation for a day, I rang him the following morning with the feedback that he was talking like a player who was ready to retire. Nothing definitive was decided, but he now knew my thoughts.

He was a professional footballer with a year to go on his contract, which, like that of many Lions players, had been heavily back-ended. Vossy eventually announced his retirement after the club agreed to pay him the vast majority of the remaining year of his contract. This meant that, while he'd officially retired, he remained on our list and in our salary cap for the 2007 season while commentating on the Channel Ten television coverage.

The Lions' premiership window closed after 2004 but the retirement of the triple premiership captain signalled the definitive end of an era. He retired with the universal respect he deserved, because no player has been more valuable to his football club than Michael Voss was to the Brisbane Lions. It also meant that history was now ready to repeat itself. Like Tony Shaw at Collingwood, from the day Vossy stopped playing he was destined to replace me as coach. The only question was when.

It was always in the back of my mind that the playing list Tony inherited from me at Collingwood was mediocre at best. Maybe I was wrong but it seemed that staying around the Lions to manage the many retiring premiership stars and to get the club started on the attempted rebuild was the right thing to do. When Michael retired, any thought of him coming onto our coaching staff was quickly dismissed. The Tony Shaw lesson had been well learnt by Gubby and myself. Firstly, two bulls in the same paddock can create a confused chain of command, and secondly, it's better to experience life away from the football home where you've grown up. Preferably at another AFL club, but working in the media allows you to watch a lot of footy and you really have to concentrate hard on what you're seeing. The media was to be Vossy's immediate future.

In total, five premiership players retired – Vossy, Brad Scott, Clark Keating, Justin Leppitsch and Mal Michael. Mal did play again but not for the Lions. His exit was very strange. He was starting to struggle and I guess the signs were ominous the day at the Gabba, when, in possession under little pressure about 15 metres out from the opposition goal, he turned and blasted a drop punt into the back of the grandstand to concede an amazing behind. The question 'What was he thinking?' crossed the mind of every person in the stadium, including me. It was one of the stranger things I have seen happen on a football field.

Mal told us just after the season ended that he was retiring, because he had some lucrative business opportunities in Papua New Guinea. He subsequently relinquished the final year of his contract, which we were quite happy about because this relieved pressure from the balancing of our salary cap. Then, to our surprise, in late October he was living back in Melbourne with his wife, Kim, when he announced a comeback with Essendon. There was a suspicion that the whole sequence of events was an elaborate plan. It didn't need to be, because Mal looked to be gone as a player and we would have cleared him to get rid of his payment from our salary cap if he'd asked. I honestly believe the PNG business opportunity fell over and playing again was his only way of earning a decent living.

The 2007 season was an improvement but we still missed the finals by a couple of wins. Along the way we had a couple of memorable victories. We were 10-to-1 outsiders against the Eagles in Perth in round 14 after not winning for seven weeks. Going into the match, the realistic aim was more about avoiding a thrashing than actually winning the game. When I looked at the time clock with five minutes to go and we were four goals in front, for the first time that whole week I thought we might win. With two minutes to go we were still four goals in front and the unlikely win was now a reality, so I went down to the interchange bench to enjoy the moment. When the siren went with the Lions 27 points in front, it was the type of enormous buzz that makes the competitive anguish totally worthwhile.

A few weeks later against Collingwood in round 17 at the MCG, we won by an amazing 15 goals. The Magpies were a good team in 2007 and restricted the rampant Geelong to a narrow five-point win in the preliminary final a couple of months later. But this Saturday night a new-look Lions team with only eight players from the premiership era completely overwhelmed Collingwood. We looked to be regrouping and ready to push towards the finals again. The crowd was officially 45,096, but late in the final term I reckon only about 5000 remained, and there was very little black and white to be seen. That was a great night at the footy. There was not a lot of joy in 2007 but, after bottoming out in 2006, we were at least looking to be on the up.

In the big picture about my personal situation, there were a couple of issues in play at the Lions that were making it difficult to assess the right time to end my coaching tenure. Firstly, as had happened at Hawthorn and Collingwood, I'd fallen in love with the club and my role within it. While I was well paid for my services, my involvement wasn't like a job. I didn't just work at the Lions, I was part of the Lions and the club was part of me. Emotionally it was more a labour of love, and voluntarily resigning was akin to ending the relationship with your family. Knowing when either the club or myself would benefit from me moving on was just too difficult to judge.

Secondly, I was still getting total support from Lions CEO Mike Bowers and the board and chairman Tony Kelly. Usually we know our time might be up by the signs coming from those who employ us, but there was no indication the club was losing faith in me as the best man for the job. However, Tony and the Kelly family had become very close friends, which would make it difficult for him to be unbiased about the situation. Consequently it was in the forefront of my thinking never to put Tony in a position where he had to sack me, because every friendship gets rocked by this scenario.

So as I entered my 10th season as Lions coach, I knew the right time was approaching but it didn't seem to be now, so we all moved on with no particular end date in mind. We did the normal post-season process of reviewing, planning and recruiting, with the urge to find a better way in everything we did as strong as ever. The annual exodus of premiership-era players continued when, after 2007, Chris Scott, Chris Johnson, Beau McDonald and Richard Hadley all departed the club.

With the salary cap squeeze easing a little, we traded a young ruckman, Cameron Wood, to Collingwood for pick 14, which we traded on to Melbourne for the experienced 27-year-old midfielder Travis Johnstone. With that pick 14, Melbourne drafted Jack Grimes, who is now one of the Demons' co-captains. Upon reflection later in the season, I concluded that swapping an early draft pick for an experienced player meant I was coaching for the present, when I should have been thinking more long term. This was one of the factors that influenced my decision to resign at season's end.

Recruiting Travis was my choice but drafting the untried talent is delegated to the recruiters. The facts are that the Lions premiership team was drafted in the '90s by Scott Clayton and Kinnear Beatson. The next decade the club has not drafted very well. Not since Jonathan Brown came to the club as a father/son pick in 2000 have the Lions drafted a player who has made an All-Australian team. The recruiters might blame the coaching/development programs, but the bottom line is that good quality teams have a big nucleus of this level of on-field performers.

Going into 2008, the Lions needed a few of our next-generation players to bridge this gap. The most likely were Mitch Clark, Jed Adcock, Jamie Charman, Daniel Merrett, Josh Drummond, Jared Brennan and, after a terrific burst of form in 2007, our livewire small forward Rhan Hooper. Rhan was the subject of a big offer from Richmond in the off-season, and while we paid overs to keep him, he became another wasted talent. His non-football mates in Ipswich were a distraction that wrecked a promising career.

The team had played some exciting footy in patches during 2007 and the future looked brighter than it had for a number of years. In the early part of the season this optimism was flowing into on-field performance. We were eight wins, five losses when we headed to the MCG to play bottom-placed Melbourne, who had won only one game for the season. When the Demons rolled us by a point after kicking the last two goals of the game, my post-match attitude was a good impersonation of the typical non-thinking yelling angry coach. That day was like Murphy's Law – what could go wrong did go wrong. We even had a 50-metre penalty paid against our physio Nathan Carloss – with a resultant goal – for running through the mark in front of the interchange bench.

The season then spiralled down badly and after throwing away late-game leads against Richmond in round 17, and again the following week against the Kangaroos, we looked like a team that was choking when the crunch came. A coach has to take that as a reflection of the effectiveness of his teaching. I thought the words were being said but the ears definitely weren't listening. I walked down to the rooms after the Kangaroos loss and berated the players for embarrassing them-selves by failing to remain composed under pressure and for a lack of on-field leadership. As I arrived in the locker room to confront the disappointed players, I yelled, 'You are the laughing stock of the whole football world.'

Almost immediately I knew I'd gone too far. I was blaming, not helping. I then tried to rebuild the shattered morale, but in hindsight the whole situation was telling me that the group was in need of the fresh start only a new coach can offer. So many times over the years, I've seen the honeymoon period that a first-year coach can give his team. The Lions of 2008 were in need of that new beginning – I just hadn't realised it yet.

On the coaching front there had been some discussions about the future and a potential succession plan. Around the middle of the season the Gold Coast Suns were being formed from scratch to join the AFL competition in 2011. The media speculation was that Michael Voss headed the list in the new club's search for its first senior coach. So I suggested to Tony Kelly that if the club wanted their premiership captain to be my successor, they'd better assess the options, because if he took the Suns job they might lose the chance. After a few weeks of due diligence and board discussions, Tony came back with the decision that the club wanted Vossy to be the Lions' next senior coach.

Tony and I met with Vossy to inform him of this development and to talk about a potential succession plan. He was open to the general concept and we decided to go our separate ways to have a think about what might be possible. At the next Lions board meeting the matter was up for discussion, but the sticking point was whether I could categorically nominate my retirement date at that time. When I hesitated about doing this, and the board didn't push me to do so, the whole idea was put on hold.

We all thought a one-year succession plan was the maximum, although Gubby wasn't a fan of the concept at all. He must have changed his mind. He is now at Greater Western Sydney as football operations manager, and the Giants embarked on a succession plan in 2013 when Leon Cameron came to the club initially as an assistant, with the agreement to replace Kevin Sheedy as senior coach in 2014.

Tony advised Vossy of the club's current position but, although there was nothing specific, Michael now knew the Lions thought of him as their next senior coach. While the exact date was uncertain, this knowledge would allow Vossy to plan his life accordingly. He accepted a position to assist John Worsfold at the West Coast Eagles in 2009. The move to Perth would never eventuate.

While the specific date for me finishing as the Lions coach was determined in the Sydney InterContinental hotel before we played the Swans that Saturday in 2008, when I look back, the sequence of events all led to that point. From that spur-of-the-moment decision to retire, it was business as usual going into that night's match. I saw no point in telling anyone, including my wife, Deb. Advising people could wait until the following day back in Brisbane. I must admit it was strange going to the footy knowing it would be the last game I'd ever coach, because I wasn't just retiring from the Lions job but from the coaching lifestyle.

When I reflect back on my two coaching stints, there were common denominators. I seemed to be good at coming in with fresh eyes and working from that starting base to create a successful environment and a successful footy team. At both Collingwood and the Brisbane Lions the success came for five or six years, but the team performance tailed off later in my tenure. So I conclude that I was not so good at critiquing and altering what my coaching/management had built. The results say that was the case. Either that or the playing talents at both clubs deteriorated in the final few seasons I was coach – who knows for sure?

I told Deb what was happening when I arrived back from Sydney and then headed to our training ground at Coorparoo, where the Lions reserves were playing an elimination final in the QAFL competition. There were two people I would tell first. My football department partner and confidant Gubby Allan, and club chairman and friend Tony Kelly.

Gubby and I found a quiet spot where he started talking about future planning until I stopped him in his tracks and blurted out that I was finishing. We then found Tony who I told the same thing. There were no ifs, buts or maybes – the decision was final. The Allan, Kelly and Matthews families had dinner together that night and have remained good friends ever since.

Tony made one stop between Coorparoo and our dinner, to advise Vossy of what had transpired. The club had already done their due diligence to know they wanted Michael to succeed me as senior coach, so his appointment would be a formality, as would the Eagles releasing him to accept the job. It's standard practice for AFL clubs to allow their assistant coaches to break an existing contract to accept a senior role. I resigned publicly at a hastily convened press conference on the Monday morning and Vossy was officially in place by the end of the following day. That Tuesday was the last time I've ever been in the Lions downstairs office and dressing-room area at the Gabba.

Once my second premiership captain had done the press conference announcing him as the new Lions coach, I hastily cleaned out my office, kept a small box of personal papers and turfed the rest. There was no angst with anyone and I left on good terms with everyone at the club. But I was still a bit melancholy walking out for the last time. One day the club is the very centre of your existence, and the next you no longer belong. I knew the deal because I'd been through it all before when I finished at Collingwood at the end of the 1995 season.

The final realisation that the time was right might seem to have come suddenly, but it had been coming for quite a while. There hasn't been one moment since when I've regretted making the call to stop coaching. For all the mixed emotions, I'd basically come to the simple realisation that I no longer wanted to accept the challenge.

43

FROM THEN TILL NOW

Being paid to go to the footy and to talk about it is like being
paid to go on holidays.

Playing, and then coaching, has dominated my existence for the whole of my adult life, so since I retired at the end of 2008 it's been refreshing to observe football without a heavy emotional stake in the result of a game. There's no doubt I had an insular and tunnel vision attitude as a player and that largely continued when I coached. Both roles involved different requirements but the common denominator was the need for a chameleon-type quality to adjust and become what I needed to be to get the job effectively done.

It's only when I finished coaching that I started to look at football without a playing or coaching bias. Removed from that week-to-week competitive cycle, I can reflect on the massive changes that have taken place in the football world during the 40-odd years since I arrived at Hawthorn as a starry-eyed teenager back in 1969.

It has been a story of non-stop evolution. From my close viewing period from about 1970, the change was constant, but over the last decade or so the speed of the evolution has accelerated rapidly. As the AFL has moved from being a pure sporting competition in the '70s and '80s into the sports entertainment industry of the last 20 years, I reckon the game has changed more in the last decade than in the previous 30 put together. The evolution will never stop, so the game's administrators and rule makers never start with a clean slate. Management would be much more effective if they could.

For example, if we could start again there's no way the AFL would plan an 18-team national competition, and definitely not with nine clubs based in Melbourne. The AFL Commission was formed out of the Victorian Football League and the national expansion began from expanding the VFL base. If we could begin from scratch, a 14-team national competition would be ideal. The Swans have been in Sydney for 30 years and have won a couple of premierships in that time, but don't seem any more elevated in the city's sporting landscape than they were in the late 1980s – likewise the Brisbane Bears/ Lions since the club started in south-east Queensland back in 1987. From my observations, both the Lions and the AFL sport in general achieved a significant rise in profile during the premiership era of the early 2000s. Unfortunately, these days neither is any higher on the popularity scale than it was prior to that period of exceptional success.

The arrogant thought that because many of us from the southern states love the sport it will automatically take over up north – on the 'If we build it, they will come' principle – has yet to be proven correct. I've lived in Brisbane now for 15 years, and even with the recent introduction of the Gold Coast Suns the status and popularity of the sport seem to show little visible growth. The hoped for future generational change that was the logic behind the AFL expanding with second clubs in Sydney and south-east Queensland is still nothing more than an optimistic theory.

So, given Australian population bases with a proven AFL interest – the southern states – and those areas that do not – New South Wales and Queensland – I would think that six clubs from Melbourne, one from Geelong, two from Perth, two from Adelaide, maybe two from Sydney – because of the city's huge population base – and one from Brisbane would be the best mix for a sustainable national competition. Even then, expecting the northern clubs ever to be financially self-sufficient over the decades as they experience inevitable performance fluctuations is extremely optimistic.

In my view, having the second team in Sydney is a calculated punt but one worth taking in an attempt to create a greater presence in Australia's largest city. The current television rights deal is to play nine games each round, so the immediate future of the 18-team competition is locked in. However, down the track removing the cost of running the extra four clubs above the 14 that I believe is the ideal number would financially balance out the reduction in the TV rights for only seven games. Surely the eighth and ninth games each round are just not that valuable to the broadcasters.

The evolution of the AFL has seen the Commission using the national competition as the cash cow to fund the whole sport, which means plenty comes off the top before the teams get their share. With the off-field arms race in non-player football department spending having skyrocketed recently, and the AFL not prepared to impose a cap to quell this explosion, the subsidising of many clubs will continue to be required into the foreseeable future.

MY BEST TEAM: 1969 TO THE PRESENT

The development of footballers from the part-time amateurs of the late '60s to the modern full-time professional has seen a mind-boggling level of improvement. Each decade, players are better than the generation before. The very best improve a little but the average player improves enormously. If we found a time machine and transferred the champions of the '70s into a current match, they'd be a long way off the pace. As the human gene pool has not altered that much, it must be totally about the vastly superior conditioning and preparation of the modern player.

When I retired from playing at the end of 1985, I nominated Malcolm Blight as the best player of my era. At the same time I picked the best team of that period. To remove any bias, I excluded my Hawthorn team-mates from being considered.

MY BEST TEAM: 1969–85

B: Ian Nankervis, Geoff Southby, Gary Dempsey
HB: Bruce Doull, Ross Glendinning, Neale Daniher
C: Robert Flower, Geoff Raines, Wayne Schimmelbusch
HF: Malcolm Blight, Royce Hart, Alex Jesaulenko
F: Roger Merrett, Bernie Quinlan, Kevin Bartlett
FOLL: Len Thompson, Tim Watson, Barry Cable
INTER: Simon Madden, Francis Bourke

To embark on the same exercise for the period from 1969 until the end of 2012, and this time also include players from the three clubs where I played or coached, I would now nominate Wayne Carey as the most valuable player I've ever seen.

It's difficult to judge players from one generation to the next, let alone over a 40-year period. Those of us whose highlights include a little of the old black-and-white footage want it all destroyed, because the speed, power, athleticism and ball skills that we currently see make us old-timers embarrassed by comparison. The modern football athlete is outstanding, and he will be even better next decade. On this basis, the current proven stars like Lance Franklin, Chris Judd and Gary Ablett junior are the best players I've ever seen.

However, when rating players, or when picking best-ever teams, I think it's fair to judge players on their performance and longevity in the era they played. That's what I've attempted to do. Given that this team is being selected in 2013, I've put it together in positional groupings more akin to modern football. This entails picking seven defenders, five forwards and 10 midfielders. The high interchange rotations mean that it is now a 22-player team (I'll ignore the substitute situation) all playing similar match time. As a coach, getting my players to chase and tackle was always the first priority. For this exercise, though, defensive abilities were largely ignored, in favour of the fantastic contest winners and superb users of the footy. The slight exception to this policy was picking Jason Dunstall at full-forward. Jason was a great goal-kicker, but it was his defensive forward work that put him ahead of Peter Hudson for the spearhead role.

MY BEST TEAM: 1969 TO THE PRESENT

Seven defenders (six on-field and one alternating off interchange): A strong defence is built around a good full-back. As a whole, the group needs to control its back 50 and then attack on the rebound. All defenders must be good one-on-one or they'll be dragged deep in defence and eventually be found wanting.

Back-fifty Defenders: Full-back: Stephen Silvagni; Second tall: Matthew Scarlett; Small: Gavin Wanganeen
Half-backs: Tall: Peter Knights; Medium/tall: Bruce Doull; Rebounders: Nathan Buckley and Andrew McLeod

Ten midfielders (a couple are designated forwards at any one time): The elite midfield needs a balance of structure organisers, strong inside getters who distribute to the fast-running and skilful ball carriers. I personally like a few big midfielders to build the group around.

Ruck: Simon Madden (picked only one – Dean Cox and Len
    Thompson would be next in line)
Organiser/Inside Getters: Michael Voss, Greg Williams
All-rounders: James Hird, Malcolm Blight, Tim Watson, Chris Judd
Ball Carriers: Kevin Bartlett, Peter Matera, Gary Ablett Junior

Five forwards (one alternating off interchange): A well-balanced forward group will have a couple of hard-running power forwards who can play either up-field or close to goal, and forward-50 targets who are strong overhead, provide good second effort at ground level, and have conversion class and flair. A high quality small forward who also has the speed and will to chase and pressure is always valuable but I can't find a spot for that type – Cyril Rioli, for example – ahead of the selected players.

Running Power Forwards: Wayne Carey, Lance Franklin
Forward-50 Targets: Jason Dunstall, Gary Ablett Senior
Medium: Peter Daicos

MY BEST TEAM (1969 TO THE PRESENT) IN TRADITIONAL TEAM-SHEET POSITIONING
B: Gavin Wanganeen, Stephen Silvagni, Matthew Scarlett
HB: Nathan Buckley, Peter Knights, Andrew McLeod
C: Peter Matera, Michael Voss, Malcolm Blight
HF: Chris Judd, Wayne Carey, Kevin Bartlett
F: Gary Ablett Senior, Jason Dunstall, Peter Daicos
FOLL: Simon Madden, Tim Watson, Gary Ablett Junior
INTER: Bruce Doull, Lance Franklin, James Hird, Greg Williams
COACH: David Parkin

I'd be happy to put this team up against any other group of players from the same era.

THE PLAYER EVOLUTION: 1969 TO THE PRESENT

As a player I never got the massive amounts of money available these days, but I wouldn't swap my time playing in the 1970s and '80s era of less onerous preparation disciplines for the pressure-cooker environment of modern footy. Playing was once a passion and a hobby; now it's a livelihood that is only poor form or a bad injury away from an abrupt ending. The mental strain is much greater on the current player. On the professional footballer issue, surely it's only a matter of time before unlimited free agency – say, four years after being drafted – is introduced. Every other worker in the community has the basic human right to choose their employer. So should footballers.

Many rules have been altered to make football safer to play, and most of the rough stuff has been officiated out of the game over the last couple of decades. At the elite AFL level there is undoubtedly less deliberate violence, but as players have become increasingly quicker, stronger and braver, the incidental contact has made the game even more dangerous. If the powerful high-speed human missiles – which is what the modern footballers have become – played under the contact rules of the 1970s, players would likely be killed.

THE CHANGING COACHING ROLE: 1969 TO THE PRESENT

The job of the senior coach has changed enormously from the 1960s and '70s era of Ron Barassi and John Kennedy to the large coaching panels of the modern AFL club. While the senior coach is still the figurehead – and the place where the buck stops – the role now is more about coordination and delegation to the numerous assistant coaches. At Collingwood in 1986 I reckon I did 95 per cent of the coaching. By 2008 at the Brisbane Lions, with four full-time assistants, my personal hands-on contribution was down to maybe 50 per cent. I much preferred the senior coaching role in the part-time era to the panel system of many assistants that has evolved with full-time football, which requires a much greater need to delegate.

In fact, some of the by-products of full-time footy have made the coach's core role of assimilating the individual into a cohesive team significantly more difficult. As player payments increased during the 1990s, player managers came into vogue. Now every player has a manager who takes 3–4 per cent of his match payments and looks out for his individual interests. There is also a well-resourced and powerful AFL Players Association now in place. These entities help the individual, but do not care much about the team cause. The latest stage in the evolution away from coach/management control is club-introduced player leadership groups, who are empowered with the responsibility of making many decisions on team rules and disciplining team-mates.

In theory, player empowerment and responsibility leading to greater ownership of the team is valid. However, greater player involvement in the running of the team – which has become normal in the modern era – can dilute the basic principle that was the John Kennedy mantra back in 1969, and which was a key plank of my football philosophy when I joined the Lions at the end of 1998. The chain of command at a football club is best served by the understanding and belief that players play, coaches coach and management manage. The power of the player has grown individually and collectively, which means that players accepting the coach's authority and instruction is no longer automatic.

To generalise a bit, with the 'me' attitude of many Generation Y players also a factor, the modern coach (as well as parents, school teachers or police, for that matter) has an enormous challenge to sell to the individual the belief that being subservient to the group cause is a necessary element in being part of a successful team.

It's difficult to judge the effectiveness of individual coaches. I find it impossible to accurately rate them, because assessing their personal contribution to the performance of the teams they coach is largely guesswork. My gut feeling tells me Paul Roos was a very good coach/manager at the Sydney Swans, but a 57 per cent winning ratio from 202 games is not particularly high. Kevin Sheedy, in his 19 seasons at Essendon, statistically tops the sustained success scale. Four premierships from seven grand finals and a winning ratio of 61 per cent from 635 games is a fantastic record.

On the basis of opponents I coached against, Denis Pagan is hard to top. Under his coaching, the Kangaroos seemed to stitch up my Collingwood teams every time in the early '90s. Denis had a 63 per cent winning ratio at North Melbourne but that dropped to 24 per cent in his five seasons at Carlton. Don't tell me his coaching talents were significantly different in his stint with the Blues. The fact is that being in the right place at the right time, or the wrong place at the wrong time, very much applies to coaching success. This is why I rate the coaching performance of David Parkin and Mick Malthouse as the very best.

David took four different groups of players to top-four finishes: Hawthorn in 1977–78, Carlton in 1981–82, Fitzroy in 1986 and Carlton again in the 1990s. Mick did the same with the Bulldogs in 1985, the Eagles in the early 1990s, and Collingwood in two bursts, 2002–03 and 2010–11. You can be lucky once but not three or four times. David and Mick have proven their coaching abilities many times over.

From my personal experience when captaining Hawthorn in the early 1980s under the coaching of Allan Jeans, it became obvious to me that Jeansy was an outstanding coach/mentor. If I had included his premiership success when coaching St Kilda in the '60s, he would have topped my list of best coaches.

THE CHAMPION TEAMS

The evolution that makes players better over the years applies equally to teams and probably their coaches, but as far as group performance is concerned, win–loss records and the premiership were of the same value back in 1970 as they are today. On this basis, the most dominant team over an extended period was Hawthorn from 1982 till 1991. I was fortunate to be part of the Hawks team for the first four years of the club's amazing 10 years at the top.

A 17-win third-position season in 1982 was followed by seven successive grand finals that netted four premierships. They were eliminated finalists in 1990 and bounced back to win the flag again in 1991. The rejuvenation of the player list from the first premiership in 1983 to the sixth in 1991 was astounding. Only four players – Gary Ayres, Dermott Brereton, Chris Mew and Michael Tuck – remained from the start of the premiership era to the finish. Recruiting and development was a well-oiled conveyor belt as numerous high-quality players joined the premiership party. How are these for names: Jason

Dunstall, John Platten, Chris Langford, Darren Pritchard, Tony Hall, Andy Collins, Paul Hudson and Darren Jarman. All joined the club during this golden decade. For the only time over the last 40 years, the Hawks achieved the footy mission impossible of replacing ageing champions with new-generation champions without suffering a drop in performance.

THE ON-FIELD EVOLUTION

As I said earlier in the book, football has changed more in the last 10 years than the previous 30 combined. The full-time era that began in the late '90s has evolved into large coaching panels heavily influenced by fresh thinking from other sports. For coaches, the objective is to increase your team's winning chances, but whether the on-field spectacle has been enhanced is a very different proposition.

Anyone who has not seen a live AFL game for a decade would immediately notice the huge change in the look of the game and the way players are positioned. When I started in 1969, the players were positioned largely in the traditional team sheet line-up and every player was expected to play every minute of the game. Until John Kennedy's Hawthorn team began congesting many players around the centre bounce, there were no lines on the field. The game's response was to introduce the centre square, with only four from each team allowed inside.

This process has been repeated many times over the years. A rule was exploited and a change was made to protect the spectacle of the game. And this occurred even in previous eras when the coaching impact on the on-field action was quite minimal.

The frantic speed, power, athleticism and skills under extreme pressure that we see in modern footy are just fantastic, but the game would be even better if the players were spread more evenly over the field. In my view the best matches to watch have the competitive tension of close scores from start to finish and 30-plus goals, which ensure that the footy goes back to the centre bounce every few minutes. These regular restarts from the middle of the ground have the important by-product of spreading players over the length of the field. When the umpire bounces the footy there is a distinct look of forwards, defenders and midfielders.

The more often this happens, the better the spectacle that results. It is radical and difficult to regulate and will therefore probably never happen, but making it compulsory to have three or four players from each team inside the 50-metre arcs at every stoppage would make for a much more entertaining game.

The on-going equalisation debate to provide an even competition is critical. As the example of soccer proves, the spectacle is irrelevant without the excitement of close scores. Because of its relatively low scoring, the winner in a soccer game is so often undecided until the final whistle. The tension of the result is the greatest attraction of any sporting contest. The rich and powerful cannot be allowed to dominate.

Until recently, the strength of the AFL's national competition has been the effectiveness of the equalisation policies of a player salary cap and the draft system. As I've mentioned, though, lately the big gap in the non-player football department spending of the wealthy clubs compared to the poorer teams is having a huge effect on winning and losing. Revenue sharing and subsidies to bolster the financially weak clubs will only further enhance the separation of the haves and have nots. If it's good enough for total player payments to be capped, it's good enough for non-player expenditure also to have a ceiling. Set it at $10 million, which is roughly what the rich clubs currently spend, and then help the less resourced clubs to eventually reach that level. If the all-important equalisation objective is to be met, the AFL must accept the challenge of making a non-player football department cap a workable reality.

LIFE OUTSIDE CLUBLAND

After retiring from coaching at the end of 2008, I was very fortunate to be able to jump over the fence back into the media. I've always been a footy fan, so my work on the Channel Seven coverage, and with radio station 3AW, allows me to see a lot of football and to earn a decent living in the process. One thing for certain, the media area at every stadium gets a terrific view and the catering is normally pretty good as well. Being paid to go to the footy and to talk about it is like being paid to go on holidays. I also enjoy the fact that my state of mind after a game is pretty much the same as it was before the match started.

My main competitive stimulation since I finished coaching has been through Sizzling, a very well-performed racehorse I part-own with some good friends in Brisbane. I've always had an interest in a horse or two but he has been the first one to win a big race. When Sizzling won the Group 1 T. J. Smith Stakes in June 2012 by a few inches, it was an adrenalin rush that, for a short time, was like winning a grand final. The feeling just doesn't last nearly as long.

One of my post-coaching roles that I really value came about when the AFL's former football operations manager, Adrian Anderson, invited me to join the AFL's Rules Review Committee of which he was chairman. This committee exists to assist the AFL's football department to monitor the on-field game. It considers the interests and views of the game's many stakeholders – mainly players, coaches and fans – and, if thought necessary, makes recommendations to the AFL Commission on potential rule changes to enhance the game and make it safer to play. The commission is the only body that has the power to alter rules. Sometimes the Rules Committee recommendations are accepted and occasionally they are not. Umpires throwing the ball up at around-the-ground stoppages, instead of bouncing it, has been a Rules Committee recommendation for many years. The commission finally introduced it in 2013.

I've only been on the committee for the last few years, so I can observe without any bias that the legacy of Adrian's work over the last decade to make the game better to watch and safer to play has been one about which he should be extremely proud.

Whether some head-in-the-sand commentators or fans accept it or not, the game as we have known it over the years has been pulled apart by the tactical innovation of the modern coaching fraternity. It is an undeniable fact that the coaching intervention on how the game is played has grown enormously since the early 2000s. For example, the game's coach-driven evolution means that, in recent years, most players spend only around 80 per cent of the game on the ground, and often the 36 players will be jammed in less than half the field. As a sport, one of AFL's unique vulnerabilities is that, with no offside rule or line of scrimmage, coaches can use their players in whatever positioning best suits the winning objective. Coaching tactics have massive repercussions on the way the game looks and is played, and when it comes to rules and regulations, from my experience the core role of players and coaches is to use and exploit them to your maximum advantage.

Someone has to remove themselves from the winning effort to look after the on-field game as a whole. This has been the critically important role of the AFL and its Laws of the Game Committee, and as a footy lover who has had a background in playing and coaching, I'm keen to play a small part in this process.

As for the future, I can't imagine not going to the football, and the involvement with my Seven and 3AW media colleagues gives me a sense of being part of a team. That loss of day-to-day team involvement is what I miss about no longer working at a club. I don't miss the tension of the contest when your whole life seems to depend on what happens in a damn game of football. I no longer have the chance to experience the extreme emotional highs that my life in a football club has provided, but to balance that out the losing lows have also disappeared.

I'll always love going to the football as a spectator and can't imagine the day I stop going. Above and beyond playing and coaching, I regard myself as a footy fan. Lately, when my media commitments permit, I take my grandson Ky along to a match. I really enjoy our time together and encouraging his footy interest is an added bonus. Sharing my love for football with the only male in my bloodline is a great bonding experience that he and I share with the numerous families who attend the footy with their loved ones of all ages and both genders. When walking into an AFL game along with the supporters of both teams, I always get the enjoyable sense that, despite the differing allegiances, we're united as part of the one football family.

In 2013 Ky is playing his first year of footy in the under-10s at Mount Martha, only a few years after I finished my life-long hands-on involvement with football clubs back in 2008. Maybe there is a small amount of karma in the grandson starting his footy as the grandfather finishes, because, like life itself, the football wheel keeps relentlessly turning. Any player who is ever tempted by the thought he is bigger than the game or bigger than his team will quickly be proven wrong.

History tells us over and over again that individuals are really only part of the passing parade, and over time will come and go.

This highlights a fact that has been emphasised constantly during my life around footy clubs. Despite the need for individuals to have an obsessively strong personal drive and ambition to succeed, ultimately the individual must always be subservient to the team cause. That is the simple but enduring life lesson from team sport that will stay with me forever.

ACKNOWLEDGEMENTS

There are many people who I would like to thank for their invaluable help and support through my life's journey. In particular those closest to me, starting from my childhood, my parents, Ray and Lorna, and my brothers, Russell and Kelvin. Then into my adulthood my first wife, Maureen, daughters Tracey and Fiona, and my second wife, Deb, and her children, Clint and Abbey. Also, along with my extended family and friends I am very appreciative of my team-mates, my coaches, players I have coached, club administrators and my media colleagues; all of whom have given me such a memorable football life. In the process of putting thoughts into words I would like to thank Peter Blucher for his assistance in writing this book, and Patrick Mangan and the team at publisher Random House for their patience and encouragement.

CAREER HIGHLIGHTS AND STATISTICS

Hawthorn premiership player 1971, 1976, 1978
Hawthorn premiership captain 1983
Collingwood premiership coach 1990
Brisbane Lions premiership coach 2001, 2002, 2003
AFL Team of the Century (forward pocket)
Australian Football Hall of Fame
    Legend (1996, inaugural)
    Player of the Century
VFLPA MVP Award: 1982
    Award renamed in Leigh's honour: 2002
Coleman Medal 1975
Victorian representative 14 times, captain 1982
Hawthorn Club Champion 1971, 1972, 1974, 1976, 1977, 1978,
    1980, 1982
Hawthorn captain 1981–1985
Hawthorn leading goal-kicker 1973, 1975, 1981–1984
All-Australian coach 2001, 2002, 2003

LEIGH MATTHEWS, THE PLAYER: 1969–1985

Season	Premiership Competition						Brownlow Medal votes	Night/ Pre Season		State		
	Mtchs	Wins	Losses	Ties	Gls	Best 6		Mtchs	Gls	Mtchs	Gls	
1969	5	3	2	0	7	2	2	3	6	0	0	Night Series Prem team selection
1970	16	7	9	0	20	11	3	2	2	0	0	
1971	23	20	3	0	43	16	10			2	4	Prem team selection/Club B&F
1972	21	13	8	0	45	19	16			2	4	All Aust selection/Club B&F
1973	19	10	9	0	51	16	23			1	0	Third in club B&F/Third in BM count/ Club LGK
1974	21	13	8	0	52	18	15			2	3	Club B&F
1975	23	17	6	0	68	20	10			2	4	Runner-up in club B&F/Club LGK/ League LGK
1976	22	17	5	0	71	21	23			1	4	Prem team selection/Club B&F
1977	24	17	7	0	91	20	0	2	5	1	2	Night Series Prem team selection/ Club B&F
1978	23	17	6	0	71	21	3	0	0	1	5	Prem team selection/Club B&F (equal)
1979	13	6	7	0	30	10	6	2	3	0	0	
1980	17	8	9	0	32	16	16	3	13	1	3	Club B&F

Year												Notes
1981	16	10	6	0	48	10	11	2	9	0	0	Club capt/Runner-up in club B&F/Club LGK
1982	22	16	6	0	74	14	17	0	0	1	0	Club capt/All Aust selection/Club B&F/Third in BM count (equal)/Club LGK
1983	22	16	6	0	79	14	5	1	1	0	0	Club capt/All Aust selection/Prem team selection/Club LGK
1984	24	18	6	0	77	15	4	2	6	0	0	Club capt/Club LGK
1985	21	12	8	1	56	6	4	0	0	0	0	Club capt
Totals	332	220	111	1	915	249	168	17	45	14	29	

LEIGH MATTHEWS, THE COACH: 1986–2008

| Club | Season | Position | Club details | | | | | | New to Club | | |
			Wins	Losses	Ties	Matches	Players Used	AFL Debut	From Other AFL Clubs	Total Players New to Club
Collingwood	1986	6	12	7	0	19	38	11	2	13
Collingwood	1987	12	7	15	0	22	45	17	4	21
Collingwood	1988	4	15	8	1	24	34	4	4	8
Collingwood	1989	5	13	10	0	23	41	7	1	8
Collingwood	1990	Premier	19	6	1	26	32	2	0	2
Collingwood	1991	7	12	9	1	22	33	6	0	6
Collingwood	1992	5	16	7	0	23	35	3	4	7
Collingwood	1993	8	11	9	0	20	34	3	1	4
Collingwood	1994	8	12	11	0	23	37	7	6	13
Collingwood	1995	10	8	12	2	22	37	10	1	11
Brisbane	1999	4	18	7	0	25	36	1	3	4
Brisbane	2000	5	13	11	0	24	36	7	2	9
Brisbane	2001	Premier	20	5	0	25	35	5	2	7
Brisbane	2002	Premier	20	5	0	25	30	2	0	2
Brisbane	2003	Premier	17	8	1	26	32	3	1	4
Brisbane	2004	2	18	7	0	25	32	5	0	5
Brisbane	2005	11	10	11	0	21	36	11	0	11
Brisbane	2006	13	7	15	0	22	39	10	1	11

Brisbane	2007	10	9	11	2	22	38	5	0	5
Brisbane	2008	10	10	12	0	22	37	7	1	8
Totals			267	186	8	461		126	33	159

Matches as Coach

Club	Span	Wins	Losses	Ties	Total	Success Rate
Collingwood	1986–95	125	94	5	224	57%
Brisbane	1999–2008	142	92	3	237	61%
Totals		267	186	8	461	59%

INDEX

Abernathy, Bruce 164

Ablett, Gary 62, 105–10, 197, 258, 274, 317, 489, 490

Ablett, Gary (Jr) 109–10, 342, 488, 489, 490

Ablett, Geoff 58, 105–6

Ablett, Kevin 105–6

Adamson, Lee 159, 244

Adcock, Jed 480

Adelaide Crows 262, 282, 302, 360, 364, 386, 390, 419, 421, 427, 428, 452

Adidas 64

AFL *v*, *xi–xii see also* VFL

  AFL Commission 66, 467, 486

  AFL Players Association Most Valuable Player Award 187

  Appeals Board 357

  blood rule 39, 363

  childhood 3

  club spending 65–7

  equalisation policies 449, 467–8, 494–5

  evolution *x*, 32, 45, 50, 62–3, 65–6, 336, 370–1, 485–7, 496

  father/son rule 340–2, 480

  full-time players and staff 370–1

  Hall of Fame 315–16

  illicit drug policy 368–9

  IV fluid replacement directive 397, 447

  Laws of the Game Committee 138

  MCG agreement 419, 444–5

  Melbourne-centric attitude 225–6, 402

  modern system 355–6

  national draft 168, 249–50, 272–3, 282, 329, 379–80, 494

  non-player expenditure 494

  performance-enhancing drugs 369

  recruitment 147, 249–50

  role in Matthews family 4–7, 9–10

  rules 191

  Rules Review Committee 495–6

  salaries and caps 62, 282, 287, 494

  scheduling of preliminary finals 419–20, 428, 443–50, 457, 463

  sustainability of national competition 486–7

  Team of the Century 314–15

  win-to-loss ratios *vii*

The Age 446, 448

Akermanis, Jason 343, 347–9, 389, 402–3, 423, 424, 430–1, 438, 439, 456, 457, 461, 471–6

Akermanis, Megan 402

Albert Oval 406, 434, 460

All-Australian team 187, 250–1, 257, 265, 271, 310, 317, 341, 343, 347, 436, 456, 480

Allan, Anne 325, 402, 455

Allan, Graeme 'Gubby' 150, 155, 156, 157–8, 166, 169, 175, 177, 188, 198, 212, 215, 239–40, 244, 254, 259, 268, 271, 273, 282, 285, 286, 295, 296, 306, 324, 326, 328, 332, 335, 337, 340, 350,

359–60, 361, 365, 379, 381, 382, 401, 402, 409, 416–17, 427, 445, 455, 466, 471, 478, 482, 483
Allan, Marcus 198, 325
Allan, Patrick 325
Alves, Stan 330
Anderson, Adrian 443, 448, 495–6
Ansett collapse 402, 405
Ansett Cup 386
Anstey, Noel 12
Anzac Day matches 289, 299–300, 302–3
  1995 300–2, 304
Apel, Isaac 63
Archer, Glenn 379
Armstrong, Matthew 337–8, 382
Arthur, Graham 62
Ashcroft, Marcus 'Choppers' 89–90, 343, 388, 389, 432, 437, 439
Assumption College 16
Austin, Rod 'Curly' 100
The Australian 320
Australian Crime Commission 2013 report 368–9, 372
Australian Football League (AFL) see AFL
Australian Institute of Sport 338
Australian International Rules coach 309–14, 335
Australian Sports Anti-Doping Authority 369
Ayres, Gary 68, 104, 115, 138, 493

Baker, Leon 141
Baker, Phil 81
Ballantyne, Jon 286
Bamford, Scott 345, 378
Banks, Denis 156, 174, 189, 201, 214, 241, 249, 251, 259, 286
Barassi, Ron 253, 314, 315, 327, 490
Barker, John 378
Barnes, John 394
Barrett, Damian 475
Bartlett, John 184

Bartlett, Kevin 487, 489, 490
Barwick, Doug 177, 206, 244, 249, 250, 260, 286
Bassett, Nathan 421
Beasley, Simon 108, 162
Beatson, Kinnear 336, 340, 342, 380, 480
Beattie, Peter 440
Beck, Judy 37
Beck, Ken 26, 27, 37
Becker, Peter 82
Belcher, Gary 344
Bennett, Andy 106
Bennett, Inspector Phil 126
Bennett, Wayne 148, 245, 343–4
best teams
  1969 to 1985 487–8
  1969 to present 488–9
  1969 to present (traditional team-sheet positioning) 489–90
Bewick, Darren 232
Bews, Andrew 330, 347
Biffin, Ray 41
Bill Patterson Cheney 64
Birt, John 147
Black, Simon 81, 90, 343, 357, 358, 361, 363, 383, 394, 412, 421, 437, 438–9, 451, 456, 468
Blake, Jason 455
Blakey, John 460
Blight, Malcolm 103, 192, 487, 489, 490
Blucher, Peter 282, 350, 403
Bolton, Craig 342, 406–7
Bonbeach Footy Club 9
Bonbeach High School 16, 21, 62
Bonney, John 30
Border, Allan 137
Bourke, Barry 41
Bourke, Brian 123
Bourke, Damian 338
Bourke, Francis 487
Bowers, Michael 415, 446–7, 448, 475, 479

Boyd, Brad 351, 378

Bradley, Craig 387

Bradshaw, Ange 366–7

Bradshaw, Daniel 343, 346, 366–7, 381, 405, 439, 458

Bradshaw, Jake 367, 405

Brandon Park Shopping Centre 55, 65

Bremner, Ian 26, 54, 143, 254

Brennan, Jared 480

Brereton, Dermott 59, 72, 93, 100–1, 103, 138, 140, 142, 178, 254, 268, 278, 298–9, 433, 467, 493

Briedis, Arnold 57

Brindley, Neil 169

Brisbane Bears 164, 165, 249, 256, 266–7, 273, 274, 282–5, 304, 329, 486 *see also* Brisbane Lions; Fitzroy

Brisbane Lions *vii, viii, xii*, 5, 8, 46, 65, 71, 81, 84, 102, 199, 211, 219, 251, 262, 278, 307, 328, 329–30, 486 *see also* Brisbane Bears; Fitzroy

   2001 grand final 409–15

   2002 grand final 389, 422–5

   2003 grand final 436–8

   2004 grand final 443, 458–62

   1999 season 345–58

   2000 season 359–67

   2001 season 376–8, 384–409

   2002 season 418–21

   2003 season 426–35

   2004 season 443–63

   2005–2008 seasons 464–83

   administrative breach fines 448

   AFL head office relationship 415–16, 446–7, 456

   age of players 452

   coach of 331–484

   coaching offer 323–8

   dehydration problems 372–5, 398

   differences in coaching role 350

   'Fab Four' 426

   finances 415–16

   go-home factors 359–60, 361–2

   hat-trick 436–42

   High Performance Reward Scheme 451

   hyperbaric chamber 375, 460

   IV saline drips 374, 396–8, 447

   off-field support 371–2

   personality profiling 84–92

   player retention allowance 359–60, 447

   playing list 1998 343

   recruitment 378–82, 480

   resignation as coach 483–4

   salary cap issues 359–60, 378, 416, 418, 451, 467

   sexual assault allegations 361

   support staff 336–9

   travel 362, 373, 400, 405, 431, 457

   weekly role-appreciation award 388

Brittain, Craig 459

Brittain, Wayne 76

Brogan, Dean 453

Brooks, David 338

Brown, Brian 340

Brown, Gavin 'Rowdy' 159, 169, 173, 177, 179–80, 190, 201, 206, 238, 240, 242, 243, 251, 257, 265, 287, 288, 291

Brown, Jonathan 89, 197, 221–2, 257, 278, 317, 340–2, 364, 367, 381, 382, 385, 394, 423, 431, 437, 438, 439, 451, 454–5, 457, 459–61, 465–6, 468–9, 471, 480

Browne and Co 323, 325

Browne, Jeff 323–4, 325, 326

Brownlow Medal *x*, 4, 27, 51, 149, 169, 227, 258, 310, 318–19, 348, 356, 402–4, 421, 431, 439, 447, 471, 474

Bruns, Neville 119–21, 129

Buckenara, Gary 59, 104, 114, 115, 140

Buckle, Frank 72, 307

Buckley, Nathan 146, 157, 273–4,

282–4, 286, 288, 291, 295, 302,
327, 337, 422, 431, 432, 436,
473, 489
Burns, John 57
Burns, Keith 159
Burns, Ronnie 347
Burns, Scott 425, 437
Bussell, Norm 26
Byrne, Michael 106, 113, 138, 140

Cable, Barry 31, 51, 79, 487
Cahill, John 149, 166, 273
Camberwell Football Club 59
Cameron, Leon 482
Camporeale, Scott 313
Canberra 10
Capper, Warwick 162
Caracella, Blake 437, 439, 440, 451,
457, 467
Carey, Stefan 360–1
Carey, Steven 141
Carey, Wayne 'Duck' 197, 257, 277–8,
311, 312, 385, 488, 489, 490
Carloss, Nathan 481
Carlton 17, 24, 51, 61, 63, 76, 82, 83,
100, 105, 113, 149, 157, 189, 260,
262, 263, 271, 278, 280, 288–9,
297, 298, 341, 356, 358, 366,
367, 376–7, 386–7, 465, 492
Carman, Phil 79
Carroll, Sean 455
Carter, Nick 378
Cartwright, Darren 456
Cerutty, Percy 18–19
Champion, Richard 'Champs' 346,
347
champion teams 492–3
Channel Nine 321, 466
Channel Seven x, 69, 102, 160, 239,
284, 317, 318, 319–21, 326–7,
327, 329, 346, 466, 495, 496
Channel Ten 15, 396, 445, 477
Charman, Jamie 71, 380, 382, 437,
439, 452–3, 480

Chelsea 2, 6–8, 18
Chelsea Primary School 7, 8
Chelsea Football Club 3, 15
under-15s 9, 12
Christian, Clare 276
Christian, Michael 'Chrisso' 168, 169,
177, 201, 204–5, 207, 213, 214,
238, 250, 259, 276–7
Clark, Mitch 480
Clarke, Matthew 360, 452–3
Clarke, Ron 64
Clarkson, Alastair 393
Clayton, Scott 112, 328, 338, 378,
480
Cloke, David 165–7, 174
Cloke, Travis 167, 342, 466
Clothier, Brian 124–5
club environment and culture 176,
252, 332–3, 418
coaches/coaching viii, xi, xii–xiii,
18–19, 194
advice 151–2
bonding themes 172, 393
career coaches 308
caring for players 215, 287
chain of command 334, 491
changing role from 1969 to present
490–2
conflict with players 471–3
culture base for team 332–3
discipline standards 109
effectiveness, judging 492
emergency players 210–11, 406,
432, 435
emotions 219–20, 233, 293, 306
fitness tests 230–2, 292
General Patton quote vi, vii, 234
influence of 32–40
intervention, increase in 216
mind games 401–2
new season build-up 265
objectives 154
over-coaching 229, 393
personality profiling 84–92

position structure 34–5, 50–1
positive reinforcement 346
reward and recognition 387–8
ruck 152
selection errors 212–16
short term outlook 295, 297
styles 76–81, 94, 95–8, 152
successful players as 147–8, 153
succession plans 146, 284, 297,
    477–8, 481–3
support role 217
tackling 200
tactical innovation 199
tactics 34–5, 97, 160–1, 178–9,
    393–4, 496
team first/individual second 214,
    249, 403–4, 474, 491
teams, picking 210, 212–15
techniques and aids 84–92
tip of the iceberg theory 266–7, 368
trust and respect building 171
veteran players 118
yelling 35, 91, 481
Coleman, Brian 72, 132
Coleman, John 47
Coleman Medal 108, 162, 196
Collingwood v, vii, 6, 19, 24, 31, 45,
    47, 62, 65, 66, 71, 79, 81, 84, 88,
    134, 144, 146, 263, 323, 330,
    354, 364–5, 381, 420, 421, 427,
    428, 429, 467, 479, 492
1990 grand final 235–47, 248, 260,
    365
2002 grand final 422–5
2003 grand final 426, 436–8
1986 season 150, 158–63
1987 season 169, 175
1988 season 176, 178, 179
1989 season 179, 180
1990 season 182–234
1991 season 265–70
1992 season 271–2
1993 season 274–81
1994 season 288–94

1995 season 295–306
Alpine National Park trek 171–6,
    186, 249
assessment of players 252–61
assistant coach 44, 145, 150
captains 164, 165–6, 168
coach 144–307
coach for life 264
Colliwobbles tag 148, 166, 181,
    182, 188, 194, 232, 264
fan base 149
finances 150, 154
first game as coach 158–9
fitness initiatives 177
leadership 252
no-alcohol-consumption rule 221–2
Operation Tackle 229–30, 233,
    240, 243
pay cuts 154–5, 249
pointing the bone jinx 276–7
post-1990 premiership 263–7
premiership hangover 266–8
premiership history 188–9, 248
recruitment 177, 249–50, 268, 273,
    282–8
sacking as coach 307
tackling award 189
under-19s 168
Collins, Andy 493
Collins, Ian 309, 314, 316, 360, 447
Colonial (Etihad) Stadium 362–3,
    384
Cometti, Denis 319
competitiveness vi–vii, ix, xiii, 3, 53,
    127–8, 267
rule-bending 368–75
sibling rivalry 3–4, 7
Conlan, Mick 112
Conway, Dr Shane 182, 236, 240,
    243, 291, 370
Cook, Bill 147, 161
Cook, Ron 82
Cooke, Michael 57
Cooke, Robert 57

Cooper, Brad 193
Copeland, Robert 386, 432, 439
Copeland Trophy 187, 252, 271, 283, 296, 307
Cort, Michelle 338, 372
Courier, Jim 319
The Courier-Mail 331, 343, 456, 465
Cox, Dean 489
Cransberg, Peter 213
Creswell, Daryn 475
Crimmins, Ben 55
Crimmins, Gwen 55
Crimmins, Peter 11, 18, 26, 29, 30, 35, 48, 54–6, 69, 71, 254
Crimmins, Sam 55
Croall, Jason 370
Crosisca, Gavin 159, 170, 177, 201, 206, 214, 250, 251, 257, 259
Crosswell, Brent 80
Cumani, Francesca 319
Cupido, Damien 360
Curran, Peter 115, 138, 140, 338

Daicos, Peter 103, 174, 179–80, 187, 189, 190, 197, 201, 206, 211–12, 218, 224, 232, 238, 243, 248, 251, 255–6, 260, 265, 272, 274, 285–6, 287, 489, 490
Dandenong 15
Daniher, Neale 487
Daniher, Terry 138, 240, 242
Davis, Barry 57, 63
Davis, Leon 420
Day, Robert 26, 27
De Wolde, Alle 58
Dear, Greg 140
Deller, Bill 52
Demetriou, Andrew 101, 415, 443, 445–6, 447–8, 449, 456
Dempsey, Gary 487
Dicker, Ian 72
Dickson, Robert 351
Dillon, Ross 22
Dimattina, Paul 363

DiPierdomenico, Robert 'Dipper' 58, 80, 98, 138, 311, 430
Ditterich, Carl 37
Doull, Bruce 105, 487, 489, 490
Downie, Graeme 325, 416
drugs in sport 368–71
Drummond, Josh 480
Dublin 309–14
Duncan, Nicole 336, 337, 400, 405
Dunlop Automotive 19, 62
Dunstall, Jason 43, 45, 47, 130–1, 135, 138, 178, 183, 255–6, 258, 273, 303, 321, 404, 488, 489, 490, 493
Dyer, Jack 238, 315

Eade, Rodney 'Rocket' 58, 88, 101, 106, 115, 138, 140, 157, 199
Edelsten, Dr Geoffrey 145–6
Elite Sports Properties 178, 259
Elliott, Herb 18, 19
Elms, Billie 410
Essendon 5, 47, 48–9, 51, 59, 63, 96, 99, 111, 112, 113, 115, 130, 133, 136, 137–42, 150, 155, 157, 165, 183, 189, 190, 192, 194, 198, 207, 209, 212, 213, 217–21, 225, 230, 262, 263, 269, 280, 289, 299, 300–2, 303, 305, 340, 376, 384, 390–1, 394, 399, 421, 445, 457, 467, 468, 492
  grand final 1990 235–44
  grand final 2001 406–13
Ezard, Alan 232

Fanning, Fred 43
Fardoulys, Jim 338, 427, 436, 459
Farmer, Graeme 'Polly' 315
Farmer, Jeff 347
Farnham, John
  'Dare to Dream' 408
Farr, Jack 68
Farr, Renee 68–9
Fellowes, Wes 162

Fielke, Grant 168
50 metre penalty introduction 138
fitness 118, 221
  comparisons 222, 488
  pre-season training 265
Fitzroy 59, 108, 112, 113, 161–2,
    162, 163, 177, 183, 189–90,
    196, 249, 260, 271 *see also*
    Brisbane Lions, 340, 492
  merger with Brisbane Lions 65,
    329, 360, 378
  Team of the Century 377
Flintoff-King, Debbie *xi*
Flower, Robert 370, 487
Football Record 267, 300
Footscray 20, 44, 59, 106, 108,
    132, 162, 336 *see also* Western
    Bulldogs
Footy Olympics 73
The Footy Show 321
Franchina, Anthony 387, 389
Francis, Tony 'Redlegs' 177, 187–8,
    189, 206, 250, 258, 288
Franklin, Lance 197, 488, 489,
    490
Frankston 5, 6
Fraser, Mark 289
Frawley, Danny 399
Freeborn, Scott 387, 389
Freedman, Richard 319
Fremantle Dockers 73, 302, 324,
    329, 355, 427
Fyfe, Nathan 73

the Gabba 96, 266, 304, 317, 328,
    330, 333, 343, 350, 356, 362,
    364, 365, 374, 386, 390, 415,
    419, 421, 444, 451, 475
Gangitano, Alphonse 158
Garden, Lorna 177
Gastev, John 256
Gay, Terry 63, 120
Gayfer, Michael 'Mick' 159, 202,
    206, 214, 259, 277, 286, 389

Geelong *vii*, 8, 33, 60–1, 63, 106, 107,
    108, 109, 119–20, 129, 150, 159,
    160, 238, 262–3, 269, 271, 274,
    314, 330, 342, 347, 385, 393, 419,
    427, 444, 445, 454, 457, 467, 479
Gieschen, Jeff 455
Giles, Ray 147, 260
Girdwood, Mal 173
Glendinning, Ross 81, 487
Glenferrie Oval 11–12, 13, 16, 17,
    30, 34, 36, 39, 41, 43, 46, 59, 76,
    134, 143, 145, 232
Goad, Alan 58
Goddard, Ken 102
Gold Coast Suns 62, 389, 481, 486
Goodes, Adam 432
Goss, Norm 80, 101–2, 382
Gough, Stephen 470
grand finals *vii, ix–x, xii*
  1970 24
  1971 23, 28–30, 58, 72
  1975 52, 58
  1976 50–1, 53–4, 75
  1978 80–1
  1983 111–15, 137
  1984 115, 137
  1985 136, 137–43
  1988 *v*
  1989 *v*
  1990 *v, vi*, 235–47, 365
  1991 73
  1995 263
  2001 376, 409–15
  2002 389, 422–5
  2003 426, 436–8
  2004 443, 458–62
  2005 409–10
  2008 393
  back-to-back 262–3, 425
  double suspensions for indiscretions
    242
  hat-trick by Lions 436–8
  preparation 139–40, 224–6,
    228–9, 399–401, 404–9

traditional parade 227, 231–2, 402, 405–6, 458, 460
week leading to 227–8
Gray, Tom 14
Greater Western Sydney Giants 169, 482
Greene, Russell 96, 104, 138, 142, 312, 365
Greig, Keith 52
Grimes, Jack 480
Group 1 T. J. Smith Stakes 495
Gunston, Norman 46

Hadley, Richard 379, 382, 432, 437, 439, 440, 480
Hafey, Tom 31, 108, 121, 146, 148, 150, 221, 468
Hall of Fame *xi*, 149
Hall, Tony 493
Hamilton, Andrew 465
Hamilton, Arthur 64–5
Hamilton, Jack 122
Handley, Robert 138
Hardie, Brad 133–4, 135, 286
Hardwick, Damian 407, 461
Harley, Tom 319
Harper, Phil 282
Harris, Leon 112
Hart, Jessy 459
Hart, Linda 459
Hart, Rick 459
Hart, Royce 16, 278, 487
Hart, Shaun 343, 388, 389–90, 409, 413, 426, 430, 438, 452, 458–9, 460, 463, 468
Harvey, Brent 55
Harvey, Mark 213
Harvey, Robert 272
Hawken, Les 26, 27
Hawking, Simon 378
Hawkins, Doug 321
Hawthorn *vii*, 16–17, 25–6, 46, 52, 151, 160, 178–9, 183, 186, 189, 192, 194, 198, 213, 215, 229, 232, 238, 249, 262, 263, 269, 273, 278, 300, 303, 307, 340, 341, 347, 364–5, 386, 399, 468, 472, 475, 492, 493
1971 season 26–30, 41, 48, 58, 72
1972 season 41, 48, 57, 59
1973 season 46, 48, 57
1974 season 47
1975 season 57, 58
1976 season 50–4
1977 season 78–9
1978 season 80–1
1982 season 100, 101, 103–4
1983 season 111–15
1984 season 115
1985 season 117–19, 129–36, 137–43
1991 season 73
captain-coach offer 83
captains 70, 71, 73, 83, 95, 112, 132
first game 19
first training session 11–12
friendships 68–70
Kennedy as coach 32–75
last season with 117–19, 129–36, 137–43
salary demands 63–4
Team of the Century 68–9, 134
training squad 13, 16–19
VFL debut 20–2
Headland, Des 330, 340, 342, 343, 406–7, 421
Heady, Brett 201, 206, 259
Heath, Kevin 16–17, 34
Henderson, Lachie 157
Hendrie, John 58
The Herald Sun 304, 317, 323, 331, 352, 475
Player of the Century 352–3
Herbert, Ken 82, 100
Heuskes, Adam 342–3, 355, 360–1, 365–6, 378, 382
Hewitt, Lleyton 319

Heywood, Doug 327
Hillgrove, Eddie 239, 242, 306, 339
Hird, James 157, 302, 406, 407, 433,
    439, 489, 490
Hobart 45–6, 47, 60
Hocking, Steven 120, 121–2, 274
Hogan, Brendan 168
Hooper, Rhan 480
Hudson, Peter 11, 18, 22, 23, 26,
    27, 28, 29, 34, 37, 41–8, 57, 72,
    78–9, 131, 255–6, 364, 488, 493
Hulme, Darren 387, 389

indigenous players 274
    All-Stars team 276
injuries
    Boyd, Brad 351
    Brown, Jonathan 459–61, 469–70
    Bruns, Neville 119–20
    Hudson, Peter 41–2, 45, 59
    Knights, Peter 51, 134
    Lappin, Nigel 426, 430–6
    Leppitsch, Justin 473
    Lions 2004 season 451
    Lynch, Alastair 453
    Matthews, Kelvin 59–60
    Millane, Darren 182–5, 190, 253
    Richardson, Alan 218, 224, 230–2
    Shaw, Tony 220, 291–2
    Voss, Michael 356, 384, 427–8, 431
International Rules competition 1998
    309–14
Ireland 309–14, 335, 350
Ireland, Andrew 282, 323, 325, 327,
    328, 335, 336, 359–60, 401, 415

Jackson, Mark 119
Jackson, Wayne 312, 326, 260, 447
Jakovich, Allen 279, 291
Jamieson, Michael 157
Jarman, Darren 493
Jauncey, Dr Phil 84–92, 336, 338,
    434
Jaworskyj, Bohdan 58

Jeans, Allan 'Yabby' x, xi, 27–8, 71,
    83, 93–104, 107–8, 112, 113,
    115, 117, 129, 130, 131, 132, 135,
    137, 139, 144, 148, 151, 153, 154,
    167, 209, 229, 344, 382, 469, 492
Jesaulenko, Alex 45, 83, 103, 487
Jock McHale coach's medal 414
Johnson, Chris 343, 378, 389, 424,
    431, 456, 480
Johnson, Mark 407
Johnson, Murray 351–2
Johnson, Shane 336, 337, 366, 402
Johnstone, Travis 480
Jones, Alan 194
Joseph, Ron 381
Judd, Chris 488, 489, 490
Judd, Robert 9
Judge, Ken 104, 115, 138
Judson, Wayne 29
Junction Oval 59, 103

Kardinia Park 107, 108, 269
Keating, Clark 'Crackers' 343, 378,
    431, 437, 439, 452, 454, 457, 478
Keating, Paul 276
Keays, Terry 268
Keddie, Bob 11, 18, 26, 28, 29
Keenan, Peter 'Crackers' 80, 152, 204,
    237
Kekovich, Sam 51
Kelly, Craig 'Ned' 168, 177–8, 213,
    238, 240, 241, 250, 251, 258–9,
    265, 271, 288, 304
Kelly, John 276, 277
Kelly, Tony 465, 475, 479–80, 481–2,
    483
Kennedy, Bernard 75
Kennedy, John x, 18, 24, 28, 30,
    32–3, 34, 35–9, 46, 53, 58, 75–6,
    77, 94, 95, 117, 127, 151, 152,
    184, 344, 384, 490, 491, 493
Kennedy, John (Jr) 59, 93–4, 115
Kennedy, Matthew 'Max' 355, 406,
    432

'Kennedy's Commandos' *see* Hawthorn
Kernahan, Stephen 268, 278
Kerrison, Shane 175, 224, 230, 232, 236, 259
Kilby, Judy 350
Kingdon, Tine 147
Knights, Peter 17, 26, 27, 34, 51, 58, 59, 106, 112, 115, 115, 134, 138, 140, 273, 489
Knocke, Daniel 408
Kokoda Track 5
Koutoufides, Anthony 377, 387
Krakouer, Jim 275
Krakouer, Phil 275

Lade, Brendon 453
Lambert, Bailey 383
Lambert, Billie 383
Lambert, Bodie 383
Lambert, Brylee 383
Lambert, Craig 102, 382, 383, 388, 409, 427, 432
Lambert, Melissa 102, 383
Lane, Tim 320
Langdon, Karl 197
Langford, Chris 104, 138, 139, 493
Langwarrin 2–6, 324, 353
Langwarrin Primary School 5, 6
Lappin, Claire 434, 435
Lappin, Nigel 46, 90, 343, 365, 383, 426, 428, 430–6, 438, 456
Larkins, Dr Peter 320
Laurie Hayden and Associates 173
Lauritz, John 139, 144
Lawrence, Barry 29, 46, 334, 380
Lawrence, Steven 334, 378, 380
leadership 186, 195, 220, 251, 348, 356, 382–4, 404, 419–20, 471–2, 475
    consultant players 251–2, 473, 474
    core players 251–2, 430, 471, 473, 474
    management principle 348–9

on-field leadership 115–16, 167
    team culture 176, 252, 332–3, 418
LeDeux, Fred 8
Lehmann, Don 373, 456
Lehmann, Troy 286
Leppitsch, Justin 90, 342, 343, 346–7, 349, 355, 381, 382, 398, 407, 412, 431, 440, 451, 471, 473–4, 476, 478
Lester-Smith, Rod 115
Lethal 145
Lewis, Chris 195, 201, 202, 203, 206–7
Lewis, Rick 358, 455, 456
Liberatore, Tony 258, 363
Licuria, Paul 424
Lloyd, Matthew 320, 407, 412
Lockett, Tony 'Plugger' 45, 47, 103, 255–6, 258, 272, 273, 295–6, 304, 305, 346
Loewe, Stewart 272, 330
Long, Michael 408
Longmire, John 146
Longmuir, Justin 330
Loveridge, Richard 59, 100, 113, 135, 138
Lowe, Barry 338, 339, 435–6
Lucas, Scott 407, 412
Luff, Michael 8, 9
Luff, Peter 8, 9
Lynch, Alastair 343, 346, 349, 355, 381, 382, 383, 385–6, 388–9, 396, 398, 406, 412, 413, 418, 421, 424, 428, 431, 432, 438, 440, 451–2, 453–4, 457, 460, 462–3, 468
Lynch, Tristan 345

McAdam, Adrian 277, 278, 279
McAlister, Allan 146, 150, 154, 155, 156, 188, 244, 254, 264, 268, 273, 275–6, 296, 307
McAvaney, Bruce 318–19, 402, 466
McBurney, Steve 455

McCarthy, Mick 113, 138, 141

McCartney, Jason 268

McConnell, Dr Paul 338, 372, 373, 437, 460

McDonald, Beau 343, 412, 422, 451, 452, 480

Macdonald, Ranald 150

McGrath, Ash 379, 382, 439

McGuane, Mick 159, 170, 177, 187, 195, 202–3, 206–7, 215, 232, 241, 243, 251, 258, 271, 288, 289, 292

McGuire, Eddie 150, 284, 303, 321, 423

McHale, Jock 160

McIvor, Scott 382

McKenna, Guy 291

McKenna, Peter 45

McKeon, Mark 173, 174, 177, 236, 238, 239, 266

McKeown, Ron 170, 189, 209–10, 212–16, 232, 259, 272

McLaren, Dylan 406, 454

McLean, Michael 'Magic' 336, 337, 382

McLeod, Andrew 489

McLeod, Jack 65

McMahon, David 112

McMullin, Ian 286

McNamara, 'Big Jim' 15

McRae, Craig 'Fly' 343, 357, 363, 388, 389, 431, 451, 452, 463, 468

Madden, Simon 96, 138, 139, 140, 213, 225, 237–8, 243, 487, 489, 490

Malaxos, Steve 140, 195

Malthouse, Mick 146, 148, 199, 284, 422, 492

Manassa, Phil 290

Manning, Andrew 213

Manson, James 'Jimmy' 71, 152, 204–6, 213, 225, 227, 237, 245, 250, 265, 286, 452

Martello, Alan 26, 54, 58, 82

Martyn, Mick 357, 358

Matera, Peter 489, 490

Matera, Phil 347

Mathews, Race 126

Matthews, Deb 325, 420, 425, 471, 482–3

Matthews, Fiona 1, 49, 127, 143, 326, 408–9, 457

Matthews, Kelvin 3, 5, 8, 9, 21, 53–4, 59–61, 352

Matthews, Leigh
    assault charge 121, 123–6, 127
    Barney nickname 48
    big-headedness lesson 8–9
    boredom, fear of 6
    Brisbane Lions, coach of *see* Brisbane Lions
    Cappy nickname 8
    challenges *vi–viii*
    childhood 1–10
    chocolate chip pavlova 48–9
    Collingwood, coach of *see* Collingwood
    'conduct unbecoming' charge 121
    confidence, loss of 132–3
    deregistration 121–3, 127, 130
    early playing days *viii–ix*
    final playing game 137–42
    first grand final 23–4
    first marriage 22
    football boots *xi*, 19–20
    grandchildren 326, 408–9, 457, 497
    Hawthorn, with *see* Hawthorn
    injury 20, 95
    jobs 64–5
    'Lethal Leigh' tag 31, 102, 127
    letters from supporters *v–vi*
    'Lips of Lethal' comments 423
    losses, accepting *vii*, 377
    marriage break-up 293, 326
    media career 309, 317–21, 324, 325, 495
    partnerships 55, 113
    playing against brother 60

premonition of sacking 303–4
salaries and earnings 62–4, 323
speech after 2003 grand final win
    441–2
state representation 30–1
Matthews, Lorna 3, 4–5, 21, 59, 143,
    326, 352–3, 470–1
Matthews, Maureen 22, 25, 40, 64,
    143, 244, 293
Matthews, Ray 3, 4–5, 8, 21, 59, 326,
    352–4
Matthews, Russell 3, 5, 21, 65, 143,
    352–3
Matthews, Tracey 1, 25, 49, 64, 127,
    129–30, 143, 326
Maxwell, Nick 473
Mayes, Robert 14
MCG 5–6, 20, 24, 31, 81, 93, 100,
    114, 140, 198, 209, 226, 278,
    279, 288, 300, 302, 376, 386,
    399, 405, 475
    Collingwood main home ground
        289–90
    Parade of Champions 470
Meagher, Des 26
media coverage 41, 45, 112, 125, 321,
    401
    south/north comparison 331
Melbourne Demons 20, 21, 41, 43,
    72, 188, 189, 190, 194, 198, 225,
    229, 278–9, 304, 314, 330, 347,
    366, 453
Melbourne Marathon 298
Melbourne Storm 8
Melbourne Velodrome 8
Mellor, Ian 388
Merrett, Daniel 480
Merrett, Roger 114, 138, 328, 329,
    330, 333, 346, 487
Mew, Chris 59, 104, 139, 493
Michael, Kim 478
Michael, Mal 381–2, 407, 412,
    422–3, 439, 478
Milburn, Darren 459

Millane, Darren 'Pants' 88, 158,
    159, 173, 182–7, 189, 190, 191,
    197, 206, 221, 227, 236, 241,
    249, 250, 251, 253–5, 258, 260,
    433–4
    AFL Players Association Most
        Valuable Player Award 187
    Best and Fairest 1987 186
    death 254, 270–1
Miller, Chief Commissioner Mick
    126
Miller, Senior Detective Doug 99
Mitchell, Barry 286
Mitchell, Kevin 469
Molloy, Jarrod 346, 364, 378, 381–2
Moncrieff, Michael 57, 58, 81
Monkhorst, Damian 152, 159, 177,
    204, 205, 213, 225, 237–8, 239,
    244, 259, 260, 452
Moorabbin Oval 44
Moore, Dr Brendan 432, 435, 437
Moore, Kelvin 26, 54, 58, 82
Mornington Peninsula League 4, 15
under-15 schoolboys' team 9, 14
Morphett, Drew 327
Morwood, Shane 159, 214, 249, 250,
    251, 259, 286
Murphy, Glenn 9, 18
Murphy, John 341
Murphy, Marc 341
Murphy, Scott 338, 371
Murphy, Shane 80
Mynott, Brian 29

Naitanui, Nic 203
Nankervis, Ian 487
Neale, Kevin 'Cowboy' 27, 28
Neitz, David 313
New Mexico State University 85
Newman, Sam 321, 472
Newton, Bob 298, 338, 340
Nicholls, John 315
Nixon, Ricky 259
Norm Smith Medal 252, 413, 438–9

North Adelaide 58

North Melbourne 5, 46, 50–1, 55, 57, 63, 66, 79, 80–1, 100, 112, 113, 132, 150, 152, 157, 177, 182, 184–5, 187, 188, 190, 192, 196, 262, 275, 277, 280, 290, 311, 337, 355, 356, 357, 358, 365, 453, 492

Northey, John 145, 329

Norwood Football Club 187–8

Notting, Tim 343, 412, 432, 435, 457

O'Bree, Shane 361–2

O'Donnell, Gary 337, 382, 424

O'Halloran, David 58, 80, 106, 138, 139, 213

O'Keefe, Bill 147

Olsson, Elle 60

Olsson, Rod 18–19, 60

on-field evolution 493–5

centre diamond, introduction of 34

Optus Oval 376–7

O'Riley, Rod 333

Osborne, Richard 112

Pagan, Denis 337, 357–8, 492

Papua New Guinea 5

Parkin, David x, 11, 18, 26, 30, 37, 55, 61, 71, 75–80, 82, 94, 95, 99–100, 151, 152, 298, 490, 492

Paton, Ian 58, 113, 138

Pendlebury, Scott 473

personality profiling 84–92, 383

Enforcers 86, 87–8, 90–1, 117, 120, 152, 186, 215, 223, 280–1, 288, 296, 336, 347, 390, 415, 434, 446, 477

Feelers 87, 90, 215, 288, 336, 434

Mozzies 86, 89

Thinkers 86–7, 89, 91, 152, 215, 223, 280–1, 288, 336, 367, 434, 477

Pert, Gary 112, 161, 162, 271, 286, 304

Petrie, Drew 157

Petrie, Rob 150

Peverall, Damien 384

Phillips, Greg 164

Pike, Martin 378–81, 382, 400, 411, 414, 429, 431, 439, 452

Piper, Alan 325, 328, 350, 364

Pirak, Oberan 145

Plain, Brad 286

Platten, John 55, 273, 493

players

attitude 266–7

evolution 490

'in the zone' 49, 223

kicking statistics 42–3, 47, 108, 118–19

peak period 52

teamsmanship 69, 230

veteran 118, 167, 349, 385–6, 452, 468

Polkinghorne, David 58, 113

Popov, Victor 338, 372, 373, 437

Port Adelaide 166, 273, 340, 341, 343, 347, 360, 374, 395–6, 397, 419, 420, 421, 427, 428, 429, 443–4, 445, 453, 457, 467, 468

grand final 2004 458–62

Porter, Mick 26

Portsea 18–19, 60

Postill, Glenn 320

Powell, Stephen 357

Power, Luke 343, 361, 409, 439, 456

Power, Peter 147, 239

Pratt, Bob 28

Predator 392–3

premierships see grand finals

Pritchard, Darren 493

Quinlan, Bernie 108, 112, 239, 487

racial abuse 274–5

Raines, Geoff 154, 165, 487

Randall, Mark 433

Rantall, John 63

Ratten, Brett 387

Ravech, Judge 126
Rendell, Matthew 112
Reynolds, Dick 315
Rhys-Jones, David 260
Ricciuto, Mark 432
Rice, Leon 26, 28, 54, 58
Richards, Lou 31, 102, 131, 246
Richards, Ron 146, 155, 156–7, 214, 244, 259, 354
Richardson, Alan 218, 224, 230–2, 236, 259
Richardson, Matthew 320, 398
Richardson, Mike 154, 165
Richardson, Wayne 354
Richmond 16, 27, 60, 65, 69, 73, 105, 130, 165, 167, 196, 262, 268, 278, 303, 323, 330, 374, 398
Riewoldt, Nick 380
Rioli, Cyril 489
Robertson, Colin 59, 104, 138, 140
Robertson, Dave 168
Rocca, Anthony 359, 422–3, 429, 431, 437
Rocca, Saverio 295, 296, 299, 301, 302, 304, 305
Romero, Jose 363
Roos, Paul 112, 146, 492
Rose, Bob 62, 144, 145, 146, 149–50, 154, 158, 354
Rowe, Brad 286
Rowlings, Barry 58
Roydan, Tony 'Shep' 173, 176
Russell, Dave 260
Russell, Scott 177, 187, 206, 250, 251, 258, 288
Russo, Peter 58, 115, 135

St Kilda 23, 27–9, 37, 44, 46–7, 53, 71, 72, 94–5, 106, 149, 162, 186, 188, 263, 271–2, 274, 295, 330, 334, 350, 352, 354, 364, 365, 444, 445, 453, 454–5, 468, 470, 492
Salmon, Paul 138, 213, 214, 238

Sanderson, Brenton 286
Scanlon, Peter 122
Scarlett, Matthew 342, 488, 489
Schimmelbusch, Wayne 487
Schwab, Alan 130
Schwab, Peter 59, 104, 115, 139
Schwarzenegger, Arnold 392
Scott, Brad 4, 90, 199, 343, 376, 378, 388, 389–90, 405, 407, 424, 451, 478
Scott, Chris 4, 90, 343, 355, 357, 405, 407, 412, 432, 434–6, 451, 471, 480
Scott, Don 24, 28–9, 44, 53, 54, 68–72, 74, 80, 82, 83, 87, 100, 112, 203, 237, 452
Scully, Phil 169
Scully, Tom 169
Second World War 5
Selwood, Joel *vii*
Seoul Olympics *xi*
September 11 terrorist attacks 396
Shattock, Aaron 342, 343, 406–7, 432, 433, 435, 467
Shaw, Jamie 151
Shaw, Ray 252
Shaw, Tony 159, 165, 168, 174, 180–1, 186, 187, 189, 195, 203, 207, 220–2, 237, 238, 241, 244, 248, 250, 251, 252–3, 254, 258, 287, 288, 291–4, 297–8, 356, 367, 384, 395, 477
The Shawshank Redemption viii
Sheahan, Mike 145, 304, 320
Sheales, Peter 29
Sheedy, Kevin 21, 99, 137, 138, 199, 232, 239–40, 308, 401–2, 406, 482, 492
Sholly, Gerard 268
Sidebottom, Garry 112
Silvagni, Stephen 488, 489
Simmonds, Roy 64
Sizzling 495
Skilton, Bob 315

sledging 206–7, 275
Smart, Graeme 332
Smith, Dr Andrew 338, 372, 433, 435, 437
Smith, Leigh *viii*
Smith, Patrick 320
South Australia 31
South Melbourne 28, 63, 101 *see also* Sydney Swans
Southby, Geoff 487
sponsors 447, 448
sport psychology *see* personality profiling
sports science 371–2
Stanton, Peter 338, 372, 373, 435, 437, 460, 465
Starcevich, Craig 168, 169, 177, 190, 201, 210, 212, 214, 242–3, 245, 250, 260, 285, 286, 327, 336, 337, 372, 373, 424, 453–4
state football 30–1
steroids 370
Stevens, Anthony 453
Stevenson, Bruce 26
Stewart, Ian 27
Stokes, Kerry 326
Stubbs, Ron 17
Stynes, Jim 310
success in sport *x–xi*
    price of 1–2
Sully, Sandra 396
Sumich, Peter 192–3, 197, 207
The Sun 21, 31, 49, 126, 131
Swan, Dane 317, 473
Sydney 17
Sydney Olympic Games 362
Sydney Swans 88, 130, 145–6, 150, 160, 162, 169, 186, 190, 249, 272, 282, 288, 296, 304–5, 330, 342, 343, 359, 426, 427, 428–30, 445, 464, 468, 470, 486, 492

tackling 152, 200
Tanner, Wayne 168

Tarrant, Chris 381
Taylor, Brian 'Barge' 69, 160, 162–3, 174, 196, 200–1, 290, 320
Taylor, Mick 179, 244
teams
    best teams 487–90
    champion 492–3
Thompson, Len 487, 489
Thompson, Lindsay 54
Thompson, Mark 157
3AW *x*, 69, 160, 200, 317, 320, 495, 496
3DB 20
time wasting penalty 137–8
Tippett, Kurt 282, 288
Toyota AFL Legendary Moments 103
training 152
    fitness 118
    Kennedy, under 38–9
    off-field preparation 118
    weights and gym work 77
Tranquilli, Andrew 291
Trezise, Neil 126
Trigg, Steven 282
Triple M 317
Tuck, Michael 53, 58, 68–70, 72–4, 138, 139, 493
Tuddenham, Des 6, 31
Turner, Jamie 159, 189, 214, 259, 286

University of Queensland 85

Van Hoboken, Jan 64
Vander Haar, Paul 138, 212–13, 214
VFA 15
VFL 5–6 *see also* AFL
    centenary year 314
    change to AFL 225, 419
    player salary cap 65, 177
    reserves teams 159
    under-14 schoolboys' team 9–10
    under-19s team 159
    zoning system 13, 34, 100, 250

VFL Commission 121, 249
  appearance before 121–2, 130
VFL Park 48, 162, 182, 190, 194,
  210, 225, 352
VFL Tribunal
  video evidence 120
Victoria Park *v*, 146, 155, 161, 183,
  185, 188, 190, 205, 215, 231, 232,
  233, 274, 277, 284, 285, 288,
  289–90, 296, 297, 324, 354–5
Victorian State of Origin coaching
  316–17
Victorian under-14 schoolboys team 3
Voss, Brett 378
Voss, Michael *x*, 90, 329, 343, 349,
  355, 356, 367, 379, 382, 383,
  384, 386, 404, 411, 412–13, 414,
  423, 425, 427–8, 429, 431, 436,
  438, 439, 451, 454, 471–3, 475,
  476–8, 481–2, 483, 489, 490

Wade, Doug 45, 57, 63
WAFL 37, 76
Waite, Vin 61
Wakelin, Darryl 396, 462
Wakelin, Shane 424
Wallace, Terry 'Plough' 58, 81, 106,
  115, 139, 140, 142, 199, 346
Wallis, Dean 408
Walls, Robert 161, 396
Wanganeen, Gavin 488, 489
Watson, Tim 259, 351, 487, 489, 490
Waverley Park 45, 69, 73, 113, 191,
  207, 226, 272, 303, 340, 347,
  364–9
weight programs 370

Wells, Stephen 467
Welsh, Peter 44
West Coast Eagles 66, 165, 177, 189,
  191–3, 194, 195, 198, 199, 200,
  203, 205–6, 209, 210, 212, 218,
  226, 249, 269, 271, 290–2, 302,
  347, 355, 395, 419, 451, 468, 478,
  482, 483, 492
Western Australia 31
Western Bulldogs 27, 53, 88, 133,
  138, 346, 356–7, 362, 363,
  366, 386, 427, 470, 492 *see also*
  Footscray
Western Oval 20, 44
White, Darryl 342, 343, 431, 452,
  460
Wiley, Robert 191
Williams, Greg 81, 169, 439, 489, 490
Williams, Julie 7, 9
Williams, Mark 164–5, 458
Wilson, Caroline 446, 448
Wilson, Garry 112
Wilson, Ray 26, 27, 63
Winmar, Nicky 274–6
Wood, Cameron 480
Woodrow, Cameron 338
Woods, Tony 286, 348
Wooller, Maureen *see* Matthews,
  Maureen
World of Sport 152
Worsfold, John 291, 482
Wright, Graham 177, 187, 250, 257,
  276, 288

Yeomans, Bob 99
Young, Dr David 427